Artificial Intelligence
Programming with Python®

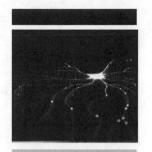

Artificial Intelligence Programming with Python®

From Zero to Hero

Perry Xiao

WILEY

This book is dedicated to my family. To my wife, May, my son, Zieger, and my daughter, Jessica, who make my life complete—without them, life would be meaningless. To my parents and my brother, who have shared their life and love with me that ultimately made me who I am today. To my friends and colleagues, who supported me throughout my career.

I would also like to dedicate this book to Grace Qing Wang, who sadly passed away during the course of writing this book. Grace Qing Wang was a young, energetic professional woman who was passionate about innovation and artificial intelligence in education. She was also a collaborator and a good friend. Through Grace I have made many professional connections that were very beneficial to my career.

About the Author

Dr. Perry Xiao is a professor and course director at the School of Engineering, London South Bank University in London, United Kingdom. He got his BEng degree in opto-electronics, MSc degree in solid-state physics, and PhD degree in photophysics. He is a charted engineering (CEng), a Fellow (FIET) from the Institution of Engineering and Technology (IET), and a Senior Fellow (SFHEA) from the Higher Education Academy (HEA). He has been teaching electronics, software, computer networks, and telecommunication subjects at both the undergraduate level and the postgraduate level for nearly two decades. He also supervises BEng final project students and MSc project students every year. His main research interest is to develop novel infrared and electronic sensing technologies for skin bioengineering applications and industrial nondestructive testing (NDT). To date, he has finished more than 12 PhD student supervisions, obtained two UK patent applications, published more than 100 scientific papers, been editorial reviewer for nine journals, and generated nearly £1 million in research grants.

He is also a director and cofounder of Biox Systems Ltd., UK, a university spin-off company that designs and manufactures state-of-the-art skin measurement instruments, AquaFlux and Epsilon, which have been used in more than 200 organizations worldwide, including leading cosmetic companies, universities, research institutes, and hospitals.

About the Technical Editors

Dr. Hongmei (Mary) He (FHEA, SIEEE) is an associate professor of cybersecurity in the School of Computer Science and Informatics at De Montfort University. Previously, she was a lecturer in AI and cyber security at Cranfield University. She received her PhD in computer science from Loughborough University in the UK in 2006 and gained sustained experience as a postdoctoral researcher at various universities. She has worked as an academic in the field of computer science and engineering for many years and has brief industrial experience at Motorola Design House in China as a senior embedded system engineer. Her research can be briefly divided into four themes: AI and data science, cognitive cybersecurity, cognitive robotics and trustworthy autonomous systems, and computing theory and optimization. Dr. He is a senior member of IEEE in the Computational Intelligence, Cybersecurity, RAS, and Women in Engineering Societies.

Dr. Weiheng Liao, DPhil (Oxon), is a computer scientist and technology entrepreneur in AI. He has authored and co-authored a number of influential papers in top journals and conferences and is the visiting scholar of several research universities. His interests include machine learning, AutoML, deep learning, explainable AI, natural language processing, and their applications in finance and investment. He cofounded YouShore, one of the world's first teams to employ deep NLP to analyze social media data, to extract alternative data, and to construct alpha signals.

If you want to know more about his recent work, please visit `www.madebydata.com`.

Acknowledgments

I would like to express my sincere gratitude to Wiley Publishing for giving me this opportunity. I would also like to thank Devon Lewis, Liz Britten, Pete Gaughan, Dr. Weiheng Liao, and Hongmei He for their support. Without them, this book would not have been possible.

Contents at a Glance

This book is accompanied by bonus content! The following extra elements can be downloaded from www.wiley.com/go/aiwithpython:

- MATLAB for AI Cheat Sheets
- Python for AI Cheat Sheets
- Python Deep Learning Cheat Sheet
- Python Virtual Environment
- Jupyter Notebook, Google Colab, and Kaggle

Contents

This book is accompanied by bonus content! The following extra elements can be downloaded from www.wiley.com/go/aiwithpython:

- MATLAB for AI Cheat Sheets
- Python for AI Cheat Sheets
- Python Deep Learning Cheat Sheet
- Python Virtual Environment
- Jupyter Notebook, Google Colab, and Kaggle

Preface

The year 2020 was a year of turmoil, conflicts, and division. The most significant event was no doubt the COVID-19 pandemic, which was, and still is, raging in more than 200 countries and affecting the lives of hundreds of millions of people. I spent a good part of the year working from home. There are many disadvantages of remote working; however, it does have at least one advantage: it saved me at least two hours a day traveling to and from work. This gave me more time to think about, to plan, and to propose this book.

I am absolutely fascinated with artificial intelligence, and I have read many artificial intelligence books. But most of the books are heavily focused on the mathematics of artificial intelligence, which makes them difficult to understand for people without mathematics or computer science backgrounds. I have always wanted to write a book that could make it easier to get into the artificial intelligence field for beginners—people from all different disciplines. Thanks to the countless researchers and developers around the world and their open source code, particularly Python-based open source code, it is much easier to use artificial intelligence now than 10 years ago. Through this book, you will find that you can do amazing things with just a few lines of code, and in some cases, you don't need to code at all.

I am a big fan of open source, and for a research field as controversial as artificial intelligence, it is better for everyone to work together. So, I want to express my ultimate gratitude to those who made their work available for the benefit of others.

We are living in an era of digital revolutions and digital technologies such as artificial intelligence, the Internet of Things, Industry 4.0, 5G technologies, digital twin, cybersecurity, big data, cloud computing, blockchains, and, on the horizon, quantum computing. They are all being developed at a breathtaking speed. In the future, the Internet of Things will provide a means to connect all things around us and to use sensors to collect data. The industry version of the Internet of Things is called Industry 4.0, which will connect all sorts of things for manufacturers. Digital twin is a digital representation of a process, product, or service updated from real-time data. With digital twin, we can predict problems before they even occur, prevent downtime, develop new opportunities for the future through simulations. 5G technologies will provide a means for fast and low-latency communications for the data. Cybersecurity will provide a means to protect the data. Big data will provide a means to analyze the data in large quantity. Cloud computing will provide the storage, display, and analysis of the data remotely, in the cloud. Blockchains will provide traceability to the data through distributed ledgers. Quantum computing will make some of the computation faster, in fact, many orders of magnitude faster. Artificial intelligence will be right at the heart of all the technologies, which allows us to analyze the data intelligently. As you can see, all these digital technologies are going to become intertwined to make us work better and live smarter.

That is why I have always said to my students, you can change your future. Your future is in your hands. The key is learning, even after graduation. Learning is a lifelong mission. In today's ever-evolving world, with all the quickly developing digital technologies, you need to constantly reinvent yourself; you will need to learn everything and learn anything. The disadvantage of fast-changing technologies is that you will need to learn all the time, but the advantage is no one has any more advantages than you; you are on the same starting line as everyone else. The rest is up to you!

I believe artificial intelligence will be just a tool for everyone in the future, just like software coding is today. Artificial intelligence will no doubt affect every aspect of our lives and will fundamentally change the way we live, how we work, and how we socialize. The more you know about artificial intelligence and the more involved you are in artificial intelligence, the better you can transform your life.

Many successful people are lifelong learners. American entrepreneur and business magnate Elon Musk is a classic example. As the world's richest man, he learned many things by himself, from computer programming, Internet, finance, to building cars and rockets. British comedian Lee Evans once said that by the end of the day, if you have learned something new, then it is a good day. I hope you will have a good day every day and enjoy reading this book!

Professor Perry Xiao

July 2021, London

Why Buy This Book

Artificial intelligence (AI) is no doubt one of the hottest buzzwords at the moment. AI has penetrated into many aspects of our lives. Knowing AI and being able to use AI will bring enormous benefits to our work and lives. However, learning AI is a daunting task for many people, largely due to the complex mathematics and sophisticated coding behind it. This book aims to demystify AI and teach readers about AI from scratch, by using plain language and simple, illustrative code examples. It is divided into three parts.

In Part I, the book gives an easy-to-read introduction about AI, including the history, the types of AI, the current status, and the possible future trends. It then introduces AI development tools and Python, the most widely used programming language for AI.

In Part II, the book introduces the machine learning and deep learning aspects of AI. Machine learning topics include classifications, regressions, and clustering. It also includes the most popular reinforcement learning. Deep learning topics include convolutional neural networks (CNNs) and long short-term memory networks (LSTMs).

In Part III, the book introduces AI case studies; topics include image classifications, transfer learning, recurrent neural networks, and the latest generative adversarial networks. It also includes the state of the art of GPUs, TPUs, cloud computing, and edge computing. This book is packed with interesting and exciting examples such as pattern recognitions, image classifications, face recognition (most controversial), age and gender detection, voice/speech recognition, chatbot, natural language processing, translation, sentiment analysis, predictive maintenance, finance and stock price analysis, sales prediction, customer segmentation, biomedical data analysis, and much more.

How This Book Is Organized

This book is divided into three parts. Part I introduces AI. Part II covers machine learning and deep learning. Part III covers the case studies, or the AI application projects. R&D developers as well as students will be interested in Part III.

Part I

Chapter 1: Introduction to AI

Chapter 2: AI Development Tools

Example Code

All the example source code is available on the website that accompanies this book.

Who This Book Is For

This book is intended for university/college students, as well as software and electronic hobbyists, researchers, developers, and R&D engineers. It assumes readers understand the basic concepts of computers and their main components such as CPUs, RAM, hard drives, network interfaces, and so forth. Readers should be able to use a computer competently, for example, can switch on and off the computer, log in and log out, run some programs, copy/move/delete files, and use terminal software such as Microsoft Windows command prompt.

It also assumes that readers have some basic programming experience, ideally in Python, but it could also be in other languages such as Java, C/C++, Fortran, MATLAB, C#, BASIC, R, and so on. Readers should know the basic syntax, the different types of variables, standard inputs and outputs, the conditional selections, and the loops and subroutines.

Finally, it assumes readers have a basic understanding of computer networks and the Internet and are familiar with some of the most commonly used Internet services such as the Web, email, file download/upload, online banking/ shopping, etc.

This book can be used as a core textbook as well as for background reading.

What This Book Is Not For

This book is not for readers to purely learn the Python programming language; there are already a lot of good Python programming books on the market. However, to appeal to a wider audience, Chapter 2 provides a basic introduction to Python and how to get started with Python programming, so even if you have never programmed Python before, you can still use the book.

If you want to learn all the technical details of Python, please refer to the following suggested prerequisite reading list and resources.

Suggested Prerequisite Readings

Computer Basics

Absolute Beginner's Guide to Computer Basics (Absolute Beginner's Guides (Que)), 5th Edition, Michael Miller, QUE, 1 Sept. 2009.

ISBN-10: 0789742535

ISBN-13: 978-0789742537

Computers for Beginners (Wikibooks)

https://en.wikibooks.org/wiki/Computers_for_Beginners

Python Programming

Python Crash Course (2nd Edition): A Hands-On, Project-Based Introduction to Programming, Eric Matthes, No Starch Press, 9 May 2019.

ISBN-10 : 1593279280

ISBN-13 : 978-1593279288

Learn Python 3 the Hard Way: A Very Simple Introduction to the Terrifyingly Beautiful World of Computers and Code, 3rd Edition, Zed A. Shaw, Addison-Wesley Professional; 10 Oct. 2013.

ISBN-10 : 0321884914

ISBN-13 : 978-0321884916

Head First Python 2e: A Brain-Friendly Guide, 2nd Edition, Paul Barry, O'Reilly; 16 Dec. 2016.

ISBN-10 : 1491919531

ISBN-13 : 978-1491919538

Think Python: How to Think Like a Computer Scientist, 2nd Edition, Allen B. Downey, O'Reilly, 25 Dec. 2015.

ISBN-10 : 1491939362

ISBN-13 : 978-1491939369

Python Pocket Reference: Python in Your Pocket, 5th edition, Mark Lutz, O'Reilly Media, 9 Feb. 2014.

ISBN-10 : 1449357016

ISBN-13 : 978-1449357016

A Beginner's Python Tutorial (Wikibooks)
https://en.wikibooks.org/wiki/A_Beginner%27s_Python_Tutorial

Python Programming (Wikibooks)
https://en.wikibooks.org/wiki/Python_Programming

Suggested Readings to Accompany the Book

Introduction to Machine Learning with Python: A Guide for Data Scientists, Sarah Guido, O'Reilly Media; 25 May 2016.

ISBN-10 : 1449369413

ISBN-13 : 978-1449369415

Hands-on Machine Learning with Scikit-Learn, Keras, and TensorFlow: Concepts, Tools, and Techniques to Build Intelligent Systems, 2nd Edition, Aurelien Geron, OReilly, 14 Oct. 2019.

ISBN-10 : 1492032646

ISBN-13 : 978-1492032649

Deep Learning with Python, Francois Chollet, Manning Publications, 30 Nov. 2017.

ISBN-10 : 9781617294433

ISBN-13 : 978-1617294433

Deep Learning (Adaptive Computation and Machine Learning Series), Illustrated edition, Ian Goodfellow, MIT Press, 3 Jan. 2017

ISBN-10 : 0262035618

ISBN-13 : 978-0262035613

Python Machine Learning: Machine Learning and Deep Learning with Python, scikit-learn, and TensorFlow 2, 3rd Edition, Sebastian Raschka, Vahid Mirjalili, Packt Publishing, 12 Dec. 2019.

ISBN-10 : 1789955750

ISBN-13 : 978-1789955750

Machine Learning Yearning (Andrew Ng's free ebook)
https://www.deeplearning.ai/machine-learning-yearning/

Dive into Deep Learning (Free ebook)
https://d2l.ai/

What You Need

In this book, you will need the following:

- A standard personal computer with a minimum 250 GB hard drive, 8 GB RAM, and Intel or AMD 2 GHz processor, running a Windows operating system (Vista/7/8/10, Internet Explorer 9 and above, or the latest Edge browser, or Google Chrome) or a Linux operating system (such as Ubuntu Linux 16.04 (or newer) and so on). You can also use a Mac (with Mac OS X 10.13 and later, administrator privileges for installation, 64-bit browser).

- Python software

  `https://www.python.org/downloads/`

- Text editors and Python IDEs (see Chapter 2)

- Raspberry Pi (optional)

  `https://www.raspberrypi.org/`

- Arduino NANO 33 BLE Sense (optional)

  `https://www.arduino.cc/en/Guide/NANO33BLESense`

This book is accompanied by bonus content! The following extra elements can be downloaded from `www.wiley.com/go/aiwithpython`:

- MATLAB for AI Cheat Sheets
- Python for AI Cheat Sheets
- Python Deep Learning Cheat Sheet
- Python Virtual Environment
- Jupyter Notebook, Google Colab, and Kaggle

Artificial Intelligence
Programming with Python®

Part

I

Introduction

In This Part:

Part I gives a bird's-eye overview of artificial intelligence (AI) and AI development resources.

Introduction to AI

*"There is no reason and no way that a human mind can keep up
with an artificial intelligence machine by 2035."*
—Gray Scott (American futurist)

1.1 What Is AI?

Artificial intelligence (AI) is no doubt one of the hottest buzzwords right now. It is in the news all the time. So, what is AI, and why is it important? When you talk about AI, the image that probably pops into most people's heads is of a human-like robot that can do complicated, clever things, as shown in Figure 1.1. AI is actually more than that.

AI is an area of computer science that aims to make machines do intelligent things, that is, learn and solve problems, similar to the natural intelligence of humans and animals. In AI, an intelligent agent receives information from the environment, performs computations to decide what action to take in order to achieve the goal, and takes actions autonomously. AI can improve its performance with learning.

For more information, see the John McCarthy's 2004 paper titled, "What Is Artificial Intelligence?"

```
https://homes.di.unimi.it/borghese/Teaching/AdvancedIntelligent
Systems/Old/IntelligentSystems_2008_2009/Old/IntelligentSystems_
2005_2006/Documents/Symbolic/04_McCarthy_whatisai.pdf
```

Figure 1.1: The common perception of AI

(Source: `https://commons.wikimedia.org/wiki/File:Artificial_
Intelligence_%26_AI_%26_Machine_Learning_-_30212411048.jpg`)

You may not be aware that AI has already been widely used in many aspects of our lives. Personal assistants such as Amazon's Alexa, iPhone's Siri, Microsoft's Cortana, and Google Assistant all rely on AI to understand what you have said and follow the instructions to perform tasks accordingly.

Online entertainment services such as Spotify and Netflix also rely on AI to figure out what you might like and recommend songs and movies. Other services such as Google, Facebook, Amazon, and eBay analyze your online activities to deliver targeted advertisements. My wife once searched *Arduino boards* at work during the day, and in the evening, after she got home, no matter which websites she visited, ads for Arduino boards kept popping up!

Have you ever used the SwiftKey program on your phone or Grammarly on your computer? They are also AI.

AI has also been used in healthcare, manufacturing, driverless cars, finance, agriculture, and more. In a recent study, researchers from Google Health and Imperial College London developed an algorithm that outperformed six human radiologists in reading mammograms for breast cancer detection. Groupe Renault is collaborating with Google Cloud to combine its AI and machine learning capabilities with automotive industry expertise to increase efficiency, improve production quality, and reduce the carbon footprint. Driverless cars use AI to identify the roads, the pedestrians, and the traffic signs. The finance industry uses AI to detect fraud and predict future growth. Agriculture is also turning to AI for healthier crops, pest control, soil and growing conditions monitoring, and so on.

AI can affect our jobs. According to the BBC, 35 percent of today's jobs will disappear in the next 20 years. You can use the following BBC website to find out how safe your workplace is:

```
https://www.bbc.co.uk/news/technology-34066941
```

1.2   The History of AI

AI can be traced back to the 1940s, during World War II, when Alan Turing, a British mathematician and computer scientist, developed a code-breaking machine called *bombe* in Bletchley Park, United Kingdom, that deciphered German Enigma–encrypted messages (see Figure 1.2). The Hollywood movie *The Imitation Game* (2014) has vividly captured this period of history. Turing's work helped the Allies to defeat the Nazis and is estimated to have shortened the war by more than two years and saved more than 14 million lives.

Figure 1.2: The bombe machine (left) and the Enigma machine (right)
(Source: https://en.wikipedia.org/wiki/Cryptanalysis_of_the_Enigma)

In October 1950, while working at the University of Manchester, Turing published a paper entitled "Computing Machinery and Intelligence" in the journal *Mind* (Oxford University Press). In this paper, he proposed an experiment that became known as the famous Turing test. The Turing test is often described as a three-person game called the *imitation game*, as illustrated in Figure 1.3, in which player C, the interrogator, tries to determine which player—A or B—is a computer and which is a human. The interrogator is limited to using the responses to written questions to make the determination. The Turing test has since been used to test a machine's intelligence to see if it is equivalent to a human. To date, no computer has passed the Turing test.

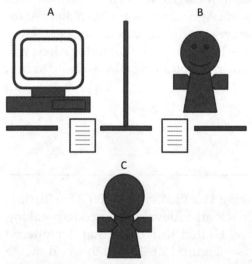

Figure 1.3: The famous Turing test, also called the *imitation game*. Player C, the interrogator, is trying to determine which player—A or B—is a computer and which is a human.

AI as a research discipline was established at a workshop at Dartmouth College in 1956, organized by John McCarthy, a young assistant professor of mathematics at the college (http://raysolomonoff.com/dartmouth/). The workshop lasted about six to eight weeks, and it was essentially an extended brainstorming session. There were about 11 mathematician attendees such as Marvin Minsky, Allen Newell, Arthur Samuel, and Herbert Simon. They were widely recognized as the founding fathers of AI. John McCarthy chose the term *artificial intelligence* for the new research field.

The history of AI can be divided into three stages, as illustrated in Figure 1.4.

- **1950s–1970s, neural networks (NNs):** During this period, neural networks, also called *artificial neural networks* (ANNs), were developed based on human brains that mimic the human biological neural networks. An NN usually has three layers: an input layer, a hidden layer, and an output layer. To use an NN, you need to train the NN with a large amount of given data. After training, the NN can then be used to predict results for unseen data. NNs attracted a lot of attention during this period. After the 1970s, when NNs failed to live up to their promises, known as *AI hype*, funding and research activities were dramatically cut. This was called an *AI winter*.

- **1980s–2010s, machine learning (ML):** This is the period when machine learning flourished. ML is a subset of AI and consists of a set of mathematical algorithms that can automatically analyze data. Classic ML can be divided into supervised learning and unsupervised learning. Supervised learning examples include speech recognition and image recognition. Unsupervised learning examples include customer segmentation, defect detection, and fraud detection. Classic ML algorithms are support vector machine (SVM), K-means clustering, decision tree, naïve Bayes, and so on.

- **2010s–present, deep learning (DL):** This is the period when deep learning (DL) was developed. DL is a special type of neural network that has more than one layer of hidden layers. This is possible only with the increase of computing power, especially graphical processing units (GPUs), and improved algorithms. DL is a subset of ML. DL has so far outperformed many other algorithms on a large dataset. But is DL hype or reality? That remains to be seen.

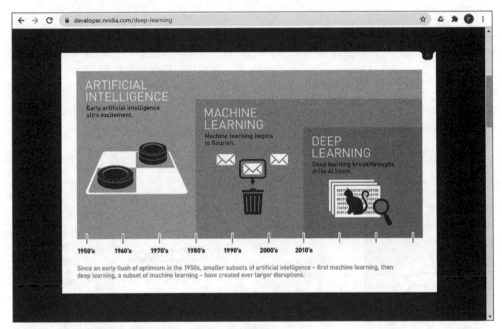

Figure 1.4: The history of AI at the NVidia website

(Source: `https://developer.nvidia.com/deep-learning`)

AI is often confused with data science, big data, and data mining. Figure 1.5 shows the relationships between AI, machine learning, deep learning, data science, and mathematics. Both mathematics and data science are related to AI but are different from AI. Data science mainly focuses on data, which includes big data and data mining. Data science can use machine learning and deep learning when processing the data.

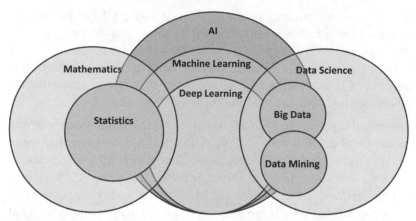

Figure 1.5: The relationships between AI, machine learning, deep learning, data science, and mathematics

Figure 1.6 shows an interesting website that explains the lifecycle of data science. It includes business understanding, data mining, data cleaning, data exploration, feature engineering, predictive modeling, and data visualization.

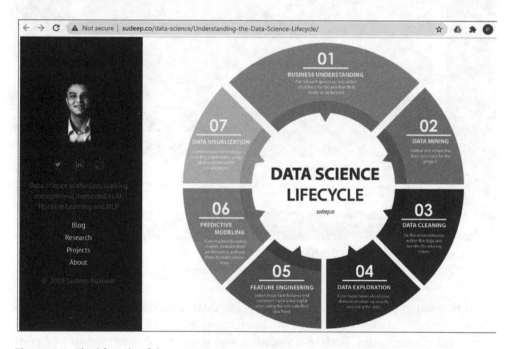

Figure 1.6: The lifecycle of data science

(Source: `http://sudeep.co/data-science/Understanding-the-Data-Science-Lifecycle/`)

In summary:

- AI means enabling a machine to do intelligent things to mimic humans. The two important aspects of AI are machine learning and deep learning.

- Machine learning is a subset of AI and consists of algorithms that can automate data analysis.

- Deep learning is a subset of machine learning. It is a neural network with more than one hidden layer.

1.3　AI Hypes and AI Winters

Like many other technologies, AI has AI hypes, as shown in Figure 1.7. An AI hype can be divided into several stages. In the first stage (1950s–1970s), called Technology Trigger, AI developed quickly, with increased funding, research activities, enthusiasm, optimism, and high expectations. In the second stage (1970s), AI reached the peak, called the Peak of Inflated Expectations. After the peak, in the third stage (1970s–1980s), when AI failed to deliver on its promises, AI reached the bottom, called the Trough of Disillusionment. This is the point at which an AI winter occurred. After the trough, AI slowly recovered; this is the fourth stage (1980s–present), which we are in now, called the Slop of Enlightenment. Finally, AI will reach the fifth stage, the Plateau of Productivity, where AI development becomes more stable.

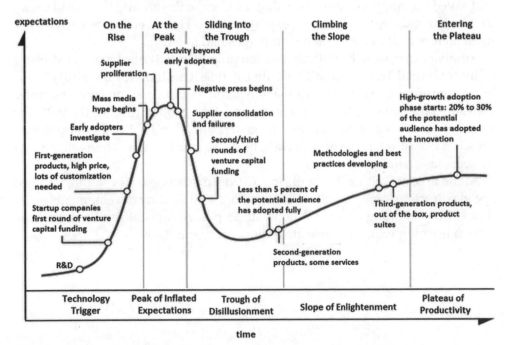

Figure 1.7: The technology hype cycle

(Source: https://en.wikipedia.org/wiki/Hype_cycle)

AI winter refers to a period of time during which public interest and research activities in artificial intelligence are significantly reduced. There have been two AI winters in history, one in the late 1970s and one in the late 1980s.

From the 1950s to the 1970s, artificial neural networks attracted a lot of attention. But since the late 1960s, after many disappointments and criticisms, funding and research activities were significantly reduced; this was the first AI winter. A famous case was the failure of machine translation in 1966. After spending $20 million to fund a research project, the National Research Council (NRC) concluded that machine translation was more expensive, less accurate, and slower than human translation, so the NRC ended all support. The careers of many people were destroyed, and the research ended.

In 1973, British Parliament commissioned Professor Sir James Lighthill to assess the state of AI research in the United Kingdom. His report, the famous Lighthill Report, criticized the utter failure of AI and concluded that nothing done in AI couldn't be done in other sciences. The report also pointed out that many of AI's most successful algorithms would not work on real-world problems. The report was contested in a debate that aired on the BBC series *Controversy* in 1973, pitting Lighthill against the team of Donald Michie, John McCarthy, and Richard Gregory. The Lighthill report virtually led to the dismantling of AI research in England in the 1970s.

In the 1980s, a form of AI program called the *expert system* became popular around the world. The first commercial expert system was developed at Carnegie Mellon for Digital Equipment Corporation. It was an enormous success and saved the company millions of dollars. Companies around the world began to develop and deploy their own expert systems. However, by the early 1990s, most commercial expert system companies had failed.

Another example is the Fifth Generation project. In 1981, the Japanese Ministry of International Trade and Industry invested $850 million for the Fifth Generation computer project to build machines that could carry on conversations, translate languages, interpret pictures, and reason like humans. By 1991, the project was discontinued, because the goals penned in 1981 had not been met. This is a classic example of expectations being much higher than what an AI project was actually capable of.

At the time of writing this book, in 2020, deep learning is developing at a fast speed, attracting lots of activities and funding, with exciting developments every day. Is deep learning a hype? When will deep learning peak, and will there be a deep learning winter? Those are billion-dollar questions.

1.4   The Types of AI

According to many resources, AI can be divided into three categories.

- **Narrow AI**, also called *weak AI* or *artificial narrow intelligence* (ANI), refers to the AI that is used to solve a specific problem. Almost all AI applications we have today are narrow AI. For example, image classification, object detection, speech recognition (such as Amazon's Alexa, iPhone's Siri, Microsoft's Cortana, and Google Assistant), translation, natural language processing, weather forecasting, targeted advertisements, sales predictions, email spam detection, fraud detection, face recognition, and computer vision are all narrow AI.

- **General AI**, also called *strong AI* or *artificial general intelligence* (AGI), refers to the AI that is for solving general problems. It is more like a human being, which is able to learn, think, invent, and solve more complicated problems. The singularity, also called *technological singularity*, is when AI overtakes human intelligence, as illustrated in Figure 1.8. According to Google's Ray Kurzweil, an American author, inventor, and futurist, AI will pass the Turing test in 2029 and reach the singularity point in 2045. Narrow AI is what we have achieved so far, and general AI is what we expect in the future.

- **Super AI**, also called *superintelligence*, refers to the AI after the singularity point. Nobody knows what will happen with super AI. One vision is human and machine integration through a brain chip interface. In August 2020, Elon Musk, the most famous American innovative entrepreneur, has already demonstrated a pig with a chip in its brain. While some people are more pessimistic about the future of AI, others are more optimistic. We cannot predict the future, but we can prepare for it.

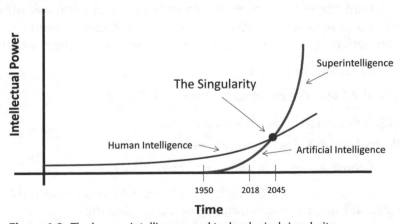

Figure 1.8: The human intelligence and technological singularity

For more details about the types of AI, see the following resources:

```
https://azure.microsoft.com/en-gb/overview/what-is-artificial-
intelligence/
https://www.ubs.com/microsites/artificial-intelligence/en/new-
dawn.html
https://doi.org/10.1016/B978-0-12-817024-3.00008-8
```

This book will mainly cover the machine learning and deep learning aspects of AI, which belong to narrow AI or weak AI.

1.5   Edge AI and Cloud AI

AI applications can be run either on the large remote servers, called *cloud AI*, or on the local machines, called *edge AI*. The advantages of cloud AI are that you don't need to purchase expensive hardware; you can upload large training datasets and fully utilize the vast computing power provided by the cloud. The disadvantages are that it might require more bandwidth and have higher latency and security issues. The top three cloud AI service providers are as follows:

Amazon AWS Machine Learning   AWS has the largest market share and the longest history and provides more cloud services than anyone else. But it is also the most expensive.

```
https://aws.amazon.com/machine-learning/
```

Microsoft Azure   Azure has the second largest market share and also provides many services. Azure can be easily integrated with Windows and many other software applications, such as .NET.

```
https://azure.microsoft.com/
```

Google Cloud Platform   Google is relatively new and has fewer different services and features than AWS and Azure. But Google Cloud Platform has attractive, "customer-friendly" pricing and is expanding rapidly.

```
https://cloud.google.com/
```

Other cloud AI service providers include the following:

- **IBM Cloud:** `https://www.ibm.com/cloud`
- **Alibaba Cloud:** `https://www.alibabacloud.com/`
- **Baidu Cloud:** `https://cloud.baidu.com/`

Figure 1.9 is an interesting website that compares AWS and Azure and Google Cloud and shows the magic quadrant of the cloud platforms.

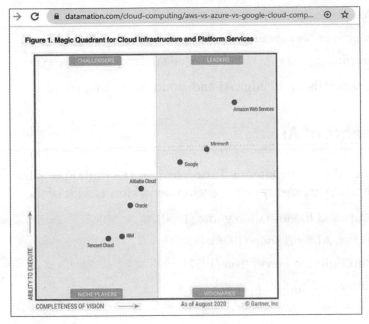

Figure 1.9: The magic quadrant of cloud platforms

(Source: `https://www.datamation.com/cloud-computing/aws-vs-azure-vs-google-cloud-comparison.html`)

The advantages of edge AI are low latency, that it can work without an Internet connection, and that it is real time and secure. The disadvantages of Edge AI are that you need purchase your own hardware, and it has limited computation power. Edge devices may have a power consumption constraint, as they are usually battery powered. The following are the most popular edge AI devices:

- **Microcontroller-based AI:** `https://www.arduino.cc/en/Guide/NANO33BLESense`

- **Raspberry Pi–based AI:** `https://magpi.raspberrypi.org/articles/learn-artificial-intelligence-with-raspberry-pi`

- **Google Edge TPU TensorFlow Processing Unit:** `https://cloud.google.com/edge-tpu`

- **NVidia Jetson GPU–based AI:** `https://developer.nvidia.com/embedded-computing`

- **Intel and Xilinx–based AI:** `https://www.intel.co.uk/content/www/uk/en/products/docs/storage/programmable/applications/machine-learning.html` and `https://www.xilinx.com/applications/industrial/analytics-machine-learning.html`

- **BeagleBone AI:** https://beagleboard.org/ai
- **96Boards AI:** https://www.96boards.ai/
- **Baidu Edgeboard:** https://ai.baidu.com/tech/hardware/deepkit

You will learn more details about edge AI and cloud AI in Chapter 12.

1.6   Key Moments of AI

Since Alan Turing introduced the famous Turing test, or the imitation game, there have been several key moments in AI development. Here is a list of them:

- Alan Turing proposed the imitation game (1950).
- Dartmouth held an AI workshop (1956).
- Frank Rosenblatt built the Perceptron (1957).
- The first AI winter (1970s).
- The second AI winter (1987).
- IBM's Deep Blue beats Kasparov (1997).
- Geoffrey Hinton unleashed deep learning networks (2012).
- AlphaGo defeated a human Go champion (2016).
- OpenAI released GPT-3 (2020).
- AlphaFold predicted protein folding (2020).

As listed, in 1997, the IBM Deep Blue computer beat the world chess champion, Garry Kasparov, in a six-game thriller. The match lasted several days, with two wins for IBM, one for Garry Kasparov, and three draws. The match received massive media coverage around the world. Although branded as "artificial intelligence," IBM Deep Blue actually played through "brute force," that is, calculating all the possible moves. Deep Blue, with its capability of evaluating 200 million positions per second, was the first and fastest computer to face a world chess champion (https://www.ibm.com/ibm/history/ibm100/us/en/icons/deepblue/).

In January 2011, IBM Watson competed against Ken Jennings and Brad Rutter, two of the most successful contestants on *Jeopardy!*, a popular American show. A practice match and the two official matches were recorded on January 13–15, 2011. In the end, IBM Watson won the first prize of $1 million, Jennings won the second place of $300,000, and Rutter won the third place of $200,000. IBM donated 50 percent of the winnings to the World Vision charity and 50 percent to the World Community Grid charity (https://en.wikipedia.org/wiki/Watson_(computer)).

In September 2012, a convolutional neural network (CNN) called AlexNet, developed by Alex Krizhevsky, Ilya Sutskever, and Geoffrey Hinton, won the ImageNet Large Scale Visual Recognition Challenge. This inspired a worldwide research interest in deep learning that is still strong today. The AlexNet paper has been cited more than 70,000 times.

In March 2016, AlphaGo of Google DeepMind competed against Lee Sedol of South Korea, the world champion Go player. Sedol has won 18 world titles and is widely considered the greatest player of that time. AlphaGo defeated Sedol in a convincing 4–1 victory in Seoul, South Korea. The matches were broadcast live and were watched by more than 200 million people worldwide. This landmark of AI achievement was a decade ahead of its predictions.

Go is a popular board game that originated in China more than 3,000 years ago (see Figure 1.10). In a Go game, two players take turns placing their stones on a board, with one player using black stones and the other using white stones. The player with black stones always starts the game. The goal of the game is to surround and capture the opponent's stones and occupy as many territories as possible. The player with the larger territory wins.

Figure 1.10: The traditional Go board game
(Source: https://en.wikipedia.org/wiki/Go_(game))

The Go board has 19×19 grids, where each grid can be a black or white stone. This gives 2^{261} (about 10 to the power of 170) possibilities. That is enormously complicated, compared with only 10 to the power of 40 possibilities in Chess. It will take the world's fastest computer (Fujitsu in Fugaku, Japan) more than 10 billion years to calculate all the possibilities. The universe is only 13.8 billion years old! Clearly, you cannot teach a machine to play Go by brute force.

Google DeepMind's AlphaGo plays the Go game through AI, by combining statistical analysis and deep learning. The calculations are done on 1,920 central processing units (CPUs), 280 graphics processing units (GPUs), and possibly Google's tensor processing units (TPUs). That is a lot of computing power (`https://www.deepmind.com/research/case-studies/alphago-the-story-so-far`)!

In June 2020, OpenAI's GPT-3 caught the attention of the world. OpenAI is a research business cofounded by Elon Musk, who also founded the famous electrical car company Tesla Inc. GPT-3 stands for Generative Pre-trained Transformer 3 and is a language prediction model, a form of deep learning neural network. GPT-3 is trained on gigabillions of text information gathered by crawling the Internet, including the text of Wikipedia. GPT-3 has 96 layers and a whopping 175 billion parameters; it is the largest language model to date. According to Google, it costs about $1 to train 1,000 parameters. This means it could cost tens of millions to train GPT-3. Once trained, GPT-3 can do many amazing things, such as generating new texts, writing essays, composing poems, answering questions, translating languages, and even creating computer code. This is hailed as one of the greatest breakthroughs in AI research and has demonstrated some mind-blowing potential applications. OpenAI made the GPT-3 application programming interface (API) available online for selected developers (`https://gpt3examples.com/`), and since then, many examples of poetry, prose, news, reports, and fiction have emerged. In September 2020, OpenAI exclusively licensed the GPT-3 language model to Microsoft (`https://openai.com/blog/openai-api/`). In January 2021, OpenAI announced DALL-E and CLIP, two impressive neural network models based on GPT-3. DALL-E is capable of generating amazing high-quality images based on text (`https://openai.com/blog/dall-e/`), while CLIP can connect text to images (`https://openai.com/blog/clip/`).

In November 2020, Google's DeepMind made a breakthrough in the protein folding problem with its AlphaFold AI system. As we all know, proteins are large complex molecules made up of chains of amino acids, and proteins are essential to our lives. What a protein can do largely depends on its unique 3D structure and on what shape a protein will fold into. These complicated chains of amino acids can have a huge number of possibilities, and yet in reality, proteins only fold into very specific shapes. This has been a grand challenge in biology for half a century. There are about 180 million known proteins, and only about 170,000 protein structures have been mapped out. AlphaFold successfully predicted two protein structures of SARS-CoV-virus, which were separately identified by researchers months later. This breakthrough could dramatically accelerate the progress in understanding how proteins work and developing treatments for diseases (`https://deepmind.com/research/case-studies/alphafold`).

In January 2021, Google announced the development of a new language model called Switch Transformer, which contains 1.6 trillion parameters. It offers up to 7x increases in pretraining speeds with the same computational resources. These improvements extend into multilingual settings, across 101 languages. For more details, see the following:

```
https://arxiv.org/pdf/2101.03961v1.pdf
https://github.com/labmlai/annotated_deep_learning_paper_
implementations
```

In June 2021, Beijing Academy of Artificial Intelligence (BAAI) unveiled a new natural language processing (NLP) model, WuDao 2.0, which was trained using 1.75 trillion parameters, the largest model to date. The model was developed with the help of more than 100 scientists from multiple organizations. For more details, see the following:

```
https://gpt3demo.com/apps/wu-dao-20
```

1.7   The State of AI

The development of AI has been gaining speed in the past decades. One of the best places to understand what is going on is an annual AI research and development report, such as the following:

- **The AI Index Report, Stanford:** `https://aiindex.stanford.edu/report/`
- **State of AI Report, Cambridge:** `https://www.stateof.ai/`

These annual reports show the realities of AI investment and development and predict future trends for the coming year. The State of AI Report, composed by Nathan Benaich and Ian Hogarth, is organized into five main sections: Research, Talent, Industry, Policies, and Predictions.

According to the 2020 "State of AI" report, new natural language processing companies raised more than $100 million in the past year. Autonomous driving companies drove millions of miles in 2019. Machine learning has been adopted for drug discovery by both large pharmaceutical companies and startups including Glaxosmithkline, Merck, and Novartis. Many universities have introduced AI degrees. Google claimed quantum supremacy in October 2019 and announced TensorFlow Quantum, an open source library for quantum machine learning, in March 2020.

For research, only 15 percent of the AI papers have published their code. Some organizations, such as OpenAI and DeepMind, never disclose their code. The most popular AI research topics are computer vision and natural language processing. Computer vision includes semantic segmentation, image classification, object detection, image generation, and pose estimation. Natural language processing includes machine translation, language modeling, question answering, sentiment analysis, and text classification. Google's TensorFlow is the most popular AI platform, but Facebook's PyTorch is catching up. Training billions of model parameters costs millions of dollars, but larger models need less data than smaller models to achieve the same performance. A new generation of transformer language models, such as GPT-3, T5, and BART, are unlocking new applications, such as translating C++ code to Java or translating Python to C++, or even debugging the code. Publications in the area of AI in biology have been growing more than 50 percent year over year since 2017. AI Papers published in 2019 and 2020 account for 25 percent of all AI publications since 2000. Graph neural networks (GNNs) are a type of emerging deep learning neural network designed to process 3D data, such as molecular structures. This enhanced the prediction of chemical properties and helped in the discovery of new drugs. By analyzing symptoms from more than 4 million people, AI can detect new disease symptoms before the public health community and can inform diagnosis without tests. In computer vision, EfficientDet-D7 has achieved the state of the art in object detection with up to 9 times fewer model parameters than the best in class and can run up to 4 times faster on GPUs and up to 11 times faster on CPUs than other object detectors.

For talent, more and more AI professors are departing US universities for technology companies such as Google, DeepMind, Amazon, and Microsoft. This has caused a reduction of graduate entrepreneurship across 69 US universities. Foreign graduates of US AI PhD programs are most likely to end up in large companies, whereas American citizens are more likely to end up in startups or academia. The Eindhoven University of Technology (TUE) has committed €100M to create a new AI institute, and Abu Dhabi opened the "world's first AI university." In the AI job market, the number of jobs posted in 2020 is declining due to the COVID-19 pandemic. But the overall demand still outstrips the supply of AI talent. According to `Indeed.com`'s US data, there are almost three times more job postings than job views for AI-related roles. Job postings also grew 12 times faster than job viewings from late 2016 to late 2018.

For industry, major pharmaceutical companies have adopted AI for drug discovery, and AI-based drug discovery startups have raised millions of dollars. Major self-driving companies have raised nearly $7 billion in investments since July 2019. UK-based Graphcore released its Mk2 intelligence processing unit (IPU) processor. IPU is a relatively new type of processors compared to the traditional CPUs and GPUs. Mk2 IPU packs about 60 billion transistors onto an 800 mm^2 die using a 7 nm process—the most complex processor ever made. IPU has 16 times faster training times for image classification than NVIDIA's GPU yet is 12 times cheaper. For enterprises, AI continues to drive revenue in sales and marketing while reducing costs in supply chain management and manufacturing.

For policy makers, the ethical issues of AI have become a mainstream. Face recognition is widely used around the world and remains to be the most controversial AI technology. There were several high-profile examples of wrongful arrests due to misuse of face recognition. The pressure has been building to regulate AI applications. Two of the leading AI conferences, NeurIPS and ICLR, have both proposed new ethical principles. AI has also promoted more nationalism with many governments increasingly planning to scrutinize the acquisitions of AI companies.

For prediction, in the coming year, the race to build larger language models continues, and soon we will have the first model with 10 trillion parameters. There will be increasing investment in military AI, and a wave of defense-based AI startups will collectively raise $100 million. One of the leading AI-first drug discovery startups will be valued at more than $1 billion. Google's DeepMind will make another major breakthrough in structural biology and drug discovery beyond AlphaFold. Facebook will make a major breakthrough in augmented and virtual reality with 3D computer vision. Finally, NVIDIA will *not* be able to complete its acquisition of Arm.

1.8   AI Resources

If you want to know more technical details of AI or just want to keep up with the latest innovations and discoveries, the following are a few good resources:

Google

```
https://ai.googleblog.com/
```

```
https://research.google/pubs/?area=algorithms-and-
    theory&team=brain&team=ai-fundamentals-applications
```

DeepMind

```
https://deepmind.com/blog?filters=%7B%22category%22:%5B%22Research
    %22%5D%7D
```

```
https://deepmind.com/research?filters=%7B%22collection%22:%5B%22
    Publications%22%5D%7D
```

Facebook AI

```
https://ai.facebook.com/results/?q&content_types[0]
   =publication&sort_by=most_recent&view=list&page=1
```

```
https://ai.facebook.com/blog/
```

Microsoft

```
https://www.microsoft.com/en-us/research/research-
   area/artificial-intelligence/?facet%5Btax%5D%5B
   msr-research-area%5D%5B0%5D=13556&sort_by=most-recent
```

MIT

```
https://news.mit.edu/topic/artificial-intelligence2
```

```
https://www.technologyreview.com/topic/artificial-intelligence/
```

Stanford

```
http://ai.stanford.edu/blog/
```

Berkeley

```
https://bair.berkeley.edu/blog/
```

Leading AI Conferences

- **NeurIPS:** `https://papers.nips.cc/`
- **RecSys:** `https://recsys.acm.org/recsys20/accepted-contributions/`
- **KDD:** `https://www.kdd.org/kdd2020/accepted-papers`
- **ICLR:** `https://iclr.cc/virtual_2020/papers.html?filter=keywords`

Latest on arXiv

```
https://arxiv.org/search/advanced
```

Paper with Code's Browse State-of-the-Art Page

This is one of my favorite web resources. At Paper with Code, you can browse
the state of AI in a number of different applications, such as computer
vision, natural language processing, medical, speech, time series, audio,
and much more. As shown in Figure 1.11, it has 3,711 benchmarks; 1,942
tasks; 3,234 datasets; and 39,567 papers with code.

Towards Data Science and Medium

This is another one of my favorite web resources. Towards Data Science is a
Medium publication for sharing concepts, ideas, and code. Towards Data
Science Inc. is a corporation registered in Canada. With Medium, it pro-
vides a platform for thousands of people to exchange ideas and expand

their understanding of data science. It is free to read a limited number of articles per month, but you have to register and pay if you want unlimited access. For more details, visit these resources:

`https://towardsdatascience.com/`

`https://medium.com/`

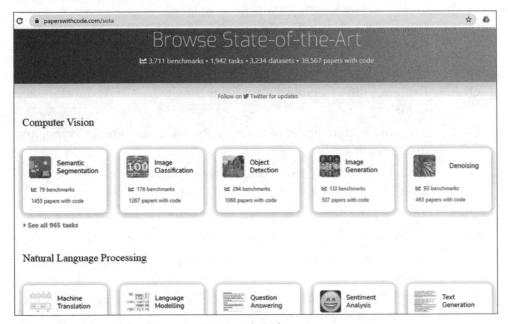

Figure 1.11: State-of-the-Art page at Paper with Code

(Source: `https://paperswithcode.com/sota`)

1.9   Summary

This chapter provided a bird's-eye overview of AI. AI is a science and technology research field that aims to make machines do intelligent things, similar to the natural intelligence exhibited by humans and animals.

AI can be traced back to the 1940s–1950s when the British mathematician Alan Turing proposed the famous Turing test, also known as the *imitation game*. AI as a research discipline was established at a workshop at Dartmouth College in 1956.

AI development can be generally divided into three periods in history; 1950–1980, focused on neural networks, or artificial neural networks; 1980–2010, focused on machine learning; and 2010–present, focused on deep learning. Deep learning is currently the hottest research topic in AI, where GPUs are widely used.

AI winters are the periods when research funding and activities have been dramatically reduced. So far, there have been two AI winters, in the 1970s and 1980s. AI hype is when AI fails to achieve what it promises.

AI can be generally divided into three types: narrow AI, general AI, and super AI. Singularity is the point at which AI overtakes human intelligence.

AI can also be divided into edge AI and cloud AI.

1.10   Chapter Review Questions

Q1.1.   What is AI? Show a few examples of AI applications in your daily life.

Q1.2.   What is the Turing test, and what is the imitation game?

Q1.3.   Explain, with a suitable diagram, the three stages of AI development in history.

Q1.4.   Explain the differences of neural networks, machine learning, and deep learning.

Q1.5.   What are AI hypes? Use a diagram to explain the different stages of an AI hype. What are AI winters?

Q1.6.   What are the three types of AI? What is the singularity?

Q1.7.   What are the differences between edge AI and cloud AI?

Q1.8.   Search the Internet and list your own top 10 key moments of AI in history.

Q1.9.   Search the Internet and list your own "current state of AI" and give your own predictions for AI.

Q1.10.   Are you optimistic or pessimistic about the future of AI, and why?

AI Development Tools

*"Success in creating AI would be the biggest event in human history.
Unfortunately, it might also be the last, unless we learn how to avoid the risks."*
—Stephen Hawking (British theoretical physicist)

2.1   AI Hardware Tools

As an old proverb says, "He who wants to do a good job must sharpen his tools first." You will also need a set of tools if you want to develop AI applications. This includes both hardware and software. Hardware mainly means the computer. As AI requires a certain amount of processing power, you will need a powerful laptop or desktop computer.

Standard Computers   For a beginner, a current standard computer is sufficient, normally including an Intel or AMD CPU with a 2 GHz clock, 8 GB RAM, 500 GB hard drive, and a current Windows, Mac, or Linux operating system. The cost is usually around $500. You can easily search the Internet for *best-selling laptops* or *best-selling desktops* to find your ideal computer.

Computers with GPUs   For a more advanced user, if you want to train more data or build more complicated, larger AI models, you will need a more advanced computer, i.e., a computer with a graphics processing unit (GPU). That typically includes a CPU with 8 cores, 32 GB RAM, 1 TB hard drive, and most importantly an NVIDIA GeForce RTX 1080 (or 2080) Series 8GB GPU. GPUs, originally developed for video games, have been increasingly used in machine learning and deep learning. GPUs can significantly speed up the calculations, thanks to their massive parallel processes. We will discuss more about GPUs in Chapter 12. A prebuilt computer with a GPU is usually around $3,000, but you can get it much cheaper if you build it yourself.

Computers with FPGAs   Field Programmable Gate Array (FPGA) is also increasingly being used in AI. Altera and Xilinx are the two most well-known FPGA manufacturers. Acquiring Altera in 2015, Intel has since developed many FPGA-based AI applications. In 2018, for example, Intel achieved 3,700 frames per second processing with its Arria 10 GX 1150 FPGA. A computer with the Intel Arria 10 GX FPGA can easily cost more than $5,000. For more details about Intel Arria FPGA, check these resources:

```
https://arxiv.org/ftp/arxiv/papers/1806/1806.11547.pdf
https://www.intel.co.uk/content/www/uk/en/products/programmable/
fpga/arria-10.html
```

We will also discuss more about FPGA in Chapter 12.

Graphcore's IPUs   In addition to GPUs and FPGAs, there is another new form of AI computing hardware: Graphcore's massively parallel intelligence processing unit (IPU). Graphcore is a young British company based in Bristol and was founded in 2016 by Simon Knowles and Nigel Toon. In July 2020, Graphcore unveiled its second-generation processor using a 7 nm process, which packs about 60 billion transistors on a 800-square-millimeter integrated circuit with 1,472 computing cores and 900 MB of local memory. As mentioned in Chapter 1, IPUs can run much faster than GPUs and cost much less. For more details, visit this resource:

```
https://www.graphcore.ai/
```

2.2   AI Software Tools

Software tools mainly depend on your choice of programming languages, such as C/C++, Java, C#, Python, Matlab, Ruby, R, Julia, Go, and so on.

C and C++ are the most popular software programming languages. Software written in C/C++ can run much faster than those written in many other

programming languages. Many AI libraries, such as OpenCV (`https://opencv`
`.org/`) for computer vision and YOLO (`https://pjreddie.com/darknet/yolo/`)
for object detection, are written in C/C++. To use C/C++ in AI development,
you can use a number of libraries:

- Google TensorFlow (`https://github.com/tensorflow/tensorflow`)
- Caffe (`https://github.com/intel/caffe`)
- Microsoft Cognitive Toolkit (CNTK) (`https://docs.microsoft.com/`
  `en-us/cognitive-toolkit/`)
- MLPACK Library (`https://www.mlpack.org/`)
- SHARK Library (`https://github.com/Shark-ML/Shark`)
- OpenNN (`https://www.opennn.net/`)

Java is another popular language. All apps on Android phones are written
in Java. To use Java in AI development, you can use the following libraries:

- Weka (`https://www.cs.waikato.ac.nz/ml/weka/`)
- Deeplearning4j (`https://deeplearning4j.org/`)

C# is popular for developing Windows desktop graphical user interface (GUI)
programs. With C#, you can use the following libraries:

- Emgu CV (`http://www.emgu.com/wiki/index.php/Main_Page`)
- ML.NET (`https://dotnet.microsoft.com/apps/machinelearning-ai/`
  `ml-dotnet`

Python is probably the most widely used programming language today.
Unlike compiled languages such as C/C++ and Java, Python is an interpreted
programming language. This means you don't need to compile the Python
code to run it. Python code is executed line by line. So even if there is an error
in the Python code, it will execute the lines before the error and stop only at
the point where the error is.

To use Python in AI development, you can use a number of libraries such
as Numpy, Pandas, Matplotlib, and NLTK. You can also use a number of open
source frameworks, such as the following:

- Scikit-Learn (`https://scikit-learn.org/stable/`)
- Keras (`https://keras.io/`)
- Google TensorFlow (`https://github.com/tensorflow/tensorflow`)
- Facebook's PyTorch (`https://pytorch.org/`)
- Caffe2 (`https://caffe2.ai/`)
- Baidu's Paddle (`https://github.com/PaddlePaddle/Paddle`)

MATLAB is popular among students as many universities/colleges have chosen the site license. This means it is free for students and staff to use. One of its best features is its workspace, which allows users to view the content and trace variables used. MATLAB is a really great tool for learning and offers a number of toolboxes for AI development.

- Statistics and Machine Learning Toolbox (`https://uk.mathworks.com/products/statistics.html`)

- Deep Learning Toolbox (`https://uk.mathworks.com/products/deep-learning.html`)

- Reinforcement Learning Toolbox (`https://uk.mathworks.com/products/reinforcement-learning.html`)

- Predictive Maintenance Toolbox (`https://uk.mathworks.com/products/predictive-maintenance.html`)

- Text Analytics Toolbox (`https://uk.mathworks.com/products/text-analytics.html`)

MATLAB Online allows you to use MATLAB from your web browser. This is excellent for online teaching and remoting learning.

`https://matlab.mathworks.com/`

MATLAB also provides support for using GPUs and FPGAs in AI development. Check out this interesting post on how to perform image classification with just 11 lines of MATLAB code:

`https://blogs.mathworks.com/pick/2017/03/03/deep-learning-in-11-lines-of-matlab-code/`

The R programming language is relatively new and is widely used for statistical analysis and graphics. R is a free software and supported by the R Foundation for Statistical Computing. It includes algorithms for machine learning, linear regression, time series, and statistical inference. For more details, visit this site:

`https://www.r-project.org/`

The Julia programming language is also relatively new and is designed for high-level, high-performance, dynamic programming. Julia is well suited for numerical analysis and computational science. For more details, visit this site:

`https://julialang.org/`

The Go programming language was developed at Google by Robert Griesemer, Rob Pike, and Ken Thompson in 2007. It is similar to the C programming language, and it was designed to build simple, reliable, and efficient software. One of main attractions of the Go programming language is that you can easily create an executable file with it. For more details, visit this site:

`https://golang.org/`

Figure 2.1 shows the interesting trends in the various programming languages in recent years. The three traditionally most common programming languages, C/C++, C#, and Java, have decreasing usage but remain prominent, while JavaScript and R are stagnant, and Python is rising fast, beginning to overtake C/C++, C#, and Java. Julia and Go usage remain relatively low. This web app was developed using Python and Streamlit (`https://www.streamlit.io/`); we will show you how to develop such apps later in this book.

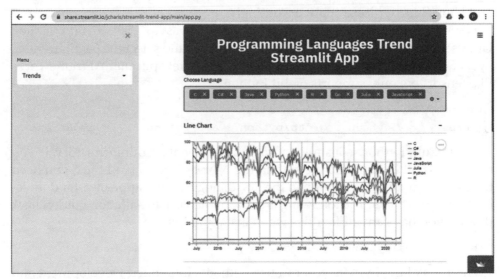

Figure 2.1: The popularity trends of different programming languages

(Source: `https://share.streamlit.io/jcharis/streamlit-trend-app/main/app.py`)

In this book, we will focus only on Python, simply because it is the most popular programming language for AI development.

2.3   Introduction to Python

Python was developed by Guido van Rossum, a Dutch programmer, at Centrum Wiskunde & Informatica (CWI) in the Netherlands in the late 1980s. Python was created as a general-purpose programming language and first released to the public in 1991. Van Rossum chose the name Python after the famous British comedy group Monty Python in the 1970s. Like MATLAB, Python is easy to use, you do not need to define variables and worry about the types of variables, and Python can automatically figure out the most appropriate variable type. Python is also an interpreted, high-level programming language. This differs from other compiled programming languages, such as C/C++, Fortran, and Java, which require you to compile your source code into binary code before it can be executed. With Python and MATLAB, your code is executed line by line. Python is the most popular programming language for machine learning and deep learning.

To use Python, you must first download and install Python on your computer. There are two main versions, version 2 and version 3. We recommend installing version 3. The latest version is 3.9.7, but since many online examples are based on older versions, we will use Python 3.6.8 in this book. We will rely on the Windows operating systems. For other operating systems, such as Mac and Unix/Linux, please adapt accordingly.

For Windows, the default installer `python-3.6.8.exe` is a 32-bit installer. Unless you are using a really old computer, you should select the 64-bit installer, `python-3.6.8-amd64.exe`. It's worth noting that a few popular AI frameworks like tensorflow only supports 64-bit Python.

```
https://www.python.org/downloads/
https://www.python.org/ftp/python/3.6.8/python-3.6.8-amd64.exe
```

By default, Python is installed into your personal account directory. If you want to install Python into the standard `C:\` or `C:\Program Files\`, you need to select Customize Installation in the first dialog box that appears after double-clicking the installer. The following is a comprehensive installation guide; check it out if you have any difficulties when installing Python:

```
https://realpython.com/installing-python/
```

After installing Python, you can use Python's Integrated Development and Learning Environment (IDLE) to edit, debug, and run Python code. See Figure 2.2.

Next, you will also need to download and install the following SciPy libraries:

- **Numpy:** For dealing with N-dimensional array data
- **Pandas:** For reading data files and analyzing data
- **Matplotlib:** For plotting data
- **SciPy:** For scientific computing
- **iPython:** For enhanced interactive console
- **Jupyter:** For a web-based Python editor
- **SymPy:** For symbolic mathematics
- **Nose:** For easier testing

See the SciPy website for more details:

```
https://www.scipy.org/install.html
```

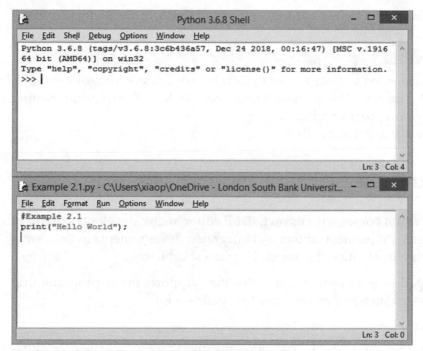

Figure 2.2: Python's IDLE (Python 3.6.8 64-bit) shell (top) and editor (bottom)

The installation process starts by typing the following commands in the Windows Command Prompt window:

```
python -m pip install numpy scipy matplotlib ipython jupyter pandas
sympy nose
```

or simply just typing the following:

```
pip install numpy scipy matplotlib ipython jupyter pandas sympy nose
```

Next, you will need to install the Scikit-Learn library for machine learning. This can be easily done by typing the following commands in the console window:

```
pip install scikit-learn
```

Finally, you will need to install the Keras, TensorFlow, and PyTorch libraries for deep learning. You can do this by typing the following commands in the console window:

```
pip install keras tensorflow torch torchvision opencv-python
```

The previous commands will install the latest version of the libraries. If you do not want the latest version, you can also specify the version you want to install. Here's an example:

```
pip install keras==2.3.1
pip install tensorflow==2.0.0
```

You can list what libraries have been installed by typing the following command in the console window:

```
pip list
```

You will also need to install other Python libraries as you progress through this book. But for now, this is enough to get you started with AI programming using the Python programming language.

You are ready to get started!

2.4   Python Development Environments

Although Python comes with its own IDLE editor, many developers prefer to use third-party Python text editors and integrated development environments (IDEs) to bring in additional features. Here is a short list:

- **Notepad++** is a popular text editor that supports many programming languages such as Python. I use Notepad++ a lot.

  ```
  https://notepad-plus-plus.org/downloads/
  ```

- **TextPad** is another similar text editor. TextPad and Notepad++ are popular with Windows users.

  ```
  https://www.textpad.com/home
  ```

- **Sublime Text** is a generic text editor, first released in 2007. It supports 44 major programming languages, including Python. It is a popular text editor among Mac and Linux users.

  ```
  http://www.sublimetext.com/
  ```

- **Atom/Atom-IDE** is a relatively new cross-platform general-purpose IDE. Atom has attractive features such as syntax highlighting, autocompletion, and a fully customizable interface.

  ```
  https://atom.io/
  ```

- **PyCharm** is a Python IDE for professional developers. It has features such as syntax highlighting, autocompletion, and live code verification.

  ```
  https://www.jetbrains.com/pycharm/
  ```

- **Spyder** is a free, cross-platform Python IDE, with features such as syntax highlighting and autocompletion. It also integrates many libraries such as Matplotlib, Numpy, IPython, and Scipy. It has a variable explorer, similar to MATLAB's workspace, which allows you to view the details of variables.

  ```
  https://github.com/spyder-ide/spyder
  ```

- **Visual Studio Code**, also called VS Code, is a cross-platform software IDE developed by Microsoft. Not to be confused with Visual Studio, VS Code is small but complete, and the software is open source under the MIT license.

  https://code.visualstudio.com/

- **Jupyter** is a web-based Python IDE that allows you to edit and run Python code from a web browser. I have found Jupyter to be remarkably easy to use. Many people believe that Jupyter is a computing notebook for data scientists. To install Jupyter, simply type the following `pip install` commands into your terminal window:

```
pip install jupyter
```

  To launch the Jupyter notebook in your web browser, simply type the following command. This will launch a web page (`http://localhost:8888/`) from which you can create, open, and run Jupyter notebooks.

```
Jupyter notebook
```

  Python program files have the extension of `.py`, and Jupyter notebooks have the extension `.ipynb`. You can make the `.ipynb` file double-clickable (i.e., so it can be opened with a double-click) in Windows by installing the following two libraries:

```
pip install nbopen
python -m nbopen.install_win
```

  For more details about Jupyter, visit this site:

  https://jupyter.org/

- **Google Colaboratory**, also called Google Colab, is a web-based Python IDE, based on Jupyter, that allows you to edit and run Python code from a web browser. This is one of my favorite Python development environments. You need a Google account to sign in to use it. Once logged in, you have everything you need and are ready to start programming in Python. You don't have to worry about which Python version to install, which Python libraries to install, and so on. One of the Google Colab features I like the most is the support for CPU, GPU, and TPU computing. So, you can run your code on GPUs and TPUs for free.

  https://colab.research.google.com/

- **Kaggle Notebook** is another web-based Python IDE, similar to Google Colab. But Kaggle also provides a huge number of datasets and runs many AI challenges, making it easier to develop new algorithms and train new models. There are also tons of other people's projects that you can copy and edit, and it is a great place to learn. Kaggle also provides support for CPU and GPU computing, so it is one of my favorites.

```
https://www.kaggle.com/
```

■ **Baidu's AI Studio** is a one-stop online development platform based on PaddlePaddle, Baidu's proprietary deep learning framework. At AI Studio, there are datasets, competitions, courses, and many projects to share. You can also create your own online projects using Jupyter notebooks, similar to Colab and Kaggle.

```
https://aistudio.baidu.com/aistudio/index?lang=en
https://www.paddlepaddle.org.cn/
```

Here are few more online Python/Jupyter editors:

■ **Deepnote** is a Google Colab alternative but has some interesting features such as real-time collaboration, no interruptions for long-running tasks, and no cost.

```
https://beta.deepnote.com/
```

■ **Binder** and **Gesis Notebooks** are also popular Jupyter online notebooks. For example, on the Scikit-Learn website, you can run many sample codes online using Binder Notebooks.

```
https://notebooks.gesis.org/
https://mybinder.org/
```

■ **Paperspace Gradient** is another Jupyter online notebook. Compared to the Google Colab alternative, it has faster memory, persistent notebooks, longer training time, and a larger dataset.

```
https://www.paperspace.com/console/gradient
```

■ When we talk about Python development environments, we have to talk about **Anaconda**. Many beginners get confused by it, but Anaconda is simply a scientific computing platform for Python and R programming languages. It also aims to simplify package management and deployment. It is cross-platform and comes with a set of libraries such as Matplotlib, Numpy, IPython, and Scipy, as well as a set of editors/IDEs such as Spyder, Jupyter, VS Code, and so on. Anaconda is basically a one-stop shop; it has everything you need for Python development. So, with many Python tutorials, the first thing you'll be asked to do is to install Anaconda. From Anaconda's graphical user interface, shown in Figure 2.3, you can launch all the tools you need. However, Anaconda is quite large and requires a lot of disk space. Therefore, it is optional for this book.

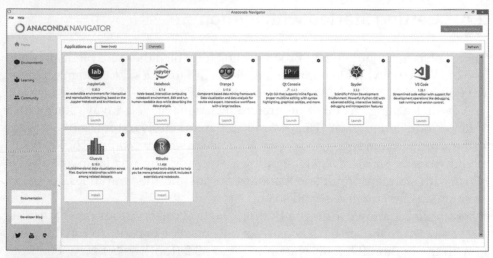

Figure 2.3: Anaconda user interface

(Source: `https://upload.wikimedia.org/wikipedia/commons/f/f4/Anaconda`
`.Starting_page.png`)

> Anaconda claims to be the most popular Python distribution platform in
> the world with more than 20 million users worldwide.
>
> `https://www.anaconda.com/`

We also need to talk about Python virtual environments. If you are writing
simple Python programs, you would not need this. But if you are writing more
complicated Python programs and need to use third-party software, you will
find that different software uses different versions of Python libraries and
packages. For example, some software code works with Google TensorFlow
version 1 and other code works with Google TensorFlow version 2. Soon you
will find yourself with many version conflicts. The solution to this is to use a
Python virtual environment, where you create an isolated Python environment
for each project so your computer can run multiple projects that require different versions of Python libraries. You can create a Python virtual environment
by using Anaconda and Virtualenv. Compared with Anaconda, Virtualenv is
much smaller and easier to use. See Appendix D for how to install and use a
Python virtual environment. For more details about Virtualenv, visit this site:

`https://virtualenv.pypa.io/en/latest/`

In this book, we will mainly use Python's IDLE, as well as a mixture of Jupyter,
Kaggle, and Google Colab.

2.4   Getting Started with Python

This book is not about Python programming for which there are plenty of good books. We do not want to reinvent the wheel. But for the sake of completeness, we will provide a simple, short introduction to Python here.

As with learning any other programming language, you always start with a "Hello World" program. A "Hello World" program simply outputs Hello World! to the screen. In computing, the screen is known as *standard output*. The keyboard is known as the *standard input*. Learning a new programming language always starts with standard input and standard output and then variables, loops, if else statements, functions, and so on.

Example 2.1 shows a simple Python "Hello World" program that prints Hello World! to the screen. It consists of only one line of code. To run this code, launch the Python IDLE (as shown in Figure 2.2 (top)), select New File from the File menu, and a new editor window will appear (as shown in Figure 2.2 (bottom)). Then type the code shown in Example 2.1, and select Run Module from the editor's Run menu, or press the F5 key, to run the code. The results will be displayed in the Python IDLE shell.

EXAMPLE 2.1: THE HELLO.PY PROGRAM

```
#Example 2.1
print("Hello World!")
```

Python uses # for a single-line comments and a pair of ''' for multiple-line comments. Example 2.2 shows an example.

EXAMPLE 2.2: THE HELLO2.PY PROGRAM

```
#Example 2.2
'''
This is a multiple line
comments.
'''
print("Hello World")
```

A cool feature of print is that you can embed mathematical functions inside it, modify the print statement as shown next, and see what you get:

```
print("Hello World"*5)
```

Python supports a number of types of variables, like MATLAB. You do not have to declare the variables, you do not have to specify the types, and you can just use them directly. Python does not require a ; at the end of each statement. Example 2.3 shows an example.

EXAMPLE 2.3: THE `HELLO3.PY` **PROGRAM**

```
#Example 2.3
a = 5
b = 7
c = a + b
print("c = " , c)

d = 'x'
e = 'y'
print(d + e)

f = "Hello"
g = "World"
l = f + " " + g
print(l)
```

For more complex structures, such as loops, selections, or functions, instead of using { and } or `Begin` and `End` to group the structure like other programming languages, Python uses `:` and indentation to distinguish different structures. This forces users to write code with proper indentations. By default, there are four spaces for each level of indentation. Example 2.4 shows a simple `for` loop; you can see the `:` character and can probably figure out that the two `print` statements are on different structural levels. The first `print` statement is inside the `for` loop, while the second `print` statement is outside the loop.

EXAMPLE 2.4: THE `LOOP.PY` **PROGRAM**

```
#Example 2.4
for i in range(5):
    print(i)
print("Finished")
```

Example 2.5 shows a nested `for` loop example; again, the three `print` statements are at different structure levels.

EXAMPLE 2.5: THE `LOOP2.PY` **PROGRAM**

```
#Example 2.5
for i in range(5):
    for j in range(5):
        x = i * j
        print(x)
    print("Inner Loop Finished")
print("Outer Loop Finished")
```

Example 2.6 shows a `while` loop example, which will continue as long as the test condition `x < 5` is satisfied.

EXAMPLE 2.6: THE `LOOP3.PY` **PROGRAM**

```
#Example 2.6
x = 0
while x < 5:
    x = x + 1
    print(x)
print("Finished")
```

Example 2.7 shows an `if else` example, which will execute different lines of the code depending on the value of `x`.

EXAMPLE 2.7: THE `IFELSE.PY` **PROGRAM**

```
#Example 2.7
x = 60
if x >= 70:
    print("Excellent")
elif x >= 60:
    print("Good")
else:
    print("OK")
```

Example 2.8 shows an example of a Python function, in which a function, `add (x,y)`, is defined, and then the function is called. The function starts with the keyword `def` and has two input parameters, `x` and `y`. The function adds `x` and `y` together, passes the value to `z`, and then returns the value z.

EXAMPLE 2.8: THE `FUNCS.PY` **PROGRAM**

```
#Example 2.8

def add (x,y):
    z = x + y
    return z

t = add(30, 20)
print(t)
```

Example 2.9 shows a Python example to find the maximum value in an array, also called a *list*. It first defines a function, called `maxarray (xs)`, which has an array-type input parameter named `xs`. The function uses a `for` loop and an `if` statement to find out the maximum value. Then it creates an array and calls the function. Python uses [and] to refer to arrays and uses , to separate each element of the array.

EXAMPLE 2.9: THE ARRAY.PY **PROGRAM**

```
#Example 2.9

def maxarray (xs):
    m = xs[0]
    for x in xs:
        if m < x:
            m = x
    return m

data = [0,1,2,3,4,5]
t = maxarray(data)
print(t)
```

EXERCISE 2.1

Modify the Python program from Example 2.9 to create a function called minarray(xs) to find out the minimum value of an array.

EXERCISE 2.2

Modify the Python program from Example 2.9 to create a function called sortarray(xs) to sort the array in ascending order.

Example 2.10 shows how to read text from the keyboard. In the print statement, a single quote (') and a double quote (") are the same.

EXAMPLE 2.10: THE INPUT.PY **PROGRAM**

```
#Example 2.10
print('What is your name? ')
x = input()
print('Hello ' + x + "!")
```

This is the output of the program:

```
What is your name?
Perry
Hello Perry!
```

Example 2.11 shows how to read text from the keyboard and then use the `int()` function to convert it to an integer, perform some calculations, and display the results. You can also use `float()` to convert text to floats, which are the numbers with decimal points, and use the `str()` function to convert the numbers to text. In Python, +, −, *, and / represent addition, subtraction, multiplication, and division, respectively. ** represents a square.

EXAMPLE 2.11: THE `INPUT2.PY` PROGRAM

```
#Example 2.11
print('Input a number: ')
x = input()
y = int(x)
y = y ** 2
print('The square of ' + str(x) + " is " + str(y))
```

This is the output of the program:

```
Input a number:
4
The square of 4 is 16
```

EXERCISE 2.3

Modify the Python programs from Example 2.11 so that it reads a float number from the keyboard. You can also use `float()` to convert text to float numbers, which are the numbers with decimal points. Then calculate the square and display it on the screen.

EXERCISE 2.4

Based on the Python programs in Examples 2.10 and 2.11, write a Python program that reads the name, the age, and the marks from the keyboard. The age should be read as an integer, and marks should be read as a float number. Then display them on the screen.

Example 2.12 shows how to read a list of numbers from the keyboard. It first reads the numbers as text into a variable called `s`, then uses the `split()` function to split it into a number of pieces, and finally uses the `map` function to map each piece into an integer.

EXAMPLE 2.12: THE `INPUTLIST.PY` PROGRAM

```
#Example 2.12
s = input("Input a list of numbers: ")
numbers = list(map(int, s.split()))
print(numbers)
```

This is the output of the program:

```
Input a list of numbers: 1 2 3 4
[1, 2, 3, 4]
```

Python has a useful Math library. Example 2.13 shows some commonly used functions of the library. You need to use `import math` to import the library first and then use dot notation, such as `math.pi` and `math.sqrt` to call the functions.

EXAMPLE 2.13: THE `MATH.PY` PROGRAM

```python
#Example 2.13
import math

r =5
cir = 2 * math.pi * r
print('The circumference is ' + str(cir))

x = 5
y = math.sqrt(x)
print("The square root of " + str(x) +" is " + str(y))

x = 7
y = math.factorial(x)
print("The factorial of " + str(x) +" is " + str(y))

x = 16.4
y = math.floor(x)
print("The floor of " + str(x) +" is " + str(y))

x = 16.4
y = math.ceil(x)
print("The ceiling of " + str(x) +" is " + str(y))
```

This is the output of the program:

```
The circumference is 31.41592653589793
The square root of 5 is 2.23606797749979
The factorial of 7 is 5040
The floor of 16.4 is 16
The ceiling of 16.4 is 17
```

For more details about the Math library, check out this interesting tutorial from `RealPython.com`:

```
https://realpython.com/python-math-module/
```

EXERCISE 2.5

Based on the Python programs from Examples 2.10 and 2.13, write a Python program that reads a list of float numbers from the keyboard, then uses the `math.sin()` function to calculate the sine value of the numbers, and finally displays the results on the screen.

Plotting is important for visualizing the data. Python has a powerful Matplotlib library, similar to MATLAB's plot function. Example 2.14 shows an example of using this library to plot. It first uses `import matplotlib.pyplot as plt` to import the library's `pyplot` function. It also imports another useful library, Numpy, which is helpful for dealing with numeric arrays. It then creates an array of 100 numbers called x using the `range` function, x = 0, 1, 2, 3 . . . 99, converts x to a Numpy array with `np.array()`, scales x between 0 and 2π, with a step size of 0.01. Numpy also has a π-function called `np.pi`, similar to `math.pi`. Then, it calculates the sine value of the array x using the `np.sin()` function. Note that `math.sin()` is not used here because it is only for scalars. Finally, it uses the `plt.plot()` function to plot the sine curve and uses the `plt.show()` function to show the plot.

EXAMPLE 2.14: THE `PLOT.PY` PROGRAM

```
#Example 2.14
import matplotlib.pyplot as plt
import numpy as np

x = [i for i in range(100)]
x = np.array(x)
x = 2 * np.pi* x * 0.01
y = np.sin(x)
plt.plot(x,y)
plt.title('Sin Plot')
plt.xlabel('x')
plt.ylabel('Sin')
plt.show()
```

Figure 2.4 shows the output of Example 2.14, which plots the `sin()` function from the range [0, 2π].

Example 2.15 shows another example of plotting. In this example, Numpy's `linspace` function is used to create an array of values x ranging from -π to π, with 50 data points in between. It then calculates the sine and cosine values of the values x and plots the data with different colors and different makers, and it also displays the legend.

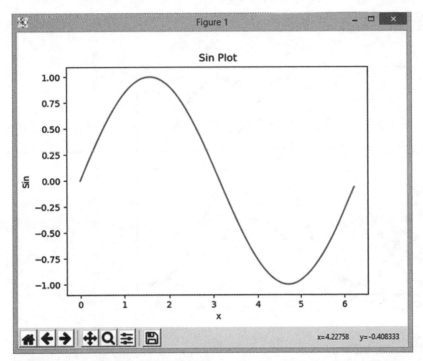

Figure 2.4: The output of Example 2.14

EXAMPLE 2.15: THE `PLOT2.PY` PROGRAM

```
#Example 2.15
import numpy as np
import matplotlib.pyplot as plt

x = np.linspace(-np.pi, np.pi, 50)
y1 = np.sin(x)
y2 = np.cos(x)
plt.plot(x, y1, color = 'blue', marker = "s", label='Sin')
plt.plot(x, y2, color = 'red', marker = "o", label='Cos')
plt.legend()
plt.show()
```

Figure 2.5 shows the output of Example 2.15, which plots the `sin()` and `cos()` functions from the range between -π and π.

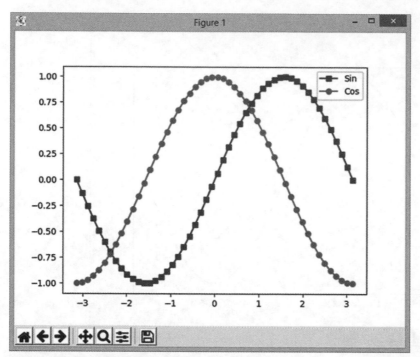

Figure 2.5: The output of Example 2.15

EXERCISE 2.6

Based on the Python programs from Examples 2.14 and 2.15, write a Python program that plots different math functions, such as $y = 3x + 4$ and $y = 2x2 + 1$ and $y = x3 + 9$ on the same graph using different colors and also displays the legend.

For more details about the Matplotlib library, access the following website: `https://matplotlib.org/tutorials/introductory/pyplot.html`

Last but not least is data file reading and writing. In machine learning and deep learning, the most commonly used data file format is Comma Separated Values (CSV). A CSV file is just plain text with many rows of data, and each row has a fixed number of columns separated by commas. CSV files can easily be imported into Microsoft Excel as a spreadsheet.

The easiest way to create a CSV file and read a CSV file is to use the Pandas library. Example 2.16 shows how to create a CSV file. It first creates an array called `data` that contains two columns of values, `Name` and `Age`. It then creates a dataframe named `df` from the array `data`. Finally, it displays the dataframe and saves the data into a CSV file named `test.csv` by using the `to_csv()` function. The dataframe has an extra index column (see Example 2.16); you can use `index=False` to avoid saving the index column in the CSV file.

EXAMPLE 2.16: THE `DATA.PY` **PROGRAM**

```
#Example 2.16
import pandas as pd

data = {'Name':    ['Tony','Robert','John','Alice'],
        'Age':     [18,24,19,21],
        }

df = pd.DataFrame (data, columns = ['Name','Age'])

print (df)
df.to_csv('test.csv', index=False)
```

The following is the output of the program, displaying the contents of the dataframe named `df`. Note that there is an additional index column.

```
     Name   Age
0    Tony    18
1  Robert    24
2    John    19
3   Alice    21
```

This is the content of the `test.csv` file:

```
Name,Age
Tony,18
Robert,24
John,19
Alice,21
```

Example 2.17 shows how to read a CSV file. It uses the `read_csv()` function to read a CSV file named `test.csv` into a dataframe named `df`.

EXAMPLE 2.17: THE `DATA2.PY` **PROGRAM**

```
#Example 2.17
import pandas
df = pandas.read_csv('test.csv')
print (df)
```

For more details about the CSV files, see this interesting tutorial from `RealPython.com`:

`https://realpython.com/python-csv/`

Excel data files are popular among Windows users. Similar to CSV files, the Python Pandas library can also easily read and write Excel files. But you need to install the xlsxwriter library by typing `pip install xlsxwriter` at the command line of your terminal program. Example 2.18 shows how to create a dataframe and save it to an Excel file. It uses the functions `ExcelWriter()` and `to_excel()` to save the dataframe variable `df` to an Excel file named `test.xlsx`.

EXAMPLE 2.18: THE `EXCEL.PY` **PROGRAM**

```
#Example 2.18
#pip install xlsxwriter

import pandas as pd

data = {'Name':     ['Tony','Robert','John','Alice'],
        'Age':      [18,24,19,21],
        }

df = pd.DataFrame (data, columns = ['Name','Age'])

print (df)
writer = pd.ExcelWriter("test.xlsx", engine='xlsxwriter')
#df.to_excel(writer, sheet_name='Sheet1',
#              startrow=7, startcol=4, header=False, index=False)
df.to_excel(writer,sheet_name = 'Sheet1', index=False)
writer.save()
```

Example 2.19 shows how to read an Excel file. It uses the `read_excel()` function to read an Excel file named `test.xlsx` into a dataframe named `df`.

EXAMPLE 2.19: THE `EXCEL2.PY` **PROGRAM**

```
#Example 2.19
#pip install xlsxwriter

import pandas

df = pandas.read_excel('test.xlsx', sheet_name='Sheet1')
print(df)
```

That is it! That is all you need to follow the exercises in this book.

If you want to learn more with Python programming, apart from books and paid courses, there are tons of free Python programming tutorials on the Internet. Here are the most popular free tutorials:

```
https://docs.python.org/3/tutorial/index.html
https://realpython.com/
https://www.learnpython.org/
https://www.geeksforgeeks.org/python-programming-language/
```

```
https://www.python.org/about/gettingstarted/
https://docs.python-guide.org/intro/learning/
https://www.w3schools.com/python/
```

The following are websites with extensive examples on Python machine learning, deep learning, and computer vision:

```
https://machinelearningmastery.com/
https://www.pyimagesearch.com/start-here/
https://pythonprogramming.net/
https://www.learnopencv.com/
https://d2l.ai/
```

2.5   AI Datasets

Many AI applications require a large amount of data. Many public datasets are available for such applications. The following is a list of datasets commonly used by AI applications:

- **UCI Machine Learning Repository** is probably the most widely used dataset for machine learning. It contains 559 datasets divided into different categories, such as classification, regression, clustering and others.

  ```
  https://archive.ics.uci.edu/ml/datasets.php
  ```

- **CIFAR-10** is a popular image dataset for image recognition. CIFAR stands for Canadian Institute for Advanced Research. The CIFAR-10 dataset consists of 60,000 32 × 32 color images in 10 classes (or categories), with 6,000 images per class. There are 50,000 training images and 10,000 test images.

  ```
  https://www.cs.toronto.edu/~kriz/cifar.html
  ```

- **ImageNet** is the largest visual database for object recognition research with more than 14 million images. At least one million of the images have object bounding boxes. The images are divided into more than 20,000 categories. However, only 1,000 non-overlapping categories are used in the ImageNet Large Scale Visual Recognition Challenge (ILSVRC).

  ```
  http://www.image-net.org/
  ```

- **COCO** (Common Objects in Context) is a large image dataset for object detection, image segmentation, and image captioning. COCO has 330,000 images (more than 200,000 labeled), 1.5 million object instances, 80 object categories, and 91 material categories.

  ```
  http://www.image-net.org/
  ```

■ **Kaggle** is a public data platform and a cloud-based workbench for data science and artificial intelligence education. Kaggle has a public data platform to provide open source datasets for researchers and runs a series of machine learning competitions. Kaggle Kernel allows users to share code and analysis in Python and R. More than 150,000 kernels (code snippets) have been shared. Kaggle also has Kaggle Learn for short AI education, as well as jobs board for employers to post machine learning and AI jobs. It has more than 1 million registered users, called Kagglers. Kaggle was acquired by Google in 2017.

```
https://www.kaggle.com/
```

■ **Google's Open Images** has a collection of 9 million images with labels from more than 6,000 categories.

```
https://ai.googleblog.com/2016/09/introducing-open-images-
dataset.html
```

■ **Labeled Faces in the Wild (LFW)** is a dataset of face photos for studying the problem of unconstrained face recognition. The original LFW dataset consists of 13,000 labeled images of faces from 5,749 people.

```
http://vis-www.cs.umass.edu/lfw/
```

■ **Quandl** is the premier source of economic and financial data. It claims to be used by more than 400,000 people, from the world's top hedge funds, asset managers, and investment banks.

```
https://www.quandl.com/
```

■ **Financial Times Market Data** provides up-to-date information on stock price indices, commodities, and foreign exchange from around the world.

```
https://markets.ft.com/data/
```

■ **US Data.Gov** is the home of U.S. government open data. The data can range from government budgets to school performance.

```
https://www.data.gov/
```

■ **US Healthcare Data** includes data about population health, diseases, drugs, and health plans.

```
https://healthdata.gov/
```

■ **EU Open Data Portal** provides access to open data published by EU institutions in the area, such as economics, employment, science, the environment, and education.

```
https://data.europa.eu/euodp/en/home
```

- **The UK Data Service** provides the UK's largest collection of social, economic, and population data.

  ```
  https://www.ukdataservice.ac.uk/
  ```

- **World Bank Open Data** covers population demographics and a huge number of economic and development indicators across the world.

  ```
  https://data.worldbank.org/
  ```

For more information about the AI datasets, check out this interesting website from Liobridge.ai, The 50 Best Free Datasets for Machine Learning:

```
https://lionbridge.ai/datasets/the-50-best-free-datasets-for-
machine-learning/
```

2.6   Python AI Frameworks

To develop Python AI applications, you need not only datasets but also open source libraries and frameworks. One of the main attractions of using Python for AI development is that there are so many resources available, many of which are open sources and free to use.

The following are commonly used Python AI frameworks:

- **Scikit-Learn** is the most widely used Python framework for machine learning. It is divided into two main categories, supervised learning and unsupervised learning. For supervised learning, it has a set of algorithms for classification and regression. For unsupervised learning, it has algorithms for clustering. You can find more details on the following website, where it is best to start with the "Getting Started" and "Tutorial" sections:

  ```
  https://scikit-learn.org/stable/
  https://scikit-learn.org/stable/getting_started.html
  https://scikit-learn.org/stable/tutorial/index.html
  ```

- **Google's TensorFlow** is undoubtedly the most widely used Python framework for AI. It is called TensorFlow because its basic data structure is a tensor, a simple multidimensional array of numbers or functions. TensorFlow is widely used for image classification, object detection, image segmentation, pose detection, text sentiment, language translation, speech recognition, and so on. It also provides TensorFlow.js, a JavsScript platform for web-based AI developments.

  ```
  https://github.com/tensorflow/tensorflow
  https://www.tensorflow.org/tutorials
  ```

- **Keras** is an open source software library that provides a Python interface for other AI libraries and frameworks. Keras is best known as the standard interface for the TensorFlow. However, Keras, as a back end, also supports many others, such as Microsoft Cognitive Toolkit, R, Theano, and PlaidML.

  https://keras.io/

- **Facebook's PyTorch** is an open source machine learning library based on the Torch library. It is developed by Facebook's AI Research Lab. PyTorch is getting more popular in recent years and has caught up with TensorFlow.

  https://pytorch.org/

- **Caffe2** (Convolutional Architecture for Fast Feature Embedding) is a well-known open source deep learning framework, originally developed by Yangqing Jia during his PhD at the University of California – Berkeley. Caffe2 is the second version of Caffe with many improvements such as large-scale distributed training, mobile deployment, and new hardware support, as well as new features such as recurrent neural networks, etc.

  https://caffe2.ai/

- **Baidu's Paddle Paddle** is an open source deep learning framework created and supported by Baidu. Paddle stands for PArallel Distributed Deep LEarning, and it provides 146 algorithms and more than 200 pretrained models. It supports the training of ultra-large deep neural networks with data sources distributed across hundreds of nodes. It is home to more than 1.5 million developers. It also offers free online AI computations, similar to Google's Colab.

  https://github.com/PaddlePaddle/Paddle

- **H2O** is a fully open source, distributed, fast, and scalable machine learning platform, and one of the best tools for any machine learning team to have when dealing with large volumes of data. It claims to be the number-one open source platform for enterprise machine learning.

  https://www.h2o.ai/

- **DeepMind** was cofounded by Demis Hassabis in September 2010. It made headlines after its AlphaGo program defeated the South Korean world champion Go player Lee Sedol in 2016. It then offered AlphaZero, a program for playing Go, chess, and shogi (Japanese chess). In 2020, it made headlines again with its AlphaFold for solving the problem of protein folding. DeepMind provides a range of examples, tools, and libraries through its GitHub site.

  https://deepmind.com/

  https://github.com/deepmind

- **OpenAI** was cofounded by Elon Musk with a more than $1 billion investment in October 2015. It is largely seen as the competitor of DeepMind. In 2016, it released the OpenAI Gym platform for reinforcement learning. In 2020, it stirred up global interest when it announced its Generative Pre-trained Transformer 3 (GPT-3) for natural language processing. GPT-3 has an astonishing 175 billion parameters.

  ```
  https://openai.com/
  ```

- **Apache MXNet** is a machine learning framework designed for both efficiency and flexibility. It has API languages such as R, Python, and Julia, and has been adopted by Amazon Web Services.

  ```
  https://github.com/dmlc/mxnet
  ```

- **OpenCV** (Open Source Computer Vision Library) is probably the most popular cross-platform and free library. It was originally developed by Intel and aimed at real-time computer vision.

  ```
  https://opencv-python-tutroals.readthedocs.io/en/latest/
  py_tutorials/py_tutorials.html
  ```

- **Scikit-image**, formerly known as Scikits.image, is a collection of algorithms for image processing. It is an open source image processing library for the Python programming language. It is built on the NumPy and SciPy libraries and contains algorithms for image segmentation, geometric transformations, color space manipulation, analysis, filtering, morphology, feature detection, and more.

  ```
  https://scikit-image.org/
  ```

There are many other libraries, platforms, and frameworks. We will introduce them in the book as we use them.

2.7   Summary

This chapter presented AI development tools, which include both hardware tools and AI software tools. For AI hardware, the concept of standard computers, computers with GPUs, computers with FPGAs, and latest IPUs from Graphcore were introduced. For AI software, a list of different programming languages was presented, such as C/C++, Java, C#, Python, Matlab, Ruby, R, Julia, and Go, with Python chosen as the main focus of this book.

This chapter also introduced the Python programming language, including download and installation, its development environments, and a short tutorial of the Python language to help you get started.

Finally, it presented commonly used AI datasets and Python AI frameworks.

2.8   Chapter Review Questions

Q2.1.   What types of computer hardware are available for AI development? Do an Internet search and find your ideal laptop/desktop computer for AI development.

Q2.2.   What programming languages can be used for AI development? List the advantages and disadvantages of each language.

Q2.3.   How is Python different from other programming languages such as C/C++ or Java?

Q2.4.   What is a Python virtual environment?

Q2.5.   What are the most commonly used datasets in AI? Search the Internet and find five other datasets.

Q2.6.   What is Scipy?

Q2.7.   What is Scikit-Learn?

Q2.8.   What is TensorFlow?

Q2.9.   What is Keras?

Q2.10.   What is PyTorch?

Q2.11.   What is Caffe2?

Q2.12.   What is the standard input and output in a Python program?

Q2.13.   What are commonly used AI datasets?

Q2.14.   What are popular Python AI frameworks?

Part

II

Machine Learning and Deep Learning

In This Part:

Part II provides a detailed introduction of machine learning and deep learning, the two most important aspects of AI.

Machine Learning

"Before we work on artificial intelligence why don't we do something about natural stupidity?"

—Steve Polyak (American Neurologist)

CHAPTER OUTLINE

3.1 Introduction

As you saw in Chapter 1, AI covers a broad area, and one of most important aspects of AI is machine learning.

Machine learning (ML) is basically a set of mathematical algorithms developed in the 1980s. Machine learning is an important subset of AI, and it is the science that aims to teach computers, or machines, to learn from data and to analyze data automatically, without human intervention. It includes a set of mathematical algorithms that can make a decision or, more accurately, predict the results for a given set of data. The term *machine learning* was coined by Arthur Samuel, an American pioneer in computer science and artificial intelligence, in 1959 when he was working at IBM. In 1997, a more modern definition of machine learning was provided by Tom Mitchell as "A computer program is said to learn from experience E with respect to some class of tasks T and performance measure P, if its performance at tasks in T, as measured by P, improves with experience E."

Machine learning can be divided into these four different categories:

- **Supervised learning:** In supervised learning, models are trained with labeled data. During the training, algorithms continuously adjust the parameters of models until the error calculated between the output and the desired output for a given input is minimized. Supervised learning is typically used in classification and regression. Classification means to identify, for a given input sample, which class (or category) something belongs to, such as dog or cat, male or female, cancer or no cancer, genuine or fake, and so on. The most popular supervised learning algorithms are the following: support vector machines, naive Bayes, linear discriminant analysis, decision trees, k-nearest neighbor algorithm, neural networks (multilayer perceptron), and similarity learning. Regression means, for the given data, fit the data with a model to get the best-fit parameters. The most popular regression algorithms are linear regression, logistic regression, and polynomial regression.

- **Unsupervised learning:** In unsupervised learning, models are fed with unlabeled data. The algorithms will study the data and divide it into groups according to features. Unsupervised learning is typically used for clustering and association. *Clustering* means dividing the data into groups. The most popular clustering algorithm is K-means clustering. *Association* means to discover rules that describe the majority portion of the data. A popular association algorithm is the Apriori algorithm.

- **Semi-supervised learning:** In semi-supervised learning, both labeled data and unlabeled data are used. This is particularly useful when not all the data can be labeled. The basic procedure is to group the data into different clusters using an unsupervised learning algorithm and then using the existing labeled data to label the rest of the unlabeled data. The most popular semi-supervised learning algorithms include self-training, generative methods, mixture models, and graph-based methods.

Semi-supervised learning can typically be used in speech analysis, internet content classification, and protein sequence classification.

■ **Reinforcement learning:** In reinforcement learning, algorithms learn to find, through trial and error, which actions can yield the maximum cumulative reward. Reinforcement learning is widely used in robotics, video gaming, and navigation.

Today, machine learning has been used in a variety of applications. In healthcare, for example, machine learning has been used for early disease detection, cancer diagnosis, and drug discovery. In social media, machine learning has been used for sentiment analysis, for example, to decide whether a comment is positive or negative. In banking, machine learning has been used for fraud detection. In e-commerce, machine learning has been used for recommending songs, movies, or products based on customers' previous shopping records.

3.2   Supervised Learning: Classifications

Supervised learning is the most important part of machine learning. Supervised learning can be used for classification and regression. We will introduce classification in this section and regression in the next section based on the popular Scikit-Learn library (`https://scikit-learn.org/`).

Classification means for a given sample you need to predict which category it belongs to. The best-known classification example in the field of machine learning is iris flower classification, which is to classify iris flowers among three species (Setosa, Versicolor, or Virginica) based on the measured length and width of the sepals and petals. Another popular classification is breast cancer classification. In this example, a set of measurement results (such as radius, area, perimeter, texture, smoothness, compactness, concavity, symmetry, and so on) of a tissue sample are given to decide whether the tissue is malignant or benign.

In machine learning, the following are commonly used terminologies. The categories of flowers, or types of breast tissue (malignant or benign), are called *classes*. The length and width of sepals and petals, or breast tissue measures, are called *features*. Data points are called *samples*, and variables in the models are called *parameters*.

■ **Class:** The categories of the data

■ **Features:** The measurements

■ **Samples:** The data points

■ **Parameters:** The variables of the model

The most popular supervised learning algorithms are support vector machines, naive Bayes, linear discriminant analysis, principal component analysis, decision trees, random forest, k-nearest neighbor, neural networks (multilayer perceptron), and so on.

Find more details about supervised learning algorithms available by using the Scikit-Learn library:

```
https://scikit-learn.org/stable/supervised_learning.html
```

Scikit-Learn Datasets

Datasets are important in machine learning. To make them easy to access, several datasets are provided with the Scikit-Learn library.

Toy Datasets

- Boston house prices dataset
- Iris plants dataset
- Diabetes dataset
- Optical recognition of handwritten digits dataset
- Linnerrud dataset
- Wine recognition dataset
- Breast cancer Wisconsin (diagnostic) dataset

Real-World Datasets

- The Olivetti faces dataset
- The 20 newsgroups text dataset
- The Labeled Faces in the Wild face recognition dataset
- Forest covertypes
- RCV1 dataset
- Kddcup 99 dataset
- California Housing dataset

There are also generated datasets; for more details, see the following:

```
https://scikit-learn.org/stable/datasets.html
```

Support Vector Machines

Support vector machine (SVM) is the best-known supervised learning algorithm. You always start machine learning with SVM. The SVM algorithm can be used for both classification and regression problems. It was developed at AT&T Bell Laboratories by Vladimir Naumovich Vapnik and his colleagues in the 1990s. It is one of the most robust prediction methods, based on the statistical learning framework.

Figure 3.1 shows a simple example of two category classification problems using SVM. You can imagine the two sets of data are two types of flowers, and horizontal and vertical axes are the values of the petals' length and width. SVM will train on this data and create a hyperplane to separate the two sets of the data. In this case, a hyperplane is a straight line. SVM adjusts the position of the hyperplane to maximize the margins to both sets of data. The data points on the margin are called the *support vectors*. This is a simple two-dimensional, linear classification problem. SVM can also work on three-dimensional, non-linear classification problems, in which cases a hyperplane could be a plain or more complex curved surface.

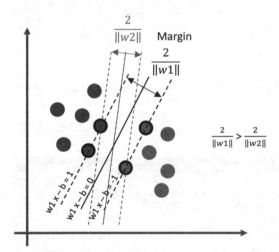

Figure 3.1: The support vector machine with two sets of data points, the hyperplane (solid line), the margin (between two dashed lines), and the support vectors (circled points on the dashed line)

The following is an interesting SVM tutorial that explains how SVM works and how to use SVM with Scikit-Learn:

```
https://www.datacamp.com/community/tutorials/svm-classification-
scikit-learn-python
```

Now let's look at some Python SVM classification examples. In this chapter, we will use the Scikit-Learn library for classification. You can install the library by typing `pip install scikit-learn` at the command line, as shown in Chapter 2.

Example 3.1 shows a simple SVM gender classification example based on height, weight, and shoe size. It first uses `from sklearn import svm` to import the SVM library. It uses an array called x to store four sets of values of height in centimeters, weight in kilos, and shoe size in UK size, and uses an array named y to store four sets of known genders, 0 for Male, 1 for Female. It then trains the SVM classifier and makes a prediction for a given height, weight, and shoe size [[160, 60, 7]].

EXAMPLE 3.1   THE `SVM.PY` PROGRAM

```
#Example 3.1 Python SVM Classifications
from sklearn import svm
X = [[170, 70, 10], [180, 80,12], [170, 65, 8],[160, 55, 7]]
#Height[cm], Weight[kg], Shoesize[UK]
y = [0, 0, 1, 1]     #Gender, 0: Male, 1: Female
clf = svm.SVC()
clf.fit(X, y)
#Predict
p = clf.predict([[160, 60, 7]])
print(p)
```

When you run the code, you will get the following output; [1] here means it is a female:

```
[1]
```

EXERCISE 3.1

Modify the Python program from Example 3.1 to use six samples of X and y.

The Iris dataset is probably the most widely used example for classification problems. Figure 3.2 shows photos of three different types of Iris flowers, Versicolor, Setosa, and Virginica, as well as the location of the sepal and petal.

Iris Versicolor and location of Sepal and Petal

Iris Setosa

(Source: `https://upload.wikimedia.org/wikipedia/commons/7/70/Iris_setosa_var._setosa_%282594194341%29.jpg`)

Iris Virginica

(Source: `https://en.wikipedia.org/wiki/Iris_virginica#/media/File:Iris_virginica_2.jpg`)

Iris Versicolor and location of Sepal and Patal
(Modified from Source: https://commons.wikimedia.org/wiki/File:Iris_versicolor_3.jpg)

Iris Setosa
(Source:
https://upload.wikimedia.org/wikipedia/commons/7/70/Iris_setosa_var._setosa_%282594194341%29
.jpg)

Iris Virginica
(Source: https://en.wikipedia.org/wiki/Iris_virginica#/media/File:Iris_virginica_2.jpg)

Figure 3.2: Example of three different types of Iris flowers, Versicolor (top), Setosa (middle), and Virginica (bottom), as well as the location of the sepal and petal (Modified from Source: `https://commons.wikimedia.org/wiki/File:Iris_versicolor_3.jpg`)

For more details, see the following interesting article about Iris flowers and machine learning:

https://medium.com/analytics-vidhya/exploration-of-iris-dataset-using-scikit-learn-part-1-8ac5604937f8

Example 3.2 shows an SVM classification example for using the Iris dataset that comes with Scikit-Learn. It uses `datasets.load_iris()` to load the Iris dataset.

EXAMPLE 3.2   THE SVM2.PY PROGRAM

```
#Example 3.2 Python SVM Iris Classifications
from sklearn import svm, datasets
iris = datasets.load_iris()
# Take the first two features: Sepal length and Sepal width
X = iris.data[:, :2]
y = iris.target #0: Setosa, 1: Versicolour, 2:Virginica
print(y)
clf = svm.SVC()
clf.fit(X, y)
#Predict the flower for a given Sepal length and width
p = clf.predict([[5.4, 3.2]])
print(p)
```

EXERCISE 3.2

Modify the Python program from Example 3.2 so that it uses the third and fourth features (petal length and width) as X. Compare the results with Example 3.2.

In machine learning, data is usually saved in CSV format. Example 3.3 shows an SVM classification example for using the Iris dataset by reading from a CSV file named `iris.csv` with the function `pd.read_csv()`.

EXAMPLE 3.3   THE SVM3.PY PROGRAM

```
#Example 3.3 Python SVM Iris CSV Classifications
from sklearn import svm, datasets
import pandas as pd

df = pd.read_csv('iris.csv')
X = df.values[:,:2]
s = df['species']
d = dict([(y,x) for x,y in enumerate(sorted(set(s)))])
y = [d[x] for x in s]

clf = svm.SVC()
clf.fit(X, y)
```

```
#Predict the flower for a given Sepal length and width
p = clf.predict([[5.4, 3.2]])
print(p)
```

Many people shared their CSV datasets on the Web, such as GitHub.com. You can use the function pd.read_csv() to read the data from a URL just as you would from a local file.

Example 3.4 shows an example of SVM classification, reading a CSV file in the Iris dataset from a URL. The data read by the pd.read_csv() function is stored in a variable called df, which is in Pandas' dataframe format. There are several useful functions in the dataframe format.

df.shape has information about the size of the data, number of rows, and number of columns.

df.head(10) shows the first five rows of the data. By default, df.head() shows the first five rows of the data.

df.tail(10) shows the last five rows of the data. By default, df.tail() shows the last five rows of the data.

df.describe shows the summary of the data.

df.isna() or df.isnull() is a function that shows Not A Number (NAN) or missing numbers. df.isna().sum() shows the number of NANs or missing numbers in each column. df.isna().sum().sum() shows the total number of NANs or missing numbers of the data.

df.dropna() removes the NANs.

df. groupby('species').size() shows the number of each species.

df.hist() plots the histogram of the data.

scatter_matrix() plots the scatter matrix of the data.

pyplot.show() shows the plot.

EXAMPLE 3.4   THE SVM4.PY PROGRAM

```
#Example 3.4 Python SVM Iris URL Classifications
from sklearn import svm, datasets
import pandas as pd
from matplotlib import pyplot
from pandas.plotting import scatter_matrix

df = pd.read_csv('https://gist.githubusercontent.com/curran/
a08a1080b88344b0c8a7/raw/0e7a9b0a5d22642a06d3d5b9bcbad9890c8ee534/
iris.csv')

print(df.shape)
print(df.head(10))
print(df.tail(10))
print(df.describe())
```

```
#count NAN
Print(df.isna().sum().sum())
#drop NAN values
df = df.dropna()

print(df.groupby('species').size())
# histograms
df.hist()
pyplot.show()
# scatter plot matrix
scatter_matrix(df)
pyplot.show()

X = df.values[:,:2]
s = df['species']
d = dict([(y,x) for x,y in enumerate(sorted(set(s)))])
y = [d[x] for x in s]

clf = svm.SVC()
clf.fit(X, y)
#Predict the flower for a given Sepal length and width
p = clf.predict([[5.4, 3.2]])
print(p)
```

The following is the output of the previous program. This shows the shape of the data, 150 rows and 5 columns.

```
(150, 5)
```

This shows the first 10 rows of the data:

```
   sepal_length  sepal_width  petal_length  petal_width  species
0           5.1          3.5           1.4          0.2  setosa
1           4.9          3.0           1.4          0.2  setosa
2           4.7          3.2           1.3          0.2  setosa
3           4.6          3.1           1.5          0.2  setosa
4           5.0          3.6           1.4          0.2  setosa
5           5.4          3.9           1.7          0.4  setosa
6           4.6          3.4           1.4          0.3  setosa
7           5.0          3.4           1.5          0.2  setosa
8           4.4          2.9           1.4          0.2  setosa
9           4.9          3.1           1.5          0.1  setosa
```

This shows the last 10 rows of the data:

```
     sepal_length  sepal_width  petal_length  petal_width    species
140           6.7          3.1           5.6          2.4  virginica
141           6.9          3.1           5.1          2.3  virginica
142           5.8          2.7           5.1          1.9  virginica
143           6.8          3.2           5.9          2.3  virginica
```

144	6.7	3.3	5.7	2.5	virginica
145	6.7	3.0	5.2	2.3	virginica
146	6.3	2.5	5.0	1.9	virginica
147	6.5	3.0	5.2	2.0	virginica
148	6.2	3.4	5.4	2.3	virginica
149	5.9	3.0	5.1	1.8	virginica

This shows the description of the data:

	sepal_length	sepal_width	petal_length	petal_width
count	150.000000	150.000000	150.000000	150.000000
mean	5.843333	3.054000	3.758667	1.198667
std	0.828066	0.433594	1.764420	0.763161
min	4.300000	2.000000	1.000000	0.100000
25%	5.100000	2.800000	1.600000	0.300000
50%	5.800000	3.000000	4.350000	1.300000
75%	6.400000	3.300000	5.100000	1.800000
max	7.900000	4.400000	6.900000	2.500000

This shows the number of rows with NAN values:

```
0
```

This shows the number of rows for different species:

```
species
setosa       50
versicolor   50
virginica    50
```

This shows the prediction result (setosa) for the given input ([[5.4, 3.2]]):

```
dtype: int64
[0]
```

Figure 3.3 shows the histogram plot (top) and matrix scatter plot (bottom) of the previous program. In the histogram, the y-axis shows the number of samples, and the x-axis shows the values of sepal length, sepal width, petal length, and petal width. The matrix scatter plot shows a matrix of 2D scatter plots of the data points with the four features (sepal length, sepal width, petal length, and petal width) against each other. This is useful as it gives an overview of all the data points in terms of all the features so that you can easily see which two features can separate the data better. For example, the scatter plot of petal length against sepal width gives the largest separation of the points into two groups, and in the scatter plot of petal width against sepal length, one group of data was close together in the corner.

On the diagonal of the matrix, as it is the same feature against the same feature, the histogram of the feature is displayed instead.

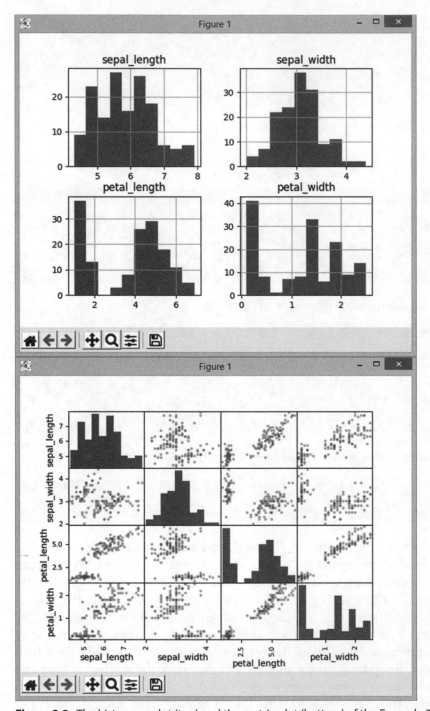

Figure 3.3: The histogram plot (top) and the matrix plot (bottom) of the Example 3.4

Modify the Python program from Example 3.4 so that it plots the first two features (sepal length and sepal width) of all the data points as a scatter plot.

The breast cancer dataset is another popular dataset for classification problems. Example 3.5 shows how to load the breast cancer data from the Scikit-Learn library using the `load_breast_cancer()` function and then print the feature names, the data, and the target names on-screen.

EXAMPLE 3.5   THE `CANCER.PY` PROGRAM

```
#Example 3.5 Breast Cancer Data
from sklearn.datasets import load_breast_cancer

cancer = load_breast_cancer()
print(cancer['feature_names'])
print(cancer['data'])
print(cancer.target_names)
```

The following is the output of feature names of the breast cancer dataset. Each feature here is a type of measurement, such as radius, size, texture, smoothness, and so on.

```
['mean radius' 'mean texture' 'mean perimeter' 'mean area'
 'mean smoothness' 'mean compactness' 'mean concavity'
 'mean concave points' 'mean symmetry' 'mean fractal dimension'
 'radius error' 'texture error' 'perimeter error' 'area error'
 'smoothness error' 'compactness error' 'concavity error'
 'concave points error' 'symmetry error' 'fractal dimension error'
 'worst radius' 'worst texture' 'worst perimeter' 'worst area'
 'worst smoothness' 'worst compactness' 'worst concavity'
 'worst concave points' 'worst symmetry' 'worst fractal dimension']
```

The following is the output of the data, which are the values of each feature of the breast cancer dataset:

```
[[1.799e+01 1.038e+01 1.228e+02 ... 2.654e-01 4.601e-01 1.189e-01]
 [2.057e+01 1.777e+01 1.329e+02 ... 1.860e-01 2.750e-01 8.902e-02]
 [1.969e+01 2.125e+01 1.300e+02 ... 2.430e-01 3.613e-01 8.758e-02]
 ...
 [1.660e+01 2.808e+01 1.083e+02 ... 1.418e-01 2.218e-01 7.820e-02]
 [2.060e+01 2.933e+01 1.401e+02 ... 2.650e-01 4.087e-01 1.240e-01]
 [7.760e+00 2.454e+01 4.792e+01 ... 0.000e+00 2.871e-01 7.039e-02]]
```

The following is the output of the target names of the breast cancer dataset. There are two classes: 0 is malignant, and 1 is benign.

```
['malignant' 'benign']
```

Example 3.6 shows an example of SVM classification for breast cancer. It first loads the breast cancer data's `load_breast_cancer()` function and then puts the data into a dataframe format, uses `features` data as X and `target` as y, and uses `train_test_split()` to split x and y into training and testing sets. Specifically, 80 percent of data is for training, and 20 percent is for testing. It uses the training data `X_train` and `y_train` to train an SVM and uses testing data `X_test` to make predictions. Finally, it prints the confusion matrix and classification report.

EXAMPLE 3.6   THE `CANCER2.PY` PROGRAM

```python
#Example 3.6 Python SVM Breast Cancer Classifications
import pandas as pd
import numpy as np
from sklearn.datasets import load_breast_cancer
from sklearn.model_selection import train_test_split
from sklearn.svm import SVC


cancer = load_breast_cancer()
X = cancer.data   # All of the features
y = cancer.target  # All of the labels
X_train, X_test, y_train, y_test = train_test_split(X, y, test_size =
0.2, random_state = 20)


clf = SVC()
clf.fit(X_train, y_train)


#Prediction
y_predict = clf.predict(X_test)


#Print Confusion Matrix and Classification Report
from sklearn.metrics import classification_report, confusion_matrix
cm = np.array(confusion_matrix(y_test, y_predict, labels=[1,0]))
confusion = pd.DataFrame(cm, index=['is_cancer', 'is_healthy'],
                         columns=['predicted_cancer','predicted_
healthy'])
print(confusion)
print(classification_report(y_test, y_predict))
```

The following is the output of confusion matrix. A confusion matrix is a simple way to show the performance of classification. The results show that there are

66 cancer tissues that have been correctly predicted as cancer, or malignant, and 40 healthy tissues have been correctly predicted as healthy, or benign. There are eight healthy tissues wrongly predicted as cancer, and zero cancer tissue wrongly predicted as healthy.

	predicted_cancer	predicted_healthy
is_cancer	66	0
is_healthy	8	40

The following is the output of the classification report, from which you can see the SVM classification has an accuracy of 93 percent:

	precision	recall	f1-score	support
0.0	1.00	0.83	0.91	48
1.0	0.89	1.00	0.94	66
accuracy			0.93	114
macro avg	0.95	0.92	0.93	114
weighted avg	0.94	0.93	0.93	114

EXERCISE 3.4

Modify the Python program from Example 3.6 so that it plots the histogram of radius, size, texture, and smoothness of all the data points.

Naive Bayes

Naive Bayes is another popular supervised learning algorithm, which applies Bayes' theorem with the naive assumption of the probabilities of features for a given dataset. Naive assumption means every feature is independent of the others.

According to Bayes' theorem, the probability of a class (C) happening for a given set of features (X) can be calculated as follows:

$$P(C|X) = \frac{P(C) \times P(X|C)}{P(X)}$$

or:

$$Posterior = \frac{Prior \times Likelihood}{Evidence}$$

where:

P(C|X)	is the posterior, the probability of class *(C)* given features *(X)*.
P(C)	is the prior, the probability of class *(C)*.
P(X|C)	is the likelihood, the probability of features *(X)* for given class *(C)*.
P(X)	is the prior, probability of features *(X)*.

To train a naive Bayes classifier, you just need to calculate all the probabilities $P(C)$ of all the classes (types of flowers) for the given features (sepals and petals' length and width) and evidence $P(X)$. For a given dataset, $P(C)$ and $P(X)$ are constants. Hence, they are saved for future use. Given a sample X, the likelihood $P(X|C)$ will be calculated, and the posterior $P(C|X)$ can be calculated.

For more details, see the following resources:

```
https://scikit-learn.org/stable/modules/naive_bayes.html
https://en.wikipedia.org/wiki/Naive_Bayes_classifier
```

Example 3.7 shows an example of a naive Bayes classification for irises. In this case, it uses `X, y = load_iris(return_X_y=True)` to load the iris data and returns the data as X and y, where X includes all four features of that data. It then trains the naive Bayes classifier model and makes a prediction for a given sample with the sepal's length and width and the petal's length and width.

EXAMPLE 3.7   THE `NAIVEBAYES.PY` **PROGRAM**

```
#Example 3.7 Naive Bayes Iris
from sklearn.datasets import load_iris
from sklearn.model_selection import train_test_split
from sklearn.naive_bayes import GaussianNB
X, y = load_iris(return_X_y=True)
print(X)
clf = GaussianNB()
clf.fit(X, y)
p = clf.predict([[5.0, 3.4, 1.5, 0.4]])
print(p)
```

For a large amount of data, you can save the trained model to a file and load the model from the file later. Saving the model to a file is called *serialization*. You can use Sklearn's `joblib` for this.

```
from sklearn.externals import joblib
joblib.dump(clf, 'model.pkl')
```

Once the model has been saved, you can then load this model into memory with a single line of code. Loading the model back into your workspace is called *deserialization*.

```
clf2 = joblib.load('model.pkl')
```

EXERCISE 3.5

Modify the Python program from Example 3.7 so that it first trains the naive Bayes model, saves the model to a file, loads the model from the file, and makes a prediction with the model.

Linear Discriminant Analysis

Linear discriminant analysis (LDA) is one of the most commonly used dimension reduction techniques in machine learning. The goal is to project a dataset onto a lower-dimensional space to separate them better into different classes and to reduce computational costs.

Figure 3.4 illustrates how LDA works. For a given set of data with three classes, measured on two features (x1 and x2), all mingled together, it is difficult to separate them; see Figure 3.4 (left). LDA will try to find new axes, see the dashed lines, and project the data to the new axes (LDA1 and LDA2); it will adjust the axes according to the means and variances of each group of data to best separate the data into different classes. After LDA, you can plot the data according to new axes (LDA1 and LDA2), which can improve the separation, as shown in Figure 3.4 (right).

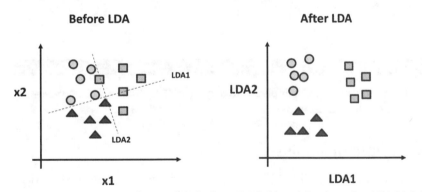

Figure 3.4: LDA: a set of given data before LDA (left) and the data after LDA (right)

LDA basically projects the data from one dimension linearly into another dimension. Apart from LDA, there is also nonlinear discriminant analysis.

- Quadratic discriminant analysis (QDA)
- Flexible discriminant analysis (FDA)
- Regularized discriminant analysis (RDA)

For more details about LDA and QDA in the Scikit-Learn library, see the following:

```
https://scikit-learn.org/stable/modules/lda_qda.html
```

Here is an interesting YouTube video from StatQuest by Josh Starmer that clearly explains LDA:

```
https://www.youtube.com/watch?v=azXCzI57Yfc
```

Example 3.8 shows a simple LDA classification example. In this example, it uses `make_classification()` to generate a simulated dataset as X and y, with 1,000 samples and 4 features. It then trains the LDA classifier model and makes a prediction for a given sample with four values.

EXAMPLE 3.8   THE `LDA.PY` PROGRAM

```python
#Example 3.8 LinearDiscriminantAnalysis Classification
from sklearn.datasets import load_iris
from sklearn.datasets import make_classification
from sklearn.discriminant_analysis import LinearDiscriminantAnalysis

X, y = make_classification(n_samples=1000, n_features=4,
                           n_informative=2, n_redundant=0,
                           random_state=0, shuffle=False)
print(X)
clf = LinearDiscriminantAnalysis()
clf.fit(X, y)
print(clf.predict([[0, 0, 0, 0]]))
```

EXERCISE 3.6

Modify the Python program from Example 3.8 so that it uses 6 features and 2,000 samples. Compare the results with Example 3.8.

Principal Component Analysis

Principal component analysis (PCA) is another common dimension reduction technique in machine learning, similar to LDA. The goal is also to project a dataset onto a lower-dimensional space. LDA aims to create new axes (called *discriminants*) to maximize class separation, while PCA aims to find new axes (called *components*) to maximize variance (the average of the squared differences from the mean). In PCA, the number of the principal components is less than or equal to the number of original variables, the first principal component will have the largest possible variance, and each succeeding component in turn has the largest variance possible under the constraint that it is orthogonal to the preceding components. Figure 3.5 illustrates the original data plotted according to its features (x1 and x2) and the data after PCA, plotted according to new axes (PCA1 and PCA2).

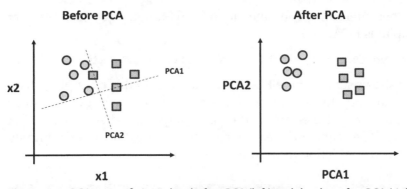

Figure 3.5: PCA: a set of given data before PCA (left) and the data after PCA (right)

Figure 3.6 shows an interesting article about LDA, which also shows a comparison of LDA and PCA. LDA can be described as a supervised algorithm, as it aims to maximize separation of the classes, while PCA can be described as an unsupervised algorithm, as it ignores the classes and aims to maximize the variance of the data. The author also provides a vivid explanation of the Iris dataset and a Python implement of LDA with step-by-step instructions. So, if you are interested in learning the mathematical background of LDA, this is an interesting article to read.

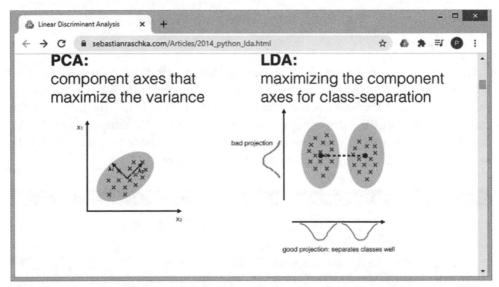

Figure 3.6: An article about linear discriminant analysis, which compares PCA and LDA

(Source: `https://sebastianraschka.com/Articles/2014_python_lda.html`)

This is another article that shows the step-by-step Python implementation of PCA:

`https://sebastianraschka.com/Articles/2014_pca_step_by_step.html`

Here is another interesting YouTube video from StatQuest by Josh Starmer that clearly explains PCA:

```
https://www.youtube.com/watch?app=desktop&v=FgakZw6K1QQ
```

Example 3.9 shows some simple PCA example code. In this example, it uses `make_classification()` to generate a simulated dataset as X and y, with 1,000 samples and 4 features. It then trains the PCA model and displays the PCA results. Although PCA cannot be used directly for classification, it is commonly used as a dimension reduction technique before classification.

EXAMPLE 3.9   THE PCA.PY PROGRAM

```python
#Example 3.9 Principal Component Analysis
from sklearn.datasets import load_iris
from sklearn.datasets import make_classification
from sklearn.decomposition import PCA

X, y = make_classification(n_samples=1000, n_features=4,
                           n_informative=2, n_redundant=0,
                           random_state=0, shuffle=False)
print(X)
clf = PCA()
clf.fit(X, y)
print(clf.explained_variance_ratio_)
print(clf.singular_values_)
```

Example 3.10 shows a simple PCA example for the Iris dataset. In this example, it loads the Iris dataset as X and y arrays, plots the original X data, trains the PCA model, and transforms the X into PCA domains. It finally displays the transformed X in PCA domains using the first two PCA components, PCA1 and PCA2. Figure 3.7 shows the output of Example 3.10, and you can clearly see the differences of original data and PCA-transformed data.

EXAMPLE 3.10   THE PCA2.PY PROGRAM

```python
#Example 3.10 Principal Component Analysis Iris
import numpy as np
import matplotlib.pyplot as plt
from mpl_toolkits.mplot3d import Axes3D
from sklearn import decomposition
from sklearn import datasets

#Load Iris data
iris = datasets.load_iris()
X = iris.data
```

```
y = iris.target

#Plot Iris data
f = plt.figure(1)
plt.scatter(X[:,0], X[:,1],   c=y)
plt.xlabel('sepals length')
plt.ylabel('sepals width')
plt.title('Original Data')
f.show()

#Perform PCA
pca = decomposition.PCA(n_components=3)
pca.fit(X)
X1 = pca.transform(X)

#Plot PCA data
g = plt.figure(2)
#y = np.choose(y, [1, 2, 0]).astype(float)
plt.scatter(X1[:, 0], X1[:, 1], c=y)
plt.xlabel('PCA1')
plt.ylabel('PCA2')
plt.title('PCA Data')
g.show()
```

EXERCISE 3.7

Modify the Python program from Example 3.10 so that it performs PCA on the breast cancer data.

Decision Tree

A decision tree is one of the most widely used, nonparametric, supervised learning methods, and it can be used for both classification and regression problems. A set of rules can be derived from a decision tree (an upside-down tree). Decisions can be made based on the derived rules. In a decision tree, a note is the query variable, and the edge is the value of the query variable. A decision process starts from the tree root and goes down to branches and leaves. Hence, each branch represents an `if-then` rule. For example, the first branch of the decision tree in Figure 3.8 represents the rule: if the weather forecast is sunny and the humidity is high, then there is no play of golf. The deeper the tree is, the more complex the rules and the model. The goal of a decision tree training algorithm is to create a decision tree based on a dataset and finally produce a set of rules for prediction given a sample.

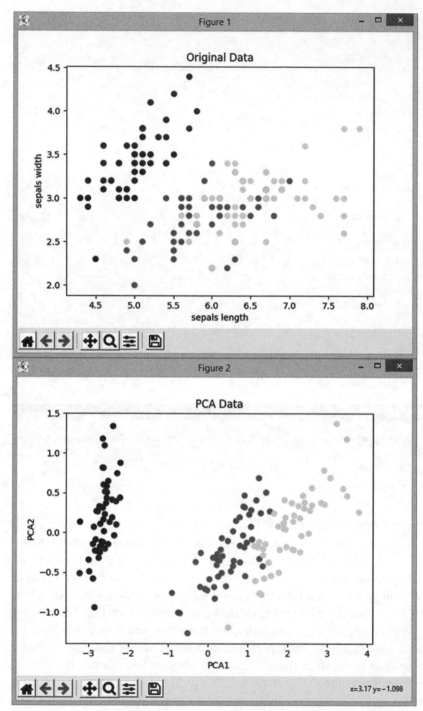

Figure 3.7: The scatter plot of the original Iris dataset (top) and the scatter plot of first two components of the corresponding PCA results (bottom)

Figure 3.8 shows a simple decision tree to determine whether to play golf.

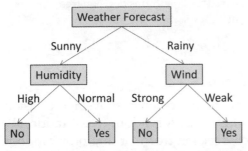

Figure 3.8: A simple decision tree to decide whether to play golf

Here is a similar example of a decision tree:

```
https://www.geeksforgeeks.org/decision-tree/
```

For more details of a decision tree in the Scikit-Learn library, see the following page:

```
https://scikit-learn.org/stable/modules/tree.html
```

Example 3.11 shows an example of decision tree classification for iris flowers. In this case, it uses X, y = load_iris(return_X_y=True) to load the Iris data and returns the data as X and y, using all four features of the data. It then splits the data into the training set and the testing set. It then trains the decision tree classifier model and makes predictions on the testing set. It also calculates and displays the total number of points, as well as the number of points that are correctly predicted.

EXAMPLE 3.11   THE DT.PY PROGRAM

```
#Example 3.11 Decision Tree Classification
from sklearn.datasets import load_iris
from sklearn.model_selection import train_test_split
from sklearn.tree import DecisionTreeClassifier

X, y = load_iris(return_X_y=True)
X_train, X_test, y_train, y_test = train_test_split(X, y, test_
size=0.5, random_state=0)
clf = DecisionTreeClassifier()
clf.fit(X_train, y_train)
y_pred = clf.predict(X_test)
N = y_test.shape[0]
C = (y_test == y_pred).sum()
print("Total points: %d Correctly labeled points : %d" %(N,C))
```

EXERCISE 3.8

Modify the Python program from Example 3.11 so that it performs decision tree classification on Scikit-Learn's wine data (https://scikit-learn.org/stable/modules/generated/sklearn.datasets.load_wine.html).

Random Forest

A random forest is an algorithm that uses multiple decision trees. A single decision tree might not be enough for some applications. A random forest randomly creates a set of decision trees, with each decision tree working on a random subset of data samples. There are different approaches to create random forests.

A random forest then combines the output of individual decision trees to generate the final output. A random forest is an ensemble learning algorithm that can be used for both classification and regression problems. Figure 3.9 illustrates a random forest algorithm; by using multiple decision trees, it can reduce overfitting and improve the performances.

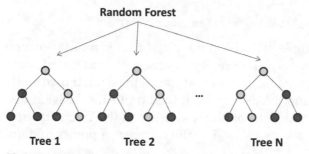

Figure 3.9: Random forest, based on multiple decision trees

Here is an interesting YouTube video from Augmented Startups that explains a random forest in a fun and easy manner:

```
https://www.youtube.com/watch?v=D_2LkhMJcfY
```

For more details of a random forest in the Scikit-Learn library, see the following:

```
https://scikit-learn.org/stable/modules/generated/sklearn.ensemble.
RandomForestClassifier.html
```

Example 3.12 shows an example of a random forest classification for iris flowers. In this case, it uses X, y = load_iris(return_X_y=True) to load the iris data and returns the data as X and y, using all four features of the data. It then trains the random forest classifier model, makes predictions on the test samples, and calculates the number of points predicted correctly.

EXAMPLE 3.12   THE RF.PY **PROGRAM**

```
#Example 3.12 Random Forest
from sklearn.datasets import load_iris
from sklearn.model_selection import train_test_split
from sklearn.ensemble import RandomForestClassifier

X, y = load_iris(return_X_y=True)
X_train, X_test, y_train, y_test = train_test_split(X, y, test_
size=0.5, random_state=0)
clf = RandomForestClassifier()
clf.fit(X_train, y_train)
y_pred = clf.predict(X_test)
print("Total points: %d Correctly labeled points : %d" %(y_test.
shape[0],(y_test == y_pred).sum()))
```

EXERCISE 3.9

Modify the Python program from Example 3.12 so that it performs random forest classification on Scikit-Learn's diabetes data (https://scikit-learn.org/stable/modules/generated/sklearn.datasets.load_diabetes.html#sklearn.datasets.load_diabetes).

K-Nearest Neighbors

K-nearest neighbors (K-NN) is a classification (or regression) algorithm that uses K number of nearest points to determine the classification of a dataset. Figure 3.10 shows an example of K-NN classification from Wikipedia. The round point is a test sample, which needs to be classified as either a square or a triangle. Regarding the three nearest neighbors, see the solid circle; it should belong to triangles as there are two triangles and only one square inside the circle. If we choose five nearest neighbors, see the dashed circle; it should belong to the squares, as there are three squares, and two triangles inside the circle. Don't confuse K-nearest neighbors with K-means. K-means is an unsupervised learning algorithm that is mainly used for clustering. We will introduce K-means in section 3.4.

Here is an interesting YouTube video from Simplilearn about K-NN:

https://www.youtube.com/watch?v=4HKqjENq9OU

For more details of K-NN in the Scikit-Learn library, visit this site:

https://scikit-learn.org/stable/modules/neighbors.html

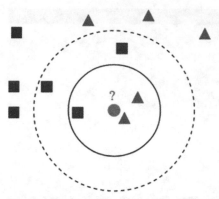

Figure 3.10: Example of K-nearest neighbors

(Source: `https://en.wikipedia.org/wiki/K-nearest_neighbors_algorithm#/media/File:KnnClassification.svg`)

Example 3.13 shows an example of K-NN classification for iris flowers. In this case, it uses `X, y = load_iris(return_X_y=True)` to load the iris data and returns the data as X and y arrays, using all four features of that data. It then trains the K-NN classifier model, makes predictions on the test samples, and calculates the number of points predicted correctly.

EXAMPLE 3.13   THE `KNN.PY` PROGRAM

```
#Example 3.13 K-Nearest Neighbors Classification
from sklearn.datasets import load_iris
from sklearn.model_selection import train_test_split
from sklearn.neighbors import KNeighborsClassifier

X, y = load_iris(return_X_y=True)
X_train, X_test, y_train, y_test = train_test_split(X, y, test_
size=0.5, random_state=0)
clf = KNeighborsClassifier()
clf.fit(X_train, y_train)
y_pred = clf.predict(X_test)
print("Total points: %d Correctly labeled points : %d" %(y_test.
shape[0],(y_test == y_pred).sum()))
```

Neural Networks

A neural network (NN), or artificial neural network (ANN), is a typical three-layer network with one input layer, one hidden layer, and one output layer. Neural networks can be used for both classification and regression. We will have a more detailed description about neural networks in Chapter 4.

For more details of neural networks, also called *multilayer perceptron*, in the Scikit-Learn library, see the following:

```
https://scikit-learn.org/stable/modules/neural_networks_super-
vised.html
```

Example 3.14 compares different classification models. It uses an array called names to store all the names of the different classifiers and an array called classifiers to store the functions of all the different classifiers. It then loads the iris data and splits it into training and testing sets. A for loop is run through all the classification models, from training the model and making a prediction to calculating the accuracy, as a ratio percentage of the number classified correctly over the total number of points.

EXAMPLE 3.14   THE CLASSIFY.PY PROGRAM

```python
#Example 3.14 Comparison of Different Classification
from sklearn.datasets import load_iris
from sklearn.model_selection import train_test_split
from sklearn.svm import SVC
from sklearn.naive_bayes import GaussianNB
from sklearn.discriminant_analysis import LinearDiscriminantAnalysis
from sklearn.tree import DecisionTreeClassifier
from sklearn.ensemble import RandomForestClassifier
from sklearn.neighbors import KNeighborsClassifier
from sklearn.neural_network import MLPClassifier
from sklearn.discriminant_analysis import
QuadraticDiscriminantAnalysis

names = [ "SVM",  "Naive Bayes", "LDA",
        "QDA", "Decision Tree", "Random Forest",
          "Nearest Neighbors", "Neural Networks"]

classifiers = [
    SVC(),
    GaussianNB(),
    LinearDiscriminantAnalysis(),
    QuadraticDiscriminantAnalysis(),
    DecisionTreeClassifier(),
    RandomForestClassifier(),
    KNeighborsClassifier(),
    MLPClassifier(alpha=1, max_iter=1000)]

X, y = load_iris(return_X_y=True)
X_train, X_test, y_train, y_test = train_test_split(X, y, test_
size=0.5, random_state=0)
```

```
for name, clf in zip(names, classifiers):
    clf.fit(X_train, y_train)
    score = clf.score(X_test, y_test)
    print(name +": " + str(score))
```

The following is the output of the program. It shows that the neural networks gives the best classification results with 98.7 percent of accuracy, compared to other models.

```
SVM: 0.9466666666666667
Naive Bayes: 0.9466666666666667
LDA: 0.96
QDA: 0.96
Decision Tree: 0.96
Random Forest: 0.9466666666666667
Nearest Neighbors: 0.96
Neural Networks: 0.9866666666666667
```

EXERCISE 3.10

Modify the Python program from Example 3.14 so that it performs the classification on Scikit-Learn's diabetes data (`https://scikit-learn.org/stable/modules/generated/sklearn.datasets.load_diabetes.html#sklearn.datasets.load_diabetes`).

3.3 Supervised Learning: Regressions

Regression is another important aspect of supervised learning. Regression means fitting the data with a mathematical model using a technique called *least squares fitting*. Regression can be divided into linear regression and nonlinear regression. In linear regression, we fit the data with a straight line ($f(x) = ax + b$), where a is the slope, and b is the intercept, as shown in Figure 3.11. For a given dataset, we calculated the sum of the squares of the errors (e_i), calculate the distances between the data points and the straight line, and adjust the slope (a) and the intercept (b) of the straight line, until we have reached the smallest sum of the squares (χ^2), which is why it's called *least squares*. Linear regression can also be extended to multiple linear regression; in this case, we fit the data with multiple straight lines.

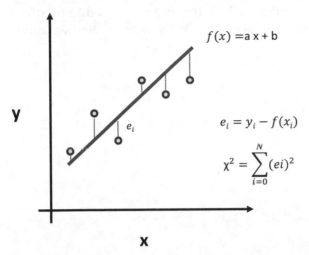

$$f(x) = a\,x + b$$

$$e_i = y_i - f(x_i)$$

$$\chi^2 = \sum_{i=0}^{N} (ei)^2$$

Figure 3.11: Linear regression and the distances between the data points and the straight line

If you are interested in the mathematical details of least squares regression, here is an interesting tutorial about least squares fitting from Wolfram MathWorld:

```
https://mathworld.wolfram.com/LeastSquaresFitting.html
```

For nonlinear regression, we fit the data with more complicated mathematical models, such as exponentials and polynomials; see Figure 3.12.

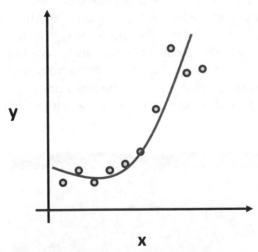

Figure 3.12: Example of nonlinear regression

A common nonlinear regression is logistic regression, where we fit the data with logistic function. Logistic regression is particularly suitable for the data that is dichotomous (binary); see Figure 3.13. It is typically used to predict a binary outcome (pass/fail, win/lose) based on a set of independent variables.

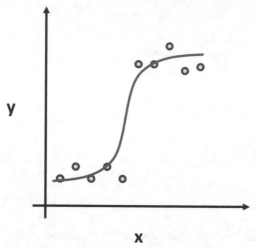

Figure 3.13: Example of logistic regression

Next, let's look at some Python regression examples.

Example 3.15 shows a simple two-dimensional (X and Y) Python linear regression example. It first creates two arrays for x and y values, then performs the linear regression by calling `linregress()`, and displays the linear regression results: the slope and the intercept. The slope represents the slope of the line, 0.9 is close to 1, which means a line with a 45° slope. The intercept represents the intersection of the line with the y-axis. It also defines a linear function called `myfunc()` and defines the functions `list()` and `map()` to calculate the values of y from the x values of the `myfunc()` function. Finally, it uses the functions `plt.scatter()` and `plt.show()` to display and plot the original x and y values and the best-fitted line.

EXAMPLE 3.15   THE `LINEARR.PY` PROGRAM

```
#Example 3.15 Linear Regression
import matplotlib.pyplot as plt
from scipy import stats

x = [0,1,2,3,4]
y = [3,5,5,6,7]

slope, intercept, r, p, std_err = stats.linregress(x, y)
print("slope: ", slope)
print("intercept: ", intercept)

def myfunc(x):
```

```
    return slope * x + intercept

mymodel = list(map(myfunc, x))

plt.scatter(x, y)
plt.plot(x, mymodel)
plt.show()
```

The following are the program outputs, the slope, and intercept values. Figure 3.14 shows the plot of the program. The round dots are the x and y values, and the straight line is the best-fit line.

```
slope:  0.9
intercept:  3.4000000000000004
```

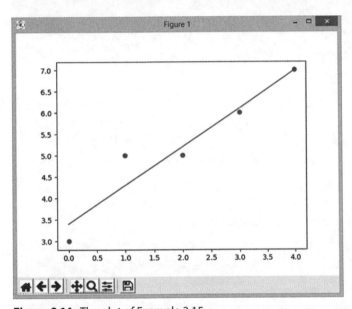

Figure 3.14: The plot of Example 3.15

EXERCISE 3.11

Modify the Python program from Example 3.15 so that it has more data points in x and y. Also, add an x label, y label, title, legend, and grids to the plot.

The Statsmodels library is a powerful statistical model library that comes with a number of mathematical functions, such as regression. To use the library, you will need to install it first, as shown here:

```
pip install statsmodels
```

For more details, see this site:

`https://www.statsmodels.org/stable/regression.html`

Example 3.15a is a similar linear regression example, using the Statsmodels library.

EXAMPLE 3.15A   THE `LINEARR2.PY` PROGRAM

```
#Example 3.15a Linear Regression
import matplotlib.pyplot as plt
import numpy as np
import statsmodels.api as sm

x = [0,1,2,3,4]
y = [3,5,5,6,7]
x1=sm.add_constant(x)

model = sm.OLS(y,x1)
results = model.fit()
print (results.params)
print (results.summary())

y_pred=results.predict(x1)
plt.scatter(x,y)
plt.xlabel("X")
plt.ylabel("Y")
plt.plot(x,y_pred, "r")
plt.show()
```

The following is the output of the program:

```
[3.4 0.9]



                            OLS Regression Results
==============================================================================
Dep. Variable:                      y   R-squared:                       0.920
Model:                            OLS   Adj. R-squared:                  0.894
Method:                 Least Squares   F-statistic:                     34.71
Date:                Sat, 09 Jan 2021   Prob (F-statistic):            0.00976
Time:                        09:46:37   Log-Likelihood:                -2.1794
No. Observations:                   5   AIC:                             8.359
Df Residuals:                       3   BIC:                             7.578
Df Model:                           1
Covariance Type:            nonrobust
==============================================================================
                 coef    std err          t      P>|t|      [0.025      0.975]
------------------------------------------------------------------------------
const          3.4000      0.374      9.087      0.003       2.209       4.591
```

x1	0.9000	0.153	5.892	0.010	0.414	1.386
===
Omnibus:		nan	Durbin-Watson:			2.914
Prob(Omnibus):		nan	Jarque-Bera (JB):			0.901
Skew:		1.031	Prob(JB):			0.637
Kurtosis:		2.729	Cond. No.			4.74
===

```
Notes:
[1] Standard Errors assume that the covariance matrix of the errors is
correctly specified.
```

Figure 3.15 is the plot output of the program.

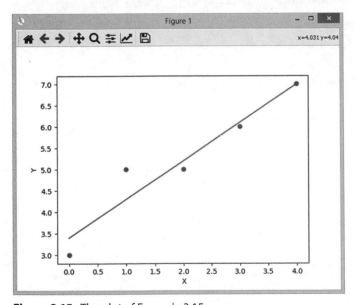

Figure 3.15: The plot of Example 3.15a

Example 3.16 shows a simple example of a two-dimensional (X and Y) Python polynomial regression. It performs the polynomial regression function by calling `np.poly1d(np.polyfit(x, y, 3))`, where the number 3 means three terms of a polynomial function, which is $y = a\,x^3 + b\,x^2 + c\,x + d$.

EXAMPLE 3.16   THE `POLYR.PY` **PROGRAM**

```
#Example 3.16 Polynomial Regression
import matplotlib.pyplot as plt
from scipy import stats
import numpy as np

x = [0,1,2,3,4,5]
```

```
y = [3,8,6,6,7,3]

mymodel = np.poly1d(np.polyfit(x, y, 3))
print(mymodel)

myline = np.linspace(0, 5, 100)
plt.scatter(x, y)
plt.plot(myline, mymodel(myline))
plt.show()
```

The following is the program output, the slope, and intercepts values. Figure 3.16 shows the plot of the program; round dots are the x and y values, and the curved line is the best polynomial curve.

```
        3           2
0.06481 x - 1.075 x + 3.749 x + 3.556
```

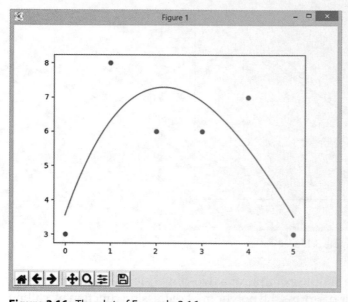

Figure 3.16: The plot of Example 3.16

Example 3.17 shows a simple example of Python least squares fitting. It first creates Numpy arrays for x values and y values. It then defines a function named `func()` that can be used to fit the x and y values. You can define your own function. Here is a simple exponential decay function: $y = a * \exp(-b\,x) + c$. It performs the least squares fitting by using the `optimization.curve_fit()` function and displays the best-fit results.

EXAMPLE 3.17   THE LSF.PY PROGRAM

```
#Example 3.17 Least Squares Fitting
import numpy as np
import scipy.optimize as optimization

x = np.array([0,1,2,3,4,5])
y = np.array([100,90,60,30,10,1])

def func(x, a, b, c):
    return a * np.exp(-b * x) + c

popt, pcov = optimization.curve_fit(func, x, y)
print ("Best fit a b c: ",popt)
print ("Best fit covariance: ",pcov)
```

The following is the output of the program:

```
Best fit a b c:  [ 4.09564212e+02  6.21466356e-02 -3.04106531e+02]
Best fit covariance:  [[ 4.92882349e+05 -8.73845292e+01 -4.95819953e+05]
 [-8.73845292e+01  1.55361498e-02  8.79409202e+01]
 [-4.95819953e+05  8.79409202e+01  4.98815648e+05]]
```

Example 3.18 shows a simple example of multiple-dimensional linear regression. It first creates Numpy arrays for x and y values. Please note the format differences of x array and y array. Here, the x array is two-dimensional, while the y array is one-dimensional. It then creates a linear regression model by using the LinearRegression() function and fits the model with the linear relation between the x array and y array. Finally, it displays the linear regression results: the coefficients and the intercept. The coefficient represents the slope of the line. 0.9 is close to 1, which means a line with a slope of 45°. The intercept represents the interception of the line with the y-axis.

EXAMPLE 3.18   THE MLR.PY PROGRAM

```
#Example 3.18 Multiple Linear Regression
from sklearn import linear_model
import numpy as np

x = np.array([[0,3,5],[1,4,6],[2,5,7],[3,6,8],[4,7,9]])
y = np.array([3,5,5,6,7])

reg = linear_model.LinearRegression()
reg.fit(x, y)
print('Coefficients: \n', reg.coef_)
print('Intercept: \n', reg.intercept_)
pred = reg.predict([[5,8,10]])
print('Predition: \n', pred)
```

The following is the output of the program:

```
Coefficients:
 [0.3 0.3 0.3]
Intercept:
 0.9999999999999991
Predition:
 [7.9]
```

EXERCISE 3.12

Modify the Python program from Example 3.18 so that it performs multiple linear regression on Scikit-Learn's Linnurd dataset; see the following:

   `https://scikit-learn.org/stable/datasets/toy_dataset`
`.html#linnerrud-dataset`
   `https://scikit-learn.org/stable/modules/generated/sklearn`
`.datasets.load_linnerud.html`

Example 3.19 shows a simple example of Python logistic regression. It first creates Numpy arrays named x and y, which contains a series of X and Y data points. It then performs logistic regression by using the `LogisticRegression()` function and the `fit()` function. Finally, it predicts the given sample and displays the result.

EXAMPLE 3.19   THE `LOGR.PY` **PROGRAM**

```python
#Example 3.19 Logistic Regression
import numpy as np
from sklearn.linear_model import LogisticRegression

X = np.array([[0],[1],[2],[3],[4],[5]])
y = np.array([1,2,3,30,32,31])

clf = LogisticRegression(random_state=0).fit(X, y)
print(clf.predict([[6]]))

print(clf.predict_proba([[6]]))
print(clf.score(X, y))
```

The following is the output of the program:

```
[31]
[[0.00111369 0.00810381 0.03285485 0.09764849 0.61051015 0.24976901]]
0.6666666666666666
```

For more details about linear regression, multiple linear regression, nonlinear regression, and logistic regression, visit the Scikit-Learn library:

```
https://scikit-learn.org/stable/modules/generated/sklearn.linear_
model.LinearRegression.html
```

```
https://scikit-learn.org/stable/modules/generated/sklearn.linear_
model.LogisticRegression.html
```

3.4   Unsupervised Learning

Unsupervised learning is a type of machine learning technique that does not require you to provide knowledge to supervise the model. The model will discover information on its own. This is different from supervised learning, where you need labeled training data to train the model. Unsupervised learning is useful when you have a large amount of unlabeled data; it can be used for applications such as clustering, association, anomaly detection, etc. Clustering means dividing data points into different groups, called *clusters*. Association means to establish associations among data points in a large dataset. Anomaly detection means detecting abnormal data points in the dataset. This can be useful for finding fraudulent transactions.

Unsupervised learning includes a number of algorithms for clustering, such as the following:

- Hierarchical clustering
- K-means clustering
- K-NN
- Principal component analysis
- Singular-value decomposition
- Independent component analysis

K-means Clustering

K-means clustering is one of the most commonly used clustering algorithms. It is an iterative algorithm that helps you to find a number of clusters for a given dataset.

The following are the steps of the algorithm, as shown in Figure 3.17:

1. Randomly select K points as the center of K clusters, called *centroids*.

2. Calculate the distance between all centroids and the data points. Separate data points into different clusters according to the distances.

3. Calculate the mean of all the data of each cluster and move the centroids to the new center of the cluster.

4. Repeat steps 2 and 3 for a specified number of iterations until all the clusters are clearly separated.

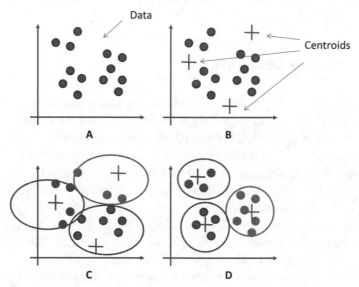

Figure 3.17: The steps of K-means clustering

For more details about K-means clustering, see the following:

```
https://www.educba.com/k-means-clustering-algorithm/
https://www.edureka.co/blog/k-means-clustering/
```

Example 3.20 shows a simple example of Python K-means clustering. It first creates a Numpy array named x, which contains two groups of values. It then performs the two-component K-means clustering by using the functions KMeans() and fit(). Finally, it displays the clustering results: the labels of the two clusters and centers of the two clusters and predicts a result for a given sample.

EXAMPLE 3.20   THE KMEANS.PY PROGRAM

```
Example 3.20 K-means Clustering
from sklearn.cluster import KMeans
import numpy as np

X = np.array([[1, 2, 3], [1, 4, 2], [1, 0, 3], \
              [10, 2, 4], [9, 4, 3], [11, 0, 2]])

kmeans = KMeans(n_clusters=2, random_state=0).fit(X)
print(kmeans.labels_)
print(kmeans.cluster_centers_)
print(kmeans.predict([[12, 3, 1]]))
```

The following is the output of the program:

```
[1 1 1 0 0 0]
[[10.          2.          3.          ]
 [ 1.          2.          2.66666667]]
[0]
```

EXERCISE 3.13

Modify the Python program from Example 3.20 so that it uses Scikit-Learn's function, `sklearn.datasets.make_blobs()`, to generate sample data points for K-means clustering. See the following links for the `sklearn.datasets.make_blobs()`:

  `https://scikit-learn.org/stable/modules/generated/sklearn`
`.datasets.make_blobs.html`

  `https://scikit-learn.org/stable/datasets/sample_generators`
`.html#sample-generators`

For more details about K-means clustering, see the Scikit-Learn library:

`https://scikit-learn.org/stable/modules/generated/sklearn.cluster`
`.KMeans.html`

For more details about unsupervised learning, see the Scikit-Learn library:

`https://scikit-learn.org/stable/unsupervised_learning.html`

3.5   Semi-supervised Learning

Semi-supervised learning lies somewhere between unsupervised learning (without labeled training data) and supervised learning (with labeled training data). Semi-supervised learning is typically used when you have a small amount of labeled data and a large amount of unlabeled data. In semi-supervised learning, data is first divided into different clusters using an unsupervised learning algorithm, and then the existing labeled data is used to label the rest of the unlabeled data.

To make the use of unlabeled data, semi-supervised learning assumes at least one of the following assumptions about the data:

- **Continuity assumption:** The data points that are closer to each other are more likely to have the same label.

- **Cluster assumption:** The data can be divided into different clusters, and each cluster shares the same label.

- **Manifold assumption:** The data lies on a much lower dimension space (called *manifold*) than the input space. This allows learning to use distances and densities defined on a manifold.

The following are four basic methods that are used in semi-supervised learning:

- **Generative models:** These are statistical models of the joint probability distribution on a given observable variable and target variable.

- **Low-density separation:** This attempts to place boundaries in regions with few data points (labeled or unlabeled).

- **Graph-based methods:** This models the problem space as a graph.

- **Heuristic approaches:** This uses a practical method to produce solutions that may not be optimal but are sufficient given a limited timeframe.

The following are three practical applications for semi-supervised learning:

- **Speech analysis:** Such as labeling audio files

- **Internet content classification:** Such as labeling web pages

- **Protein sequence classification:** Such as classifying protein families based on their sequence of aminoacids

For more details about semi-supervised learning, visit the following:

```
https://www.geeksforgeeks.org/ml-semi-supervised-learning/
https://scikit-learn.org/stable/modules/semi_supervised.html
```

Example 3.21 shows a simple example of Python semi-supervised learning. It first creates a Numpy array named x, which contains two groups of values. It then creates a label variable named `labels`. All the data points are not labeled, with a value of -1, except the first point labeled as 0, and the last point labeled as 1. This then creates the semi-supervised learning model by calling the `Label-Spreading()` function, trains the model by calling the `label_spread.fit()` function, spreads the label by calling the `label_spread.transduction_` function, and finally displays the label results.

EXAMPLE 3.21   THE `SEMIL.PY` PROGRAM

```
#Example 3.21 Semi-supervised Learning
import numpy as np
import matplotlib.pyplot as plt
from sklearn.semi_supervised import LabelSpreading
from sklearn.datasets import make_circles

X = np.array([[0,1],[1,1],[2,0],[3,1],[10,5],[11,6],[12,4],[13,5]])
y = np.array([0,0,0,0,1,1,1,1])

labels = np.full(8, -1.)
labels[0] = 0
labels[-1] = 1
print(labels)
```

```
label_spread = LabelSpreading(kernel='knn', alpha=0.8)
label_spread.fit(X, labels)
output_labels = label_spread.transduction_
print(output_labels)
```

The following is the program output with the labels before and the labels after the execution of the `LabelSpreading()` function. As you can see, all the data points have been correctly labeled.

```
[ 0. -1. -1. -1. -1. -1. -1.  1.]
[0. 0. 0. 0. 1. 1. 1. 1.]
```

EXERCISE 3.14

Sketch the X data points on a piece of paper, add two more points to each group, and modify the Python program from Example 3.20 accordingly.

EXERCISE 3.15

Sketch the X data points on a piece of paper, add the third group of points, and modify the Python program from Example 3.20 accordingly. Make sure in each group only one point is labeled.

3.6 Reinforcement Learning

Reinforcement learning (RL) is another type of machine learning technique that enables software agents to learn in an interactive environment by trial and error using feedback to maximize accumulative rewards. You have probably already used reinforcement learning in real life; for example, a dog can be taught tricks using reinforcement learning. The dog is the software agent, and the environment is where you teach it tricks. The dog does not understand what you want it to do; it simply tries different actions, and every time when it gets a right action, it gets a reward, or a treat. The next time, the dog learns to do the same thing again and gets the treat again. This is how training a dog works and how reinforcement learning works. Reinforcement learning is currently one of the hottest research topics.

Figure 3.18 shows a schematic diagram of reinforcement learning. In this case, an agent takes actions in an environment. The interpreter interprets these actions into a reward and a state, which are fed back into the agent. The agent adjusts its actions accordingly. This process is repeated many times to maximize the reward.

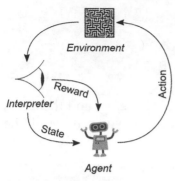

Figure 3.18: A schematic diagram of reinforcement learning, which includes an agent, actions, an environment, a reward, and a state

(Source: `https://en.wikipedia.org/wiki/Reinforcement_learning`)

Some key terms are often used in reinforcement learning, listed here:

- **Environment:** Physical world in which the agent operates
- **State:** Current situation of the agent
- **Reward:** Positive or negative feedback from the environment
- **Policy:** The rules that change agent's state to actions
- **Value:** Future reward that an agent would receive

Q-Learning and SARSA (State-Action-Reward-State-Action) are two commonly used model-free reinforcement learning algorithms. Q-Learning is an off-policy method in which the agent learns the value based on action derived from another policy. SARSA is an on-policy method where it learns the value based on its current action derived from its current policy. These two methods are simple to implement but lack the ability to estimate values for unseen states.

This can be solved by more advanced algorithms such as Deep Q-Networks (DQN) and Deep Deterministic Policy Gradient (DDPG). However, DQNs can handle only discrete, low-dimensional action spaces. DDPG tackles this problem by learning policies in high-dimensional, continuous action spaces.

The following are some practical applications of reinforcement learning:

- **Games:** Reinforcement learning is widely used for computer games. The best example is Google's AlphaGo, which defeated a world champion in the ancient Chinese game of Go. AlphaGo does not understand the rules of Go; it just learns to play the Go game by trial and error over many times.

- **Robotics:** Reinforcement learning is also widely used in robotics and industrial automation to enable the robot to create an efficient adaptive control system for itself that learns from its own experience and behavior.

- **Natural language processing:** Reinforcement learning is used for text summarization engines and dialog agents that can learn from user interactions and improve over time. This is commonly used in healthcare and online stock trading.

The following are a few popular online platforms for reinforcement learning:

- **DeepMind Lab:** This is an open source 3D game-like platform, created for reinforcement learning simulated environments.
  https://deepmind.com/blog/article/open-sourcing-deepmind-lab

- **Project Malmo:** This is another experimentation platform for reinforcement learning.
  https://www.microsoft.com/en-us/research/project/project-malmo/

- **OpenAI Gym:** This is a toolkit for building and comparing reinforcement learning algorithms.
  https://gym.openai.com/

Q-Learning

Q-learning is one of the most commonly used reinforcement learning algorithms. Let's look at an example to explain how Q-learning works. Take a simple routing example, as shown in Figure 3.19. It contains seven nodes (0–6), called *states*, and the aim is to choose the best route to go from the Start state (0) to the Goal state (6).

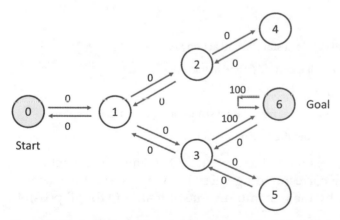

Figure 3.19: A simple routing problem with seven states, with 0 as the start state and 6 as the goal state

Based on Figure 3.19, you can construct a corresponding matrix R, which indicates the reward values from a state to take an action to the next state, as shown in Figure 3.20. The value 0 means it is possible to go from one state to another state, for example, from state 0 to state 1, from state 1 to state 2, and so on. The value -1 means it is not possible, for example, from state 0 to state 3, or from state 2 to state 6, and so on. The value 100 indicates reaching the Goal state; there are only two possibilities, from state 3 to state 6, and from state 6 to state 6.

Action

$$
R = \begin{array}{c} \\ \mathbf{0} \\ \mathbf{1} \\ \mathbf{2} \\ \mathbf{3} \\ \mathbf{4} \\ \mathbf{5} \\ \mathbf{6} \end{array}
\begin{array}{c}
\begin{array}{ccccccc} \mathbf{0} & \mathbf{1} & \mathbf{2} & \mathbf{3} & \mathbf{4} & \mathbf{5} & \mathbf{6} \end{array} \\
\left[\begin{array}{ccccccc}
-1 & 0 & -1 & -1 & -1 & -1 & -1 \\
0 & -1 & 0 & 0 & -1 & -1 & -1 \\
-1 & -1 & -1 & -1 & 0 & -1 & -1 \\
-1 & 0 & -1 & -1 & -1 & 0 & 100 \\
-1 & -1 & 0 & -1 & -1 & -1 & -1 \\
-1 & -1 & -1 & 0 & -1 & -1 & -1 \\
-1 & -1 & -1 & 0 & -1 & -1 & 100
\end{array}\right]
\end{array}
$$

State

Figure 3.20: The corresponding reward value R matrix of the routing problem

Based on the reward matrix R you can also construct a similar matrix Q, and you update the values of matrix Q iteratively by using the following formula:

$$Q(s,a) = R(s,a) + \gamma \times \max(Q(ns, aa))$$

where:

Q(s, a)	is the Q matrix value at state *(s)* and action *(a)*.
R(s, a)	is the R matrix value at state *(s)* and action *(a)*.
γ	is the learning rate.
Q(ns, aa)	is the Q matrix values at next state *(ns)* and all actions *(aa)*.
Max()	is the function to get the maximum values.

The formula basically says the value of matrix Q at state *(s)* and action *(a)* is equal to the sum of the corresponding value in matrix R and the learning parameter γ, multiplied by the maximum value of matrix Q for all possible actions in the next state.

Example 3.22 shows a simple example of Q-learning for the previous routing problem. It contains two programs, `Q_test.py` and `Q_Utils.py`. The following is the `Q_test.py` program.

EXAMPLE 3.22   THE Q_TEST.PY PROGRAM

```python
#Example 3.22 - Q_test.py
#Modified from:
#https://amunategui.github.io/reinforcement-learning/index.html
#http://firsttimeprogrammer.blogspot.com/2016/09/getting-ai-smarter-
with-q-learning.html
#http://mnemstudio.org/path-finding-q-learning-tutorial.htm
import numpy as np
import pylab as plt
from Q_Utils import *

# Setting up Parameters ==========================================
# Create a routing list and set the goal
points_list = [(0,1),(1,2),(1,3),(2,4),(3,5),(3,6)]
goal = 6

# Show the routing graph
showgraph(points_list)

# The number of points of the R matrix
MATRIX_SIZE = 7

# create matrix R
R = createRmat(MATRIX_SIZE,points_list,goal)

# Create matrix Q
Q = np.matrix(np.zeros([MATRIX_SIZE,MATRIX_SIZE]))

# Learning parameter
gamma = 0.8

# Training ================================================
scores = []
for i in range(700):
    #Select a random current_state (starting point)
    current_state = np.random.randint(0, int(Q.shape[0]))
    #Work out all the available next step actions
    available_act = available_actions(R, current_state)
    #Choose a random next step action
    action = sample_next_action(available_act)
    #Update the Q matrix
    score = update(R,Q,current_state,action,gamma)
    scores.append(score)
    print ('Score:', str(score))

print("Trained Q matrix:")
print(Q/np.max(Q)*100)
```

```
# Testing =========================================================
current_state = 0
steps = [current_state]

while current_state != goal:

    next_step_index = np.where(Q[current_state,] == np.max(Q[current_
state,]))[1]

    if next_step_index.shape[0] > 1:
        next_step_index = int(np.random.choice(next_step_index, size
= 1))
    else:
        next_step_index = int(next_step_index)

    steps.append(next_step_index)
    current_state = next_step_index

# Display Results ==================================================
print("Most efficient path:")
print(steps)

plt.plot(scores)
plt.show()
```

The following is the Q_Utils.py program, which contains the functions needed for Q-learning:

```
#Example 3.22 - Q_Utils.py
#Modified from:
#https://amunategui.github.io/reinforcement-learning/index.html
#http://firsttimeprogrammer.blogspot.com/2016/09/getting-ai-smarter-
with-q-learning.html
#http://mnemstudio.org/path-finding-q-learning-tutorial.htm
import numpy as np
import pylab as plt
import networkx as nx

def showgraph(points_list):
    G=nx.Graph()
    G.add_edges_from(points_list)
    pos = nx.spring_layout(G)
    nx.draw_networkx_nodes(G,pos)
    nx.draw_networkx_edges(G,pos)
    nx.draw_networkx_labels(G,pos)
    plt.show()

def createRmat(MATRIX_SIZE,points_list,goal):
    # create matrix x*y
```

```python
    R = np.matrix(np.ones(shape=(MATRIX_SIZE, MATRIX_SIZE)))
    R *= -1

    # assign zeros to paths and 100 to goal-reaching point
    for point in points_list:
        print(point)
        if point[1] == goal:
            R[point] = 100
        else:
            R[point] = 0

        if point[0] == goal:
            R[point[::-1]] = 100
        else:
            # reverse of point
            R[point[::-1]]= 0

    # add goal point round trip
    R[goal,goal]= 100
    print(R)
    return R

def available_actions(R, state):
    current_state_row = R[state,]
    av_act = np.where(current_state_row >= 0)[1]
    return av_act

def sample_next_action(available_act):
    next_action = int(np.random.choice(available_act,1))
    return next_action

def update(R, Q, current_state, action, gamma):

  max_index = np.where(Q[action,] == np.max(Q[action,]))[1]

  if max_index.shape[0] > 1:
      max_index = int(np.random.choice(max_index, size = 1))
  else:
      max_index = int(max_index)
  max_value = Q[action, max_index]

  Q[current_state, action] = R[current_state, action] + gamma * max_value
  print('max_value', R[current_state, action] + gamma * max_value)

  if (np.max(Q) > 0):
    return(np.sum(Q/np.max(Q)*100))
  else:
    return (0)
```

Figure 3.21 and Figure 3.22 show the corresponding outputs of Example 3.22.

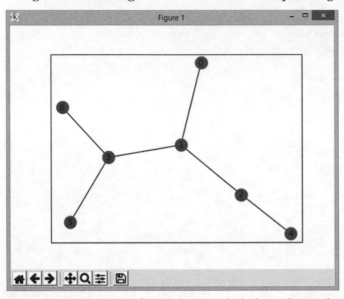

Figure 3.21: The output of Example 3.22, which shows the graph of the network

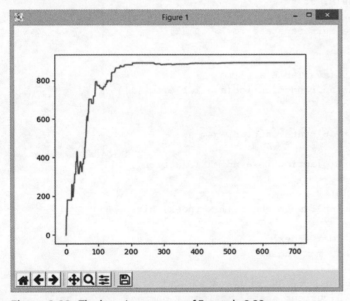

Figure 3.22: The learning process of Example 3.22

The following are the text output of the example, which shows the possible routes from node 0 to node 6, the R matrix with reward values, the training process (mostly omitted), and final trained Q matrix.

```
(0, 1)
(1, 2)
(1, 3)
```

```
(2, 4)
(3, 5)
(3, 6)
[[ -1.    0.   -1.   -1.   -1.   -1.   -1.   -1.]
 [  0.   -1.    0.    0.   -1.   -1.   -1.   -1.]
 [ -1.    0.   -1.   -1.    0.   -1.   -1.   -1.]
 [ -1.    0.   -1.   -1.   -1.    0.  100.   -1.]
 [ -1.   -1.    0.   -1.   -1.   -1.   -1.   -1.]
 [ -1.   -1.   -1.    0.   -1.   -1.   -1.   -1.]
 [ -1.    1.   -1.    0.   -1.   -1.  100.   -1.]
 [ -1.   -1.   -1.   -1.   -1.   -1.   -1.   -1.]]
max_value 0.0
max_value 0.0
Score: 0
max_value 0.0
max_value 0.0
Score: 0
max_value 0.0
Score: 0
max_value 0.0
Score: 0


... ...

max_value 255.93353860021085
Score: 890.5013677573843
Trained Q matrix:
[[  0.          64.           0.            0.            0.
     0.           0.        ]
 [ 51.2          0.          51.18893731  80.            0.
     0.           0.        ]
 [  0.          63.98617164   0.            0.           40.95114985
     0.           0.        ]
 [  0.          63.98617164   0.            0.            0.
    64.         100.        ]
 [  0.           0.          51.18893731   0.            0.
     0.           0.        ]
 [  0.           0.           0.           80.            0.
     0.           0.        ]
 [  0.           0.           0.           80.            0.
     0.         100.        ]]
Most efficient path:
[0, 1, 3, 6]
```

EXERCISE 3.16

Based on the example program from Example 3.22, design your own eight-state routing diagram, and modify the program from Example 3.22 accordingly to solve your routing problem.

Example 3.23 shows a simple program of Python reinforcement learning for balancing a cart pole, using the OpenAI Gym library. Figure 3.23 shows its output.

EXAMPLE 3.23   THE `GYM.PY` **PROGRAM**

```
# Example 3.23 OpenAI Gym CartPole
#https://gym.openai.com/docs/
#https://gym.openai.com/envs/CartPole-v0/

import gym
env = gym.make('CartPole-v0')
for i_episode in range(20):
    observation = env.reset()
    for t in range(100):
        env.render()
        print(observation)
        action = env.action_space.sample()
        observation, reward, done, info = env.step(action)
        if done:
            print("Episode finished after {} timesteps".format(t+1))
            break
env.close()
```

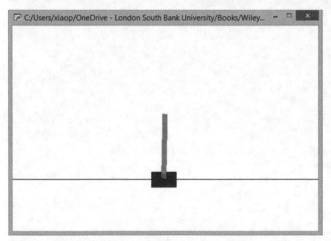

Figure 3.23: The output of Example 3.23, which shows the balancing of a cart pole by using reinforcement learning

3.7   Ensemble Learning

Ensemble learning is a process that uses multiple learning algorithms, or multiple models, to obtain better performance than could be obtained from a single learning algorithm or model. Ensemble learning is mainly used to improve the performance of applications such as classifications, regressions, predictions, and so on.

Two methods are usually used in ensemble learning:

- **Averaging methods:** In this method, multiple estimators are created independently, and then their predictions are averaged. On average, the combined estimator is usually better than any of the individual base estimators because its variance is reduced. Examples of averaging methods include bagging, forests of randomized trees, and so on.

- **Boosting methods:** This method builds the base estimators sequentially and tries to reduce the bias of the combined estimator. By combining multiple weak models, it is possible to produce a powerful ensemble. Examples of boosting methods are AdaBoost, gradient tree boosting, and so on.

For more details of ensemble learning in the Scikit-Learn library, visit this page:

```
https://scikit-learn.org/stable/modules/ensemble.html
```

Example 3.24 shows a simple program of Python ensemble learning for iris classification. It uses four different classifiers: logistic regression, random forest, naive Bayes, and SVM. It then uses VotingClassifier to choose the best classifier.

EXAMPLE 3.24   THE ENSEMBLE1.PY PROGRAM

```python
# Example 3.24 Ensemble1.py
from sklearn import datasets
from sklearn.model_selection import cross_val_score
from sklearn.linear_model import LogisticRegression
from sklearn.naive_bayes import GaussianNB
from sklearn.ensemble import RandomForestClassifier
from sklearn.ensemble import VotingClassifier
from sklearn.svm import SVC

iris = datasets.load_iris()
X, y = iris.data[:, 1:3], iris.target

clf1 = LogisticRegression(random_state=1)
clf2 = RandomForestClassifier(n_estimators=50, random_state=1)
clf3 = GaussianNB()
clf4 = SVC()

eclf = VotingClassifier(
    estimators=[('lr', clf1), ('rf', clf2), ('gnb', clf3), ('svc', clf4)],
    voting='hard')
```

```
for clf, label in zip([clf1, clf2, clf3, clf4, eclf], ['Logistic
Regression', 'Random Forest', 'naive Bayes', 'SVM', 'Ensemble']):
    scores = cross_val_score(clf, X, y, scoring='accuracy', cv=5)
    print("Accuracy: %0.2f (+/- %0.2f) [%s]" % (scores.mean(),
scores.std(), label))
```

The following is the output of the program, which shows the accuracy of each model.

```
Accuracy: 0.95 (+/- 0.04) [Logistic Regression]
Accuracy: 0.94 (+/- 0.04) [Random Forest]
Accuracy: 0.91 (+/- 0.04) [naive Bayes]
Accuracy: 0.95 (+/- 0.04) [SVM]
Accuracy: 0.95 (+/- 0.04) [Ensemble]
```

EXERCISE 3.17

Modify the Python program from Example 3.24 to add another classifier to the ensemble learning, for example, K-nearest neighbor (`https://scikit-learn.org/stable/modules/generated/sklearn.neighbors.KNeighborsClassifier.html`).

Example 3.25 shows a simple program of Python ensemble learning for diabetes data regression. It first loads the diabetes dataset as X and y, where X contains the values of age, sex, body mass index, average blood pressure, and six blood serum measurements of 442 diabetes patients, and y is the response variable with a range of 25–346; it is a measure of disease progression one year after baseline. It uses four different regressors: gradient boosting, random forest, linear regression, and MLP (neural networks). It then uses `VotingRegressor` to choose the best regressor. Figure 3.24 shows its output.

EXAMPLE 3.25 THE `ENSEMBLE2.PY` PROGRAM

```
# Example 3.25 Ensemble2.py

import matplotlib.pyplot as plt

from sklearn.datasets import load_diabetes
from sklearn.ensemble import GradientBoostingRegressor
from sklearn.ensemble import RandomForestRegressor
from sklearn.linear_model import LinearRegression
from sklearn.ensemble import VotingRegressor
from sklearn.neural_network import MLPRegressor
```

```
X, y = load_diabetes(return_X_y=True)

# Train classifiers
reg1 = GradientBoostingRegressor(random_state=1)
reg2 = RandomForestRegressor(random_state=1)
reg3 = LinearRegression()
reg4 = MLPRegressor()

reg1.fit(X, y)
reg2.fit(X, y)
reg3.fit(X, y)
reg4.fit(X, y)
ereg = VotingRegressor(estimators=[('gb', reg1), ('rf', reg2), ('lr',
reg3), ('NN', reg4)])
print(ereg.fit(X, y))

# %%
# Making predictions
# --------------------------------
#
# Now we will use each of the regressors to make the 20 first
predictions.

xt = X[:20]

pred1 = reg1.predict(xt)
pred2 = reg2.predict(xt)
pred3 = reg3.predict(xt)
pred4 = reg4.predict(xt)
pred5 = ereg.predict(xt)


plt.figure()
plt.plot(pred1, 'gd', label='GradientBoostingRegressor')
plt.plot(pred2, 'b^', label='RandomForestRegressor')
plt.plot(pred3, 'ys', label='LinearRegression')
plt.plot(pred4, 'mo', label='NeuralNetworks')
plt.plot(pred5, 'r*', ms=10, label='VotingRegressor')

plt.tick_params(axis='x', which='both', bottom=False, top=False,
                labelbottom=False)
plt.ylabel('predicted')
plt.xlabel('training samples')
plt.legend(loc="best")
plt.title('Regressor predictions and their average')

plt.show()
```

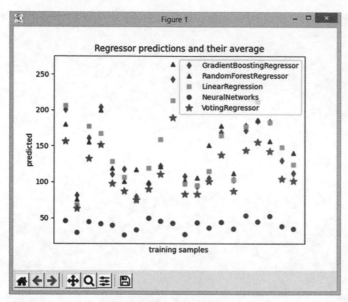

Figure 3.24: The output of Example 3.25, which shows the results of different regression algorithms

3.8 AutoML

Automated machine learning (AutoML) is the process of automating machine learning, from a raw dataset to a deployable model, for easily solving real-world problems. With AutoML, you can use machine learning without having to become an expert in the field.

For more details about AutoML, visit this site:

```
https://www.automl.org/automl/
```

There are several AutoML frameworks available, as listed here:

- **AutoWEKA** is automated machine learning for the WEKA package.

```
http://www.cs.ubc.ca/labs/beta/Projects/autoweka/
https://github.com/automl/pyautoweka
```

- **Auto-sklearn** is automated machine learning for the Python Scikit-Learn library.

```
https://automl.github.io/auto-sklearn/master/
```

- **TPOT** stands for tree-based pipeline optimization tool. It is built on the Scikit-Learn library and optimizes machine learning pipelines using genetic programming.

```
http://epistasislab.github.io/tpot/
```

- **H2O AutoML** provides automated model selection and ensemble learning for the H2O platform. H2O is an open source, machine learning platform for big data and enterprise applications.

  `http://docs.h2o.ai/h2o/latest-stable/h2o-docs/automl.html`

- **TransmogrifAI** is an AutoML library written in Scala running on the top of Apache Spark.

  `https://github.com/salesforce/TransmogrifAI`

- **MLBoX** is an AutoML library with three components: preprocessing, optimization, and prediction.

  `https://github.com/AxeldeRomblay/MLBox`

Let's look at some AutoML example code to demonstrate how to use the AutoML library, called AutoML. You can install the library using the `pip` command, as shown here:

```
pip install automl
```

For more details about the library, check out the following:

`https://pypi.org/project/automl/`

Example 3.26 shows a simple test program of Python AutoML for Boston housing price regression using the AutoML library.

EXAMPLE 3.26   THE `AUTO_ML_TEST.PY` **PROGRAM**

```python
# Example 3.26 Auto_ml_test.py
from auto_ml import Predictor
from auto_ml.utils import get_boston_dataset

df_train, df_test = get_boston_dataset()

column_descriptions = {
    'MEDV': 'output',
    'CHAS': 'categorical'
}

ml_predictor = Predictor(type_of_estimator='regressor',
column_descriptions=column_descriptions)
ml_predictor.train(df_train)
ml_predictor.score(df_test, df_test.MEDV)
```

The following is the output:

```
[360] random_holdout_set_from_training_data's score is: -3.019
The number of estimators that were the best for this training dataset: 260
The best score on the holdout set: -3.0164762974861277
Finished training the pipeline!
Total training time:
0:00:02


Here are the results from our GradientBoostingRegressor
predicting MEDV
Calculating feature responses, for advanced analytics.
The printed list will only contain at most the top 100 features.
+----+----------------+--------------+----------+------------------+----------------
----+----------+----------+----------+----------+
|    | Feature Name   |  Importance  |  Delta   |  FR_Decrementing |  FR_
Incrementing |  FRD_abs  |  FRI_abs  |  FRD_MAD  |  FRI_MAD |
|----+----------------+--------------+----------+------------------+----------------
----+----------+----------+----------+----------|
| 12 | CHAS=0.0       |      0.0002  | nan      |        nan       |       nan
|  nan      | nan      | nan      | nan      |
| 1  | ZN             |      0.0004  | 11.5619  |       -0.0076    |
0.0274  |   0.0111  |   0.0373  |   0.0000  |   0.0000 |
| 13 | CHAS=1.0       |      0.0006  | nan      |        nan       |       nan
|  nan      | nan      | nan      | nan      |
| 7  | RAD            |      0.0026  | 4.2895   |       -0.7435    |
0.1468  |   0.7463  |   0.1506  |   0.4483  |   0.0000 |


... ...


**************************************************
Advanced scoring metrics for the trained regression model on this
particular dataset:

Here is the overall RMSE for these predictions:
2.6904150974597933

Here is the average of the predictions:
21.162475591449812

Here is the average actual value on this validation set:
21.488235294117654

Here is the median prediction:
20.198866346944087
```

```
Here is the median actual value:
20.15

Here is the mean absolute error:
1.9106331359259123

Here is the median absolute error (robust to outliers):
1.3878228036848688

Here is the explained variance:
0.9027431327637244

Here is the R-squared value:
0.9012960591325954
Count of positive differences (prediction > actual):
46
Count of negative differences:
56
Average positive difference:
1.7571422846991702
Average negative difference:
-2.03671490657645


**************************************************
```

EXERCISE 3.18

Modify the Python program from Example 3.26 to use the California housing dataset for regression (`https://scikit-learn.org/stable/modules/generated/sklearn.datasets.fetch_california_housing.html`).

3.9   PyCaret

PyCaret is an impressive open source machine learning library in Python that allows you to use multiple models to analyze your data automatically. PyCaret is basically a wrapper around several machine learning libraries such as Scikit-Learn, XGBoost, Microsoft LightGBM, spaCy, and more. PyCaret is a low-code library, and it is best known for its ease of use and efficiency.

To use the PyCaret library, you need to install the library using the `pip` command, as shown here:

```
pip install pycaret
```

Example 3.27 shows a simple Python PyCaret classification demo program for the iris dataset. It is remarkably simple, requiring only one line of code to set up the classification environment and one line of code to compare all the models.

EXAMPLE 3.27   THE `PYCARET_DEMO.PY` **PROGRAM**

```
#Example 3.27 The PyCaret_demo.py
#!pip install pycaret
import pandas as pd
from sklearn import datasets

iris = datasets.load_iris(as_frame=True)
iris.data['Target'] = iris.target
iris   = iris.data
iris.head()

from pycaret import classification
classification.setup(data= iris, target='Target')
classification.compare_models()
```

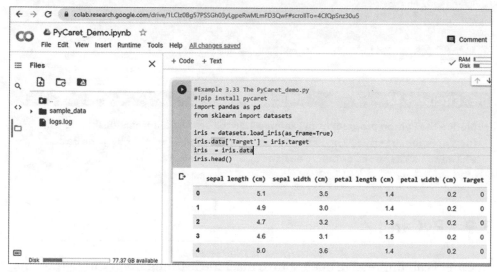

Figure 3.25: The first part of the output of Example 3.27, which shows the Iris dataset

It is easier to run the previous code in Google Colab. Just log in to Google Colab and load the file `PyCaret_Demo.ipynb`. Figure 3.25 shows the code to load the iris dataset, the code to format it into the required dataframe, and the first five rows of the data. Figure 3.26 shows the code for setting up the classification environment and comparing the models. The results show that linear discriminant analysis gives the best results, with more than 99 percent accuracy.

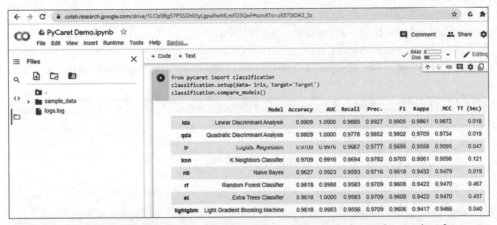

Figure 3.26: The second part of the output of Example 3.27, which shows the results of different regression algorithms

---

EXERCISE 3.19

Modify Example 3.27's Python PyCaret demo program to use the breast cancer dataset for classification (`https://scikit-learn.org/stable/modules/generated/sklearn.datasets.load_breast_cancer.html#sklearn.datasets.load_breast_cancer`).

You can use PyCaret for both classification problems and regression problems. For more details about PyCaret, see the following:

```
https://pycaret.org/
https://pycaret.org/create-model/
```

3.10   LazyPredict

LazyPredict is another cool library that can perform classification and regression, using a list of algorithms. For more details, see the following:

```
https://github.com/shankarpandala/lazypredict
```

To install the LazyPredict library, use this:

```
pip install lazypredict
```

Example 3.28 (a, b, c, d and e) is a simple demo example program of Python LazyPredict. Again, it can be easily run on Google Colab. Just go to Google Colab and upload the file called `lazypredict.ipynb`.

Example 3.28a shows the first section of the code that simply installs the LazyPredict library on Google Colab.

EXAMPLE 3.28A   THE `LAZYPREDICT.IPYNB` PROGRAM (PART 1)

```
!pip install lazypredit
```

Example 3.28b is the second section of the code that uses the iris dataset as an example to demonstrate the use of LazyPredict for a classifier with the function `LazyClassifier()`. Again, it is remarkably simple, just one line of code to create the LazyPredict classifier and one line of code to fit and compare the models.

EXAMPLE 3.28B   THE `LAZYPREDICT.IPYNB` PROGRAM (PART 2)

```
import lazypredict
from lazypredict.Supervised import LazyClassifier
from sklearn.datasets import load_iris
from sklearn.model_selection import train_test_split

X, y = load_iris(return_X_y=True)
X_train, X_test, y_train, y_test = train_test_split(X, y,test_
size=.25,random_state =1)

clf = LazyClassifier()
models,predictions = clf.fit(X_train, X_test, y_train, y_test)
print(models)
```

Figure 3.27 shows the Google Colab code of the first two sections of the program. Figure 3.28 shows the output of the second section's classification code. The results show that LabelSpreading gives the best classification results, with 100 percent accuracy!

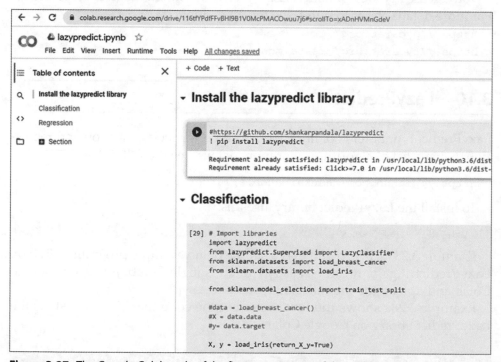

Figure 3.27: The Google Colab code of the first two sections of the program

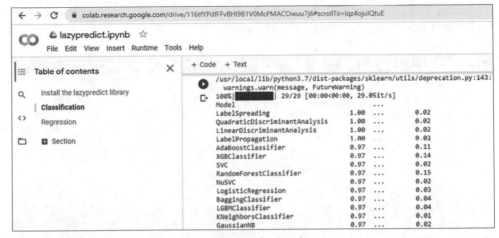

Figure 3.28: The output of the LazyPredict classifier results

Example 3.28c shows the section of code that plots the accuracy of different models. Figure 3.29 shows the output of the plot.

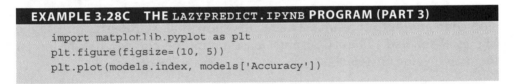

EXAMPLE 3.28C   THE LAZYPREDICT.IPYNB PROGRAM (PART 3)

```
import matplotlib.pyplot as plt
plt.figure(figsize=(10, 5))
plt.plot(models.index, models['Accuracy'])
```

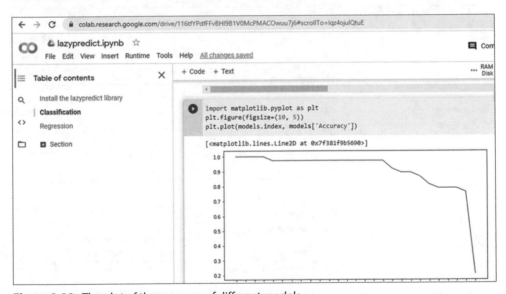

Figure 3.29: The plot of the accuracy of different models

Example 3.28d shows how to use LazyPredict for regression. It uses the California housing price dataset as the example.

EXAMPLE 3.28D THE `LAZYPREDICT.IPYNB` PROGRAM (PART 4)

```
import lazypredict
from lazypredict.Supervised import LazyRegressor
from sklearn import datasets
from sklearn.utils import shuffle
import numpy as np
from sklearn.datasets import fetch_california_housing

X, y = fetch_california_housing(return_X_y=True, as_frame=True)
X_train, X_test, y_train, y_test = train_test_split(X, y,test_
size=.1,random_state =1)


reg = LazyRegressor()
models, predictions = reg.fit(X_train, X_test, y_train, y_test)
print(models)
```

Figure 3.30 shows the Google Colab California housing price dataset regression code and output results. The results show that XGBRegressor has the highest R-squared value of 0.84, and GaussianProcessRegressor has the lowest R-squared value of -4467.92.

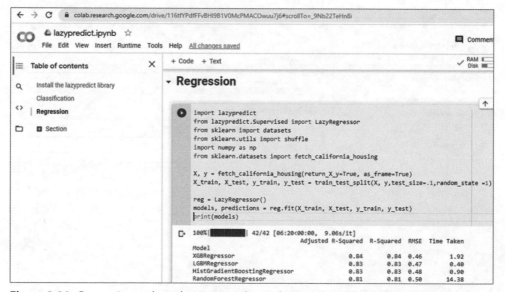

Figure 3.30: Regression code and output results on the Google Colab California housing price dataset

Example 3.28e plots the R-squared values of different models. Figure 3.31 shows the plot of R-squared values of different models.

EXAMPLE 3.28E   THE `LAZYPREDICT.IPYNB` **PROGRAM (PART 5)**

```
import matplotlib.pyplot as plt
plt.figure(figsize=(10, 5))
plt.plot(models.index, models['R-Squared'],'-s')
```

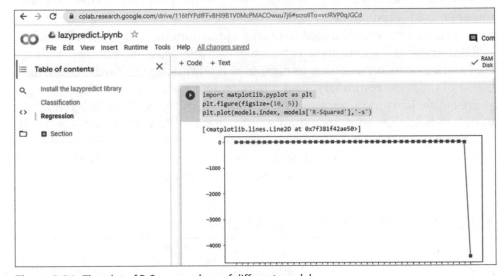

Figure 3.31: The plot of R-Square values of different models

EXERCISE 3.20

Modify the Python program from Example 3.28 using a different dataset for classification.

EXERCISE 3.21

Modify the Python program from Example 3.28 using a different dataset for regression.

3.11   Summary

This chapter provides a comprehensive overview of machine learning. Machine learning is an important aspect of AI and can be divided into supervised learning, unsupervised learning, semi-supervised learning, and reinforcement learning.

Supervised learning can be generally divided into classification and regression. Classification means predicting the class or category to which the data belongs. Commonly used classification algorithms include support vector machines, naive Bayes, linear discriminant analysis, decision tree, random forest, K-nearest neighbors, neural networks. and so on. Regression means predicting the output values for a given set of input values.

Unsupervised learning is mainly used for clustering data, and K-means clustering is a popular algorithm.

Semi-supervised learning is somewhere between supervised learning and unsupervised learning. Semi-supervised learning is typically used when you have a small amount of labeled data and a large amount of unlabeled data.

Reinforcement learning involves learning in an interactive environment through trial and error using feedback to maximize accumulative rewards. Q-learning is one of the most commonly used reinforcement learning algorithms.

Ensemble learning uses multiple learning algorithms, or multiple models, to obtain better performance than would be possible with a single learning algorithm or model.

AutoML, PyCaret, and LazyPredict are some popular libraries that can automatically use multiple learning algorithms to analyze the data.

3.12   Chapter Review Questions

Q3.1.   What is machine learning?

Q3.2.   What is supervised learning?

Q3.3.   What is the difference between classification and regression in supervised learning?

Q3.4.   What is SVM? What can it be used for?

Q3.5.   What is naive Bayes, and how does it work?

Q3.6.   What is linear discriminant analysis, and what is principal component analysis?

Q3.7.   What is the difference between decision tree and random forest?

Q3.8.   How does K-nearest neighbors work?

Q3.9.   What is unsupervised learning?

Q3.10.   What is K-means clustering?

Q3.11.   What is semi-supervised learning?

Q3.12.   What is reinforcement learning, and what can it be used for?

Q3.13.   What is Q-learning?

Q3.14.   What is ensemble learning?

Q3.15.   What are the AutoML, PyCaret, and LazyPredict libraries?

Deep Learning

"Our intelligence is what makes us human, and AI is an extension of that quality."

—Yann LeCun (French computer scientist)

CHAPTER OUTLINE

4.1 Introduction

Deep learning (DL) has attracted the world's attention since 2012, when AlexNet won the famous ImageNet challenge. Since then, deep learning has been the hottest research topic in AI. Most of the AI research news you hear today is based on deep learning.

Deep learning is largely considered a subset of machine learning, and it is built on traditional artificial neural networks. As illustrated in Figure 4.1 (left), traditional artificial neural networks typically have one input layer, one output layer, and one hidden layer. The reason they have only one hidden layer is that as the number of hidden layers increases, the complexity also increases, which makes computations unstable and impossible. Deep learning neural networks have an input layer, an output layer, and more than one layer of hidden layers. Deep learning neural networks can have more than one hidden layer due to improved algorithms and higher computing power.

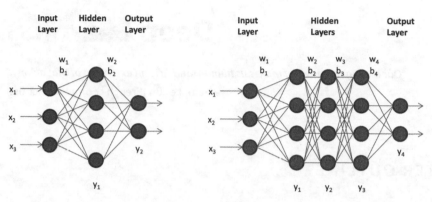

Figure 4.1: Traditional artificial neural networks (left) and deep learning neural networks (right)

Deep learning neural networks can be generally divided into two types:

- Convolutional neural networks
- Recurrent neural networks

Convolutional neural networks are mainly for images, while recurrent neural networks are mainly for sequence data, such as text and time series.

Deep learning can be dated back to 1989, when Yann LeCun and his colleagues proposed a structure for a convolutional neural network, called LeNet. LeNet was successfully used in handwritten digit recognition.

In 2010, Professor Feifei Li of Stanford University created the ImageNet (http://image-net.org/), the largest image database that contains more than 14 million images of daily objects, divided into more than 20,000 categories, such as cats, dogs, cars, tables, chairs, and so on. ImageNet then launched an annual challenge on image classification, called ImageNet Large Scale Visual Recognition Challenge (ILSVRC). The ImageNet challenges only use 1,000 categories. The competitions ran from 2010 to 2017, and moved to Kaggle (https://www.kaggle.com/c/imagenet-object-localization-challenge) after 2017.

The breakthrough came in 2012, when Alex Krizhevsky, Ilya Sutskever, and Geoffrey Hinton from the University of Toronto developed AlexNet. AlexNet won the competition with an impressive top-five accuracy of 85 percent. The next best result was far behind at 74 percent.

In image classification, top-one accuracy is the accuracy with which the best prediction must match the expected answer. Top-five accuracy means that each of the top five answers has the highest probability of matching the expected answer.

The key finding of the original AlexNet publication was that the depth of the model was critical to its high performance. This was computationally expensive but was made feasible by the utilization of graphics processing units (GPUs) during training.

Geoffrey Hinton, Yann LeCun, and Yoshua Bengio, a Canadian computer scientist, are sometimes referred to as the Godfathers of AI or the Godfathers of Deep Learning for their work on deep learning.

In 2014, Christian Szegedy and colleagues at Google achieved top results in object detection with its GoogLeNet model that used the inception module and architecture. This approach was described in its 2014 paper titled "Going Deeper with Convolutions." GoogLeNet (later known as Inception) becomes the nearest neural network counterpart with a top-five error rate of 6.66 percent. Karen Simonyan and Andrew Zisserman in the Oxford Vision Geometry Group (VGG) achieved top results for image classification and localization with their VGG model. VGG is second place with a top-five error rate of 7.3 percent. The best human-level error rate for classifying ImageNet data is 5.1 percent.

In 2015, Kaiming He and colleagues from Microsoft Research achieved top results in object detection and object detection with localization tasks using their residual network (ResNet). ResNet outperformed human recognition and classified images with a top-five error rate of 3.7 percent.

EfficientNet claims to have achieved a top-five classification accuracy of 97.1 percent in 2019. Figure 4.2 shows the state of the art in image classification on ImageNet, published by Papers with Code.

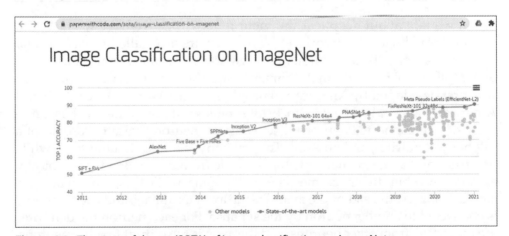

Figure 4.2: The state of the art (SOTA) of image classification on ImageNet

(Source: https://paperswithcode.com/sota/image-classification-on-imagenet)

Figure 4.3 shows typical performances of traditional machine learning algorithms, conventional neural networks (also known as shallow neural networks), and the performance of deep learning neural networks.

Initially, when there is less data, the traditional machine learning algorithms were very efficient and effective. But when the amount of data reaches millions, their performance reaches a plateau, and the performance maintains a stable level even if the data size increases. The traditional neural networks perform better with a larger data set, but still reach a plateau at some point. Only deep learning neural networks continue to increase their performance as data size increases. This is the reason why deep learning neural networks are attracting much research attention.

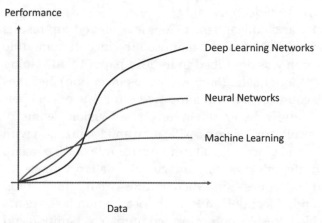

Figure 4.3: The typical performances of traditional machine learning algorithms, traditional neural networks, and deep learning neural networks against the data

4.2   Artificial Neural Networks

When we talk about deep learning neural networks, we have to start with the traditional neural networks (NNs), which are also called *artificial neural networks* (ANNs). Traditional neural networks are computer simulations of biological neural networks in the human brain. The concept of neural networks was first developed by American neurophysiologist Warren McCulloch and American logician Walter Pitts in 1943. A biological neural network is a network of interconnected neurons. The biological neuron typically consists of a cell body, dendrites, and an axon. The cell body is also called the *soma*, while dendrites and axon are filaments that extrude from it. The dendrites typically extrude a few hundred micrometers from the soma, while the axon can be up to a meter long. At the end of the axon are the axon terminals, and each terminal is connected to another neuron by the synapse. For each neuron the dendrites are the inputs from other neurons, and the axon is the output to other neurons. A human brain typically has 100 billion neurons.

There are three types of neurons: sensory neurons respond to stimuli such as touch, sound, or light and send signals to the brain. Motor neurons receive signals from the brain to control muscle. Interneurons connect neurons to other neurons.

Similar to biological neurons, artificial neurons also have an input and an output, as shown in Figure 4.4. Artificial neurons take input signals, multiply them by weights, add them together, and then pass them to a nonlinear activation function for output. The activation function of a node defines the output of that node as a function of an input or a set of inputs. Similar to biological neuron networks, artificial neural networks consist of interconnected artificial neurons. They usually have three layers, as shown in Figure 4.4: an input layer, an output layer, and a hidden layer. The reason they have only one hidden layer is that the computation complexity increases as the number of layers increases.

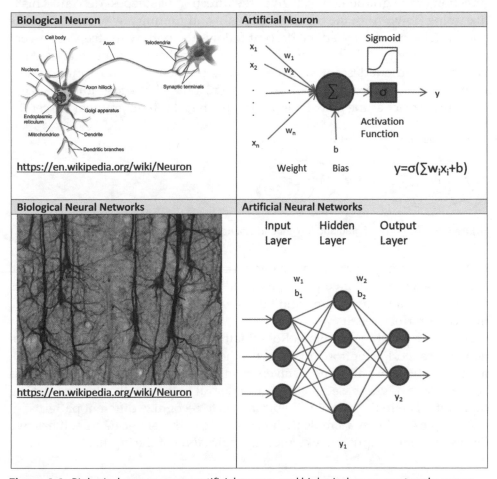

Figure 4.4: Biological neuron versus artificial neuron, and biological neuron networks versus artificial neuron networks

To train an artificial neural network, we first initialize the neural network's weights randomly, and then we feed the network a set of training data, with certain inputs and outputs. Each time the network produces an output from the inputs, it uses a loss function to compare the computed output with the desired output and then returns the differences, called *errors*, to the network to adjust the weights accordingly. This is called *backpropagation*, short for "backward propagation of errors." The weights are adjusted according to the errors using a method called *gradient descent*, which calculates the gradient of the errors with respect to the neural network weights and adjusts the weights to reduce the errors. This process is then repeated many times until the neural network weights are stabilized. Training an artificial neural network is essentially an optimization problem.

Gradient descent is a commonly used iterative optimization algorithm to find a local minimum of a function. The idea is to take repeated steps in the opposite direction of the gradient, which gives the direction of steepest descent. This is like going down from the top of a mountain and finding a way to explore the bottom. The standard gradient descent follows the path with steepest descent and tends to get stuck at a local minimum. The Stochastic gradient descent is a variant of gradient descent, which solves this problem by adding randomness to the path, as illustrated in Figure 4.5. As a result, stochastic gradient descent converges (reaches the global minimum) much faster than gradient descent.

Gradient Decent   Stochastic Gradient Decent

Figure 4.5: The paths of gradient descent and stochastic gradient descent

After training, you can feed the network with a set of unseen data as input, and the network will give you a predicted output. Artificial neural networks usually need a lot of training and take a long time to train, but once trained, they can produce results very quickly.

American psychologist Frank Rosenblatt developed the first artificial neural network called Perceptron in 1958, when he was working at the Cornell Aeronautical Laboratory at Cornell University in Buffalo, New York. Perceptron was an electronic device based on biological neural networks that had a learning capability. The main goal of Perceptron was to recognize different patterns.

Example 4.1 shows a simple Python example with a single neuron. It has two inputs and one output and executes the logic AND of the inputs.

EXAMPLE 4.1   THE NEURON.PY **PROGRAM**

```
#Example 4.1 Neuron.py

from numpy import exp, array, random, dot

#Set up parameters ==================================================
inputs = array([[0, 0], [1, 1], [1, 0], [0, 1]])
outputs = array([[0, 1, 1, 1]]).T
random.seed(1)
weights = 2 * random.random((2, 1)) - 1

#Define a Single Neuron function ===================================
def neuron(inputs, weights):
    output = 1 / (1 + exp(-(dot(inputs, weights))))
    return output

#Train the Neuron ==================================================
for iteration in range(50000):
    output = 1 / (1 + exp(-(dot(inputs, weights))))
    weights += dot(inputs.T, (outputs - output) * output *
(1 - output))

#Test the Neuron ==================================================
x = array([1, 0])
print (neuron (x,weights))
```

EXERCISE 4.1

Modify Python program from the Example 4.1 so that it performs a logical OR of the inputs.

Example 4.2 shows a Python multiple layer perceptron using the Scikit-Learn library. It has two inputs and one output and performs the logical AND of the inputs.

EXAMPLE 4.2   THE MLP.PY **PROGRAM**

```
#Example 4.2 Multiple Layer Perceptron
#https://scikit-learn.org/stable/modules/neural_networks_supervised
.html
from sklearn.neural_network import MLPClassifier
X = [[0., 0.], [1., 1.], [0., 1.], [1., 0.]]
y = [0, 1, 1, 1]
```

```
clf = MLPClassifier(solver='lbfgs', alpha=1e-5,
                    hidden_layer_sizes=(5, 2), random_state=1)
clf.fit(X, y)
print(clf.predict([[2., 2.], [-1., -2.]]))
print([coef.shape for coef in clf.coefs_])
```

EXERCISE 4.2

Modify the Python program from Example 4.2 so that it has three inputs, instead of two inputs.

Example 4.3 shows a simple Keras multiple layer perceptron for the breast cancer classification. It has an input layer, a hidden layer (dense layer) of 10 neurons, and an output layer. The dense layer is a neural network layer that each neuron in the dense layer receives input from all neurons of its previous layer.

EXAMPLE 4.3   THE MPL2.PY PROGRAM

```
#Example 4.4 Multiple Layer Perceptron Classification
from keras.models import Sequential
from keras.layers import Activation, Dense
from keras import optimizers
from sklearn.datasets import load_breast_cancer
from sklearn.model_selection import train_test_split

whole_data = load_breast_cancer()
X_data = whole_data.data
y_data = whole_data.target
X_train, X_test, y_train, y_test = train_test_split(X_data, y_data,
test_size = 0.3, random_state = 7)

features = X_train.shape[1]


#MPL 3-layer Model ==============================================
model = Sequential()
model.add(Dense(10, activation='relu', input_shape=[X_train
.shape[1]]))
model.add(Dense(10, activation='relu'))
model.add(Dense(1))
print(model.summary())
print(model.get_config())

model.compile(optimizer = 'adam', loss = 'mean_squared_error',
metrics = ['mse'])
```

```
model.fit(X_train, y_train, batch_size = 50, validation_split=0.2,
epochs = 100, verbose = 1)

results = model.evaluate(X_test, y_test)

print('loss: ', results[0])
print('accuracy: ', results[1])
```

EXERCISE 4.3

Modify the Python program from Example 4.3 so that it uses five neurons for the dense layer, instead of 10 neurons. Compare the performances, such as the training time and the accuracy.

For more information about traditional neural network, also called multiple layer perceptron, check the following links:

https://scikit-learn.org/stable/modules/neural_networks_
supervised.html

https://scikit-neuralnetwork.readthedocs.io/en/latest/module_
mlp.html

https://docs.oracle.com/javase/8/docs/technotes/guides/swing/index
.html

https://keras.io/guides/sequential_model/

4.3   Convolutional Neural Networks

The convolutional neural network (CNN, or ConvNet) is probably the most widely used deep learning neural network. CNN is mainly used for image analysis, e.g., image classification, object detection, and image segmentation. It can also be used in recommendation systems, natural language processing, brain-computer interfaces, and financial time series. To date, a number of CNNs have been developed, such as LeNet, AlexNet, GoogLeNet (now Inception), VGG, ResNet, DenseNet, MobileNet, EffecientNet, YOLO, and so on.

Figure 4.6 shows a typical architecture of convolutional neural network that contains an input layer, convolutional layers, pooling layers (subsampling, or down sampling), activation layers, fully connected layers, and an output layer.

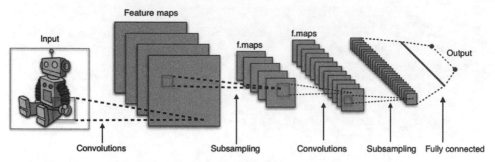

Figure 4.6: Typical convolutional neural network architecture

(Source: `https://en.wikipedia.org/wiki/Convolutional_neural_network`)

Input Layer   This is the layer that takes images as input. It typically has a size of 32 × 32 × 1 for handwriting digit images in grayscale, and 224 × 224 × 3 for color photo images.

Convolutional Layer   This is the core structure of a convolutional neural network. It uses feature filters (also called *kernels*) to extra feature information from the input. Figure 4.7a shows some commonly used image filters, or image kernels, that can perform sharpening, blurring, and edge detection of an input image. Figure 4.7b shows the convolution process of an image and a kernel. The convolution process is essentially to multiply the image matrix values with kernel values as an element-wise product and then add all the values to get the convoluted results.

Pooling Layer   Pooling layer is another core structure of CNN. The pooling layer is used for downsampling. Max pooling is the most commonly used pooling. As shown in Figure 4.8, max pooling divides the input image into a series of nonoverlapping rectangles and outputs the maximum for each of these subregions. In this example, a 4 × 48 × 8 image has been mapped by a 2 × 2 window with the stride size of 2. Within the 2 × 2 window, each region (2 × 2) is collapsed into a single pixel by choosing the maximum value. In this way, the entire 4 × 4 image is downsampled into a 2 × 2 image. Another commonly used pooling is average pooling.

Activation Layer   The activation function of a node defines the output of that node as a function of an input or a set of inputs. There are three commonly used activation functions: REctified Linear Unit (ReLU), hyperbolic tangent, and sigmoid function, as shown in Figure 4.9. In deep learning, ReLU is often preferred because it makes neural network training much faster.

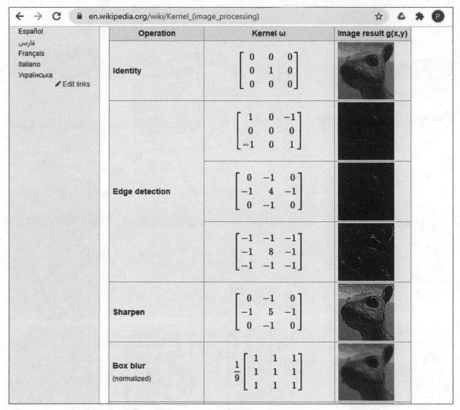

Figure 4.7a: Commonly used image convolution filters (kernels)

(Source: https://en.wikipedia.org/wiki/Kernel_(image_processing))

Fully Connected Layer After several convolutional layers and max pooling layers, the high-level reasoning in the neural network is done via fully connected layers. The neurons in a fully connected layer have connections to all activations in the previous layer, as shown in regular (nonconvolutional) artificial neural networks. Fully connected layer is also called *dense layer*.

Dropout Layer The dropout layer drops out some of nodes in the neural network to prevent overfitting. Dropout layer can be used with most types of layers, typically after the fully connected layer.

Output Layer This layer gives the final output of the CNN. For classification, neural networks the number of outputs depends on the number of classes. For regression neural networks, there is only one output that is a floating-point number, a number with a decimal point.

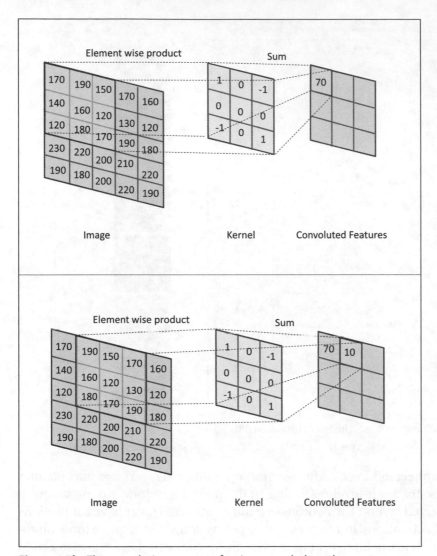

Figure 4.7b: The convolution process of an image and a kernel

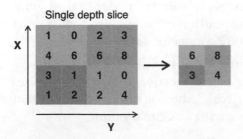

Figure 4.8: Max pooling with a 2×2 filter and stride = 2

(Source: https://en.wikipedia.org/wiki/Convolutional_neural_network)

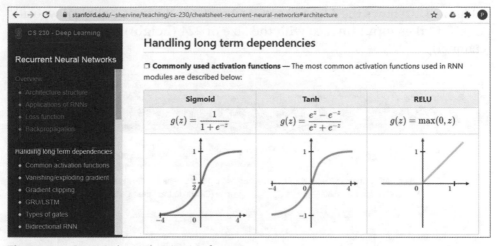

Figure 4.9: Commonly used activation functions

(Source: `https://stanford.edu/~shervine/teaching/cs-230/cheatsheet-recurrent-neural-networks#architecture`)

The following link shows a simple CNN example implemented with Keras.

`https://github.com/buomsoo-kim/Easy-deep-learning-with-Keras/blob/master/2.%20CNN/1-Basic-CNN/1-basic-cnn.py`

4.3.1   LeNet, AlexNet, GoogLeNet

LeNet, often referred to LeNet-5, is probably the best known first convolutional neural network. Developed by Yann LeCun and his colleagues in 1989, LeNet is a seven-layer convolutional neural network. LeNet is famous for classifying handwritten digits, and input images must have the size of 28 (height) × 28 (width) × 1 (channel). See the following LeNet official website details.

`http://yann.lecun.com/exdb/lenet/`

AlexNet is a convolutional neural network, developed by Alex Krizhevsky in collaboration with Ilya Sutskever and Geoffrey Hinton. Krizhevsky was then a PhD research student of Geoffrey Hinton.

AlexNet made a name for itself when it won the ImageNet Large Scale Visual Recognition Challenge on September 30, 2012. It achieved a top-five error rate of 15.3 percent, more than 10 percentage points lower than the runner-up.

AlexNet has eight layers; the first five were convolutional layers, followed by max-pooling layers, and the last three were fully connected layers. It is divided into two branches, designed for two GPUs. It also uses the nonsaturating ReLU activation function, which showed better training performance than the hyperbolic tangent (Tanh) and sigmoid activation functions. AlexNet has a total of about 61 million parameters and more than 600 million connections.

Figure 4.10 shows the AlexNet architecture from the missinglink.ai website. AlexNet takes input images with the size of 224 (height) × 224 (width) × 3 (channel).

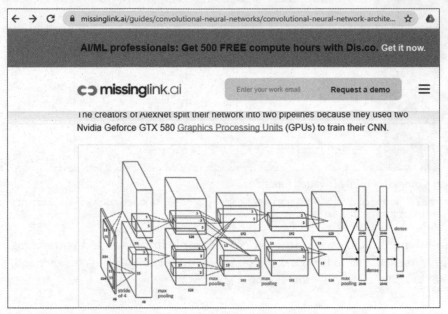

Figure 4.10: The AlexNet architecture from missinglink.ai website

(Source: `https://missinglink.ai/guides/convolutional-neural-networks/ convolutional-neural-network-architecture-forging-pathways-future/`)

See the following link for the AlexNet original paper, which is considered one of the most influential papers in computer vision. The AlexNet original paper has been cited more than 70,000 times according to Google Scholar.

`https://papers.nips.cc/paper/4824-imagenet-classification-with- deep-convolutional-neural-networks.pdf`

GoogLeNet, now known as Inception, is another impressive deep learning neural network. Inception v3 is the third edition of Google's Inception con- volutional neural network. GoogLeNet takes input images with the size of 224 (height) × 224 (width) × 3 (channel), while Inception takes input images with the size of 299 (height) × 299 (width) × 3 (channel).

Compared to AlexNet, Inception has a concept of Inception modules that perform different-sized convolutions and concatenate the filters for the next layer, as shown in Figure 4.11. Inception v3 has 48 layers and 24 million param- eters. Although Inception has more layers than AlexNet, it has many fewer parameters.

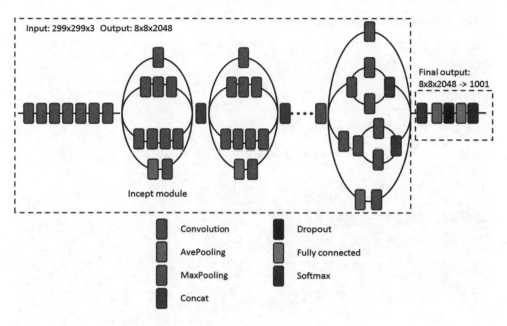

Figure 4.11: The schematic diagram of the Inception v3 architecture

For more details, check the GoogLeNet original paper:

```
https://static.googleusercontent.com/media/research.google.com/
en//pubs/archive/43022.pdf
```

```
https://cloud.google.com/tpu/docs/inception-v3-advanced
```

Example 4.4 shows a Keras implementation of the LeNet-5 deep learning neural network and the output of the summary of the model.

EXAMPLE 4.4   THE `LENET.PY` **PROGRAM**

```
#Example 4.4 LeNet-5 Keras
from keras.models import Sequential
from keras.layers import Dense, Conv2D, Flatten,AveragePooling2D
from keras import optimizers

model = Sequential()
model.add(Conv2D(filters=6, kernel_size=(3, 3), activation='relu',
input_shape=(32,32,1)))
model.add(AveragePooling2D())
model.add(Conv2D(filters=16, kernel_size=(3, 3), activation='relu'))
model.add(AveragePooling2D())
model.add(Flatten())
model.add(Dense(units=120, activation='relu'))
model.add(Dense(units=84, activation='relu'))
model.add(Dense(units=10, activation = 'softmax'))
model.summary()
```

The following is the output:

```
Using TensorFlow backend.
Model: "sequential_1"

Layer (type)                 Output Shape              Param #
=================================================================
conv2d_1 (Conv2D)            (None, 30, 30, 6)         60

average_pooling2d_1 (Average (None, 15, 15, 6)         0

conv2d_2 (Conv2D)            (None, 13, 13, 16)        880

average_pooling2d_2 (Average (None, 6, 6, 16)          0

flatten_1 (Flatten)          (None, 576)               0

dense_1 (Dense)              (None, 120)               69240

dense_2 (Dense)              (None, 84)                10164

dense_3 (Dense)              (None, 10)                850
=================================================================
Total params: 81,194
Trainable params: 81,194
Non-trainable params: 0
```

EXERCISE 4.4

Modify Python LeNet program from the Example 4.4 to use a different number of filters and see how this affects the total number of parameters.

Example 4.5 shows a Keras implementation of the AlexNet deep learning neural network and the output of the summary of the model.

EXAMPLE 4.5   THE `ALEXNET.PY` PROGRAM

```
#Example 4.5 AlexNet with Keras
#Modified from:
#https://engmrk.com/alexnet-implementation-using-keras/

import keras
from keras.models import Sequential
from keras.layers import Dense, Dropout, Flatten, Conv2D,
MaxPooling2D
from keras.layers.normalization import BatchNormalization
```

```
#Create the AlexNet model
model = Sequential()

# 1st Convolutional Layer
model.add(Conv2D(filters=96, input_shape=(224,224,3), kernel_
size=(11,11), activation='relu', strides=(4,4), padding='valid'))
model.add(MaxPooling2D(pool_size=(2,2), strides=(2,2),
padding='valid'))

# 2nd Convolutional Layer
model.add(Conv2D(filters=256, kernel_size=(11,11), activation='relu',
strides=(1,1), padding='valid'))
model.add(MaxPooling2D(pool_size=(2,2), strides=(2,2),
padding='valid'))

# 3rd Convolutional Layer
model.add(Conv2D(filters=384, kernel_size=(3,3), activation='relu',
strides=(1,1), padding='valid'))

# 4th Convolutional Layer
model.add(Conv2D(filters=384, kernel_size=(3,3), activation='relu',
strides=(1,1), padding='valid'))

# 5th Convolutional Layer
model.add(Conv2D(filters=256, kernel_size=(3,3), activation='relu',
strides=(1,1), padding='valid'))
model.add(MaxPooling2D(pool_size=(2,2), strides=(2,2),
padding='valid'))

# 1st Fully Connected layer
model.add(Flatten())
model.add(Dense(4096, activation='relu', input_shape=(224*224*3,)))
model.add(Dropout(0.4))

# 2nd Fully Connected Layer
model.add(Dense(4096,activation='relu'))
model.add(Dropout(0.4))

# 3rd Fully Connected Layer
model.add(Dense(1000,activation='relu'))
model.add(Dropout(0.4))

# Output Layer
model.add(Dense(17,activation='softmax'))

model.summary()

# Compile the model
model.compile(loss=keras.losses.categorical_crossentropy,
optimizer='adam', metrics=["accuracy"])
```

```
# Fit the model
#model.fit()

# Prediction with the model
#model.evaluate()
```

The following is the output:

```
Using TensorFlow backend.
Model: "sequential_1"

Layer (type)                  Output Shape              Param #
=================================================================
conv2d_1 (Conv2D)             (None, 54, 54, 96)        34944

max_pooling2d_1 (MaxPooling2  (None, 27, 27, 96)        0

conv2d_2 (Conv2D)             (None, 17, 17, 256)       2973952

max_pooling2d_2 (MaxPooling2  (None, 8, 8, 256)         0

conv2d_3 (Conv2D)             (None, 6, 6, 384)         885120

conv2d_4 (Conv2D)             (None, 4, 4, 384)         1327488

conv2d_5 (Conv2D)             (None, 2, 2, 256)         884992

max_pooling2d_3 (MaxPooling2  (None, 1, 1, 256)         0

flatten_1 (Flatten)           (None, 256)               0

dense_1 (Dense)               (None, 4096)              1052672

dropout_1 (Dropout)           (None, 4096)              0

dense_2 (Dense)               (None, 4096)              16781312

dropout_2 (Dropout)           (None, 4096)              0

dense_3 (Dense)               (None, 1000)              4097000

dropout_3 (Dropout)           (None, 1000)              0

dense_4 (Dense)               (None, 17)                17017
=================================================================
Total params: 28,054,497
Trainable params: 28,054,497
Non-trainable params: 0
```

EXERCISE 4.5

Modify the Python AlexNet program from Example 4.5, to use a different number of dense layer units and see how this affects the total number of parameters.

Example 4.6 shows a Python code that can load Google Inception V3 and show the summary of the models using the Keras built-in functions. It is just three lines of code!

EXAMPLE 4.6   THE `INCEPT.PY` PROGRAM

```
#Example 4.6
from tensorflow.keras.applications import inception_v3

# init the models
model = inception_v3.InceptionV3(weights='imagenet')
print(model.summary())
```

The following is the truncated output, which shows the first few layers and the last few layers:

```
Model: "inception_v3"

Layer (type)                    Output Shape          Param #     Connected to
==================================================================================
input_1 (InputLayer)            [(None, 299, 299, 3)  0

conv2d (Conv2D)                 (None, 149, 149, 32)  864         input_1[0][0]


... ...


mixed10 (Concatenate)           (None, 8, 8, 2048)    0           activation_85[0][0]
                                                                  mixed9_1[0][0]
                                                                  concatenate_1[0][0]
                                                                  activation_93[0][0]

avg_pool (GlobalAveragePooling2 (None, 2048)          0           mixed10[0][0]

predictions (Dense)             (None, 1000)          2049000     avg_pool[0][0]
==================================================================================
Total params: 23,851,784
Trainable params: 23,817,352
Non-trainable params: 34,432

None
```

Example 4.7 shows a Python code that you can use to create a simple custom-built deep learning neural network and output the summary of the model. It contains an input layer (28, 28, 1), a convolution layer, a max-pooling layer, a dropout layer, a flatten layer, a dense layer, and an output layer. The dense layer is a neural network layer that each neuron in the dense layer receives input from all neurons of its previous layer. The flatten layer flattens the data into a one-dimensional array, which is typically used before the dense layer in convolutional neural networks.

EXAMPLE 4.7 THE DLMODEL.PY **PROGRAM**

```
#Example 4.7

from keras.models import Sequential
from keras.layers import Dense, Dropout, Flatten
from keras.layers.convolutional import Conv2D, MaxPooling2D
# Create model
model = Sequential()
model.add(Conv2D(32, (5, 5), input_shape=(28, 28, 1),
activation='relu'))
model.add(MaxPooling2D())
model.add(Dropout(0.2))
model.add(Flatten())
model.add(Dense(128, activation='relu'))
model.add(Dense(2, activation='softmax'))
# Compile model
model.compile(loss='categorical_crossentropy', optimizer='adam',
metrics=['accuracy'])
print(model.summary())
```

This is the output of the example, showing the summary of the customized neural network:

```
Using TensorFlow backend.
Model: "sequential_1"
```

Layer (type)	Output Shape	Param #
conv2d_1 (Conv2D)	(None, 24, 24, 32)	832
max_pooling2d_1 (MaxPooling2	(None, 12, 12, 32)	0
dropout_1 (Dropout)	(None, 12, 12, 32)	0
flatten_1 (Flatten)	(None, 4608)	0
dense_1 (Dense)	(None, 128)	589952

```
dense_2 (Dense)                    (None, 2)                    258
=================================================================
Total params: 591,042
Trainable params: 591,042
Non-trainable params: 0
```

None

Modify the Python program from Example 4.7, and add another Conv2D, MaxPooling, and Dropout layer before the Flatten layer. Compare the number of parameters.

Example 4.8 shows Python code for loading the MNIST handwriting images and displaying them.

EXAMPLE 4.8   THE `MNIST.PY` PROGRAM

```python
#Example 4.8

from keras.datasets import mnist
import matplotlib.pyplot as plt

# load data
(X_train, y_train), (X_test, y_test) = mnist.load_data()
# plot 4 images as gray scale
plt.subplot(141)
plt.imshow(X_train[0])
plt.subplot(142)
plt.imshow(X_train[1])
plt.subplot(143)
plt.imshow(X_train[2])
plt.subplot(144)
plt.imshow(X_train[3])
plt.show()
```

Figure 4.12 shows a few sample images of MNIST handwriting images.

Example 4.9 shows an improved version of the previous code. It creates a simple deep learning neural network, which is used to classify MNIST handwriting digits.

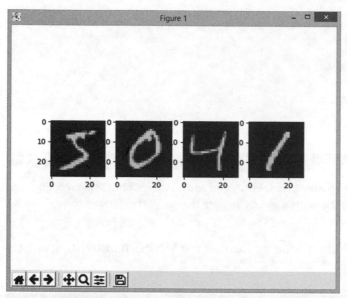

Figure 4.12: The sample images of MNIST handwriting digits images

EXAMPLE 4.9   THE `MNIST2.PY` **PROGRAM**

```
#Example 4.9

# Simple CNN for the MNIST Dataset
from keras.datasets import mnist
from keras.models import Sequential
from keras.layers import Dense, Dropout, Flatten
from keras.layers.convolutional import Conv2D, MaxPooling2D
from keras.utils import np_utils
# load data
(X_train, y_train), (X_test, y_test) = mnist.load_data()
# plot 4 images as gray scale
plt.subplot(141)
plt.imshow(X_train[0])
plt.subplot(142)
plt.imshow(X_train[1])
plt.subplot(143)
plt.imshow(X_train[2])
plt.subplot(144)
plt.imshow(X_train[3])
plt.show()

# reshape to be [samples][width][height][channels]
X_train = X_train.reshape((X_train.shape[0], 28, 28, 1))
.astype('float32')
X_test = X_test.reshape((X_test.shape[0], 28, 28, 1))
.astype('float32')
```

```
# normalize inputs from 0-255 to 0-1
X_train = X_train / 255
X_test = X_test / 255
# one hot encode outputs
y_train = np_utils.to_categorical(y_train)
y_test = np_utils.to_categorical(y_test)
num_classes = y_test.shape[1]
# Create model
model = Sequential()
model.add(Conv2D(32, (5, 5), input_shape=(28, 28, 1),
activation='relu'))
model.add(MaxPooling2D())
model.add(Dropout(0.2))
model.add(Flatten())
model.add(Dense(128, activation='relu'))
model.add(Dense(num_classes, activation='softmax'))
# Compile model
model.compile(loss='categorical_crossentropy', optimizer='adam',
metrics=['accuracy'])

# Fit the model
model.fit(X_train, y_train, validation_data=(X_test, y_test),
epochs=10, batch_size=200)
# Evaluation of the model
scores = model.evaluate(X_test, y_test, verbose=0)
print("CNN Error: %.2f%%" % (100-scores[1]*100))
```

This is the output of the example, showing the summary of the neural network:

```
Using TensorFlow backend.
Model: "sequential_1"

_____
Layer (type)                 Output Shape              Param #
=================================================================
conv2d_1 (Conv2D)            (None, 24, 24, 32)        832

max_pooling2d_1 (MaxPooling2 (None, 12, 12, 32)        0

dropout_1 (Dropout)          (None, 12, 12, 32)        0

flatten_1 (Flatten)          (None, 4608)              0

dense_1 (Dense)              (None, 128)               589952

dense_2 (Dense)              (None, 2)                 258
=================================================================
Total params: 591,042
Trainable params: 591,042
Non-trainable params: 0
_____
None
```

EXERCISE 4.7

Modify the Python program from Example 4.9, change the kernel size of 32 to 64 in the Conv2D layer, and compare their performances. Change the filter size (5,5) to (3,3) and compare the performances.

EXERCISE 4.8

Modify the Example 4.9 Python program, add another Conv2D, MaxPooling, and Dropout layer before the flatten layer. Compare the performances.

4.3.2 VGG, ResNet, DenseNet, MobileNet, EffecientNet, and YOLO

The VGG deep learning neural network was developed by the Visual Geometry Group at the University of Oxford. There are two versions, VGG 16 and VGG 19. VGG 16 is a 16-layer architecture with a pair of convolutional layers, a pooling layer, and fully connected layer at the end. A VGG network is the idea of much deeper networks and with much smaller filters. A VGG takes input images with the size of 224 (height) × 224 (width) × 3 (channel).

The following link shows an interesting VGG practice website from the University of Oxford, where you can learn to build VGG networks step-by-step using MATLAB software (www.mathworks.com).

```
https://www.robots.ox.ac.uk/~vgg/practicals/cnn/index.html
```

Figure 4.13 shows the architecture of VGG16 neural networks. It has an input of 224 × 224 × 3, followed by a convolutional layer and a ReLU layer that reduce the size to 224 × 224 × 64, then to 112 × 112 × 128, 56 × 56 × 256, and finally to 1 × 1 × 1000.

A **ResNet** (Residual Network) is a convolutional neural network developed by Microsoft. It took the deep learning world by storm in 2015, as the first neural network that could train hundreds or thousands of layers without succumbing to the "vanishing gradient" problem.

ResNet builds on constructs known from pyramidal cells in the cerebral cortex. This is done by utilizing jump connections or shortcuts to skip some layers. Typical ResNet models are implemented with double- or triple-layer jumps that contain nonlinearities (ReLU) and batch normalization in between; see Figure 4.14. ResNet takes input images with the size of 224 (height) × 224 (width) × 3 (channel).

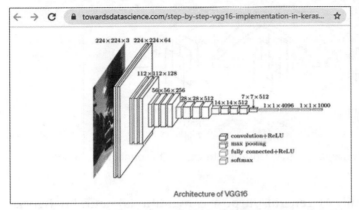

Figure 4.13: The architecture of VGG16 neural networks

(Source: `https://towardsdatascience.com/step-by-step-vgg16-implementation-in-keras-for-beginners-a833c686ae6c`)

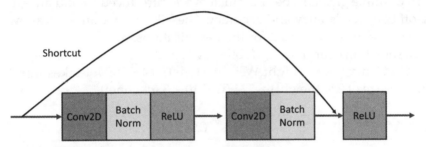

Figure 4.14: The schematic diagram of the ResNet structure with a double layer skip

For more details of ResNet, see the following:

`https://arxiv.org/abs/1512.03385v1`
`https://paperswithcode.com/method/resnet`

DenseNet is a convolutional neural network that uses dense connections between layers, where all layers are directly connected; see Figure 4.15. DenseNet has several compelling advantages over other neural networks. It can mitigate the vanishing-gradient problem, enhance feature propagation, promote feature reuse, and significantly reduce the number of parameters. DenseNet takes input images with the size of 224 (height) × 224 (width) × 3 (channel).

For more details of DenseNet, see the following:

`https://arxiv.org/abs/1608.06993`
`https://paperswithcode.com/method/densenet`

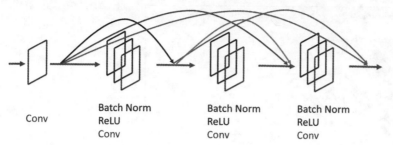

Conv   Batch Norm   Batch Norm   Batch Norm
              ReLU   ReLU   ReLU
              Conv   Conv   Conv

Figure 4.15: The schematic diagram of the DenseNet structure with connections between layers

MobileNet is a family of general-purpose convolutional neural networks designed for use on mobile devices. MobileNet comes in two versions and can be used for image classification, object detection, and more. MobileNets are based on a streamlined architecture for building lightweight deep neural networks. Two simple global hyper-parameters are introduced to find an efficient trade-off between latency and accuracy. These hyper-parameters allow modelers to choose the right model for their applications.

Figure 4.16 shows an overview of MobileNetV1 and the structure of Depthwise Separable Convolution (Light Weight Model). MobileNet takes input images with the size of 224 (height) × 224 (width) × 3 (channel).

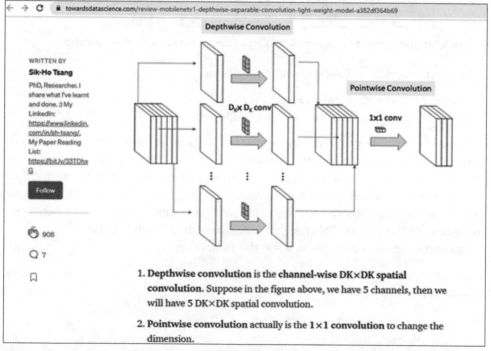

Figure 4.16: Review: MobileNetV1 — Depthwise Separable Convolution (Light Weight Model)

(Source: `https://towardsdatascience.com/review-mobilenetv1-depthwise-separable-convolution-light-weight-model-a382df364b69`)

For more details of MobileNet, see the following:

```
https://arxiv.org/abs/1704.04861
https://ai.googleblog.com/2019/11/introducing-next-generation-on-
device.html
https://github.com/tensorflow/models/tree/master/research/slim/
nets/mobilenet
```

EfficientNet is a relatively new deep learning neural network developed by Mingxing Tan, at Google AI, in May 2019. It was developed based on AutoML and Compound Scaling. First, a mobile-size baseline network called EfficientNet-B0 was developed using AutoML MNAS Mobile framework. Then, the compound scaling method was used to scale up this baseline to obtain EfficientNet-B1 to B7. EfficientNet has achieved much better accuracy and efficiency than previous convolutional neural networks. EfficientNet-B7 has achieved a top-one accuracy of 84.3 percent on ImageNet; see Figure 4.17. Efficient takes input images with the size of 224 (height) × 224 (width) × 3 (channel),

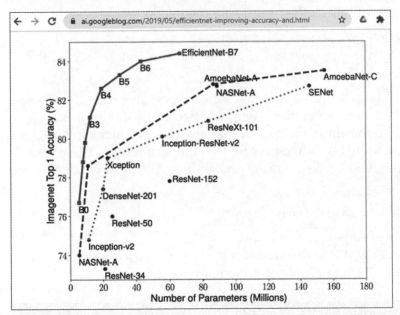

Figure 4.17: Accuracies of different deep learning neural networks on ImageNet
(Source: `https://ai.googleblog.com/2019/05/efficientnet-improving-accuracy-and.html`)

EfficientNet is also at the top on the ImageNet classification leaderboard, as shown in Figure 4.18.

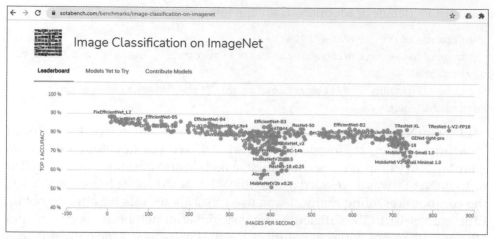

Figure 4.18: The SOTA board for image classification on ImageNet

(Source: `https://sotabench.com/benchmarks/image-classification-on-imagenet`)

For more details of EfficientNet, see the following:

```
https://arxiv.org/abs/1905.11946
https://github.com/tensorflow/tpu/tree/master/models/official/
efficientnet
```

YOLO (you only look once) is a state-of-the-art system for real-time object detection. Unlike other convolutional neural networks, YOLO applies a single neural network to the entire image and then divides the image into regions and predicts bounding boxes and probabilities for each region. These bounding boxes are weighted by the predicted probabilities. For more detail, visit the YOLO website:

```
https://pjreddie.com/darknet/yolo/
```

Now let's look at some example code.

Example 4.10 shows the Python code for loading a deep learning neural network, such as VGG16, and printing the summary of the model.

EXAMPLE 4.10   THE `VGG16.PY` **PROGRAM**

```
#Example 4.10
from tensorflow.keras.preprocessing import image
from tensorflow.keras.applications.vgg16 import VGG16
from tensorflow.keras.applications.vgg16 import preprocess_input
from keras.applications.imagenet_utils import decode_predictions
import numpy as np

model = VGG16(weights='imagenet')
print(model.summary())
```

This is the output of the example, showing the summary of VGG16 network:

```
Using TensorFlow backend.
Model: "vgg16"

Layer (type)                    Output Shape              Param #
=================================================================
input_1 (InputLayer)            [(None, 224, 224, 3)]     0

block1_conv1 (Conv2D)           (None, 224, 224, 64)      1792

block1_conv2 (Conv2D)           (None, 224, 224, 64)      36928

block1_pool (MaxPooling2D)      (None, 112, 112, 64)      0

block2_conv1 (Conv2D)           (None, 112, 112, 128)     73856

block2_conv2 (Conv2D)           (None, 112, 112, 128)     147584

block2_pool (MaxPooling2D)      (None, 56, 56, 128)       0

block3_conv1 (Conv2D)           (None, 56, 56, 256)       295168

block3_conv2 (Conv2D)           (None, 56, 56, 256)       590080

block3_conv3 (Conv2D)           (None, 56, 56, 256)       590080

block3_pool (MaxPooling2D)      (None, 28, 28, 256)       0

block4_conv1 (Conv2D)           (None, 28, 28, 512)       1180160

block4_conv2 (Conv2D)           (None, 28, 28, 512)       2359808

block4_conv3 (Conv2D)           (None, 28, 28, 512)       2359808

block4_pool (MaxPooling2D)      (None, 14, 14, 512)       0

block5_conv1 (Conv2D)           (None, 14, 14, 512)       2359808

block5_conv2 (Conv2D)           (None, 14, 14, 512)       2359808

block5_conv3 (Conv2D)           (None, 14, 14, 512)       2359808

block5_pool (MaxPooling2D)      (None, 7, 7, 512)         0

flatten (Flatten)               (None, 25088)             0

fc1 (Dense)                     (None, 4096)              102764544

fc2 (Dense)                     (None, 4096)              16781312
```

```
predictions (Dense)              (None, 1000)              4097000
=================================================================
Total params: 138,357,544
Trainable params: 138,357,544
Non-trainable params: 0


None
```

EXERCISE 4.9

Modify the Python program from Example 4.10 so that it loads the VGG19 model, instead of the VGG16 model.

Example 4.11 shows an improved version of the previous example code. In this case, it also uses the model to classify an image.

EXAMPLE 4.11   THE VGG16A.PY PROGRAM

```python
#Example 4.11
from tensorflow.keras.preprocessing import image
from tensorflow.keras.applications.vgg16 import VGG16
from tensorflow.keras.applications.vgg16 import preprocess_input
from keras.applications.imagenet_utils import decode_predictions
import numpy as np

model = VGG16(weights='imagenet')

img_path = 'Elephant.jpg'
img = image.load_img(img_path, target_size=(224, 224))
x = image.img_to_array(img)
x = np.expand_dims(x, axis=0)
x = preprocess_input(x)

# prediction
predictions = model.predict(x)
results = decode_predictions(predictions)

print(results)
```

This is the output of the example, showing the classification results:

```
[[('n02504458', 'African_elephant', 0.80238396), ('n01871265',
'tusker', 0.12562281), ('n02504013', 'Indian_elephant', 0.07094732),
('n02099849', 'Chesapeake_Bay_retriever', 0.00035384137), ('n02437312',
'Arabian_camel', 0.00018172464)]]
```

EXERCISE 4.10

Modify the Python program from Example 4.11 to use VGG19 for classification and compare its performance with VGG16.

Example 4.12 shows a Python code that can load a set of deep learning neural network models, such as VGG16, ResNet50, MobileNet, and Inception V3, display the summary of the models, and use the model to classify an image.

EXAMPLE 4.12   THE MULTICLASSIFY.PY **PROGRAM**

```
#Example 4.12
from tensorflow.keras.preprocessing import image
from keras.applications.imagenet_utils import decode_predictions
import numpy as np

from tensorflow.keras.applications import (
        vgg16,
        resnet50,
        mobilenet,
        inception_v3
    )

# init the models
#model = vgg16.VGG16(weights='imagenet')
#model = resnet50.ResNet50(weights='imagenet')
model = mobilenet.MobileNet(weights='imagenet')
#model = inception_v3.InceptionV3(weights='imagenet')
print(model.summary())

img_path = 'Elephant.jpg'
img = image.load_img(img_path, target_size=(224, 224))
x = image.img_to_array(img)
x = np.expand_dims(x, axis=0)
#processed_image = vgg16.preprocess_input(x)
#processed_image = resnet50.preprocess_input(x)
processed_image = mobilenet.preprocess_input(x)
#processed_image = inception_v3.preprocess_input(x)

# prediction
predictions = model.predict(x)
results = decode_predictions(predictions)
print(results)
```

A web camera, or webcam, is a useful tool to capture images to provide data resource for image classification using deep learning. Example 4.13 shows a Python code for image classification based on the image array from a web camera (webcam), using VGG16 deep learning neural network.

EXAMPLE 4.13   THE `WEBCAMCLASSIFY.PY` **PROGRAM**

```
#Example 4.13

import cv2
from tensorflow.keras.preprocessing.image import img_to_array
from keras.applications.imagenet_utils import decode_predictions
from tensorflow.keras.applications import vgg16
import numpy as np

image_size = 224
model = vgg16.VGG16(weights='imagenet')
print(model.summary())

camera = cv2.VideoCapture(0)

while camera.isOpened():
    ok, cam_frame = camera.read()

    frame= cv2.resize(cam_frame, (image_size, image_size))
    numpy_image = img_to_array(frame)
    image_batch = np.expand_dims(numpy_image, axis=0)
    processed_image = vgg16.preprocess_input(image_batch.copy())

    # get the predicted probabilities for each class
    predictions = model.predict(processed_image)
    label = decode_predictions(predictions)

    # format final image visualization to display the results of
experiments
    cv2.putText(cam_frame, "VGG16: {}, {:.1f}".format(label[0][0][1],
label[0][0][2]) , (10, 30), cv2.FONT_HERSHEY_SIMPLEX, 1, (255, 0, 0),
2)


    cv2.imshow('video image', cam_frame)

    key = cv2.waitKey(30)
    if key == 27: # press 'ESC' to quit
        break

camera.release()
cv2.destroyAllWindows()
```

Figure 4.19 shows the output of the previous VGG16 classifier based on the images from a webcam, which correctly identifies a computer mouse with 90 percent confidence.

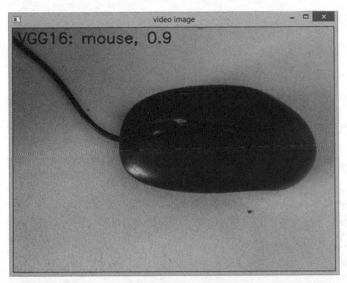

Figure 4.19: The output of VGG16 webcam classification program

---

EXERCISE 4.11

Modify the Python VGG16 webcam program to use VGG19 to classify webcam images. Compare the performances.

Example 4.14 shows a Python code for image classification based on a web camera using different deep learning neural networks such as VGG16, ResNet50, MobileNet, and Google's Inception V3.

EXAMPLE 4.14   THE WEBCAMCLASSIFY2.PY **PROGRAM**

```
# Example 4.14
import cv2
from tensorflow.keras.preprocessing.image import img_to_array
from keras.applications.imagenet_utils import decode_predictions
from tensorflow.keras.applications import (
        vgg16,
        resnet50,
        mobilenet,
        inception_v3
    )
import numpy as np

# init the models
#model = vgg16.VGG16(weights='imagenet')
model = resnet50.ResNet50(weights='imagenet')
#model = mobilenet.MobileNet(weights='imagenet')
#model = inception_v3.InceptionV3(weights='imagenet')
```

```
print(model.summary())

camera = cv2.VideoCapture(0)
image_size = 224
#image_size = 299
while camera.isOpened():
    ok, cam_frame = camera.read()

    frame= cv2.resize(cam_frame, (image_size, image_size))
    numpy_image = img_to_array(frame)
    image_batch = np.expand_dims(numpy_image, axis=0)

    #processed_image = vgg16.preprocess_input(image_batch.copy())
    processed_image = resnet50.preprocess_input(image_batch.copy())
    #processed_image = mobilenet.preprocess_input(image_batch.copy())
    #processed_image = inception_v3.preprocess_input(image_batch
.copy())

    # get the predicted probabilities for each class
    predictions = model.predict(processed_image)
    label = decode_predictions(predictions)

    # format final image visualization to display the results of
experiments
    cv2.putText(cam_frame, "{}, {:.1f}".format(label[0][0][1],
label[0][0][2]) , (10, 30), cv2.FONT_HERSHEY_SIMPLEX, 1, (255, 0, 0),
2)


    cv2.imshow('video image', cam_frame)

    key = cv2.waitKey(30)
    if key == 27: # press 'ESC' to quit
        break
```

EXERCISE 4.12

Modify the Python program from Example 4.14 and add DenseNet to the model to classify webcam images. Compare the performances.

The Image-Classifier library is a classification model zoo library that supports 13 different types of deep learning neural networks. It is based on Keras and TensorFlow (https://pypi.org/project/image-classifiers/). To use the library, you must first install it.

```
pip install image-classifiers
```

Example 4.15 shows a Python code for image classification based on a web camera using Image-Classifier library, which supports a number of different deep learning neural networks such as VGG, ResNet, MobileNet, and Google's Inception, etc.

EXAMPLE 4.15   THE `WEBCLASSIFY3.PY` **PROGRAM**

```
# Example 4.15
#https://pypi.org/project/image-classifiers/

!pip install image-classifiers
from keras.applications.imagenet_utils import decode_predictions
from keras.applications.imagenet_utils import preprocess_input
from classification_models.keras import Classifiers

import numpy as np
import cv2

#Set up a model
clf, preprocess_input = Classifiers.get('vgg16')
#clf, preprocess_input = Classifiers.get('resnet50')
#clf, preprocess_input = Classifiers.get('mobilenetv2')
#clf, preprocess_input = Classifiers.get('densenet201')
sz = 224
#clf, preprocess_input = Classifiers.get('inceptionv3')
#sz = 299
model = clf(input_shape=(sz,sz,3), weights='imagenet', classes=1000)

model.summary()
while True:
    ret, cam_frame = camera.read()
    frame= cv2.resize(cam_frame, (image_size, image_size))
    image = np.asarray(frame)
    image = np.expand_dims(image, 0)
    image = preprocess_input(image)

    preds = model.predict(image)
    label = decode_predictions(preds)


    cv2.putText(cam_frame, "{}, {:.1f}".format(label[0][0][1],
label[0][0][2]),
        (10, 30),cv2.FONT_HERSHEY_SIMPLEX, 0.9, (0, 255, 0), 2)
    cv2.imshow("Classification", cam_frame)
    key = cv2.waitKey(30)
    if key == 27: # press 'ESC' to quit
        break

camera.release()
cv2.destroyAllWindows()
```

EXERCISE 4.13

Modify the Python program from Example 4.15, uncomment the different models, and compare the performances.

EXERCISE 4.14

Modify the Python program from Example 4.15 to use an `if-else` statement to select the models for classification.

4.3.3   U-Net

U-Net is a convolutional neural network, developed for biomedical image segmentation at the Computer Vision Group, Department of Computer Science, the University of Freiburg, Germany. Figure 4.20 shows the U-Net website with its architecture.

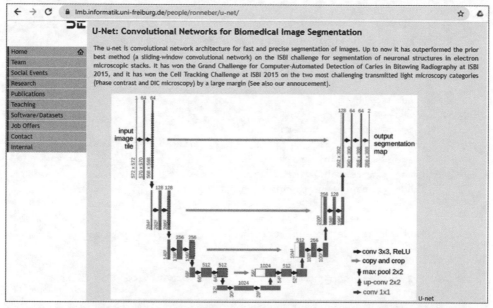

Figure 4.20: The U-Net website at Computer Vision Group, Department of Computer Science, the University of Freiburg, Germany

(Source: `https://lmb.informatik.uni-freiburg.de/people/ronneber/u-net/`)

U-Net is based on a fully convolutional network and has an input size of 572 × 572. It uses three convolution layers and pooling layers to reduce the input image to a 1,024-feature vector. It then uses three pooling and convolution layers to bring the feature vector back to 382 × 382 as a segmented image. The architecture looks like a *U*, which is where it gets its name.

To date, U-Net has been used in many applications in biomedical image segmentation, such as brain image segmentation, liver image segmentation, and medical image reconstruction

The easiest way to implement U-Net is to use the Keras-Unet library. See the following links for more details:

```
https://pypi.org/project/keras-unet/
https://github.com/karolzak/keras-unet
```

To install the Keras-Unet library, do this:

```
pip install keras-unet
```

To create a simple vanilla U-Net model and display a summary of the model, use the following code:

```
from keras_unet.models import vanilla_unet
model = vanilla_unet(input_shape=(512, 512, 3))
model.summary()
```

The following is the model summary of a vanilla U-Net. As you can see, the U-Net has changed from the input size (512 × 512 × 3) gradually down to (44 × 44 × 512) and then back up to (324 × 324 × 1).

```
Model: "model"
```

Layer (type)	Output Shape	Param #	Connected to
input_1 (InputLayer)	[(None, 512, 512, 3)	0	
conv2d (Conv2D)	(None, 510, 510, 64)	1792	input_1[0][0]
conv2d_1 (Conv2D)	(None, 508, 508, 64)	36928	conv2d[0][0]
max_pooling2d (MaxPooling2D)	(None, 254, 254, 64)	0	conv2d_1[0][0]
conv2d_2 (Conv2D)	(None, 252, 252, 128	73856	max_pooling2d[0][0]
conv2d_3 (Conv2D)	(None, 250, 250, 128	147584	conv2d_2[0][0]
max_pooling2d_1 (MaxPooling2D)	(None, 125, 125, 128	0	conv2d_3[0][0]
conv2d_4 (Conv2D)	(None, 123, 123, 256	295168	max_pooling2d_1[0][0]
conv2d_5 (Conv2D)	(None, 121, 121, 256	590080	conv2d_4[0][0]
max_pooling2d_2 (MaxPooling2D)	(None, 60, 60, 256)	0	conv2d_5[0][0]

Layer	Output Shape	Param #	Connected to
conv2d_6 (Conv2D)	(None, 58, 58, 512)	1180160	max_pooling2d_2[0][0]
conv2d_7 (Conv2D)	(None, 56, 56, 512)	2359808	conv2d_6[0][0]
max_pooling2d_3 (MaxPooling2D)	(None, 28, 28, 512)	0	conv2d_7[0][0]
dropout (Dropout)	(None, 28, 28, 512)	0	max_pooling2d_3[0][0]
conv2d_8 (Conv2D)	(None, 26, 26, 1024)	4719616	dropout[0][0]
conv2d_9 (Conv2D)	(None, 24, 24, 1024)	9438208	conv2d_8[0][0]
conv2d_transpose (Conv2DTranspo	(None, 48, 48, 512)	2097664	conv2d_9[0][0]
cropping2d (Cropping2D)	(None, 48, 48, 512)	0	conv2d_7[0][0]
concatenate (Concatenate)	(None, 48, 48, 1024)	0	conv2d_transpose[0][0] cropping2d[0][0]
conv2d_10 (Conv2D)	(None, 46, 46, 512)	4719104	concatenate[0][0]
conv2d_11 (Conv2D)	(None, 44, 44, 512)	2359808	conv2d_10[0][0]
conv2d_transpose_1 (Conv2DTrans	(None, 88, 88, 256)	524544	conv2d_11[0][0]
cropping2d_1 (Cropping2D)	(None, 88, 88, 256)	0	conv2d_5[0][0]
concatenate_1 (Concatenate)	(None, 88, 88, 512)	0	conv2d_transpose_1[0][0] cropping2d_1[0][0]
conv2d_12 (Conv2D)	(None, 86, 86, 256)	1179904	concatenate_1[0][0]
conv2d_13 (Conv2D)	(None, 84, 84, 256)	590080	conv2d_12[0][0]
conv2d_transpose_2 (Conv2DTrans	(None, 168, 168, 128	131200	conv2d_13[0][0]
cropping2d_2 (Cropping2D)	(None, 168, 168, 128	0	conv2d_3[0][0]
concatenate_2 (Concatenate)	(None, 168, 168, 256	0	conv2d_transpose_2[0][0] cropping2d_2[0][0]
conv2d_14 (Conv2D)	(None, 166, 166, 128	295040	concatenate_2[0][0]
conv2d_15 (Conv2D)	(None, 164, 164, 128	147584	conv2d_14[0][0]
conv2d_transpose_3 (Conv2DTrans	(None, 328, 328, 64)	32832	conv2d_15[0][0]

cropping2d_3 (Cropping2D)	(None, 328, 328, 64) 0	conv2d_1[0][0]
concatenate_3 (Concatenate) [0]	(None, 328, 328, 128 0	conv2d_transpose_3[0]
		cropping2d_3[0][0]
conv2d_16 (Conv2D)	(None, 326, 326, 64) 73792	concatenate_3[0][0]
conv2d_17 (Conv2D)	(None, 324, 324, 64) 36928	conv2d_16[0][0]
conv2d_18 (Conv2D)	(None, 324, 324, 1) 65	conv2d_17[0][0]

```
Total params: 31,031,745
Trainable params: 31,031,745
Non-trainable params: 0
```

The following code shows how to plot the U-Net model and save the model into a Portable Network Graphics (PNG) file. Figure 4.21 shows the plot of the U-Net.

```
from keras.utils import plot_model
plot_model(model, to_file='model.png')
```

You can also create a customized U-Net model and display the model summary using the following code:

```
from keras_unet.models import custom_unet

model = custom_unet(
input_shape=(512, 512, 3),
use_batch_norm=False,
num_classes=1,
filters=64,
dropout=0.2,
output_activation='sigmoid')
model.summary()
```

The quickest way to try image segmentation with the Keras-Unet library is through its GitHub repository. It uses Keras U-Net to segment images from a serial section Transmission Electron Microscopy (ssTEM) dataset of the Drosophila first instar larva ventral nerve cord (VNC), as shown in Figure 4.22. Just follow the code in this IPython Notebook:

```
https://github.com/karolzak/keras-unet/blob/master/notebooks/kz-isbi-challenge.ipynb
```

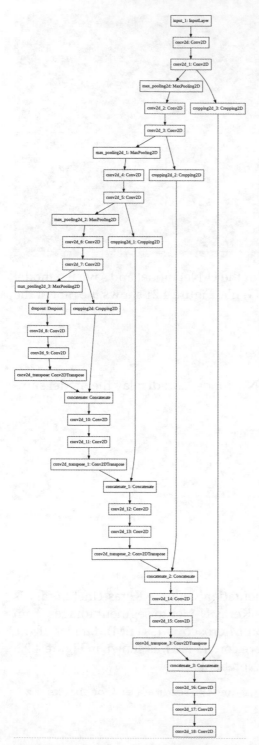

Figure 4.21: The plot of vanilla U-Net model

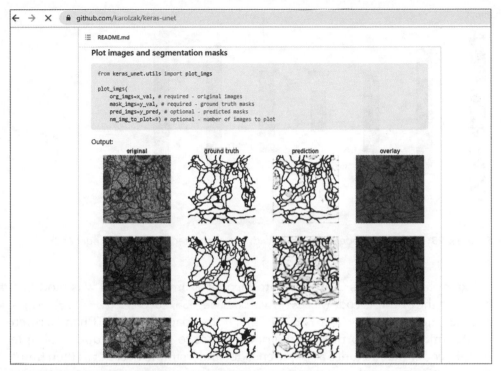

Figure 4.22: The Keras-Unet library GitHub website with serial section Transmission Electron Microscopy images

(Source: `https://github.com/karolzak/keras-unet`)

The following are more examples of U-Net projects:

`https://github.com/zhixuhao/unet`

`https://github.com/Hsankesara/DeepResearch`

`https://github.com/devswha/keras-Unet`

`http://deeplearning.net/tutorial/unet.html`

`https://www.kaggle.com/phoenigs/u-net-dropout-augmentation-stratification`

`https://www.kaggle.com/kmader/baseline-u-net-model-part-1`

4.3.4   AutoEncoder

AutoEncoder is a neural network architecture, consisting of two connected networks: Encoder and Decoder, as illustrated in Figure 4.23. The Encoder receives the input image and encodes it into a latent spatial vector of a lower dimension. The network is trained to ignore signal noise during this dimensionality reduction. The Decoder takes this vector and decodes it to produce an output that is as close as possible to the original input. Autoencoders are developed with the goal of learning the low-dimensional feature representations of the input data.

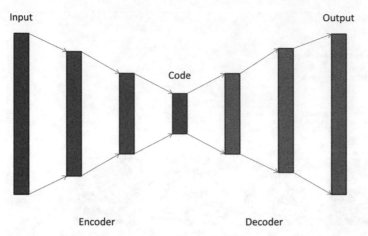

Figure 4.23: The AutoEncoder architecture with two connected networks: Encoder and Decoder

Example 4.16 shows a Python AutoEncoder example code. It was modified based on the example code (`https://stackabuse.com/autoencoders-for-image-reconstruction-in-python-and-keras/`). It first loads the MNIST handwritten digital images and normalizes the pixel values to 1. Then it builds a simple AutoEncoder that includes a simple encoder and a simple decoder. It then trains the AutoEncoder and uses the trained AutoEncoder to reconstruct the digits.

EXAMPLE 4.16   THE `AUTOENCODERKERAS.PY` PROGRAM

```python
# Example 4.16 AutoencoderKeras.py
# Modified from:
# https://stackabuse.com/autoencoders-for-image-reconstruction-in-python-
and-keras/
#
# Load the MNIST handwritten digital images ===============================
from keras.datasets import mnist
import numpy as np
(x_train, _), (x_test, _) = mnist.load_data()
x_train = x_train.astype('float32') / 255.
x_test = x_test.astype('float32') / 255.
print(x_train.shape)
print(x_test.shape)


# Build Autoencoder =======================================================
from keras.layers import Dense, Flatten, Reshape, Input, InputLayer
from keras.models import Sequential, Model

def build_autoencoder(img_shape, code_size):
    # The encoder
    encoder = Sequential()
    encoder.add(InputLayer(img_shape))
```

```
        encoder.add(Flatten())
        encoder.add(Dense(code_size))

        # The decoder
        decoder = Sequential()
        decoder.add(InputLayer((code_size,)))
        decoder.add(Dense(np.prod(img_shape)))
        decoder.add(Reshape(img_shape))

        return encoder, decoder

IMG_SHAPE = x_train[0].shape
encoder, decoder = build_autoencoder(IMG_SHAPE, 32)

inp = Input(IMG_SHAPE)
code = encoder(inp)
reconstruction = decoder(code)

autoencoder = Model(inp,reconstruction)
autoencoder.compile(optimizer='adamax', loss='mse')

print(autoencoder.summary())

# Train Autoencoder ========================================================
history = autoencoder.fit(x=x_train, y=x_train, epochs=20,
                validation_data=(x_test, x_test))

# Plot the training results ================================================
import matplotlib.pyplot as plt

plt.plot(history.history['loss'])
plt.plot(history.history['val_loss'])
plt.title('model loss')
plt.ylabel('loss')
plt.xlabel('epoch')
plt.legend(['train', 'test'], loc='upper left')
plt.show()

# Plot the original, encoded and decoded images ============================
import matplotlib.pyplot as plt
def show_image(x):
    plt.imshow(np.clip(x + 0.5, 0, 1))

def visualize(img,encoder,decoder):
    """Draws original, encoded and decoded images"""
    # img[None] will have shape of (1, 32, 32, 3) which is the same as the
model input
    code = encoder.predict(img[None])[0]
    reco = decoder.predict(code[None])[0]
```

```
        plt.subplot(1,3,1)
        plt.title("Original")
        show_image(img)

        plt.subplot(1,3,2)
        plt.title("Code")
        plt.imshow(code.reshape([code.shape[-1]//2,-1]))

        plt.subplot(1,3,3)
        plt.title("Reconstructed")
        show_image(reco)
        plt.show()

    for i in range(5):
        img = x_test[i]
        visualize(img,encoder,decoder)
```

This is the output of the example, showing the structures of AutoEncoder:

```
(60000, 28, 28)
(10000, 28, 28)
Model: "model"
_____
Layer (type)                 Output Shape              Param #
=================================================================
input_3 (InputLayer)         [(None, 28, 28)]          0

sequential (Sequential)      (None, 32)                25120

sequential_1 (Sequential)    (None, 28, 28)            25872
=================================================================
Total params: 50,992
Trainable params: 50,992
Non-trainable params: 0
_____
None
```

Figure 4.24 shows the example outputs of the AutoEncoder program, which includes the original digit images (left), the output of the encoder called code (middle), and the reconstructed digit images by the decoder.

For more information about AutoEncoders, see the following:

```
https://blog.keras.io/building-autoencoders-in-keras.html
https://stackabuse.com/autoencoders-for-image-reconstruction-in-
python-and-keras/
```

```
https://www.analyticsvidhya.com/blog/2020/02/what-is-autoencoder-
enhance-image-resolution/
    https://www.kaggle.com/shivamb/how-autoencoders-work-intro-and-
usecases
    https://theaisummer.com/Autoencoder/
```

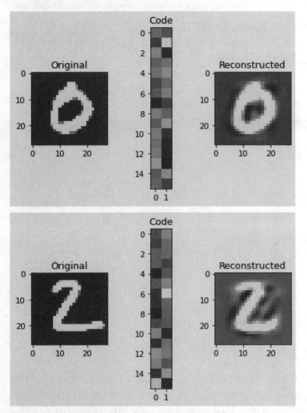

Figure 4.24: The example output of AutoEncoder program, which includes the original digit images (left), the output of the encoder called code (middle), and the reconstructed digit images by decoder (right).

4.3.5   Siamese Neural Networks

When I first started looking into deep learning, one thing always puzzled me. Take image classification, for example. Deep learning neural networks require a large amount of labeled training data to achieve high performance. However, we humans are able to learn things with just a glance at the object. Even if we have never seen passion fruits, we don't need to see thousands and thousands of images before we can recognize them.

Can deep learning neural networks learn the same way? The answer is yes, this is called *one-shot learning*. In one-shot learning, we need only a single training example for each class instead of training a large set of images. The most commonly used one-shot learning neural network is the Siamese network.

Figure 4.25 shows an interesting introduction of one-shot learning and Siamese networks in Keras. It describes a typical architecture of a convolutional Siamese network as an example of classifying pairs of omniglot images (`https://github.com/brendenlake/omniglot`). The omniglot data contains 1,623 different hand-written characters from 50 different alphabets.

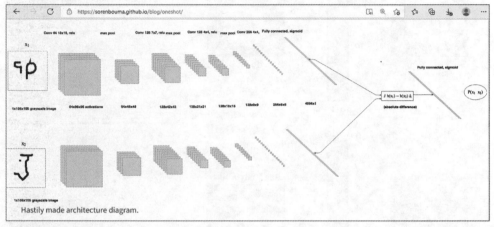

Figure 4.25: One-shot learning and Siamese networks in Keras

(Source: `https://sorenbouma.github.io/blog/oneshot/`)

The Siamese network contains two convolutional neural networks, called *twin neural network*. The two neural networks reduce the inputs to lower-dimension tensors; finally, there is a fully connected layer with 4,096 units. The absolute difference between the two vectors is used as input to a linear classifier. A linear classifier performs a classification decision based on the value of a linear combination of the characteristics. The network has 38,951,745 parameters, 96 percent of which belong to the fully connected layer. Training Siamese networks in this way with comparative loss functions can give better performances. Siamese networks have also been used for face recognition.

To try a Siamese network for classifying omniglot images, just follow this interesting IPython notebook:

```
https://github.com/sorenbouma/keras-oneshot/blob/master/SiameseNet
.ipynb
```

For more information about Siamese networks, visit the following websites:

```
https://github.com/tensorfreitas/Siamese-Networks-for-One-Shot-
Learning
https://towardsdatascience.com/one-shot-learning-with-siamese-
networks-using-keras-17f34e75bb3d
https://github.com/hlamba28/One-Shot-Learning-with-Siamese-Networks
https://github.com/akshaysharma096/Siamese-Networks
https://github.com/sorenbouma/keras oneshot
https://github.com/aspamers/siamese
https://www.cs.cmu.edu/~rsalakhu/papers/oneshot1.pdf
https://machinelearningmastery.com/one-shot-learning-with-siamese-
networks-contrastive-and-triplet-loss-for-face-recognition/
```

Apart from one-shot learning, there are also few-shot learning and zero-shot learning. Few-shot learning means that the neural network is trained with a few (one to five) images. Zero-shot learning means that the neural network is trained with zero images. This is fascinating! Few-shot learning and zero-shot learning are sometimes categorized as N-shot learning, which means that the neural network is trained with N images.

The key concept of n-shot learning is the prototypical network. Unlike typical deep learning neural networks, prototypical networks do not classify the image directly; instead, they learn the mapping of images in the metric space and group the images into different clusters, called *prototypes*. In metric space, there is no distinguished "origin" point; instead, you just calculate the distance from one point to another. Prototypical networks then use the distances between prototypes and encoded query images to classify them.

N-shot learning is a learning algorithm that allows the network to learn more with less data. It is typically used when it is hard to find training data, for example, rare diseases, or when the cost of labeling data is too high.

For more details, check the following interesting blog and the GitHub code to the blog:

```
https://blog.floydhub.com/n-shot-learning/
https://github.com/Hsankesara/Prototypical-Networks
```

4.3.6 Capsule Networks

Convolutional neural networks perform best when the image to be classified is similar to the training image dataset. If the image to be classified is different (e.g., rotated, tilted, or transitioned), then the performance drops. Take face detection as an example; if the eyes, nose, and mouth are detected, the image is classified as a face, even if they are in the wrong place. Because of this, there are many shocking errors in image classification.

How can this problem be solved? The answer is a capsule network. A capsule network is a new deep learning network architecture proposed by Sara Sabour, Nicholas Frost, and Geoffrey Hinton in their paper titled "Dynamic Routing Between Capsules" in 2017. See Figure 4.26 for the original paper and a simple three-layer capsule network architecture called CapsNet. In this model, there are modules called *capsules* that are particularly good at handling different types of visual stimuli such as position, size, orientation, deformation, texture, and so on. As a result, the performance is significantly improved.

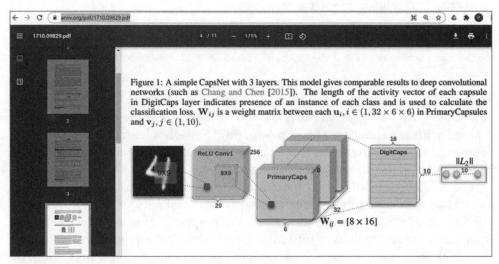

Figure 4.26: The original capsule network paper and a three-layer simple capsule network architecture

(Source: https://arxiv.org/pdf/1710.09829.pdf)

The following website shows an interesting simple introduction of a capsule network, which provides the full capsule network source code implemented in TensorFlow.

https://hackernoon.com/what-is-a-capsnet-or-capsule-network-2bfbe48769cc

This is the corresponding Github site for the source code.

https://github.com/debarko/CapsNet-Tensorflow

The following website shows the capsule network implementation in TensorFlow.

https://github.com/debarko/CapsNet-Tensorflow

Figure 4.27 shows the PyTorch implementation of a capsule graph neural network.

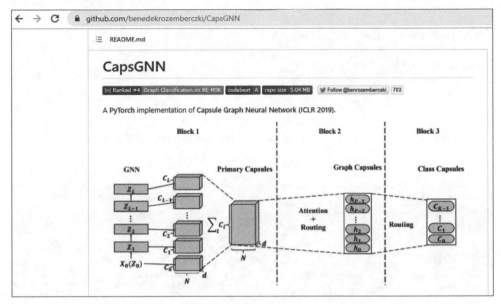

Figure 4.27: A PyTorch implementation of a capsule graph neural network
(Source: `https://github.com/benedekrozemberczki/CapsGNN`)

4.3.7   CNN Layers Visualization

During the development, you may want to see the output of each layer of a convolutional neural network (CNN), whether for debugging purposes or just out of curiosity.

The easiest way to do this is to visualize each layer individually. The following example shows how you can visualize the output of the different convolutional layers in the VGG19 model; it is modified based on an excellent article on visualizing the filters and feature maps in convolutional neural networks (`https://machinelearningmastery.com/how-to-visualize-filters-and-feature-maps-in-convolutional-neural-networks/`).

We will show the code section by section. You can find the full code in a file called `CNN_Visualize_Filters.ipynb`. We will run it by uploading it to Google Colab.

Example 4.17 is the first section of the code that shows how to load a VGG19 model and display the summary of the model.

EXAMPLE 4.17   THE `CNN VISUALIZE FILTERS.IPYNB` PROGRAM (PART 1)

```
# Example 4.17 CNN Visualize Filters.ipynb
#Modified from:
#https://machinelearningmastery.com/how-to-visualize-filters-and-
feature-maps-in-convolutional-neural-networks/
```

```
# load vgg model
from keras.applications.vgg19 import VGG19
# load the model
model = VGG19()
# summarize the model
model.summary()
```

The following is the output that shows the summary of the model:

```
Model: "vgg19"

Layer (type)                 Output Shape              Param #
=================================================================
input_31 (InputLayer)        [(None, 224, 224, 3)]     0

block1_conv1 (Conv2D)        (None, 224, 224, 64)      1792

block1_conv2 (Conv2D)        (None, 224, 224, 64)      36928

block1_pool (MaxPooling2D)   (None, 112, 112, 64)      0

block2_conv1 (Conv2D)        (None, 112, 112, 128)     73856

block2_conv2 (Conv2D)        (None, 112, 112, 128)     147584

block2_pool (MaxPooling2D)   (None, 56, 56, 128)       0

block3_conv1 (Conv2D)        (None, 56, 56, 256)       295168

block3_conv2 (Conv2D)        (None, 56, 56, 256)       590080

block3_conv3 (Conv2D)        (None, 56, 56, 256)       590080

block3_conv4 (Conv2D)        (None, 56, 56, 256)       590080

block3_pool (MaxPooling2D)   (None, 28, 28, 256)       0

block4_conv1 (Conv2D)        (None, 28, 28, 512)       1180160

block4_conv2 (Conv2D)        (None, 28, 28, 512)       2359808

block4_conv3 (Conv2D)        (None, 28, 28, 512)       2359808

block4_conv4 (Conv2D)        (None, 28, 28, 512)       2359808

block4_pool (MaxPooling2D)   (None, 14, 14, 512)       0

block5_conv1 (Conv2D)        (None, 14, 14, 512)       2359808
```

```
block5_conv2 (Conv2D)        (None, 14, 14, 512)       2359808

block5_conv3 (Conv2D)        (None, 14, 14, 512)       2359808

block5_conv4 (Conv2D)        (None, 14, 14, 512)       2359808

block5_pool (MaxPooling2D)   (None, 7, 7, 512)         0

flatten (Flatten)            (None, 25088)             0

fc1 (Dense)                  (None, 4096)              102764544

fc2 (Dense)                  (None, 4096)              16781312

predictions (Dense)          (None, 1000)              4097000
=================================================================
Total params: 143,667,240
Trainable params: 143,667,240
Non-trainable params: 0
```

Example 4.17 shows how to display all the layers in a VGG19 model and show the layer numbers.

EXAMPLE 4.17   THE CNN VISUALIZE FILTERS.IPYNB **PROGRAM (PART 2)**

```
n=0
for layer in model.layers:
  print(n,layer.name)
  n+=1
```

The following is the output, showing the layer number and the layer name of all the 25 layers:

```
0 input_16
1 block1_conv1
2 block1_conv2
3 block1_pool
4 block2_conv1
5 block2_conv2
6 block2_pool
7 block3_conv1
8 block3_conv2
9 block3_conv3
10 block3_conv4
11 block3_pool
12 block4_conv1
13 block4_conv2
14 block4_conv3
```

```
15 block4_conv4
16 block4_pool
17 block5_conv1
18 block5_conv2
19 block5_conv3
20 block5_conv4
21 block5_pool
22 flatten
23 fc1
24 fc2
25 predictions
```

The following section of the code shows the filter shape and bias shape for the convolutional layers in the VGG16 model. It uses the function `layer.get_weights()` to get the filter and bias parameters.

EXAMPLE 4.17   THE `CNN VISUALIZE FILTERS.IPYNB` **PROGRAM (PART 3)**

```
n=0
for layer in model.layers:
  if 'conv' in layer.name:
    filters, biases = layer.get_weights()
    print(n,layer.name, filters.shape, biases.shape)
  n+=1
```

The following output shows all the convolutional layers, their layer number, and their filter and bias parameters. There are 20 convolutional layers. For layer 1, there are 3 color channels; the filter kernel is (3,3), the total number of filters is 64, and total number of bias is also 64.

```
1 block1_conv1 (3, 3, 3, 64) (64,)
2 block1_conv2 (3, 3, 64, 64) (64,)
4 block2_conv1 (3, 3, 64, 128) (128,)
5 block2_conv2 (3, 3, 128, 128) (128,)
7 block3_conv1 (3, 3, 128, 256) (256,)
8 block3_conv2 (3, 3, 256, 256) (256,)
9 block3_conv3 (3, 3, 256, 256) (256,)
10 block3_conv4 (3, 3, 256, 256) (256,)
12 block4_conv1 (3, 3, 256, 512) (512,)
13 block4_conv2 (3, 3, 512, 512) (512,)
14 block4_conv3 (3, 3, 512, 512) (512,)
15 block4_conv4 (3, 3, 512, 512) (512,)
17 block5_conv1 (3, 3, 512, 512) (512,)
18 block5_conv2 (3, 3, 512, 512) (512,)
19 block5_conv3 (3, 3, 512, 512) (512,)
20 block5_conv4 (3, 3, 512, 512) (512,)
```

The following section of the code shows the filters in the first convolutional layers (n = 1) in VGG19 model. Again, the function `layer.get_weights()` is used to get the filter and bias parameters. Also, the filter is normalized to 0–1 for the purpose of visualization. Then, the first four filters (n_filters, ix = 4, 1) of the total 64 filters are displayed in the first layer.

EXAMPLE 4.17 THE `CNN VISUALIZE FILTERS.IPYNB` **PROGRAM (PART 4)**

```
from matplotlib import pyplot
# retrieve weights from the first hidden layer
n = 1
filters, biases = model.layers[n].get_weights()
s = filters.shape
print("Color channels: ", s[0])
print("Filter size: ", s[1],s[2])

print("Total number of filters : ", s[3])
# normalize filter values to 0-1 so we can visualize them
f_min, f_max = filters.min(), filters.max()
filters = (filters - f_min) / (f_max - f_min)
# plot first few filters
#n_filters, ix = s[3], 1
n_filters, ix = 4, 1

pyplot.figure(figsize=(10,10))
for i in range(n_filters):
        # get the filter
  f = filters[:, :, :, i]

  # plot each channel separately
  for j in range(s[0]):
    ax = pyplot.subplot(n_filters, s[0], ix)
    ax.set_xticks([])
    ax.set_yticks([])
    pyplot.imshow(f[j,:, :], cmap='gray')
    ix += 1
# show the figure
pyplot.show()
```

Figure 4.28 shows the output of the previous code, which shows there are 3 color channels, (3,3) filter size, and total 64 filters in layer 1. It also displays the (3,3) filters in layer 1.

EXERCISE 4.15

Modify the Python code from the previous example, select the second convolutional layer to visualize by changing n = 1 to n = 2, and comment on the results.

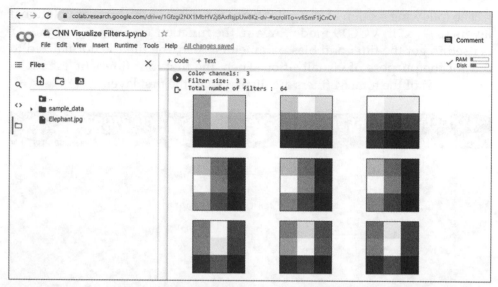

Figure 4.28: The output of the previous example code that displays the filters in layer 1

EXERCISE 4.16

Modify the Python code from the previous example, display all the filters by changing `n_filters, ix = 4, 1` to `n_filters, ix = s[3], 1`, and comment on the results.

The following shows a simple function to draw feature maps in a subplot with multiple rows and columns. The number of columns is set to eight, `col = 8`.

EXAMPLE 4.17   THE CNN VISUALIZE FILTERS.IPYNB PROGRAM (PART 5)

```
def plot_feature_maps(feature_maps):
  # plot all feature maps
  col = 8
  row = int(feature_maps.shape[3]/col)
  ix = 1
  plt.figure(figsize=(20,20))
  for _ in range(row):
    for _ in range(col):
      # specify subplot and turn of axis
      ax = plt.subplot(row, col, ix)
      ax.set_xticks([])
      ax.set_yticks([])
      # plot filter channel in grayscale
      plt.imshow(feature_maps[0, :, :, ix-1], cmap='gray')
      ix += 1
  # show the figure
  plt.show()
```

You can visualize the output of the first layer of the VGG19 model by setting the output of layer 1 (n = 1) as the model output; see `Model(inputs=model.inputs, outputs=model.layers[n].output)` in the following section of the code. Then `feature_maps = model.predict(img)` is used to get the output of layer 1. We call this layer 1 output as feature maps. Then, it calls `plot_feature_maps(feature_maps)` to display feature maps. The feature maps basically show what the image looks like after applying all the layer 1 filters. You can change to other layers by changing `n = 1`.

EXAMPLE 4.17   THE `CNN VISUALIZE FILTERS.IPYNB` **PROGRAM (PART 6)**

```
from keras.applications.vgg19 import VGG19
from keras.applications.vgg19 import preprocess_input
from keras.preprocessing.image import load_img
from keras.preprocessing.image import img_to_array
from keras.models import Model
import matplotlib.pyplot as plt
from numpy import expand_dims
# load the model
model = VGG19()
#Select the hidde layer to visualize
n = 1
# redefine model to output right after the hidden layer
model = Model(inputs=model.inputs, outputs=model.layers[n].output)
model.summary()

# load the image with the required shape
img = load_img('Elephant.jpg', target_size=(224, 224))
# convert the image to an array
img = img_to_array(img)
# expand dimensions so that it represents a single 'sample'
img = expand_dims(img, axis=0)
# prepare the image (e.g. scale pixel values for the vgg)
img = preprocess_input(img)
# get feature map for first hidden layer
feature_maps = model.predict(img)
print("Feature maps: ", feature_maps.shape)
#plot all the feature maps
plot_feature_maps(feature_maps)
```

Figure 4.29 shows the output of the previous code, which shows the structure of the VGG19 model with the first layer as the output. It also shows the feature maps (the output) of layer 1.

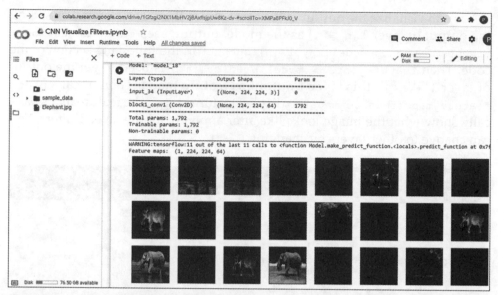

Figure 4.29: The output of the previous code, which shows the structure of the VGG19 model with the first layer as the output. It also shows the feature maps (the output) of layer 1.

EXERCISE 4.17

Modify the previous example Python code, select the second or third or fourth convolutional layer for visualization by changing $n = 1$ to $n = 2$ and so on, and comment on the results.

Another way to visualize each layer is to use the Keras Visualization Toolkit, see the following link for details.

```
https://raghakot.github.io/keras-vis/
```

Figure 4.30 shows the examples of convolution filter visualization, dense layer visualization, and attention maps in Keras Visualization Toolkit.

The following are a few more examples on the visualization of intermediate layers in convolutional neural networks:

```
https://keras.io/examples/conv_filter_visualization/
https://www.analyticsvidhya.com/blog/2018/03/essentials-of-deep-
learning-visualizing-convolutional-neural-networks/
https://github.com/JGuillaumin/DeepLearning-NoBlaBla/blob/master/
KerasViz.ipynb
https://towardsdatascience.com/visualizing-intermediate-activation-
in-convolutional-neural-networks-with-keras-260b36d60d0
https://github.com/gabrielpierobon/cnnshapes/blob/master/README.md
https://www.kaggle.com/amarjeet007/visualize-cnn-with-keras
```

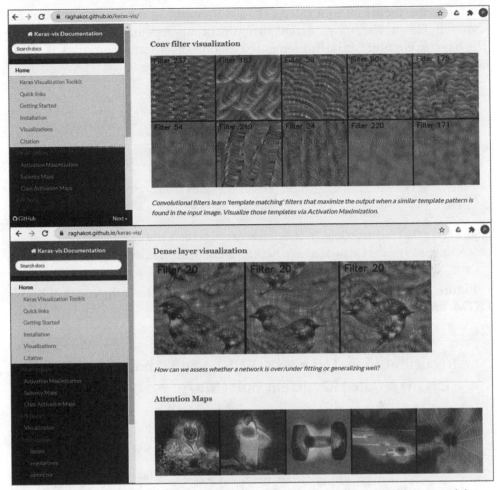

Figure 4.30: The convolutional filter visualization (top), the dense layer visualization, and the attention maps (bottom) in the Keras Visualization Toolkit

(Source: `https://raghakot.github.io/keras-vis/`)

4.4   Recurrent Neural Networks

Recurrent neural networks (RNNs) are another popular deep learning neural network, along with convolutional neural networks. Convolutional neural networks specialize in processing images, while RNNs specialize in processing sequences. RNNs are derived from feedforward neural networks and can use their internal state (memory) to process variable-length sequences of inputs. RNNs have been applied in sequence prediction, text analysis, and speech recognition.

Figure 4.31 shows the schematic diagram of a recurrent neural network and its unfolded structure. X is the sequential input data, O is the sequential output data, h is the recurrent unit (also called cell), and v is the feedback loop. As shown in Figure 4.31, the recurrent structure occurs repeatedly in the network. The h recurrent unit can be implemented as long short-term memory k (LSTM) network unit and a gated recurrent unit (GRU).

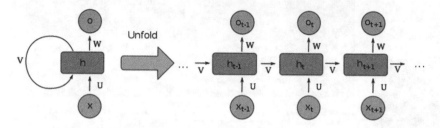

Figure 4.31: The schematic diagram of recurrent neural network and its unfolded structure
(Source: `https://en.wikipedia.org/wiki/Recurrent_neural_network`)

Figure 4.32 shows an interesting article that explains the differences of RNN, LSTM, and GRU.

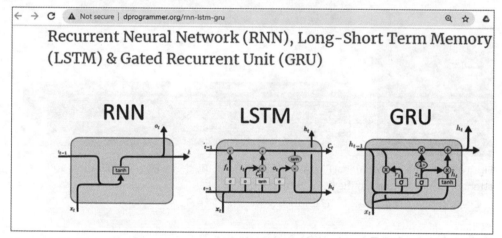

Figure 4.32: The schematic diagram of RNN, LSTM, and GRU
(Source: `http://dprogrammer.org/rnn-lstm-gru`)

Figure 4.33 shows the four types of recurrent neural networks.

- **One to one:** One input and one output
- **One to many:** One input and multiple outputs
- **Many to one:** Multiple inputs and one output
- **Many to many:** Multiple inputs and multiple outputs

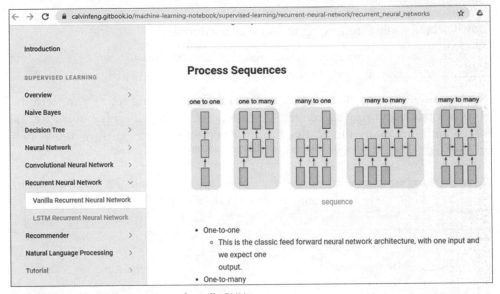

Figure 4.33: The different types of vanilla RNN

(Source: `https://calvinfeng.gitbook.io/machine-learning-notebook/ supervised-learning/recurrent-neural-network/recurrent_neural_ networks`)

For more details about recursive neural networks, see the following:

`https://stanford.edu/~shervine/teaching/cs-230/cheatsheet-recurrent- neural-networks`

`https://www.simplilearn.com/tutorials/deep-learning-tutorial/rnn`

4.4.1   Vanilla RNNs

A vanilla RNN is the simplest recurrent neural network that has an input vector, an output vector, and a recurrent unit or cell, as shown in Figure 4.34. Within the recurrent unit, there is an activation function, called *tanh*. You can also use a different activation function.

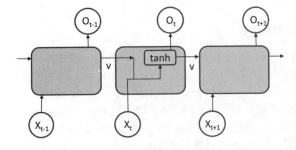

Vanilla RNN

Figure 4.34: The vanilla RNN structure

(Source: `https://subscription.packtpub.com/book/data/9781789340990/5/ ch05lvl1sec21/vanilla-rnns`)

The easiest way to implement vanilla RNN is to use the Keras function called SimpleRNN; see the following links for more details:

```
https://www.tensorflow.org/api_docs/python/tf/keras/layers/SimpleRNN
https://keras.io/api/layers/recurrent_layers/simple_rnn/
```

The following is another example of vanilla RNNs using Keras SimpleRNN. It comes from an impressive website called Easy-deep-learning-with-Keras, which contains many illustrative example codes on deep learning neural networks; see Figure 4.35.

```
https://github.com/buomsoo-kim/Easy-deep-learning-with-Keras/blob/
master/3.%20RNN/1-Basic-RNN/1-1-vanilla-rnn.py
```

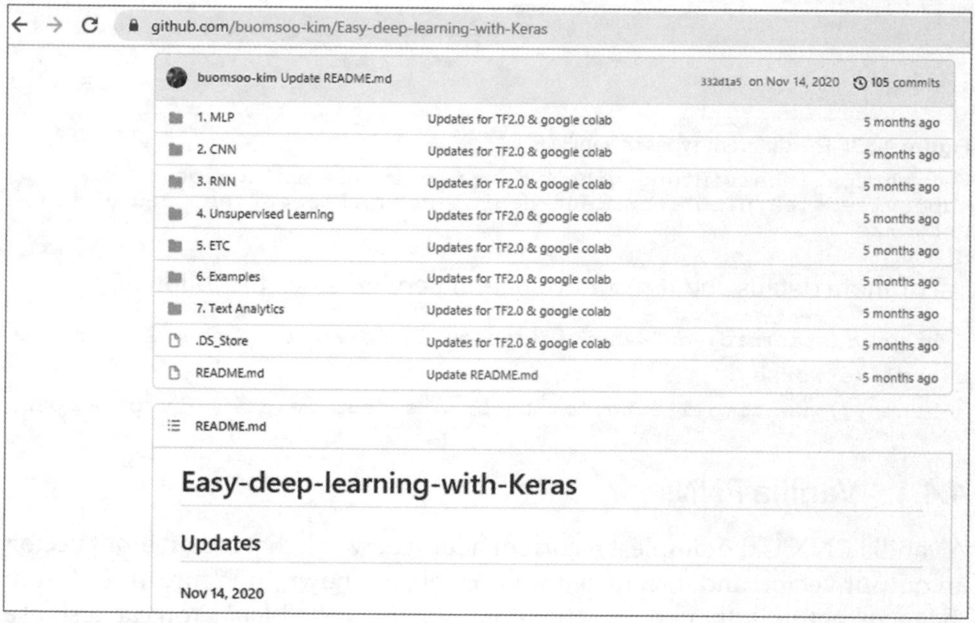

Figure 4.35: The Easy-deep-learning-with-Keras website

(Source: `https://github.com/buomsoo-kim/Easy-deep-learning-with-Keras`)

4.4.2   Long-Short Term Memory

Long short-term memory (LSTM) is the most popular recurrent neural network architecture. Unlike conventional feedforward neural networks, LSTM has feedback connections. It can process both single input data (e.g., an image) and a sequence of data (e.g., sequences of images in a video). LSTM networks were developed to deal with the vanishing gradient problem and are well-suited for classification and prediction based on time-series data.

Figure 4.36 shows an ordinary LSTM unit, consisting of a cell, an input gate, an output gate, and a forgetting gate. The cell remembers values over arbitrary time intervals, and the three gates regulate the flow of information in and out of the cell.

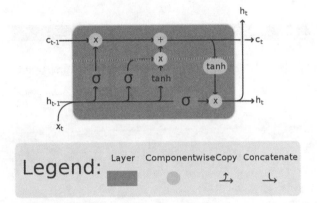

Figure 4.36: The long short memory unit structure
(Source: `https://en.wikipedia.org/wiki/Long_short-term_memory`)

LSTM has been commonly used in the following:

■ Time-series prediction

■ Time-series anomaly detection

■ Speech recognition

■ Language translation

■ Music composition

■ Text generation

■ Handwriting recognition

■ Human action recognition

■ Robot control

There are five types of LSTM networks:

■ LSTM classic

■ Peephole connections

■ Gated recurrent unit

■ Multiplicative LSTM (2017)

■ LSTMs with attention

See the following website about the five types of LSTM networks:

```
https://blog.exxactcorp.com/5-types-lstm-recurrent-neural-network/
```

Now, let's look at some RNN Python example code. Example 4.18 shows a simple Keras SimpleRNN example.

EXAMPLE 4.18   THE `SIMPLERNN.PY` PROGRAM

```
#Example 4.18 SimpleRNN.py
#https://www.tensorflow.org/api_docs/python/tf/keras/layers/SimpleRNN
import tensorflow as tf
import numpy as np

i = 4
s = 5
n = 1
inputs = np.random.random([i, s, n]).astype(np.float32)
simple_rnn = tf.keras.layers.SimpleRNN(i)
print(inputs)


output = simple_rnn(inputs)   # The output has shape `[32, 4]`.
print(output)
```

This is the output of the example, showing the inputs and the outputs of the SimpleRNN:

```
[[[0.62100476]
  [0.6268874 ]
  [0.29603383]
  [0.7806354 ]
  [0.2677117 ]]

 [[0.07438648]
  [0.4314253 ]
  [0.8583106 ]
  [0.37769878]
  [0.6659656 ]]

 [[0.7893332 ]
  [0.52695924]
  [0.7091379 ]
  [0.7229491 ]
  [0.4395296 ]]

 [[0.7297753 ]
  [0.9190028 ]
  [0.16167772]
  [0.24619947]
  [0.00972256]]]
```

```
tf.Tensor(
[[ 0.74350387   0.14273308  -0.606336      0.03686696]
 [ 0.9149856   -0.29274157  -0.41164276  -0.18939926]
 [ 0.86783993  -0.00522089  -0.5399761   -0.09883117]
 [ 0.2526757    0.2733288   -0.5457421    0.54237866]], shape=(4, 4),
dtype=float32)
```

Example 4.19 is another example of Keras SimpleRNN, showing how to create an RNN model and show the model summary.

EXAMPLE 4.19   THE SIMPLERNN2.PY PROGRAM

```python
#Example 4.19 SimpleRNN2.py
from keras.models import Sequential
from keras.layers import Dense, SimpleRNN, Activation
from keras import optimizers

model = Sequential()
model.add(SimpleRNN(50, input_shape = (49,1), return_sequences =
False))
model.add(Dense(46))
model.add(Activation('softmax'))

adam = optimizers.Adam(lr = 0.001)
model.compile(loss = 'categorical_crossentropy', optimizer = adam,
metrics = ['accuracy'])
print(model.summary())
```

This is the output of the previous example, showing the inputs and the outputs of the SimpleRNN:

```
Model: "sequential_1"

_____
Layer (type)                 Output Shape              Param #
=================================================================
simple_rnn_1 (SimpleRNN)     (None, 50)                2600

_____
dense_1 (Dense)              (None, 46)                2346

_____
activation_1 (Activation)    (None, 46)                0
=================================================================
Total params: 4,946
Trainable params: 4,946
Non-trainable params: 0
_____
None
  [0.2677117 ]]
```

The following is another Keras SimpleRNN example, predicting the airline passenger numbers, which is modified based on the example code at `https://www.datatechnotes.com/2018/12/rnn-example-with-keras-simplernn-in.html`. First, the airline passenger numbers are retrieved from a website:

```
df = pd.read_csv('https://raw.githubusercontent.com/jbrownlee/
Datasets/master/airline-passengers.csv', usecols=[1], engine='python')
```

Then put the first 80 percent of the data as training data and use the remaining 20 percent for prediction.

```
Tp = int(df.shape[0]*0.8)
```

Then build a simple RNN model, train the model with the training data (first 80 percent of the total data), predict the data, and finally plot the results.

EXAMPLE 4.20   THE `SIMPLERNN3A.PY` **PROGRAM**

```
#Example 4.20
#Modified based on:
#https://www.datatechnotes.com/2018/12/rnn-example-with-keras-
simplernn-in.html
import pandas as pd
import numpy as np
import matplotlib.pyplot as plt
from keras.models import Sequential
from keras.layers import Dense, SimpleRNN

# convert into dataset matrix
def convertToMatrix(data, step):
 X, Y =[], []
 for i in range(len(data)-step):
  d=i+step
  X.append(data[i:d,])
  Y.append(data[d,])
 return np.array(X), np.array(Y)

# https://www.kaggle.com/rakannimer/air-passengers
#df = pd.read_csv('AirPassengers.csv', usecols=[1], engine='python')
df = pd.read_csv('https://raw.githubusercontent.com/jbrownlee/
Datasets/master/airline-passengers.csv', usecols=[1], engine='python')
df.head()
plt.plot(df)
plt.show()

step = 4
N = df.shape[0]
Tp = int(df.shape[0]*0.8)
```

```python
values=df.values
train,test = values[0:Tp,:], values[Tp:N,:]

# add step elements into train and test
test = np.append(test,np.repeat(test[-1,],step))
train = np.append(train,np.repeat(train[-1,],step))

trainX,trainY =convertToMatrix(train,step)
testX,testY =convertToMatrix(test,step)
trainX = np.reshape(trainX, (trainX.shape[0], 1, trainX.shape[1]))
testX = np.reshape(testX, (testX.shape[0], 1, testX.shape[1]))

model = Sequential()
model.add(SimpleRNN(units=32, input_shape=(1,step),
activation="relu"))
model.add(Dense(8, activation="relu"))
model.add(Dense(1))
model.compile(loss='mean_squared_error', optimizer='rmsprop')
model.summary()

model.fit(trainX,trainY, epochs=10, batch_size=16, verbose=2)
trainPredict = model.predict(trainX)
testPredict= model.predict(testX)
predicted=np.concatenate((trainPredict,testPredict),axis=0)

trainScore = model.evaluate(trainX, trainY, verbose=0)
print(trainScore)

index = df.index.values

plt.plot(df,label='Data')
plt.plot(predicted,label='Prediction')
plt.axvline(df.index[Tp], c="r")
plt.legend()
plt.show()
```

This is the output of the example, showing the inputs and the outputs of SimpleRNN:

```
Model: "sequential_1"
```

Layer (type)	Output Shape	Param #
simple_rnn_1 (SimpleRNN)	(None, 32)	1184
dense_1 (Dense)	(None, 8)	264
dense_2 (Dense)	(None, 1)	9

```
Total params: 1,457
Trainable params: 1,457
Non-trainable params: 0


Epoch 1/10
 - 0s - loss: 41144.4444
Epoch 2/10
 - 0s - loss: 17512.6174
Epoch 3/10
 - 0s - loss: 8119.1773
Epoch 4/10
 - 0s - loss: 4370.8642
Epoch 5/10
 - 0s - loss: 2613.2462
Epoch 6/10
 - 0s - loss: 2054.8084
Epoch 7/10
 - 0s - loss: 1925.8166
Epoch 8/10
 - 0s - loss: 1789.0628
Epoch 9/10
 - 0s - loss: 1733.9799
Epoch 10/10
 - 0s - loss: 1731.7953
1606.9956946331522
```

Figure 4.37 shows the output of Example 4.20, showing the original data, the predictions, and the vertical red line representing the 80 percent prediction point. The x-axis consists of data points at different time, and the y-axis consists of the number of air passengers. The predicted result after the 80 percent prediction point agrees well with the original data, even though the model has never seen the data before.

Example 4.21 shows how to create a simple Keras LSTM network. It was modified based on the TensorFlow RNN website (`https://www.tensorflow.org/guide/keras/rnn`).

EXAMPLE 4.21   THE `SIMPLELSTM.PY` PROGRAM

```
#Example 4.21 SimpleLSTM.py
#Based on
#https://www.tensorflow.org/guide/keras/rnn
from tensorflow import keras
from tensorflow.keras import layers
model = keras.Sequential()
model.add(layers.Embedding(input_dim=100, output_dim=32))
model.add(layers.LSTM(64))
model.add(layers.Dense(1))
model.summary()
```

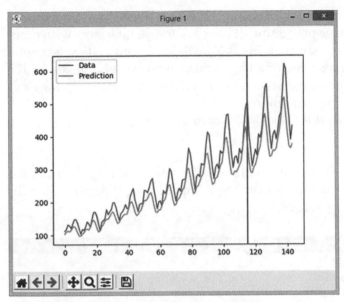

Figure 4.37: The plot output of the Example 4.17

This is the output of the example, showing the summary of the LSTM network:

```
Model: "sequential"

Layer (type)                 Output Shape              Param #
=================================================================
embedding (Embedding)        (None, None, 32)          3200

lstm (LSTM)                  (None, 64)                24832

dense (Dense)                (None, 1)                 65
=================================================================
Total params: 28,097
Trainable params: 28,097
Non-trainable params: 0
```

4.4.3   Natural Language Processing and Python Natural Language Toolkit

Natural language processing (NLP) is a form of artificial intelligence that deals with human (natural) languages, in particular with the processing and analysis of large amounts of natural language data. The main challenges in NPL are speech recognition, natural language understanding, and natural language generation.

The Python Natural Language Toolkit (NLKT) is a leading open source library for natural language processing. It has easy-to-use interfaces with more than 50 corpora lexical resources (such as WordNet). In linguistics, a corpus is a language resource consisting of a large and structured set of texts. NLKT has a number of libraries for classification, tokenization, stemming, tagging, parsing, semantic reasoning, and more.

For more details about NLKT, see the following:

```
https://www.nltk.org/
```

Example 4.22 shows a Python example code for using the NLTK library for text analysis. The text in the code is from the Wikipedia page "Artificial Intelligence" (`https://en.wikipedia.org/wiki/Artificial_intelligence`).

EXAMPLE 4.22 THE `NLTK.PY` PROGRAM

```python
# Example 4.22 The NLTK.py Program
# https://www.nltk.org/
# pip install nltk
import nltk
nltk.download('maxent_ne_chunker')
nltk.download('words')

sentence = """
Artificial intelligence (AI), is intelligence demonstrated by
machines,
  unlike the natural intelligence displayed by humans and animals.
  Leading AI textbooks define the field as the study of "intelligent
agents":
  any device that perceives its environment and takes actions that
maximize its
  chance of successfully achieving its goals.[3] Colloquially, the
term
  "artificial intelligence" is often used to describe machines (or
computers)
  that mimic "cognitive" functions that humans associate with the
human mind,
  such as "learning" and "problem solving".[4]
"""
tokens = nltk.word_tokenize(sentence)
print(tokens)
tagged = nltk.pos_tag(tokens)
print(tagged)
entities = nltk.chunk.ne_chunk(tagged)
print(entities)
```

The following are the outputs of the example, showing the tokens, tags, and entities of the text. This block shows the token entities of the text.

```
 ['Artificial', 'intelligence', '(', 'AI', ')', ',', 'is',
'intelligence', 'demonstrated', 'by', 'machines', ',', 'unlike',
'the', 'natural', 'intelligence', 'displayed', 'by', 'humans', 'and',
'animals', '.', 'Leading', 'AI', 'textbooks', 'define', 'the', 'field',
'as', 'the', 'study', 'of', '``', 'intelligent', 'agents', "''",
':', 'any', 'device', 'that', 'perceives', 'its', 'environment',
'and', 'takes', 'actions', 'that', 'maximize', 'its', 'chance', 'of',
'successfully', 'achieving', 'its', 'goals', '.', '[', '3', ']',
'Colloquially', ',', 'the', 'term', '``', 'artificial', 'intelligence',
"''", 'is', 'often', 'used', 'to', 'describe', 'machines', '(', 'or',
'computers', ')', 'that', 'mimic', '``', 'cognitive', "''", 'functions',
'that', 'humans', 'associate', 'with', 'the', 'human', 'mind', ',',
'such', 'as', '``', 'learning', "''", 'and', '``', 'problem', 'solving',
"''", '.', '[', '4', ']']
```

The following block shows the tags entities of the text:

```
 [('Artificial', 'JJ'), ('intelligence', 'NN'), ('(', '('), ('AI',
'NNP'), (')', ')'), (',', ','), ('is', 'VBZ'), ('intelligence',
'NN'), ('demonstrated', 'VBN'), ('by', 'IN'), ('machines', 'NNS'),
(',', ','), ('unlike', 'IN'), ('the', 'DT'), ('natural', 'JJ'),
('intelligence', 'NN'), ('displayed', 'VBN'), ('by', 'IN'), ('humans',
'NNS'), ('and', 'CC'), ('animals', 'NNS'), ('.', '.'), ('Leading',
'VBG'), ('AI', 'NNP'), ('textbooks', 'NNS'), ('define', 'VBP'),
('the', 'DT'), ('field', 'NN'), ('as', 'IN'), ('the', 'DT'), ('study',
'NN'), ('of', 'IN'), ('``', '``'), ('intelligent', 'JJ'), ('agents',
'NNS'), ("''", "''"), (':', ':'), ('any', 'DT'), ('device', 'NN'),
('that', 'WDT'), ('perceives', 'VBZ'), ('its', 'PRP$'), ('environment',
'NN'), ('and', 'CC'), ('takes', 'VBZ'), ('actions', 'NNS'), ('that',
'IN'), ('maximize', 'VB'), ('its', 'PRP$'), ('chance', 'NN'), ('of',
'IN'), ('successfully', 'RB'), ('achieving', 'VBG'), ('its', 'PRP$'),
('goals', 'NNS'), ('.', '.'), ('[', '$'), ('3', 'CD'), (']', 'NNP'),
('Colloquially', 'NNP'), (',', ','), ('the', 'DT'), ('term', 'NN'),
('``', '``'), ('artificial', 'JJ'), ('intelligence', 'NN'), ("''",
"''"), ('is', 'VBZ'), ('often', 'RB'), ('used', 'VBN'), ('to', 'TO'),
('describe', 'VB'), ('machines', 'NNS'), ('(', '('), ('or', 'CC'),
('computers', 'NNS'), (')', ')'), ('that', 'IN'), ('mimic', 'JJ'),
('``', '``'), ('cognitive', 'JJ'), ("''", "''"), ('functions', 'NNS'),
('that', 'WDT'), ('humans', 'NNS'), ('associate', 'VBP'), ('with',
'IN'), ('the', 'DT'), ('human', 'JJ'), ('mind', 'NN'), (',', ','),
('such', 'JJ'), ('as', 'IN'), ('``', '``'), ('learning', 'VBG'), ("''",
"''"), ('and', 'CC'), ('``', '``'), ('problem', 'NN'), ('solving',
'NN'), ("''", "''"), ('.', '.'), ('[', 'VB'), ('4', 'CD'), (']', 'NN')]
```

The following block shows the sections of entities of the text:

```
(S
  (GPE Artificial/JJ)
  intelligence/NN
  (/(
  AI/NNP
  )/)
  ,/,
```

```
is/VBZ
intelligence/NN
demonstrated/VBN
by/IN
machines/NNS
,/,
unlike/IN
the/DT
natural/JJ
intelligence/NN
displayed/VBN
by/IN
humans/NNS
and/CC
animals/NNS
./.
Leading/VBG

... ...

functions/NNS
that/WDT
humans/NNS
associate/VBP
with/IN
the/DT
human/JJ
mind/NN
,/,
such/JJ
as/IN
``/``
learning/VBG
''/''
and/CC
``/``
problem/NN
solving/NN
''/''
./.
[/VB
4/CD
]/NN)
```

EXERCISE 4.18

Modify the previous example Python code and choose a different piece of text for text analysis. Comment on the results.

More examples about natural language processing will be available in Chapter 10.

4.5   Transformers

Transformers are new deep learning neural networks introduced by Hugging Face in 2017, mainly used in the field of natural language processing. Transformers are based on a concept called *attention*, a mechanism for weighting different parts of the input based on their importance. The creation and development of transformers has demonstrated the effectiveness of large pre-trained models for tackling NLP tasks such as machine translation and question answering. Transformers are starting to make recurrent neural networks obsolete.

Transformers consist of a number of stacked encoders that form the encoder layer, a number of stacked decoders that form the decoder layer, and a bunch of attention layers that form self-attentions and encoder-decoder attentions.

Like recurrent neural networks, transformers are designed to handle sequential data. But, unlike RNNs, transformers do not need to process sequential data in the correct order. For example, if the input data is a natural language sentence, the transformer does not need to process the beginning before the end. Because of this, transformers allow for much more parallelization and thus shorter training time.

The following are the three main types of transformers:

- **BERT:** Bidirectional Encoder Representations from Transformers
- **ALBERT:** A Lite BERT
- **GPT:** Generative Pre-trained Transformer

Transformers have been implemented in both TensorFlow and PyTorch. See the following Transformers GitHub site for details:

```
https://github.com/huggingface/transformers
```

4.5.1   BERT and ALBERT

BERT (Bidirectional Encoder Representations from Transformers) is a library for natural language processing. BERT was created and published in 2018 by Jacob Devlin and his colleagues at Google. Google uses BERT to better understand user search queries. The original English-language BERT model used two corpora in pre-training: BookCorpus and English Wikipedia, which together contain around 16GB of uncompressed text.

ALBERT is a "lite" version of BERT. ALBERT uses two parameter-reduction techniques to reduce memory requirements and increase training speed.

Google's ALBERT has achieved top scores on three popular benchmark tests for natural language understanding: GLUE, RACE, and SQuAD 2.0. Google has introduced three outstanding innovations with ALBERT: factorized embedding parameterization, cross-layer parameter sharing, and inter-sentence coherence loss. As a result, the large ALBERT model has about 18x fewer parameters compared to BERT-large.

Figure 4.38 shows the performance of the machine on the RACE challenge, where ALBERT has outperformed other models.

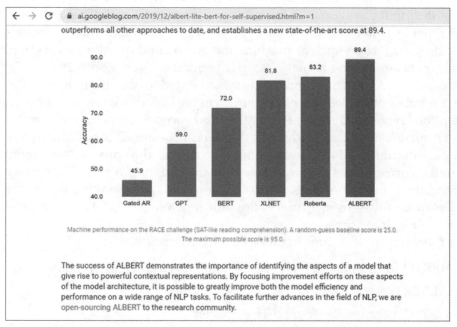

Figure 4.38: The machine performance on the RACE challenge

(Source: `https://ai.googleblog.com/2019/12/albert-lite-bert-for-self-supervised.html?m=1`)

Example 4.23 shows a Python example code of using transformers for text sentiment analysis.

EXAMPLE 4.23   THE `TRANSFORMERS.PY` PROGRAM

```
# Example 4.23
# https://github.com/huggingface/transformers
# pip install transformers
# https://aka.ms/vs/16/release/vc_redist.x64.exe


from transformers import pipeline
classifier = pipeline('sentiment-analysis')
classifier('This is a good movie.')
```

This is the output of the example, showing the classification result as positive:

```
[{'label': 'POSITIVE', 'score': 0.9998612999916077}]
```

EXERCISE 4.19

Modify the previous example Python code, choose some different sentences, and make sure some are positive and some are negative. Comment on the results.

Example 4.24 shows a Python example code for using transformers for question answering.

EXAMPLE 4.24   THE TRANSFORMERS2.PY **PROGRAM**

```
#Example 4.24
from transformers import pipeline
question_answerer = pipeline('question-answering')
question_answerer({
 'question': 'What is the name of the company?',
 'context': 'We created Biox Systems Ltd company back in the year of
2000.'
})
```

This is the output of the example, showing the answer to the question:

```
{'answer': 'Biox Systems Ltd',
 'end': 27,
 'score': 0.7553602457046509,
 'start': 11}
```

EXERCISE 4.20

Modify the previous example Python code, choose a different piece of text, and ask different questions. Comment on the results.

4.5.2   GPT-3

Generative Pre-trained Transformer (GPT) is an autoregressive natural language processing model that uses deep learning neural networks to produce human-like text. GPT was created by OpenAI, a San Francisco–based artificial intelligence research laboratory. There are three versions so far:

- GPT
- GPT-2
- GPT-3

The latest GPT-3 has 175 billion machine learning parameters and has caught the attention of the world in July 2020 with its amazing capabilities. Here is an impressive YouTube video about the GPT-3 demo:

```
https://www.youtube.com/watch?v=8V20HkoiNtc&t=502s
```

Before GPT-3, the largest language model was Microsoft's Turing-NLG with 17 billion parameters, released in February 2020.

There are already startups using GPT-3 to provide cool services.

Dover.io allows users to create job descriptions based on simple key words. See the following for more details about the Job Descriptions Creator - Dover.io.

```
https://www.dover.io/tools/job-description-rewriter
```

Fitness AI is an iPhone app that uses artificial intelligence to generate personalized workouts. Ask GPT-3 health-related or fitness-related questions for free.

```
https://www.fitnessai.com/
```

OthersideAI allows users to generate email messages with a list of a few bullet points.

```
https://www.othersideai.com/
```

Philosopher AI allows users to ask philosophical questions. You need to pay for the service.

```
https://philosopherai.com/
```

CopyAI helps users to automatically generate professional marketing copy based on your input. It claims to be able to automate the tedious and often frustrating aspects of copy creation.

```
https://www.copy.ai/
```

4.5.3   Switch Transformers

In early 2021, researchers at Google Brain developed a new, open source AI model for NLP, called Switch Transformer, which has a whopping 1.6T parameters, nearly ten times that of GPT-3. The training speed of Switch Transformer has also been improved by seven times compared to previous architectures.

Switch Transformer uses a switch feed-forward neural network (FFN) layer to replace the standard FFN layer in the transformer architecture. Instead of a single FFN, each switch layer contains multiple FFNs, called *experts*. The Switch Transformer architecture is based on the concept of Mixture of Experts (MoE). This approach simplifies the computations and reduces the communication cost.

At the time of writing this book, Google has not released the pretrained model weights for Switch Transformer; for more details about Switch Transformer, visit the following:

```
https://arxiv.org/abs/2101.03961
https://github.com/tensorflow/mesh/blob/master/mesh_tensorflow/
transformer/
```

4.6   Graph Neural Networks

Although recurrent neural networks have been superseded by transformers in natural language processing, they are still useful in many areas that require sequential decision-making and in reinforcement learning. Recurrent neural networks typically take input data in a sequence, such as time-series data or language text. A graph neural network (GNN) is a special type of recurrent neural network that can take graphs as input data. GNN has been used in many applications such as analyzing social media data, and molecular structures. There is also the quantum graph neural networks (QGNNs) for quantum chemistry analysis. QGNNs have been applied to learning quantum dynamics, graph clustering, and graph isomorphism classification.

Convolutional neural networks work well on data with a regular grid structure, such as images, but not on graphs because they are arbitrarily large and have a complex topology.

The following website shows a friendly introduction to the GNN. It also covers the future of GNN including Quantum Graph Neural Networks (QGNNs).

```
https://www.kdnuggets.com/2020/11/friendly-introduction-graph-
neural-networks.html
```

The following website shows the introduction to a GNN and its applications, such as modeling real-world physical systems, molecular fingerprints, protein interface prediction, modeling social interactions, and so on.

```
https://neptune.ai/blog/graph-neural-network-and-some-of-gnn-
applications
```

The following is a GNN implementation by Google's DeepMind:

```
https://github.com/deepmind/graph_nets
```

The following is a GNN implementation by Facebook's PyTorch:

```
https://github.com/rusty1s/pytorch_geometric
```

For more details about GNNs, visit the following website:

```
https://theaisummer.com/Graph_Neural_Networks/
https://www.dgl.ai/
```

4.6.1 SuperGLUE

SuperGlue is a CVPR 2020 research project, being conducted at Magic Leap. CVPR (Conference on Computer Vision and Pattern Recognition) is the premier annual event on computer vision, including several co-located workshops and short courses in addition to the main conference. The SuperGlue network is a GNN combined with an optimal matching layer that is trained to match two sets of sparse image features. This repo includes PyTorch code and pre-trained weights for running the SuperGlue matching network based on SuperPoint key points and descriptors. Given a pair of images, you can use this repo to extract matching features for the image pair. See the following links for details.

```
https://github.com/magicleap/SuperGluePretrainedNetwork
https://psarlin.com/superglue/
```

4.7 Bayesian Neural Networks

Traditional deep learning neural networks have a fixed value for their parameters; hence, they are also called *deterministic neural networks*. Traditional deep learning neural networks have been successful in many applications. However, they also have some drawbacks. For example, mere knowledge of the input-output mapping is inadequate when it comes to generating predictive uncertainty in their predictions. This can be important when the available data is limited or the data does not span the whole space of interest.

Bayesian neural networks (BNNs) have been developed to address these issues. Bayesian neural networks are neural networks whose weights or parameters are expressed as a distribution rather than a deterministic value and are learned using Bayesian inference. The output of Bayesian neural networks is also a distribution rather than a fixed value.

Figure 4.39 shows the differences between traditional neural networks and Bayesian neural networks.

Traditional Neural Networks   Bayesian Neural Networks

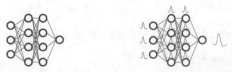

Figure 4.39: The traditional neural networks and Bayesian neural networks

The following is the Keras website on probabilistic Bayesian neural networks, providing a detailed introduction and a Google Colab IPython Notebook with the source code. You can access the code by clicking the View in Colab link.

```
https://keras.io/examples/keras_recipes/bayesian_neural_networks/
```

Figure 4.40 shows the modified version of the Google Colab code. You can access the modified code by using the following link or by uploading a file named `Copy_of_bayesian_neural_networks_wine.ipynb` to your Google Colab.

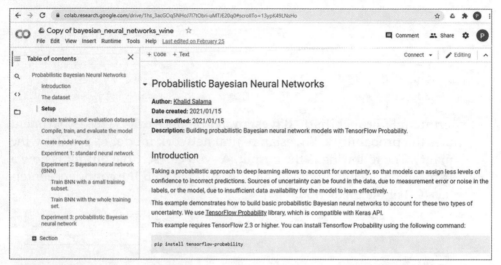

Figure 4.40: The corresponding Google Colab code for the Keras website on probabilistic Bayesian neural networks

(Source: `https://colab.research.google.com/drive/1hs_3acGOq5NHoJ7l7t Obri-uMTJE20q0#scrollTo=13ypK49LNsHo`)

The modified code performs three experiments to predict wine quality.

Experiment 1: standard neural network   In this experiment, the basic deterministic model is used to predict the wine quality. From the following outputs, you can see that only one fixed value is predicted for each input:

```
Predicted: 5.8 - Actual: 6.0
Predicted: 5.6 - Actual: 6.0
Predicted: 6.1 - Actual: 6.0
Predicted: 5.4 - Actual: 6.0
Predicted: 5.5 - Actual: 5.0
Predicted: 5.5 - Actual: 6.0
Predicted: 5.8 - Actual: 5.0
Predicted: 5.6 - Actual: 8.0
Predicted: 6.6 - Actual: 6.0
Predicted: 6.1 - Actual: 7.0
```

Experiment 2: Bayesian neural network (BNN)   In this experiment, the Bayesian neural network model is used to predict wine quality.

The following outputs show that for each input a mean value, a minimum value, and a maximum value are predicted:

```
Predictions mean: 6.08, min: 5.47, max: 6.34, range: 0.86 - Actual: 6.0
Predictions mean: 5.46, min: 4.78, max: 5.96, range: 1.17 - Actual: 6.0
Predictions mean: 6.11, min: 5.75, max: 6.38, range: 0.63 - Actual: 6.0
Predictions mean: 5.19, min: 4.58, max: 5.81, range: 1.23 - Actual: 6.0
Predictions mean: 5.25, min: 4.76, max: 5.84, range: 1.08 - Actual: 5.0
Predictions mean: 5.15, min: 4.49, max: 5.79, range: 1.29 - Actual: 6.0
Predictions mean: 5.89, min: 5.23, max: 6.26, range: 1.03 - Actual: 5.0
Predictions mean: 5.53, min: 4.7, max: 6.15, range: 1.46 - Actual: 8.0
Predictions mean: 6.36, min: 6.12, max: 6.52, range: 0.4 - Actual: 6.0
Predictions mean: 6.02, min: 5.57, max: 6.31, range: 0.74 - Actual: 7.0
```

Experiment 3: Probabilistic Bayesian neural network   This experiment uses the probabilistic Bayesian neural network model to predict wine quality. The following is the output. As you can see, the output is now a distribution, including the mean, the variance, and the confidence intervals (CI) of the prediction.

```
Prediction mean: 5.99, stddev: 0.75, 95% CI: [7.47 - 4.52] - Actual: 6.0
Prediction mean: 5.3, stddev: 0.7, 95% CI: [6.68 - 3.93] - Actual: 6.0
Prediction mean: 6.05, stddev: 0.77, 95% CI: [7.57 - 4.54] - Actual: 6.0
Prediction mean: 5.22, stddev: 0.69, 95% CI: [6.58 - 3.86] - Actual: 6.0
Prediction mean: 5.2, stddev: 0.69, 95% CI: [6.56 - 3.85] - Actual: 5.0
Prediction mean: 5.15, stddev: 0.69, 95% CI: [6.5 - 3.8] - Actual: 6.0
Prediction mean: 6.02, stddev: 0.75, 95% CI: [7.5 - 4.55] - Actual: 5.0
Prediction mean: 5.93, stddev: 0.74, 95% CI: [7.38 - 4.47] - Actual: 8.0
Prediction mean: 6.61, stddev: 0.87, 95% CI: [8.32 - 4.9] - Actual: 6.0
Prediction mean: 5.77, stddev: 0.75, 95% CI: [7.24 - 4.29] - Actual: 7.0
```

You can also plot the mean, the maximum, and the minimum on a graph. Figure 4.41 shows the code for plotting the mean, the maximum, and the minimum of the predictions (top), and the corresponding plot (bottom).

The following is a list of interesting tutorials and projects about Bayesian neural networks:

```
https://github.com/JavierAntoran/Bayesian-Neural-Networks
https://davidstutz.de/a-short-introduction-to-bayesian-neural-
networks/
https://sanjaykthakur.com/2018/12/05/the-very-basics-of-bayesian-
neural-networks/
http://edwardlib.org/tutorials/bayesian-neural-network
http://krasserm.github.io/2019/03/14/bayesian-neural-networks/
https://nbviewer.jupyter.org/github/krasserm/bayesian-machine-
learning/blob/dev/bayesian-neural-networks/bayesian_neural_networks
.ipynb
https://github.com/krasserm/bayesian-machine-learning
https://inferpy.readthedocs.io/en/0.0.3/notes/guidebayesian.html
```

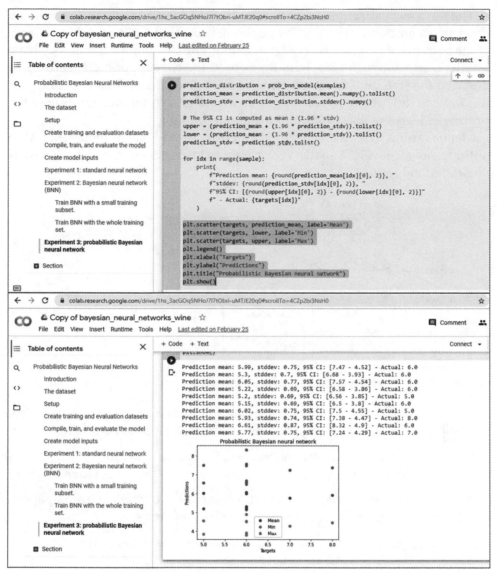

Figure 4.41: The code for plotting the mean, the maximum, and the minimum of the predictions (top), and the corresponding plot (bottom)

(Source: `https://colab.research.google.com/drive/1hs_3acGOq5NHoJ7l7tObri-uMTJE20q0#scrollTo=13ypK49LNsHo`)

4.8   Meta Learning

Meta learning is another approach in AI that has become popular in recent years. *Meta* is a Greek word meaning "after" or "beyond." When used as a prefix, *meta* means "about." So, meta learning is "learning about learning" or "learn to learn."

The term *meta learning* was coined by Donald Maudsley in 1979, where he described a mechanism by which people are becoming "increasingly in charge of the patterns of perception, inquiry, learning, and development that they have internalized." Later in 1985, John Biggs used the concept of meta learning to describe the state of "being conscious of one's learning and taking control of it." You can describe meta learning as an awareness and understanding of the process of learning itself, like thinking about thinking.

Meta learning in AI is essentially about using high-level or meta-level AI to optimize lower-level AI, so that it can learn to learn effectively and quickly, as illustrated in Figure 4.42.

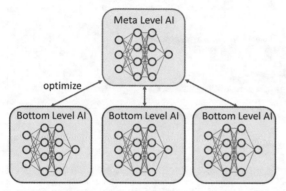

Figure 4.42: The schematic architecture of meta learning

The following are two interesting articles that give a comprehensive introduction to the meta learning, including all the mathematics behind it:

```
https://jameskle.com/writes/meta-learning-is-all-you-need
https://lilianweng.github.io/lil-log/2018/11/30/meta-learning.html
```

The following two GitHub sites give a curated list of meta learning papers, codes, books, blogs, videos, datasets, and other resources.

```
https://github.com/sudharsan13296/Awesome-Meta-Learning
https://github.com/dragen1860/awesome-meta-learning
```

The following GitHub site gives all the code examples for the book:

```
https://github.com/sudharsan13296/Hands-On-Meta-Learning-With-Python
```

The following two GitHub sites are meta learning projects implemented by PyTorch.

```
https://github.com/learnables/learn2learn
https://github.com/yaoyao-liu/meta-transfer-learning
https://github.com/facebookresearch/LearningToLearn/tree/main/ml3
```

4.9   Summary

This chapter gave a comprehensive overview of deep learning. Deep learning is the most important aspect of AI and a subset of machine learning. Deep learning is the hottest research topic in AI.

Deep learning neural networks are built on traditional neural networks, which are also called artificial neural networks. Deep learning neural networks can be generally divided into two types: convolutional neural networks and recurrent neural networks. Convolutional neural networks are the most popular deep learning neural networks, which include networks such as LeNet, AlexNet, GoogLeNet (Inception), VGG, ResNet, DenseNet, MobileNet, YOLO, and so on.

Apart from traditional convolutional neural networks, there are also new types of networks, such as U-Net, AutoEncoder, siamese neural networks, and capsule networks.

Recurrent neural networks are another popular deep learning neural network. Convolutional neural networks are specialized in processing images, while recurrent neural networks are specialized in processing sequences.

Transformers are new deep learning neural networks that are mainly used in the field of natural language processing. Transformers are gradually making recurrent neural networks obsolete.

Graph neural networks are a special type of recurrent neural network that can take graphs as input data.

Bayesian neural networks are neural networks whose weights or parameters are expressed as a distribution rather than a deterministic value. The learning of Bayesian neural networks is done by Bayesian inference.

4.10   Chapter Review Questions

Q4.1.   What is the difference between machine learning and deep learning?

Q4.2.   What is an artificial neural network?

Q4.3.   What is a convolutional neural network?

Q4.4.   Explain the terms of convolutional layer, pooling layer, activation layer, dropout layer, and fully connected layer, in the context of convolutional neural networks.

Q4.5.   Compare the features of three commonly used activation functions: REctified Linear Unit (ReLU), hyperbolic tangent, and the sigmoid function.

Q4.6.   Use a table to compare the characteristic features of AlexNet, Inception, VGG, ResNet, DenseNet, MobileNet, and EffecientNet.

Q4.7.   What is U-Net, and what is it best used for?

Q4.8.   What is AutoEncoder?

Q4.9.   What is a Siamese neural network? Draw a schematic diagram of a Siamese neural network.

Q4.10.   What are differences between zero-shot learning, one-shot learning, few-shot learning, and n-shot learning?

Q4.11.   What is a capsule network, and how does it differ from a convolutional neural network?

Q4.12.   What is a recurrent neural network?

Q4.13.   What is a long-short term memory (LSTM) network?

Q4.14.   What is a transformer?

Q4.15.   What is BERT and ALBERT?

Q4.16.   What is GPT-3?

Q4.17.   What is a graph neural network?

Q4.18.   What is a Bayesian neural network?

Part

III

AI Applications

In This Part:

This part covers popular AI applications, including some of the latest developments. This part aims to give you a snapshot of what we can do with AI today.

Image Classification

"If our era is the next Industrial Revolution, as many claim, AI is surely one of its driving forces."

—Fei-Fei Li (American computer scientist)

CHAPTER OUTLINE

5.1 Introduction

Image analysis or image processing is the most researched topic in deep learning. *Image processing* simply means extracting information from images and learning from images. This is an important aspect of computer vision. In deep learning, image processing is largely done using convolutional neural networks (CNNs) and can be generally divided into image classification, object detection, image segmentation, and so on.

Figure 5.1 illustrates the differences between image classification, object detection, and image segmentation. *Image classification* is about identifying the image or classifying the image. Image classification can be typically done by using deep learning neural networks such as AlexNet, GoogLeNet, VGG, ResNet, MobileNet, and so on. *Object detection* is about identifying a particular object in the image. Object detection can be typically done by using deep learning neural networks such as region-based convolutional neural networks (R-CNNs), you only look once (YOLO), and so on. *Image segmentation* means dividing the image into different segments according to the content. Image segmentation can be typically done by using Detectron, Gluon, PixelLib libraries, and so on. Chapter 7 contains more details about object detection and image segmentation.

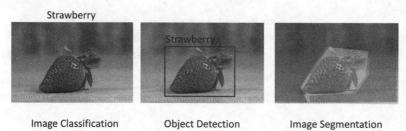

Image Classification   Object Detection   Image Segmentation

Figure 5.1: The differences between image classification, object detection, and image segmentation

Image classification is the simplest and most commonly used image processing technique. Image classification allows you to identify the content of an image, for example, whether an image is a dog or a cat, a type of flower, cancer or noncancer, and so on. Image classification is done by two steps called *training* and *inference*, as shown in Figure 5.2. During training, you feed the deep learning neural networks with training images and targets (also called *labels*) and adjust the weights of the neural network until it maximizes the recognition rate, called *accuracy*. The more training images and the more complex the neural networks, the higher the training accuracy. After training, you can feed a query image to the network, and it will predict the result. The process of using a trained deep learning model to make predictions against previously unseen data is called *inference*.

For image classification, you can either use pre-trained models or custom trained models. Pre-trained models are trained on a data source such as the ImageNet dataset (`http://www.image-net.org/`) or the CIFAR-10 dataset (`https://www.cs.toronto.edu/~kriz/cifar.html`). ImageNet has 1,000 classes, and CIFAR-10 consists of 10 classes; the pre-trained model will therefore only recognize the 1,000 classes or 10 classes. You can also re-train the pre-trained models with your own datasets, which is called *transfer learning*. You can find more details on transfer learning in section 5.3.

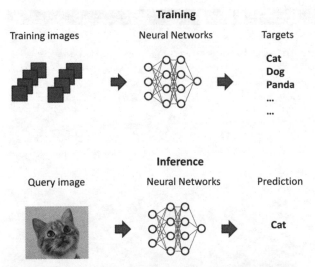

Figure 5.2: Training and inference in image classification

Image classification has countless real-life applications. For example, take a picture of a skin mole; image classification can tell you whether it is benign or malignant. Or, take a picture of a flower or a plant; it can tell you what type of flower or plant it is. For tourists, it can tell you what building or what attraction is in your photo. For fashionistas, it can tell what brand of cloth or shoes the photo is about. In healthcare, it can also classify X-ray images, CT images, and MRI images. The potential is really endless!

In this chapter, we will first look at image classifications with pre-trained models, then at image classifications with custom trained models, and at some applications for image classification in medical imaging. We will also look at federated learning for image classification, and finally, we will look at how to develop web-based image classification applications.

5.2   Classification with Pre-trained Models

As shown in Chapter 4, there are a number of deep learning neural networks available. The easiest way to use them for image classification is through the TensorFlow and Keras libraries.

Example 5.1 shows some Python code that can load deep learning neural network models, such as VGG16, ResNet50, MobileNet, Inception V3, and EfficientNet, and show the summary of the models. These models are pre-trained on the ImageNet dataset with 1,000 classes.

EXAMPLE 5.1:   THE `KERASMODEL.PY` PROGRAM

```
#Example 5.1
#https://www.tensorflow.org/api_docs/python/tf/keras/applications

from tensorflow.keras.preprocessing import image
from keras.applications.imagenet_utils import decode_predictions
import numpy as np

from tensorflow.keras.applications import (
        vgg16,
        resnet50,
        mobilenet_v2,
        inception_v3,
        efficientnet
    )

# init the models
#model = vgg16.VGG16(weights='imagenet')
#model = resnet50.ResNet50(weights='imagenet')
#model = mobilenet_v2.MobileNetV2(weights='imagenet')
#model = inception_v3.InceptionV3(weights='imagenet')
model = efficientnet.EfficientNetB0(weights='imagenet')
print(model.summary())
```

You will need the latest TensorFlow version 2.4 to view EfficientNet. So it is best to run the previous code in Google Colab, as shown in Figure 5.3. Just go to the Google Colab website (`https://colab.research.google.com/`), sign in with your Google account, create a new notebook, copy and paste the previous code, and run it. You can comment out each model individually to see the summary of each model's structure.

EXERCISE 5.1

Modify the Python program from Example 5.1 to use an `if-else` structure to select which model to display.

    You can find more predefined models on the Keras application website, as shown in the following link. If you are interested, you can find more details about each model here.

    `https://keras.io/api/applications/`

EXERCISE 5.2

Continue with the previous exercise, based on the models shown in Keras application website, and add a few more models, such as VGG19, DenseNet201, and EfficientNetB7, to the Python program.

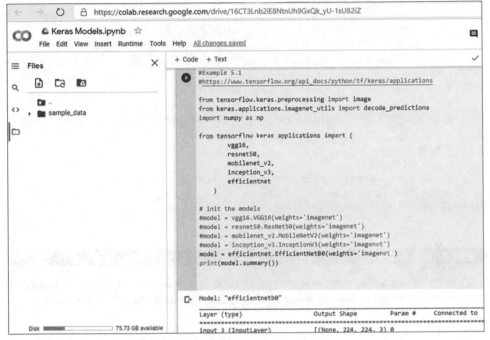

Figure 5.3: The previous program on Google Colab

Example 5.2 shows a revised version of the previous Python code. It selects a deep learning neural network model, shows the summary of the model, and uses the model to classify an image file named `elephant.jpg`. Again, you can comment out each model individually to see how each model performs.

EXAMPLE 5.2: THE `KERASMODEL2.PY` **PROGRAM**

```
#Example 5.2
from tensorflow.keras.preprocessing import image
from keras.applications.imagenet_utils import decode_predictions
import numpy as np

from tensorflow.keras.applications import (
        vgg16,
        resnet50,
        mobilenet,
        inception_v3
    )

# init the models
#model = vgg16.VGG16(weights='imagenet')
#model = resnet50.ResNet50(weights='imagenet')
model = mobilenet.MobileNet(weights='imagenet')
#model = inception_v3.InceptionV3(weights='imagenet')
print(model.summary())
```

```
img_path = 'Elephant.jpg'
img = image.load_img(img_path, target_size=(224, 224))
x = image.img_to_array(img)
x = np.expand_dims(x, axis=0)
#processed_image = vgg16.preprocess_input(x)
#processed_image = resnet50.preprocess_input(x)
processed_image = mobilenet.preprocess_input(x)
#processed_image = inception_v3.preprocess_input(x)


# prediction
predictions = model.predict(x)
results = decode_predictions(predictions)
print(results)
```

EXERCISE 5.3

Go to the Internet, find some more animal pictures, and download them. Try to identify them using Example 5.2, and comment on the performance of the different models.

In Google Colab, you do not have to download the images to your computer and then upload them to Colab; you can use the wget command to load the images directly from the Internet into Colab using their uniform resource locators (URLs). Since wget is an external command, you must prefix it with an exclamation mark, i.e., !wget. The following is an example to get a cat image from the Internet and save it as cat.jpg in Colab:

```
!wget -O cat.jpg
'https://upload.wikimedia.org/wikipedia/commons/thumb/b/bb/Kittyply_
edit1.jpg/1024px-Kittyply_edit1.jpg'
img_path = 'cat.jpg'
```

The following commands show how to load and view the cat.jpg file in Colab:

```
import cv2
from google.colab.patches import cv2_imshow
image = cv2.imread(img_path)
cv2_imshow(image)
```

For many computer users, a web camera, or *webcam*, is a useful tool for working with images. Example 5.3 shows how to scan and open all available webcams on your computer. It goes through the first five possible webcams in a for loop, creates a webcam object in each loop using the cv2.VideoCapture() function, and then checks to see if it can be opened. If you have more than five webcams, just increase the number 5 to the appropriate value. You must run this program on your local computer.

EXAMPLE 5.3:   THE WEBCAMSCAN.PY **PROGRAM**

```
# Example 5.3
import cv2
for i in range(5):
    print ("Checking camera #{0}...".format(i))
    cap = cv2.VideoCapture(i)
    if cap.isOpened():
        print ("Camera found!")
    if not cap.isOpened():
        print ("Camera not found!")
```

Once you know which webcam is available on your computer, you can use the code in Example 5.4 to open the webcam and show live images. First, use the cv2.VideoCapture() function to create a webcam object. id = 0 means the first webcam on your computer. Then, it uses a while loop to continuously read images from the webcam, as long as the webcam is open. Inside the while loop, it first uses the camera.read() function to read an image from the webcam. If the reading was successful, it continues; otherwise, it stops. Then, it uses the cv2.imshow() function to display the image frame. After displaying the image, it uses the cv2.waitKey() function to wait for 30ms to see if a key was pressed; if the Esc key was pressed, the while loop is stopped. After the while loop is stopped, the webcam object is released, and all windows are closed.

EXAMPLE 5.4:   THE WEBCAM.PY **PROGRAM**

```
# Example 5.4
import cv2
id = 0
camera = cv2.VideoCapture(id)
# image_size = 224

while camera.isOpened():
    ok, cam_frame = camera.read()
    if not ok:
        break
    #cam_frame= cv2.resize(cam_frame, (image_size, image_size))
    cv2.imshow('video image', cam_frame)
    key = cv2.waitKey(30)
    if key == 27: # press 'ESC' to quit
        break

camera.release()
cv2.destroyAllWindows()
```

Example 5.5 is the webcam version of the image classification code. It first uses a web camera (webcam) to get the image and then uses a deep learning neural network to classify the webcam image. You can comment out each model separately to see how each model performs.

EXAMPLE 5.5:   THE `KERASMODEL3.PY` **PROGRAM**

```
# Example 5.5
import cv2
from tensorflow.keras.preprocessing.image import img_to_array
from keras.applications.imagenet_utils import decode_predictions
from tensorflow.keras.applications import (
        vgg16,
        resnet50,
        mobilenet,
        inception_v3
    )
import numpy as np

# init the models
#model = vgg16.VGG16(weights='imagenet')
model = resnet50.ResNet50(weights='imagenet')
#model = mobilenet.MobileNet(weights='imagenet')
#model = inception_v3.InceptionV3(weights='imagenet')
print(model.summary())

camera = cv2.VideoCapture(0)
image_size = 224
#image_size = 299
while camera.isOpened():
    ok, cam_frame = camera.read()
    frame= cv2.resize(cam_frame, (image_size, image_size))
    numpy_image = img_to_array(frame)
    image_batch = np.expand_dims(numpy_image, axis=0)
    #processed_image = vgg16.preprocess_input(image_batch.copy())
    processed_image = resnet50.preprocess_input(image_batch.copy())
    #processed_image = mobilenet.preprocess_input(image_batch.copy())
    #processed_image = inception_v3.preprocess_input(image_batch.copy())
    # get the predicted probabilities for each class
    predictions = model.predict(processed_image)
    label = decode_predictions(predictions)
    # format final image visualization to display the results of
experiments
    cv2.putText(cam_frame, "{}, {:.1f}".format(label[0][0][1],
label[0][0][2]) , (10, 30), cv2.FONT_HERSHEY_SIMPLEX, 1, (255, 0, 0),
2)


    cv2.imshow('video image', cam_frame)
    key = cv2.waitKey(30)
    if key == 27: # press 'ESC' to quit
        break
```

EXERCISE 5.4

Modify the Python program from Example 5.5, choose a different model each time, run the program, and compare the results. Instead of reading images from the webcam, you can also modify the code to read images from a video file. Hint: modify the `cv2.VideoCapture(0)` function and replace 0 with the name of the video file.

5.3   Classification with Custom Trained Models: Transfer Learning

Although classifying images with a pre-trained model is useful, it can only classify the images that have been previously specified. For example, if a model has been trained on ImageNet, then the model can classify only the 1,000 types of images defined by ImageNet. If a model has been trained on CIFAR-10, then it can classify only 10 classes of images defined by CIFAR-10.

Therefore, if you want to classify new types of images, you can use the pre-trained deep learning neural network model as the starting point for a model on the second task of interest, for example, on your own image data. This is called *transfer learning*. Transfer learning is popular because it can train deep learning neural networks with comparatively little data. The potential of transfer learning is enormous and can really bring image classification to life.

Example 5.6 shows how to create a customized deep learning neural network for training your own image datasets. In this example, all the training images are stored in a folder, and the different classes are stored in different subfolders, which are named by class names. It is a long program, so we will go through it section by section.

Example 5.6a contains the first section and shows how to load all the libraries needed. Note that the preferred version of the H5PY library is 2.10.0. You can install it by typing **pip install h5py==2.10.0**.

EXAMPLE 5.6A: THE TRANSFERLEARNINGKERAS.IPYNB **PROGRAM (PART 1)**

```
# Example 5.6a
# Load all the libraries
=====================================================================
# pip install h5py==2.10.0
import matplotlib
from sklearn.model_selection import train_test_split
from keras.preprocessing.image import img_to_array
from keras.utils import to_categorical
from imutils import paths
import matplotlib.pyplot as plt
```

```
import numpy as np
import argparse
import random
import cv2
import os
```

Example 5.6b shows how to specify the folder for the training images and create the appropriate class labels and class names. In this example, all the training images are stored in a folder named `SkinArea`. Within the folder, skin images from six different skin areas, namely, Face, Forearm, Forehead, Lower Leg, Neck, and Palm, are stored in six subfolders. The folders are named by the class names.

EXAMPLE 5.6B: THE `TRANSFERLEARNINGKERAS.IPYNB` **PROGRAM (PART 2)**

```
# Select the image folder
======================================================================
datapath=os.getcwd() + "\SkinArea"

# grab the image paths and randomly shuffle them
imagePaths = sorted(list(paths.list_images(datapath)))
random.seed()
random.shuffle(imagePaths)

# initialize the number of epochs to train for, initia learning rate,
# and batch size
batch_size=32
epochs=50
lr = 1e-3         # Initial Learning rate

image_size = 224 # For Inception use 299
num_classes=0    #number of classes for classification

# initialize the data and labels
data = []
labels = []
classNum=[]
classNames=[]


#Get a list of subfolders as labels
subfolders = [ f.path for f in os.scandir(datapath) if f.is_dir() ]
i=0
for folder in subfolders:
    s = folder.split("\\")[-1]
    #print(s)
    classNum.append(i)
    classNames.append(s)
```

```
    i=i+1

num_classes=len(classNum)
print(classNum)
print(classNames)
print(num_classes)
```

The following is the output of the previous code, showing the numerical values of the classes, the names of the classes, and the total number of classes (six).

```
[0, 1, 2, 3, 4, 5]
['Face', 'Forearm', 'Forehead', 'LowerLeg', 'Neck', 'Palm']
6
```

Example 5.6c shows how to go through all the images in the training image folder including the subfolders, read in the images, get the class names, and map the class names into numerical values. This is essential as deep learning models can use numeric values only as targets during training.

EXAMPLE 5.6C: THE TRANSFERLEARNINGKERAS.IPYNB **PROGRAM (PART 3)**

```
# Create training data and labels
========================================================================
for imagePath in imagePaths:
    # load the image, pre-process it, and store it in the data list
    image = cv2.imread(imagePath)
    image = cv2.resize(image, (image_size, image_size))
    image = img_to_array(image)
    data.append(image)

    # extract the class label from the image path and update the
    # labels list
    label = imagePath.split(os.path.sep)[-2]

    i=0
    for name in classNames:
      if label == name:
            label = classNum[i]
            #print(name)
            break
      i = i+1
    labels.append(label)
    #print(label)

print(labels[0:20])
```

The following output shows the first 20 numeric values of class labels:

```
[1, 0, 3, 3, 0, 2, 1, 2, 4, 2, 1, 4, 4, 0, 2, 4, 3, 0, 2, 0]
```

Example 5.6d shows how to split the image data into X training data, Y training data, X test data, and Y test data. X is the input for the model, and Y is the output of the model. Here, all images are randomly divided into training data (75 percent) and test data (25 percent).

EXAMPLE 5.6D: THE TRANSFERLEARNINGKERAS.IPYNB PROGRAM (PART 4)

```
data = np.array(data, dtype="float") / 255.0
labels = np.array(labels)
print(labels[0:30])

#Split the data into training (75%) and testing (25%)
(trainX, testX, trainY, testY) = train_test_split(data, labels,
test_size=0.25, random_state=42)

# convert the labels from integers to vectors
trainY = to_categorical(trainY, num_classes=len(classNum))
testY = to_categorical(testY, num_classes=len(classNum))
```

Example 5.6e shows how to create and train a model with X and Y data. It uses a pre-trained VGG16 model as the base model and then adds Flatten, Dense, and final output layers. By using a pre-trained base model, re-training can be more efficient and faster. There are a number of pre-trained deep learning neural networks, such as VGG16, ResNet50, DenseNet, MobileNet V2, Inception V3 (GoogLeNet), and EfficientNet. For EfficientNet you need TensorFlow 2.4.

EXAMPLE 5.6E: THE TRANSFERLEARNINGKERAS.IPYNB PROGRAM (PART 5)

```
#Create and train the model
=====================================================================
from keras.models import Model, load_model, Sequential
from keras.layers import Activation, Dropout, Flatten, Dense

from keras.applications import (
        vgg16,
        resnet50,
        densenet,
        mobilenet_v2,
        inception_v3,
#        efficientnet
)


#Keras Models: https://keras.io/api/applications/
base_model = vgg16.VGG16(weights='imagenet', include_top=False,
input_shape=(image_size, image_size, 3))
```

```
#base_model = mobilenet_v2.MobileNetV2(weights='imagenet', include_
top=False, input_shape=(image_size, image_size, 3))
#base_model = densenet.DenseNet201(weights='imagenet', include_
top=False, input_shape=(image_size, image_size, 3))
#base_model = resnet50.ResNet50(weights='imagenet', include_
top=False, input_shape=(image_size, image_size, 3))
#base_model = inception_v3.InceptionV3(weights='imagenet', include_
top=False, input_shape=(image_size, image_size, 3))
#base_model = efficientnet.EfficientNetB0(weights='imagenet',
include_top=False, input_shape=(image_size, image_size, 3))
#print(base_model.summary())

    # Freeze the layers
for layer in base_model.layers:
    layer.trainable = False
# # Create the model
model = Sequential()

# # Add the convolutional base model
model.add(base_model)

# # Add new layers
model.add(Flatten())
model.add(Dense(1024, activation='relu'))
model.add(Dense(1024, activation='relu'))
model.add(Dense(num_classes, activation='softmax'))
print(model.summary())

# # Compile the model
model.compile(optimizer= 'adam' , loss= keras.losses.categorical_
crossentropy, metrics=['accuracy'])
#model.compile(optimizer= 'sgd' , loss= keras.losses.categorical_
crossentropy, metrics=['accuracy'])
#from keras.optimizers import SGD
#model.compile(loss='categorical_crossentropy',
#      optimizer=SGD(lr=1e-3),
#      metrics=['accuracy'])

# Start the training process
model.fit(trainX, trainY, validation_split=0.30, batch_size=32,
epochs=50, verbose=2)
# Verbosity mode. 0 = silent, 1 = progress bar, 2 = one line per
epoch.

#save the model
model.save('model.h5')
```

The following is the output of the previous example program. It first shows the summary of the VGG16 base model and the layers added to the base model, and then it trains the model on X and Y training data. Depending on your computer and the number of training images, this training can take a long time.

```
Model: "sequential_6"

Layer (type)                    Output Shape              Param #
=================================================================
vgg16 (Model)                   (None, 7, 7, 512)         14714688

flatten_5 (Flatten)             (None, 25088)             0

dense_13 (Dense)                (None, 1024)              25691136

dense_14 (Dense)                (None, 1024)              1049600

dense_15 (Dense)                (None, 6)                 6150
=================================================================
Total params: 41,461,574
Trainable params: 26,746,886
Non-trainable params: 14,714,688
_____
None
Train on 46 samples, validate on 21 samples
Epoch 1/50
 - 25s - loss: 4.6965 - accuracy: 0.1957 - val_loss: 4.2004 - val_accuracy: 0.3333
Epoch 2/50
 - 27s - loss: 5.0228 - accuracy: 0.3043 - val_loss: 5.6886 - val_accuracy: 0.1905
Epoch 3/50
 - 29s - loss: 4.2033 - accuracy: 0.4348 - val_loss: 3.1784 - val_accuracy: 0.3810
Epoch 4/50
 - 31s - loss: 1.7474 - accuracy: 0.5652 - val_loss: 1.7178 - val_accuracy: 0.3810
Epoch 5/50
 - 31s - loss: 1.0725 - accuracy: 0.5435 - val_loss: 0.3896 - val_accuracy: 0.9048


... ...


 - 33s - loss: 1.7668e-04 - accuracy: 1.0000 - val_loss: 0.1156 - val_accuracy: 0.9048
Epoch 49/50
 - 34s - loss: 1.6812e-04 - accuracy: 1.0000 - val_loss: 0.1155 - val_accuracy: 0.9048
Epoch 50/50
 - 35s - loss: 1.6058e-04 - accuracy: 1.0000 - val_loss: 0.1147 - val_accuracy: 0.9048
```

After training, you would be able to classify your own images using the trained neural network model. Example 5.6f shows how to load the newly trained model and evaluate its performances using X and Y test images:

EXAMPLE 5.6F: THE `TRANSFERLEARNINGKERAS.IPYNB` **PROGRAM (PART 6)**

```
model = load_model('model.h5')
score = model.evaluate(testX, testY, verbose=0)
print('Test loss:', score[0])
print('Test accuracy:', score[1])
```

The following is the output, showing the loss and accuracy. The accuracy is 39 percent in this case. You can improve the accuracy by increasing the sample size or having more epochs, that is, more rounds of trainings.

```
Test loss: 2.6502907276153564
Test accuracy: 0.39130434
```

Example 5.6g is the code for predictions on X test image data.

EXAMPLE 5.6G: THE `TRANSFERLEARNINGKERAS.IPYNB` **PROGRAM (PART 7)**

```
names = model.predict(testX)
print(len(testX))
print((trainX[0,:].shape))
print(name)
print(testY)
```

The following is the output:

```
23
(224, 224, 3)
Forearm
[[0. 0. 1. 0. 0. 0.]
 [0. 0. 1. 0. 0. 0.]
 [0. 0. 0. 0. 1. 0.]
 [1. 0. 0. 0. 0. 0.]
 [1. 0. 0. 0. 0. 0.]
 [0. 0. 0. 0. 1. 0.]
 [1. 0. 0. 0. 0. 0.]
 [0. 1. 0. 0. 0. 0.]
 [0. 0. 1. 0. 0. 0.]
 [0. 0. 0. 1. 0. 0.]
 [0. 0. 0. 0. 0. 1.]
 [0. 0. 0. 1. 0. 0.]
 [0. 1. 0. 0. 0. 0.]
 [1. 0. 0. 0. 0. 0.]
 [0. 0. 0. 1. 0. 0.]
 [0. 0. 0. 0. 0. 1.]
 [0. 0. 1. 0. 0. 0.]
 [0. 0. 1. 0. 0. 0.]
 [1. 0. 0. 0. 0. 0.]
```

```
[0. 1. 0. 0. 0. 0.]
[0. 0. 0. 0. 1. 0.]
[1. 0. 0. 0. 0. 0.]
[0. 0. 1. 0. 0. 0.]]
```

Example 5.6h is the code for predictions on a particular image file:

EXAMPLE 5.6H: THE `TRANSFERLEARNINGKERAS.IPYNB` **PROGRAM (PART 8)**

```
import numpy as np
from keras.preprocessing import image
base_dir = datapath
testfile = base_dir +'\Face\elen_f4-r02-03.jpg'
image_size = 224
test_image = image.load_img(testfile , target_size=(image_size,
image_size))
test_image = image.img_to_array(test_image)
test_image = np.expand_dims(test_image, axis=0)
results = model.predict(test_image)
print(results)
i=0
prediction="Unknown"
for name in classNames:
    if results[0][i]>0.4:
        prediction=name
        break
    i += 1
print(prediction)

plt.figure()
plt.title(str(testfile))
plt.imshow(image.load_img(testfile ))
plt.show()
```

The following is the output, and Figure 5.4 is the image that is used for prediction:

```
[[0.0000000e+00 1.4933567e-10 0.0000000e+00 0.0000000e+00 1.0000000e+00
  0.0000000e+00]]
Neck
```

The complete code for the example can be found in the Jupyter Notebook file, `TransferLearningKeras.ipynb`, in the Chapter 6 folder of the example code that accompanies this book. You can edit and run the file from a web browser, as shown in Figure 5.5.

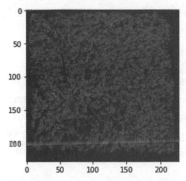

Figure 5.4: The test image for classification

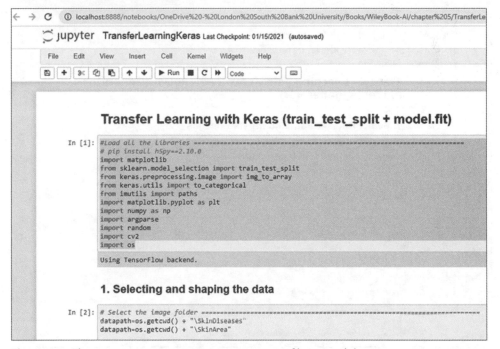

Figure 5.5: The `TransferLearningKeras.ipynb` file in a web browser

EXERCISE 5.5

Run the previous Python program with different pre-trained models, and comment on the performances, i.e., the time required for training and the accuracy that can be achieved.

EXERCISE 5.6

Add more base models to the previous Python program, and comment on the performances.

Model optimizers are one of the key factors for transfer learning. For more details, see the following:

```
https://keras.io/api/optimizers/
```

Example 5.7 shows another version of the transfer learning for skin cancer image classification. In this case, the function `ImageDataGenerator()` is used to store the images, and the function `model.fit_generator()` is used to train the models. Again, we will show the code section by section. The full code is available in an IPython Jupyter Notebook file, named `TransferLearningKeras2 .ipynb`, as shown in Figure 5.6.

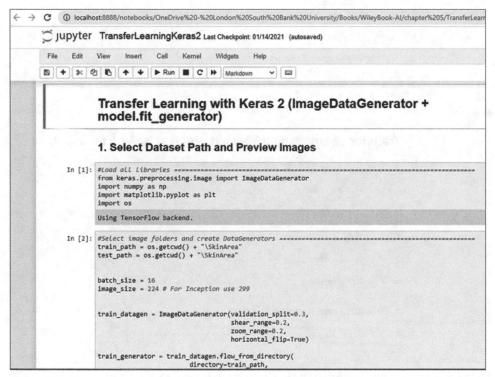

Figure 5.6: The `TransferLearningKeras2.ipynb` file in a web browser

The first section, shown in Example 5.7a, shows how to load all the libraries you need.

EXAMPLE 5.7A: THE `TRANSFERLEARNINGKERAS2.IPYNB` **PROGRAM (PART 1)**

```
from keras.preprocessing.image import ImageDataGenerator
import numpy as np
import matplotlib.pyplot as plt
import os
```

The second section, shown in Example 5.7b, shows how to specify the folder for the training images and the folder for the test images, in this case, `SkinArea`. Then the function `ImageDataGenerator()` is used to generate the training image data.

EXAMPLE 5.7B: THE `TRANSFERLEARNINGKERAS2.IPYNB` PROGRAM (PART 2)

```python
train_path = os.getcwd() + "\SkinArea"
test_path = os.getcwd() + "\SkinArea"


batch_size = 16
image_size = 224 # For Inception use 299


train_datagen = ImageDataGenerator(validation_split=0.3,
                                   shear_range=0.2,
                                   zoom_range=0.2,
                                   horizontal_flip=True)

train_generator = train_datagen.flow_from_directory(
                      directory=train_path,
                      target_size=(image_size,image_size),
                      batch_size=batch_size,
                      class_mode='categorical',
                      color_mode='rgb',
                      shuffle=True)

x_batch, y_batch = train_generator.next()

it = train_generator.class_indices
print(it.items())
print(train_generator.n)
print(np.unique(train_generator.classes))
num_classes = len(np.unique(train_generator.classes))

fig=plt.figure(figsize=(15,6))
columns = 4
rows = 4
for i in range(1, columns*rows):
    num = np.random.randint(batch_size)
    image = x_batch[num].astype(np.int)
    fig.add_subplot(rows, columns, i)
    plt.title(y_batch[num])
    plt.imshow(image)
plt.show()
```

Figure 5.7 shows the plot of some sample training images.

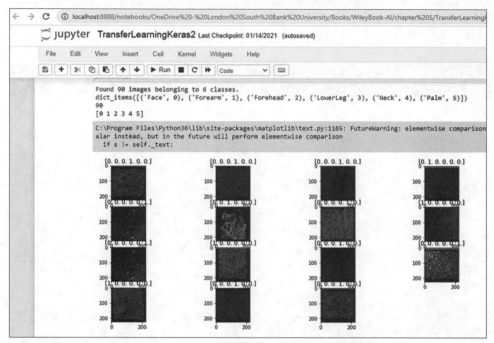

Figure 5.7: The sample training images

The third section, in Example 5.7c, shows how to create the customized deep learning model based on VGG16, ResNet50, and so on; train the model; and store it.

EXAMPLE 5.7C: THE `TRANSFERLEARNINGKERAS2.IPYNB` **PROGRAM (PART 3)**

```
from tensorflow.keras.models import Model, load_model,Sequential
from tensorflow.keras.layers import Activation, Dropout, Flatten,
Dense

from tensorflow.keras.applications import (
        vgg16,
        resnet50,
        densenet,
        mobilenet_v2,
        inception_v3,
        inception_resnet_v2,
#        efficientnet
)

#Keras Models: https://keras.io/api/applications/
base_model = vgg16.VGG16(weights='imagenet', include_top=False,
input_shape=(image_size, image_size, 3))
```

```
#base_model = mobilenet_v2.MobileNetV2(weights='imagenet', include_
top=False, input_shape=(image_size, image_size, 3))
#base_model = densenet.DenseNet201(weights='imagenet', include_
top=False, input_shape=(image_size, image_size, 3))
#base_model = resnet50.ResNet50(weights='imagenet', include_
top=False, input_shape=(image_size, image_size, 3))
#base_model = inception_v3.InceptionV3(weights='imagenet', include_
top=False, input_shape=(image_size, image_size, 3))
#base_model = inception_resnet_v2.InceptionResNetV2(weights='image
net', include_top=False, input_shape=(image_size, image_size, 3))
#base_model = efficientnet.EfficientNetB0(weights='imagenet',
include_top=False, input_shape=(image_size, image_size, 3))
#print(base_model.summary())

# Freeze the layers
for layer in base_model.layers:
    layer.trainable = False

# # Create the model
model = Sequential()

# # Add the vgg convolutional base model
model.add(base_model)

# # Add new layers
model.add(Flatten())
model.add(Dense(128, activation='relu'))
model.add(Dense(128, activation='relu'))
model.add(Dense(num_classes, activation='softmax'))
print(model.summary())

# # Compile the model
model.compile(optimizer= 'adam' , loss= keras.losses.categorical_
crossentropy, metrics=['accuracy'])
#model.compile(optimizer= 'sgd' , loss= keras.losses.categorical_
crossentropy, metrics=['accuracy'])
#from keras.optimizers import SGD
#model.compile(loss='categorical_crossentropy',
#      optimizer=SGD(lr=1e-3),
#      metrics=['accuracy'])

history = model.fit_generator(
        train_generator,
        steps_per_epoch=train_generator.n/batch_size,
        epochs=3)

model.save('fine_tune.h5')

# summarize history for accuracy
import matplotlib.pyplot as plt
```

```
plt.plot(history.history['loss'])
plt.title('loss')
plt.ylabel('loss')
plt.xlabel('epoch')
plt.legend(['loss'], loc='upper right')
plt.show()
```

Figure 5.8 shows the model structure and the model training output.

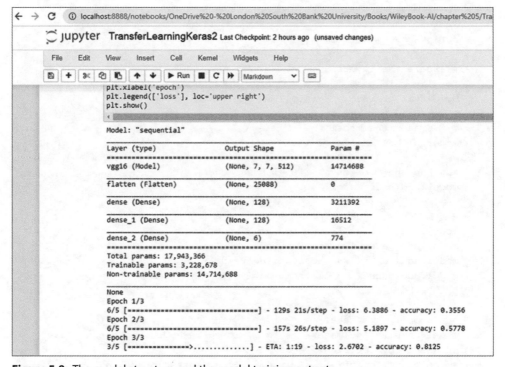

Figure 5.8: The model structure and the model training output

The fourth section, in Example 5.7d, shows how to predict the test images. Again, the function `ImageDataGenerator()` is used to generate test image data, and the predictions are made on the test data generator. Finally, some test images are plotted in a 4 × 4 grid.

EXAMPLE 5.7D: **THE** `TRANSFERLEARNINGKERAS2.IPYNB` **PROGRAM (PART 4)**

```
import keras
from keras.models import Model, load_model
from keras.layers import Activation, Dropout, Flatten, Dense
from keras.preprocessing.image import ImageDataGenerator
```

```
#test image classified
#model = load_model('fine_tune.h5')

test_datagen = ImageDataGenerator()
test_generator = test_datagen.flow_from_directory(
                    directory=test_path,
                    target_size=(image_size, image_size),
                    color_mode='rgb',
                    shuffle=False,
                    class_mode='categorical',
                    batch_size=1)

filenames = test_generator.filenames
nb_samples = len(filenames)
test_generator.reset()

fig=plt.figure(figsize=(15,6))
columns = 4
rows = 4
for i in range(1, columns*rows -1):
    x_batch, y_batch = test_generator.next()

    name = model.predict(x_batch)
    name = np.argmax(name, axis=-1)
    true_name = y_batch
    true_name = np.argmax(true_name, axis=-1)

    label_map = (test_generator.class_indices)
    label_map = dict((v,k) for k,v in label_map.items()) #flip k,v
    predictions = [label_map[k] for k in name]
    true_value = [label_map[k] for k in true_name]

    image = x_batch[0].astype(np.int)
    fig.add_subplot(rows, columns, i)
    plt.title(str(predictions[0]) + ':' + str(true_value[0]))
    plt.imshow(image)
plt.show()
```

Figure 5.9 shows the plot of some test sample images. It also displays the predicted results compared to the ground truth at the top of the images.

The fifth section, Example 5.7e, shows how to calculate the accuracy of the model. See Figure 5.10.

EXAMPLE 5.7E: THE TRANSFERLEARNINGKERAS2.IPYNB **PROGRAM (PART 5)**

```
score = model.evaluate_generator(test_generator, STEP_SIZE_TEST,
workers=12)
print("Loss: ", score[0], "Accuracy: ", score[1])
```

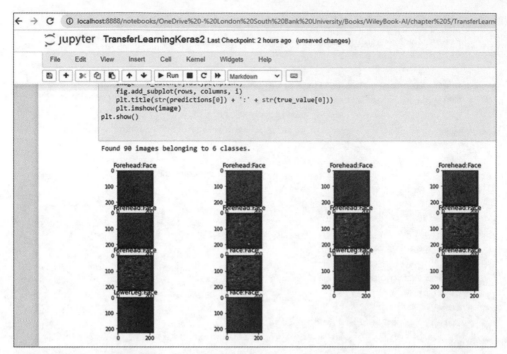

```
        fig.add_subplot(rows, columns, i)
        plt.title(str(predictions[0]) + ':' + str(true_value[0]))
        plt.imshow(image)
plt.show()
```

Found 90 images belonging to 6 classes.

Figure 5.9: The sample test images and the predicted results against the ground truth

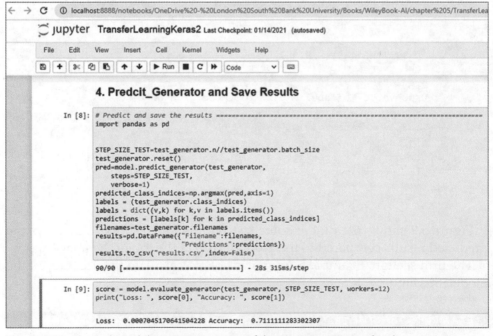

4. Predcit_Generator and Save Results

```
In [8]:  # Predict and save the results ==================================================
         import pandas as pd

         STEP_SIZE_TEST=test_generator.n//test_generator.batch_size
         test_generator.reset()
         pred=model.predict_generator(test_generator,
             steps=STEP_SIZE_TEST,
             verbose=1)
         predicted_class_indices=np.argmax(pred,axis=1)
         labels = (test_generator.class_indices)
         labels = dict((v,k) for k,v in labels.items())
         predictions = [labels[k] for k in predicted_class_indices]
         filenames=test_generator.filenames
         results=pd.DataFrame({"Filename":filenames,
                         "Predictions":predictions})
         results.to_csv("results.csv",index=False)

         90/90 [==============================] - 28s 315ms/step
```

```
In [9]:  score = model.evaluate_generator(test_generator, STEP_SIZE_TEST, workers=12)
         print("Loss: ", score[0], "Accuracy: ", score[1])

         Loss:  0.0007045170641504228 Accuracy:  0.7111111283302307
```

Figure 5.10: The code and the output accuracy of the previous section of code

You can also build deep learning models yourself. Example 5.8 shows how to build a customized deep learning model layer by layer. The rest of the code is similar to the previous example `TransferLearningKeras2.ipynb`. The full code is available in an IPython Jupyter Notebook file named `Transfer-LearningKeras3.ipynb`, as shown in Figure 5.11.

EXAMPLE 5.8: THE `TRANSFERLEARNINGKERAS3.IPYNB` **PROGRAM**

```
# Example 5.8
from tensorflow.keras.models import Model, load_model, Sequential
from tensorflow.keras.layers import Activation, Dropout, Flatten,
Dense,Conv2D,MaxPooling2D

model = Sequential()
model.add(Conv2D(32, (3, 3),  input_shape=(image_size, image_size,
3)))
model.add(Activation('relu'))
model.add(MaxPooling2D(pool_size=(2, 2)))

model.add(Conv2D(32, (3, 3)))
model.add(Activation('relu'))
model.add(MaxPooling2D(pool_size=(2, 2)))

model.add(Conv2D(64, (3, 3)))
model.add(Activation('relu'))
model.add(MaxPooling2D(pool_size=(2, 2)))

model.add(Flatten())
model.add(Dense(64))
model.add(Activation('relu'))
model.add(Dropout(0.5))
model.add(Dense(num_classes))
model.add(Activation('sigmoid'))
print(model.summary())

# # Compile the model
model.compile(optimizer= 'adam' , loss= keras.losses.categorical_
crossentropy, metrics=['accuracy'])
#model.compile(optimizer= 'sgd' , loss= keras.losses.categorical_
crossentropy, metrics=['accuracy'])

history = model.fit_generator(
        train_generator,
        steps_per_epoch=train_generator.n/batch_size,
        epochs=1)

model.save('fine_tune.h5')

# summarize history for accuracy
```

```
import matplotlib.pyplot as plt

plt.plot(history.history['loss'])
plt.title('loss')
plt.ylabel('loss')
plt.xlabel('epoch')
plt.legend(['loss'], loc='upper right')
plt.show()
```

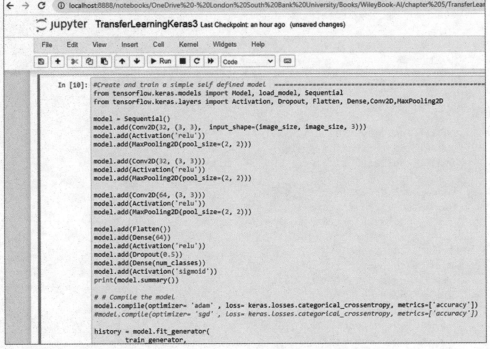

Figure 5.11: The `TransferLearningKeras3.ipynb` file in a web browser

If you do not like programming, many web services also offer transfer learning on image classification without having to write any code.

The following link shows an impressive website called Vize.ai that allows users to perform image classification in three simple steps:

1. **Define:** This is where you define your problem and upload your own image data.

2. **Train:** This allows you to train the model using your data.

3. **Recognize:** This allows you to perform image classification using your trained model.

```
https://vize.ai
```

For more details, check out this interesting article, titled How to train custom image classifier in 5 minutes, which shows you step-by-step how to use Vize. ai for gender classification.

```
https://towardsdatascience.com/how-to-train-custom-image-classifier-
in-5-minutes-4efa61255fc7
```

5.4   Cancer/Disease Detection

In this section, we will show some examples classifying medical images. In healthcare, there are many different imaging modalities, such as X-ray images, computerized tomography (CT) scan images, magnetic resonance imaging (MRI) images, retinal images, and so on. Examining these images manually is slow and requires years of experience. Using deep learning neural networks to classify these images is much easier and faster. In January 2020, Google and Imperial College London have already demonstrated that their algorithm can outperform six human radiologists in reading mammograms to detect breast cancer. Image classification is probably the best example of how AI can be used in healthcare.

5.4.1   Skin Cancer Image Classification

Skin cancer affects millions of people around the world. The effectiveness of treatment depends largely on early detection. Image classification is a very effective method to improve early detection as there are many digital images of skin cancer. There have already been several skin diagnostic apps for this purpose.

■ UMSkinCheck

```
https://www.uofmhealth.org/paticnt%20and%20visitor%20guide/my-
skin-check-app
```

■ SkinVision

```
www.skinvision.com/
```

■ MoleCare

```
https://www.nhs.uk/apps-library/molecare/
```

So, how can you develop your own skin disease/cancer classification software? First you will need skin disease/cancer images, and lots of them. The most commonly cited source of skin disease/cancer images is the International Skin Imaging Collaboration (ISIC); see the following link. There are tons of skin disease/cancer images, and annual ISIC challenges are held on skin lesion analysis for melanoma detection.

```
https://www.isic-archive.com/
```

You can also find skin images from various other places, such as the following:

```
https://www.cancer.org/cancer/skin-cancer/skin-cancer-image-gallery
.html
https://www.skincancer.org/
https://www.medicinenet.com/image-collection/skin_cancer_picture/
picture.htm
```

Once you get your skin disease/cancer images, you can basically use the transfer learning examples from the previous section to train the models and classify the images.

If you want to learn from other people's projects for skin disease/cancer image classification, the best place is Kaggle, where you can get both the dataset (skin images) and other people's projects (also called a *repository*) that you can copy and edit. You can create an account by using your Google account.

The following shows a skin cancer dataset on Kaggle that contains 2.7GB of skin pigmented images. From the Code menu, you can see there are 176 projects based on this dataset. You can sort the projects by Hotness, Most Votes, Recently Run, and so on. Once you find a project you like, you have the choice to copy it and edit it on Kaggle in your own account, download a copy, or open it in the Google Cloud.

```
https://www.kaggle.com/kmader/skin-cancer-mnist-ham10000
```

The following are two interesting example projects based on the skin cancer dataset:

```
https://www.kaggle.com/ingbiodanielh/skin-cancer-classification-
with-resnet-50-fastai
https://www.kaggle.com/mikeleske/2-stage-densenet201-fine-tuning-
98-4-accuracy
```

EXERCISE 5.7

Log in to your Kaggle account via a web browser, find one of the previous Kaggle projects, make a copy of the project, and then modify the code to use VGG16 as the base model. Compare the performances.

5.4.2   Retinopathy Classification

Retinal imaging is commonly used to examine eye health, especially in diabetic patients. Retinal imaging takes a digital image of the back of the eye, showing the retina, the optic disk, and the blood vessels. The retina is the tissue that is sensitive to light, and the optic disk is a dark spot on the retina that contains the optic nerve, which sends information to the brain.

Figure 5.12 shows an image database of diabetic retinopathy on Kaggle. It has 3,663 retinal images divided into five categories: Mild, Moderate, No_DR (no diabetic retinopathy), Proliferate_ DR, and Severe.

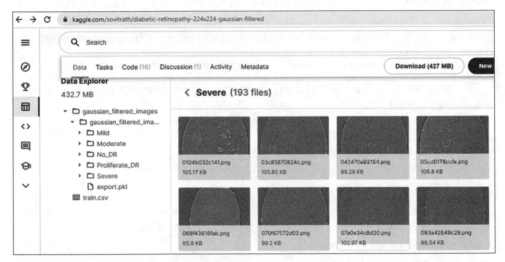

Figure 5.12: The image dataset of diabetic retinopathy on Kaggle and some sample images
(Source: `https://www.kaggle.com/sovitrath/diabetic-retinopathy-224x224-gaussian-filtered`)

EXERCISE 5.8

Log in to your Kaggle account via a web browser, locate the previous Kaggle dataset, choose an appropriate project, make a copy of the project, and modify the code to use VGG16 as the base model. Comment on the results.

The following are three interesting example projects based on the previous diabetic retinopathy image dataset:

`https://www.kaggle.com/mattmcfee/retinopathy-classification-with-vgg16`

`https://www.kaggle.com/akshat0007/diabetic-retinopathy-detection-and-classification`

`https://www.kaggle.com/huseyinefe/diabetic-retinopathy-with-cnn-by-keras`

5.4.3   Chest X-Ray Classification

X-ray images are commonly used in hospitals to detect broken bones and pneumonia. When X-rays pass through our bodies, they produce an image on a metal film. Soft tissues, such as skin and organs, absorb very few X-rays, while dense tissues, like the bones, absorb the radiation. Similar to camera film, X-ray film develops depending on which areas have been exposed to the X-rays. Black areas on an X-ray image represent soft tissues, where X-rays are not absorbed. White areas represent the bones, where X-rays are absorbed.

The following shows a dataset of chest X-ray images on Kaggle. There are nearly 6,000 images divided into three subfolders: `test`, `train`, and `val` (for "validate"). In each subfolder, the images are divided into two categories: normal and pneumonia. There are more than 900 projects based on this dataset.

```
https://www.kaggle.com/paultimothymooney/chest-xray-pneumonia
```

The following two projects based on the previous datasets have the highest number of votes:

```
https://www.kaggle.com/aakashnain/beating-everything-with-depthwise-
convolution
https://www.kaggle.com/amyjang/tensorflow-pneumonia-classification-
on-x-rays
```

During the COVID-19 pandemic, there was a lot of interest in applying deep learning for COVID-19 detection. The following shows the COVID-19 Chest X-ray Image dataset on Kaggle.

```
https://www.kaggle.com/alifrahman/covid19-chest-xray-image-dataset
```

The following shows a simple transfer learning project on an X-ray image classification by using the previous two datasets on Kaggle. It uses a customized mode, based on VGG16, similar to what we did in section 5.3, and uses X-ray images for the customized model.

```
https://www.kaggle.com/alifrahman/covid-19-detection-using-transfer-
learning
```

EXERCISE 5.9

From a web browser, log in to your Kaggle account, locate the previous Kaggle project, make a copy of the project, and finally modify the code so that it uses MobileNet as the base model, instead of VGG16. Compare the performances.

5.4.5   Brain Tumor MRI Image Classification

Magnetic resonance imaging (MRI) is a medical imaging technique that uses strong magnetic fields and radio waves to produce detailed images of the inside of the body. As we know, the human body is mostly made up of water, and the water molecule is composed of hydrogen and oxygen atoms. At the heart of the hydrogen atom is a positively charged particle called a *proton*. A proton is like a tiny magnet and is sensitive to magnetic fields. When the human body is in a strong magnetic field, such as an MRI scanner, all the protons align with the magnetic field. During the MRI scan, a series of short radio wave pulses is sent to specific areas of the body, causing the protons out of alignment. When the radio wave pulses disappear, the protons realign themselves in their original positions. This sends out radio signals that are picked up by the MRI receiver coils. These signals provide information not only about the exact location of the protons in the body but also about the different types of tissue (such as fat and water) in the body, as the protons align at different rates in different types of tissue and can be identified separately. Different from X-rays, which are mainly used to image bones, an MRI is mainly used to image soft tissues, such as the brain.

The following shows a dataset of brain MRI images for brain tumor detection on Kaggle. There are 98 brain MRI images, labeled as `no`, i.e., without tumor, and 155 images, labeled as `yes`, i.e., with tumor.

```
https://www.kaggle.com/navoneel/brain-mri-images-for-brain-tumor-detection
```
The following are some interesting projects for brain MRI tumor detection:

```
https://www.kaggle.com/ruslankl/brain-tumor-detection-v1-0-cnn-vgg-16
https://www.kaggle.com/ethernext/brain-tumour-detection-with-cnn-96-accuracy
https://www.kaggle.com/monkira/brain-mri-segmentation-using-unet-keras
```

5.4.5   RSNA Intracranial Hemorrhage Detection

CT is another medical imaging technique that uses X-rays to take a series of images of the body from different angles and combines the images with the help of computing technology to create detailed images of the structures inside the body. During a CT scan, the X-ray tube rotates around the patient and shoots narrow beams of X-rays through the body. The X-rays are then picked up by special X-ray detectors. When the X-rays leave the patient, they are picked up by the X-ray detectors, which are located directly opposite the X-ray tube, and transmitted to a computer. The computer will use complicated mathematical algorithms to construct 2D slice images of the patient, including the internal organs, blood vessels, and bones. Compared to MRI imaging, CT is cheaper and quicker. But an MRI can provide soft tissue images with higher image resolution than CT.

The following shows the Radiological Society of North America (RSNA) Intracranial Hemorrhage Detection dataset on Kaggle. It has an impressive 427GB of brain CT images.

```
https://www.kaggle.com/c/rsna-intracranial-hemorrhage-detection/data
```

The following are two highly voted projects based on the previous dataset:

```
https://www.kaggle.com/marcovasquez/basic-eda-data-visualization
https://www.kaggle.com/akensert/rsna-inceptionv3-keras-tf1-14-0
```

EXERCISE 5.10

Log in to your Kaggle account using a web browser, find one of the previous Kaggle projects, make a copy of the project, and then modify the code to use VGG16 as the base model. Compare the performances.

5.5 Federated Learning for Image Classification

Conventional deep learning requires all the data to be uploaded to the computer doing the computation, whether it is a server in the cloud or your local computer. In the case of mobile users, there could be millions of mobile phones, generating tons of data every day and making it impractical to upload all the data to perform the computation. This is where federated learning comes into play.

Federated learning is a new technique for model training that enables mobile devices to train and learn collaboratively from a shared model. A central server is used to create and train a shared model using proxy data, and then it distributes the shared model to the mobile devices. Each mobile device trains the shared model using its own data and sends the updates back. The server is then able to improve the shared model, as illustrated in Figure 5.13. This process is called *federated learning*, because the server uses federated data—mobile data—to improve its model. Federated learning can be used for both image classification and regression.

This approach presents several benefits. First, it does not require a large amount of bandwidth to transfer the data. Second, a large storage space is not required on the server. Last but not the least, users' privacy is protected, as the data never leaves the mobile devices.

Server

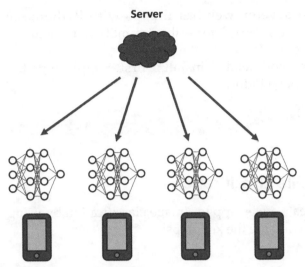

Figure 5.13: The federated learning architecture

The following shows how you can use TensorFlow to perform federated learning for image classification. You can find both the GitHub site for the full source code and a Google Colab online example to try.

```
https://www.tensorflow.org/federated/tutorials/federated_learning_
for_image_classification
```

EXERCISE 5.11

In a web browser, find the Google Colab Notebook of the previous website. Make a copy of the notebook in your own Google Colab account. Run the code and comment on the results.

The following shows another example of federated learning by using Baidu's PaddlePaddle. You can also find the GitHub site for the full source code there.

```
https://github.com/PaddlePaddle/PaddleFL
```

5.6   Web-Based Image Classification

Web-based applications, or web apps, have gained popularity in recent years. Different from mobile apps, which you have to download and install on your mobile phone, web apps are accessed via the Internet browser, so you don't have to download and install them. Mobile apps are run on mobile phones, while web apps are run on a remote server. Different types of mobile phones, such as Android and iPhones, require different mobile apps, while web apps adapt to whichever device you're viewing them on.

There are several ways to develop web-based apps with Python; see Chapter 12 for more details. The quickest way is to use the Streamlit library (`https://docs.streamlit.io/en/stable/`).

To use the Streamlit library, you need to install it first. Simply type the following command in a terminal window:

```
pip install --upgrade protobuf
pip install streamlit
```

5.6.1   Streamlit Image File Classification

Example 5.9 shows how to create a web app for image classification by using the Streamlit library. The following are the key steps.

Load the Streamlit library.

```
import streamlit as st
```

Define a function to use VGG16 for image classification and run the function in the Streamlit cache.

```
@st.cache(allow_output_mutation=True)
def vgg16_predict(cam_frame, image_size):
... ...
```

Create a VGG16 model and specify the image size.

```
model = vgg16.VGG16(weights='imagenet')
image_size = 224
```

Create an empty Streamlit web app that defaults to a main page and a left sidebar, and specify the title and sidebar.

```
frameST = st.empty()
```

Specify the title of the main page and the Markdown of the left sidebar. Markdown is a lightweight markup language designed to make formatting plaintext easier for a web page. Markdown claims to be one of the most popular markup languages in the world (`https://www.markdownguide.org/`).

```
st.title("Image Classification")
st.sidebar.markdown("# Image Classification")
```

Allow users to upload a file for classification. If the file does not exist, an error message is displayed; if it is successful, image classification is performed.

```
file_image = st.sidebar.file_uploader("Upload your Images", type=['jpeg',
'jpg','png','gif'])
if file_image is None:
```

```
        st.write("No image file!")
else:
... ...
```

Create a Download button that, when clicked, saves the image to a file named output.jpg.

```
    if st.button("Download"):
```

Example 5.9 shows the complete code.

EXAMPLE 5.9: THE STREAMLITIMAGECLASSIFICATION0.PY **PROGRAM**

```
#Example 5.9
#pip install --upgrade protobuf
#pip install streamlit

import streamlit as st
import cv2
import numpy as np
import pandas as pd
from PIL import Image
from tensorflow.keras.preprocessing.image import load_img
from tensorflow.keras.preprocessing.image import img_to_array
from keras.applications.imagenet_utils import decode_predictions
import time
import matplotlib.pyplot as plt
import random
import os

# import the models for further classification experiments
from tensorflow.keras.applications import vgg16

@st.cache(allow_output_mutation=True)
def vgg16_predict(cam_frame, image_size):
    frame= cv2.resize(cam_frame, (image_size, image_size))
    numpy_image = img_to_array(frame)
    image_batch = np.expand_dims(numpy_image, axis=0)
    processed_image = vgg16.preprocess_input(image_batch.copy())

    # get the predicted probabilities for each class
    predictions = model.predict(processed_image)
    label_vgg = decode_predictions(predictions)
    cv2.putText(cam_frame, "VGG16: {}, {:.2f}".format(label_vgg[0][0]
[1], label_vgg[0][0][2]) , (10, 30), cv2.FONT_HERSHEY_SIMPLEX, 0.7,
(255, 0, 0), 1)
    return cam_frame


model = vgg16.VGG16(weights='imagenet')
image_size = 224
```

```
frameST = st.empty()
st.title("Image Classification")
st.sidebar.markdown("# Image Classification")

file_image = st.sidebar.file_uploader("Upload your Images", type=['jp
eg','jpg','png','gif'])
if file_image is None:
    st.write("No image file!")
else:
    img = Image.open(file_image)
    img = np.asarray(img)[:,:,::-1].copy()
    #imcv = cv2.cvtColor(np.asarray(im), cv2.COLOR_RGB2BGR)
    st.write("Image")

    img = vgg16_predict(img, image_size)
    img = img[:,:,::-1]
    st.image(img, use_column_width=True)
    if st.button("Download"):
        im_pil = Image.fromarray(img)
        im_pil.save('output.jpg')
        st.write('Download completed')
```

To run it, simply type the following command in a terminal window:

```
streamlit run StreamlitImageClassification0.py
```

Figure 5.14 shows the output results. As you can see, the apple is not only correctly identified but also identified as a Granny Smith. The image file `apple`.`jpeg` and other image files used in this chapter are royalty-free images from the `Pexels.com` website (`https://www.pexels.com/search/apple/`). When you run the program for the first time, it may take a while, as it needs to download the VGG16 model first.

Example 5.9a shows an improved version of the previous image classification web app, allowing you to select different models to classify images. The following are the main differences.

It loads four different deep learning models: VGG16, ResNet50, MobileNet, and Inception V3.

```
from tensorflow.keras.applications import (
    vgg16,
    resnet50,
    mobilenet,
    inception_v3
)
```

Create four functions to use the four models for image classification and run the functions in the Streamlit cache.

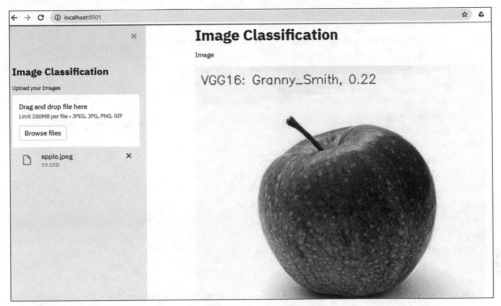

Figure 5.14: The Streamlit Image Classification web page using VGG16 to classify an apple image

```
@st.cache(allow_output_mutation=True)
def vgg16_predict(cam_frame, image_size):
... ...

@st.cache(allow_output_mutation=True)
def resnet50_predict(cam_frame, image_size):
... ...

@st.cache(allow_output_mutation=True)
def mobilenet_predict(cam_frame, image_size):
... ...
@st.cache(allow_output_mutation=True)
def inception_v3_predict(cam_frame, image_size):
... ...
```

Create an empty web app and specify the main page title and sidebar Markdown.

```
frameST = st.empty()
st.title("Image Classification")
st.sidebar.markdown("# Image Classification")
```

Create a drop-down list to allow users to select and create different models and specify image sizes. It uses `K.clear_session()` to clear the session for each model so that each model runs from a clean start. It also uses the `mode` variable to distinguish between models.

```
option = st.sidebar.selectbox(
    'Select a Deep Learning Model:',
    ["VGG16","RESNET50","MOBILENET","INCEPTION_V3"], index=0)
st.sidebar.write('You selected:', option)
if option == "VGG16":
    K.clear_session()
    model = vgg16.VGG16(weights='imagenet')
    image_size = 224
    mode = 1
elif option == "RESNET50":
    K.clear_session()
    model = resnet50.ResNet50(weights='imagenet')
    image_size = 224
    mode = 2
elif option == "MOBILENET":
... ...
elif option == "INCEPTION_V3":
... ...
```

Once an image file is uploaded, various functions are called to classify the image, depending on the value of the mode variable.

```
if mode == 1:
    img = vgg16_predict(img, image_size)
elif mode == 2:
    img = resnet50_predict(img, image_size)
elif mode == 3:
    img = mobilenet_predict(img, image_size)
elif mode == 4:
    img = inception_v3_predict(img, image_size)
```

Example 5.9a shows the complete code of the program.

EXAMPLE 5.9A: THE STREAMLITIMAGECLASSIFICATION.PY **PROGRAM**

```
#Example 5.9a
#https://github.com/streamlit/streamlit/issues/511
#pip install --upgrade protobuf
#pip install streamlit

import streamlit as st
import cv2
import numpy as np
import pandas as pd
from PIL import Image
from tensorflow.keras.preprocessing.image import load_img
from tensorflow.keras.preprocessing.image import img_to_array
from keras.applications.imagenet_utils import decode_predictions
import time
import matplotlib.pyplot as plt
```

```python
import random
import os
# imports for reproducibility
from keras import backend as K

# import the models for further classification experiments
from tensorflow.keras.applications import (
        vgg16,
        resnet50,
        mobilenet,
        inception_v3
)

@st.cache(allow_output_mutation=True)
def vgg16_predict(cam_frame, image_size):
    frame= cv2.resize(cam_frame, (image_size, image_size))
    numpy_image = img_to_array(frame)
    image_batch = np.expand_dims(numpy_image, axis=0)
    # prepare the image for the VGG16 model
    processed_image = vgg16.preprocess_input(image_batch.copy())
    predictions = model.predict(processed_image)
    label_vgg = decode_predictions(predictions)
    cv2.putText(cam_frame, "VGG16: {}, {:.2f}".format(label_vgg[0][0]
[1], label_vgg[0][0][2]) , (10, 30), cv2.FONT_HERSHEY_SIMPLEX, 0.7,
(255, 0, 0), 1)
    return cam_frame

@st.cache(allow_output_mutation=True)
def resnet50_predict(cam_frame, image_size):
    frame= cv2.resize(cam_frame, (image_size, image_size))
    numpy_image = img_to_array(frame)
    image_batch = np.expand_dims(numpy_image, axis=0)
    # prepare the image for the ResNet50 model
    processed_image = resnet50.preprocess_input(image_batch.copy())
    predictions = model.predict(processed_image)
    label_resnet = decode_predictions(predictions, top=3)
    cv2.putText(cam_frame, "ResNet50: {}, {:.2f}".format(label_
resnet[0][0][1], label_resnet[0][0][2]) , (10, 30), cv2.FONT_HERSHEY_
SIMPLEX, 0.7, (255, 0, 0), 1)
    return cam_frame

@st.cache(allow_output_mutation=True)
def mobilenet_predict(cam_frame, image_size):
    frame= cv2.resize(cam_frame, (image_size, image_size))
    numpy_image = img_to_array(frame)
    image_batch = np.expand_dims(numpy_image, axis=0)
    # prepare the image for the MobileNet model
    processed_image = mobilenet.preprocess_input(image_batch.copy())
    predictions = model.predict(processed_image)
    label_mobilenet = decode_predictions(predictions)
```

```
        cv2.putText(cam_frame, "MobileNet: {}, {:.2f}".format(label_
mobilenet[0][0][1], label_mobilenet[0][0][2]) , (10, 30), cv2.FONT_
HERSHEY_SIMPLEX, 0.7, (255, 0, 0), 1)
        return cam_frame
@st.cache(allow_output_mutation=True)
def inception_v3_predict(cam_frame, image_size):
        frame= cv2.resize(cam_frame, (image_size, image_size))
        numpy_image = img_to_array(frame)
        image_batch = np.expand_dims(numpy_image, axis=0)
        # prepare the image for the Inception model
        processed_image = inception_v3.preprocess_input(image_batch
.copy())
        predictions = model.predict(processed_image)
        label_inception = decode_predictions(predictions)
        cv2.putText(cam_frame, "Inception: {}, {:.2f}".format(label_
inception[0][0][1], label_inception[0][0][2]) , (10, 30), cv2.FONT_
HERSHEY_SIMPLEX, 0.7, (255, 0, 0), 1)
        return cam_frame


mode = 1
#model = vgg16.VGG16(weights='imagenet')
#image_size = 224

frameST = st.empty()
st.title("Image Classification")
st.sidebar.markdown("# Image Classification")
option = st.sidebar.selectbox(
        'Select a deep learning Model:',
        ["VGG16","RESNET50","MOBILENET","INCEPTION_V3"], index=0)
st.sidebar.write('You selected:', option)
if option == "VGG16":
        K.clear_session()
        model = vgg16.VGG16(weights='imagenet')
        image_size = 224
        mode = 1
elif option == "RESNET50":
        K.clear_session()
        model = resnet50.ResNet50(weights='imagenet')
        image_size = 224
        mode = 2
elif option == "MOBILENET":
        K.clear_session()
        model = mobilenet.MobileNet(weights='imagenet')
        image_size = 224
        mode = 3
elif option == "INCEPTION_V3":
        K.clear_session()
        model = inception_v3.InceptionV3(weights='imagenet')
```

```
        image_size = 299
        mode = 4



file_image = st.sidebar.file_uploader("Upload your Images",
type=['jpeg','jpg','png','gif'])

if file_image is None:
    st.write("No image file!")

else:
    img = Image.open(file_image)
    img = np.asarray(img)[:,:,::-1].copy()
    #imcv = cv2.cvtColor(np.asarray(im), cv2.COLOR_RGB2BGR)
    st.write("Image")

    if mode == 1:
        img = vgg16_predict(img, image_size)
    elif mode == 2:
        img = resnet50_predict(img, image_size)
    elif mode == 3:
        img = mobilenet_predict(img, image_size)
    elif mode == 4:
        img = inception_v3_predict(img, image_size)

    img = img[:,:,::-1]
    st.image(img, use_column_width=True)
    if st.button("Download"):
        im_pil = Image.fromarray(img)
        im_pil.save('output.jpg')
        st.write('Download completed')
```

Again, just type the following command in a terminal window to run it:

```
streamlit run StreamlitImageClassification.py
```

Figure 5.15 shows the output results using MobileNet. As you can see, it correctly identifies the orange. When you run the program using the different models for the first time, it may take a while, as it needs to download the model first.

EXERCISE 5.12

Modify the previous Python program, and add another deep learning model, such as VGG19. Run the code and comment on the results.

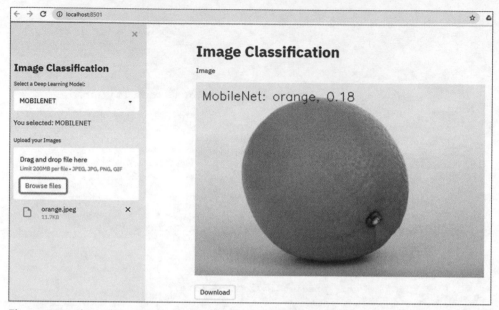

Figure 5.15: The image classification results by using MobileNet on an orange image

5.6.2 Streamlit Webcam Image Classification

One of the coolest things you can do with the Streamlit library is to access the webcam from the web app. Example 5.10 shows how to create a web app to perform image classification on live images from a webcam. The following are the key steps.

Create a function for a webcam and run the function in the Streamlit cache for optimal performance.

```
@st.cache(allow_output_mutation=True)
def get_cap():
    return cv2.VideoCapture(0)
```

Create an empty web app and create two sliders in the left sidebar to control the contrast and brightness of the webcam image.

```
frameST = st.empty()
contrast=st.sidebar.slider('Contrast')/50.0
brightness=st.sidebar.slider('Brightness')
```

Use a `while` loop to read the webcam image.

```
while True:
    ret, frame = cap.read()
```

Convert the image to the HSV color space, adjust the contrast and brightness, and convert the image back to the RGB color space.

```
frame = cv2.cvtColor(frame, cv2.COLOR_BGR2HSV)
frame[:,:,2] = np.clip(contrast * frame[:,:,2] + brightness, 0, 255)
frame = cv2.cvtColor(frame, cv2.COLOR_HSV2BGR)
```

Example 5.10 shows the complete code of the program.

EXAMPLE 5.10:   THE STREAMLITWENCAM.PY PROGRAM

```
#Example 5.10
#pip install --upgrade protobuf
#pip install streamlit

import streamlit as st
import cv2
import numpy as np

@st.cache(allow_output_mutation=True)
def get_cap():
    return cv2.VideoCapture(0)


cap = get_cap()

frameST = st.empty()
contrast=st.sidebar.slider('Contrast')/50.0
brightness=st.sidebar.slider('Brightness')

while True:
    ret, frame = cap.read()
    frame = cv2.cvtColor(frame, cv2.COLOR_BGR2HSV)
    frame[:,:,2] = np.clip(contrast * frame[:,:,2] + brightness, 0,
255)
    frame = cv2.cvtColor(frame, cv2.COLOR_HSV2BGR)
    # Stop the program if reached end of video
    if not ret:
        print("Done processing !!!")
        cv2.waitKey(3000)
        # Release device
        cap.release()
        break

    frameST.image(frame, channels="BGR")
```

Figure 5.16 shows the output of the program from Example 5.10, which has live images from a webcam and two sliders for contrast and brightness control.

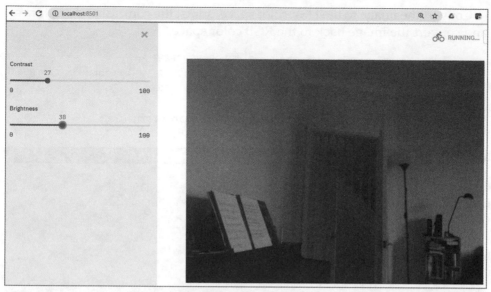

Figure 5.16: The output of the Example 5.10 program, which shows live images from a webcam and two sliders for contrast and brightness control

---

EXERCISE 5.13

Modify the previous Python program to read images from a video file, instead of reading images from the webcam. Hint: modify `cv2.VideoCapture(0)` and replace 0 with the name of the video file.

Example 5.10a shows how to create a web app that performs image classification for live images from a webcam.

EXAMPLE 5.10A: THE STREAMLITWEBCAMIMAGECLASSIFICATION.PY
PROGRAM

```
#Example 5.10a
#pip install --upgrade protobuf
#pip install streamlit

import streamlit as st
import cv2
import numpy as np
import pandas as pd

from tensorflow.keras.preprocessing.image import load_img
from tensorflow.keras.preprocessing.image import img_to_array
from keras.applications.imagenet_utils import decode_predictions
import time
```

```
# import the models for further classification experiments
from tensorflow.keras.applications import (
        vgg16,
        resnet50,
        mobilenet,
        inception_v3
    )

import matplotlib.pyplot as plt

# imports for reproducibility
import tensorflow as tf
import random
import os
from keras import backend as K

@st.cache(allow_output_mutation=True)
def get_cap():
    return cv2.VideoCapture(0)

@st.cache(allow_output_mutation=True)
def vgg16_predict(cam_frame, image_size):
    frame= cv2.resize(cam_frame, (image_size, image_size))
    numpy_image = img_to_array(frame)
    image_batch = np.expand_dims(numpy_image, axis=0)
    processed_image = vgg16.preprocess_input(image_batch.copy())
    predictions = model.predict(processed_image)
    label_vgg = decode_predictions(predictions)
    cv2.putText(cam_frame, "VGG16: {}, {:.2f}".format(label_vgg[0][0]
[1], label_vgg[0][0][2]) , (10, 30), cv2.FONT_HERSHEY_SIMPLEX, 0.7,
(255, 0, 0), 1)
    return cam_frame

@st.cache(allow_output_mutation=True)
def resnet50_predict(cam_frame, image_size):
    frame= cv2.resize(cam_frame, (image_size, image_size))
    numpy_image = img_to_array(frame)
    image_batch = np.expand_dims(numpy_image, axis=0)
    processed_image = resnet50.preprocess_input(image_batch.copy())
    predictions = model.predict(processed_image)
    label_resnet = decode_predictions(predictions, top=3)
    cv2.putText(cam_frame, "ResNet50: {}, {:.2f}".format(label_
resnet[0][0][1], label_resnet[0][0][2]) , (10, 30), cv2.FONT_HERSHEY_
SIMPLEX, 0.7, (255, 0, 0), 1)
    return cam_frame

@st.cache(allow_output_mutation=True)
def mobilenet_predict(cam_frame, image_size):
    frame= cv2.resize(cam_frame, (image_size, image_size))
    numpy_image = img_to_array(frame)
```

```python
        image_batch = np.expand_dims(numpy_image, axis=0)
        processed_image = mobilenet.preprocess_input(image_batch.copy())
        predictions = model.predict(processed_image)
        label_mobilenet = decode_predictions(predictions)
        cv2.putText(cam_frame, "MobileNet: {}, {:.2f}".format(label_
mobilenet[0][0][1], label_mobilenet[0][0][2]) , (10, 30), cv2.FONT_
HERSHEY_SIMPLEX, 0.7, (255, 0, 0), 1)
        return cam_frame
@st.cache(allow_output_mutation=True)
def inception_v3_predict(cam_frame, image_size):
        frame= cv2.resize(cam_frame, (image_size, image_size))
        numpy_image = img_to_array(frame)
        image_batch = np.expand_dims(numpy_image, axis=0)
        processed_image = inception_v3.preprocess_input(image_batch
.copy())
        predictions = model.predict(processed_image)
        label_inception = decode_predictions(predictions)
        cv2.putText(cam_frame, "Inception: {}, {:.2f}".format(label_
inception[0][0][1], label_inception[0][0][2]) , (10, 30), cv2.FONT_
HERSHEY_SIMPLEX, 0.7, (255, 0, 0), 1)
        return cam_frame


cap = get_cap()

mode = 1
frameST = st.empty()
st.title("Image Classification")
st.sidebar.markdown("# Image Classification")
option = st.sidebar.selectbox(
        'Select a Deep Learning Model:',
        ["VGG16","RESNET50","MOBILENET","INCEPTION_V3"], index=0)
st.sidebar.write('You selected:', option)
if option == "VGG16":
    K.clear_session()
    model = vgg16.VGG16(weights='imagenet')
    image_size = 224
    mode = 1
elif option == "RESNET50":
    K.clear_session()
    model = resnet50.ResNet50(weights='imagenet')
    image_size = 224
    mode = 2
elif option == "MOBILENET":
    K.clear_session()
    model = mobilenet.MobileNet(weights='imagenet')
    image_size = 224
    mode = 3
elif option == "INCEPTION_V3":
    K.clear_session()
    model = inception_v3.InceptionV3(weights='imagenet')
```

```
        image_size = 299
        mode = 4

while True:
    ret, frame = cap.read()
    if mode == 1:
        frame = vgg16_predict(frame, image_size)
    elif mode == 2:
        frame = resnet50_predict(frame, image_size)
    elif mode == 3:
        frame = mobilenet_predict(frame, image_size)
    elif mode == 4:
        frame = inception_v3_predict(frame, image_size)

    # Stop the program if reached end of video
    if not ret:
        cv2.waitKey(3000)
        # Release device
        cap.release()
        break

    frameST.image(frame, channels="BGR")
```

To run it, simply type the following command in a terminal window:

```
streamlit run StreamlitWebcamImageClassification.py
```

Figure 5.17 shows the output results.

Figure 5.17: Image classification through a webcam by using the VGG16 model

5.6.3   Streamlit from GitHub

GitHub (`https://github.com/`) is an online platform that is popular among software developers. With GitHub, you can easily create, share, and collaborate on projects. You can also run your Streamlit program directly from your GitHub site.

To create your own project on GitHub, simply log in to GitHub, and follow the instructions to create your project. The project on GitHub is also called a *repository*. Figure 5.18 shows my GitHub site for the `streamlit-file-image-classification` repository.

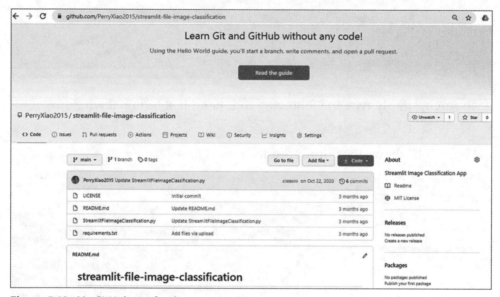

Figure 5.18: My GitHub site for the `streamlit-file-image-classification` repository

(Source: `https://github.com/PerryXiao2015/streamlit-file-image-classification`)

After creating your GitHub repository, you can run Streamlit directly from your GitHub site. The following is an example of how to run the code on your GitHub site:

```
streamlit run https://raw.githubusercontent.com/PerryXiao2015/streamlit-file-image-classification/main/StreamlitFileImageClassification.py
```

5.6.4   Streamlit Deployment

You can also deploy your GitHub repository through `https://share.streamlit.io`.

Just go to the website, log in using your GitHub account, and input the name of your GitHub directory, in this case, `PerryXiao2015/streamlit-file-image-classification`, and input the Python Streamlit file, in this case, `StreamlitFileImageClassification.py`. Then click the Deploy button. It will take quite a while; see Figure 5.19.

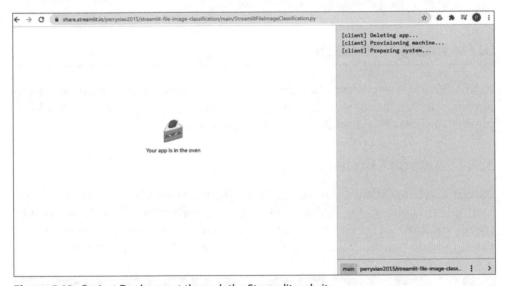

Figure 5.19: Project Deployment through the Streamlit website

After deployment, you will see your project on the website, as shown in Figure 5.20. Now you can share the web link to your friends so that they can also run your program online.

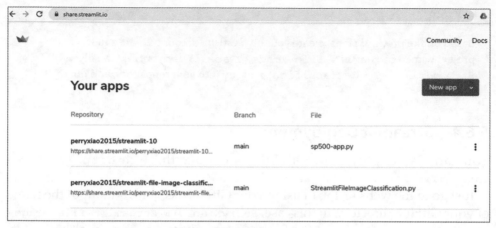

Figure 5.20: My projects on the Streamlit website

For more details, examples, and documents, please visit the following:
`https://docs.streamlit.io/en/stable/`

5.7   Image Processing

In this section we will introduce some commonly used image processing techniques, such as image stitching, template matching, photo inpaint, de-oldify photos, and black-and-white photo colorization.

5.7.1   Image Stitching

Image stitching allows you to stitch multiple images into a single image. Example 5.11 shows the Python code for image stitching. This allows you to specify multiple image files and stitch them together. The two image files `London_left.jpg` and `London_right.jpg` are from the website `www.pexels.com/`.

EXAMPLE 5.11:   THE `IMAGESTITCHING.PY` PROGRAM

```
#Example 5.11 Image Stitching
import numpy as np
import cv2 as cv
import sys

modes = (cv.Stitcher_PANORAMA, cv.Stitcher_SCANS)
names=['London_left.jpg','London_right.jpg']
imgs = []
for img_name in names:
    img = cv.imread(cv.samples.findFile(img_name))
    cv.imshow(img_name,img)
```

```
    if img is None:
        print("can't read image " + img_name)
        sys.exit(-1)
    imgs.append(img)

stitcher = cv.Stitcher.create(modes[0])
status, pano = stitcher.stitch(imgs)

if status != cv.Stitcher_OK:
    print("Can't stitch images, error code = %d" % status)
    sys.exit(-1)

cv.imwrite('result.jpg', pano)
cv.imshow('result', pano)
```

Figure 5.21 shows the image of the file `London_left.jpg`. Figure 5.22 shows the image of the file `London_right.jpg`. Figure 5.23 shows the final composite result image.

Figure 5.21: The image `London_left.jpg`

Figure 5.22: The image `London_right.jpg`

Figure 5.23: The final stitched result image

EXERCISE 5.17

Modify the previous Python program so that it can stitch three images together. Comment on the results.

5.7.2   Image Inpainting

Image inpainting is a process to repair and restore the damaged, deteriorated, or missing parts of the image. Example 5.12 shows the Python code to allow you to select a region of interest (ROI) in an image and remove it from the image using image inpainting. The file `church.jpeg` is again from the website `www.pexels.com/`.

EXAMPLE 5.12:   THE `IMAGEINPAINTING.PY` **PROGRAM**

```python
#Example 5.12 Photo Inpaint Example
import numpy as np
import cv2

img = cv2.imread('church.jpeg')
rows,cols,channels = img.shape
print(rows, cols)
cv2.imshow('Orignial',img)

height,width,depth = img.shape
mask = np.zeros(shape=img.shape, dtype="uint8")
r = cv2.selectROI(img)
left = int(r[0])
top = int(r[1])
right= int(r[0]+r[2])
bottom= int(r[1]+r[3])

cv2.rectangle(img=mask,
            pt1=(left, top), pt2=(right, bottom),
            color=(255, 255, 255),
            thickness=-1)
# Apply the mask and display the result
maskedImg = cv2.bitwise_and(src1=img, src2=mask)
cv2.imshow("Masked", maskedImg)
mask = cv2.cvtColor(mask, cv2.COLOR_BGR2GRAY)
(thresh, mask) = cv2.threshold(mask, 127, 255, cv2.THRESH_BINARY)
cv2.imshow('Mask',mask)

dst = cv2.inpaint(img,mask,3,cv2.INPAINT_TELEA)
cv2.imshow('Result',dst)
cv2.waitKey(0)
cv2.destroyAllWindows()
```

Figure 5.24 shows the original image file `church.jpeg`. Figure 5.25 shows the ROI selected on the `church.jpeg` image. Figure 5.26 shows the image inpainting effect. As you can see, the top part of the church has magically disappeared!

Figure 5.24: The original `church.jpeg` image file

Figure 5.25: The ROI selected on the `church.jpeg` image

Figure 5.26: The image inpainting effect

5.7.3 Image Coloring

Adding colors to old black-and-white photos has become popular recently. Figure 5.27 shows an impressive GitHub project for old photo coloring with Python. It uses PySimpleGUI to create a graphical user interface and select old black-and-white photos to convert them into color ones.

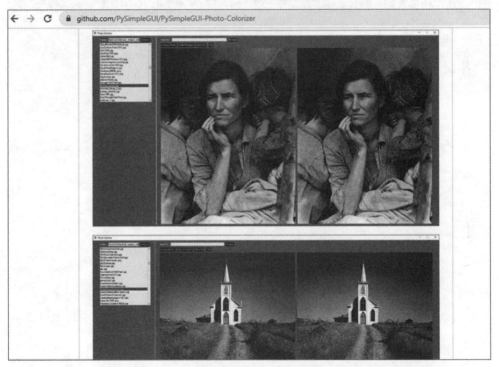

Figure 5.27: The GitHub site for the `PySimpleGUI-Photo-Colorizer` repository
(Source: `https://github.com/PySimpleGUI/PySimpleGUI-Photo-Colorizer`)

5.7.4   Image Super Resolution

With a deep learning neural network, you can also improve the image resolution. This process is called *image super resolution*. This is important if you want to improve image quality before performing image classification.

Example 5.13 shows the Python code for image super resolution. It has been modified from `https://www.pyimagesearch.com/2020/11/09/opencv-super-resolution-with-deep-learning/`. It reads an image from the webcam and enlarges the image using the model `LapSRN_x8.pb`, which enlarges the image eight times.

EXAMPLE 5.13:   THE `IMAGESUPERRESOLUTION.PY` **PROGRAM**

```
#Example 5.13 Image Super Resolution
#Modified from:
#https://www.pyimagesearch.com/2020/11/09/opencv-super-resolution-
with-deep-learning/
# pip install opencv-contrib-python
from imutils.video import VideoStream
import imutils
import time
import cv2
import os

modelfile = 'LapSRN_x8.pb'
modelName = modelfile.split(os.path.sep)[-1].split("_")[0].lower()
modelScale = modelfile.split("_x")[-1]
modelScale = int(modelScale[:modelScale.find(".")])

sr = cv2.dnn_superres.DnnSuperResImpl_create()
sr.readModel(modelfile)
sr.setModel(modelName, modelScale)

vs = VideoStream(src=0).start()
time.sleep(2.0)
while True:
        frame = vs.read()
        frame = imutils.resize(frame, width=100)

        upscaled = sr.upsample(frame)
        bicubic = cv2.resize(frame,
            (upscaled.shape[1], upscaled.shape[0]),
            interpolation=cv2.INTER_CUBIC)

        cv2.imshow("Original", frame)
        cv2.imshow("Bicubic", bicubic)
        cv2.imshow("Super Resolution", upscaled)
        key = cv2.waitKey(1) & 0xFF
        # if the `q` key was pressed, break from the loop
```

```
        if key == ord("q"):
            break

cv2.destroyAllWindows()
vs.stop()
```

You can also download the following different models:

- **EDSR_x4.pb EDSR:** Enhanced Deep Residual Networks for Single Image Super-Resolution (`https://github.com/Saafke/EDSR_Tensorflow`)

- **ESPCN_x4.pb ESPCN:** Real-Time Single Image and Video Super-Resolution Using an Efficient Sub-Pixel Convolutional Neural Network (`https://github.com/fannymonori/TF-ESPCN`)

- **FSRCNN_x3.pb FSRCNN:** Accelerating the Super-Resolution Convolutional Neural Network (`https://github.com/Saafke/FSRCNN_Tensorflow`)

- **LapSRN_x8.pb LapSRN:** Fast and Accurate Image Super-Resolution with Deep Laplacian Pyramid Networks (`https://github.com/fannymonori/TF-LAPSRN`)

EXERCISE 5.20

Modify the previous Python program, use different deep learning models, run the program, and comment on the results.

5.7.5   Gabor Filter

The Gabor filter is a linear filter that is commonly used for image texture analysis. It is named after Dennis Gabor, a Hungarian-British electrical engineer and physicist. The Gabor filter uses the concept of frequency (or wavelength) and orientation of a wavelet (small wave) to analyze image texture. Frequency and orientation in Gabor filters are similar to those of the human visual system. The Gabor filter has been found to be particularly useful for texture representation and discrimination. Visit the following links for more details on the Gabor filter and wavelet:

```
https://en.wikipedia.org/wiki/Gabor_filter
https://en.wikipedia.org/wiki/Gabor_transform
https://en.wikipedia.org/wiki/Wavelet
```

Example 5.14 shows a Python code displaying Gabor filters with four different wavelengths (or frequencies) and four different orientations.

Wavelengths: 4, 8, 12, 16

Orientation: $0, \pi/4, \pi/2, 3\pi/4$

EXAMPLE 5.14: THE `GABORFILTER.PY` **PROGRAM**

```
#Example 5.14
import math
import cv2
import numpy as np
import matplotlib.pyplot as plt

# cv2.getGaborKernel(ksize, sigma, theta, lambda, gamma, psi, ktype)
# ksize - size of gabor filter (n, n)
# sigma - standard deviation of the gaussian function
# theta - orientation of the normal to the parallel stripes
# lambda - wavelength of the sunusoidal factor
# gamma - spatial aspect ratio
# psi - phase offset
# ktype - type and range of values that each pixel in the gabor
kernel can hold


No = 4
Nw = 4
N = No*Nw
n = 0
plt.figure(figsize=(20,20))
for j in range(Nw): #wavelength
    for i in range(No):  #Orientation
        kernel = cv2.getGaborKernel((21, 21), 5, np.pi/4*i, 4*(j+1),
1, 0, cv2.CV_32F)
        kernel /= math.sqrt((kernel * kernel).sum())

        n = n + 1
        plt.subplot(Nw,No,n)
        plt.imshow(kernel, cmap='rainbow')
plt.show()
```

Figure 5.28 shows the wavelets of the Gabor filters at four different wavelengths (rows) and four different orientations (columns).

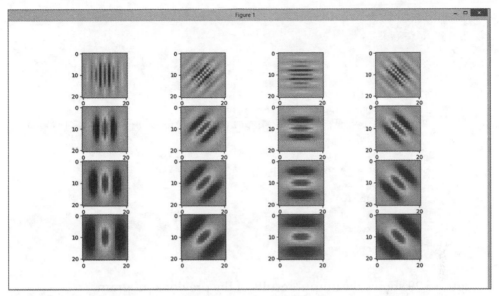

Figure 5.28: The wavelets of the Gabor filters at four different wavelengths (rows) and four different orientations (columns)

EXERCISE 5.21

Modify the previous Python program, use six different wavelengths (4, 8, 12, 16, 20, 24) and 6 different orientations (0, $\pi/6$, $2\pi/6$, $3\pi/6$, $4\pi/6$, $5\pi/6$), run the program, and comment on the results.

Example 5.15 shows a Python code for applying Gabor filters to an image. The Gabor filter has four different wavelengths and four different orientations. The file `pineapple.jpeg` is again from the website `www.pexels.com/`.

EXAMPLE 5.15:   THE `GABORFILTER2.PY` **PROGRAM**

```
# Example 5.15
import math
import cv2
import numpy as np
import matplotlib.pyplot as plt

image = cv2.imread('pineapple.jpeg', 0).astype(np.float32) / 255
cv2.imshow('Image', image)

No = 4
```

```
Nw = 4
N = No*Nw
n = 0

plt.figure(figsize=(20,20))
for j in range(Nw): #wavelength
    for i in range(No):  #Orientation
        kernel = cv2.getGaborKernel((21, 21), 5, np.pi/5*i, 4*(j+1),
1, 0, cv2.CV_32F)
        kernel /= math.sqrt((kernel * kernel).sum())
        filtered = cv2.filter2D(image, -1, kernel)
        n = n + 1
        plt.subplot(Nw,No,n)
        plt.imshow(filtered, cmap='rainbow')
        plt.axis('off')
plt.show()
```

Figure 5.29 shows the output results of the previous program.

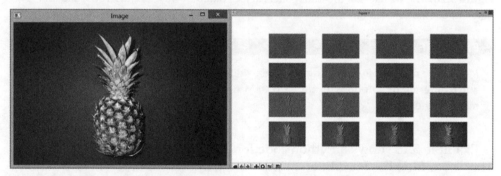

Figure 5.29: The original grayscale image (top) and the corresponding filtered images (bottom) with Gabor filters at four different wavelengths (rows) and four different orientations (columns)

You can use the Gabor filter to create artistic images with what is called the Fractalius effect. Example 5.16 shows the Python code for applying Gabor filters to a color image to generate the Fractalius effect. The Gabor filter has a fixed wavelength and four different orientations $(0, \pi/4, \pi/2, 3\pi/4)$. It selects the maximum values of all filters at each pixel and generates a filtered image. The files `bird2.jpeg` and `pineapple.jpeg` are again from the website `www.pexels.com/`.

EXAMPLE 5.16:   THE `GABORFILTER3.PY` **PROGRAM**

```
# Example 5.16
import math
import cv2
```

```python
import numpy as np
import matplotlib.pyplot as plt

#image = cv2.imread('bird2.jpg').astype(np.float32) / 255
image = cv2.imread('pineapple.jpeg').astype(np.float32) / 255
image = cv2.cv2.cvtColor(image, cv2.COLOR_BGR2RGB)
No = 4
j = 1
size = image.shape #h, w, c = im.shape
filtered = np.zeros(size, np.int8)

for i in range(No):  #Orientation
    kernel = cv2.getGaborKernel((21, 21), 4, np.pi/4*i, 4*(j+1), 1,
0, cv2.CV_32F)
    kernel /= math.sqrt((kernel * kernel).sum())
    fimg = cv2.filter2D(image, -1, kernel)
    filtered = np.maximum(filtered, fimg)
plt.figure()
plt.subplot(1,2,1)
plt.imshow(image)
plt.axis('off')
plt.title('Original Image')
plt.subplot(1,2,2)
plt.imshow(filtered)
plt.axis('off')
plt.title('Gabor Filtered Image')
plt.show()
```

Figure 5.30 and Figure 5.31 show the original color images and the corresponding Gabor filtered images with the Fractalius effect.

Figure 5.30: The original color image of the `pineapple.jpeg` file and the corresponding Gabor filtered image with the Fractalius effect

Figure 5.31: The original color image of the `bird2.jpeg` file and the corresponding Gabor filtered image with the Fractalius effect

---

EXERCISE 5.22

Modify the previous Python program, use six different orientations (0, $\pi/6$, $2\pi/6$, $3\pi/6$, $4\pi/6$, $5\pi/6$), run the program, and comment on the results.

5.8   Summary

This chapter covered image classifications, one of the most researched topics, in artificial intelligence. You can perform image classifications using pre-trained deep learning neural network models or using custom trained models, this is also called *transfer learning*.

With pre-trained models, such as AlexNet, GoogLeNet, VGG, ResNet, MobileNet, EfficientNet, and so on, you can classify images with predefined classes. For example, when you train the deep neural networks on ImageNet, you can recognize 1,000 types of daily objects.

With transfer learning, you can train the models with your own image data to recognize new image classes. Transfer learning can be used in many areas, such as skin cancer classification, retinopathy classification, chest X-ray classification, MRI classification, and so on.

Federated learning is a new technique for model training. It enables mobile devices to train together and to learn collaboratively from a shared model.

With the Streamlit library, you can easily build web-based image classification applications.

In image processing, image stitching allows you to merge multiple images into a single image. With image template matching, you can search the same regions of interest in different images. Image inpainting allows you to fix the damaged, deteriorated, or missing parts of the image. Image coloring allows you to add colors to old black-and-white photos. Image super resolution allows you to improve the image resolutions. Gabor filters use frequency and orientation to analyze the image texture.

5.9   Chapter Review Questions

Q5.1.   What is image classification?

Q5.2.   What are the differences between image classification, object detection, and image segmentation?

Q5.3.   What is transfer learning?

Q5.4.   What are medical imaging technologies?

Q5.5.   Use a suitable table to compare the characteristic features of X-ray, MRI, and CT imaging.

Q5.6.   What is federated learning?

Q5.7.   What is the Streamlit library?

Q5.8.   What is meant by image stitching, template matching, region of interest, and photo inpainting in the context of image processing?

Q5.9.   What is the PySimpleGUI library?

Q5.10.   What is the image super resolution?

Q5.11.   What is a Gabor filter? What are the effects of different wavelengths (or frequencies) and different orientations on Gabor wavelets?

Q5.12.   What is the Fractalius effect?

Face Detection and Face Recognition

"Why are there so many shocking results in AI? Because AI is the new electricity."

—Andrew Ng (American computer scientist)

CHAPTER OUTLINE

6.1   Introduction

Face detection and face recognition are probably the most controversial AI technologies and yet are still widely adopted in many areas. With face detection, smart phones and many digital cameras can identify faces while photos and videos are being taken. With face recognition, people can unlock their phones, find and track missing people or criminals, and provide access control in airports and stations. Many of the big companies, such as Facebook, Google, Amazon,

Microsoft, IBM, and so on, have worked on their own face recognition technologies. Face recognition has outperformed humans with an accuracy of close to 100 percent in many cases. The main controversies around face recognition are ethical and privacy issues, which will be the research focus for coming years.

Face recognition can be dated back to the 1960s, when Woody Bledsoe, Helen Chan Wolf, and Charles Bisson worked on using the computer to recognize human faces in photographs. In their project, coordinates of the facial features in a photograph had to be established first, and then 20 distances of key feature points were calculated. In 2001, Kaiqi Cen published a paper titled "Study of Viola-Jones Real Time Face Detector," which was the first scientific study relating to the use of algorithms in detecting faces (`https://web.stanford.edu/class/cs231a/prev_projects_2016/cs231a_final_report.pdf`).

Many people get confused about the difference between face detection and face recognition. Face detection simply means to detect faces in an image, while face recognition means to identify a person by their face. You will need to detect the faces first and then perform the recognition. A typical face recognition paradigm can include these four steps:

1. **Face detection**: Detect faces in an image.

2. **Face alignment**: Align the face (size, orientation) with the database faces.

3. **Face feature extraction**: Analyze the face and extract distinguishable landmarks, also called *nodal points*, from each face. Each face can have up to 80 nodal points, such as eyes, nose, cheeks, and lips. Other features include the distance between your eyes or the shape of your cheekbones.

4. **Face matching**: Match the face against a database of known faces according to the nodal point values and return the best match(es).

In this chapter, we will introduce how to detect faces in an image, either from an image file or from a webcam, and then how to recognize faces.

6.2 Face Detection and Face Landmarks

The most popular method to detect faces in real time is to use the Haar cascade classifier, an effective object detection method proposed by Paul Viola and Michael Jones in 2001. In this approach, a cascade function is trained from a lot of positive and negative images and then used to detect faces in other images.

Example 6.1 shows a simple face detection program by using OpenCV. It loads a face image from a file called `face0.jpeg` (`https://www.pexels.com/search/face/`). Please note that OpenCV reads the image file as BGR (blue, green, red) format, not the commonly used RGB (red, green, blue) format, which can cause problems when you are using different image processing libraries.

You will also need to download the Haar cascade XML file from `https://github.com/Itseez/opencv/tree/master/data/haarcascades`.

EXAMPLE 6.1   THE `FACE.PY` PROGRAM

```
#Example 6.1 OpenCV face detection
import cv2
img = cv2.imread('face0.jpg')
cascade_classifier = cv2.CascadeClassifier('haarcascade frontalface_
default.xml')
gray =cv2.cvtColor(img, cv2.COLOR_BGR2GRAY)
faces= cascade_classifier.detectMultiScale(gray, minNeighbors=5)

for (x,y,w,h) in faces:
    cv2.rectangle(img,(x,y),(x+w,y+h),(255,255,0),2)
    cv2.putText(img,'face', (x + 10, y + 10), cv2.FONT_HERSHEY_
SIMPLEX, 1, (255,0,255), 2)

cv2.imshow('face', img)
cv2.waitKey(0)
```

Figure 6.1 shows the output of the program, which includes the image of the `face0.jpeg` file and the face detected in the image.

Figure 6.1: The image of the `face0.jpeg` file and the face detected in the image

As you try different photos, you will find that sometimes face detection can misidentify faces. Unfortunately, for AI, this is not an uncommon problem. To solve this problem, OpenCV's face detection function (`faceCascade` `.detectMultiScale()`) allows you to adjust its parameters, such as `scaleFactor`, `minNeighbors`, and `minSize`, as shown here:

```
faces = faceCascade.detectMultiScale(
    gray,
    scaleFactor=1.3,
    minNeighbors=5,
    minSize=(30, 30)
)
```

EXERCISE 6.1

Modify the Example 6.1 Python program. Try different face images and comment on the accuracy of the face detection. Adjust the `scaleFactor`, `minNeighbors`, and `minSize` parameters to see how they affect the results.

For more information on OpenCV face detection, see the following:

https://realpython.com/face-recognition-with-python/

https://opencv-python-tutroals.readthedocs.io/en/latest/ py_tutorials/py_objdetect/py_face_detection/py_face_detection.html

Example 6.2 shows a different version of the previous face detection program that uses OpenCV. It uses a webcam to get the image and perform face detection on the webcam image.

EXAMPLE 6.2 THE `FACEWEBCAM.PY` PROGRAM

```
#Example 6.2 OpenCV Face Detection with Webcam
import cv2

cascade_classifier = cv2.CascadeClassifier('haarcascade_frontalface_
default.xml')
camera = cv2.VideoCapture(0)

while camera.isOpened():
    ok, cam_frame = camera.read()
    if not ok:
        break

    gray_img=cv2.cvtColor(cam_frame, cv2.COLOR_BGR2GRAY)
    faces= cascade_classifier.detectMultiScale(gray_img, minNeighbors=5)
```

```
       for (x,y,w,h) in faces:
            cv2.rectangle(cam_frame,(x,y),(x+w,y+h),(255,255,0),2)
            cv2.putText(cam_frame,'face', (x + 10, y + 10), cv2
.FONT_HERSHEY_SIMPLEX, 1, (255,0,255), 2)

        cv2.imshow('video image', cam_frame)
        key = cv2.waitKey(30)
        if key == 27: # press 'ESC' to quit
            break

camera.release()
cv2.destroyAllWindows()
```

EXERCISE 6.2

Modify the Example 6.2 Python program so that it reads images from a video file. Hint: Modify `cv2.VideoCapture(0)` **and replace 0 with the video filename.**

Example 6.3 shows a simple face and eye detection program that uses OpenCV. It loads a face image from a file called `face1.jpeg` (`https://www.pexels.com/search/face/`). The smile detection is based on the `haarcascade_eye.xml` file.

EXAMPLE 6.3   THE `FACEEYE.PY` PROGRAM

```
#Example 6.3 OpenCV Faces and Eyes detection
import cv2
img = cv2.imread('face1.jpeg')
faceCascade = cv2.CascadeClassifier('haarcascade_frontalface_default
.xml')
eyeCascade = cv2.CascadeClassifier('haarcascade_eye.xml')

gray =cv2.cvtColor(img, cv2.COLOR_BGR2GRAY)
faces = faceCascade.detectMultiScale(
    gray,
    scaleFactor=1.3,
    minNeighbors=5,
    minSize=(30, 30)
)

for (x,y,w,h) in faces:
    cv2.rectangle(img,(x,y),(x+w,y+h),(255,255,0),2)
    cv2.putText(img,'face', (x + 10, y + 10), cv2.FONT_HERSHEY_
SIMPLEX, 1, (255,0,255), 2)
    face_gray = gray[y:y+h, x:x+w]
    face_color = img[y:y+h, x:x+w]
```

```
    eyes = eyeCascade.detectMultiScale(
        face_gray,
        scaleFactor= 1.1,
        minNeighbors=10,
        minSize=(10, 10),
    )

    for (ex, ey, ew, eh) in eyes:
        cv2.rectangle(face_color, (ex, ey), (ex + ew, ey + eh),
(0, 255, 0), 2)

cv2.imshow('face', img)
cv2.waitKey(0)
```

Figure 6.2 shows the output of the program, which includes the image of the `face1.jpeg` file and the face and the eyes detected in the image.

Figure 6.2: The image of the `face1.jpeg` file and the face and the eyes detected in the image

EXERCISE 6.3

Modify the Example 6.3 Python program, trying different images and commenting on the accuracy of the detections.

Example 6.4 shows a simple face, eye, and smile detection program by using OpenCV. It loads a face image from the file called `face2.jpeg` (`https://www.pexels.com/search/face/`). The smile detection is based on the `haarcascade_smile.xml` file.

EXAMPLE 6.4   THE `FACEEYESMILE.PY` PROGRAM

```python
#Example 6.4 OpenCV Face, Eye and Smile detection
import cv2
img = cv2.imread('face2.jpeg')
faceCascade = cv2.CascadeClassifier('haarcascade_frontalface_default
.xml')
eyeCascade = cv2.CascadeClassifier('haarcascade_eye.xml')
smileCascade = cv2.CascadeClassifier('haarcascade_smile.xml')

gray =cv2.cvtColor(img, cv2.COLOR_BGR2GRAY)
faces = faceCascade.detectMultiScale(
    gray,
    scaleFactor=1.3,
    minNeighbors=5,
    minSize=(30, 30)
)

for (x,y,w,h) in faces:
    cv2.rectangle(img,(x,y),(x+w,y+h),(255,255,0),2)
    cv2.putText(img,'face', (x + 10, y + 10), cv2.FONT_HERSHEY_
SIMPLEX, 1, (255,0,255), 2)
    face_gray = gray[y:y+h, x:x+w]
    face_color = img[y:y+h, x:x+w]

    eyes = eyeCascade.detectMultiScale(
        face_gray,
        scaleFactor= 1.1,
        minNeighbors=10,
        minSize=(10, 10),
    )

    for (ex, ey, ew, eh) in eyes:
        cv2.rectangle(face_color, (ex, ey), (ex + ew, ey + eh),
(0, 255, 0), 2)

    smile = smileCascade.detectMultiScale(
        face_gray,
        scaleFactor= 1.5,
        minNeighbors=5,
        minSize=(10, 10),
    )
```

```
     for (xx, yy, ww, hh) in smile:
          cv2.rectangle(face_color, (xx, yy), (xx + ww, yy + hh),
(0, 0, 255), 2)

cv2.imshow('face', img)
cv2.waitKey(0)
```

Figure 6.3 shows the output of the previous program, which shows the image of the face2.jpeg file and the face, the eyes, and the smile detected in the image.

Figure 6.3: The image of the face2.jpeg file and the face, the eyes, and the smile detected in the image

---

EXERCISE 6.4

Modify the Example 6.4 Python program, trying different images and commenting on the accuracy of the detections.

Example 6.5 is the webcam version of the previous face, eye, and smile detection program that uses OpenCV.

EXAMPLE 6.5   THE FACEEYESMILEWEBCAM.PY PROGRAM

```python
#Example 6.5 OpenCV Face, Eye and Smile detection with Webcam
import cv2

faceCascade = cv2.CascadeClassifier('haarcascade_frontalface_default
.xml')
eyeCascade = cv2.CascadeClassifier('haarcascade_eye.xml')
smileCascade = cv2.CascadeClassifier('haarcascade_smile.xml')


camera = cv2.VideoCapture(0)

while camera.isOpened():
    ok, frame = camera.read()
    if not ok:
        break
    gray =cv2.cvtColor(frame, cv2.COLOR_BGR2GRAY)
    faces = faceCascade.detectMultiScale(
        gray,
        scaleFactor=1.3,
        minNeighbors=5,
        minSize=(30, 30)
    )

    for (x,y,w,h) in faces:
        cv2.rectangle(frame,(x,y),(x+w,y+h),(255,255,0),2)
        cv2.putText(frame,'face', (x + 10, y + 10), cv2.FONT_HERSHEY_
SIMPLEX, 1, (255,0,255), 2)
        face_gray = gray[y:y+h, x:x+w]
        face_color = frame[y:y+h, x:x+w]

        eyes = eyeCascade.detectMultiScale(
            face_gray,
            scaleFactor= 1.1,
            minNeighbors=10,
            minSize=(10, 10),
        )

        for (ex, ey, ew, eh) in eyes:
            cv2.rectangle(face_color, (ex, ey), (ex + ew, ey + eh),
(0, 255, 0), 2)

        smile = smileCascade.detectMultiScale(
            face_gray,
            scaleFactor= 1.6,
            minNeighbors=5,
            minSize=(10, 10),
        )
```

```
            for (xx, yy, ww, hh) in smile:
                cv2.rectangle(face_color, (xx, yy), (xx + ww, yy + hh),
    (0, 0, 255), 2)


        cv2.imshow('face', frame)
        key = cv2.waitKey(30)
        if key == 27: # press 'ESC' to quit
            break

    camera.release()
    cv2.destroyAllWindows()
```

EXERCISE 6.5

Modify the previous Python program so that it read images from a video file. Hint: Modify `cv2.VideoCapture(0)` and replace 0 with the video filename.

Besides OpenCV, you can use many other libraries for face detection and face recognition. Among them, the Face_Recognition library (`https://github.com/ageitgey/face_recognition`) is probably the simplest and the most accurate way to perform face detection and face recognition. It is built on the well-known DLib library (`http://dlib.net/`). It not only can detect faces, it can also identify nine landmarks with 72 key points on face.

To use the Face_Recognition library, you need to install it first.

```
pip install face-recognition
```

See the following PyPi website for more details:

```
https://pypi.org/project/face-recognition/
```

Example 6.6 is a simple example of a face detection program using the Face_Recognition library. It uses the PIL library's `Image` function to read the image, as the Face_Recognition library needs the image in RGB format. Again, the image file `faces.jpeg` is from `https://www.pexels.com/search/face/`.

EXAMPLE 6.6   THE `FACEDETECT.PY` **PROGRAM**

```
#Example 6.6 Face detection by face_recognition library
from PIL import Image
import face_recognition

image = face_recognition.load_image_file("faces.jpg")
face_locations = face_recognition.face_locations(image)
```

```
count = 0
for face_location in face_locations:
    count = count + 1
    top, right, bottom, left = face_location
    print("Face {} Top: {}, Left: {}, Bottom: {}, Right: {}".
format(count, top, left, bottom, right))

    face_image = image[top:bottom, left:right]
    pil_image = Image.fromarray(face_image)
    pil_image.show()
```

Example 6.6a is the OpenCV version of the previous face detection program using the Face_Recognition library. As OpenCV reads the image file in BGR (blue, green, red) format, you need to convert it to RGB format first, before calling the Face_Recognition library functions.

EXAMPLE 6.6A   THE `FACEDETECT2.PY` **PROGRAM**

```
#Example 6.6a Face detection by face_recognition library
import cv2
import face_recognition

image = cv2.imread("faces.jpg")
cv2.imshow('photo', image)

rgb_frame = image[:, :, ::-1]   #Convert to RGB format
face_locations = face_recognition.face_locations(rgb_frame)

count = 0
for face_location in face_locations:
    count = count + 1
    top, right, bottom, left = face_location
    print("Face {} Top: {}, Left: {}, Bottom: {}, Right: {}"
.format(count, top, left, bottom, right))

    face_image = image[top:bottom, left:right]
    title = 'face' + str(count)
    cv2.imshow(title, face_image)

cv2.waitKey(0)
cv2.destroyAllWindows()
```

Figure 6.4 shows the original image of the `faces.jpg` file, and Figure 6.5 shows the corresponding faces detected in the image.

Figure 6.4: The original image of the `faces.jpg` file

Figure 6.5: The corresponding faces detected in the image of the `faces.jpg` file

---

EXERCISE 6.6

Modify the previous Python program, trying different images with multiple faces. Then run the program and comment on the accuracy.

Example 6.7 is an example that detects face landmarks by using the Face_Recognition library. It uses the OpenCV library to read and display the image from a file. It can detect nine face landmarks with 72 key points:

- chin
- left_eyebrow
- right_eyebrow
- nose_bridge
- nose_tip
- left_eye
- right_eye
- top_lip
- bottom_lip

EXAMPLE 6.7   THE FACEMARKS.PY PROGRAM

```
#Example 6.7 Face Landmarks detection by face_recognition library
import cv2
import face_recognition
```

```
image = cv2.imread("face1.jpeg")
cv2.imshow('photo', image)

rgb_frame = image[:, :, ::-1]
face_landmarks_list = face_recognition.face_landmarks(rgb_frame)
count = 0
for face_landmarks in face_landmarks_list:
    for facial_feature in face_landmarks.keys():
        print( facial_feature)
        a = face_landmarks[facial_feature]
        for index, item in enumerate(a):
            if index == len(a) -1:
                break
            cv2.line(image, item, a[index + 1], [0, 255, 0], 2)
        for pt in face_landmarks[facial_feature]:
            image = cv2.circle(image, pt, 2, (0, 0, 255), 2)
            count = count +1
            print(pt)

print(count)
cv2.imshow('Face Landmarks', image)
cv2.waitKey(0)
cv2.destroyAllWindows()
```

Figure 6.6 shows the output of the previous program, which shows the face landmark key points detected on the image of the `face1.jpeg` file.

Figure 6.6: The face landmark key points detected on the image of the `face1.jpeg` file

EXERCISE 6.7

Modify the previous Python program so that it uses the `print()` function to print out the face landmark names and the corresponding coordinate values.

Example 6.8 is the webcam version of the previous face landmarks detection program using the Face_Recognition library.

EXAMPLE 6.8   THE `FACEMARKSWEBCAM.PY` **PROGRAM**

```python
#Example 6.8 Face Landmarks detection by face_recognition library
using Webcam
import cv2
import face_recognition

# Get a reference to webcam
video_capture = cv2.VideoCapture(0)

# Initialize variables
face_locations = []

while True:
    # Grab a single frame of video
    ret, frame = video_capture.read()
    rgb_frame = frame[:, :, ::-1]
    face_landmarks_list = face_recognition.face_landmarks(rgb_frame)
    for face_landmarks in face_landmarks_list:
        for facial_feature in face_landmarks.keys():
            a = face_landmarks[facial_feature]
            for index, item in enumerate(a):
                if index == len(a) -1:
                    break
                cv2.line(frame, item, a[index + 1], [0, 255, 0], 2)
            for pt in face_landmarks[facial_feature]:
                frame = cv2.circle(frame, pt, 2, (0, 0, 255), 2)


    cv2.imshow('Face Landmarks', frame)

    # Hit 'q' on the keyboard to quit!
    if cv2.waitKey(1) & 0xFF == ord('q'):
        break

# Release handle to the webcam
video_capture.release()
cv2.destroyAllWindows()
```

EXERCISE 6.8

Modify the previous Python program so that it uses the `cv2.putText()` function to display the face landmark names at the corresponding positions on the webcam live images.

6.3   Face Recognition

Face recognition is a hot topic and has been increasingly used, from unlocking a phone such as with iPhone X's Face ID to granting employees entry to their offices such as at Baidu. There are several open source libraries for face recognition. We will be mainly focused on the Face_Recognition library and the OpenCV library.

6.3.1   Face Recognition with Face_Recognition

Example 6.9 is a face recognition program by using the Face_Recognition library. It uses a webcam to load the image. It can recognize three different faces. The three known faces are stored in three files, `face0.jpeg`, `face1.jpeg`, and `face2.jpeg`. The filenames are used as labels; they are `face0`, `face1`, and `face2`.

EXAMPLE 6.9   THE `FACERECWEBCAM.PY` **PROGRAM**

```
#Example 6.9 Face Recognition by face_recognition library using Webcam
import face_recognition
import cv2
import numpy as np

video_capture = cv2.VideoCapture(0)

face0_image = face_recognition.load_image_file("face0.jpeg")
face1_image = face_recognition.load_image_file("face1.jpeg")
face2_image = face_recognition.load_image_file("face2.jpeg")
face0_encoding = face_recognition.face_encodings(face0_image)[0]
face1_encoding = face_recognition.face_encodings(face1_image)[0]
face2_encoding = face_recognition.face_encodings(face2_image)[0]

# Create arrays of known face encodings and their names
known_face_encodings = [
    face0_encoding,
    face1_encoding,
    face2_encoding
]
```

```
known_face_names = [
    "Face 0",
    "Face 1",
    "Face 2"
]

while True:
    ret, frame = video_capture.read()
    rgb_frame = frame[:, :, ::-1]

    face_locations = face_recognition.face_locations(rgb_frame)
    face_encodings = face_recognition.face_encodings(rgb_frame,
face_locations)

    for (top, right, bottom, left), face_encoding in zip(face_
locations, face_encodings):
        matches = face_recognition.compare_faces(known_face_
encodings, face_encoding)
        name = "Unknown"
        face_distances = face_recognition.face_distance(known_face_
encodings, face_encoding)
        best_match_index = np.argmin(face_distances)
        if matches[best_match_index]:
            name = known_face_names[best_match_index]
        cv2.rectangle(frame, (left, top), (right, bottom), (0, 0,
255), 2)

        cv2.rectangle(frame, (left, bottom - 35), (right, bottom),
(0, 0, 255), cv2.FILLED)
        font = cv2.FONT_HERSHEY_DUPLEX
        cv2.putText(frame, name, (left + 6, bottom - 6), font, 1.0,
(255, 255, 255), 1)

    # Display the resulting image
    cv2.imshow('Video', frame)

    # Hit 'q' on the keyboard to quit!
    if cv2.waitKey(1) & 0xFF == ord('q'):
        break

# Release handle to the webcam
video_capture.release()
cv2.destroyAllWindows()
```

Figure 6.7 shows the output of the previous program. It shows the face recognized on the webcam image.

Figure 6.7: The face recognized on the webcam image

Example 6.9a is another version of the previous face recognition program that uses the Face_Recognition library. All the known images are saved in a directory specified by the `path` variable. It uses the `def getFaces(path)` function to go through all the files in the folder, collects all the faces and the labels, and saves them in the `faces` and `IDs` list variables.

EXAMPLE 6.9A   THE `FACEREC2.PY` **PROGRAM**

```
#Example 6.9a Face Recognition by face_recognition library using
Webcam
import face_recognition
import cv2
import numpy as np
import os


path='.'

def getFaces(path):
    imagepaths=[os.path.join(path,f) for f in os.listdir(path)]
    faces=[]
```

```
        IDs=[]
        count = 0
        for imagepath in imagepaths:
            if (os.path.split(imagepath)[-1].split('.')[1]!='jpeg'):
                continue
            print(imagepath)
            face_image = face_recognition.load_image_file(imagepath)
            face_encoding = face_recognition.face_encodings(face_image)[0]
            faces.append(face_encoding)
            ID=os.path.split(imagepath)[-1].split('.')[0]
            IDs.append(ID)
            count = count + 1
        return IDs,faces


known_face_names, known_face_encodings = getFaces(path)
print(known_face_names)
testpath = "face2.jpeg";

frame = cv2.imread(testpath)
rgb_frame = frame[:, :, ::-1]

face_locations = face_recognition.face_locations(rgb_frame)
face_encodings = face_recognition.face_encodings(rgb_frame, face_locations)

for (top, right, bottom, left), face_encoding in zip(face_locations,
face_encodings):
    matches = face_recognition.compare_faces(known_face_encodings,
face_encoding)
    name = "Unknown"
    face_distances = face_recognition.face_distance(known_face_
encodings, face_encoding)
    best_match_index = np.argmin(face_distances)
    if matches[best_match_index]:
        name = known_face_names[best_match_index]
    cv2.rectangle(frame, (left, top), (right, bottom), (0, 0, 255), 2)

    cv2.rectangle(frame, (left, bottom - 35), (right, bottom), (0, 0,
255), cv2.FILLED)
    font = cv2.FONT_HERSHEY_DUPLEX
    cv2.putText(frame, name, (left + 6, bottom - 6), font, 1.0, (255,
255, 255), 1)

# Display the resulting image
cv2.imshow('Video', frame)
cv2.waitKey(0)
cv2.destroyAllWindows()
```

The following is the text output, which shows the three known face image files used and their labels extracted from the names of the images.

```
.\face0.jpeg
.\face1.jpeg
.\face2.jpeg
['face0', 'face1', 'face2']
```

Figure 6.8 shows the webcam output of the previous program. It shows the face recognized on the webcam image.

Figure 6.8: The face recognized on the webcam image

Example 6.9b is the webcam version of the previous face recognition program. Again, all the known face images are saved in a directory specified by the `path` variable.

EXAMPLE 6.9B   THE `FACERECWEBCAM2.PY` **PROGRAM**

```
#Example 6.9b Face Recognition by face_recognition library using Webcam
import face_recognition
import cv2
import numpy as np
import os
```

```
path='.'

def getFaces(path):
    imagepaths=[os.path.join(path,f) for f in os.listdir(path)]
    faces=[]
    IDs=[]
    count = 0
    for imagepath in imagepaths:
        if (os.path.split(imagepath)[-1].split('.')[1]!='jpeg'):
            continue
        print(imagepath)
        face_image = face_recognition.load_image_file(imagepath)
        face_encoding = face_recognition.face_encodings(face_image)[0]
        faces.append(face_encoding)
        ID=os.path.split(imagepath)[-1].split('.')[0]
        IDs.append(ID)
        count = count + 1
    return IDs,faces


known_face_names, known_face_encodings = getFaces(path)
print(known_face_names)

video_capture = cv2.VideoCapture(0)
while True:
    ret, frame = video_capture.read()
    rgb_frame = frame[:, :, ::-1]

    face_locations = face_recognition.face_locations(rgb_frame)
    face_encodings = face_recognition.face_encodings(rgb_frame,
face_locations)

    for (top, right, bottom, left), face_encoding in zip(face_
locations, face_encodings):
        matches = face_recognition.compare_faces(known_face_
encodings, face_encoding)
        name = "Unknown"
        face_distances = face_recognition.face_distance(known_face_
encodings, face_encoding)
        best_match_index = np.argmin(face_distances)
        if matches[best_match_index]:
            name = known_face_names[best_match_index]
        cv2.rectangle(frame, (left, top), (right, bottom), (0, 0,
255), 2)

        cv2.rectangle(frame, (left, bottom - 35), (right, bottom),
(0, 0, 255), cv2.FILLED)
```

```
        font = cv2.FONT_HERSHEY_DUPLEX
        cv2.putText(frame, name, (left + 6, bottom - 6), font, 1.0,
(255, 255, 255), 1)

    # Display the resulting image
    cv2.imshow('Video', frame)

    # Hit 'q' on the keyboard to quit!
    if cv2.waitKey(1) & 0xFF == ord('q'):
        break

# Release handle to the webcam
video_capture.release()
cv2.destroyAllWindows()
```

6.3.2   Face Recognition with OpenCV

OpenCV also provides several methods for face recognition. You will need to install the opencv-contrib-python library first.

```
pip install opencv-contrib-python
```

To use OpenCV for face recognition, you need to do two steps: train the recognizer, and use the trained recognizer to recognize faces. Example 6.10 is a face recognition training program that uses the OpenCV library. Example 6.11 is a face recognizer program.

Example 6.10 trains three different faces by using the Local Binary Patterns Histograms Recognizer (LBPHFaceRecognizer) and saves the training result in a file called cvtraining.yml. The three known faces are stored in three files: face0.jpeg, face1.jpeg, and face2.jpeg. The filenames are used as labels; they are face0, face1, and face2.

EXAMPLE 6.10   THE FACERECCV.PY PROGRAM

```
#Example 6.10 Train a Face Recognition model with OpenCV

#pip install opencv-contrib-python
import os
import cv2
import numpy as np
import os

recognizer=cv2.face.LBPHFaceRecognizer_create()

imagePaths = ["face0.jpeg", "face1.jpeg", "face2.jpeg"]
```

```
faceCascade = cv2.CascadeClassifier('haarcascade_frontalface_default
.xml')
X = []
ids = []
count = 0
for imagePath in imagePaths:
    image = cv2.imread(imagePath)
    gray = cv2.cvtColor(image, cv2.COLOR_BGR2GRAY)
    img_numpy = np.array(gray,'uint8')
    faces = faceCascade.detectMultiScale(
        img_numpy ,
        scaleFactor=1.3,
        minNeighbors=10,
        minSize=(100, 100)
    )

    for (x,y,w,h) in faces:
        X.append(img_numpy[y:y+h,x:x+w])
        ids.append(count)
        print(ids)
        break
    count = count + 1

recognizer.train(X,np.array(ids))
recognizer.save('cvtraining.yml')
```

Example 6.11 is a face recognizer program that uses the OpenCV library. It loads the training data from a file called `cvtraining.yml` and recognizes different faces by using `LBPHFaceRecognizer`.

EXAMPLE 6.11   THE `FACERECCV2.PY` PROGRAM

```
#Example 6.11 Image Face Recognition with model trained in OpenCV

#pip install opencv-contrib-python
import os
import cv2
import numpy as np
import os

recognizer=cv2.face.LBPHFaceRecognizer_create()
recognizer.read('cvtraining.yml')

testpath = "face2.jpeg";

faceCascade = cv2.CascadeClassifier('haarcascade_frontalface_default
.xml')
image = cv2.imread(testpath)
gray = cv2.cvtColor(image, cv2.COLOR_BGR2GRAY)
```

```
img_numpy = np.array(gray,'uint8')
faces = faceCascade.detectMultiScale(
    img_numpy ,
    scaleFactor=1.3,
    minNeighbors=10,
    minSize=(100, 100)
)
for (x,y,w,h) in faces:
    id, confidence = recognizer.predict(gray[y:y+h,x:x+w])
    print(id)
    print(confidence)
```

The following is the output, which shows that the face ID is 2 and the confidence is 0. The confidence is more like an error here; the lower the value the better. A confidence between 0 and 50 normally means a perfect match.

```
2
0.0
```

For more information about face recognition using OpenCV, see the following:
`https://docs.opencv.org/2.4/modules/contrib/doc/facerec/facerec_tutorial.html`

EXERCISE 6.10

Modify the previous Python program, trying the different OpenCV face recognizers, such as EigenFaceRecognizer, FisherFaceRecognizer, **and** LBPHFaceRecognizer, **and comment on the accuracy.**

Example 6.12 is a webcam version of the previous face recognizer program that uses the OpenCV library. It loads the training data and recognizes different faces by using the LBPHFaceRecognizer function.

EXAMPLE 6.12   THE FACERECCVWEBCAM.PY PROGRAM

```
#Example 6.12 Webcam Face Recognition with model trained in OpenCV

import os
import cv2
import numpy as np
import os

recognizer=cv2.face.LBPHFaceRecognizer_create()
recognizer.read('cvtraining.yml')
```

```
faceCascade = cv2.CascadeClassifier('haarcascade_frontalface_default
.xml')

cam = cv2.VideoCapture(0)
font = cv2.FONT_HERSHEY_SIMPLEX

while True:

    ret, img =cam.read()
    gray = cv2.cvtColor(img, cv2.COLOR_BGR2GRAY)

    img_numpy = np.array(gray,'uint8')
    faces = faceCascade.detectMultiScale(
        img_numpy ,
        scaleFactor=1.3,
        minNeighbors=10,
        minSize=(100, 100)
    )
    for (x,y,w,h) in faces:
        cv2.rectangle(img, (x,y), (x+w,y+h), (0,255,0), 2)
        id, confidence = recognizer.predict(gray[y:y+h,x:x+w])
        print(confidence)
        cv2.putText(img, str(id), (x+5,y-5), font, 1, (255,255,255), 2)
        cv2.putText(img, str(int(confidence)), (x+5,y+h-5), font, 1,
(255,255,0), 1)

    cv2.imshow('camera',img)

    k = cv2.waitKey(10) & 0xff # Press 'ESC' for exiting video
    if k == 27:
        break

cam.release()
cv2.destroyAllWindows()
```

Figure 6.9 shows the output of the previous program. It shows the face recognized on the webcam image.

6.3.3   GUI-Based Face Recognition System

By using libraries such as PySimpleGUI, you can also develop a face recognition system with a graphical user interface (GUI). For more details about the PySimpleGUI library, visit this website:

```
https://pysimplegui.readthedocs.io/en/latest/
```

Figure 6.9: The face recognized on the webcam image

Example 6.13 shows an example of a complete, fully functional GUI-based face recognition system for student records. The face recognition is achieved by using OpenCV, and the GUI is achieved by using the PySimpleGUI library. You find the program in the `FaceRecSystem1` subdirectory in the Chapter 6 directory of the code that accompanies this book. It has the following file structures. The `data` directory is for storing face image files. The `database.txt` file is for storing the information of each student, such as ID, name, and course. The `FaceRecSystem1` `.py` file is the main Python program. The `haarcascade_frontalface_default` `.xml` file is the Haar cascade classifier for detecting frontal faces. The `Trainner` `.yml` file holds a trained `OpenCV` face recognizer model.

```
FaceRecSystem1\
    |--data
        |--perry.0.0.jpg
        |--perry.0.1.jpg
... ...
        |--tony.1.0.jpg
        |--tony.1.1.jpg
... ...
    |--database.txt
    |--FaceRecSystem1.py
    |--haarcascade_frontalface_default.xml
    |--Trainner.yml
```

In the `FaceRecSystem1.py` file, the `createImages` function takes an image frame from the webcam as input and then uses the OpenCV Haar cascade code to find and locate the faces and save the faces into the `data` directory. The face filenames have the following format: `name.ID.count.jpg`.

```
def createImages(frame,count):
... ...
```

This `writeDatabase()` function saves the student information such as the ID, name, and course into the `database.txt` file.

```
def writeDatabase(databaseFile,row):
... ...
```

This `getImagesAndLabels()` function goes through the `data` directory, gets all the face file images and their IDs, puts them into `faces` and `Id` list variables, and returns them.

```
def getImagesAndLabels(path):
... ...
```

This `Train()` function trains the `OpenCV` face recognizer using the `faces` and `Id` data and saves the trained model into a file called `Trainner.yml`.

```
def Train(path):
... ...
```

This `TrackImages()` function loads the trained model from the `Trainner.yml` file, detects the faces in the image, and uses the trained recognizer to recognize faces.

```
def TrackImages(frame):
... ...
```

`main()` is the main of the program. It first creates a GUI window by using the PySimpleGUI library, and then it uses a `while` loop to catch the window events, read images from the webcam, and perform the corresponding tasks.

```
def main():
... ...
```

This program is run in three simple steps through three buttons on the window:

1. **Register**: This allows you to detect faces in the webcam images, save the face images into files, and save the corresponding student information such as ID, name, and course into the `database.txt` file.

2. **Train**: This is to train the OpenCV face recognizer, such as LBPHFaceRecognizer, using the face image files and IDs, and save the trained model into the Trainner.yml file.

3. **Recognize**: This is to load the trained model from the Trainner.yml file, recognize faces, and display the corresponding information in the webcam live images.

Example 6.13 shows the complete code of the FaceRecSystem1.py file.

EXAMPLE 6.13   THE FACERECSYSTEM1.PY PROGRAM

```
#Example 6.13 Face Recognition System OpenCV
import cv2
import numpy as np
import PySimpleGUI as sg
import sys
import os
from PIL import Image
import pandas as pd
import csv

dataPath = "data"
databaseFile = "database.txt"

register = False
recognizeFrame = False
sampleNum = 20
name = ""
Id = ""
course = ""

faces=[]
Id =[]
# Local Binary Pattern Histogram is an Face Recognizer
recognizer = cv2.face.LBPHFaceRecognizer_create()
#recognizer = cv2.face.EigenFaceRecognizer_create()
#recognizer = cv2.face.FisherFaceRecognizer_create()

# creating detector for faces
detector = cv2.CascadeClassifier("haarcascade_frontalface_default.xml")

def createImages(frame,count):
    global dataPath,name,Id,detector
    gray = cv2.cvtColor(frame, cv2.COLOR_BGR2GRAY)
    faces = detector.detectMultiScale(gray, 1.3, 5)
    for (x, y, w, h) in faces:
        cv2.rectangle(frame, (x, y), (x + w, y + h), (255, 0, 0), 2)
```

```python
            cv2.imwrite(dataPath+"\\"+name +"."+Id +'.'+ str(count) +
".jpg", gray[y:y + h, x:x + w])
    return frame
def writeDatabase(databaseFile,row):
    #Create a student record file if does not exist
    if not os.path.exists(databaseFile):
        with open(databaseFile, 'a+') as csvFile:
            writer = csv.writer(csvFile)
            writer.writerow(["Id","Name","Course"])
        csvFile.close()
    with open(databaseFile, 'a+') as csvFile:
        writer = csv.writer(csvFile)
        writer.writerow(row)
    csvFile.close()
    return "Saved to database"
def getImagesAndLabels(path):
    imagePaths =[os.path.join(path, f) for f in os.listdir(path)]
    faces =[]
    Ids =[]
    for imagePath in imagePaths:
        extension = os.path.splitext(imagePath)[1]
        if extension != '.jpg':
            print(extension)
            continue
        pilImage = Image.open(imagePath).convert('L')
        imageNp = np.array(pilImage, 'uint8')
        Id = int(os.path.split(imagePath)[-1].split(".")[1])
        faces.append(imageNp)
        Ids.append(Id)
    return faces, Ids


def Train(path):
    global recognizer,detector
    faces, Id = getImagesAndLabels(path)
    recognizer.train(faces, np.array(Id))
    recognizer.save("Trainner.yml")
    return "Training finished..."


# For testing phase
def TrackImages(frame):
    global recognizer,detector
    recognizer.read("Trainner.yml")
    df = pd.read_csv(databaseFile,delimiter=',')
    font = cv2.FONT_HERSHEY_SIMPLEX
    gray = cv2.cvtColor(frame, cv2.COLOR_BGR2GRAY)
    faces = detector.detectMultiScale(gray, 1.2, 5)
    person = ""
    person_to_show = ""
    for(x, y, w, h) in faces:
```

```
            cv2.rectangle(frame, (x, y), (x + w, y + h), (225, 0, 0), 2)
            Id, conf = recognizer.predict(gray[y:y + h, x:x + w])
            #print("ID:" + str(Id) + " conf:" + str(conf))
            #print(df['Id'] )

            #If confidence is less than 100 ==>"0" perfect match
            if(conf < 50):
                person = df.loc[df['Id'] == Id]['Name'].values
                cr = df.loc[df['Id'] == Id]['Course'].values
                print(person)
                person = str(Id)+"-"+person+"-"+cr
            else:
                Id ='Unknown'
                person = str(Id)
            person = (str(person)+" " +str(int(conf))+"%")
            #cv2.putText(frame, person, (x, y + h),
            #            font, 1, (255, 255, 255), 2)
            if(conf < 50):
                person_to_show = person # only shows a recognized person,
useful when multiple faces are detected


    return frame, person_to_showcount = 0
def main():
    global register,sampleNum,dataPath,name,Id,course,recognizeFrame
    sg.ChangeLookAndFeel('LightGreen')

    # define the window layout
    leftpanel = [
                [sg.Text('Face Recognition', size=(20, 1),
justification='center', font='Helvetica 20',key='title')],
                [sg.Image(filename='', key='image')],
                ]
    rightpanel =[[sg.Text('Id:', size =(10, 1))],
                [sg.InputText("", key="Id")],
                [sg.Text('Name:', size =(10, 1))],
                [sg.InputText("", key="name")],
                [sg.Text('Course:', size =(10, 1))],
                [sg.InputText("", key="course")],
                [sg.Button('1.Register', size=(15, 1),
font='Helvetica 14')],
                [sg.Button('2.Train', size=(15, 1), font='Any 14')],
                [sg.Button('3.Recognize', size=(15, 1),
font='Helvetica 14')],
                ]
    layout = [
        [   sg.Column(leftpanel),
            sg.VSeperator(),
            sg.Column(rightpanel),
        ]
    ]
```

```python
        window = sg.Window('Face Recognition System',location=(100, 100))
        window.Layout(layout).Finalize()


    info =""
    cap = cv2.VideoCapture(0)
    while True:
        event, values = window.read(timeout=20, timeout_key='timeout')
        if event == sg.WIN_CLOSED:
            break
        elif event == '1.Register':
            register = True
            count = 0
        elif event == '2.Train':
            info = Train(dataPath)
        elif event == '3.Recognize':
            recognizeFrame = True

        name = values["name"]
        Id = values["Id"]
        course = values["course"]

        ret, frame = cap.read()

        if register:
            createImages(frame,count)
            info = "Saving "+str(count)
            count = count + 1
            if count > sampleNum:  # for each student, we take
multiple samples
                row = [Id, name,course]
                info = writeDatabase(databaseFile,row)
                register = False
        if recognizeFrame:
            frame,info =  TrackImages(frame)

        imgbytes = cv2.imencode('.png', frame)[1].tobytes()
        window['image'].update(data=imgbytes)
        window['title'].update(info)

    # Release the webcam and close the window
    cap.release()
    cv2.destroyAllWindows()
    window.close()

# Start the main program ==============
main()
```

Figure 6.10 and Figure 6.11 show the output of the previous GUI-based face recognition system program. Figure 6.10 shows the register step, and Figure 6.11 shows the recognize step.

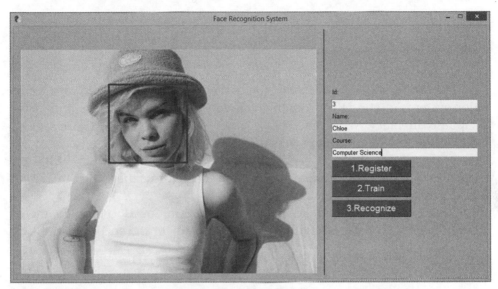

Figure 6.10: The GUI-based face recognition system program, register step

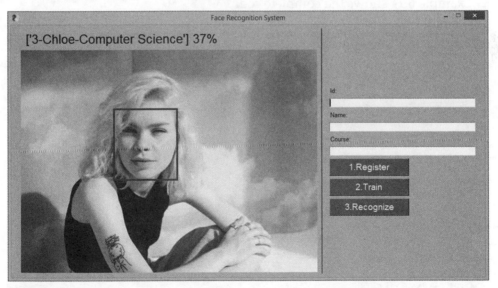

Figure 6.11: The GUI-based face recognition system program, recognize step

EXERCISE 6.11

Modify the previous Python program so that it also stores the address of the student.

For more details about the PySimpleGUI library, see the following:

```
https://pysimplegui.readthedocs.io/en/latest/
https://github.com/PySimpleGUI/PySimpleGUI
```

Example 6.14 shows another version of the previous GUI-based face recognition system. You find the program in the `FaceRecSystem2` subdirectory in the Chapter 6 directory.

This time the face recognition is achieved by using the Face_Recognition library. The GUI is still achieved by using the PySimpleGUI library. It has the same file structures and the same functions and performs the same three steps: register, update, and recognize.

The difference is in step 2, update, where you don't need to train the model anymore; instead, it uses the following function to get the encoding of all the faces and their IDs:

```
def getFaces(path):
... ...
```

Example 6.14 shows the complete code.

EXAMPLE 6.14   THE `FACERECSYSTEM2.PY` PROGRAM

```python
#Example 6.14 Face Recognition System face_recognition
#pip install face-recognition
import cv2
import numpy as np
import PySimpleGUI as sg
import sys
import os

import pandas as pd
import csv
import face_recognition

dataPath = "data"
databaseFile = "database.txt"

register = False
recognizeFrame = False
sampleNum = 1
name = ""
Id = ""
course = ""
```

```python
faces=[]
Id =[]
def getFaces(path):
    imagepaths=[os.path.join(path,f) for f in os.listdir(path)]
    faces=[]
    IDs=[]
    count = 0
    for imagepath in imagepaths:
        ext = os.path.split(imagepath)[-1].split('.')[-1]
        if (ext!='jpg'):
            continue

        face_image = face_recognition.load_image_file(imagepath)
        face_encoding = face_recognition.face_encodings(face_image)
        if len(face_encoding)<1:
            continue
        faces.append(face_encoding[0])
        ID=os.path.split(imagepath)[-1].split('.')[0]

        #Id = int(os.path.split(imagePath)[-1].split(".")[1])
        IDs.append(ID)
        count = count + 1
    print(IDs)
    return IDs,faces


def createImages(frame,count):
    global dataPath,name,Id
    rgb_frame = frame[:, :, ::-1]

    face_locations = face_recognition.face_locations(rgb_frame)
    face_encodings = face_recognition.face_encodings(rgb_frame,
face_locations)

    for (top, right, bottom, left), face_encoding in zip(face_
locations, face_encodings):
        cv2.imwrite(dataPath+"\\"+name +"."+Id +'.'+ str(count) +
".jpg", frame)
        cv2.rectangle(frame, (left, top), (right, bottom), (0, 0,
255), 2)
    return frame

def writeDatabase(databaseFile,row):
    #Create a student record file if does not exist
    if not os.path.exists(databaseFile):
        with open(databaseFile, 'a+') as csvFile:
            writer = csv.writer(csvFile)
            writer.writerow(["Id","Name","Course"])
        csvFile.close()
    with open(databaseFile, 'a+') as csvFile:
```

```python
        writer = csv.writer(csvFile)
        writer.writerow(row)
    csvFile.close()
    return "Saved to database"


# For testing phase
def recogImages(frame,known_face_names, known_face_encodings):
    global recognizer,detector
    rgb_frame = frame[:, :, ::-1]
    df = pd.read_csv(databaseFile,delimiter=',')
    face_locations = face_recognition.face_locations(rgb_frame)
    face_encodings = face_recognition.face_encodings(rgb_frame,
face_locations)
    name = "Unknown"
    for (top, right, bottom, left), face_encoding in zip(face_
locations, face_encodings):
        matches = face_recognition.compare_faces(known_face_
encodings, face_encoding)
        if (len(matches)<1):
            continue

        face_distances = face_recognition.face_distance(known_face_
encodings, face_encoding)
        best_match_index = np.argmin(face_distances)
        if matches[best_match_index]:
            name = known_face_names[best_match_index]
            cr = df.loc[df['Name'] == name]['Course'].values
            name = name + "-" + cr[0]
            print(name)

        cv2.rectangle(frame, (left, top), (right, bottom), (0, 0,
255), 2)
        cv2.rectangle(frame, (left, bottom - 35), (right, bottom),
(0, 0, 255), cv2.FILLED)
        font = cv2.FONT_HERSHEY_DUPLEX
        cv2.putText(frame, name, (left + 6, bottom - 6), font, 1.0,
(255, 255, 255), 1)
    return frame,name


count = 0
def main():
    global register,sampleNum,dataPath,name,Id,course,recognizeFrame
    sg.ChangeLookAndFeel('LightGreen')

    # define the window layout
    leftpanel = [
                [sg.Text('Face Recognition', size=(20, 1),
justification='center', font='Helvetica 20',key='title')],
                [sg.Image(filename='', key='image')],
                ]
```

```
      rightpanel =[[sg.Text('Id:', size =(10, 1))],
                   [sg.InputText("", key="Id")],
                   [sg.Text('Name:', size =(10, 1))],
                   [sg.InputText("", key="name")],
                   [sg.Text('Course:', size =(10, 1))],
                   [sg.InputText("", key="course")],
                  [sg.Button('1.Register', size=(15, 1), font='Helvetica
14')],
                   [sg.Button('2.Update', size=(15, 1), font='Any 14')],
                   [sg.Button('3.Recognize', size=(15, 1), font='Helvetica
14')],
                   ]
   layout = [
       [   sg.Column(leftpanel),
           sg.VSeperator(),
           sg.Column(rightpanel),
       ]
   ]
   window = sg.Window('Face Recognition System',location=(100, 100))
   window.Layout(layout).Finalize()

   known_face_names, known_face_encodings = getFaces(dataPath)

   info =""
   cap = cv2.VideoCapture(0)
   #frame = cv2.imread('./data/face 0.0.0.jpg')
   while True:
       event, values = window.read(timeout=20, timeout_key='timeout')
       if event == sg.WIN_CLOSED:
           break
       elif event == '1.Register':
           register = True
           count = 0
       elif event == '2.Update':
           known_face_names, known face_encodings = getFaces(dataPath)
           info = "Update done!"
       elif event == '3.Recognize':
           recognizeFrame = True

       name = values["name"]
       Id = values["Id"]
       course = values["course"]

       ret, frame = cap.read()

       if register:
           createImages(frame,count)
```

```
                        info = "Saving "+str(count)
                        count = count + 1
                        if count >= sampleNum:
                            row = [Id, name,course]
                            info = writeDatabase(databaseFile,row)
                            register = False
                if recognizeFrame:
                        frame,info =  recogImages(frame,known_face_names,
known_face_encodings)

                imgbytes = cv2.imencode('.png', frame)[1].tobytes()
                window['image'].update(data=imgbytes)
                window['title'].update(info)

        # Release the webcam and close the window
        cap.release()
        cv2.destroyAllWindows()
        window.close()

# Start the main program =============
main()
```

EXERCISE 6.12

Modify the previous Python program; instead of using `database.txt`, add another text box so that users can specify a filename.

Other GUI Development Libraries

Besides the PySimpleGUI library, there are several other GUI libraries for Python.

- **WxPython** is an open source Python interface that brings its wxWidgets cross-platform GUI library from its native C++ to Python.

  ```
  https://www.wxpython.org/
  https://www.tutorialspoint.com/wxpython/index.htm
  ```

- **Tkinter** is the Python interface to the Tk GUI toolkit shipped with Python.

  ```
  https://wiki.python.org/moin/TkInter
  https://docs.python.org/3/library/tkinter.html
  ```

- **JPython** is a Java implementation of Python that gives Python scripts seamless access to Java class libraries on the local machine.

  ```
  http://www.jython.org
  ```

- **PyQt** is a Python binding of the open source widget toolkit Qt, a popular C++ cross-platform application development framework.

  ```
  https://wiki.python.org/moin/PyQt
  https://www.guru99.com/pyqt-tutorial.html
  https://realpython.com/qt-designer-python/
  https://www.tutorialspoint.com/python/python_gui_programming.htm
  ```

- **Python GTK+ 3** provides Python bindings to GTK objects (windows, widgets, and so on).

  ```
  https://python-gtk-3-tutorial.readthedocs.io/en/latest/
  ```

- **Pyramid** is a simple web framework for Python.

  ```
  https://trypyramid.com/
  ```

- **Pywebview** is a lightweight cross-platform wrapper for displaying web HTML content in its own native GUI window.

  ```
  https://github.com/r0x0r/pywebview
  ```

- **Pyforms** is a Python 3 framework to develop applications for Desktop GUI, Terminal, and web environments.

  ```
  https://pyforms.readthedocs.io/en/latest/
  ```

6.3.4   Google FaceNet

Google's FaceNet (`https://github.com/davidsandberg/facenet`) has achieved state-of-the-art performances in face recognition by using *siamese* networks. Siamese networks have an architecture with two parallel neural networks, each taking a different input and whose outputs are combined to make predictions.

For more details about Google's FaceNet, see the following resources:

```
https://thedatamage.com/face-recognition-tensorflow-tutorial/
https://missinglink.ai/guides/tensorflow/tensorflow-
face-recognition-three-quick-tutorials/
https://machinelearningmastery.com/one-shot-learning-with-
siamese-networks-contrastive-and-triplet-loss-for-face-recognition/
https://github.com/davidsandberg/facenet
```

6.4   Age, Gender, and Emotion Detection

In this section we'll talk about age, gender, and emotion detection.

6.4.1   DeepFace

Another interesting application is age, gender, and emotion detection. The DeepFace repository is a cool library that allows you to use different deep learning models to detect faces, identify faces, verify and analyze faces, and get age, gender, race, and emotion information.

To use it, just install the library like so:

```
pip install deepface
```

Example 6.15 is a simple DeepFace demo example. It first shows how to detect faces in the image file `oldwoman.jpeg`; then shows how to verify two images, `face11a.jpeg` and `face11b.jpeg`, to see if they are the same person; and finally shows how to analyze image file `face10.jpeg` to get age, gender, race, and emotion information. Again, all the images are from `https://www.pexels.com/`.

EXAMPLE 6.15   THE `DEEPFACEDEMO.PY` **PROGRAM**

```python
#Example 6.15
from deepface import DeepFace


#Detect Faces =========================================================
detected_face = DeepFace.detectFace("oldwoman.jpeg")


#Verify images========================================================
result = DeepFace.verify("face11a.jpeg", "face11b.jpeg")
print("Is verified: ", result["verified"])


# Get age, gender, race, emotion ===================================
#from deepface import DeepFace
#demography = DeepFace.analyze("perry1.jpg") #passing nothing as 2nd
argument will find everything
#demography = DeepFace.analyze("face5.jpeg", ['age', 'gender', 'race',
'emotion']) #identical to the line above
demography = DeepFace.analyze("face10.jpeg") #passing nothing as 2nd
argument will find everything


print("Age: ", int(demography["age"]))
print("Emotion: ", demography["dominant_emotion"])
print("Gender: ", demography["gender"])
print("Race: ", demography["dominant_race"])
```

Figure 6.12 shows shows the original image from the `oldwoman.jpeg` file (left) and the face detected (right).

Figure 6.12: The original image from the `oldwoman.jpeg` file (left) and the face detected (right)

Figure 6.13 shows the two images `face11a.jpeg` and `face11b.jpeg` for verification to see if they are the same person.

Figure 6.13: The two images `face11a.jpeg` and `face11b.jpeg` for same-person verification

The following is the corresponding text output, which confirms that the `face11a.jpeg` and `face11b.jpeg` images are the same person.

```
Is verified:   True
```

Figure 6.14 shows `face10.jpeg`, which is the input file for age, gender, race, and emotion detection.

The following is the corresponding text output, which shows the age, gender, race, and emotion information from the `face10.jpeg` file:

```
Actions to do:   ['emotion', 'age', 'gender', 'race']

Finding actions:   0%|            | 0/4 [00:00<?, ?it/s]
Action: emotion:   0%|            | 0/4 [00:00<?, ?it/s]
```

```
Action: emotion:  25%|##5          | 1/4 [00:00<00:00,  3.34it/s]
Action: age:  25%|##5              | 1/4 [00:00<00:00,  3.34it/s]
Action: age:  50%|#####            | 2/4 [00:01<00:00,  2.09it/s]
Action: gender:  50%|#####         | 2/4 [00:01<00:00,  2.09it/s]
Action: gender:  75%|#######5      | 3/4 [00:02<00:00,  1.72it/s]
Action: race:  75%|#######5        | 3/4 [00:02<00:00,  1.72it/s]
Action: race: 100%|##########|       4/4 [00:02<00:00,  1.51it/s]
Action: race: 100%|##########|       4/4 [00:02<00:00,  1.39it/s]
Age:  29
Gender:  Woman
Emotion:  happy
Race:   asian
```

Figure 6.14: The `face10.jpeg` file for age, gender, race, and emotion detection

---

EXERCISE 6.13

Modify the previous Python program, try different photos for face detection, face identification, and age, gender, race, and emotion detection. Comment on the results.

You can also use this program with a webcam. It will read an image from the webcam; analyze image to get age, gender, race, and emotion information; then wait for five seconds and start again. It takes just one line of code! See Example 6.15a and Figure 6.15.

EXAMPLE 6.15A   THE `DEEPFACESTREAM.PY` **PROGRAM**

```
# https://github.com/serengil/deepface
# pip install deepface
#Example 6.15a Online Face Analysis with DeepFace

from deepface import DeepFace
DeepFace.stream(".")
```

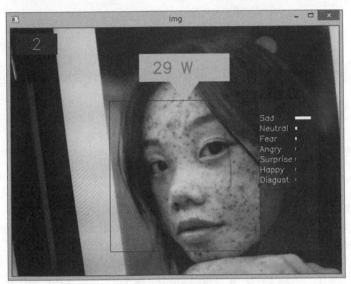

Figure 6.15: The webcam version of the previous program for age, gender, race, and emotion detection

For more details about the DeepFace library, see the following:
`https://github.com/serengil/deepface`

6.4.2   TCS-HumAIn-2019

The following repository is an interesting example of age, gender, emotion, and ethnicity detection. It is a submission for the TCS-HumAIn-2019 contest, which is organized by Tata Consultancy Services (TCS) (`https://www.tcs.com/`).

To use the code, just download the entire repository as a zipped file, as shown in Figure 6.16. By default, the zipped file is called `TCS-HumAIn-2019-Age-Emotions-Ethnicity-Gender-Predictions-Using-Computer-Vision-master.zip`. Just unzip the file into a folder; then from the terminal software, such as the Windows Command Prompt, go into the folder and run the following Python program:

```
Python data_preprocessing_and_model_training.py
```

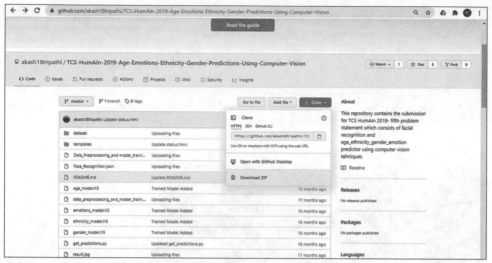

Figure 6.16: The TCS-HumAIn-2019-Age-Emotions-Ethnicity-Gender-Predictions-Using-Computer-Vision GitHub website

(Source: `https://github.com/akash18tripathi/TCS-HumAIn-2019-Age-Emotions-Ethnicity-Gender-Predictions-Using-Computer-Vision`)

This program will first download a range of training human face images of different age, gender, emotion, and ethnicity according to the `Face_Recognition.json` file and then use four different deep learning models to train on the data. The face images are reshaped to 70×70 pixels in size. Finally, save the trained models. There is also a Jupyter notebook version of the same code named `data_preprocessing_and_model_training.ipynb`.

After training, you can run the following program to perform age, gender, emotion, and ethnicity predictions:

```
Python get_predictions.py
```

However, there are two typos in the code, which set the face size to 25×25, on line 78:

```
image = img.load_img('face.jpg',target_size=(25,25))
```

as well as on line 82:

```
image = image.reshape(1,25,25,3)
```

You need to change 25 to 70 in those two places. This program will run the prediction through a web page using the Flask library, where you can upload an image, and it will give you the results. So you will need to install the Flask library first, as shown here, and it runs on TensorFlow version 1:

```
pip install flask
```

Example 6.15b is a revised version of the `get_predictions.py` program, which runs as a normal Python program, and can work for both TensorFlow version 1 and version 2.

EXAMPLE 6.15B   THE `GET_PREDICTIONS0.PY` PROGRAM

```
#Example 6.15b
#Modified from:
#https://github.com/akash18tripathi/TCS-HumAIn-2019-Age-Emotions-
Ethnicity-Gender-Predictions-Using-Computer-Vision/blob/master/get_
predictions.py

from tensorflow.keras.models import load_model
from PIL import Image
import numpy as np
import cv2
import tensorflow as tf
from tensorflow.keras.models import load_model
from tensorflow.keras.preprocessing import image as img
import cv2
import matplotlib.pyplot as plt

age_dict={
    0:'below_20',
    1:'20-30',
    2:'30-40',
    3:'40-50',
    4:'above_50'
}

gender_dict = {
    0:'Male',
    1:'Female'
}
ethnicity_dict={
    0:'arab',
    1:'asian',
    2:'black',
    3:'hispanic',
    4:'indian',
    5:'white'
}
emotion_dict={
    0:'angry',
    1:'happy',
    2:'neutral',
    3:'sad'
}
```

```
def predict(file):

    #image = img.load_img(file)
    #image = np.array(image,dtype='uint8')
    image = cv2.imread(file)

    gray = cv2.cvtColor(image,cv2.COLOR_BGR2GRAY)
    faces = face_cascade.detectMultiScale(gray,1.3,10)
    for (x,y,w,h) in faces:
        cv2.rectangle(image,(x,y),(x+w,y+h),(0,255,0),2)
        roi_color = image[y:y+h,x:x+w]
        roi_color = cv2.resize(roi_color, (70,70), interpolation =
cv2.INTER_AREA)
        face = np.array(roi_color,dtype='uint8')
        face = face/255
        face = face.reshape(1,70,70,3)
        #Predicting
        g_pred = gender_pred(face)
        e_pred = ethnicity_pred(face)
        a_pred = age_pred(face)
        emo_pred = emotions_pred(face)
        cv2.putText(image,"Age:"+str(a_pred),(x,y+h+20),cv2.FONT_
HERSHEY_SIMPLEX,0.8,(0,255,0),1,cv2.LINE_AA)
        cv2.putText(image,"Gender:  "+str(g_pred),(x,y+h+40),cv2
.FONT_HERSHEY_SIMPLEX,0.8,(0,255,0),1,cv2.LINE_AA)
        cv2.putText(image,"Emotion: "+str(emo_pred),(x,y+h+60),cv2
.FONT_HERSHEY_SIMPLEX,0.8,(0,255,0),1,cv2.LINE_AA)
        cv2.putText(image,"Ethnicity: "+str(e_pred),(x,y+h+80),cv2
.FONT_HERSHEY_SIMPLEX,0.8,(0,255,0),1,cv2.LINE_AA)
    cv2.imwrite('output.jpg',image)
    cv2.imshow('output',image)

def gender_pred(image):
        gen = gender_model.predict(image).argmax()
        return gender_dict[gen]


def emotions_pred(image):
        emotion = emotions_model.predict(image).argmax()
        return emotion_dict[emotion]


def ethnicity_pred(image):
        eth = ethnicity_model.predict(image).argmax()
        return ethnicity_dict[eth]

def age_pred(image):
        age = age_model.predict(image).argmax()
        return age_dict[age]
```

```
ethnicity_model = load_model('ethnicity_model.h5')
gender_model = load_model('gender_model.h5')
age_model = load_model('age_model.h5')
emotions_model = load_model('emotions_model.h5')
face_cascade = cv2.CascadeClassifier('haarcascade_frontalface_
default.xml')

file = 'image2.jpeg'
predict(file)
```

Figure 6.17 shows the output of the previous program, which predicts age, gender, race, and emotion. As you can see, it is pretty accurate.

Figure 6.17: The output of the `get_predictions0.py` program

EXERCISE 6.14

Modify the previous Python program, and try different photos for age, gender, race, and emotion detection. Comment on the results.

6.5   Face Swap

Face swap is a controversial but popular AI application, which allows you to swap faces in photos and videos. There are already many apps that implement face swap, such as Snapchat, B612, Cupace, Face Swap by Microsoft, Face App, Face Swap, MSQRD, Face Swap Booth, MixBooth, and so on. The Face Swap Live app can even allow you to swap faces in real time in live videos. The simplest way to achieve this is to use the Face_Recognition and OpenCV libraries.

6.5.1 Face_Recognition and OpenCV

Example 6.16 shows a face swap example, which is modified from `https://github.com/spmallick/learnopencv/blob/master/FaceSwap/faceSwap.py`. It basically loads images from two image files, `face0.jpeg` and `face1.jpeg`, and detects and locates the faces by using the Face_Recognition library; this includes finding the face landmarks. Then it masks the face in the `face0.jpeg` file and blends it into the face location of the `face1.jpeg` file.

EXAMPLE 6.16 THE `FACESWAP.PY` PROGRAM

```python
#Example 6.16 Face Swap with OpenCV and Face_Recognition
#Modified from:
#https://github.com/spmallick/learnopencv/blob/master/FaceSwap/
faceSwap.py
import sys
import numpy as np
import cv2
import face_recognition

# Read points from text file
def readPoints(path) :
    # Create an array of points.
    points = [];


    image = cv2.imread(path)


    rgb_frame = image[:, :, ::-1]
    face_landmarks_list = face_recognition.face_landmarks(rgb_frame)
    for face_landmarks in face_landmarks_list:
        for facial_feature in face_landmarks.keys():
            #print( facial_feature)
            a = face_landmarks[facial_feature]
            for index, item in enumerate(a):
                if index == len(a) -1:
                    break
                cv2.line(image, item, a[index + 1], [0, 255, 0], 2)
            for pt in face_landmarks[facial_feature]:
                image = cv2.circle(image, pt, 2, (0, 0, 255), 2)
                points.append(pt)
    cv2.imshow(path, image)
```

```
        print(points)
        return points


# Apply affine transform calculated using srcTri and dstTri to src and
# output an image of size.
def applyAffineTransform(src, srcTri, dstTri, size) :

    # Given a pair of triangles, find the affine transform.
    warpMat = cv2.getAffineTransform( np.float32(srcTri),
np.float32(dstTri) )

    # Apply the Affine Transform just found to the src image
    dst = cv2.warpAffine( src, warpMat, (size[0], size[1]), None,
flags=cv2.INTER_LINEAR, borderMode=cv2.BORDER_REFLECT_101 )

    return dst


# Check if a point is inside a rectangle
def rectContains(rect, point) :
    if point[0] < rect[0] :
        return False
    elif point[1] < rect[1] :
        return False
    elif point[0] > rect[0] + rect[2] :
        return False
    elif point[1] > rect[1] + rect[3] :
        return False
    return True


#calculate delanauy triangle
def calculateDelaunayTriangles(rect, points):
    #create subdiv
    subdiv = cv2.Subdiv2D(rect);

    # Insert points into subdiv
    for p in points:
        subdiv.insert(p)

    triangleList = subdiv.getTriangleList();

    delaunayTri = []

    pt = []

    for t in triangleList:
        pt.append((t[0], t[1]))
        pt.append((t[2], t[3]))
        pt.append((t[4], t[5]))
```

```
            pt1 = (t[0], t[1])
            pt2 = (t[2], t[3])
            pt3 = (t[4], t[5])

            if rectContains(rect, pt1) and rectContains(rect, pt2) and
rectContains(rect, pt3):
                ind = []
                #Get face-points (from 68 face detector) by coordinates
                for j in range(0, 3):
                    for k in range(0, len(points)):
                        if(abs(pt[j][0] - points[k][0]) < 1.0 and
abs(pt[j][1] - points[k][1]) < 1.0):
                            ind.append(k)
                # Three points form a triangle. Triangle array
corresponds to the file tri.txt in FaceMorph
                if len(ind) == 3:
                    delaunayTri.append((ind[0], ind[1], ind[2]))

            pt = []


    return delaunayTri



# Warps and alpha blends triangular regions from img1 and img2 to img
def warpTriangle(img1, img2, t1, t2) :

    # Find bounding rectangle for each triangle
    r1 = cv2.boundingRect(np.float32([t1]))
    r2 = cv2.boundingRect(np.float32([t2]))

    # Offset points by left top corner of the respective rectangles
    t1Rect = []
    t2Rect = []
    t2RectInt = []

    for i in range(0, 3):
        t1Rect.append(((t1[i][0] - r1[0]),(t1[i][1] - r1[1])))
        t2Rect.append(((t2[i][0] - r2[0]),(t2[i][1] - r2[1])))
        t2RectInt.append(((t2[i][0] - r2[0]),(t2[i][1] - r2[1])))


    # Get mask by filling triangle
    mask = np.zeros((r2[3], r2[2], 3), dtype = np.float32)
    cv2.fillConvexPoly(mask, np.int32(t2RectInt), (1.0, 1.0, 1.0), 16, 0);
```

```python
        # Apply warpImage to small rectangular patches
        img1Rect = img1[r1[1]:r1[1] + r1[3], r1[0]:r1[0] + r1[2]]
        #img2Rect = np.zeros((r2[3], r2[2]), dtype = img1Rect.dtype)

        size = (r2[2], r2[3])

        img2Rect = applyAffineTransform(img1Rect, t1Rect, t2Rect, size)

        img2Rect = img2Rect * mask

        # Copy triangular region of the rectangular patch to the output
image
        img2[r2[1]:r2[1]+r2[3], r2[0]:r2[0]+r2[2]] = img2[r2[1]:r2[1]+r2[3],
r2[0]:r2[0]+r2[2]] * ( (1.0, 1.0, 1.0) - mask )

        img2[r2[1]:r2[1]+r2[3], r2[0]:r2[0]+r2[2]] = img2[r2[1]:r2[1]+r2[3],
r2[0]:r2[0]+r2[2]] + img2Rect


if __name__ == '__main__' :

    # Make sure OpenCV is version 3.0 or above
    (major_ver, minor_ver, subminor_ver) = (cv2.__version__).split('.')

    if int(major_ver) < 3 :
        print >>sys.stderr, 'ERROR: Script needs OpenCV 3.0 or higher'
        sys.exit(1)

    # Read images
    filename1 = 'face1.jpeg'
    filename2 = 'face2.jpeg'

    img1 = cv2.imread(filename1);
    img2 = cv2.imread(filename2);
    img1Warped = np.copy(img2);

    # Read array of corresponding points
    points1 = readPoints(filename1 )
    points2 = readPoints(filename2 )

    # Find convex hull
    hull1 = []
    hull2 = []

    hullIndex = cv2.convexHull(np.array(points2), returnPoints = False)
```

```
for i in range(0, len(hullIndex)):
    hull1.append(points1[int(hullIndex[i])])
    hull2.append(points2[int(hullIndex[i])])


# Find Delanauy Triangulation for convex hull points
sizeImg2 = img2.shape
rect = (0, 0, sizeImg2[1], sizeImg2[0])

dt = calculateDelaunayTriangles(rect, hull2)

if len(dt) == 0:
    quit()

# Apply affine transformation to Delaunay triangles
for i in range(0, len(dt)):
    t1 = []
    t2 = []

    #get points for img1, img2 corresponding to the triangles
    for j in range(0, 3):
        t1.append(hull1[dt[i][j]])
        t2.append(hull2[dt[i][j]])

    warpTriangle(img1, img1Warped, t1, t2)


# Calculate Mask
hull8U = []
for i in range(0, len(hull2)):
    hull8U.append((hull2[i][0], hull2[i][1]))

mask = np.zeros(img2.shape, dtype = img2.dtype)

cv2.fillConvexPoly(mask, np.int32(hull8U), (255, 255, 255))

r = cv2.boundingRect(np.float32([hull2]))

center = ((r[0]+int(r[2]/2), r[1]+int(r[3]/2)))


# Clone seamlessly.
output = cv2.seamlessClone(np.uint8(img1Warped), img2, mask, center,
cv2.NORMAL_CLONE)

cv2.imshow("Face Swapped", output)
cv2.waitKey(0)

cv2.destroyAllWindows()
```

The program outputs the 72 face landmark key points of the two images.

```
 [(162, 194), (163, 216), (166, 239), (171, 261), (178, 282), (191, 300),
(206, 316), (223, 330), (243, 334), (263, 331), (282, 319), (298, 305),
(311, 290), (320, 271), (324, 250), (328, 228), (329, 206), (175, 171),
(189, 165), (204, 166), (218, 170), (231, 178), (266, 179), (279, 174),
(294, 173), (308, 174), (319, 181), (248, 199), (247, 216), (247, 234),
(247, 251), (231, 258), (238, 262), (246, 265), (254, 263), (261, 259),
(192, 195), (202, 190), (215, 191), (225, 202), (213, 203), (200, 202),
(270, 204), (280, 195), (293, 195), (303, 202), (294, 207), (281, 207),
(215, 286), (227, 281), (237, 278), (246, 281), (254, 279), (264, 282),
(276, 287), (270, 288), (254, 287), (245, 288), (237, 287), (221, 287),
(276, 287), (265, 298), (254, 302), (245, 302), (236, 301), (226, 296),
(215, 286), (221, 287), (237, 288), (245, 289), (254, 289), (270, 288)]
 [(127, 306), (131, 330), (136, 354), (144, 378), (155, 399), (172, 417),
(192, 433), (216, 445), (243, 444), (270, 434), (291, 416), (310, 393),
(322, 369), (327, 341), (325, 312), (321, 285), (315, 258), (131, 286),
(137, 271), (153, 266), (170, 266), (187, 270), (223, 262), (239, 251),
(256, 244), (274, 243), (290, 248), (208, 282), (211, 300), (214, 318),
(218, 336), (202, 351), (212, 352), (223, 352), (233, 347), (243, 342),
(152, 298), (161, 289), (174, 287), (186, 291), (176, 297), (163, 300),
(237, 279), (247, 269), (260, 267), (270, 270), (263, 276), (251, 279),
(193, 387), (206, 379), (218, 374), (228, 374), (239, 369), (255, 368),
(270, 366), (265, 369), (241, 376), (229, 380), (220, 381), (198, 387),
(270, 366), (259, 379), (246, 389), (234, 393), (223, 395), (210, 395),
(193, 387), (198, 387), (221, 381), (231, 379), (242, 375), (265, 369)]
```

Figure 6.18 shows the first input face image from the `face0.jpeg` file. Figure 6.19 shows the second input face image from the `face1.jpeg` file. Figure 6.20, the output image, shows the `face1.jpeg` file image with the face swapped with the `face0.jpeg` face. The face swap result is impressive; it even re-aligns the swapped face accordingly.

EXERCISE 6.15

Modify the previous Python program, trying different photos for the face swap. Comment on the results.

6.5.2   Simple_Faceswap

Here is another interesting face swap Python repository (`https://github.com/Jacen789/simple_faceswap`), which uses Dlib to get 68 face landmarks and uses OpenCV to perform the face swap on live video images from a webcam. Example 6.17 is a revised version of the program.

Figure 6.18: The first face image from the `face0.jpeg` file

Figure 6.19: The second face image from the `face1.jpeg` file

Figure 6.20: The `face1.jpeg` file image with the face swapped with the `face0.jpeg` face

Example 6.17 is the main program `FaceSwap2.py`. It uses a file called `face1.jpeg` as the face template, detects the face in the webcam image, and swaps the webcam face with the template face.

EXAMPLE 6.17   THE `FACESWAP2.PY` PROGRAM

```
#Example 6.17 Face Swap with dlib and OpenCV
#Modified from:
#https://raw.githubusercontent.com/Jacen789/simple_faceswap/master/
faceswap.py


#pip install opencv-python, dlib
#Download dlib face landmarks detection model:shape_predictor_68_
face_landmarks.dat.bz2
#and unzip it
#http://dlib.net/files/shape_predictor_68_face_landmarks.dat.bz2


import os
import cv2
import dlib
import numpy as np
from FaceSwap_Utils import * # see Example 6.17b
```

```python
here = os.path.dirname(os.path.abspath(__file__))

models_folder_path = os.path.join(here)
faces_folder_path = os.path.join(here)
predictor_path = os.path.join(models_folder_path, 'shape_
predictor_68_face_landmarks.dat')
image_face_path = os.path.join(faces_folder_path, 'face1.jpeg')

detector = dlib.get_frontal_face_detector()
predictor = dlib.shape_predictor(predictor_path)



def main():
    im1 = cv2.imread(image_face_path)
    im1 = cv2.resize(im1, (600, im1.shape[0] * 600 // im1.shape[1]))
    landmarks1 = get_face_landmarks(im1, detector, predictor)  # 68_
face_landmarks
    if landmarks1 is None:
        print('{}:Face not detected'.format(image_face_path))
        exit(1)
    im1_size = get_image_size(im1)
    im1_mask = get_face_mask(im1_size, landmarks1)

    cam = cv2.VideoCapture(0)
    while True:
        ret_val, im2 = cam.read()  # camera_image
        landmarks2 = get_face_landmarks(im2, detector, predictor)  #
68_face_landmarks
        if landmarks2 is not None:
            im2_size = get_image_size(im2)
            im2_mask = get_face_mask(im2_size, landmarks2)

            affine_im1 = get_affine_image(im1, im2, landmarks1,
landmarks2)
            affine_im1_mask = get_affine_image(im1_mask, im2,
landmarks1, landmarks2)

            union_mask = get_mask_union(im2_mask, affine_im1_mask)


            affine_im1 = skin_color_adjustment(affine_im1, im2,
mask=union_mask)
            point = get_mask_center_point(affine_im1_mask)
            seamless_im = cv2.seamlessClone(affine_im1, im2,
mask=union_mask, p=point, flags=cv2.NORMAL_CLONE)
            cv2.imshow('seamless_im', seamless_im)
        else:
            cv2.imshow('seamless_im', im2)
        if cv2.waitKey(1) == 27:
```

```
            break
    cv2.destroyAllWindows()


if __name__ == '__main__':
    main()
```

Example 6.17 makes use of the FaceSwap_Utils package, shown in Example 6.17a.

EXAMPLE 6.17A   THE FACESWAP_UTILS.PY **PROGRAM**

```
#Example 6.17a FaceSwap_Utils for Example 6.17a
#Modified from:
#https://raw.githubusercontent.com/Jacen789/simple_faceswap/master/
faceswap.py

import os
import cv2
import dlib
import numpy as np

def get_image_size(image):
    """
    :param image: image
    :return: (height,width)
    """
    image_size = (image.shape[0], image.shape[1])
    return image_size


def get_face_landmarks(image, face_detector, shape_predictor):
    """
    Get face landmark, 68 key points
    :param image: image
    :param face_detector: dlib.get_frontal_face_detector
    :param shape_predictor: dlib.shape_predictor
    :return: np.array([[],[]]), 68 key points
    """
    dets = face_detector(image, 1)
    num_faces = len(dets)
    if num_faces == 0:
        print("Sorry, there were no faces found.")
        return None
    shape = shape_predictor(image, dets[0])
    face_landmarks = np.array([[p.x, p.y] for p in shape.parts()])
    return face_landmarks
```

```python
def get_face_mask(image_size, face_landmarks):
    """
    Get Face Mask
    :param image_size: Image Size
    :param face_landmarks: 68 key points
    :return: image_mask, Face Mask
    """
    mask = np.zeros(image_size, dtype=np.uint8)
    points = np.concatenate([face_landmarks[0:16],
face_landmarks[26:17:-1]])
    cv2.fillPoly(img=mask, pts=[points], color=255)

    # mask = np.zeros(image_size, dtype=np.uint8)
    # points = cv2.convexHull(face_landmarks)  # 凸包
    # cv2.fillConvexPoly(mask, points, color=255)
    return mask


def get_affine_image(image1, image2, face_landmarks1,
face_landmarks2):
    """
    Get Affine Image
    :param image1: Image 1
    :param image2: Image 2
    :param face_landmarks1: Image 1 face landmarks
    :param face_landmarks2: Image 2 face landmarks
    :return: The Affine Image 1
    """
    three_points_index = [18, 8, 25]
    M = cv2.getAffineTransform(face_landmarks1[three_points_index].
astype(np.float32),
                               face_landmarks2[three_points_index].
astype(np.float32))
    dsize = (image2.shape[1], image2.shape[0])
    affine_image = cv2.warpAffine(image1, M, dsize)
    return affine_image.astype(np.uint8)


def get_mask_center_point(image_mask):
    """
    Get Mask Center Point
    :param image_mask: Image mask
    :return: center point
    """
    image_mask_index = np.argwhere(image_mask > 0)
    miny, minx = np.min(image_mask_index, axis=0)
    maxy, maxx = np.max(image_mask_index, axis=0)
    center_point = ((maxx + minx) // 2, (maxy + miny) // 2)
    return center_point
```

```
def get_mask_union(mask1, mask2):
    """
    Get Mask Union
    :param mask1: mask_image, Mask 1
    :param mask2: mask_image, Mask 2
    :return: The union of two masks
    """
    mask = np.min([mask1, mask2], axis=0)
    mask = ((cv2.blur(mask, (5, 5)) == 255) * 255).astype(np.uint8)
    mask = cv2.blur(mask, (3, 3)).astype(np.uint8)
    return mask


def skin_color_adjustment(im1, im2, mask=None):
    """
    Skin Color Adjustment
    :param im1: Image 1
    :param im2: Image 2
    :param mask: Face mask.
    :return: Adjusted Image 1
    """
    if mask is None:
        im1_ksize = 55
        im2_ksize = 55
        im1_factor = cv2.GaussianBlur(im1, (im1_ksize, im1_ksize),
0).astype(np.float)
        im2_factor = cv2.GaussianBlur(im2, (im2_ksize, im2_ksize),
0).astype(np.float)
    else:
        im1_face_image = cv2.bitwise_and(im1, im1, mask=mask)
        im2_face_image = cv2.bitwise_and(im2, im2, mask=mask)
        im1_factor = np.mean(im1_face_image, axis=(0, 1))
        im2_factor = np.mean(im2_face_image, axis=(0, 1))

    im1 = np.clip((im1.astype(np.float) * im2_factor / np.clip(im1_
factor, 1e-6, None)), 0, 255).astype(np.uint8)
    return im1
```

Figure 6.21 shows the webcam output of Example 6.17, which shows the face in the webcam has been swapped.

EXERCISE 6.16

Modify the previous Python program, choosing a different file template for the face swap. Comment on the results.

Figure 6.21: The webcam output of Example 6.17, which shows the face has been swapped

6.5.3 DeepFaceLab

In computer science, a *deepfake* means to use deep learning neural networks to generate fake images. This is often done by training the deep learning neural network models with a large quantity of face images of two people to learn the features and to swap the faces. Deepfakes are highly controversial and have attracted widespread attention for their uses in pornography, celebrity photos/videos, fake news, hoaxes, and so on.

DeepFaceLab claims to be the leading software for creating deepfakes. With DeepFaceLab, you can replace the face or head, de-age the face, or even manipulate someone's lips. It even created a realistic fake Queen Speech in 2020 that broadcast on Channel 4 in the United Kingdom. See the following link for more details.

```
https://github.com/iperov/DeepFaceLab
```

For more details about DeepFaceLab, see the following:

```
https://arxiv.org/abs/2005.05535
```

Here are other Python face swap repositories:

```
https://awesomeopensource.com/project/deepfakes/faceswap
https://faceswap.dev/
https://github.com/topics/faceswap
```

6.6 Face Detection Web Apps

With the Streamlit library (`https://docs.streamlit.io/en/stable/`) you can develop a web-based app for face detection.

Example 6.18 shows how to create a web app to perform face detection. It first allows users to upload an image file and then performs face detection by clicking the Detect Faces button.

EXAMPLE 6.18   THE `STREAMLITFACE.PY` **PROGRAM**

```
#Example 6.18 Face Detection web app with Streamlit
#pip install --upgrade protobuf
#pip install streamlit

import streamlit as st
import cv2
from PIL import Image
import numpy as np

face_cascade = cv2.CascadeClassifier('haarcascade_frontalface_
default.xml')


def detect_faces(our_image):
        new_img = np.array(our_image.convert('RGB'))
        img = cv2.cvtColor(new_img,1)
        gray = cv2.cvtColor(new_img, cv2.COLOR_BGR2GRAY)
        # Detect faces
        faces = face_cascade.detectMultiScale(gray, 1.1, 4)
        # Draw rectangle around the faces
        for (x, y, w, h) in faces:
            cv2.rectangle(img, (x, y), (x+w, y+h), (255, 0, 0), 2)
        return img,faces

def main():
        st.title("Face Detection")
        st.text("Built with Streamlit and OpenCV")

        image_file = st.file_uploader("Upload Image",type=['jpg','jpeg',
'png','gif'])

        if image_file is not None:
            our_image = Image.open(image_file)
            st.text("Original Image")
            st.image(our_image)

        if st.button("Detect Faces"):
            result_img,result_faces = detect_faces(our_image)
            st.image(result_img)
            st.success("Found {} faces".format(len(result_faces)))

if __name__ == '__main__':
    main()
```

To run it, just type the following command in a Command Prompt window:

```
streamlit run StreamlitFace.py
```

Figure 6.22 shows the output results.

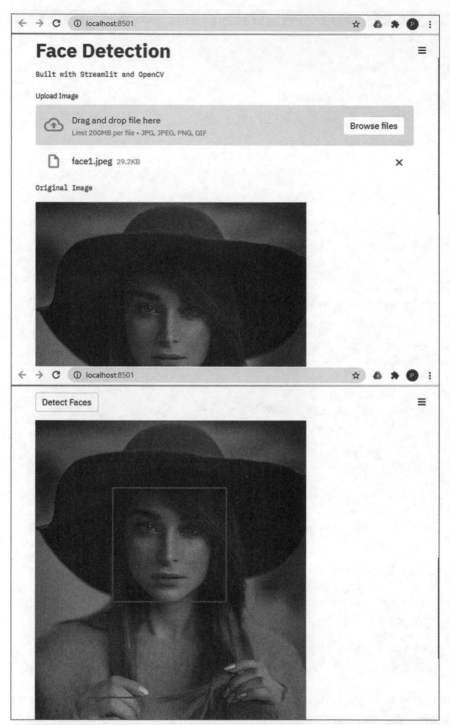

Figure 6.22: The output of the `StreamlitFace.py` program, which shows the original image of a file (top) and a face detected in the image (bottom)

EXERCISE 6.17

Modify the previous Python program, adding another Save Face button that, when clicked, will save the face-detected image into a file.

Example 6.19 is a webcam-based version of Example 6.18. It also has three slider bars to allow users to adjust the `scaleFactor`, `minNeighbours`, and `minSize` parameters. Those parameters will affect the results and accuracy of the face detection. This example allows you to work on both a webcam file or a video file. You can comment and uncomment the corresponding lines, `return cv2.VideoCapture(0)` and `return cv2.VideoCapture('Roller Coaster.mp4')`. Here `Roller Coaster.mp4` is a video clip you can download from this location:

https://www.pexels.com/video/roller-coaster-852415/

EXAMPLE 6.19 THE `STREAMLITWEBFACE.PY` PROGRAM

```
#Example 6.19 Face Detection in webcam - web app with Streamlit
#pip install --upgrade protobuf
#pip install streamlit

import streamlit as st
import cv2

cascade_classifier = cv2.CascadeClassifier('haarcascade_frontalface_
default.xml')


@st.cache(allow_output_mutation=True)
def get_cap():
    #from webcam
#    return cv2.VideoCapture(0)
    #from a video file
    return cv2.VideoCapture('Roller Coaster.mp4')


cap = get_cap()

frameST = st.empty()
st.title("Face Detection")
st.text("Built with Streamlit and OpenCV")

scale=st.sidebar.slider('Scale Factor:', 1.0, 2.0, 1.3)
mn=st.sidebar.slider('minNeighbors:', 5, 20, 5)
msize=st.sidebar.slider('minSize:', 10, 200, 30)

while True:
    ret, frame = cap.read()
    # Stop the program if reached end of video
```

```
        if not ret:
            cv2.waitKey(3000)
            cap.release()
            break

        gray_img=cv2.cvtColor(frame, cv2.COLOR_BGR2GRAY)
        faces= cascade_classifier.detectMultiScale(gray_img,
                                            scaleFactor=scale,
                                            minNeighbors=mn,
                                            minSize=(msize, msize)
        )

        for (x,y,w,h) in faces:
            cv2.rectangle(frame,(x,y),(x+w,y+h),(255,255,0),2)
            cv2.putText(frame,'face', (x + 10, y + 10), cv2.FONT_HERSHEY_
SIMPLEX, 1, (255,0,255), 2)


        frameST.image(frame, channels="BGR")
```

To run it, just type the following command in a Command Prompt window:

```
streamlit run StreamlitWebcamFace.py
```

Figure 6.23 shows the output of the previous program, which shows the face detection in the `Roller Coaster.mp4` video clip. There are the three sliders for adjusting the `scaleFactor`, `minNeighbours`, and `minSize` parameters, and with a face detected in the image.

Figure 6.23: The output of the `StreamlitWebcamFace.py` program, which shows the three sliders for adjusting the `scaleFactor`, `minNeighbours`, and `minSize` parameters, and with a face detected in the image

EXERCISE 6.18

Modify the previous Python program, adding another Save Face button that, when clicked, will save the webcam image into a file.

Example 6.20 is a webcam-based beauty web app. It also has slider bars to allow users to adjust different parameters of a live feed from the webcam.

EXAMPLE 6.20   THE STREAMLITWEBCAMBEAUTY **PROGRAM**

```python
#Example 6.20 Webcam Beautify web app with Streamlit
#pip install --upgrade protobuf
#pip install streamlit

from PIL import Image
from PIL import ImageEnhance
import streamlit as st
import cv2
import numpy as np
import pandas as pd


@st.cache(allow_output_mutation=True)
def get_cap():
    return cv2.VideoCapture(0)


brightness = 1.5
contrast = 0.2
color=1.9
sharpness=0.1
whiteness = 1

cap = get_cap()

frameST = st.empty()
st.subheader("Webcam Beauty App")
st.sidebar.markdown("# Brightness Contrast ")
brightness = st.sidebar.slider("Brightness", 0, 255, 0, 1)
contrast = st.sidebar.slider("Contrast", 0, 255, 0, 1)
smothness = st.sidebar.slider("Smothness", 0.0, 5.0, 1.0, 0.1)

st.sidebar.markdown("# Alpha * frame + Beta")
alpha = st.sidebar.slider("Alpha", 0.0, 5.0, 2.0, 0.1)
beta = st.sidebar.slider("Beta", 0, 100, 10, 1)

def apply_brightness_contrast(input_img, brightness = 0, contrast = 0):

    if brightness != 0:
        if brightness > 0:
```

```
                shadow = brightness
                highlight = 255
            else:
                shadow = 0
                highlight = 255 + brightness
            alpha_b = (highlight - shadow)/255
            gamma_b = shadow

            buf = cv2.addWeighted(input_img, alpha_b, input_img, 0,
gamma_b)
        else:
            buf = input_img.copy()

        if contrast != 0:
            f = 131*(contrast + 127)/(127*(131-contrast))
            alpha_c = f
            gamma_c = 127*(1-f)

            buf = cv2.addWeighted(buf, alpha_c, buf, 0, gamma_c)

        return buf

while True:
    ret, frame = cap.read()
    # Stop the program if reached end of video
    if not ret:
        cv2.waitKey(3000)
        # Release device
        cap.release()
        break

    #Alpha and Beta =================================================
    frame2 = np.uint8(np.clip((alpha * frame + beta), 0, 255))

    #Ajust the Smoothness of the Image===============================
    level = int(smothness*10)
    frame2 = cv2.bilateralFilter(frame2, level, 75, 75)

    #Adjust the brightness and contrast =============================
    frame2 = apply_brightness_contrast(frame2, brightness , contrast )

    #concatanate image Vertically ==================================
    result=np.concatenate((frame,frame2),axis=0)


    frameST.image(result, channels="BGR")
```

To run it, just type the following command in a Command Prompt window:

```
streamlit run StreamlitWebcamBeauty.py
```

Figure 6.24 shows the output of the previous program; on the right are the sliders for adjusting different parameters.

Figure 6.24: The output of the `StreamlitWebcamBeauty.py` program, which shows the sliders for adjusting different parameters

Example 6.21 is a photo pencil sketch program.

EXAMPLE 6.21   THE `PENCILSKETCH_WEBAPP.PY` **PROGRAM**

```python
#Example 6.21 Pencil Sketch web app with Streamlit
import streamlit as st
import numpy as np
from PIL import Image
import cv2


def pencilSketch(inp_img):
    img_gray = cv2.cvtColor(inp_img, cv2.COLOR_BGR2GRAY)
    img_invert = cv2.bitwise_not(img_gray)
    img_smoothing = cv2.GaussianBlur(img_invert, (21, 21),sigmaX=0,
sigmaY=0)
    final_img = cv2.divide(img_gray, 255 - img_smoothing, scale=256)
    return(final_img)
```

```
st.title("Photo Pencil Sketch")
st.write("Convert your photos to pencil sketches")

file_image = st.sidebar.file_uploader("Upload your Photos",
type=['jpeg','jpg','png','gif'])

if file_image is None:
    st.write("No image file!")

else:
    input = Image.open(file_image)
    final_sketch = pencilSketch(np.array(input))
    st.write("Original Photo")
    st.image(input, use_column_width=True)
    st.write("Pencil Sketch")
    st.image(final_sketch, use_column_width=True)
    if st.button("Download"):
        im_pil = Image.fromarray(final_sketch)
        im_pil.save('output.jpg')
        st.write('Download completed')
```

To run it, just type the following command in a Command Prompt window:

```
streamlit run pencilsketch_webapp.py
```

Figure 6.25 shows the output of the proevious program, which shows an impressive pencil sketch of a photo image.

Figure 6.25: The output of the `pencilsketch_webapp.py` program

EXERCISE 6.19

Modify the previous Python program, add sliders for adjusting the parameters in the `cv2.GaussianBlur(img_invert, (21, 21),sigmaX=0, sigmaY=0)` function. Comment on the results.

TensorFlow.js Facemesh   TensoFlow.js is Google's solution for deploying Python code through web apps by using JavaScript. The following is the TensorFlow.js Facemesh repository GitHub site, with an impressive Facemesh example.

```
https://github.com/tensorflow/tfjs-models/tree/master/face-landmarks-
detection
```

It also has a live demo website (`https://storage.googleapis.com/tfjs-models/demos/face-landmarks-detection/index.html`), as shown in Figure 6.26, where you use your own webcam for generating a face mesh.

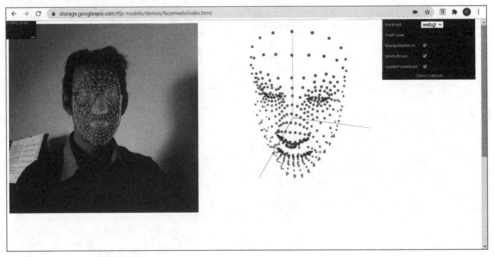

Figure 6.26: The TensorFlow.js Facemesh live demo site

(Source: `https://storage.googleapis.com/tfjs-models/demos/face-landmarks-detection/index.html`)

Mediapipe   Mediapipe is another impressive library that provides a range of deep learning functionalities, including face detection and face meshing; see the following link for more details.

```
https://github.com/google/mediapipe
```

To use it, you will need to install it first.

```
pip install mediapipe
```

With Mediapipe, you can also detect faces and generate face meshes. Example 6.22 shows a simple Mediapipe example for detecting faces in a file.

EXAMPLE 6.22 THE `MEDIAPIPE_FACEMESH.PY` **PROGRAM**

```python
#Example 6.22 mediapipe facemesh
#Modified based on:
#https://google.github.io/mediapipe/solutions/face_mesh.html
#pip install mediapipe

import cv2
import mediapipe as mp
mp_drawing = mp.solutions.drawing_utils
mp_face_mesh = mp.solutions.face_mesh


# For static images:
face_mesh = mp_face_mesh.FaceMesh(
    static_image_mode=True,
    max_num_faces=1,
    min_detection_confidence=0.5)
drawing_spec = mp_drawing.DrawingSpec(thickness=1, circle_radius=1)

file_list = ['emotion10.jpeg']
for idx, file in enumerate(file_list):
  image = cv2.imread(file)
  # Convert the BGR image to RGB before processing.
  results = face_mesh.process(cv2.cvtColor(image, cv2.COLOR_BGR2RGB))

  # Print and draw face mesh landmarks on the image.
  if not results.multi_face_landmarks:
    continue
  annotated_image = image.copy()
  for face_landmarks in results.multi_face_landmarks:
    print('face_landmarks:', face_landmarks)
    mp_drawing.draw_landmarks(
        image=annotated_image,
        landmark_list=face_landmarks,
        connections=mp_face_mesh.FACEMESH_CONTOURS,
        landmark_drawing_spec=drawing_spec,
        connection_drawing_spec=drawing_spec)
```

```
        cv2.imwrite('annotated_image' + str(idx) + '.png', annotated_image)
        cv2.imshow(file,annotated_image)
face_mesh.close()


cv2.waitKey(-1)
cv2.destroyAllWindows()
```

EXERCISE 6.20

Modify the previous Python program, at `file_list = ['emotion10.jpeg']`, so that it has more than one file. Run the program and comment on the results.

Example 6.23 shows a simple Mediapipe example for detecting faces in the live feed of a webcam.

EXAMPLE 6.23   THE `MEDIAPIPE_FACEMESH_WEBCAM.PY` PROGRAM

```
#Example 6.23 mediapipe facemesh from webcam feed
#Modified based on:
#https://google.github.io/mediapipe/solutions/face_mesh.html
#pip install mediapipe

import cv2
import mediapipe as mp
mp_drawing = mp.solutions.drawing_utils
mp_face_mesh = mp.solutions.face_mesh

# For webcam input:
face_mesh = mp_face_mesh.FaceMesh(
    min_detection_confidence=0.5, min_tracking_confidence=0.5)
drawing_spec = mp_drawing.DrawingSpec(thickness=1, circle_radius=1)
cap = cv2.VideoCapture(0)
#image = cv2.imread('emotion10.jpeg')

#while cap.isOpened():
while True:

    success, image = cap.read()
    if not success:
```

```
        print("Ignoring empty camera frame.")
        # If loading a video, use 'break' instead of 'continue'.
        continue

    # Flip the image horizontally for a later selfie-view display, and
convert
    # the BGR image to RGB.
    image = cv2.cvtColor(cv2.flip(image, 1), cv2.COLOR_BGR2RGB)
    # To improve performance, optionally mark the image as not
writeable to
    # pass by reference.
    image.flags.writeable = False
    results = face_mesh.process(image)

    # Draw the face mesh annotations on the image.
    image.flags.writeable = True
    image = cv2.cvtColor(image, cv2.COLOR_RGB2BGR)
    if results.multi_face_landmarks:
      for face_landmarks in results.multi_face_landmarks:
        mp_drawing.draw_landmarks(
            image=image,
            landmark_list=face_landmarks,
            connections=mp_face_mesh. FACEMESH_CONTOURS,
            landmark_drawing_spec=drawing_spec,
            connection_drawing_spec=drawing_spec)
    cv2.imshow('MediaPipe FaceMesh', image)
    if cv2.waitKey(5) & 0xFF == 27:
      break
face_mesh.close()
cap.release()
```

EXERCISE 6.21

Modify the previous Python program and use the `print ()` function to print all the face landmarks and corresponding locations. Run the program and comment on the results.

6.7 How to Defeat Face Recognition

As we explained, face recognition is highly controversial. If you don't want your face to be detected and recognized, there are a range of things you can do, for example, wearing certain patterns on your clothes, wearing certain types of glasses or makeup, or having certain types of hair styles.

For more details, check out the Survivopedia website for six ways to defeat facial recognition.

```
https://www.survivopedia.com/6-ways-to-defeat-facial-recognition/
```

6.8   Summary

This chapter covered face detection and face recognition. Face detection means to detect faces in an image, while face recognition, one of the most controversial research topics in artificial intelligence, means to identify the person of each face. Face recognition can be divided into four steps: face detection, face alignment, face feature attraction, and face matching.

A popular way to detect faces is to use the Haar cascade classifier, an effective object detection method proposed by Paul Viola and Michael Jones in 2001. Face detection can also be achieved by using many deep learning neural network model libraries, such as DLib library and Face_Recognition library, which not only detect faces but also identify face landmarks such as eyebrows, eyes, nose, chin, and mouth.

Face recognition can be achieved by using the Face_Recognition library or OpenCV (for example, with its Local Binary Patterns Histograms Recognizer, LBPHFaceRecognizer). We also presented a GUI-based face recognition system example, where you can register, detect, and recognize faces.

- With the DeepFace library, you can perform age, gender, race, and emotion detection.
- With OpenCV and DLib, you can detect faces in two images and swap the faces.
- With the Streamlit library, you can easily turn those programs into web-based apps.
- With the TensorFlow.js and Mediapipe libraries, you can create face meshes, even within a web browser.

Finally, remember there are also ways to defeat face recognition, which is also increasingly difficult to achieve thanks to the continuing advancement of the technology.

6.9 Chapter Review Questions

Q6.1. What is face detection?

Q6.2. What is face recognition? How many steps are there in face recognition?

Q6.3. What are face landmarks?

Q6.4. How does age detection work?

Q6.5. How does gender detection work?

Q6.6. How does emotion detection work?

Q6.7. What is the DeepFace library?

Q6.8. What is face swap, and how does it work?

Q6.9. What is the PySimpleGUI library?

Q6.10. What is TensorFlow.js? What can it do?

Q6.11. What is the Mediapipe library? What can you achieve with it?

Q6.12. Do an Internet search, and find out more about how to defeat face recognition.

Object Detections and Image Segmentations

"AI doesn't have to be evil to destroy humanity—if AI has a goal and humanity just happens to come in the way, it will destroy humanity as a matter of course without even thinking about it, no hard feelings."

—Elon Musk (American entrepreneur, industrial designer, and engineer)

CHAPTER OUTLINE

7.1 Introduction
7.2 Object Detections with Pretrained Models
7.3 Object Detections with Custom Trained Models
7.4 Object Tracking
7.5 Image Segmentation
7.6 Background Removal
7.7 Depth Estimation
7.8 Augmented Reality
7.9 Summary
7.10 Chapter Review Questions

7.1   Introduction

Object detection is another important aspect of image analysis or image processing. Different from image classification, which identifies the content of the whole image, object detection detects and locates different objects within an image, for example, to detect dogs and cats in an image or to detect cyclists, vehicles, and pedestrians in an image.

Traditionally, object detection is achieved by detecting colors, shapes, and contours, and you can typically implement this by using the popular OpenCV library. In Hollywood, people have long been using green-colored backgrounds during filming, which can then be easily replaced with different scenes later. However, this approach is suitable only for detecting simple objects.

A much more modern approach is to use deep learning neural network models, which are suitable for detecting more complex objects. Object detection with deep learning is essentially dividing the whole image into small regions and performing image classification with each region.

The following are some commonly used deep learning neural network models for object detection:

- **R-CNN:** Region-based convolutional neural network (two-step approach)
- **YOLO:** You only look once (one-step approach)
- **SSD:** Single-shot detector (one-step approach)

R-CNN is a two-step approach, first to identify regions and then to detect objects in those regions using convolutional neural networks (CNNs). YOLO and SSD are one-step approaches, which use a CNN that is able to find all objects within an image in one step.

R-CNN Family

R-CNNs are a family of techniques for addressing object localization and recognition tasks, which include R-CNN, Fast R-CNN, Faster R-CNN, and the latest Mask R-CNN. Facebook's Mesh R-CNN is also a cool implementation that can even predict the full 3D shape of each detected object.

R-CNN was introduced in 2013 by Ross Girshick and colleagues from University of California – Berkeley, in a paper titled "Rich feature hierarchies for accurate object detection and semantic segmentation." Traditionally, object detection is done through sliding windows, that is, scanning through the image with sliding windows of different sizes and trying to find if there is an object inside the window. As you can see, this process is extremely time-consuming. A much more efficient approach is selective search, which is an advanced algorithm that seeks to merge similar pixels and to find regions of an image that could contain an object. R-CNN first uses selective search to generate 2,000 regions from the image, called *regions of interest* (ROIs). It then extracts features from these regions by using CNNs and checks whether any of these regions contain any object by classifying features as one of the known classes using the Support Vector Machines (SVM) classifier. In other words, R-CNN divides the image into 2,000 proposed regions and performs image classification on each region. For every region with known objects, it labels the region and puts a box around the region. R-CNN achieved then state-of-the-art results on the VOC-2012 dataset and the 200-class ILSVRC-2013 object detection dataset.

However, R-CNN is also very slow. It takes around 40 to 50 seconds to make predictions for each image, which makes it impossible for real-time object detection.

Fast R-CNN was introduced, also by Ross Girshick, to reduce the computational burden of R-CNN. Instead of dividing the image into 2,000 regions and running a CNN for each region, it runs a CNN on the whole image first, generates the convolutional feature maps, and then uses a ROI pooling layer to reshape all the proposed regions (region proposals) into a fixed size so that it can be fed into a fully connected network. As a result, Fast R-CNN has dramatically reduced the time from 40 to 50 seconds to around 2 seconds per image to detect objects. However, 2 seconds per image is still not good enough for real-time detection. Here enters Faster R-CNN.

Faster R-CNN is the modified version of Fast RCNN. Instead of using selective search for generating regions of interest, Faster RCNN uses a region proposal network (RPN), which takes image feature maps as an input and generates a set of object proposals, each with an object score as output.

Mask R-CNN is basically an extension of Faster R-CNN. It is built on top of Faster R-CNN. In addition to the class label and bounding box coordinates for each object, Mask R-CNN will also return the object mask.

Mesh R-CNN is from Facebook AI Research (FAIR). Mesh R-CNN takes an input image, predicts object instances in that image, and infers their 3D shape. The implementation of Mesh R-CNN is based on Detectron2 and PyTorch3D (`https://github.com/facebookresearch/meshrcnn`).

YOLO

YOLO was first developed by Joseph Redmon and Ross Girshick in 2015, in a paper titled "You Only Look Once: Unified, Real-Time Object Detection." YOLO uses a single neural network trained from end to end to predict objects in an image with bounding boxes and class labels. It first splits the image into a grid of nonoverlapping NxN cells. Then for each cell, it predicts a bounding box if the center of a bounding box falls within the cell. It also predicts the class and the confidence. YOLO uses a technique called *nonmax suppression* to remove overlapping boxes by returning the boxes with maximum probability and suppressing the close-by boxes with nonmax probabilities. YOLO is less accurate and not good at detecting small objects, but YOLO is orders of magnitude faster than other object detection algorithms. YOLO can remarkably process images at 45 frames per second and up to 155 frames per second for a speed-optimized version of the model. YOLO has four official versions: v1, v2, v3, and v4.

SSD

SSD was developed by Wei Liu and colleagues in 2016 in a paper titled "SSD: Single Shot MultiBox Detector." Unlike YOLO, SSD does not split the image into grids of arbitrary size but uses a convolutional neural network's pyramidal feature hierarchy for efficient detection of objects of various sizes. SSD has two components, a feature extraction network and a detection network. The feature extraction network usually is a pretrained image classification network used as a feature extractor, such as a ResNet trained on an ImageNet. The detection network is just one or more convolutional layers added to this feature extraction network. The detection network's outputs are the bounding boxes and classes of objects.

Table 7.1 compares different object detection algorithms.

Table 7.1: Comparison of Different Object Detection Algorithms

ALGORITHM	FEATURES	PREDICTION TIME PER IMAGE	PROS AND CONS
R-CNN	Uses selective search to generate 2,000 regions from each image and extracts features using CNN from each region.	40 to 50 seconds	Accurate but slow. Long computation time, as well as using three different models for predictions. Not suitable for real-time detection.
Fast R-CNN	Uses CNN only once on the image to extract feature maps and use selective search on the maps to detect objects.	2.3 seconds	Computation time is still long for real-time detection. Selective search is slow.
Faster R-CNN	Uses RPN to extract features. RPN is much faster.	0.2 seconds	Very accurate and reasonably fast.
Mask R-CNN	Built on top of Faster R-CNN; returns not only object class, label, bounding box, but also its mask.	0.2 seconds	Very accurate and with object mask.
YOLO	Divides the image into grids and uses a single neural network to predict objects in an image	0.02 seconds	Less accurate but very fast.
SSD	Uses a pretrained feature extraction network and a detection network to detect objects.	0.02 seconds	Less accurate but very fast.

In summary, if you look for accurate object detection, choose Faster R-CNN or Mask R-CNN, and if you look for fast object detection, choose YOLO or SSD. In fact, variants of YOLO and SSD can achieve comparable accuracies as Faster R-CNN; see the following article for a detailed accuracy comparison:

https://jonathan-hui.medium.com/object-detection-speed-and-
accuracy-comparison-faster-r-cnn-r-fcn-ssd-and-yolo-5425656ae359

7.2 Object Detections with Pretrained Models

Object detection can be done by using either pretrained models or customized trained models. Pretrained models are trained on large object image datasets, such as a COCO image dataset (https://cocodataset.org/).

7.2.1 Object Detection with OpenCV

OpenCV is the most widely used for object detections. To use OpenCV, you need to install the library first.

```
pip install opencv-python
```

OpenCV can detect objects by using shapes, contours, colors, or Haar cascade codes.

Example 7.1 is a simple Python circle detection code. It first reads the image from a file called `ball.jpeg`, changes to grayscale, and then uses the `cv2.HoughCircles()` function to detect the circles. The image file `ball.jpeg` is again from `http://www.pexels.com`.

EXAMPLE 7.1 THE `OPENCV1.PY` PROGRAM

```
#Example 7.1 Circle Detection
import cv2

img = cv2.imread("ball.jpeg")
width,height,c=img.shape
print(img.shape)

gray = cv2.cvtColor(img, cv2.COLOR_BGR2GRAY)
gray = cv2.medianBlur(gray, 5)
circles = cv2.HoughCircles(gray,cv2.HOUGH_GRADIENT,1,20,
                        param1=50,param2=30,minRadius=35,maxRadius=50)

for co, i in enumerate(circles[0, :], start=1):
    cv2.circle(img,(int(i[0]),int(i[1])),int(i[2]),(0,255,0),2)
    cv2.circle(img,(int(i[0]),int(i[1])),2,(0,0,255),3)
print("Number of circles detected:", co)
cv2.imshow('Circle Detection',img)
```

Figure 7.1 shows the output. You can use `minRadius` and `maxRadius` to control the number of circles detected.

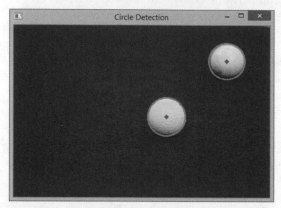

Figure 7.1: The output of the Example 7.1 program with two circles detected

EXERCISE 7.1

Modify the Example 7.1 Python program, trying different images, and comment on the accuracy of detection. Adjust the parameters of the `cv2.HoughCircles()` function, and see how they affect the results.

Example 7.2 is a simple Python shape detection code. It reads the image from a file called `shapes1.jpeg`, changes it to grayscale, blurs the image using the `cv2.medianBlur()` function, uses the `cv2.findContours()` function to detect the different shapes, and then selects only the contours whose area is greater than 10. The image file `shapes1.jpeg` is again from `http://www.pexels.com`.

EXAMPLE 7.2   THE `OPENCV2.PY` **PROGRAM**

```
#Example 7.2 Shape Detection
import cv2
import numpy as np

img = cv2.imread("shapes1.jpeg")
width,height,c=img.shape
print(img.shape)

gray = cv2.cvtColor(img, cv2.COLOR_BGR2GRAY)
gray = cv2.medianBlur(gray, 5)
ret, thresh = cv2.threshold(gray, 0, 255, cv2.THRESH_BINARY | cv2
.THRESH_OTSU)
cnts, _ = cv2.findContours(thresh.copy(), cv2.RETR_EXTERNAL, cv2
.CHAIN_APPROX_SIMPLE)
cnts = np.array(cnts)[[cv2.contourArea(c)>10 for c in cnts]]
```

```
for c in cnts:
    area = cv2.contourArea(c)
    if area > 10:
        cv2.drawContours(img, [c], -1, (0, 255, 0), 2)
        M = cv2.moments(c)
        if M["m00"] != 0:
            cX = int((M["m10"] / M["m00"]) )
            cY = int((M["m01"] / M["m00"]) )
        # Find the Center of a Blob (detected contour)
        cv2.circle(img, (cX,cY), 2, (255, 255,0), 2)
cv2.imshow("Output", img)
cv2.waitKey(0)
```

Figure 7.2 shows the output.

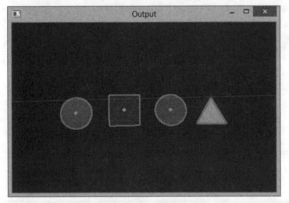

Figure 7.2: The output of the Example 7.2 program with different shapes detected

EXERCISE 7.2

Modify the Example 7.2 Python program, trying different images, and comment on the accuracy of detection.

Example 7.2a is a different version of the earlier Python shape detection code. It first reads the image from a file, changes to grayscale, then uses the cv2 .Canny() function to find the edges, uses the cv2.findContours() function to detect the different shapes, and uses the cv2.drawContours() function to draw the different contours.

EXAMPLE 7.2A   THE OPENCV2A.PY PROGRAM

```
#Example 7.2a Identifying and Drawing Contours with OpenCV
import cv2
import numpy as np

image = cv2.imread('shapes.jpeg')
gray = cv2.cvtColor(image, cv2.COLOR_BGR2GRAY)
```

```
edged = cv2.Canny(gray, 30, 200)
contours, hierarchy = cv2.findContours(edged,
    cv2.RETR_EXTERNAL, cv2.CHAIN_APPROX_NONE)

print("Number of Contours found = " + str(len(contours)))

# contourIdx=-1signifies drawing all contours  3: thickness
cv2.drawContours(image=image, contours=contours, contourIdx=-1,
color=(0, 255, 0), thickness=2, lineType=cv2.LINE_AA)cv2
.imshow('Contours', image)
cv2.waitKey(0)
```

EXERCISE 7.3

Modify the Example 7.2a Python program, trying different images and commenting on the accuracy of detection. Adjust the parameters of the `cv2.Canny()` function to see how they affect the results.

Example 7.3 is a simple Python object detection code based on color. It uses a webcam to read in the image, uses a tracker bar to select the range of HSV values, uses HSV ranges to generate a mask, and then uses the mask to mask out the background of the image. We are left with the detected object. You can use this program to select the desired color range for your object, such as skin or a hand.

EXAMPLE 7.3   THE `OPENCV3.PY` PROGRAM

```
#Example 7.3 Color Detection
import cv2
import numpy as np

def callback(x):
    pass

cap = cv2.VideoCapture(0)
cv2.namedWindow('HSV Color')

# create trackbars for HSV color
cv2.createTrackbar('H0','HSV Color',0,179,callback)
cv2.createTrackbar('H1','HSV Color',179,179,callback)

cv2.createTrackbar('S0','HSV Color',0,255,callback)
cv2.createTrackbar('S1','HSV Color',255,255,callback)

cv2.createTrackbar('V0','HSV Color',0,255,callback)
cv2.createTrackbar('V1','HSV Color',255,255,callback)
```

```
while(1):
    ret, frame = cap.read()
    h0 = cv2.getTrackbarPos('H0', 'HSV Color')
    h1 = cv2.getTrackbarPos('H1', 'HSV Color')
    s0 = cv2.getTrackbarPos('S0', 'HSV Color')
    s1 = cv2.getTrackbarPos('S1', 'HSV Color')
    v0 = cv2.getTrackbarPos('V0', 'HSV Color')
    v1 = cv2.getTrackbarPos('V1', 'HSV Color')

    hsv = cv2.cvtColor(frame, cv2.COLOR_BGR2HSV)
    cv2.imshow('HSV', hsv)
    lower = np.array([h0, s0, v0])
    higher = np.array([h1, s1, v1])
    mask = cv2.inRange(hsv, lower, higher)
    frame = cv2.bitwise_and(frame, frame, mask=mask)

    cv2.imshow('frame', frame)

    if(cv2.waitKey(1) & 0xFF == ord('q')):
        break
cv2.destroyAllWindows()
cap.release()
```

Figure 7.3 shows the output of the earlier program including the masked image, the image in HSV color space, and the HSV sliders.

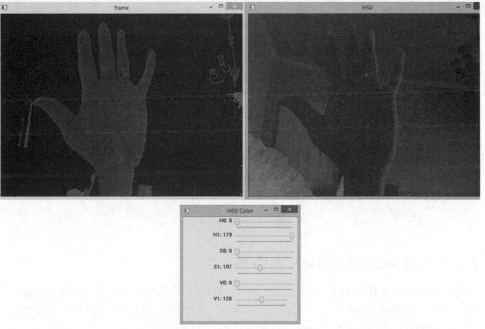

Figure 7.3: The output of the Example 7.3 program that shows the original webcam image (top left), the masked image (top right), and the HSV sliders (bottom)

Modify the Example 7.3 Python program, using the `cv2.imshow()` function to display the mask as well.

Example 7.4 is a simple Python full body detection code based on the Haar cascade code. You can find more about the Haar cascade code from `https://github.com/opencv/opencv/tree/master/data/haarcascades`.

EXAMPLE 7.4   THE `OPENCV4.PY` **PROGRAM**

```
#Example 7.4 Haar Cascade Code Detection
import time
import numpy as np
import cv2
classifier = cv2.CascadeClassifier('haarcascade_fullbody.xml')
cap = cv2.VideoCapture(0)

while cap.isOpened():
    ret, frame = cap.read()
    gray = cv2.cvtColor(frame, cv2.COLOR_BGR2GRAY)

    # Pass frame to the classifier
    bodys = classifier.detectMultiScale(gray, 1.5, 10)

    # Extract bounding boxes for any bodies identified
    for (x,y,w,h) in bodys:
        cv2.rectangle(frame, (x, y), (x+w, y+h), (0, 255, 255), 2)

    cv2.imshow('Body', frame)
    if cv2.waitKey(1) == 13: #13 is the Enter Key
        break
cap.release()
cv2.destroyAllWindows()
```

Modify the Example 7.4 Python program so that it can detect the upper body by using the upper body Haar cascade code, in `haarcascade_upperbody.xml`.

7.2.2   Object Detection with YOLO

YOLO is one of the most popular object detection libraries. You can detect 20 different classes of objects with YOLO. For more details, see the following:

```
https://github.com/pjreddie/darknet
```

Example 7.5 is a simple Python YOLO program that works for both YOLOv3 and YOLOv4. It is modified from this GitHub repository: `https://github.com/iArunava/YOLOv3-Object-Detection-with-OpenCV`. It has two files, `yolov3 .py` and `yolo_util.py`. To run this program, you also need to download the YOLOv3 weights and CFG and COCO label files from the following links and save them into a subfolder called `yolov3-coco`:

`https://pjreddie.com/media/files/yolov3.weights`

`https://github.com/pjreddie/darknet/blob/master/cfg/yolov3.cfg`

`https://github.com/pjreddie/darknet/blob/master/data/coco.names`

`https://github.com/iArunava/YOLOv3-Object-Detection-with-OpenCV/blob/master/yolov3-coco/coco-labels`

This is the `yolov3.py` program.

EXAMPLE 7.5   THE `YOLOV3.PY` PROGRAM

```python
#Example 7.5 YOLOv3 Detection
import numpy as np
import argparse
import cv2 as cv
import subprocess
import time
import os
from yolo_utils import infer_image, show_image
from types import SimpleNamespace

d = {'confidence':0.5,'threshold':0.3,
     'weights':'./yolov3-coco/yolov3.weights',
     'config':'./yolov3-coco/yolov3.cfg',
     'show_time':False}
FLAGS = SimpleNamespace(**d)
cocolabels='./yolov3-coco/coco-labels'
labels = open(cocolabels).read().strip().split('\n')
print(FLAGS)


colors = np.random.randint(0, 255, size=(len(labels), 3), dtype='uint8')
net = cv.dnn.readNetFromDarknet(FLAGS.config, FLAGS.weights)

layer_names = net.getLayerNames()
layer_names = [layer_names[i[0] - 1] for i in net
.getUnconnectedOutLayers()]

vid = cv.VideoCapture(0)

while True:
    _, frame = vid.read()
```

```
        #frame = cv.resize(frame, (1280,720), interpolation = cv.INTER_AREA)
        #1920, 1080
        frame = cv.resize(frame, (640,360), interpolation = cv.INTER_AREA)
        height, width = frame.shape[:2]
        frame, boxes, confidences, classids, idxs = infer_image(net,
layer_names, \
                        height, width, frame, colors, labels, FLAGS)
        cv.imshow('webcam', frame)

        if cv.waitKey(1) & 0xFF == ord('q'):
            break
    vid.release()
    cv.destroyAllWindows()
```

This is the `yolo_utils.py` program:

```python
#Example 7.5 yolo_utils.py
import numpy as np
import argparse
import cv2 as cv
import subprocess
import time
import os



def show_image(img):
    cv.imshow("Image", img)
    cv.waitKey(0)

def draw_labels_and_boxes(img, boxes, confidences, classids, idxs, colors,
labels):
    # If there are any detections
    if len(idxs) > 0:
        for i in idxs.flatten():
            # Get the bounding box coordinates
            x, y = boxes[i][0], boxes[i][1]
            w, h = boxes[i][2], boxes[i][3]

            # Get the unique color for this class
            color = [int(c) for c in colors[classids[i]]]

            # Draw the bounding box rectangle and label on the image
            cv.rectangle(img, (x, y), (x+w, y+h), color, 2)
            text = "{}: {:4f}".format(labels[classids[i]], confidences[i])
            cv.putText(img, text, (x, y-5), cv.FONT_HERSHEY_SIMPLEX, 0.5,
color, 2)
    return img
```

```python
def generate_boxes_confidences_classids(outs, height, width, tconf):
    boxes = []
    confidences = []
    classids = []

    for out in outs:
        for detection in out:
            #print (detection)
            #a = input('GO!')

            # Get the scores, classid, and the confidence of the prediction
            scores = detection[5:]
            classid = np.argmax(scores)
            confidence = scores[classid]

            # Consider only the predictions that are above a certain
confidence level
            if confidence > tconf:
                # TODO Check detection
                box = detection[0:4] * np.array([width, height, width,
height])
                centerX, centerY, bwidth, bheight = box.astype('int')

                # Using the center x, y coordinates to derive the top
                # and the left corner of the bounding box
                x = int(centerX - (bwidth / 2))
                y = int(centerY - (bheight / 2))

                # Append to list
                boxes.append([x, y, int(bwidth), int(bheight)])
                confidences.append(float(confidence))
                classids.append(classid)

    return boxes, confidences, classids

def infer_image(net, layer_names, height, width, img, colors, labels, FLAGS,
            boxes=None, confidences=None, classids=None, idxs=None,
infer=True):

    if infer:
        # Contructing a blob from the input image
        blob = cv.dnn.blobFromImage(img, 1 / 255.0, (416, 416),
                    swapRB=True, crop=False)

        # Perform a forward pass of the YOLO object detector
        net.setInput(blob)
```

```
            # Getting the outputs from the output layers
            start = time.time()
            outs = net.forward(layer_names)
            end = time.time()

            if FLAGS.show_time:
                print ("[INFO] YOLOv3 took {:6f} seconds".format(end - start))



            # Generate the boxes, confidences, and classIDs
            boxes, confidences, classids = generate_boxes_confidences_
classids(outs, height, width, FLAGS.confidence)

            # Apply Non-Maxima Suppression to suppress overlapping bounding
boxes
            idxs = cv.dnn.NMSBoxes(boxes, confidences, FLAGS.confidence,
FLAGS.threshold)

        if boxes is None or confidences is None or idxs is None or classids
is None:
            raise '[ERROR] Required variables are set to None before drawing
boxes on images.'

        # Draw labels and boxes on the image
        img = draw_labels_and_boxes(img, boxes, confidences, classids, idxs,
colors, labels)

        return img, boxes, confidences, classids, idxs
```

EXERCISE 7.6

Modify the Example 7.5 Python program so that it uses a YOLOv3-Tiny model for object detection. Comment on the accuracy and speed. You can get the YOLOv3-Tiny model weights and CFG files from here:

```
https://pjreddie.com/media/files/yolov3-tiny.weights
https://github.com/pjreddie/darknet/blob/master/cfg/
yolov3-tiny.cfg
```

EXERCISE 7.7

Modify the Example 7.5 Python program so that it uses the YOLOv4 model for object detection. Comment on the accuracy and speed. You can get the YOLOv4 model weights and CFG files from here:

```
https://github.com/AlexeyAB/darknet/releases/download/
darknet_yolo_v3_optimal/yolov4.weights
https://raw.githubusercontent.com/AlexeyAB/darknet/master/
cfg/yolov4.cfg
```

For more details about YOLOv4, see the following:

`https://github.com/AlexeyAB/darknet`

PySimpleGUI-YOLO   You can also use PySimpleGUI library to create a YOLO object detection program; see a ready example in Figure 7.4.

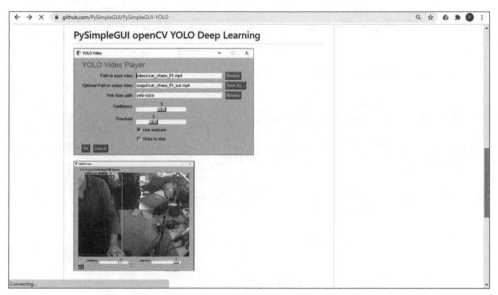

Figure 7.4: The GitHub website for the PySimpleGUI-YOLO project

(Source: `https://github.com/PySimpleGUI/PySimpleGUI-YOLO`)

For more examples about using PySimpleGUI library, see the following:

`https://pysimplegui.readthedocs.io/en/latest/`

7.2.3   Object Detection with OpenCV and Deep Learning

Example 7.6 is an object detection Python program that uses OpenCV and deep learning neural networks. It uses OpenCV to load the MobileNet SSD deep learning model to detect 20 different objects from webcam images.

You need to download the MobileNet SSD model files, `MobileNetSSD_deploy .prototxt` and `MobileNetSSD_deploy.caffemodel`, from here:

`https://github.com/TheNsBhasin/DNN_Object_Detection/`

In the program, this is to specify the deep learning model files and the confidence for detection:

```
prototxt = 'MobileNetSSD_deploy.prototxt'
model = 'MobileNetSSD_deploy.caffemodel'
confidence = 0.1
```

This is to specify all the object labels:

```
CLASSES = ["background", "aeroplane", "bicycle", "bird", "boat",
       "bottle", "bus", "car", "cat", "chair", "cow", "diningtable",
       "dog", "horse", "motorbike", "person", "pottedplant", "sheep",
       "sofa", "train", "tvmonitor"]
```

This is to use OpenCV to load the deep learning model:

```
net = cv2.dnn.readNetFromCaffe(prototxt, model)
```

This is to use the deep learning model to detect objects in the image:

```
net.setInput(blob)
detections = net.forward()
```

This is to display all the detected objects whose confidence is greater than 0.1 on the image:

```
for i in np.arange(0, detections.shape[2]):
    conf = detections[0, 0, i, 2]

    if conf > confidence:
    ... ...
```

Example 7.6 shows the complete code.

EXAMPLE 7.6   THE OBJECTDETECTIONDNNOPENCV.PY **PROGRAM**

```
# Example 7.6 MobileNet SSD Object Detection
# Modified based on:
# https://www.pyimagesearch.com/2017/09/18/
real-time-object-detection-with-deep-learning-and-opencv/

# import the necessary packages
from imutils.video import VideoStream
from imutils.video import FPS
import numpy as np
import argparse
import imutils
import time
import cv2

prototxt = 'MobileNetSSD_deploy.prototxt'
model = 'MobileNetSSD_deploy.caffemodel'
confidence = 0.1

CLASSES = ["background", "aeroplane", "bicycle", "bird", "boat",
       "bottle", "bus", "car", "cat", "chair", "cow", "diningtable",
       "dog", "horse", "motorbike", "person", "pottedplant", "sheep",
       "sofa", "train", "tvmonitor"]
```

```python
COLORS = np.random.uniform(0, 255, size=(len(CLASSES), 3))

net = cv2.dnn.readNetFromCaffe(prototxt, model)

vf=0
vs = VideoStream(vf).start()

time.sleep(2.0)
fps = FPS().start()


while True:
    frame = vs.read()
    frame = imutils.resize(frame, width=400)
    (h, w) = frame.shape[:2]
    blob = cv2.dnn.blobFromImage(cv2.resize(frame, (300, 300)),
    0.007843, (300, 300), 127.5)
    net.setInput(blob)
    detections = net.forward()

    for i in np.arange(0, detections.shape[2]):
        conf = detections[0, 0, i, 2]

        if conf > confidence:
            idx = int(detections[0, 0, i, 1])
            box = detections[0, 0, i, 3:7] * np.array([w, h, w, h])
            (startX, startY, endX, endY) = box.astype("int")
            label = "{}: {:.2f}%".format(CLASSES[idx],
                conf * 100)
            cv2.rectangle(frame, (startX, startY), (endX, endY),
                COLORS[idx], 2)
            y = startY - 15 if startY - 15 > 15 else startY + 15
            cv2.putText(frame, label, (startX, y),
            cv2.FONT_HERSHEY_SIMPLEX, 0.5, COLORS[idx], 2)
    cv2.imshow("Frame", frame)
    key = cv2.waitKey(1) & 0xFF
    # if the `q` key was pressed, break from the loop
    if key == ord("q"):
        break
    fps.update()

fps.stop()
print("[INFO] elapsed time: {:.2f}".format(fps.elapsed()))
print("[INFO] approx. FPS: {:.2f}".format(fps.fps()))
# do a bit of cleanup
cv2.destroyAllWindows()
vs.stop()

Example output below:
```

7.2.4   Object Detection with TensorFlow, ImageAI, Mask RNN, PixelLib, Gluon

In this section, we'll talk about object detection with even more libraries.

TensorFlow Object Detection

You can also use TensorFlow for object detection. The following link shows the GitHub website for object detection using TensorFlow 2.

```
https://github.com/TannerGilbert/Tensorflow-Object-Detection-with-Tensorflow-2.0
```

More details are also available from here:

```
https://gilberttanner.com/blog/object-detection-with-tensorflow-2
```

There is also a Google Colab tutorial on object detection using TensorFlow 2 for you to try; see the following link.

```
https://colab.research.google.com/github/tensorflow/models/blob/
master/research/object_detection/colab_tutorials/object_detection_
tutorial.ipynb
```

The following link shows an interesting example code for using TensorFlow object detection through the webcam.

```
https://tensorflow-object-detection-api-tutorial.readthedocs.io/
en/latest/auto_examples/object_detection_camera.html
```

ImageAI Object Detection

ImageAI is an object detection library built on TensorFlow version 1.x. See the following links for more details:

```
https://imageai.readthedocs.io/en/latest/
https://github.com/OlafenwaMoses/ImageAI
```

Example 7.7 shows some simple code for object detection that uses the ImageAI library. As you can see, it has only eight lines of code. It is based on ResNet50 deep learning neural networks. You need to download the ResNet50 library from here:

```
https://github.com/OlafenwaMoses/ImageAI/releases/download/
essentials-v5/resnet50_imagenet_tf.2.0.h5
https://github.com/OlafenwaMoses/ImageAI/releases/download/1.0/
resnet50_coco_best_v2.0.1.h5
```

EXAMPLE 7.7   THE `IMAGEAI1.PY` PROGRAM

```python
# Example 7.7 Object Detection with ImageAI
# https://github.com/OlafenwaMoses/ImageAI
# Only works for TensorFlow 1.X
# pip install imageai

from imageai.Detection import ObjectDetection
import cv2
import time;

t0 = time.time();
detector = ObjectDetection()
detector.setModelTypeAsRetinaNet()
detector.setModelPath("resnet50_coco_best_v2.0.1.h5")
detector.loadModel()
detections = detector.detectObjectsFromImage("fruits.jpeg", output_
image_path="imagenew.jpg")
print(detections)
t1 = time.time() - t0;
print(t1)
```

EXERCISE 7.11

Modify the earlier Python program to use the YOLOv3 model; see the model file to download here. Run the program and comment on the accuracy and speed.

```
https://github.com/OlafenwaMoses/ImageAI/releases/
download/1.0/yolo.h5/
```

Example 7.8 is a longer version of the earlier program. It not only detects the objects but also prints out the x,y locations of the objects.

EXAMPLE 7.8   THE `IMAGEAI2.PY` PROGRAM

```python
# Example 7.8 Object Detection with ImageAI
# https://github.com/OlafenwaMoses/ImageAI
# Only works for TensorFlow 1.X
# pip install imageai

import matplotlib.pyplot as plt
from imageai.Detection import ObjectDetection
import os
import cv2

import tensorflow.compat.v1 as tf
tf.disable_v2_behavior

execution_path = os.getcwd()
print(execution_path)
input_image=os.path.join(execution_path , "fruits.jpeg")

detector = ObjectDetection()
detector.setModelTypeAsRetinaNet()
detector.setModelPath( os.path.join(execution_path ,
"resnet50_coco_best_v2.0.1.h5"))
#detector.setModelTypeAsYOLOv3()
#detector.setModelPath(os.path.join(execution_path , "yolo.h5")) #
Download the model via this link https://github.com/OlafenwaMoses/
ImageAI/releases/tag/1.0

detector.loadModel()
detections = detector.detectObjectsFromImage(input_image, output_
image_path=os.path.join(execution_path , "imagenew.jpg"))


for eachObject in detections:
    print(eachObject["name"] , " : " , eachObject["percentage_
probability"] , " : ", eachObject["box_points"] )
    x1= int(eachObject["box_points"][0])
    y1= int(eachObject["box_points"][1])
    x2= int(eachObject["box_points"][2])
    y2= int(eachObject["box_points"][3])
    start_point = (x1,y1)
    end_point = (x2,y2)
    image = cv2.rectangle(image, start_point, end_point, color,
thickness)
    cv2.putText(image, eachObject["name"] , (x1, y1-10), cv2.FONT_
HERSHEY_SIMPLEX, 0.9, color , thickness)
```

```
# Displaying the image
cv2.imshow(window_name, image)
```

EXERCISE 7.12

Modify the earlier Python program to use the YOLOv3-Tiny model; see the model file to download here. Run the program and comment on the accuracy and speed.
https://github.com/OlafenwaMoses/ImageAI/releases/
download/1.0/yolo-tiny.h5/

Example 7.9 is a webcam version of the earlier program.

EXAMPLE 7.9   THE IMAGEAIWEBCAM.PY PROGRAM

```
# Example 7.9 Object Detection from live webcam feed with ImageAI
from imageai.Detection import VideoObjectDetection
import os
import cv2

camera = cv2.VideoCapture(0)

detector = VideoObjectDetection()
detector.setModelTypeAsRetinaNet()
detector.setModelPath("resnet50_coco_best_v2.0.1.h5")
detector.loadModel()

video_path = detector.detectObjectsFromVideo(camera_input=camera,
    output_file_path=os.path.join(execution_path, "camera_detected_video")
    , frames_per_second=20, log_progress=True, minimum_percentage_
probability=40, detection_timeout=120)
```

EXERCISE 7.13

Modify the earlier Python program to use the YOLOv3 or YOLOv3-Tiny model. Run the program and comment on the accuracy and speed.

MaskRCNN Object Detection

MaskRCNN is also a popular Python library for object detection. It is based on the Mask R-CNN algorithm; see the following GitHub site for more details:

```
https://github.com/matterport/Mask_RCNN/
```

To use it, you need to install it first, as well as scikit-image, which it relies upon, by typing this:

```
pip install mrcnn scikit-image
```

Example 7.10 is a code for object detection that uses the MaskRCNN library. It is modified based on the following:

https://machinelearningmastery.com/how-to-perform-object-detection-in-photographs-with-mask-r-cnn-in-keras/

Note this example requires TensorFlow version 1.

EXAMPLE 7.10   THE MASK R-CNN.PY **PROGRAM**

```
# Example 7.10 Object Detection with MaskRCNN
# Modified based on:
# https://machinelearningmastery.com/how-to-perform-object-detection-
in-photographs-with-mask-r-cnn-in-keras/
# example of inference with a pre-trained coco model: download from
https://github.com/matterport/Mask_RCNN/releases/download/v2.0/mask_
rcnn_coco.h5


from keras.preprocessing.image import load_img
from keras.preprocessing.image import img_to_array
from mrcnn.config import Config
from mrcnn.model import MaskRCNN
from mrcnn import model as modellib
from mrcnn import visualize

from matplotlib import pyplot
from matplotlib.patches import Rectangle
import cv2
import numpy as np
import imutils
import colorsys
import random
import os

# load the class label names from disk, one label per line
#The content does not seem to be correct
#CCLASS_NAMES = open('coco_labels.txt').read().strip().split("\n")

CLASS_NAMES = ['BG', 'person', 'bicycle', 'car', 'motorcycle', 'airplane',
               'bus', 'train', 'truck', 'boat', 'traffic light',
               'fire hydrant', 'stop sign', 'parking meter', 'bench', 'bird',
               'cat', 'dog', 'horse', 'sheep', 'cow', 'elephant', 'bear',
               'zebra', 'giraffe', 'backpack', 'umbrella', 'handbag', 'tie',
               'suitcase', 'frisbee', 'skis', 'snowboard', 'sports ball',
               'kite', 'baseball bat', 'baseball glove', 'skateboard',
               'surfboard', 'tennis racket', 'bottle', 'wine glass', 'cup',
```

```
                    'fork', 'knife', 'spoon', 'bowl', 'banana', 'apple',
                    'sandwich', 'orange', 'broccoli', 'carrot', 'hot dog', 'pizza',
                    'donut', 'cake', 'chair', 'couch', 'potted plant', 'bed',
                    'dining table', 'toilet', 'tv', 'laptop', 'mouse', 'remote',
                    'keyboard', 'cell phone', 'microwave', 'oven', 'toaster',
                    'sink', 'refrigerator', 'book', 'clock', 'vase', 'scissors',
                    'teddy bear', 'hair drier', 'toothbrush']
#
# generate random (but visually distinct) colors for each class label
# (thanks to Matterport Mask R-CNN for the method!)
hsv = [(i / len(CLASS_NAMES), 1, 1.0) for i in
range(len(CLASS_NAMES))]
COLORS = list(map(lambda c: colorsys.hsv_to_rgb(*c), hsv))
random.seed(42)
random.shuffle(COLORS)


# define the test configuration
class TestConfig(Config):
    NAME = "test"
    GPU_COUNT = 1
    IMAGES_PER_GPU = 1
    NUM_CLASSES = 1 + 80


# define the model
rcnn = MaskRCNN(mode='inference', model_dir='./',
config=TestConfig())
# load coco model weights
rcnn.load_weights('mask_rcnn_coco.h5', by_name=True)


image = cv2.imread("./apple.jpeg")
image = cv2.cvtColor(image, cv2.COLOR_BGR2RGB)
image = imutils.resize(image, width=512)
r = rcnn.detect([image], verbose=1)[0]


for i in range(0, r["rois"].shape[0]):
        classID = r["class_ids"][i]
        mask = r["masks"][:, :, i]
        color = COLORS[classID][::-1]
        # visualize the pixel-wise mask of the object
        image = visualize.apply_mask(image, mask, color, alpha=0.5)


mage = cv2.cvtColor(image, cv2.COLOR_RGB2BGR)
for i in range(0, len(r["scores"])):
        (startY, startX, endY, endX) = r["rois"][i]
        classID = r["class_ids"][i]
        label = CLASS_NAMES[classID]
```

```
                    score = r["scores"][i]
                    color = [int(c) for c in np.array(COLORS[classID]) * 255]
                    # draw the bounding box, class label, and score of the object
                    cv2.rectangle(image, (startX, startY), (endX, endY), color, 2)
                    text = "{}: {:.3f}".format(label, score)
                    y = startY - 10 if startY - 10 > 10 else startY + 10
                    cv2.putText(image, text, (startX, y), cv2.
FONT_HERSHEY_SIMPLEX,
                                    0.6, color, 2)
            cv2.imshow('image', image)
```

EXERCISE 7.14

Modify the earlier Python program, trying different images. Run the program and comment on the accuracy and speed.

Example 7.11 is a webcam version of the earlier code for object detection that uses the MaskRCNN library. It works on TensorFlow 1.x, and it is very slow.

EXAMPLE 7.11   THE MASK R-CNN WEBCAM.PY PROGRAM

```
# Example 7.11 Object Detection from live webcam feed with MaskRCNN
# Modified based on:
# https://machinelearningmastery.com/how-to-perform-object-detection-
in-photographs-with-mask-r-cnn-in-keras/
# example of inference with a pretrained coco model

from keras.preprocessing.image import load_img
from keras.preprocessing.image import img_to_array
from mrcnn.config import Config
from mrcnn.model import MaskRCNN
from mrcnn import model as modellib
from mrcnn import visualize


from matplotlib import pyplot
from matplotlib.patches import Rectangle
import cv2
import numpy as np
import imutils
import colorsys
import random
import os

# load the class label names from disk, one label per line
#The content does not seem to be correct
#CCLASS_NAMES = open('coco_labels.txt').read().strip().split("\n")
```

```
CLASS_NAMES = ['BG', 'person', 'bicycle', 'car', 'motorcycle', 'airplane',
               'bus', 'train', 'truck', 'boat', 'traffic light',
               'fire hydrant', 'stop sign', 'parking meter', 'bench', 'bird',
               'cat', 'dog', 'horse', 'sheep', 'cow', 'elephant', 'bear',
               'zebra', 'giraffe', 'backpack', 'umbrella', 'handbag', 'tie',
               'suitcase', 'frisbee', 'skis', 'snowboard', 'sports ball',
               'kite', 'baseball bat', 'baseball glove', 'skateboard',
               'surfboard', 'tennis racket', 'bottle', 'wine glass', 'cup',
               'fork', 'knife', 'spoon', 'bowl', 'banana', 'apple',
               'sandwich', 'orange', 'broccoli', 'carrot', 'hot dog', 'pizza',
               'donut', 'cake', 'chair', 'couch', 'potted plant', 'bed',
               'dining table', 'toilet', 'tv', 'laptop', 'mouse', 'remote',
               'keyboard', 'cell phone', 'microwave', 'oven', 'toaster',
               'sink', 'refrigerator', 'book', 'clock', 'vase', 'scissors',
               'teddy bear', 'hair drier', 'toothbrush']
#
# generate random (but visually distinct) colors for each class label
# (thanks to Matterport Mask R-CNN for the method!)
hsv = [(i / len(CLASS_NAMES), 1, 1.0) for i in range(len(CLASS_NAMES))]
COLORS = list(map(lambda c: colorsys.hsv_to_rgb(*c), hsv))
random.seed(42)
random.shuffle(COLORS)




# define the test configuration
class TestConfig(Config):
     NAME = "test"
     GPU_COUNT = 1
     IMAGES_PER_GPU = 1
     NUM_CLASSES = 1 + 80

# define the model
rcnn = MaskRCNN(mode='inference', model_dir-'./', config=TestConfig())
# load coco model weights
rcnn.load_weights('mask_rcnn_coco.h5', by_name=True)

# Read video
cap = cv2.VideoCapture(0)
vf='./Vehicle Detection/vehicle-detection-master/examples/
PedalPostIncident20200821.mp4'
#cap = cv2.VideoCapture(vf)
#while cap.isOpened():
#    ok, image = cap.read()
#    if not ok:
#        break

while True:
```

```
#    image = cv2.imread("images/3ft.jpg")
    image = cv2.imread("./apple.jpeg")
    image = cv2.cvtColor(image, cv2.COLOR_BGR2RGB)
    image = imutils.resize(image, width=512)
    # perform a forward pass of the network to obtain the results
    print("[INFO] making predictions with Mask R-CNN...")
    r = rcnn.detect([image], verbose=1)[0]


    # loop over of the detected object's bounding boxes and masks
    for i in range(0, r["rois"].shape[0]):
        # extract the class ID and mask for the current detection, then
        # grab the color to visualize the mask (in BGR format)
        classID = r["class_ids"][i]
        mask = r["masks"][:, :, i]
        color = COLORS[classID][::-1]
        # visualize the pixel-wise mask of the object
        image = visualize.apply_mask(image, mask, color, alpha=0.5)


    # convert the image back to BGR so we can use OpenCV's drawing
    # functions
    mage = cv2.cvtColor(image, cv2.COLOR_RGB2BGR)
    # loop over the predicted scores and class labels
    for i in range(0, len(r["scores"])):
        # extract the bounding box information, class ID, label,
predicted
        # probability, and visualization color
        (startY, startX, endY, endX) = r["rois"][i]
        classID = r["class_ids"][i]
        label = CLASS_NAMES[classID]
        score = r["scores"][i]
        color = [int(c) for c in np.array(COLORS[classID]) * 255]
        # draw the bounding box, class label, and score of the object
        cv2.rectangle(image, (startX, startY), (endX, endY), color, 2)
        text = "{}: {:.3f}".format(label, score)
        y = startY - 10 if startY - 10 > 10 else startY + 10
        cv2.putText(image, text, (startX, y), cv2.FONT_HERSHEY_SIMPLEX,
                    0.6, color, 2)
    # show the output image
    cv2.imshow('video image', image)
    key = cv2.waitKey(30)
    if key == 27: # press 'ESC' to quit
        break

cap.release()
cv2.destroyAllWindows()
```

EXERCISE 7.15

Modify the earlier Python program, trying different images. Run the program, and comment on the accuracy and speed.

Gluon Object Detection

The Gluon library in Apache MXNet is another popular library that provides a clear, concise, and simple API for deep learning. It makes it easy to prototype, build, and train deep learning models without sacrificing training speed.

Example 7.12 shows some simple code for object detection by using the Gluon library. It is modified based on the following:

```
https://cv.gluon.ai/build/examples_detection/demo_webcam.html
```

EXAMPLE 7.12   THE GLUONWEBCAM.PY **PROGRAM**

```python
# Example 7.12 Object Detection from live webcam feed with Gluon
# Modified based on:
# https://cv.gluon.ai/build/examples_detection/demo_webcam.html
import gluoncv as gcv
import cv2
import mxnet as mx

# Load the model
net = gcv.model_zoo.get_model('ssd_512_mobilenet1.0_voc', pretrained=True)
# Compile the model for faster speed
net.hybridize()

# Load the webcam handler
cap = cv2.VideoCapture(0)

while(cap.isOpened()):
    ret, frame = cap.read()
    frame = mx.nd.array(cv2.cvtColor(frame, cv2.COLOR_BGR2RGB))
.astype('uint8')
    rgb_nd, frame = gcv.data.transforms.presets.ssd.transform_
test(frame, short=512, max_size=700)
    class_IDs, scores, bounding_boxes = net(rgb_nd)

    # Display the result
    img = gcv.utils.viz.cv_plot_bbox(frame, bounding_boxes[0],
scores[0], class_IDs[0], class_names=net.classes)
    gcv.utils.viz.cv_plot_image(img)
```

```
        if cv2.waitKey(1) & 0xFF == ord('q'):
            break

    cap.release()
    cv2.destroyAllWindows()
```

In the program, the following will load the deep learning model and compile it for faster speed:

```
net = gcv.model_zoo.get_model('ssd_512_mobilenet1.0_voc', pretrained=True)
net.hybridize()
```

This is to prepare the webcam frame into the required format and detect the object in the frame:

```
    frame = mx.nd.array(cv2.cvtColor(frame, cv2.COLOR_BGR2RGB)).
astype('uint8')
    rgb_nd, frame = gcv.data.transforms.presets.ssd.transform_
test(frame, short=512, max_size=700)
    class_IDs, scores, bounding_boxes = net(rgb_nd)
```

This is to draw the box around the objects in the frame:

```
    img = gcv.utils.viz.cv_plot_bbox(frame, bounding_boxes[0],
scores[0], class_IDs[0], class_names=net.classes)
    gcv.utils.viz.cv_plot_image(img)
```

EXERCISE 7.16

Modify the earlier Python program, and use the different model, such as YOLOv3, as shown here:

```
  net = model_zoo.get_model('yolo3_darknet53_voc',
pretrained=True)
```

Run the program and comment on the accuracy and speed.

7.2.5   Object Detection with Colab OpenCV

Google Colab is a great platform for Python programming on machine learning and deep learning. But one of the difficulties is to work with a webcam. The following example shows how to work with a webcam in Google Colab and perform object detection. We will show the code section by section, and you can get the full code from the `Camera_Capture.ipynb` notebook file. To use it, just log in to your Google Colab account, and upload the notebook file.

Figure 7.5 shows the Section 1 code to start the webcam (top) and the webcam image displayed (bottom). After running the section, you will see live images from the webcam.

Figure 7.5: The Section 1 code to start the webcam (top) and the webcam image displayed (bottom)

Figure 7.6 shows the Section 2 code to record a video from the webcam (top) and the video recorded (bottom). When you run the section, it will start recording; click the button to stop recoding. After it's stopped, the video will be saved in a file called `test.mp4`, and you will be able to view the video.

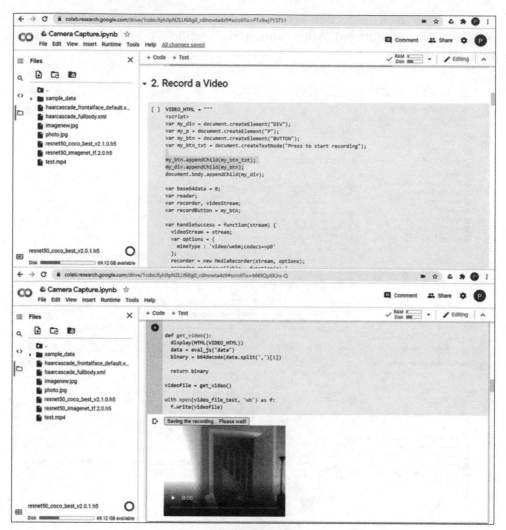

Figure 7.6: The Section 2 code to record a video from a webcam (top) and the video recorded (bottom)

Figure 7.7 shows the Section 3 code to capture an image from a webcam (top) and the image captured (bottom). After you run the section, it will start showing the webcam image; click the Capture button to capture an image.

Figure 7.8 shows the Section 4 code to use OpenCV to perform full body detection from the webcam video file called `test.mp4`.

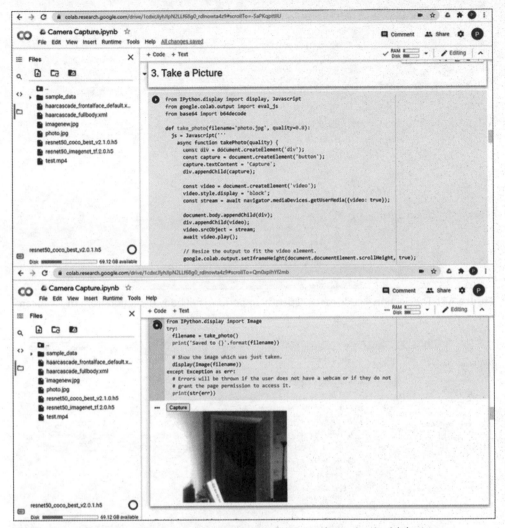

Figure 7.7: The Section 3 code to capture an image from a webcam (top) and the image captured (bottom)

Figure 7.9 shows the Section 5 code to perform object detection by using the ImageAI library on an image. It first installs the ImageAI library, then uses the !wget command to download the ResNet model to Google Colab, and finally performs the object detection on the photo.jpg image file.

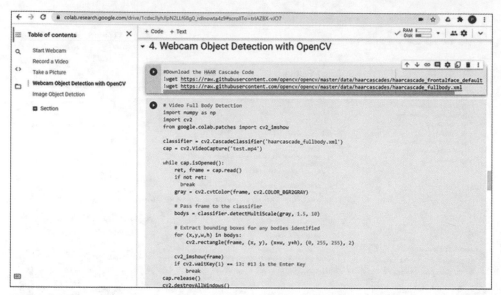

Figure 7.8: The Section 4 code to use OpenCV to perform full body detection from the webcam video image

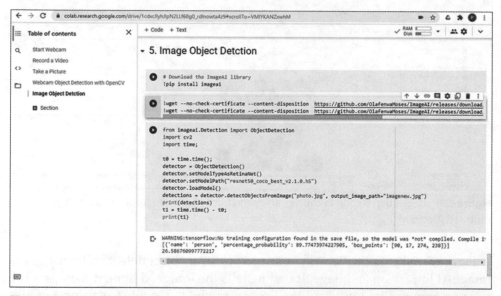

Figure 7.9: The Section 5 code to perform object detection by using the ImageAI library on an image file called `photo.jpg`

EXERCISE 7.17

Log in to your Google Colab account, and upload the `Camera_Capture.ipynb` file. Run the program and comment on the results.

7.3   Object Detections with Custom Trained Models

With pretrained models, you can only recognize the objects that have been predefined. To recognize your own objects in your own images, you will need to retrain/update the pretrained models with your own data; this is a type of transfer learning. This is exactly the same as the image classification we covered in Chapter 5. In this section, we will introduce how to retrain models on your own objects by using OpenCV, YOLO, TensorFlow, Gluon, and ImageAI.

7.3.1   OpenCV

As you have seen, you can use Haar cascade code for detecting objects in OpenCV. You can also train the Haar cascade code for your own customized objects. In the following example, we will show how to train Haar cascade code to detect an otter in an image.

Step 1

To train Haar cascade code from scratch, you will require software. So, download the `Cascade-Trainer-GUI` software using the following link:

    https://amin-ahmadi.com/cascade-trainer-gui/

After downloading, install it and launch it.

Step 2

For training a custom object detector using Haar cascade code, you will need a training image dataset. In this example, we get the otter image dataset from Bing Images (`https://www.bing.com/images/`) by using a Python library named `icrawler`.

Besides Bing Images, you can also use it for Google and Baidu Images. For more details about `icrawler`, visit its website:

    https://icrawler.readthedocs.io/en/latest/builtin.html

To install `icrawler`, type the following command:

```
pip install icrawler
```

Step 3

To create a dataset XML file, you will need to classify the images you have into positive images and negative images. Positive images are images with the object you want to predict, and negative images are images without the object you want to predict.

Example 7.13 shows how to search and download positive images (otter) as well as negative images (not otter) from the Bing Images website.

EXAMPLE 7.13   THE OPENCVHAARCASCADE.PY **PROGRAM**

```
# Example 7.13 Training Haar Cascade Code - Prepare Images
# pip install icrawler
from icrawler.builtin import BingImageCrawler
# Find some Otter images and save them in the /p directory
classes=['otter']
number=100
for c in classes:
    bing_crawler=BingImageCrawler(storage={'root_dir':f'p/'})
    bing_crawler.crawl(keyword=c,filters=None,max_num=number,offset=0)

# Find some non-Otter images and save them in the /n directory
classes=['trees','roads','cars']
number=100
for c in classes:
    print(number)
    bing_crawler=BingImageCrawler(storage={'root_dir':f'n/'})
    bing_crawler.crawl(keyword=c,filters=None,m
ax_num=number,offset=0)
    number = number + number
```

After running the program, you will see two folders created, a p folder for positive images and an n folder for negative images. The following are the file structures, assuming your current folder is E:/Chapter 7/:

```
E:/Chapter 7/
    |--p/
       |--000001.jpg
       |--000002.jpg
       ... ...
    |--n/
       |--000001.jpg
       |--000002.jpg
       ... ...
```

Step 4

Open the Cascade-Trainer-GUI program, and paste the current folder path E:/Chapter 7/ into a sample folder location. Please also count the number of negative images and put it in the negative image count, as shown in Figure 7.10. Then click the Start button to train and generate the otter Haar cascade code.

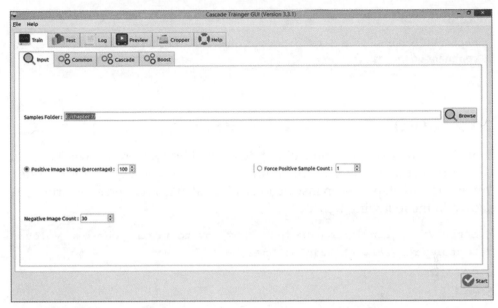

Figure 7.10: The `Cascade-Trainer-GUI` program with the sample folder input and the negative image count input

Step 5

After running it, a new directory named `classifier` will be created, and a new file named `cascade.xml` will be created.

From the Bing Images website, find an otter image, and save it to a file. Example 7.14 shows how to use the `cascade.xml` file to detect an otter in the file.

EXAMPLE 7.14   THE `OPENCVHAARCASCADE.PY` **PROGRAM**

```
# Example 7.14 Training Haar Cascade Code - Testing the Trained Code

import cv2
face_cascade=cv2.CascadeClassifier(r"./classifier/cascade.xml")
img= cv2.imread(r"Otter_6336.jpeg")
scale_percent = 60 # percent of original size
width = int(img.shape[1] * scale_percent / 100)
height = int(img.shape[0] * scale_percent / 100)
dim = (width, height)
resized = cv2.resize(img,dim)
gray=cv2.cvtColor(resized,cv2.COLOR_BGR2GRAY)
faces=face_cascade.detectMultiScale(gray,6.5,17)
for(x,y,w,h) in faces:
    resized=cv2.rectangle(resized,(x,y),(x+w,y+h),(0,255,0),2)
cv2.imshow('img',resized)
cv2.waitKey(0)
cv2.destroyAllWindows()
```

EXERCISE 7.18

Repeat the earlier steps, and create your own object dataset. Run the program and comment on the results.

7.3.2 YOLO

YOLO is an amazing real-time object detection library. Here we will use skin cancer detection as an example to illustrate training your YOLOv3 model. We will follow step-by-step instructions, illustrated in an interesting article, as shown in the following website.

```
https://blog.insightdatascience.com/how-to-train-your-own-yolov3-
detector-from-scratch-224d10e55de2
```

Step 1

Clone the GitHub repository onto the local computer, as shown in the following linking.

```
https://github.com/AntonMu/TrainYourOwnYOLO
```

Step 2

Create your own skin cancer image dataset from `https://www.isic-archive.com` and put into the `TrainYourOwnYOLO/Data/Source_Images/` folder, as shown next. The training images are stored in the `Training_Images` folder. The testing images are stored in the `Test_Images` folder.

```
TrainYourOwnYOLO/
      |--Data/
            |--Source_Images/
                  |--Training_Images/
                        |--actinic_keratorsis_0024468.jpg
                        |--actinic_keratorsis_0024470.jpg
                        ... ...
                        |--carcinoma_0001120.jpg
                        |--carcinoma_0001149.jpg
                        ... ...
                        |--nevus_0000000.jpg
                        |--nevus_0000001.jpg
                        |--nevus_0000003.jpg
                        ... ...
```

```
|--Test_Images/
        |--actinic_keratorsis_0032437.jpg

    ... ...

        |--carcinoma_0028542.jpg

    ... ...

        |--nevus_0000075.jpg

    ... ...
```

Step 3

Annotate your own image dataset by using Microsoft's Visual Object Tagging Tool (VoTT). From the following link, download and install the VoTT software.

```
https://github.com/Microsoft/VoTT/releases
```

Run the VoTT software and create a new project by clicking the New Project button, as shown in Figure 7.11.

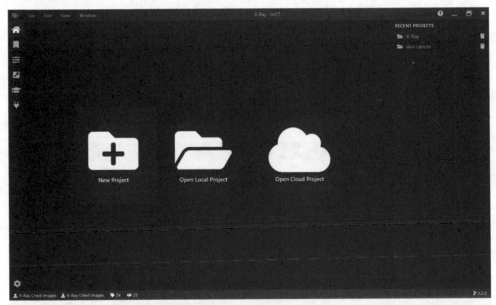

Figure 7.11: The VoTT software for creating a new project

You will then be brought to the new Project Settings page, as shown in Figure 7.12. Put **Annotations** for the display name. Then click the Add Connection button for Source Connection.

You will then be brought to the Connection Settings page, as shown in Figure 7.13. Choose Skin Cancer as the display name, choose Local File System

Figure 7.12: The VoTT software for new project settings

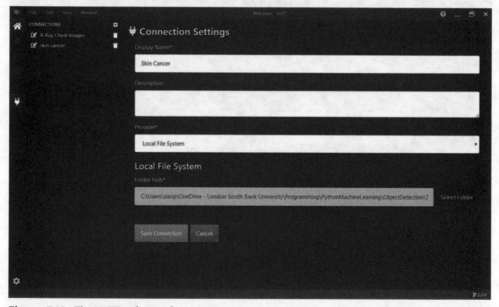

Figure 7.13: The VoTT software for creating a new connection setting

as the provider, and choose the `TrainYourOwnYOLO/Data/Source_Images/ Training_Images` folder as the folder path. Click the green Save Connection button to save the settings.

This will bring you back to the Project Setting page, as shown in Figure 7.12. Select Skin Cancer for both Source Connection and Target Connection. Click the green Save Project button at the bottom of the page to save the project settings.

Next, you will be brought to the image annotation page, as shown in Figure 7.14. This is the most time-consuming part; just go through images and select and label the objects in the images. In this example, three types of skin cancer objects are labeled.

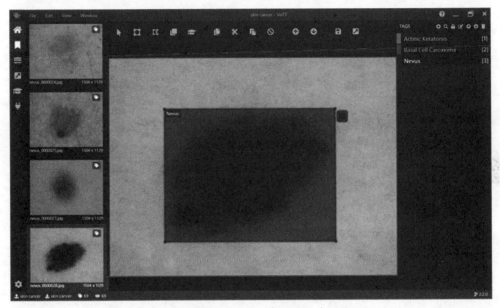

Figure 7.14: The VoTT software for annotating the objects in the images

Step 4

Go to the `TrainYourOwnYOLO/1_Image_Annotation` folder and run the Python program to convert the annotations to YOLO format.

```
python Convert_to_YOLO_format.py
```

Step 5

Go to the `TrainYourOwnYOLO/2_Training` folder and run the following Python to download the pretrained YOLOv3 weights:

```
python Download_and_Convert_YOLO_weights.py
```

After that's finished, run the following Python program to train your YOLOv3 model:

```
python TrainYourOwnYOLO/2_Training/Train_YOLO.py
```

After training, run the following Python program to test your YOLOv3 model. This will use the images in the `TrainYourOwnYOLO/Data/Source_Images/Test_Images` folder for detecting the skin cancer objects.

```
python TrainYourOwnYOLO/3_Inference/Train_YOLO.py
```

EXERCISE 7.19

Repeat the earlier steps, creating your own object dataset. Run the program and comment on the results.

7.3.3   TensorFlow, Gluon, and ImageAI

You can also train your own object detection models by using other libraries or frameworks, such as TensorFlow, Gluon, and ImageAI.

TensorFlow

The following shows how to also train your own object detection models by using TensorFlow:

```
https://tensorflow-object-detection-api-tutorial.readthedocs.io/
en/latest/training.html
https://neptune.ai/blog/how-to-train-your-own-object-detector-
using-tensorflow-object-detection-api
```

EXERCISE 7.20

Use the earlier links, create your own object dataset, and train your own TensorFlow object detection model. Run the program and comment on the results.

Gluon

The following shows how to also train your own object detection models by using Gluon:

```
https://cv.gluon.ai/build/examples_datasets/detection_custom.html
```

ImageAI

The following shows how to also train your own object detection models by using ImageAI:

```
https://github.com/OlafenwaMoses/ImageAI/blob/master/imageai/
Detection/Custom/CUSTOMVIDEODETECTION.md
```

7.4   Object Tracking

Object detection in images is simple and straightforward. Object detection in video is a different story. The simplest way is to perform object detection frame by frame. As a standard video typically has 30 frames per second, this approach is obviously inefficient and cumbersome. A much more elegant approach is through object tracking, which means you detect the object in the first frame and then simply track the same object in consequent frames. In this section, we will show how to do object tracking with OpenCV, YOLO, and Gluon.

7.4.1   Object Size and Distance Detection

Let's start with object size and distance detection first. With a webcam, you can easily detect the object size, distances, and speed. This may have many applications in real life. Figure 7.15 shows the simple camera imaging system and the relationships between object height (H), object distance (D), image height (h), and focal length (f).

If we know the object height (H), object distance (D), and image height (h), we can calculate the focal length (f). Once we know the focal length (f), we can calculate the object height (H) if we know object distance (D), or we can calculate the object distance (D), if we know object height (H).

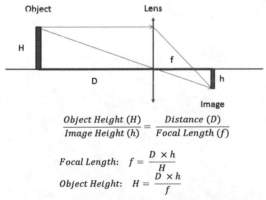

$$\frac{Object\ Height\ (H)}{Image\ Height\ (h)} = \frac{Distance\ (D)}{Focal\ Length\ (f)}$$

$$Focal\ Length:\quad f = \frac{D \times h}{H}$$

$$Object\ Height:\quad H = \frac{D \times h}{f}$$

Figure 7.15: The simple camera imaging system and the relationships between object height (H), object distance (D), image height (h), and focal length (f).

Example 7.15 shows a simple Python program to calculate the focal length of a webcam. It uses a standard A4 paper (210×297 mm) at 1040 mm distance to calculate the camera focal length.

EXAMPLE 7.15   THE `GETWEBCAMFOCALLENGTH.PY` **PROGRAM**

```python
# Example 7.15
# Use a standard A4 paper (210 x 297 mm),at 1040 mm distance,
# to calculate the Camera Focal Length

import cv2
import imutils

#sideway A4 paper size in mm
paperHeight = 210
paperWidth = 297
#Distance of A4 paper to camera in mm
distance = 1040

def find_paper(image):
    x,y,w,h = -1, -1, -1, -1
    gray = cv2.cvtColor(image, cv2.COLOR_BGR2GRAY)
    gray = cv2.GaussianBlur(gray, (5, 5), 0)

    mask  = cv2.Canny(gray, 35, 125)
    cv2.imshow('Mask', mask)
    #ret,mask = cv2.threshold(gray,127,255,0)
    contours, _ = cv2.findContours(mask, cv2.RETR_TREE, cv2
.CHAIN_APPROX_NONE)
    if len(contours)>0:
        c = max(contours, key = cv2.contourArea)
        cv2.drawContours(image, [c], 0, (0, 255, 0), 3)
        area = cv2.contourArea(c)
        #print(area)
        c = cv2.boundingRect(c)
        x,y,w,h = int(c[0]), int(c[1]),int(c[2]),int(c[3])
    return x,y,w,h

def getFocalLength(image, KNOWN_DISTANCE, KNOWN_WIDTH):
    focalLength = -1
    x,y,w,h = find_paper(image)
    focalLength = (w * KNOWN_DISTANCE) / KNOWN_WIDTH
    return x,y,w,h, focalLength


# capture frame from a video
cap = cv2.VideoCapture(0)
while True:
    # reads frame from a video
    ret, frame = cap.read()
```

```
      x,y,w,h, f = getFocalLength(frame, distance,paperWidth)

      if (f>0):
          cv2.rectangle(frame,(x,y),(x+w,y+h),(0,0,255),2)
          text = "Width: {:0.1f} Height: {:0.1f} pixels".format(w,h)
          cv2.putText(frame, text, (x, y-20), cv2.FONT_HERSHEY_SIMPLEX,
0.5, (0,0,255), 2)
          text = "Focal Length: {:0.1f}mm".format(f)
          cv2.putText(frame, text, (x, y-5), cv2.FONT_HERSHEY_SIMPLEX,
0.5, (0,0,255), 2)

      # Display frame in a window
      cv2.imshow('Webcam', frame)

      # Wait for Esc key to stop
      if cv2.waitKey(33) == 27:
          break

# close the already opened camera
cap.release()

# De-allocate any associated memory usage
cv2.destroyAllWindows()
```

Figure 7.16 shows the output of the program, including the detected A4 paper mask, the A4 paper width and height in pixels, and the calculated focal length in mm.

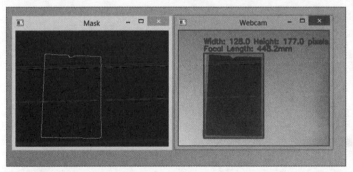

Figure 7.16: The detected A4 paper mask (left), the A4 paper width and height in pixels, and the calculated focal length in mm (right)

Once you know the focal length of the webcam, you will be then able to calculate the distance of A4 paper from the webcam.

Example 7.16 shows a simple Python program to calculate the distance of A4 paper to a webcam.

EXAMPLE 7.16   THE GETWEBCAMDISTANCE.PY **PROGRAM**

```
# Example 7.16
# Use a standard A4 paper (210 x 297 mm),at 1040 mm distance,
# to calculate the Camera Focal Length

import cv2
import imutils

focalLength = 448 #mm
#sideway A4 paper size in mm
paperHeight = 210
paperWidth = 297

def find_paper(image):
    x,y,w,h = -1, -1, -1, -1
    gray = cv2.cvtColor(image, cv2.COLOR_BGR2GRAY)
    gray = cv2.GaussianBlur(gray, (5, 5), 0)

    mask  = cv2.Canny(gray, 35, 125)
    cv2.imshow('Mask', mask)
    #ret,mask = cv2.threshold(gray,127,255,0)
    contours, _ = cv2.findContours(mask, cv2.RETR_TREE, cv2
.CHAIN_APPROX_NONE)
    if len(contours)>0:
        c = max(contours, key = cv2.contourArea)
        cv2.drawContours(image, [c], 0, (0, 255, 0), 3)
        area = cv2.contourArea(c)
        #print(area)
        c = cv2.boundingRect(c)
        x,y,w,h = int(c[0]), int(c[1]),int(c[2]),int(c[3])
    return x,y,w,h
def distance_to_camera(image, focalLength, KNOWN_WIDTH):
    x,y,w,h = find_paper(image)
    distance = (KNOWN_WIDTH * focalLength) / w
    return x,y,w,h, distance

# capture frame from a video
cap = cv2.VideoCapture(0)
while True:
    # reads frame from a video
    ret, frame = cap.read()

    x,y,w,h, D = distance_to_camera(frame, focalLength, paperWidth)

    if (D>0):
        cv2.rectangle(frame,(x,y),(x+w,y+h),(0,0,255),2)
        text = "Width: {:0.1f} Height: {:0.1f} pixels".format(w,h)
        cv2.putText(frame, text, (x, y-20), cv2.FONT_HERSHEY_SIMPLEX,
0.5, (0,0,255), 2)
```

```
        text = "Distance: {:0.1f}mm".format(D)
        cv2.putText(frame, text, (x, y-5), cv2.FONT_HERSHEY_SIMPLEX,
0.5, (0,0,255), 2)

    # Display frame in a window
    cv2.imshow('Webcam', frame)

    # Wait for Esc key to stop
    if cv2.waitKey(33) == 27:
        break

# close the already opened camera
cap.release()

# De-allocate any associated memory usage
cv2.destroyAllWindows()
```

Figure 7.17 shows two example outputs of the earlier program, including the detected A4 paper mask, the A4 paper width and height in pixels, and the calculated distance of A4 paper to the webcam in mm.

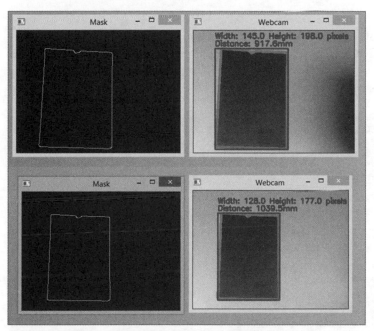

Figure 7.17: The detected A4 paper mask (left), the A4 paper width and height in pixels, and the calculated distance of A4 paper to the webcam in mm (right)

EXERCISE 7.22

Modify the earlier two programs so that they can work on a cycle shape object. Run the program and comment on the results.

You can find more details about detecting the object size, distance, and camera focus length from the following websites:

`http://emaraic.com/blog/distance-measurement`

`https://www.pyimagesearch.com/2015/01/19/find-distance-camera-objectmarker-using-python-opencv/`

`https://www.pyimagesearch.com/2016/04/04/measuring-distance-between-objects-in-an-image-with-opencv/`

7.4.2 Object Tracking with OpenCV

This section talks about object tracking with OpenCV.

Single Object Tracking with OpenCV

Example 7.17 is an example of single object tracking using a mouse to select a region of interest. It is modified from `https://www.learnopencv.com/object-tracking-using-opencv-cpp-python/`. It first opens the webcam, reads a frame, waits for you to select an ROI, and then performs the object tracking by using OpenCV's tracker. This program works only for single object tracking.

EXAMPLE 7.17 THE `WEBCAM OBJECTTRACKING ROI.PY` **PROGRAM**

```
# Example 7.17 webcam ObjectTracking ROI
# Modified based on:
# https://www.learnopencv.com/object-tracking-using-opencv-cpp-python/
import cv2
import sys

#OpenCV Trackers:
#tracker = cv2.TrackerBoosting_create()
tracker = cv2.TrackerMIL_create()
#tracker = cv2.TrackerKCF_create()
#tracker = cv2.TrackerTLD_create()
#tracker = cv2.TrackerMedianFlow_create()
#tracker = cv2.TrackerGOTURN_create()
#tracker = cv2.TrackerMOSSE_create()
#tracker = cv2.TrackerCSRT_create()
```

```
#Open Webcam and select a ROI box
video = cv2.VideoCapture(0)
ok, frame = video.read()
bbox = cv2.selectROI(frame, True)

# Initialize tracker with first frame and bounding box
ok = tracker.init(frame, bbox)

while True:
    ok, frame = video.read()
    # Start timer
    timer = cv2.getTickCount()

    if bbox is not None:
        ok, bbox = tracker.update(frame)
        # Calculate Frames per second (FPS)
        fps = cv2.getTickFrequency() / (cv2.getTickCount() - timer);
        # Draw bounding box
        if ok:
            p1 = (int(bbox[0]), int(bbox[1]))
            p2 = (int(bbox[0] + bbox[2]), int(bbox[1] + bbox[3]))
            cv2.rectangle(frame, p1, p2, (0,255,0), 2, 1)
        else :
            cv2.putText(frame, "Tracking failure detected", (100,80),
cv2.FONT_HERSHEY_SIMPLEX, 0.75,(0,0,255),2)

        # Display FPS on frame
        cv2.putText(frame, "FPS : " + str(int(fps)), (100,50),
cv2.FONT_HERSHEY_SIMPLEX, 0.75, (50,170,50), 2);
        # Display result
        cv2.imshow("Tracking", frame)
        # Exit if ESC pressed
        k = cv2.waitKey(1) & 0xff
        if k == 27 : break

video.release()
# close all windows
cv2.destroyAllWindows()
```

Figure 7.18 shows the output of the earlier program. In this case, a golf ball was selected in the first frame and was tracked in the subsequent frames. The program is capable of running 14 frames per second.

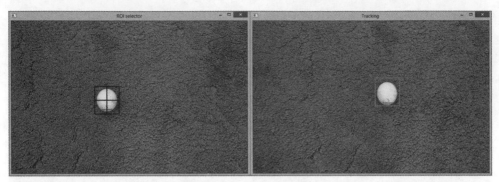

Figure 7.18: The object tracking through a webcam. A golf ball was selected in the first frame (left) and was tracked in the subsequent frames (right).

EXERCISE 7.23

Modify the earlier program, and try a different OpenCV tracker. Run the program and comment on the results.

Here are more examples of object tracking:

https://www.pyimagesearch.com/2018/07/23/simple-object-tracking-with-opencv/

https://www.pyimagesearch.com/2018/07/30/opencv-object-tracking/

https://learnopencv.com/object-tracking-using-opencv-cpp-python/

Multiple Object Tracking with OpenCV

Example 7.18 shows an example of multiple object tracking using a mouse to select a region of interest. It is modified from `https://stackoverflow.com/questions/54730427/multi-object-tracking-initialization-in-opencv-using-multitracker-object`. In this program, you press the S key to select an ROI on the webcam image, and you press the R key to clear all the selections.

EXAMPLE 7.18 THE `OBJECTOPENCV.PY` **PROGRAM**

```
# Example 7.18 OpenCV multi-objects tracking
# Modified based on:
# https://stackoverflow.com/questions/54730427/multi-object-tracking-
initialization-in-opencv-using-multitracker-object
# Worked for multi Object tracking
# This programe doesn't work for OpenCV > 4.5.0

import imutils
import cv2
```

```python
from random import randint

trackerName = 'csrt'

OPENCV_OBJECT_TRACKERS = {
    "csrt": cv2.TrackerCSRT_create,
    "kcf": cv2.TrackerKCF_create,
    "boosting": cv2.TrackerBoosting_create,
    "mil": cv2.TrackerMIL_create,
    "tld": cv2.TrackerTLD_create,
    "medianflow": cv2.TrackerMedianFlow_create,
    "mosse": cv2.TrackerMOSSE_create
}

# initialize OpenCV's special multi-object tracker
trackers = cv2.MultiTracker_create()
cap = cv2.VideoCapture(0)

while cap.isOpened():

    ret, frame = cap.read()

    if frame is None:
        break

    frame = imutils.resize(frame, width=600)
    (success, boxes) = trackers.update(frame)

    # loop over the bounding boxes and draw them on the frame
    count = 1
    for box in boxes:
        (x, y, w, h) = [int(v) for v in box]
        cv2.rectangle(frame, (x, y), (x + w, y + h), (0, 255, 0), 2)
        cv2.putText(frame, str(count) , (x,y), cv2.FONT_HERSHEY_
SIMPLEX, 0.75, (50,170,50), 2)
        print(count)
        count = count + 1
    cv2.imshow("Frame", frame)
    key = cv2.waitKey(1) & 0xFF

    # if the 's' key is selected, we are going to "select" a bounding
    # box to track
    if key == ord("s"):
        colors = []
        # select the bounding box of the object we want to track (make
        # sure you press ENTER or SPACE after selecting the ROI)
        box = cv2.selectROIs("Frame", frame, fromCenter=False,
                             showCrosshair=True)
        box = tuple(map(tuple, box))
        for bb in box:
```

```
                  tracker = OPENCV_OBJECT_TRACKERS[trackerName]()
                  trackers.add(tracker, frame, bb)


        # if you want to reset bounding box, select the 'r' key
        elif key == ord("r"):
            trackers.clear()
            trackers = cv2.MultiTracker_create()

            box = cv2.selectROIs("Frame", frame, fromCenter=False,
                            showCrosshair=True)
            box = tuple(map(tuple, box))
            for bb in box:
                  tracker = OPENCV_OBJECT_TRACKERS[trackerName]()
                  trackers.add(tracker, frame, bb)


        elif key == ord("q"):
            break
    cap.release()
    cv2.destroyAllWindows()
```

Figure 7.19 shows the output of the earlier program. When run the program, press s key to freeze the video, select a region of a golf ball (top), press Enter key, select another region of another golf ball (middle), press Enter key, and then press the Esc key to start tracking (bottom). You can also press s key to reset the selection.

7.4.2   Object Tracking with YOLOv4 and DeepSORT

You can also implement object tracking with YOLO. The following link shows an interesting object tracking project implemented with YOLOv4, called DeepSORT:

```
https://github.com/theAIGuysCode/yolov4-deepsort
```

YOLOv4 is a state-of-the-art algorithm for object detection. Built on the output of YOLOv4, DeepSORT has to be able to create a highly accurate object tracker.

An IPython notebook called YOLOv4_DeepSORT.ipynb has been created, which you can upload to Google Colab to play with.

Example 7.19 highlights some of the code. It first clones the DeepSORT project into your Google Colab and installs all the required libraries. Download the YOLOv4 weights, put it in the /yolov4-deepsort/data/ directory, convert it to a TensorFlow model, and run the DeepSORT object tracker on a video called car.mp4. The result is saved in a file called car.avi. The code also supports YOLOv4 tiny weights; just download the tiny weights and follow the same procedure. The result is saved in a file called car.avi. The video file car.mp4 is also from www.pexels.com.

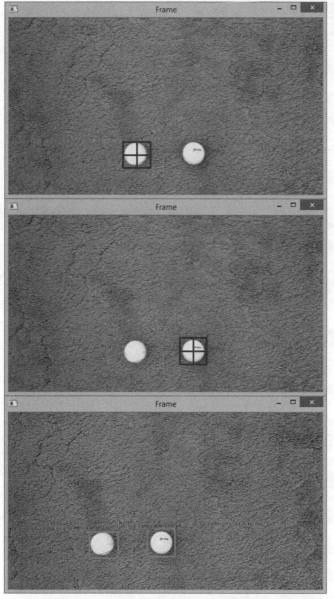

Figure 7.19: The multiple objects tracking through a webcam. Two golf balls were selected (top and middle) and were tracked (bottom).

EXAMPLE 7.19   THE `YOLOV4_DEEPSORT.IPYNB` **PROGRAM**

```
# Example 7.19 YOLOv4_DeepSORT on Google Colab
#https://github.com/theAIGuysCode/yolov4-deepsort
#!git clone https://github.com/theAIGuysCode/yolov4-deepsort
!git clone https://github.com/PerryXiao2015/yolov4-deepsort

# TensorFlow GPU
!pip install -r requirements-gpu.txt

!curl -L "https://drive.google.com/u/0/uc?export=download&confirm=T6-
x&id=1cewMfusmPjYWbrnuJRuKhPMwRe_b9PaT" > yolov4.weights

!mv yolov4.weights /content/yolov4-deepsort/data/

# Convert darknet weights to tensorflow model
!python save_model.py --model yolov4

# Run yolov4 deep sort object tracker on video
!python object_tracker.py --video ./data/video/car.mp4 --output
./outputs/car.avi --model yolov4

# Run yolov4 deep sort object tracker on webcam (set video flag to 0)
#!python object_tracker.py --video 0 --output ./outputs/webcam.avi
--model yolov4

!wget https://github.com/AlexeyAB/darknet/releases/download/darknet_
yolo_v4_pre/yolov4-tiny.weights
!mv yolov4-tiny.weights /content/yolov4-deepsort/data/

import os
os.environ["CUDA_VISIBLE_DEVICES"] = "1"
from google.colab.patches import cv2_imshow
#cv2_imshow(img)

# save yolov4-tiny model
!python save_model.py --weights ./data/yolov4-tiny.weights --output
./checkpoints/yolov4-tiny-416 --model yolov4 --tiny

# Run yolov4-tiny object tracker
!python object_tracker.py --weights ./checkpoints/yolov4-tiny-416
--model yolov4 --video ./data/video/cars.mp4 --output ./outputs/
cartiny.avi --tiny
```

Figure 7.20 shows the output of the video tracking results of the earlier program. As you can see, it can identify and track different cars; the tracking tails from the center of each car box shows relative movement of the car within the frame.

Figure 7.20: The video tracking result of the YOLOv4-DeepSORT project

(Source: `https://colab.research.google.com/drive/1EnaiYUrH-M8ZDKJPCX_D7_9tNziPICf0`)

EXERCISE 7.24

Following the information earlier, try to run the DeepSORT project program on your own videos. Comment on the results.

7.4.3   Object Tracking with Gluon

You can also perform object tracking with the Gluon library; see the following link for more information.

```
https://cv.gluon.ai/build/examples_tracking/index.html
```

7.5   Image Segmentation

Image segmentation is important for many applications. Image segmentation can be divided into image semantic segmentation and image instance segmentation. *Image semantic segmentation* is to find out which object category each pixel belongs to.

Image instance segmentation is similar to image semantic segmentation but goes even further; it not only identifies each pixel which object category it belongs to but also identifies each pixel which object instance it belongs.

Figure 7.21 shows the differences between image semantic segmentation and image instance segmentation.

Original Image   Semantic Segmentation   Instance Segmentation

Figure 7.21: The differences between semantic segmentation and instance segmentation

When semantic segmentation is applied, all the pears belong to the same category and therefore are colored the same. In instance segmentation, it goes even further; different pears belong to different instances and hence are colored differently.

7.5.1   Image Semantic Segmentation and Image Instance Segmentation

This section covers different tools for image semantic segmentation and image instance segmentation.

PexelLib

PexelLib is a Python library that can perform object detection, image semantic segmentation, and image instance segmentation; see `https://github.com/ayoolaolafenwa/PixelLib`.

Example 7.20 is an image semantic segmentation example. You need to download the DeepLab V3 Xception model library from `https://github.com/ayoolaolafenwa/PixelLib/releases/download/1.1/deeplabv3_xception_tf_dim_ordering_tf_kernels.h5`.

EXAMPLE 7.20   THE `PIXELLIB SEMANTIC SEGMENT.PY` **PROGRAM**

```
#Example 7.20 Pixellib Semantic Segmentation
#pip install pixellib
import pixellib
from pixellib.semantic import semantic_segmentation
import cv2
```

```
segment_image = semantic_segmentation()
segment_image.load_pascalvoc_model("deeplabv3_xception_tf_dim_
ordering_tf_kernels.h5")

f = "city0.jpeg"
segment_image.segmentAsPascalvoc(f, output_image_name = "output.jpg",
overlay = True)
image = cv2.imread(f)
cv2.imshow("Original", image)
output = cv2.imread("output.jpg")
cv2.imshow("Semantic Segment", output)
```

EXERCISE 7.25

Modify the earlier program, trying different images. Run the program and comment on the results.

You can also apply semantic segmentation on webcam or video files, as shown in Example 7.21. As you can see, it is quite slow to apply semantic segmentation on a webcam and video.

EXAMPLE 7.21   THE `PIXELLIB SEMANTIC WEBCAM.PY` PROGRAM

```
#Example 7.21 Pixellib Semantic Segmentation - Webcam Feed
#Model download
#https://github.com/ayoolaolafenwa/PixelLib/releases/download/1.1/
deeplabv3_xception_tf_dim_ordering_tf_kernels.h5

import pixellib
from pixellib.semantic import semantic_segmentation
import cv2

capture = cv2.VideoCapture(0)
segment_video = semantic_segmentation()
segment_video.load_pascalvoc_model("deeplabv3_xception_tf_dim_
ordering_tf_kernels.h5")
#Webcam
segment_video.process_camera_pascalvoc(capture, overlay = True,
frames_per_second= 15, output_video_name="output_video.mp4", show_
frames= True,frame_name= "frame", check_fps = True)
#Video
#segment_video.process_video("cityscene.mp4", show_bboxes = True,
frames_per_second= 15, output_video_name="output_video.mp4")
```

EXERCISE 7.26

Modify the earlier program, trying it on a webcam first; then try it on a video file. Run the program and comment on the results.

Example 7.22 shows a different version of the earlier example on a webcam. In this example, it processes frame by frame from the webcam, saving the results to a file. Then load in the file, and display the file. As you will see, this approach is even slower.

EXAMPLE 7.22 THE `PIXELLIB SEMANTIC WEBCAM 2.PY` **PROGRAM**

```
import pixellib
from pixellib.semantic import semantic_segmentation
import cv2

segment_frame = semantic_segmentation()
segment_frame.load_pascalvoc_model("deeplabv3_xception_tf_dim_
ordering_tf_kernels.h5")

cap = cv2.VideoCapture(0)
count = 0
while True:
    ret, frame = cap.read()
    outfile = str(count) + ".jpg"
    segment_frame.segmentFrameAsPascalvoc(frame, output_frame_name=
outfile, overlay = True)
    image = cv2.imread(outfile)
    cv2.imshow("Semantic Segmentation",image)
    count = count + 1
    k = cv2.waitKey(1) & 0xff
    if k == 27 :
        breakcap.release()
cv2.destroyAllWindows()
```

Example 7.23 is an image instance segmentation example that uses PixelLib.

EXAMPLE 7.23 THE `PIXELLIB INSTANCE SEGMENT.PY` **PROGRAM**

```
#Example 7.23 Pixellib Instance Segment
#pip install pixellib
import pixellib
from pixellib.instance import instance_segmentation
import cv2
```

```
segment_frame = instance_segmentation()
segment_frame.load_model("mask_rcnn_coco.h5")

image = cv2.imread("strawberrys2.jpeg")
cv2.imshow("Original", image)

segmask, output =segment_frame.segmentFrame(image)
cv2.imshow("Instance Segment", output)
```

Example 7.24 is the webcam version of the earlier image instance segmentation example.

EXAMPLE 7.24   THE `PIXELLIB INSTANCE WEBCAM.PY` **PROGRAM**

```python
#Example 7.24 Pixellib Instance Webcam Feed
import time
import pixellib
from pixellib.instance import instance_segmentation
import cv2

segment_frame = instance_segmentation()
segment_frame.load_model("mask_rcnn_coco.h5")

capture = cv2.VideoCapture(0)
while True:
    start = time.time()
    ret, frame = capture.read()
    segmask, output =segment_frame.segmentFrame(frame)
    # Display result
    cv2.imshow("Webcam", output)

    # Exit if ESC pressed
    k = cv2.waitKey(1) & 0xff
    if k == 27 :
        break     end = time.time()
    print(f"Inference Time: {end-start:.2f}seconds")
```

EXERCISE 7.27

Modify the earlier program, trying different instance segmentation models. Run the program and comment on the results.

One of the major advantages of PixelLib is simplicity. You can also build your own custom trained object detector by using PixelLib with just seven lines of code; see the following link for details.

```
https://github.com/ayoolaolafenwa/PixelLib#Custom-Training-with-
7-Lines-of-Code
```

Detectron2

Facebook's Detectron2 is another popular image segmentation library. Detectron2 is based on the PyTorch framework. It also provides a Google Colab notebook file for you to try; see the following links for details.

```
https://github.com/facebookresearch/detectron2
https://colab.research.google.com/drive/16jcaJoc6bCFAQ96jDe2HwtX
j7BMD_-m5
```

Gluon CV

Another powerful deep learning framework is Gluon CV, which can do a range of things, including image segmentation and object detection. See the following link for the Gluon GitHub website.

```
https://github.com/gluon-api/gluon-api
```

The following link shows the Gluon documentation site on Mxnet.

```
https://gluon.mxnet.io/)
```

The following link shows the Gluon examples on semantic segmentation.

```
https://cv.gluon.ai/build/examples_segmentation/index.html
```

The following link shows the Gluon examples on instance segmentation.

```
https://cv.gluon.ai/build/examples_instance/index.html
```

Gluon has also published an open source textbook called *Dive into Deep Learning*, which covers all the aspects of deep learning; see the following website for details.

```
https://d2l.ai/
```

7.5.2   K-means Clustering Image Segmentation

K-means clustering is another popular technique for image segmentation. It groups the image pixels into different clusters, by minimizing the sum of squared distances between all points and the cluster center.

Example 7.25 shows some simple code for image segmentation by using K-means clustering.

EXAMPLE 7.25   THE KMEANS IMAGE.PY **PROGRAM**

```python
#Example 7.25 K-means Clustering for Image Segmentation
import numpy as np
import matplotlib.pyplot as plt
import cv2


# Load image and Change RGB color
image = cv2.imread('strawberry.jpeg')
cv2.imshow('Original',image)
image = cv2.cvtColor(image, cv2.COLOR_BGR2RGB)


# Reshaping the image and Convert to float type
pixel_vals = np.float32(image.reshape((-1,3)))


# Criteria for the algorithm to stop: 100 iterations or 85% accuracy
criteria = (cv2.TERM_CRITERIA_EPS + cv2.TERM_CRITERIA_MAX_ITER, 100,
0.85)


# K-means clustering with 3 clusters and random initial centres
k = 3
retval, labels, centers = cv2.kmeans(pixel_vals, k, None, criteria,
10, cv2.KMEANS_RANDOM_CENTERS)


# convert data into 8-bit values
centers = np.uint8(centers)
segmented_data = centers[labels.flatten()]


# reshape data into the original image dimensions
segmented_image = segmented_data.reshape((image.shape))
segmented_image = cv2.cvtColor(segmented_image, cv2.COLOR_RGB2BGR)
cv2.imshow('Segmented', segmented_image)
```

Figure 7.22 shows the output of the earlier program, with the original image (top) and segmented image (bottom) by using K-means clustering.

EXERCISE 7.28

Modify the earlier program, trying different parameters in K-means clustering and different images. Run the program and comment on the results.

Figure 7.22: The original image (top) and segmented image (bottom) by using K-means clustering

7.5.3   Watershed Image Segmentation

In image processing, a watershed is an algorithm for processing grayscale images. It treats the image grayscale like a topographic map, with the brightness representing the height. A watershed algorithm finds the ridge lines that are then used to separate the images into segments. In this section, we will show how to do watershed image segmentation by using the OpenCV library and the Scikit-image library. For more details, see the following:

- OpenCV library

  ```
  https://opencv-python-tutroals.readthedocs.io/en/latest/
  py_tutorials/py_imgproc/py_watershed/py_watershed.html
  ```

- Scikit-image library

  ```
  https://scikit-image.org/docs/stable/index.html
  ```

Example 7.26 shows a simple watershed image segmentation example that uses the OpenCV library.

EXAMPLE 7.26   THE `WATERSHED DEMO.PY` **PROGRAM**

```python
#Example 7.26 Watershed Image Segmentation with OpenCV
# Modified based on:
# https://opencv-python-tutroals.readthedocs.io/en/latest/py_
tutorials/py_imgproc/py_watershed/py_watershed.html

import numpy as np
import cv2
from matplotlib import pyplot as plt
import urllib.request as urllib
#from urllib.request import Request, urlopen

#get image by url
#req = urllib.Request('https://opencv-python-tutroals.readthedocs.
io/en/latest/_images/water_coins.jpg', headers={'User-Agent':
'Mozilla/5.0'})
#req = urllib.Request('https://images.wisegeek.com/skin-mole.jpg',
headers={'User-Agent': 'Mozilla/5.0'})
#req = urllib.Request('http://www.anti-aging-skin-care-illusions.com/
images/Dry-Skin.jpg', headers={'User-Agent': 'Mozilla/5.0'})

#req = urllib.Request('https://jooinn.com/images/human-skin-4.jpg',
headers={'User-Agent': 'Mozilla/5.0'})
#req = urllib.Request('https://images.pexels.com/photos/4046561/
pexels-photo-4046561.jpeg?auto=compress&cs=tinysrgb&dpr=2&h=
650&w=940', headers={'User-Agent': 'Mozilla/5.0'})
req = urllib.Request('https://images.pexels.com/photos/4046567/
pexels-photo-4046567.jpeg?auto=compress&cs=tinysrgb&dpr=2&h=
650&w=940', headers={'User-Agent': 'Mozilla/5.0'})
#req = urllib.Request('https://images.pexels.com/photos/2709386/
pexels-photo-2709386.jpeg?auto=compress&cs=tinysrgb&dpr=3&h=
750&w=1260', headers={'User-Agent': 'Mozilla/5.0'})
#req = urllib.Request('https://images.pexels.com/photos/2683373/
pexels-photo-2683373.jpeg?auto=compress&cs=tinysrgb&dpr=1&w=500',
headers={'User-Agent': 'Mozilla/5.0'})
#req = urllib.Request('https://images.pexels.com/photos/952360/
pexels-photo-952360.jpeg?auto=compress&cs=tinysrgb&dpr=2&h=
650&w=940', headers={'User-Agent': 'Mozilla/5.0'})

resp = urllib.urlopen(req)

image = np.asarray(bytearray(resp.read()), dtype="uint8")
img = cv2.imdecode(image, cv2.IMREAD_COLOR)
img = cv2.resize(img, (520,480), interpolation = cv2.INTER_AREA)

cv2.imshow('Original',img)
gray = cv2.cvtColor(img,cv2.COLOR_BGR2GRAY)
ret, thresh = cv2.threshold(gray,127,255,cv2.THRESH_BINARY_INV+cv2
.THRESH_OTSU)
```

```
#thresh = cv2.adaptiveThreshold(gray,255,cv2.ADAPTIVE_THRESH_MEAN_C,
cv2.THRESH_BINARY,11,2)
#thresh = cv2.adaptiveThreshold(gray,255,cv2.ADAPTIVE_THRESH_
GAUSSIAN_C, cv2.THRESH_BINARY,11,2)

cv2.imshow('Thresh',thresh)

# noise removal
kernel = np.ones((3,3),np.uint8)
opening = cv2.morphologyEx(thresh,cv2.MORPH_OPEN,kernel,
iterations = 2)

# sure background area
sure_bg = cv2.dilate(opening,kernel,iterations=3)
cv2.imshow('Sure BG',sure_bg)

# Finding sure foreground area
dist_transform = cv2.distanceTransform(opening,cv2.DIST_L2,5)
ret, sure_fg = cv2.threshold(dist_transform,0.7*dist_transform
.max(),255,0)
cv2.imshow('Sure FG',sure_fg)
# Finding unknown region
sure_fg = np.uint8(sure_fg)
unknown = cv2.subtract(sure_bg,sure_fg)

# Marker labelling
ret, markers = cv2.connectedComponents(sure_fg)

# Add one to all labels so that sure background is not 0, but 1
markers = markers+1

# Now, mark the region of unknown with zero
markers[unknown==255] = 0


markers = cv2.watershed(img,markers)
img[markers == -1] = [255,0,0]
cv2.imshow('Watershed',img)
```

Figure 7.23 shows the original image.

Figure 7.24 shows the normal threshold (left) and segmented image (right) by using OpenCV watershed image segmentation. We chose a skin image in the example to show the effect of watershed image segmentation using the different thresholds techniques.

Figure 7.25 shows the adaptive threshold (left) and segmented image (right) by using OpenCV watershed image segmentation.

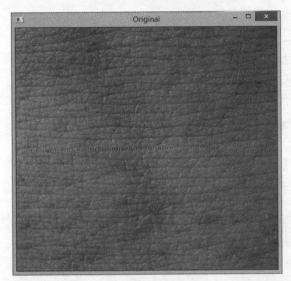

Figure 7.23: The original image for Scikit watershed image segmentation

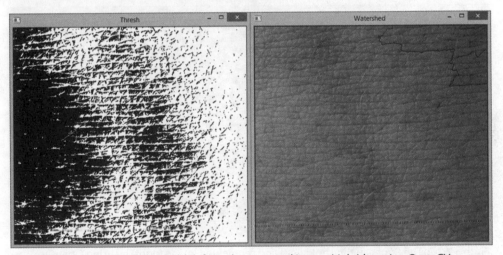

Figure 7.24: The normal threshold (left) and segmented image (right) by using OpenCV watershed image segmentation

Figure 7.26 shows the Gaussian threshold (left) and segmented image (right) by using OpenCV watershed image segmentation.

EXERCISE 7.29

Modify the earlier program, trying different threshold methods and trying different images. Run the program and comment on the results.

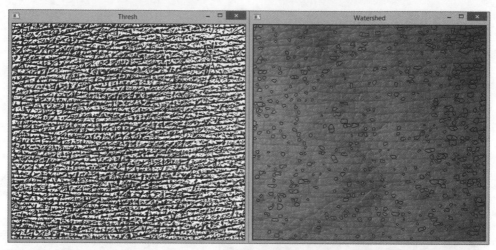

Figure 7.25: The adaptive threshold (left) and segmented image (right) by using OpenCV watershed image segmentation

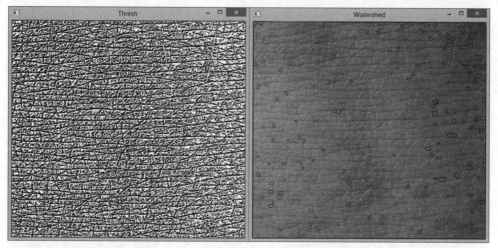

Figure 7.26: The Gaussian threshold (left) and segmented image (right) by using OpenCV watershed image segmentation

Example 7.27 is a simple watershed image segmentation by using the Scikit-image library.

EXAMPLE 7.27   THE `SCIKIT WATERSHED.PY` **PROGRAM**

```
#Example 7.27 Watershed Image Segmentation with using Scikit-image
import numpy as np
from skimage import data, util, filters, color
from skimage.segmentation import watershed
```

```
import matplotlib.pyplot as plt
import cv2

image = cv2.imread('skin.jpeg',0)
edges = filters.sobel(image)

grid = util.regular_grid(image.shape, n_points=200)

seeds = np.zeros(image.shape, dtype=int)
seeds[grid] = np.arange(seeds[grid].size).reshape(seeds[grid].shape) + 1

w0 = watershed(edges, seeds)

image0 = color.label2rgb(w0, image, bg_label=-1)
cv2.imshow('Classical watershed', image0)
```

Figure 7.27 show the image segmentation results of using the Scikit-image library, with 200 points in the util.regular_grid() function.

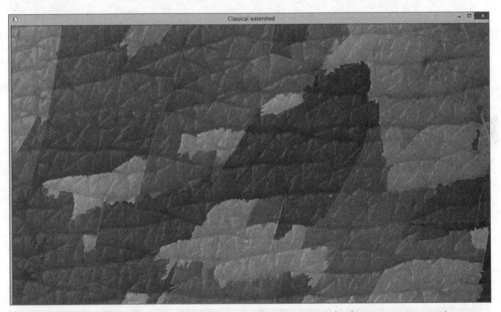

Figure 7.27: The segmented image by using Scikit-image watershed image segmentation

EXERCISE 7.30

Modify the earlier program, trying different points in the util.regular_grid() function and trying different images. Run the program and comment on the results.

Example 7.28 is the webcam version of the earlier simple watershed image segmentation that uses the Scikit-image library.

EXAMPLE 7.28   THE `SCIKIT WATERSHED WEBCAM.PY` **PROGRAM**

```
# Example 7.28 Scikit Watershed Webcam
import numpy as np
from skimage import data, util, filters, color
from skimage.segmentation import watershed
import matplotlib.pyplot as plt
import cv2

cap = cv2.VideoCapture(0)
while True:
    ret, frame = cap.read()
    image = cv2.cvtColor(frame, cv2.COLOR_BGR2GRAY)

    edges = filters.sobel(image)

    grid = util.regular_grid(image.shape, n_points=468)

    seeds = np.zeros(image.shape, dtype=int)
    seeds[grid] = np.arange(seeds[grid].size).reshape(seeds[grid]
.shape) + 1

    w0 = watershed(edges, seeds)

    image0 = color.label2rgb(w0, image, bg_label=-1)
    cv2.imshow('Classical watershed', image0)

    if cv2.waitKey(25) & 0xFF == ord('q'):
        cap.release()
        cv2.destroyAllWindows()
        break
```

Example 7.29 is a simple watershed image segmentation that uses the Scikit-image library. The full code is saved in a file called `plot_watershed.ipynb`. The simplest way to run it is from Google Colab.

EXAMPLE 7.29   THE `PLOT_WATERSHED.IPYNB` **PROGRAM**

```
#Example 7.29 plot_watershed with Scikit-image
#import necessary packages
import numpy as np
import urllib.request as urllib
import cv2
import matplotlib.pyplot as plt
```

```python
from scipy import ndimage as ndi
from skimage.segmentation import watershed
from skimage.feature import peak_local_max

#get image by url
#resp = urllib.urlopen("https://jooinn.com/images/human-skin-4.jpg")

image = np.asarray(bytearray(resp.read()), dtype="uint8")
image = cv2.imdecode(image, cv2.IMREAD_COLOR)

#show image
#cv2.imshow("Image", image)

image_rgb = cv2.cvtColor(image, cv2.COLOR_BGR2RGB)
gray = cv2.cvtColor(image, cv2.COLOR_BGR2GRAY)
thresh = cv2.adaptiveThreshold(gray,255,cv2.ADAPTIVE_THRESH_MEAN_C,
cv2.THRESH_BINARY,11,2)

# Now we want to separate the two objects in image
# Generate the markers as local maxima of the distance to the
background
distance = ndi.distance_transform_edt(thresh)
coords = peak_local_max(distance, footprint=np.ones((3, 3)),
labels=gray)
mask = np.zeros(distance.shape, dtype=bool)
mask[tuple(coords.T)] = True
markers, _ = ndi.label(mask)
labels = watershed(-distance, markers, mask=thresh)

fig, axes = plt.subplots(ncols=3, figsize=(9, 3), sharex=True,
sharey=True)
ax = axes.ravel()

ax[0].imshow(image_rgb, cmap=plt.cm.gray)
ax[0].set_title('Overlapping objects')
ax[1].imshow(-distance, cmap=plt.cm.gray)
ax[1].set_title('Distances')
ax[2].imshow(labels, cmap=plt.cm.nipy_spectral)
ax[2].set_title('Separated objects')

for a in ax:
    a.set_axis_off()

fig.tight_layout()
plt.show()
```

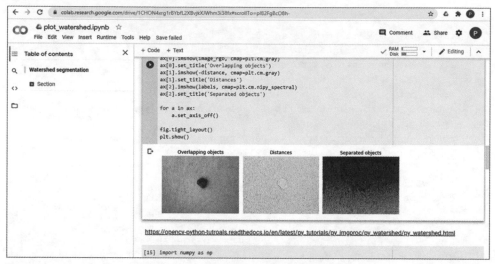

Figure 7.28: The Google Colab outputs of the `plot_watershed.ipynb` file

Figure 7.28 shows the Google Colab outputs of the `plot_watershed.ipynb` file.

Example 7.30 is a simple watershed image segmentation by using the SNOW filter from the PoreSpy library (`https://github.com/PMEAL/porespy`). PoreSpy is a popular library used to extract information from 3D images of porous materials.

EXAMPLE 7.30   THE `PORESPY SNOW.PY` PROGRAM

```
#Example 7.30 Image segmentation by using SNOW filter from Porespy
#https://www.researchgate.net/post/Watershed-segmentation-
implementation-using-scikit-image
#pip install porespy
import porespy as ps
import os
import matplotlib.pyplot as plt
import cv2
import numpy as np
```

```
# Import image
file="blueberrys.jpeg"
gray= cv2.imread(file,0)
plt.imshow(gray)
plt.show()
#ret,thresh = cv2.threshold(gray,164,255,cv2.THRESH_BINARY)
thresh = cv2.adaptiveThreshold(gray,255,cv2.ADAPTIVE_THRESH_MEAN_C,
cv2.THRESH_BINARY,11,2)


#cv2.imshow('Thresh',thresh)
plt.imshow(thresh)
plt.show()
# Perform SNOW on Binarized image
watershed = ps.filters.snow_partitioning(thresh > 0, randomize=True,
                                         return_all=True)

# Display and Load
plt.imshow(watershed.regions)
plt.show()
```

Figure 7.29 shows the output of the watershed segmentation by using the SNOW filter.

7.6   Background Removal

During the COVID-19 pandemic in 2020, many people were forced to work from home. Online meeting tools such as Zoom, Microsoft Teams, WebEx, Google Meet, and so on, hence became popular. One of the features of online meeting software is the ability to set the background. In this section, we will show you how to remove a background and set a background using Python.

7.6.1   Background Removal with OpenCV

Example 7.31 shows some simple code for background subtraction by using OpenCV. OpenCV provides three different background subtractors; you can try to see which one works for your video. See Figure 7.30.

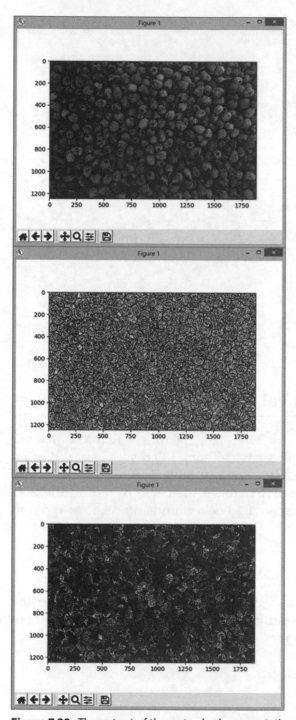

Figure 7.29: The output of the watershed segmentation by using SNOW filter. The top is original grayscale image, the middle is the corresponding threshold, and the bottom is segmented images.

EXAMPLE 7.31   THE BACKGROUNDSUBTRACTIONOPENCV.PY **PROGRAM**

```
#Example 7.31 OpenCV Background Substractor

# importing libraries
import numpy as np
import cv2

# creating background subtractor object
fgbg = cv2.bgsegm.createBackgroundSubtractorMOG();
#fgbg = cv2.createBackgroundSubtractorMOG2();
#fgbg = cv2.bgsegm.createBackgroundSubtractorGMG();

#cap = cv2.VideoCapture(0);
cap = cv2.VideoCapture('vtest.avi')

while(1):
    # read frames
    ret, img = cap.read();
    fgmask = fgbg.apply(img);
    output = cv2.bitwise_and(img, img, mask=fgmask)

    cv2.imshow("Video", output)

    k = cv2.waitKey(30) & 0xff;
    if k == 27:
        break;

cap.release();
cv2.destroyAllWindows();
```

EXERCISE 7.31

Modify the earlier program, trying different background removal methods and trying different images. Run the program and comment on the results.

After you remove the video background, you can also add the new background. Example 7.32 is a revised version of the earlier code; it reads the background from an image file and sets the background to the video. See Figure 7.31.

Figure 7.30: The output of the background subtraction program. The top is the original video, and the bottom is the video with the background removed.

EXAMPLE 7.32 **THE** BACKGROUNDSUBTRACTIONOPENCV **PROGRAM**

```
#Example 7.32 OpenCV Background Substractor

# importing libraries
import numpy as np
import cv2

# creating background subtractor object
fgbg = cv2.bqsegm.createBackgroundSubtractorMOG();
#fgbg = cv2.createBackgroundSubtractorMOG2();
#fgbg = cv2.bgsegm.createBackgroundSubtractorGMG();
# Kernel for denoise
kernel = cv2.getStructuringElement(cv2.MORPH_ELLIPSE, (3, 3));

#cap = cv2.VideoCapture(0);
cap = cv2.VideoCapture('vtest.avi')
bg=cv2.imread("londoneye.jpg")
while(1):
    # read frames
    ret, img = cap.read();
    fgmask = fgbg.apply(img);
    fgmask = cv2.morphologyEx(fgmask, cv2.MORPH_OPEN, kernel);
    output = cv2.bitwise_and(img, img, mask=fgmask)
    #Change the background=========================================
    height,width,depth = output.shape
    dim = (width, height)
    bg = cv2.resize(bg, dim, interpolation = cv2.INTER_AREA)
    fgmask1a = cv2.bitwise_not(fgmask)
    bg2 = cv2.bitwise_and(bg, bg, mask=fgmask1a)
    output = cv2.add(output,bg2)
    cv2.imshow("Video", output)

    k = cv2.waitKey(30) & 0xff;
    if k == 27:
        break;

cap.release();
cv2.destroyAllWindows();
```

Example 7.33 is an example to evaluate the effect of different OpenCV background subtraction methods. See Figure 7.32 and Figure 7.33.

Figure 7.31: The output of the background subtraction program with background reset

EXAMPLE 7.33   THE BACKGROUNDSUBTRACTIONOPENCV2 **PROGRAM**

```
# https://www.geeksforgeeks.org/background-subtraction-opencv/?ref=rp
# OpenCV Background Substraction
# Worked on TensorFlow 2.0 23/10/2020

# importing libraries
import numpy as np
import cv2

# creating object
fgbg1 = cv2.bgsegm.createBackgroundSubtractorMOG();
fgbg2 = cv2.createBackgroundSubtractorMOG2();
fgbg3 = cv2.bgsegm.createBackgroundSubtractorGMG();
# Kernel for denoise
kernel = cv2.getStructuringElement(cv2.MORPH_ELLIPSE, (3, 3));

#Create a tracker bars================================================
def nothing(x):
    # any operation
    pass
cv2.namedWindow("Trackbars")
cv2.createTrackbar("Alpha", "Trackbars", 4, 10, nothing)

# capture frames from a camera  or a video ======================
#cap = cv2.VideoCapture(0);
cap = cv2.VideoCapture('vtest.avi')
#load background image
```

```python
bg = cv2.imread("bg.jpg")
#cv2.imshow("background", bg)
while(1):
    # read frames
    ret, img = cap.read();

    # apply mask for background subtraction =====================
    fgmask1 = fgbg1.apply(img);
    fgmask2 = fgbg2.apply(img);
    fgmask3 = fgbg3.apply(img);

    # apply transformation to remove noise =====================
    fgmask4 = cv2.morphologyEx(fgmask3, cv2.MORPH_OPEN, kernel);

    #Bitwise AND the image and mask
    output = cv2.bitwise_and(img, img, mask=fgmask1)
    #Change the background=====================================
    height,width,depth = output.shape
    dim = (width, height)
    # resize background image
    bg = cv2.resize(bg, dim, interpolation = cv2.INTER_AREA)
    fgmask1a = cv2.bitwise_not(fgmask1)
    bg2 = cv2.bitwise_and(bg, bg, mask=fgmask1a)

    alpha=cv2.getTrackbarPos("Alpha", "Trackbars")/10
    output2 = cv2.addWeighted(output,alpha,bg2,1-alpha,0)
    output3 = cv2.add(output,bg2)

    #Display the images ======================================
    res1 = np.hstack((fgmask1, fgmask2,fgmask3, fgmask4))
    res2 = np.hstack((img, output,output2,output3))

    cv2.namedWindow("Mask", 0)
    cv2.resizeWindow("Mask", 640, 480)
    cv2.imshow("Mask", res1)

    cv2.namedWindow("Video", 0)
    cv2.resizeWindow("Video", 640, 480)
    cv2.imshow("Video", res2)

    k = cv2.waitKey(30) & 0xff;
    if k == 27:
        break;

cap.release();
cv2.destroyAllWindows();
```

Figure 7.32: The slider for adjusting

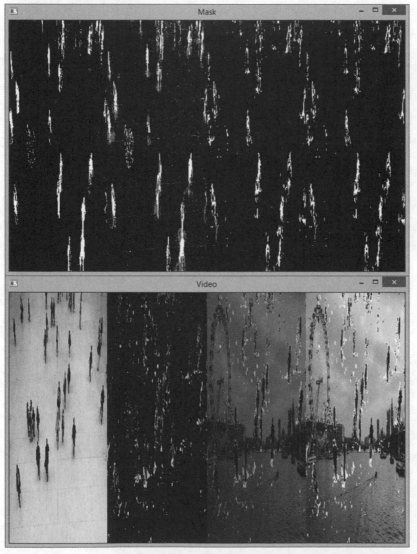

Figure 7.33: The output of the background subtraction program with background reset

Example 7.34 is another approach for background removal that uses OpenCV. In this case, it first uses a threshold to change the color image to a black-and-white image, then uses the cv.findContours() method to find the contours of the image, and then uses the cv.copyMakeBorder() method to create borders around the contours. Finally, it removes the background based on the borders. See Figure 7.34.

EXAMPLE 7.34   THE BGREMOVAL.PY **PROGRAM**

```python
# Example 7.34 BGRemoval with OpenCV
import cv2 as cv

def remove_background(image, thresh, scale_factor=.25, kernel_
range=range(1, 15), border=None):
    gray = cv.cvtColor(image, cv.COLOR_BGR2GRAY)

    im_bw = cv.threshold(gray, thresh, 255, cv.THRESH_BINARY)[1]
    im_bw_inv = cv.bitwise_not(im_bw)

    contour, _ = cv.findContours(im_bw_inv, cv.RETR_CCOMP,
cv.CHAIN_APPROX_SIMPLE)
    for cnt in contour:
        cv.drawContours(im_bw_inv, [cnt], 0, 255, -1)

    nt = cv.bitwise_not(im_bw)
    im_bw_inv = cv.bitwise_or(im_bw_inv, nt)

    border = border or kernel_range[-1]

    small = cv.resize(im_bw_inv, None, fx=scale_factor, fy=scale_factor)
    bordered = cv.copyMakeBorder(small, border, border, border,
border, cv.BORDER_CONSTANT)

    for i in kernel_range:
        kernel = cv.getStructuringElement(cv.MORPH_ELLIPSE, (2*i+1,
2*i+1))
        bordered = cv.morphologyEx(bordered, cv.MORPH_CLOSE, kernel)

    unbordered = bordered[border: -border, border: -border]
    mask = cv.resize(unbordered, (image.shape[1], image.shape[0]))
    fg = cv.bitwise_and(image, image, mask=mask)
    return fg


img = cv.imread('person_football.jpeg')
cv.imshow('image',img)
nb_img = remove_background(img, 100)
cv.imshow('bg rm',nb_img)
```

Figure 7.34: The original image and the image with background removed

Example 7.35 is another example code for background removal from webcam images by using OpenCV. In this example, it first converts the webcam images to grayscale, uses the `cv2.Canny()` method to find the edges using the Canny Edge filter, and uses the `cv2.dilate()` and `cv2.erode()` methods to blur the image. It then uses the `cv.findContours()` method to find out all the contours and sort the contours according to area. It then uses the largest contour to remove the background.

EXAMPLE 7.35   THE `BACKBROUNDREMOVALWEBCAM.PY` PROGRAM

```python
#Example 7.35 Webcam Feed BGRemoval with OpenCV
import keyboard  # using module keyboard

import cv2
import numpy as np
import imutils

#== Parameters
MASK_COLOR = (0.0,0.0,1.0) # In BGR format

#-- Get the background mask
def getBackgroundMask(img):
    gray = cv2.cvtColor(img,cv2.COLOR_BGR2GRAY)

    #-- Edge detection
    edges = cv2.Canny(gray, 10, 100)
    edges = cv2.dilate(edges, None)
    edges = cv2.erode(edges, None)

    #-- Find contours in edges, sort by area
    contour_info = []
    contours, _ = cv2.findContours(edges, cv2.RETR_LIST, cv2
.CHAIN_APPROX_NONE)

    for c in contours:
        contour_info.append((
            c,
            cv2.isContourConvex(c),
            cv2.contourArea(c),
        ))
    contour_info = sorted(contour_info, key=lambda c: c[2],
reverse=True)
    max_contour = contour_info[0]

    #-- Create empty mask, draw filled polygon on it corresponding to
largest contour ----
    # Mask is black, polygon is white
    mask = np.zeros(edges.shape)
    cv2.fillConvexPoly(mask, max_contour[0], (255))

    #-- Smooth mask, then blur it
    mask = cv2.dilate(mask, None, iterations=10)
    mask = cv2.erode(mask, None, iterations=10)
    mask = cv2.GaussianBlur(mask, (21, 21), 0)
    mask_stack = np.dstack([mask]*3)    # Create 3-channel alpha mask
    return mask_stack
```

```
camera = cv2.VideoCapture(0)
bolMask = False
while camera.isOpened():
    ok, img = camera.read()
    if not ok:
        break

    if keyboard.is_pressed('t'):  # if key 't' is pressed, bolMask =
not bolMask
        bolMask = not bolMask
    if (bolMask==True):
        mask_stack  = getBackgroundMask(img)
        #-- Blend masked img into MASK_COLOR background
        mask_stack  = mask_stack.astype('float32') / 255.0
        img         = img.astype('float32') / 255.0
        masked = (mask_stack * img) + ((1-mask_stack) * MASK_COLOR)
        img = (masked * 255).astype('uint8')

    cv2.imshow('video image', img)
    key = cv2.waitKey(30)
    if key == 27: # press 'ESC' to quit
        break

camera.release()
cv2.destroyAllWindows()
```

Figure 7.35 shows the output of the earlier code.

Figure 7.35: The original webcam image (left) and the image with background removed, shown in red (right)

Example 7.36 shows the code for background removal from webcam images and blends the background with another video by using OpenCV.

EXAMPLE 7.36 THE WEBCAMBGVIDEO.PY PROGRAM

```python
# Example 7.36 Webcam background blending with video
import cv2
import numpy as np
import time

# get captures
cap = cv2.VideoCapture(0)
background_capture = cv2.VideoCapture(r'./londoneye.mp4')
#background = cv2.imread('green.jpg')

counter = -1
while cap.isOpened():
    counter += 1
    start_time_extract_figure = time.time()
    # extract your figure
    _, frame = cap.read()
    frame = cv2.resize(frame, (640, 480), interpolation=cv2.INTER_AREA)
    cv2.imshow('original', frame)
    frame = cv2.cvtColor(frame, cv2.COLOR_BGR2RGB)
    mask = np.zeros(frame.shape[:2], np.uint8)
    bgdModel = np.zeros((1, 65), np.float64)
    fgdModel = np.zeros((1, 65), np.float64)
    rect = (10, 10, 300, 400)
    start_time_grabCut = time.time()
    cv2.grabCut(frame, mask, rect, bgdModel, fgdModel, 1, cv2
.GC_INIT_WITH_RECT)
    during_time_grabCut = time.time() - start_time_grabCut
    print('{}-th t_time: {}'.format(counter, during_time_grabCut))
    mask2 = np.where((mask == 2) | (mask == 0), (0,), (1,)).astype('uint8')
    frame = frame * mask2[:, :, np.newaxis]
    elapsed_time_extract_figure = time.time() - start_time_extract_figure
    print('{}-th extract_figure_time: {}'.format(counter,
elapsed_time_extract_figure))

    # extract the background
    start_time_combination = time.time()
    ret, background = background_capture.read()
    background = cv2.resize(background, (640, 480), interpolation=cv2
.INTER_AREA)

    # combine the figure and background using mask instead of iteration
    mask_1 = frame > 0
    mask_2 = frame <= 0
    combination = cv2.cvtColor(frame, cv2.COLOR_BGR2RGB) * mask_1 +
background * mask_2
    elapsed_time_combination = time.time() - start_time_combination
    print('{}-th combination_time: {}'.format(counter,
elapsed_time_combination))
```

```
        cv2.imshow('combination', combination)

        k = cv2.waitKey(30) & 0xff
        if k == 27:
            break

cap.release()
cv2.destroyAllWindows()
```

Figure 7.36 shows the original webcam image (top) and the image with the background removed and blended with another video (bottom).

Figure 7.36: The original webcam image (top) and the image with background removed and blended with another video (bottom)

Example 7.37 shows another version of the earlier code for background removal from webcam images and blends the background with a `green.jpg` background file by using OpenCV. See Figure 7.37.

EXAMPLE 7.37   THE `WEBCAMBGFILE.PY` **PROGRAM**

```python
# Example 7.37 Webcam background blending with picture
import cv2
import numpy as np
import time

# get captures
cap = cv2.VideoCapture(0)
background = cv2.imread('green.jpg')


counter = -1
while cap.isOpened():
    counter += 1
    start_time_extract_figure = time.time()
    # extract your figure
    _, frame = cap.read()
    frame = cv2.cvtColor(frame, cv2.COLOR_BGR2RGB)
    mask = np.zeros(frame.shape[:2], np.uint8)
    bgdModel = np.zeros((1, 65), np.float64)
    fgdModel = np.zeros((1, 65), np.float64)
    rect = (20, 20, 300, 400)
    start_time_grabCut = time.time()
    cv2.grabCut(frame, mask, rect, bgdModel, fgdModel, 1, cv2
.GC_INIT_WITH_RECT)
    during_time_grabCut = time.time() - start_time_grabCut
    print('{}-th t_time: {}'.format(counter, during_time_grabCut))
    mask2 = np.where((mask == 2) | (mask == 0), (0,), (1,))
.astype('uint8')
    frame = frame * mask2[:, :, np.newaxis]
    elapsed_time_extract_figure = time.time() - start_time_extract_figure
    print('{}-th extract_figure_time: {}'.format(counter,
elapsed_time_extract_figure))

    # extract the background
    start_time_combination = time.time()
    background = cv2.resize(background, (320, 240), interpolation=cv2
.INTER_AREA)
    # maybe the default size of embedded camera is 640x480

    # combine the figure and background using mask instead of
iteration
    mask_1 = frame > 0
    mask_2 = frame <= 0
```

```
    combination = cv2.cvtColor(frame, cv2.COLOR_BGR2RGB) * mask_1 +
background * mask_2
    elapsed_time_combination = time.time() - start_time_combination
    print('{}-th combination_time: {}'.format(counter,
elapsed_time_combination))

    cv2.imshow('combination', combination)

    k = cv2.waitKey(30) & 0xff
    if k == 27:
        break

cap.release()
cv2.destroyAllWindows()
```

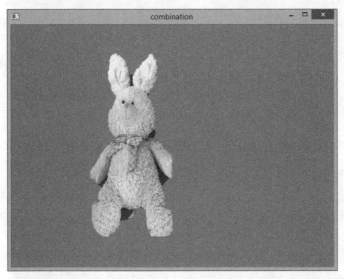

Figure 7.37: The webcam image with background removed and blended with a green color image file

In the Hollywood blockbuster movie *Harry Potter*, Harry has an invisible cloak that he can hide inside and became invisible. Example 7.38 shows some example Python code that can achieve this amazing invisible cloak effect based on the same background removal principle we showed earlier. It first takes 30 frames as a background; then when a person enters, it uses an HSV color mask to identify the region that matches the color and then replaces the region with the background to generate an illusion that the person covered by the region becomes transparent, or invisible. See Figure 7.38.

EXAMPLE 7.38   THE CLOAK.PY PROGRAM

```python
# Example 7.38 Harry's Cloak

import cv2
import numpy as np
import time
print(cv2.__version__)


# Select Webcam or a video
#capture_video = cv2.VideoCapture("video1.mp4")
capture_video = cv2.VideoCapture(0)

# Warm up the Webcam
time.sleep(1)
count = 0
background = 0

# Get the background
for i in range(30):
    return_val, background = capture_video.read()
    if return_val == False :
        continue
    background = np.flip(background, axis = 1)

# Start the Webcam
while (capture_video.isOpened()):
    return_val, img = capture_video.read()
    if not return_val :
        break

    count = count + 1
    img = np.flip(img, axis = 1)

    # Convert the image from BGR to HSV
    hsv = cv2.cvtColor(img, cv2.COLOR_BGR2HSV)

    # Select the Red color range in HSV space
    lower_red = np.array([0,120,70])
    upper_red = np.array([10,255,255])
    mask1 = cv2.inRange(hsv, lower_red, upper_red)

    # mask2
    lower_red = np.array([170,120,70])
    upper_red = np.array([180,255,255])
    mask2 = cv2.inRange(hsv, lower_red, upper_red)

    # Apply the masks to image
    mask1 = mask1 + mask2
    mask1 = cv2.morphologyEx(mask1, cv2.MORPH_OPEN, np.ones((3, 3),np
.uint8), iterations = 2)
```

```
    mask1 = cv2.dilate(mask1, np.ones((3, 3), np.uint8),
iterations = 1)
    mask2 = cv2.bitwise_not(mask1)

    # Final Output
    res1 = cv2.bitwise_and(background, background, mask = mask1)
    res2 = cv2.bitwise_and(img, img, mask = mask2)
    final_output = cv2.addWeighted(res1, 1, res2, 1, 0)
    cv2.imshow("INVISIBLE CLOAK", final_output)

    k = cv2.waitKey(30) & 0xff
    if k == 27:
        break

capture_video.release()
cv2.destroyAllWindows()
```

Figure 7.38: The webcam image with red color notebook (top) and the corresponding image with the red color notebook made invisible (bottom)

7.6.2   Background Removal with PaddlePaddle

PaddlePaddle is a deep learning framework from Baidu. It is powerful and yet still simple to use; see the following link for its GitHub site.

```
https://github.com/PaddlePaddle/Paddle
```

You can use the following command to install PaddlePaddle through a terminal or Windows Command Prompt:

```
pip install paddlehub paddlepaddle
hub install deeplabv3p_xception65_humanseg==1.0.0
```

You can use the following command to check the installation:

```
C:\python
>>> import paddle
>>> paddle.utils.run_check()
```

Example 7.39 shows some simple code for photo background removal by using the PaddlePaddle framework. It has only four lines of code. It performs background removal on the file `./img/01.jpg` and saves the results in the `humanseg_output` folder.

EXAMPLE 7.39   THE `PADDLEPADDLE1.PY` PROGRAM

```
# Example 7.39 paddlepaddle background removal
import os, paddlehub as hub
huseg = hub.Module(name='deeplabv3p_xception65_humanseg')
files = ['./imgs/01.jpg']
results = huseg.segmentation(data={'image': files} ,
visualization=True, output_dir='humanseg_output/')
```

Example 7.40 shows the improved version of the earlier code. It can get all the files in a folder and remove their background. It has only five lines of code.

EXAMPLE 7.40   THE `PADDLEPADDLE2.PY` PROGRAM

```
# Example 7.40 paddlepaddle batch background removal
import os, paddlehub as hub
huseg = hub.Module(name='deeplabv3p_xception65_humanseg')
path = './imgs/'
files = [path + i for i in os.listdir(path)]
results = huseg.segmentation(data={'image': files} ,
visualization=True, output_dir='humanseg_output/')
```

This further improved version selects all the image files with an extension of jpg, jpeg, bmp, png, and gif from a folder and removes their background. See Example 7.41.

EXAMPLE 7.41   THE PADDLEPADDLE3.PY **PROGRAM**

```
# Example 7.41 paddlepaddle batch background removal
import os, paddlehub as hub
module = hub.Module(name='deeplabv3p_xception65_humanseg')
path = './imgs/'
included_extensions = ['jpg','jpeg', 'bmp', 'png', 'gif']
files = [path + i for i in os.listdir(path)
         if any(i.endswith(ext) for ext in included_extensions)]
results = module.segmentation(data={'image': files} ,
visualization=True, output_dir='humanseg_output/')
```

Example 7.42 shows some simple code for photo background removal by using the PaddlePaddle framework.

EXAMPLE 7.42   THE PADDLEPADDLE4.PY **PROGRAM**

```
# Example 7.42 PaddlePaddle background removal
import matplotlib.pyplot as plt
import matplotlib.image as mpimg
from matplotlib import animation
import cv2
import paddlehub as hub
from PIL import Image, ImageSequence
from IPython.display import display, HTML
import numpy as np
import imageio
import os

# 1. Define the input and output image folder
test_path = 'imgs/'
output_path = 'humanseg_output/'
# Get all the input images
test_img_path = ['01.jpg', '02.jpg']
test_img_path = [test_path + img for img in test_img_path]
# Display the first image
img = mpimg.imread(test_img_path[0])
plt.figure(figsize=(10,10))
plt.imshow(img)
plt.axis('off')
plt.show()
#2. Get the Deep Learning model
```

```
# PaddleHub DeepLabv3+(deeplabv3p_xception65_humanseg)
module = hub.Module(name="deeplabv3p_xception65_humanseg")
input_dict = {"image": test_img_path}
# execute predict and print the result
results = module.segmentation(data=input_dict, visualization=True,
output_dir=output_path)for result in results:
    print(result)
    out_img_path = result['save_path']
    img = mpimg.imread(out_img_path)
    plt.figure(figsize=(10,10))
    plt.imshow(img)
    plt.axis('off')
    plt.show()
```

EXERCISE 7.32

Modify the earlier program, trying different deep learning models and trying different images. Run the program and comment on the results.

7.6.3   Background Removal with PixelLib

Learn about using PixelLib background editing in images and videos here:

`https://github.com/ayoolaolafenwa/PixelLib`

You can download the model here:

`https://github.com/ayoolaolafenwa/PixelLib/releases/download/1.1/xception_pascalvoc.pb`

Example 7.43 shows a program that uses PixelLib to blur the background.

EXAMPLE 7.43   THE `PIXELLIB BG.PY` PROGRAM

```
# Example 7.43 Pixellib background editing
import pixellib
from pixellib.tune_bg import alter_bg

change_bg = alter_bg(model_type = "pb")
change_bg.load_pascalvoc_model("xception_pascalvoc.pb")
change_bg.blur_bg("person1.jpeg", extreme = True, detect = "person",
output_image_name="out.jpg")
```

PixelLib can also set the background of videos with five lines of code. See Example 7.44.

EXAMPLE 7.44   THE `PIXELLIB BG VIDEO` **PROGRAM**

```
# Example 7.44 Pixellib background editing

import pixellib
from pixellib.tune_bg import alter_bg

change_bg = alter_bg(model_type="pb")
change_bg.load_pascalvoc_model("xception_pascalvoc.pb")
change_bg.change_video_bg("person.mp4", "londoneye.jpg", frames_per_
second = 10, output_video_name="output_video.mp4", detect = "person")
```

Figure 7.39 is the video output of the earlier code.

EXERCISE 7.33

Modify the earlier program, trying deep learning models and trying different videos. Run the program and comment on the results.

7.7   Depth Estimation

Depth estimation is a technique to estimate the depth information from images. Depth estimation can be achieved by using a single image or two images, also called *stereo images*. When estimating depth from a single image, it is also called *monocular depth estimation*. Depth estimation has many practical applications, such as self-driving technology. See the following site for more details:

```
https://paperswithcode.com/task/monocular-depth-estimation
```

7.7.1   Depth Estimation from a Single Image

The following link shows an interesting GitHub project called High Quality Monocular Depth Estimation via Transfer Learning (arXiv 2018), which can estimate the depth information from a single image in a video. Just follow the instructions to run the code.

```
https://github.com/priya-dwivedi/Deep-Learning/tree/master/depth_
estimation
```

The following link shows another GitHub project called MonoDepth2, which is the PyTorch implementation for training and testing depth estimation models. It also has an IPython notebook for you to run the code easily.

```
https://github.com/nianticlabs/monodepth2
```

Figure 7.39: The original video (top) and the video with background removed and replaced with the London Eye image (bottom)

You can also perform depth estimation with Gluon library. The following website shows the Gluon examples for depth prediction.

```
https://cv.gluon.ai/build/examples_depth/index.html
```

7.7.2   Depth Estimation from Stereo Images

Similarly, you can estimate the depth information by using two images, or stereo images. See the following link for details on how to create a depth map using OpenCV:

```
https://opencv-python-tutroals.readthedocs.io/en/latest/
py_tutorials/py_calib3d/py_depthmap/py_depthmap.html
```

Example 7.45 shows an example of how to get the depth map from stereo images.

EXAMPLE 7.45   THE OPENCVDEPTHMAP.PY **PROGRAM**

```python
# Example 7.45 OpenCV Depth Estimation from Stereo Images
import numpy as np
import cv2
from matplotlib import pyplot as plt

imgL = cv2.imread('tsukuba_l.png',0)
imgR = cv2.imread('tsukuba_r.png',0)

stereo = cv2.cv2.StereoBM_create(numDisparities=16, blockSize=15)
disparity = stereo.compute(imgL,imgR)
plt.imshow(disparity,'nipy_spectral')
plt.show()
```

EXERCISE 7.34

Modify the earlier program so that it allows users to select two image files. Run the program and comment on the results. Hint: You can use the Tkinter library to select files through a file open dialog box, as shown here:

import tkinter as tk

from tkinter import filedialog as fd

root = tk.Tk()

root.withdraw()

filenames = fd.askopenfilenames()

Example 7.46 shows the webcam version of the earlier code, which takes a left image and a right image from two webcams, combines them, and creates a live depth map.

EXAMPLE 7.46   THE OPENCVDEPTHMAPWEBCAM.PY **PROGRAM**

```python
# Example 7.46 depth map using two live webcams
import numpy as np
import cv2
from matplotlib import pyplot as plt

capL = cv2.VideoCapture(0)
capR = cv2.VideoCapture(1)

while capL.isOpened() and capR.isOpened():
    ok, imgL = capL.read()
    if not ok:
        break
    ok, imgR = capR.read()
    if not ok:
        break

    # stereo.compute() requires input images converted to single
channel, i.e. of type CV_8UC1
    imgL=cv2.cvtColor(imgL, cv2.COLOR_BGR2GRAY)
    imgR=cv2.cvtColor(imgR, cv2.COLOR_BGR2GRAY)

    stereo = cv2.cv2.StereoBM_create(numDisparities=16, blockSize=15)
    disparity = stereo.compute(imgL,imgR)

    disparity = (disparity - np.amin(disparity))/(np.amax(disparity)-np
.amin(disparity))*255
    w,h, = imgR.shape
    img = np.zeros([w,h,3])
    img[:,:,0] = np.ones([w,h])*0/255.0
    img[:,:,1] = np.ones([w,h])*0/255.0
    img[:,:,2] = np.ones([w,h])*disparity/255.0

    cv2.imshow('Depth Map',img)
    key = cv2.waitKey(30)
    if key == 27: # press 'ESC' to quit
        break

capL.release()
capR.release()
cv2.destroyAllWindows()
```

7.8   Augmented Reality

Augmented reality (AR) and virtual reality (VR) are two of the hottest technologies at the moment. Augmented reality means to blend the virtual object into real-world video images, while virtual reality means to replace the real world with a virtual world. This is typically achieved by wearing VR goggles.

Augmented reality can be used in many real-life applications. One of the examples is Microsoft's HoloLens 2, which is an amazing kit that can used in engineering, healthcare, and more. See the following link for more details:

```
https://www.microsoft.com/en-us/hololens/
```

The following links show an interesting GitHub site for an augmented-reality project. This is an interesting two-part tutorial on how to create augmented reality by using OpenCV. This tutorial shows you how to detect and recognize the target flat surface in an image, estimate the homography, derive from the homography the transformation from the target surface coordinate system to the target image coordinate system, and finally project a 3D model onto the target surface in the image and draw it.

```
https://github.com/juangallostra/augmented-reality
https://bitesofcode.wordpress.com/2017/09/12/augmented-reality-
with-python-and-opencv-part-1/
```

The following link shows another example of augmented reality by using OpenCV. It is a project called augmented reality using AruCo Markers in OpenCV from the LearnOpenCV GitHub site. This project shows you how to use the AruCo markers to replace the image inside a picture to display new images or videos in the frame.

```
https://github.com/spmallick/learnopencv/tree/master/Augmented-
RealityWithArucoMarkers
```

ArUco markers are synthetic square markers composed by a wide black border and an inner binary matrix which determines its identifier (id). See the following link for more details.

```
https://docs.opencv.org/4.x/d5/dae/tutorial_aruco_detection.html
```

The following link shows another OpenCV augmented reality example from the PyImageSearch website. This tutorial shows you how to perform real-time augmented reality in video streams.

```
https://www.pyimagesearch.com/2021/01/11/opencv-video-augmented-
reality/
```

7.9   Summary

This chapter covered object detection and image segmentation, which are heavily researched artificial intelligence areas. Image classification means to classify the whole image into different categories, object detection means to detect and locate different objects with the image, and image segmentation means to divide the image into different segments.

Object detection can be achieved by detecting colors, shapes, and contours, and you can implement this by using the popular OpenCV library. Object detection can also be achieved by using pretrained deep learning models, such as those trained on the COCO image dataset. You can detect multiple classes of predefined objects. You can also retrain or update existing deep learning models on your own image data to detect new objects, a type of transfer learning. You can perform this kind of transfer learning with OpenCV, YOLO, ImageAI, and so on.

Object tracking is also an interesting area, where you can detect and track objects from a series of images, such as video.

Image segmentation includes image semantic segmentation and image instance segmentation. Image semantic segmentation divides the image into different segments according to content and treats multiple objects within a single category as one entity. Image instance segmentation, on the other hand, identifies individual objects and divides the image into segments accordingly.

K-means clustering is another popular algorithm for image segmentation. It is used to divide the image into segments based on how similar the pixel data is to different centers. The pixel data points in the same cluster are more similar than those in other clusters.

The watershed algorithm treats the image like a topographic map, with the brightness of each point representing its height, and finds the lines that run along the tops of ridges. The watershed algorithm then uses ridges and troughs to segment the image.

Background removal detects and removes the background of the image.

Depth estimation estimates the depth from single or multiple 2D images.

Augmented reality mixes the computer generated patterns with the live camera image in real time.

7.10   Chapter Review Questions

Q7.1.   What is object detection?

Q7.2.   What is the difference between R-CNN, YOLO, and SSD in object detection?

Q7.3.   What is R-CNN?

Q7.4.   What is Fast R-CNN?

Q7.5.   What is Faster R-CNN?

Q7.6.   What is Mask R-CNN?.

Q7.7.   What is YOLO?

Q7.8.   What is SSD?

Q7.9.   What is Haar cascade code?

Q7.10.   What is the COCO dataset?

Q7.11.   What is object detection with transfer learning?

Q7.12.   What is object tracking?

Q7.13.   What is image semantic segmentation, and what is image instance segmentation?

Q7.14.   What is K-means clustering image segmentation?

Q7.15.   What is watershed image segmentation?

Q7.16.   What is image background removal?

Q7.17.   What is image depth estimation?

Q7.18.   What is augmented reality?

Pose Detection

"Software is eating the world, but AI is going to eat software."

—Jensen Huang (cofounder and CEO of Nvidia)

CHAPTER OUTLINE

8.1   Introduction

Pose detection, also called *human pose detection* or *human pose estimation*, is a hot research topic that has attracted the attention of the computer vision community for the past few decades. The key to pose detection is to detect and locate human joints, also known as *keypoints* in images or videos, such as heads, necks, shoulders, hips, elbows, wrists, knees, ankles, and so on. The pose estimation problem is often referred to as the *perspective-n-point problem*, in which the goals are to find the pose of an object with a calibrated camera and to find the locations of *n* 3D points on the object and the corresponding 2D projections in the image.

With pose detection, you can do many cool things, such as recognizing people's activities, teaching people online (sports, workouts, yoga), and gaming. During the 2020 COVID-19 pandemic, there was a rise of yoga apps that use pose detection to help teach people yoga online.

In this chapter, we will first show you how to detect and recognize hand gestures and, related to that, sign language. Then we will introduce body pose detections and, finally, human activity recognition (HAR).

The following are some pose detection datasets and challenges:

- COCO Keypoints challenge

  ```
  https://cocodataset.org/#keypoints-2020
  ```

- MPII Human Pose Dataset

  ```
  http://human-pose.mpi-inf.mpg.de/
  ```

- VGG Pose Dataset

  ```
  https://www.robots.ox.ac.uk/~vgg/data/pose_evaluation/
  ```

- The Cambridge-Imperial APE (Action-Pose-Estimation) Dataset

  ```
  https://labicvl.github.io/APE.html
  ```

See the following links for more information about human pose detection:

```
https://learnopencv.com/tag/human-pose-estimation/
https://learnopencv.com/deep-learning-based-human-pose-estimation-
using-opencv-cpp-python/
https://github.com/garyzhao/SemGCN
https://docs.openvinotoolkit.org/latest/omz_demos_python_demos_
human_pose_estimation_3d_demo_README.html
```

8.2   Hand Gesture Detection

Hand gesture detection is one of the most popular solutions for human computer interaction. It has found wide application in video gaming, medicine, accessibility support, and so on. It has also become popular on devices such as smart phones, tablets, and laptops. In this section, we will introduce how to do hand gesture detection by using the OpenCV library and the TensorFlow. js library.

8.2.1   OpenCV

The following shows an example of hand gesture detection using OpenCV. This is a two-part tutorial. In Part 1, it basically recognizes a hand by subtracting the background and therefore requires a plain, simple background. It also requires the hand to be in a certain area of the camera.

```
https://github.com/Gogul09/gesture-recognition
```

Example 8.1 shows the `segment.py` code in Part 1 that can separate the hand from the background (`https://github.com/Gogul09/gesture-recognition/blob/master/segment.py`), with minor modifications.

EXAMPLE 8.1   THE SEGMENT.PY **PROGRAM**

```
# Example 8.1 segment.py
# https://github.com/Gogul09/gesture-recognition/blob/master/segment
.py
# With minor modifications.
#-----------------------------------------
# SEGMENT HAND REGION FROM A VIDEO SEQUENCE
#-----------------------------------------


# organize imports
import cv2
import imutils
import numpy as np

# global variables
bg = None


#----------------------------------------------------
# To find the running average over the background
#----------------------------------------------------
def run_avg(image, aWeight):
    global bg
    # initialize the background
    if bg is None:
        bg = image.copy().astype("float")
        return

    # compute weighted average, accumulate it and update the
background
    cv2.accumulateWeighted(image, bg, aWeight)

#---------------------------------------------
# To segment the region of hand in the image
#---------------------------------------------
def segment(image, threshold=25):
    global bg
    # find the absolute difference between background and current
frame
    diff = cv2.absdiff(bg.astype("uint8"), image)
```

```
    # threshold the diff image so that we get the foreground
    thresholded = cv2.threshold(diff, threshold, 255, cv2.THRESH_
BINARY)[1]

    # get the contours in the thresholded image
    #(_, cnts, _) = cv2.findContours(thresholded.copy(), cv2.RETR_
EXTERNAL, cv2.CHAIN_APPROX_SIMPLE)
    (cnts, _) = cv2.findContours(thresholded.copy(), cv2.RETR_
EXTERNAL, cv2.CHAIN_APPROX_SIMPLE)

    # return None, if no contours detected
    if len(cnts) == 0:
        return
    else:
        # based on contour area, get the maximum contour which is the
hand
        segmented = max(cnts, key=cv2.contourArea)
        return (thresholded, segmented)

#-----------------
# MAIN FUNCTION
#-----------------
if __name__ == "__main__":
    # initialize weight for running average
    aWeight = 0.5

    # get the reference to the webcam
    camera = cv2.VideoCapture(0)

    # region of interest (ROI) coordinates
    #top, right, bottom, left = 10, 350, 225, 590
    top, right, bottom, left = 10, 10, 250, 300

    # initialize num of frames
    num_frames = 0

    # keep looping, until interrupted
    while(True):
        # get the current frame
        (grabbed, frame) = camera.read()

        # resize the frame
        frame = imutils.resize(frame, width=700)

        # flip the frame so that it is not the mirror view
        frame = cv2.flip(frame, 1)

        # clone the frame
        clone = frame.copy()
```

```
        # get the height and width of the frame
        (height, width) = frame.shape[:2]

        # get the ROI
        roi = frame[top:bottom, right:left]

        # convert the roi to grayscale and blur it
        gray = cv2.cvtColor(roi, cv2.COLOR_BGR2GRAY)
        gray = cv2.GaussianBlur(gray, (9, 9), 0)

        # to get the background, keep looking till a threshold is
reached
        # so that our running average model gets calibrated
        if num_frames < 30:
            run_avg(gray, aWeight)
        else:
            # segment the hand region
            hand = segment(gray)

            # check whether hand region is segmented
            if hand is not None:
                # if yes, unpack the thresholded image and
                # segmented region
                (thresholded, segmented) = hand

                # draw the segmented region and display the frame
                cv2.drawContours(clone, [segmented + (right, top)], -1,
(0, 0, 255))
                cv2.imshow("Thesholded", thresholded)

        # draw the segmented hand
        cv2.rectangle(clone, (left, top), (right, bottom), (0,255,0), 2)

        # increment the number of frames
        num_frames += 1

        # display the frame with segmented hand
        cv2.imshow("Video Feed", clone)

        # observe the keypress by the user
        keypress = cv2.waitKey(1) & 0xFF

        # if the user pressed "q", then stop looping
        if keypress == ord("q"):
            break

# free up memory
camera.release()
cv2.destroyAllWindows()
```

Figure 8.1 shows the output of the `segment.py` code in Part 1 of the tutorial, which shows how to extract a hand from the image.

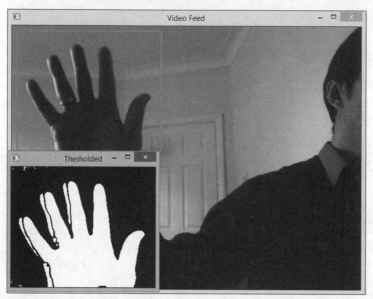

Figure 8.1: The output of the `segment.py` code in Part 1 of the tutorial of the Gesture-Recognition project

In the Part 2 tutorial, we recognize and count the number of fingers. Example 8.2 shows the `recognize.py` code in Part 2 that can recognize and count the number of fingers (`https://github.com/Gogul09/gesture-recognition/blob/master/recognize.py`), with minor modifications.

EXAMPLE 8.2   THE `RECOGNIZE.PY` **PROGRAM**

```
# Example 8.2
# https://github.com/Gogul09/gesture-recognition/blob/master/recognize.py
# With minor modifications.
#-------------------------------------------------------------
# SEGMENT, RECOGNIZE and COUNT fingers from a video sequence
#-------------------------------------------------------------

# organize imports
import cv2
import imutils
import numpy as np
from sklearn.metrics import pairwise

# global variables
bg = None
```

```
#----------------------------------------------------
# To find the running average over the background
#----------------------------------------------------
def run_avg(image, accumWeight):
    global bg
    # initialize the background
    if bg is None:
        bg = image.copy().astype("float")
        return

    # compute weighted average, accumulate it and update the background
    cv2.accumulateWeighted(image, bg, accumWeight)

#---------------------------------------------
# To segment the region of hand in the image
#---------------------------------------------
def segment(image, threshold=25):
    global bg
    # find the absolute difference between background and current frame
    diff = cv2.absdiff(bg.astype("uint8"), image)

    # threshold the diff image so that we get the foreground
    thresholded = cv2.threshold(diff, threshold, 255, cv2.THRESH_BINARY)[1]

    # get the contours in the thresholded image
    #(_, cnts, _) = cv2.findContours(thresholded.copy(), cv2.RETR_
EXTERNAL, cv2.CHAIN_APPROX_SIMPLE)
    (cnts, _) = cv2.findContours(thresholded.copy(), cv2.RETR_EXTERNAL,
cv2.CHAIN_APPROX_SIMPLE)

    # return None, if no contours detected
    if len(cnts) == 0:
        return
    else:
        # based on contour area, get the maximum contour which is the hand
        segmented = max(cnts, key=cv2.contourArea)
        return (thresholded, segmented)

#------------------------------------------------------------
# To count the number of fingers in the segmented hand region
#------------------------------------------------------------
def count(thresholded, segmented):
    # find the convex hull of the segmented hand region
    chull = cv2.convexHull(segmented)

    # find the most extreme points in the convex hull
    extreme_top    = tuple(chull[chull[:, :, 1].argmin()][0])
```

```
        extreme_bottom = tuple(chull[chull[:, :, 1].argmax()][0])
        extreme_left   = tuple(chull[chull[:, :, 0].argmin()][0])
        extreme_right  = tuple(chull[chull[:, :, 0].argmax()][0])

        # find the center of the palm
        cX = int((extreme_left[0] + extreme_right[0]) / 2)
        cY = int((extreme_top[1] + extreme_bottom[1]) / 2)

        # find the maximum euclidean distance between the center of the palm
        # and the most extreme points of the convex hull
        distance = pairwise.euclidean_distances([(cX, cY)], Y=[extreme_left,
extreme_right, extreme_top, extreme_bottom])[0]
        maximum_distance = distance[distance.argmax()]

        # calculate the radius of the circle with 80% of the max euclidean
distance obtained
        radius = int(0.8 * maximum_distance)

        # find the circumference of the circle
        circumference = (2 * np.pi * radius)

        # take out the circular region of interest which has
        # the palm and the fingers
        circular_roi = np.zeros(thresholded.shape[:2], dtype="uint8")

        # draw the circular ROI
        cv2.circle(circular_roi, (cX, cY), radius, 255, 1)

        # take bit-wise AND between thresholded hand using the circular ROI
as the mask
        # which gives the cuts obtained using mask on the thresholded hand
image
        circular_roi = cv2.bitwise_and(thresholded, thresholded,
mask=circular_roi)

        # compute the contours in the circular ROI
        #(_, cnts, _) = cv2.findContours(circular_roi.copy(), cv2.RETR_
EXTERNAL, cv2.CHAIN_APPROX_NONE)
        ( cnts, _) = cv2.findContours(circular_roi.copy(), cv2.RETR_
EXTERNAL, cv2.CHAIN_APPROX_NONE)

        # initalize the finger count
        count = 0

        # loop through the contours found
        for c in cnts:
            # compute the bounding box of the contour
            (x, y, w, h) = cv2.boundingRect(c)
```

```python
            # increment the count of fingers only if -
            # 1. The contour region is not the wrist (bottom area)
            # 2. The number of points along the contour does not exceed
            #      25% of the circumference of the circular ROI
            if ((cY + (cY * 0.25)) > (y + h)) and ((circumference * 0.25)
> c.shape[0]):
                count += 1

    return count

#-----------------
# MAIN FUNCTION
#-----------------
if __name__ == "__main__":
    # initialize accumulated weight
    accumWeight = 0.5

    # get the reference to the webcam
    camera = cv2.VideoCapture(0)

    # region of interest (ROI) coordinates
    #top, right, bottom, left = 10, 350, 225, 590
    top, right, bottom, left = 10, 10, 250, 300

    # initialize num of frames
    num_frames = 0

    # calibration indicator
    calibrated = False

    # keep looping, until interrupted
    while(True):
        # get the current frame
        (grabbed, frame) = camera.read()

        # resize the frame
        frame = imutils.resize(frame, width=700)

        # flip the frame so that it is not the mirror view
        frame = cv2.flip(frame, 1)

        # clone the frame
        clone = frame.copy()

        # get the height and width of the frame
        (height, width) = frame.shape[:2]

        # get the ROI
        roi = frame[top:bottom, right:left]
```

```python
            # convert the roi to grayscale and blur it
            gray = cv2.cvtColor(roi, cv2.COLOR_BGR2GRAY)
            gray = cv2.GaussianBlur(gray, (9, 9), 0)

            # to get the background, keep looking till a threshold is
reached
            # so that our weighted average model gets calibrated
            if num_frames < 30:
                run_avg(gray, accumWeight)
                if num_frames == 1:
                    print("[STATUS] please wait! calibrating...")
                elif num_frames == 29:
                    print("[STATUS] calibration successfull...")
            else:
                # segment the hand region
                hand = segment(gray)

                # check whether hand region is segmented
                if hand is not None:
                    # if yes, unpack the thresholded image and
                    # segmented region
                    (thresholded, segmented) = hand

                    # draw the segmented region and display the frame
                    cv2.drawContours(clone, [segmented + (right, top)], -1,
(0, 0, 255))

                    # count the number of fingers
                    fingers = count(thresholded, segmented)

                    cv2.putText(clone, str(fingers), (70, 45), cv2.FONT_
HERSHEY_SIMPLEX, 1, (0,0,255), 2)

                    # show the thresholded image
                    cv2.imshow("Thesholded", thresholded)

            # draw the segmented hand
            cv2.rectangle(clone, (left, top), (right, bottom), (0,255,0), 2)

            # increment the number of frames
            num_frames += 1

            # display the frame with segmented hand
            cv2.imshow("Video Feed", clone)

            # observe the keypress by the user
            keypress = cv2.waitKey(1) & 0xFF
```

```
            # if the user pressed "q", then stop looping
            if keypress == ord("q"):
                break

    # free up memory
    camera.release()
    cv2.destroyAllWindows()
```

Figure 8.2 shows the output of the `recognize.py` code in Part 2 of the tutorial, which shows the result of recognizing the number of fingers captured in the region of interest (ROI).

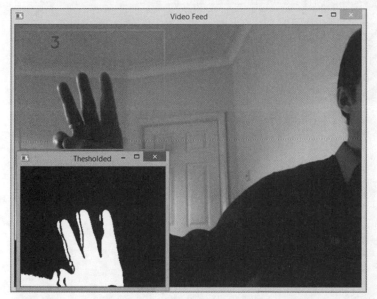

Figure 8.2: The output of the `recognize.py` code in Part 2 or the tutorial for the Gesture-Recognition project

EXERCISE 8.1

Download the previous Python GitHub project. Run the programs and comment on the results.

The following shows a similar hand gesture recognition based on OpenCV. It is based on the same principle of the previous example, and it can recognize the hand as pointing, stone, paper, scissors; you also need to put the hand in a certain area of the camera.

```
https://github.com/ishfulthinking/Python-Hand-Gesture-Recognition
```

Example 8.3 shows the `checkpoint5.py` example code based on (https://github.com/ishfulthinking/Python-Hand-Gesture-Recognition/blob/master/checkpoint5.ipynb), with minor modifications.

EXAMPLE 8.3   THE `CHECKPOINT5.PY` **PROGRAM**

```
# Example 8.3 checkpoint5.py
# https://github.com/ishfulthinking/Python-Hand-Gesture-Recognition/
blob/master/checkpoint5.ipynb
# With minor modifications.
#!/usr/bin/env python
# coding: utf-8

# # Python Hand Gesture Recognition (Checkpoint 5)

# This checkpoint is at the end of Objective 5.
#
# At this point, your code should be fully functional -- it'll recognize
waving, pointing, a peace sign (scissors), and a fist (rock). Congrats
on making it here!

# ### Header: Importing libraries and creating global variables

# In[21]:


import numpy as np
import cv2


# Hold the background frame for background subtraction.
background = None
# Hold the hand's data so all its details are in one place.
hand = None
# Variables to count how many frames have passed and to set the size of
the window.
frames_elapsed = 0
FRAME_HEIGHT = 480
FRAME_WIDTH = 640
# Humans come in a ton of beautiful shades and colors.
# Try editing these if your program has trouble recognizing your skin
tone.
CALIBRATION_TIME = 30
BG_WEIGHT = 0.5
OBJ_THRESHOLD = 18


# ### HandData: A class to hold all the hand's details and flags

# In[22]:
```

```python
class HandData:
    top = (0,0)
    bottom = (0,0)
    left = (0,0)
    right = (0,0)
    centerX = 0
    prevCenterX = 0
    isInFrame = False
    isWaving = False
    fingers = None
    gestureList = []

    def __init__(self, top, bottom, left, right, centerX):
        self.top = top
        self.bottom = bottom
        self.left = left
        self.right = right
        self.centerX = centerX
        self.prevCenterX = 0
        isInFrame = False
        isWaving = False

    def update(self, top, bottom, left, right):
        self.top = top
        self.bottom = bottom
        self.left = left
        self.right = right

    def check_for_waving(self, centerX):
        self.prevCenterX = self.centerX
        self.centerX = centerX

        if abs(self.centerX - self.prevCenterX > 3):
            self.isWaving = True
        else:
            self.isWaving = False


# ### write_on_image(): Write info related to the hand gesture and
outline the region of interest

# In[23]:


# Here we take the current frame, the number of frames elapsed, and how
many fingers we've detected
# so we can print on the screen which gesture is happening (or if the
camera is calibrating).
def write_on_image(frame):
    text = "Searching..."
```

```
          if frames_elapsed < CALIBRATION_TIME:
              text = "Calibrating..."
          elif hand == None or hand.isInFrame == False:
              text = "No hand detected"
          else:
              if hand.isWaving:
                  text = "Waving"
              elif hand.fingers == 0:
                  text = "Rock"
              elif hand.fingers == 1:
                  text = "Pointing"
              elif hand.fingers == 2:
                  text = "Scissors"


      cv2.putText(frame, text, (10,20), cv2.FONT_HERSHEY_COMPLEX, 0.4,( 0
  , 0 , 0 ),2,cv2.LINE_AA)
      cv2.putText(frame, text, (10,20), cv2.FONT_HERSHEY_COMPLEX,
  0.4,(255,255,255),1,cv2.LINE_AA)

      # Highlight the region of interest.
      cv2.rectangle(frame, (region_left, region_top), (region_right,
  region_bottom), (255,255,255), 2)


  # ### get_region(): Separate the region of interest and preps it for
  edge detection

  # In[24]:


  def get_region(frame):
      # Separate the region of interest from the rest of the frame.
      region = frame[region_top:region_bottom, region_left:region_right]
      # Make it grayscale so we can detect the edges more easily.
      region = cv2.cvtColor(region, cv2.COLOR_BGR2GRAY)
      # Use a Gaussian blur to prevent frame noise from being labeled as
  an edge.
      region = cv2.GaussianBlur(region, (5,5), 0)

      return region


  # ### get_average(): Create a weighted average of the background for
  image differencing

  # In[25]:
```

```python
def get_average(region):
    # We have to use the global keyword because we want to edit the
global variable.
    global background
    # If we haven't captured the background yet, make the current region
the background.
    if background is None:
        background = region.copy().astype("float")
        return
    # Otherwise, add this captured frame to the average of the
backgrounds.
    cv2.accumulateWeighted(region, background, BG_WEIGHT)


# ### segment(): Use image differencing to separate the hand from the
background

# In[26]:


# Here we use differencing to separate the background from the object of
interest.
def segment(region):
    global hand
    # Find the absolute difference between the background and the
current frame.
    diff = cv2.absdiff(background.astype(np.uint8), region)

    # Threshold that region with a strict 0 or 1 ruling so only the
foreground remains.
    thresholded_region = cv2.threshold(diff, OBJ_THRESHOLD, 255, cv2
.THRESH_BINARY)[1]

    # Get the contours of the region, which will return an outline of
the hand.
    #(_, contours, _) = cv2.findContours(thresholded_region.copy(), cv2
.RETR_EXTERNAL, cv2.CHAIN_APPROX_SIMPLE)
    (contours, _) = cv2.findContours(thresholded_region.copy(), cv2
.RETR_EXTERNAL, cv2.CHAIN_APPROX_SIMPLE)

    # If we didn't get anything, there's no hand.
    if len(contours) == 0:
        if hand is not None:
            hand.isInFrame = False
        return
    # Otherwise return a tuple of the filled hand (thresholded_region),
along with the outline (segmented_region).
    else:
        if hand is not None:
            hand.isInFrame = True
```

```
        segmented_region = max(contours, key = cv2.contourArea)
        return (thresholded_region, segmented_region)


# ### get_hand_data(): Find the extremities of the hand and put them in
the global hand object

# In[27]:


def get_hand_data(thresholded_image, segmented_image):
    global hand

    # Enclose the area around the extremities in a convex hull to
connect all outcroppings.
    convexHull = cv2.convexHull(segmented_image)

    # Find the extremities for the convex hull and store them as points.
    top    = tuple(convexHull[convexHull[:, :, 1].argmin()][0])
    bottom = tuple(convexHull[convexHull[:, :, 1].argmax()][0])
    left   = tuple(convexHull[convexHull[:, :, 0].argmin()][0])
    right  = tuple(convexHull[convexHull[:, :, 0].argmax()][0])

    # Get the center of the palm, so we can check for waving and find
the fingers.
    centerX = int((left[0] + right[0]) / 2)

    # We put all the info into an object for handy extraction (get it?
HANDy?)
    if hand == None:
        hand = HandData(top, bottom, left, right, centerX)
    else:
        hand.update(top, bottom, left, right)

    # Only check for waving every 6 frames.
    if frames_elapsed % 6 == 0:
        hand.check_for_waving(centerX)

    # We count the number of fingers up every frame, but only change
hand.fingers if
    # 12 frames have passed, to prevent erratic gesture counts.
    hand.gestureList.append(count_fingers(thresholded_image))
    if frames_elapsed % 12 == 0:
        hand.fingers = most_frequent(hand.gestureList)
        hand.gestureList.clear()


# ### count_fingers(): Count the number of fingers using a line
intersecting fingertips

# In[28]:
```

```python
def count_fingers(thresholded_image):

    # Find the height at which we will draw the line to count fingers.
    line_height = int(hand.top[1] + (0.2 * (hand.bottom[1] - hand.
top[1])))

    # Get the linear region of interest along where the fingers would
be.
    line = np.zeros(thresholded_image.shape[:2], dtype=int)

    # Draw a line across this region of interest, where the fingers
should be.
    cv2.line(line, (thresholded_image.shape[1], line_height), (0, line_
height), 255, 1)

    # Do a bitwise AND to find where the line intersected the hand --
this is where the fingers are.
    line = cv2.bitwise_and(thresholded_image, thresholded_image, mask =
line.astype(np.uint8))

    # Get the line's new contours. The contours are basically just
little lines formed by gaps
    # in the big line across the fingers, so each would be a finger
unless it's very wide.
    #(_, contours, _) = cv2.findContours(line.copy(), cv2.RETR_EXTERNAL,
cv2.CHAIN_APPROX_NONE)
    (contours, _) = cv2.findContours(line.copy(), cv2.RETR_EXTERNAL,
cv2.CHAIN_APPROX_NONE)

    fingers = 0

    # Count the fingers by making sure the contour lines are "finger-
sized", i.e. not too wide.
    # This prevents a "rock" gesture from being mistaken for a finger.
    for curr in contours:
        width = len(curr)

        if width < 3 * abs(hand.right[0] - hand.left[0]) / 4 and width > 5:
            fingers += 1

    return fingers


# ### most_frequent(): Returns the value in a list that appears most
frequently

# In[29]:
```

```
def most_frequent(input_list):
    dict = {}
    count = 0
    most_freq = 0

    for item in reversed(input_list):
        dict[item] = dict.get(item, 0) + 1
        if dict[item] >= count :
            count, most_freq = dict[item], item

    return most_freq


# ### Main function: Get input from camera and call functions to
understand it

# In[30]:


# Our region of interest will be the top right part of the frame.
region_top = 0
region_bottom = int(2 * FRAME_HEIGHT / 3)
region_left = int(FRAME_WIDTH / 2)
region_right = FRAME_WIDTH

frames_elapsed = 0

capture = cv2.VideoCapture(0)

while (True):
    # Store the frame from the video capture and resize it to the window
size.
    ret, frame = capture.read()
    frame = cv2.resize(frame, (FRAME_WIDTH, FRAME_HEIGHT))
    # Flip the frame over the vertical axis so that it works like a
mirror, which is more intuitive to the user.
    frame = cv2.flip(frame, 1)

    # Separate the region of interest and prep it for edge detection.
    region = get_region(frame)
    if frames_elapsed < CALIBRATION_TIME:
        get_average(region)
    else:
        region_pair = segment(region)
        if region_pair is not None:
            # If we have the regions segmented successfully, show them
in another window for the user.
            (thresholded_region, segmented_region) = region_pair
```

```
            cv2.drawContours(region, [segmented_region], -1, (255, 255,
    255))

            cv2.imshow("Segmented Image", region)

            get_hand_data(thresholded_region, segmented_region)

    # Write the action the hand is doing on the screen, and draw the
    region of interest.
    write_on_image(frame)
    # Show the previously captured frame.
    cv2.imshow("Camera Input", frame)
    frames_elapsed += 1
    # Check if user wants to exit.
    if (cv2.waitKey(1) & 0xFF == ord('x')):
        break

# When we exit the loop, we have to stop the capture too.
capture.release()
cv2.destroyAllWindows()
```

Figure 8.3 shows the output.

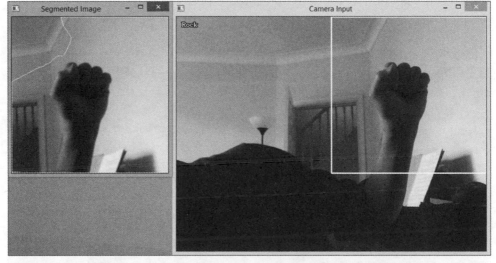

Figure 8.3: The output of the `checkpoint5.py` code for the Python-Hand-Gesture-Recognition project

EXERCISE 8.2

Download the previous Python GitHub project. Run the programs and comment on the results. Then add a three-finger salute gesture, as shown in the blockbuster movie *The Hunger Games*.

The following website shows another hand gesture example project called: Hand Gesture Recognition. This Python project first creates three template images to present three hand signs for victory, like, and respect. Then it uses a webcam to capture the hand in the image and uses OpenCV's `cv2 .matchTemplate()` function to find the best match with the hand sign template image.

```
https://github.com/adilsofficial/HandGesture
```

The following shows a GitHub project called Training a Neural Network to Detect Gestures with OpenCV in Python; it basically builds Microsoft Kinect functionality with just a webcam.

```
https://github.com/athena15/project_kojak
```

8.2.2 TensorFlow.js

Google's TensorFlow.js is a library for machine learning in JavaScript. With the TensorFlow.js library, you can develop ML models in JavaScript and use ML directly in the browser or in Node.js.

The following shows the GitHub site for Google's TensorFlow.js MediaPipe Handpose Project. It has an impressive live demo website (see Figure 8.4), which can use your webcam to detect hand poses in real time.

```
https://github.com/tensorflow/tfjs-models/tree/master/handpose
```

Figure 8.4: The live demo website for the MediaPipe Handpose project

(Source: `https://storage.googleapis.com/tfjs-models/demos/handpose/ index.html`)

TensorFlow.js provides models for a range of applications; such as image classifications, object detection, body segmentation, pose detection, hand pose detection and so on. See the following link for details.

```
https://www.tensorflow.org/js/models
```

There is also a Hand Gesture Recognition Database and corresponding projects on Kaggle. For more information, see the following:

```
https://www.kaggle.com/gti-upm/leapgestrecog
https://www.kaggle.com/benenharrington/hand-gesture-recognition-
database-with-cnn
```

8.3   Sign Language Detection

Related to hand gesture detection is sign language detection. A good starting point is Kaggle, which has a Sign Language MNIST dataset and a collection of sign language projects; see the following link for details.

```
https://www.kaggle.com/datamunge/sign-language-mnist/kernels
```

The following shows an interesting Kaggle project called "CNN using Keras (100% Accuracy)." This repository uses CNN Keras and achieved 100 percent accuracy on the Sign Language MNIST dataset.

```
https://www.kaggle.com/madz2000/cnn-using-keras-100-accuracy
```

Figure 8.5 shows another example of the sign language project called Sign Language Recognition Using OpenCV.

The following is the corresponding GitHub site of the project, where you can get all the source code:

```
https://github.com/Arshad221b/Sign-Language-Recognition
```

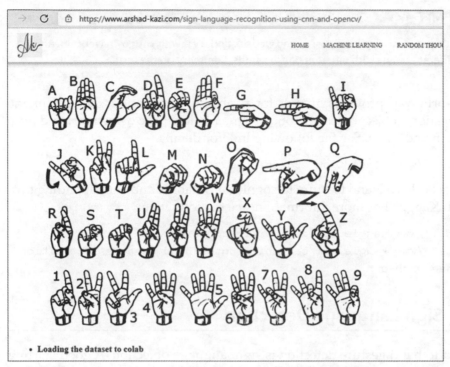

Figure 8.5: A project called Sign Language Recognition Using OpenCV for the Sign Language MNIST dataset

(Source: `https://www.arshad-kazi.com/sign-language-recognition-using-cnn-and-opencv/`)

8.4   Body Pose Detection

In this section, we will show how to detect human body poses by using different libraries, such as OpenPose, OpenCV, Gluon, PoseNet, ML5JS, MediaPipe, and so on.

8.4.1   OpenPose

OpenPose, an open source library for body pose detection developed at Carnegie Mellon University, is one of the most accurate libraries for human pose estimation. It is the first real-time multiperson system to jointly detect human body, hand, facial, and foot keypoints (in total 135 keypoints) on single images.

OpenPose uses a convolutional neural network–based approach and attacks the pose estimation problem using a multistage classifier. Each stage improves the results of the previous one. The first stage takes the input image and predicts the possible locations of each keypoint in the image with a confidence score, called the *confidence map*. Each subsequent stage takes not only the image data but also the confidence map of the previous stage. This improves the prediction after each step.

A confidence map is good for single-person pose estimation, but not so good in multiperson pose estimation, where overlapping body parts make it difficult to uniquely identify the limbs of each person. To solve this problem, OpenPose introduces the idea of part affinity maps, where another convolutional neural network branch is introduced that predicts the location and orientation of the limbs.

In the final stage, it just connects these points using greedy inference to generate the pose keypoints for all the people in the image.

The following shows the GitHub site of the OpenPose project, where you can just follow the instructions to run the code.

```
https://github.com/CMU-Perceptual-Computing-Lab/openpose
```

EXERCISE 8.5

Download the previous Python GitHub project. Run the programs and comment on the results.

8.4.2   OpenCV

The following website shows an interesting tutorial on how to perform human pose estimation by using OpenCV and deep learning networks. In this tutorial, it uses a pretrained Caffe model that won the COCO keypoints challenge in 2016 for detecting keypoint locations.

```
https://learnopencv.com/deep-learning-based-human-pose-estimation-
using-opencv-cpp-python/
```

The following shows the corresponding IPython Notebook on its GitHub site, where you can try the example code.

```
https://github.com/spmallick/learnopencv/blob/master/OpenPose/
OpenPose_Notebook.ipynb
```

EXERCISE 8.6

From a web browser, log in to your Google Colab account, and upload the previous IPython Notebook. Run the code and comment on the results.

8.4.3   Gluon

Gluon is another open source library that can be used for pose estimation. The following link shows the Gluon website for pose estimation examples.

```
https://cv.gluon.ai/build/examples_pose/index.html
```

The following shows the Gluon example of a simple pose demo.

`https://cv.gluon.ai/build/examples_pose/demo_simple_pose.html`

The following shows the Gluon webcam demo example for pose estimation.

`https://cv.gluon.ai/build/examples_pose/cam_demo.html`

EXERCISE 8.7

Download the previous Gluon webcam demo code. Run the code and comment on the results.

8.4.4 PoseNet

Google's PoseNet is a library for running real-time pose estimation in the browser using the TensorFlow.js library. The recently released version 2.0 has a new ResNet model and API.

The following link shows the TensorFlow.js site for PoseNet.

`https://github.com/tensorflow/tfjs-models/tree/master/posenet`

PoseNet also has an impressive web demo site, where you can run the pose detection on your own webcam; see Figure 8.6. The demo supports both MobileNet and ResNet50.

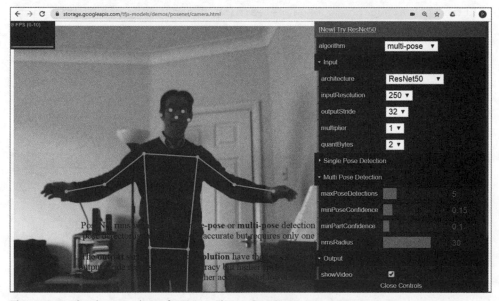

Figure 8.6: The demo website for TensorFlow.js PoseNet

(Source: `https://storage.googleapis.com/tfjs-models/demos/posenet/camera.html`)

8.4.5   ML5JS

ML5JS is a user-friendly machine learning library, which allows you to run a range of machine learning algorithms through the web browser. The following is the ML5JS website, where you can get all the instructions.

```
https://ml5js.org/
```

The following shows the ML5JS - PoseNet website, where you can run Google's PoseNet through a simple, friendly web browser.

```
https://learn.ml5js.org/#/reference/posenet
```

The following shows an example of running ML5JS - PoseNet through a webcam.

```
https://github.com/ml5js/ml5-library/tree/main/examples/p5js/
PoseNet/PoseNet_webcam
```

It essentially has just two files.

```
index.html
sketch.js
```

The `index.html` file is for creating the web page (Figure 8.7), and the `sketch .js` file is for running the machine learning code for PoseNet (Figure 8.8). To run the code, just use a web browser to open the `index.html` file, as shown in Figure 8.9. Simple! As you can see, you don't need to install any libraries; everything is automatically handled by the `sketch.js` file.

Figure 8.7: The `index.html` file of ML5JS - PoseNet webcam example

(Source: `https://github.com/ml5js/ml5-library/blob/main/examples/p5js/PoseNet/PoseNet_webcam/index.html`)

```
1   // Copyright (c) 2019 ml5
2   //
3   // This software is released under the MIT License.
4   // https://opensource.org/licenses/MIT
5
6   /* ===
7   ml5 Example
8   PoseNet example using p5.js
9   === */
10
11  let video;
12  let poseNet;
13  let poses = [];
14
15  function setup() {
16    createCanvas(640, 480);
17    video = createCapture(VIDEO);
18    video.size(width, height);
19
20    // Create a new poseNet method with a single detection
21    poseNet = ml5.poseNet(video, modelReady);
22    // This sets up an event that fills the global variable "poses"
23    // with an array every time new poses are detected
24    poseNet.on("pose", function(results) {
25      poses = results;
26    });
27    // Hide the video element, and just show the canvas
28    video.hide();
29  }
30
31  function modelReady() {
32    select("#status").html("Model Loaded");
33  }
```

Figure 8.8: The `sketch.js` file of ML5JS - PoseNet webcam example

(Source: `https://github.com/ml5js/ml5-library/blob/main/examples/p5js/PoseNet/PoseNet_webcam/sketch.js`)

Figure 8.9: The ML5JS - PoseNet webcam example through a web browser

ML5JS also allows you to run the examples online, through the `https://editor.p5js.org` website. Figure 8.10 shows all the ML5JS examples available on the `https://editor.p5js.org` website.

Figure 8.11 shows the ML5JS PoseNet webcam example on the `https://editor.p5js.org` website.

8.4.6   MediaPipe

Google's MediaPipe is a library that offers cross-platform, customizable ML solutions for live and streaming media. Example solutions include face detection, face mesh, iris within an eye, hands, pose, holistic, hair segmentation, object detection, box tracking, instant motion tracking, and so on. The following link shows the GitHub website for the MediaPipe pose project.

```
https://google.github.io/mediapipe/solutions/pose.html
```

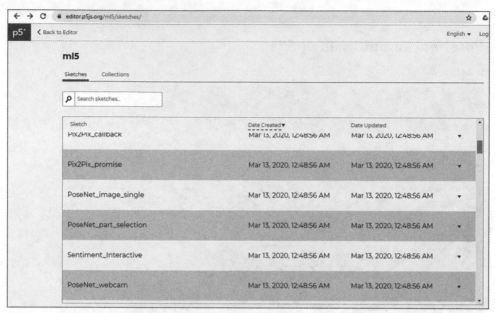

Figure 8.10: The ML5JS examples on the `https://editor.p5js.org` website

(Source: `https://editor.p5js.org/ml5/sketches/`)

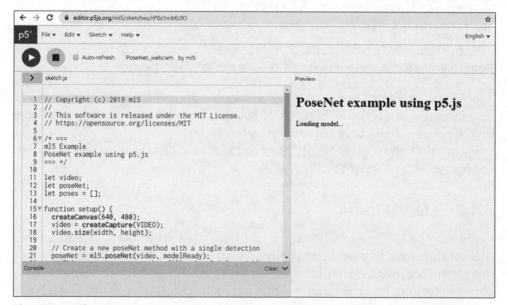

Figure 8.11: The ML5JS PoseNet webcam example on the `https://editor.p5js.org` website

(Source: `https://editor.p5js.org/ml5/sketches/rP8x1mML0O`)

8.5   Human Activity Recognition

This section covers human activity recognition.

ActionAI

ActionAI is an open source library for human activity recognition. See the following link for the GitHub site of ActionAI.

```
https://github.com/smellslikeml/ActionAI
```

Gluon Action Detection

The following link shows the Gluon examples for the action recognition.

```
https://cv.gluon.ai/build/examples_action_recognition/index.html
```

Accelerometer Data HAR

The following website shows an interesting tutorial on using long short-term memory (LSTM) recurrent neural networks to perform human activity recognition based on the University of California, Irvine (UCI) smart phone accelerometer dataset.

```
https://machinelearningmastery.com/how-to-develop-rnn-models-for-
human-activity-recognition-time-series-classification/
```

An accelerometer is a device that measures dynamic acceleration or proper acceleration. Acceleration is the rate of change of velocity. Dynamic acceleration is the acceleration of a body in its own coordinate, which is different from fixed coordinate acceleration. For example, an accelerometer resting on the earth's surface will measure an acceleration of g ≈ 9.81 m/s2 (Earth's gravity), while an accelerometer in free fall will measure zero. An accelerometer measures in meters per second squared (m/s2) or in gravitational forces (G-forces, g). A gyroscope is a device used for measuring orientation and angular velocity. A conventional gyroscope typically contains a spinning wheel in which the axis of rotation is free to assume any orientation by itself. The microelectro-mechanical system (MEMS) gyroscopes generally use a vibrating mechanical element as a sensing element for detecting the angular velocity. They do not have rotating parts, which allows an easy miniaturization and manufacturing. The microelectromechanical system accelerometers and gyroscopes are small, are inexpensive, and are commonly available in modern smart phones.

In this HAR recognition tutorial, a group of 30 volunteers (19–48 years) performed six activities with a smartphone on their waists. Their movement was recorded as the x, y, and z accelerometer data (linear acceleration) and gyroscopic data (angular velocity) from the smart phone, at 50 Hz (i.e., 50 data points per second). The preprocessed, denoised data was split into fixed windows of 2.56 seconds (128 data points) with 50 percent overlap. The data was also randomly partitioned into two sets, 70 percent for training and 30 percent for test.

These were the six activities performed:

- Walking
- Walking upstairs
- Walking downstairs
- Sitting
- Standing
- Laying

EXERCISE 8.13

From a web browser, go to the previous website, follow the instructions, run the example code, and comment on the results.

The following website shows another interesting HAR project based on the same UCI smart phone accelerometer dataset, also using LSTM recurrent neural networks.

```
https://github.com/guillaume-chevalier/LSTM-Human-Activity-
Recognition
```

Compared to classical ML methods, this example using recurrent neural networks requires no feature engineering. Data can be fed directly into the neural network like a black box. This project is built on TensorFlow 1.x.

A modified `LSTM.ipynb` has been created based on the original (`https://github.com/guillaume-chevalier/LSTM-Human-Activity-Recognition/blob/master/LSTM.ipynb`). To run the code, just log in to your Google Colab, upload the file, and run the code.

EXERCISE 8.14

From a web browser, log in to your Google Colab, and upload the file `LSTM.ipynb`. Run the programs and comment on the results.

The following link shows another GitHub project for human activity recognition; it is implemented with a CNN in TensorFlow.

`https://aqibsaeed.github.io/2016-11-04-human-activity-recognition-cnn/`

EXERCISE 8.15

Download the previous Python GitHub project. Run the programs and comment on the results.

The following link shows a GitHub project for the HAR project. In this project, it compares the accuracy of different deep learning networks, such as CNN, LSTM, CNN+LSTM, CNN+Inception, and Xgboost. Xgboost gives the highest accuracy of 96 percent.

`https://github.com/JohnnyHaan/HumanActivityRecognition_HAR`

EXERCISE 8.16

Download the previous Python GitHub project. Run the programs and comment on the results.

The following shows the GitHub project for the health data science HAR. This project discusses the HAR problem using deep learning algorithms and compares the results with standard machine learning algorithms that use engineered features.

`https://github.com/healthDataScience/deep-learning-HAR`

EXERCISE 8.17

Download the previous Python GitHub project. Run the programs and comment on the results.

8.6   Summary

This chapter covered pose detection, or pose estimation, which is defined as the problem of locating human joints, also known as keypoints, such as elbows, wrists, shoulders, waist, and legs, in images or videos.

Hand gesture detection is for detecting and recognizing the different hand gestures.

Sign language detection is for detecting sign language.

Body pose detection, human pose detection, or human pose estimation, is for detecting and recognizing human body positions.

Human activity recognition is for detecting and recognizing human activities via camera or accelerometer data.

8.7   Chapter Review Questions

Q8.1.   What is pose detection?

Q8.2.   What is hand gesture detection?

Q8.3.   What is sign language detection?

Q8.4.   What is body pose detection?

Q8.5.   What is OpenPose?

Q8.6.   What PoseNet?

Q8.7.   What is ML5JS?

Q8.8.   What is MediaPipe?

Q8.9.   What is human activity recognition?

Q8.10.   What is ActionAI?

GAN and Neural-Style Transfer

"A year spent in artificial intelligence is enough to make one believe in God."

—Alan Perlis (American computer scientist)

CHAPTER OUTLINE

9.1 Introduction

Over the years, there have been many exciting developments in the field of deep learning, such as generative adversarial networks (GANs) and neural-style transfer. In this chapter, we will first introduce GAN and neural-style transfer and then introduce adversarial machine learning and music generation.

9.2   Generative Adversarial Network

A generative adversarial network (GAN) is probably one of the most exciting developments in deep learning. A GAN is a class of new deep learning neural networks designed by Ian Goodfellow and his colleagues from the Université de Montréal in 2014. Ian Goodfellow was doing his PhD in machine learning under the supervision of Yoshua Bengio and Aaron Courville.

In a GAN architecture, two neural networks (*agents*) compete against each other in the form of a zero-sum game, where one agent's gain is another agent's loss. A GAN is an approach to generate new images using deep learning methods, such as convolutional neural networks.

Figure 9.1 shows the schematic diagram of a GAN, including two key components: Generator and Discriminator. In this example, both Generator and Discriminator are built on convolutional neural networks. A GAN uses the Generator to generate a fake image from a random noise input, and it uses the Discriminator to compare the fake image with the real image. It then feeds the comparison results back and fine-tunes the Generator. After a number of iterations, the Generator will be able to generate realistic images.

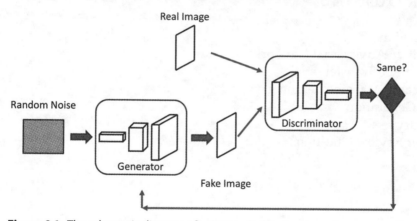

Figure 9.1: The schematic diagram of a GAN including two key components: Generator and Discriminator

Figure 9.2 shows the Wikipedia page for a GAN and a realistic image generated by the GAN. You can see more of this kind of images by visiting the This Person Does Not Exist website (`https://thispersondoesnotexist.com/`).

The following website shows a simple tutorial on how to develop a GAN for a 1D function from scratch with Keras.

```
https://machinelearningmastery.com/how-to-develop-a-generative-
adversarial-network-for-a-1-dimensional-function-from-scratch-in-
keras/
```

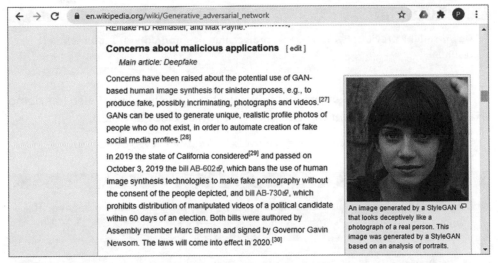

Figure 9.2: The Wikipedia page for the GAN and a very realistic image generated by GAN

(Source: `https://en.wikipedia.org/wiki/Generative_adversarial_network`)

EXERCISE 9.1

From a web browser, go to the previous website, follow the instructions, run the code, and comment on the results.

9.2.1 CycleGAN

The Cycle Generative Adversarial Network (CycleGAN) is an approach to training a deep convolutional neural network for image-to-image translation tasks. CycleGAN uses a cycle consistency loss to enable training without the need for paired data. The following is the GitHub site of Torch implementation of the CycleGAN project.

`https://github.com/junyanz/CycleGAN`

The following is their PyTorch implementation:

`https://github.com/junyanz/pytorch-CycleGAN-and-pix2pix`

With CycleGAN, you can turn horses to zebras or turn zebras to horses, you can turn paintings to photos or turn photos to paintings, and you can turn a summer scene in the photo to a winter scene or turn a winter scene to a summer scene. It is really cool!

EXERCISE 9.2

Download the previous Python GitHub project. Run the programs and comment on the results.

The following is the TensorFlow tutorial site for CycleGAN. It also has demo example code, which you can download or run in Google Colab.

```
https://www.tensorflow.org/tutorials/generative/cyclegan
```

EXERCISE 9.3

Download the previous Python GitHub project. Run the programs and comment on the results.

The following link shows a simple tutorial on how to develop a CycleGAN for image-to-image translation with Keras.

```
https://machinelearningmastery.com/cyclegan-tutorial-with-keras/
```

An IPython Notebook called `CycleGAN.ipynb` has been created based on the previous tutorial code. To use the code, just log in to your Google Colab, and upload the file.

EXERCISE 9.4

From a web browser, go to Google Colab, upload the `CycleGAN.ipynb` file, run the code, and comment on the results.

The following link shows another CycleGAN project implemented with PyTorch, which is remarkably simple and has only a few lines to use:

```
https://cyxu.tv/portfolio/simplified-cyclegan-implementation-in-pytorch/
```

```
#Clone the project
git clone https://github.com/cy-xu/simple_CycleGAN
cd simple_CycleGAN

pip install -r requirements.txt

#Download a CycleGAN dataset from the authors (e.g. horse2zebra):
bash ./util/download_cyclegan_dataset.sh horse2zebra
#Train a model (different from original implementation):
python simple_cygan.py train
#Test the model:
python simple_cygan.py test
```

9.2.2   StyleGAN

The style-based GAN architecture (StyleGAN) is a novel GAN introduced by Nvidia in December 2018. A StyleGAN yields state-of-the-art results in data-driven unconditional generative image modeling. StyleGAN2 is the second version of StyleGAN.

The following is the GitHub site for a StyleGAN2 project implemented in TensorFlow. With StyleGAN and StyleGAN2, you can turn a person in the photo from young to old and from female to male. It does this by projecting the photo images into latent space, which contains a compressed representation of the image. From latent space, you can change the variables such as age and gender.

```
https://github.com/NVlabs/stylegan2
```

The following are two interesting IPython Notebooks for StyleGAN2; you can simply upload them into Google Colab to run them:

```
https://github.com/Puzer/stylegan-encoder/blob/master/Play_with_
latent_directions.ipynb
https://github.com/pbaylies/stylegan-encoder/blob/master/Style
GAN_Encoder_Tutorial.ipynb
```

EXERCISE 9.5

From a web browser, log in to your Google Colab account, upload the previous IPython Notebooks, run the code, and comment on the results.

1. **StyleGAN_Encoder_Notebook.ipynb**   Figure 9.3 shows an interesting Google Colab Notebook called 1. `StyleGAN_Encoder_Notebook.ipynb` for StyleGAN implemented in TensorFlow. See the following links for more details of this example code:

   ```
   https://colab.research.google.com/drive/1jrSki9OXahtnS2Okcf7_
   ubvLkPnboJey
   https://www.youtube.com/watch?v=dCKbRCUyop8
   ```

To run the code, just log in to your Google Colab and upload the previous IPython Notebook.

Upload a high-quality photo into a subfolder called `raw_images`. Run the following commands in the IPython Notebook to convert the raw photo images to aligned photo images:

```
!python align_images.py raw_images/ aligned_images/ --output_size=1024
```

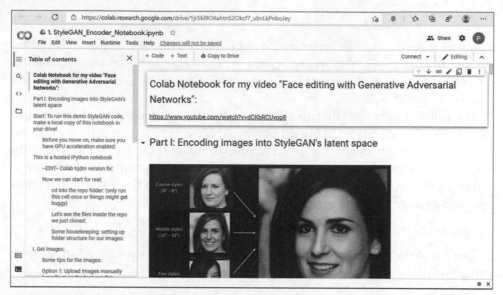

Figure 9.3: The Google Colab Notebook `1. StyleGAN_Encoder_Notebook.ipynb` for StyleGAN implemented in TensorFlow

(Source: `https://colab.research.google.com/drive/1jrSki9OXahtnS2Okcf7_ubvLkPnboJey`)

Run the following commands in the IPython Notebook to convert the aligned photo images into latent photo images:

```
!python encode_images.py --optimizer=lbfgs --face_mask=True
--iterations=6 --use_lpips_loss=0 --use_discriminator_loss=0 --output_
video=True aligned_images/ generated_images/ latent_representations/
```

Figure 9.4 shows the original photo image (right) and latent (encoded) photo image generated by StyleGAN (left).

Figure 9.4: The original photo image (right) and latent (encoded) photo image generated by StyleGAN (left)

A latent photo image is generated by a StyleGAN that is as close as possible to real photo images. With latent photo images, you can vary the different parameters, such as age and gender, to generate images at different ages and different genders.

Figure 9.5 shows the different ages of the latent photo, from young to old.

Figure 9.6 shows the different genders of the latent photo, from female to male.

Figure 9.5: The different ages of the latent photo image, from young to old

Figure 9.6: The different genders of the latent photo image, from female to male

StyleGAN_Encoder_Tutorial.ipynb   The following link shows another interesting example, which has an IPython Notebook called `StyleGAN_Encoder_Tutorial.ipynb`:

```
https://github.com/pbaylies/stylegan-encoder/blob/master/
StyleGAN_Encoder_Tutorial.ipynb
```

To use this example code, log in to your Google Colab, and upload the previous IPython Notebook; then upload two high-quality photo images into a subfolder called `raw_images`. Figure 9.7 shows two example photo images uploaded and displayed in Google Colab.

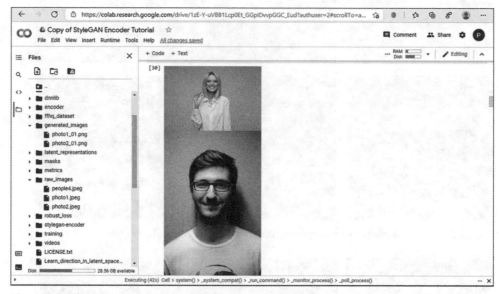

Figure 9.7: The two photo images uploaded to Google Colab

Then run the following commands in the IPython Notebook to convert the raw photo images into aligned photo images:

```
!python align_images.py raw_images/ aligned_images/
```

Run the following commands in the IPython Notebook to convert the aligned photo images into latent photo images. The latent photo images are the images reconstructed by the GAN.

```
!python encode_images.py --batch_size=2 --output_video=True aligned_images/ generated_images/ latent_representations/
```

Figure 9.8 shows the two corresponding generated latent photo images. As you can see, they really look like the original photo images, as shown in Figure 9.8.

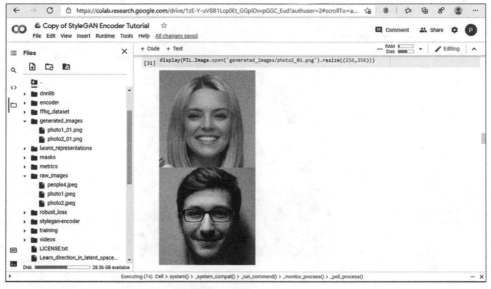

Figure 9.8: The two generated latent photo images

Figure 9.9 shows the second latent photo image blended with the first latent photo image. Figure 9.10 shows the first latent photo image blended with the second latent photo image.

Figure 9.9: The second latent photo image blended with the first latent photo image

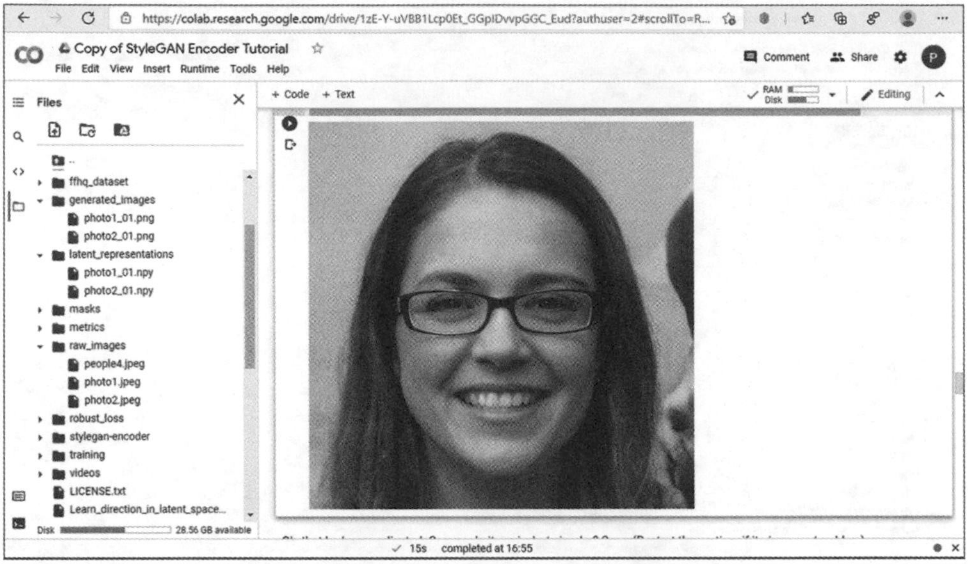

Figure 9.10: The first latent photo image blended with the second latent photo image

9.2.3   Pix2Pix

The Pix2Pix model is a type of conditional GAN for image-to-image translation. Pix2Pix is the brainchild of the Dutch public broadcasting network NPO. It was developed as part of the NPO's desire to create its own artificial intelligence system and see how well machines would do at analyzing human creations and turning them into lifelike paintings.

Pix2Pix uses a range of features, including an algorithm to interpret information, a discriminator that can analyze both the original and the output when it's created, and a neural network that it relies on to guess what the image should look like. For example, Pix2Pix can convert a simple line drawing into an oil painting, based on its understanding of shapes, human drawings, and the real world. And if you're an accomplished artist, it might actually spit out something interesting.

The following is the GitHub site for the Pix2Pix project, implemented with Torch, which shows examples of how to convert labels to street scenes, satellite aerial images to street maps, and sketches to photos.

```
https://github.com/phillipi/pix2pix
```

EXERCISE 9.6

Download the previous GitHub project, follow the instructions, run the code, and comment on the results.

The following website is an interesting tutorial on how to develop a Pix2Pix GAN for image-to-image translation.

```
https://machinelearningmastery.com/how-to-develop-a-pix2pix-gan-
for-image-to-image-translation/
```

EXERCISE 9.7

From a web browser, go to the previous website, follow the instructions, run the code, and comment on the results.

9.2.4   PULSE

Self-Supervised Photo Upsampling via Latent Space Exploration of Generative Models (PULSE) is an impressive library that can turn low-resolution images into high-resolution images. It uses a low-resolution image as the input and uses the StyleGAN generative model to search the high-resolution natural image manifold for images that are perceptually realistic and downscale correctly.

The following is the GitHub site for the PULSE project.

```
https://github.com/adamian98/pulse
```

EXERCISE 9.8

Download the previous GitHub project, follow the instructions, run the code, and comment on the results.

9.2.5   Image Super-Resolution

Image Super-Resolution (ISR) is a project aimed to upscale and improve the quality of low-resolution images by using novel residual dense networks. The following is the GitHub site for the ISR project.

```
https://github.com/idealo/image-super-resolution
```

This project contains Keras implementations of different residual dense networks for single ISR as well as scripts to train these networks using content and adversarial loss components.

To use the ISR library, you will need to install it first.

```
pip install ISR
```

Example 9.1 shows the Python code that uses ISR to magnify images using deep learning models. It opens a small fly image called `pexels-thierry-fillieul-1046492.jpg` (from `www.pixels.com`) and amplifies the image with super resolution. When you run it for the first time, it takes a while to download the model. It will be much faster the second time.

EXAMPLE 9.1   THE `ISR1.PY` PROGRAM

```
#Example 9.1 ISR to magnify images
#https://github.com/idealo/image-super-resolution
#pip install ISR

import numpy as np
from PIL import Image

#pip install 'h5py<3.0.0'
#pip install h5py==2.10.0
#import h5py
#h5py.run_tests()

img = Image.open(pexels-thierry-fillieul-1046492.jpg')
img.show()
lr_img = np.array(img)
from ISR.models import RDN

rdn = RDN(weights='psnr-small')
#rdn = RDN(weights='psnr-large')
#rdn = RDN(weights='noise-cancel')
sr_img = rdn.predict(lr_img)
sr_img =Image.fromarray(sr_img)
sr_img.show()
```

Figure 9.11 shows the output of Example 9.1 with the original image and the amplified image (top) with super resolution (bottom).

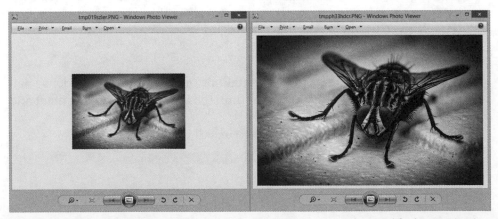

Figure 9.11: The output of Example 9.1 with the original image and the amplified image (top) with super resolution (bottom)

If you are using version h5py 3.0.0 and higher, you may need to down-grade it to version 2, such as 2.10.0. You can downgrade the h5py library by the following `pip` commands:

```
pip install 'h5py<3.0.0'
```

or

```
pip install h5py==2.10.0
```

EXERCISE 9.9

Run the previous program on your own images and comment on the results. Try different RDN weights, such as `psnr-small`, `psnr-large`, `noise-cancel`, and comment on the effects.

Example 9.2 is the webcam version of the previous ISR program.

EXAMPLE 9.2   THE `ISR2.PY` PROGRAM

```
#Example 9.2 ISR webcam
#https://github.com/idealo/image-super-resolution
#pip install ISR

import numpy as np
from PIL import Image
from imutils.video import VideoStream
import cv2
import imutils

#pip install 'h5py<3.0.0'
#pip install h5py==2.10.0
#import h5py
#h5py.run_tests()

from ISR.models import RDN

#rdn = RDN(weights='psnr-small')
#rdn = RDN(weights='psnr-large')
rdn = RDN(weights='noise-cancel')


vs = VideoStream(src=0).start()
while True:
    frame = vs.read()
    #frame = imutils.resize(frame, width=50)
    lr_img = np.array(frame)
    sr_img = rdn.predict(lr_img)
    #sr_img =Image.fromarray(sr_img)
```

```
        cv2.imshow("Original", frame)
        cv2.imshow("ISR", sr_img)
        key = cv2.waitKey(1) & 0xFF
        # if the `q` key was pressed, break from the loop
        if key == ord("q"):
            break

    cv2.destroyAllWindows()
    vs.stop()
```

See Figure 9.12 for the output.

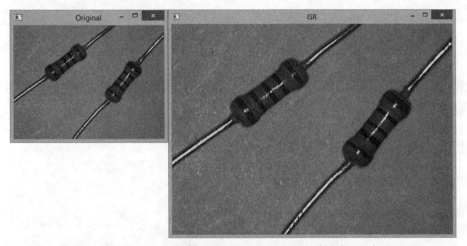

Figure 9.12: The webcam output of low-resolution image and high-resolution image

EXERCISE 9.10

From a web browser, go to the previous website, follow the instructions, run the code, and comment on the results.

9.2.6   2D to 3D

"PIFuHD - Multi-Level Pixel-Aligned Implicit Function for High-Resolution 3D Human Digitization" (CVPR 2020), developed by Facebook, is a library that can convert 2D images into 3D images. It can generate an impressive 3D human shape construction from a single photo by using deep neural networks.

The following is the GitHub site for the PIFuHD project.

```
https://github.com/facebookresearch/pifuhd
```

It also has a Google Colab Notebook example for you to play with, see the link below.

```
https://colab.research.google.com/drive/11z58bl3meSzo6kFqkahMa35
G5jmh2Wgt?usp=sharing
```

9.3   Neural-Style Transfer

Neural-style transfer is an optimization technique that uses deep learning to compose one image in the style of another image. It typically takes two images as inputs; one image is used as a content image and another as a style reference image (such as an artwork by a famous painter) and blends them together so the output image looks like the content image, but in the style of the style reference image.

The following is the Keras website for neural-style transfer.

```
https://keras.io/examples/generative/neural_style_transfer/
```

It also has a Google Colab Notebook example; see the link below.

```
https://colab.research.google.com/github/keras-team/keras-io/blob/
master/examples/generative/ipynb/neural_style_transfer.ipynb
```

Figure 9.13 shows an article about painting like Van Gogh with convolutional neural networks.

Figure 9.13: An article on how to paint like Van Gogh by using neural-style transfer

(Source: `http://www.subsubroutine.com/sub-subroutine/2016/11/12/ painting-like-van-gogh-with-convolutional-neural-networks`)

The following link shows an article on how to do neural-style transfer with Baidu's PaddlePaddle library:

```
https://www.pythonf.cn/read/103549
```

Figure 9.14 shows an IPython Notebook example on how to do neural-style transfer with Baidu's PaddlePaddle library. It is based on Baidu's AIStudio, which you can register or use your GitHub account to log in.

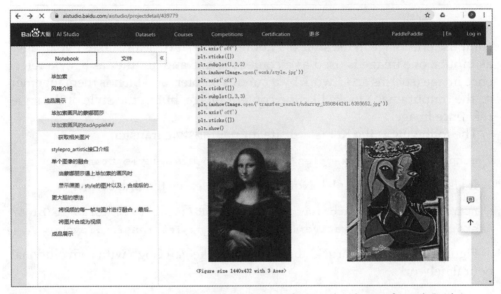

Figure 9.14: An IPython Notebook example on how to do neural-style transfer with Baidu's PaddlePaddle library

(Source: `https://aistudio.baidu.com/aistudio/projectdetail/439779`)

If you are interested in trying different painting styles, you may try Pinterest (Figure 9.15), where you can find different styles of painting from different artists, such as Picasso and Van Gogh.

Example 9.3 shows a Python code that uses the PaddleHub framework to perform neural-style transfer with only a few lines of code.

EXAMPLE 9.3   THE `PADDLE1.PY` PROGRAM

```python
#Example 9.3 Neural-style Transfer with PaddleHub

import cv2
import paddlehub as hub

stylepro_artistic = hub.Module(name="stylepro_artistic")
result = stylepro_artistic.style_transfer(
        images=[{
            'content': cv2.imread('people1.jpeg'),
            'styles': [cv2.imread('style2.jpg')],
            'weights':[1]
```

```
        }],
        alpha = 1.0,
        use_gpu = False,
        visualization=True,
        output_dir='result')
import matplotlib.pyplot as plt
plt.imshow(result[0]['data'])
plt.show()
```

Figure 9.15: The Pinterest website that has different styles of painting from different artists, such as Picasso and Van Gogh

(Source: `https://www.pinterest.co.uk/pin/29203097574051641/`)

See Figure 9.16 for the output.

Figure 9.16: The output of the PaddlePaddle neural-style transfer example. The left is a Picasso painting, used as a style. The middle is the original photo. The right is a style-transferred photo.

EXERCISE 9.11

Modify the previous Python program, try different styles on different photos, run the code, and comment on the results.

PaddleHub can also work on video. Just read out all the frames in the video, do the neural-style transfer for all the frames, and then put the frames back together as a video.

Example 9.4a shows how to read out all the frames in the video file `work/person.mp4` and save the frames as JPEG images in the folder `work/target`.

EXAMPLE 9.4A   THE `PADDLE2.PY` **PROGRAM**

```
#Example 9.4a
# Read out all the frames in the video
import cv2
from tqdm import tqdm
video = cv2.VideoCapture("work/person.mp4")
fps = video.get(cv2.CAP_PROP_FPS)
frameCount = video.get(cv2.CAP_PROP_FRAME_COUNT)
size = (int(video.get(cv2.CAP_PROP_FRAME_WIDTH)), int(video.get(cv2
.CAP_PROP_FRAME_HEIGHT)))
print("Total Frames:",frameCount)
success, frame = video.read()
index = 0
for i in tqdm(range(int(frameCount)),desc='Progress'):
    if success:
        cv2.imwrite('work/target/'+str(index)+'.jpg', frame)
    success, frame = video.read()
    index += 1
```

Example 9.4b shows how to perform the neural-style transfer for all the frames and save all the transferred frames as JPG files in the subfolder `work/result`; this could take a long time.

EXAMPLE 9.4B   THE `PADDLE2B.PY` **PROGRAM**

```
#Example 9.4b
# Perform the Neural Style Transfer for all the frames
import cv2
import paddlehub as hub
from tqdm import tqdm
stylepro_artistic = hub.Module(name="stylepro_artistic")
video = cv2.VideoCapture("work/person.mp4")
fps = video.get(cv2.CAP_PROP_FPS)
frameCount = video.get(cv2.CAP_PROP_FRAME_COUNT)
```

```
size = (int(video.get(cv2.CAP_PROP_FRAME_WIDTH)), int(video.get(cv2
.CAP_PROP_FRAME_HEIGHT)))
print("Total Frames:",frameCount)
success, frame = video.read()
file_paths = []
index = 0
for i in tqdm(range(int(frameCount))):
    if success and index > 33:
            result = stylepro_artistic.style_transfer(
                images=[{
                    'content': frame,
                    'styles': [cv2.imread('work/style.jpg')]
                }],
                visualization=True,
                output_dir='work/result')
            file_paths.append(result[0]['save_path'])
    elif success:
        filep = 'work/result/'+str(index)+'.jpg'
        cv2.imwrite(filep, frame)
        file_paths.append(filep)
    success, frame = video.read()
    index += 1
```

Example 9.4c shows how to put all the transferred frames saved in the previous code back into a video.

EXAMPLE 9.4C   THE PADDLE2C.PY **PROGRAM**

```
# Example 9.4c
# Next put all the frames back into a video
import os
import cv2
import datetime
file_dict = {}
video = cv2.VideoCapture("work/person.mp4")
fps = video.get(cv2.CAP_PROP_FPS)
frameCount = video.get(cv2.CAP_PROP_FRAME_COUNT)
size = (int(video.get(cv2.CAP_PROP_FRAME_WIDTH)),
int(video.get(cv2.CAP_PROP_FRAME_HEIGHT)))
for i in os.listdir('work/ result/'):
    filename, file_extension = os.path.splitext(i)
    if file_extension != '.jpg':
        continue
    file_dict['work/ result/'+i] = float(i.replace('ndarray_','')
.replace('.jpg',''))
file_dict = sorted(file_dict.items(),key = lambda x:x[1])
videoWriter = cv2.VideoWriter('trans.avi', cv2.VideoWriter_
fourcc(*"MJPG"), fps, size)
flag = True
```

```
for i in file_dict:
    if flag:
        for j in range(34):
            videoWriter.write(cv2.imread('work/target/0.jpg'))
        flag = False
    videoWriter.write(cv2.imread(i[0]))
videoWriter.release()
cv2.destroyAllWindows()
```

Figure 9.17 shows the output of the previous code with the original video frame (left), the Picasso painting used as a style (middle), and the style transferred frame image (right).

Figure 9.17: The original video frame (left), the Picasso painting used as a style (middle), and the style transferred frame image (right)

EXERCISE 9.12

Modify the previous Python codes, merge them into one Python program, try different styles on different videos, run the code, and comment on the results.

9.4   Adversarial Machine Learning

Adversarial machine learning is a research area that attempts to fool machine learning models by supplying deceptive input. It arranges the input data to exploit specific vulnerabilities and compromise the results. For example, it can modify the input image with small, intentional feature perturbations that cause a machine learning model to make a false prediction.

For more details, see the following:

```
https://en.wikipedia.org/wiki/Adversarial_machine_learning
https://openai.com/blog/adversarial-example-research/
```

Figure 9.18 shows an article on breaking neural networks with adversarial attacks, in which it added a small noise (0.007x) to a panda image, which causes the machine learning model to falsely classify it as Gibbon with 99.3 percent confidence.

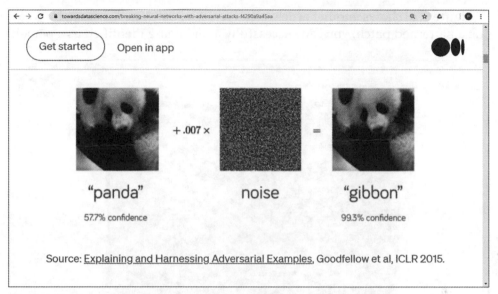

Figure 9.18: An article on breaking neural networks with adversarial attacks

(Source: `https://towardsdatascience.com/breaking-neural-networks-with-adversarial-attacks-f4290a9a45aa`)

Figure 9.19 shows another article on what adversarial machine learning is; a slightly modified tortoise photo makes the classifier falsely identify it as a rifle.

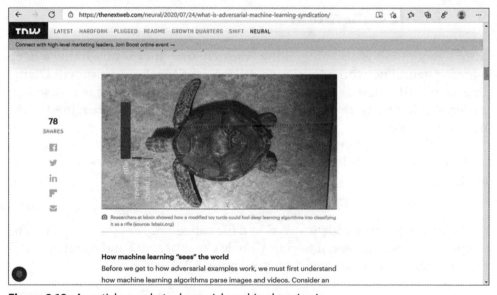

Figure 9.19: An article on what adversarial machine learning is

(Source: `https://thenextweb.com/neural/2020/07/24/what-is-adversarial-machine-learning-syndication/`)

Figure 9.20 shows another article on adversarial machine learning; by wearing a patterned patch, you can successfully avoid being identified as a person.

Figure 9.20: An article on adversarial machine learning

(Source:`https://blog.floydhub.com/introduction-to-adversarial-machine-learning/`)

9.5 Music Generation

Music generation is also an exciting research area. It typically trains a deep learning neural network model on a collection of Musical Instrument Digital Interface (MIDI) files, such as music by Mozart. The training is focused on patterns of harmony, rhythm, and style. After training, it can then predict the new music notes.

The following is an interesting article on how to use LSTM networks to train and create music. It is based on the Music21 library (`https://web.mit.edu/music21/`).

`https://www.toutiao.com/i6797601979804680717/?channel=news_tech`

The corresponding code is saved in a file called `Music21_Midi.ipynb`. The simplest way is to upload it to your Google Colab account and run it on GPU, as the training will take some time; see Figure 9.21.

Figure 9.21: The Google Colab Notebook for the `Music21_Midi.ipynb` file

WaveNet is another powerful generative model developed by Google Deep-Mind for creating your own audio; see the following link for more details about the DeepMind WaveNet website. However, DeepMind does not provide any source code for the WaveNet.

`https://deepmind.com/blog/article/wavenet-generative-model-raw-audio`

There are several attempts for implementing WaveNet. The following GitHub repository, the WaveNet Keras implementation, contains a basic implementation of WaveNet, as described in the paper `https://arxiv.org/pdf/1609.03499.pdf` published by DeepMind.

`https://github.com/peustr/wavenet`

Figure 9.22 shows the Google Colab Notebook example for the WaveNet Keras implementation. You can find the full code in a file called `WaveNet_Keras.ipynb`.

The following is another GitHub project called "A TensorFlow implementation of DeepMind's WaveNet." This project is a TensorFlow implementation of the WaveNet generative neural network architecture for audio generation.

`https://github.com/ibab/tensorflow-wavenet`

Figure 9.22: The Google Colab Notebook for the `WaveNet_Keras.ipynb` file

Apart from generating music, WaveNet can be used to generate text and images. See the following GitHub repositories:

```
https://github.com/Zeta36/tensorflow-tex-wavenet
https://github.com/Zeta36/tensorflow-image-wavenet
```

Figure 9.23 shows the Google Colab Notebook example for using WaveNet for text generation. You can find the full code in a file called `WaveNet_Text.ipynb`.

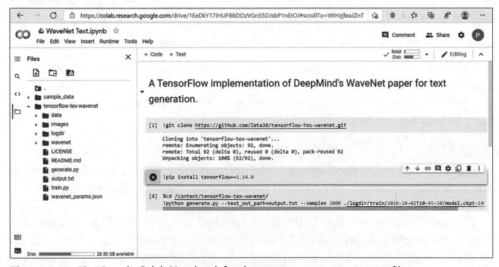

Figure 9.23: The Google Colab Notebook for the `WaveNet_Text.ipynb` file

EXERCISE 9.14

From a web browser, log in to your Google Colab account, upload the `WaveNet_ Text.ipynb` file, run the code, and comment on the results.

9.6   Summary

This chapter covered some of the exciting topics of AI, such as generative adversarial network (GAN), neural-style transfer, adversarial machine learning, and music generation.

A generative adversarial network (GAN) is arguably one of the most exciting AI research topics, which uses a Generator and a Discriminator to generate realistic output (typically images). The commonly implemented types of GANs are CycleGAN and StyleGAN.

Pix2Pix is a type of conditional GAN for image-to-image translation.

Neural-style transfer is an optimization technique to take two images, a content image and a style reference image, and blend them together into one image.

Adversarial machine learning is a technique that attempts to fool a machine learning model by supplying deceptive input.

Music generation is also an exciting research area, where training can be done on a collection of music files to generate new music notes from them.

9.7   Chapter Review Questions

Q9.1. What is a generative adversarial network (GAN), and how does it work?

Q9.2. What is a CycleGAN?

Q9.3. What is a StyleGAN?

Q9.4. What is Pix2Pix?

Q9.5. What is PULSE?

Q9.6. What is neural-style transfer?

Q9.7. What is adversarial machine learning?

Q9.8. In what ways can you fool the image classification models?

Q9.9. How do you avoid being detected in face or person detection?

Q9.10. What is music generation?

Natural Language Processing

"Some people call this artificial intelligence, but the reality is this technology will enhance us. So instead of artificial intelligence, I think we'll augment our intelligence."

—Ginni Rometty (American business executive, former chairman, president, and CEO of IBM)

CHAPTER OUTLINE

10.1   Introduction

Natural language processing (NLP) is another popularly researched subfield of artificial intelligence. It is all about developing applications and services that are able to process and understand the human language, retrieve meaningful pieces of information from it, or even generate text output/conversations. Some practical examples of NLP are text summarization, text sentiment analysis, text generation, speech recognition, translation, chatbot, and so on. NLP has been widely used in business, finance, insurance, and healthcare.

The development of NLP can be generally divided into three stages:

- **Symbolic NLP (1950s to the early 1990s):** This is rule-based NLP, where the computer processes the language by applying a collection of rules.

- **Statistical NLP (1990s to 2010s):** This is the process that uses large amounts of data and machine learning algorithms to train NLP models. Once trained, the model will be able to process the text automatically.

- **Neural NLP (2010s to the present):** This is when deep learning neural networks are used in natural language processing.

NLP has the following common tasks:

- **Lexical analysis:** It divides a whole chunk of text into paragraphs, sentences, and words, through identifying and analyzing words' structure.

- **Syntactic analysis:** This involves the analysis of words in a sentence for grammar and arranging words in a manner that shows the relationship among the words.

- **Semantic analysis:** This extracts the language-independent meaning from the text.

- **Disclosure analysis:** Disclosure integration takes into account the context of the text. It considers the meaning of the sentence before it ends. For example: "He works at Google." In this sentence, "he" must be referenced in the sentence before it.

- **Pragmatic analysis:** Pragmatic analysis deals with overall communication and interpretation of language. It deals with deriving meaningful use of language in various situations.

The following are popular and easy-to-use NLP libraries.

10.1.1   Natural Language Toolkit

Natural Language Toolkit (NLTK) is a suite of Python libraries for symbolic and statistical natural language processing. NLTK is generally used as an education and research tool. It's not usually used on production applications. However, it can be used to build exciting programs due to its ease of use.

NLTK supports the following features:

- Tokenization
- Part-of-speech tagging (POS)

- Named entity recognition (NER)
- Classification
- Sentiment analysis
- Packages of chatbots

NLTK can be used in the following examples:

- Recommendation systems
- Sentiment analysis
- Building chatbots

10.1.2   spaCy

spaCy is a free open source NLP library, written in the programming languages Python and Cython. It is designed to be fast and production-ready. spaCy focuses on providing software for production usage.

spaCy supports the following features:

- Tokenization
- Part-of-speech tagging
- Named entity recognition
- Classification
- Sentiment analysis
- Dependency parsing
- Word vectors

spaCy can be used in the following examples:

- Autocomplete and autocorrect
- Analyzing reviews
- Summarization

10.1.3   Gensim

Gensim is an NLP Python framework generally used in unsupervised topic modeling and similarity detection. It is not a general-purpose NLP library, but it now supports a variety of other NLP tasks such as converting words to vectors (word2vec), document to vectors (doc2vec), finding text similarity, and text summarization.

Gensim supports the following features:

- Latent semantic analysis

- Non-negative matrix factorization
- TF-IDF

Gensim can be used in the following examples:

- Converting documents to vectors
- Finding text similarity
- Text summarization

10.1.4 TextBlob

TextBlob is a simple Python library designed for processing textual data. TextBlob supports complex analysis and operations on textual data, such as part-of-speech tagging, noun phrase extraction, sentiment analysis, classification, translation, and more.

TextBlob supports the following features:

- Part-of-speech tagging
- Noun phrase extraction
- Sentiment analysis
- Classification
- Language translation
- Parsing
- Wordnet integration

TextBlob can be used in the following examples:

- Sentiment analysis
- Spelling correction
- Translation and language detection

10.2 Text Summarization

Text summarization is one of the most important tasks in NLP; it is a technique for generating a concise and precise summary of long texts without losing the overall meaning.

Example 10.1 shows some Python example code of using the SpaCy library for NLP. To use the SpaCy library, you will need to install it.

```
pip install spacy
```

To download the English dictionary, use this:

```
python -m spacy download en_core_web_sm
```

For Windows users, you also need to download and install Microsoft Visual C++ Redistributable.

```
https://aka.ms/vs/16/release/vc_redist.x64.exe
```

The following example, based on spaCy, first reads a piece of text and then finds out all the sentences, tokens (or keywords), and lemmas. In NLP, *lemmatization* is the process of reducing inflected forms of a word while still ensuring that the reduced form belongs to the language. This reduced form or root word is called a *lemma*. Finally, it finds out the most frequently used words and unique words.

EXAMPLE 10.1:   THE `SPACY1.PY` PROGRAM

```
# Example 10.1 spaCy example - finding common and unique words from texts
# pip install spacy
# python -m spacy download en_core_web_sm
# https://aka.ms/vs/16/release/vc_redist.x64.exe

import spacy
nlp = spacy.load('en_core_web_sm')

introduction_text = ('London is the capital of the UK,'
                     ' with a population of nearly 9 millions people.'
                     ' London is one of the most diverse cities in the
world.'
                     ' London has over 100 museums, galleries and
exhibitions.'
                     ' London has 40 universities and higher education
institutions.'
                     ' London has over 15,500 restaurants, serving Italian,
Indian, Thai and Chinese cuisines.'
                     ' London is also one of the world''s capitals of
finance, fashion, arts and entertainment.')

#file_name = 'london.txt'
#introduction_text = open(file_name).read()

introduction_doc = nlp(introduction_text)

print("#Sentences ======================================================")
sentences = list(introduction_doc.sents)
print(len(sentences))
for sentence in sentences:
    print (sentence)
```

```
# Extract tokens for the given doc
print("#Tokens ========================================================")
for token in introduction_doc:
    print (token, token.idx)
print("#Tokens not in the stop list ==================================")
for token in introduction_doc:
    if not token.is_stop:
        print (token)


print("#Lemmatization ================================================")
for token in introduction_doc:
    print (token, token.lemma_)



print("#Word Frequency ===============================================")
from collections import Counter
# Remove stop words and punctuation symbols
words = [token.text for token in introduction_doc
        if not token.is_stop and not token.is_punct]
word_freq = Counter(words)
# 5 commonly occurring words with their frequencies
common_words = word_freq.most_common(5)
print (common_words)


print("#Unique words =================================================")
unique_words = [word for (word, freq) in word_freq.items() if freq == 1]
print (unique_words)
```

The following are the selected outputs, which show the sentences, tokens, lemmatization, and word frequency.

```
#Sentences =====================================================
6
London is the capital of the UK, with a population of nearly 9 millions
people.
London is one of the most diverse cities in the world.
London has over 100 museums, galleries and exhibitions.
London has 40 universities and higher education institutions.
London has over 15,500 restaurants, serving Italian, Indian, Thai and
Chinese cuisines.
London is also one of the worlds capitals of finance, fashion, arts and
entertainment.
#Tokens =====================================================
London 0
is 7
the 10
capital 14
of 22
```

```
the 25
UK 29
, 31
with 33
a 38
population 40
of 51
nearly 54
9 61
millions 63
... ...
.
#Lemmatization ==================================================
London London
is be
the the
capital capital
... ...
. .
#Word Frequency ==================================================
[('London', 6), ('capital', 1), ('UK', 1), ('population', 1), ('nearly',
1)]
#Unique words ==================================================
['capital', 'UK', 'population', 'nearly', '9', 'millions', 'people',
'diverse', 'cities', 'world', '100', 'museums', 'galleries', 'exhibitions',
'40', 'universities', 'higher', 'education', 'institutions', '15,500',
'restaurants', 'serving', 'Italian', 'Indian', 'Thai', 'Chinese',
'cuisines', 'worlds', 'capitals', 'finance', 'fashion', 'arts',
'entertainment']
```

EXERCISE 10.1

Modify the previous code, try different text, run the code, and comment on the results.

Example 10.2 shows some more Python example code of using the SpaCy library for text summarization. It works in several steps. Step 1 is to get all the keywords. Step 2 is to calculate the sentence strength according to most common words. Step 3 is to summarize the text using the top three sentences based on their sentence strength.

EXAMPLE 10.2: THE `SPACY2.PY` **PROGRAM**

```
#Example 10.2 Summarizing based on sentence strength
# pip install spacy
# python -m spacy download en_core_web_sm
# https://aka.ms/vs/16/release/vc_redist.x64.exe
```

```
import spacy
from spacy.lang.en.stop_words import STOP_WORDS
from string import punctuation
from collections import Counter
from heapq import nlargest

#nlp = spacy.load('en')
nlp = spacy.load('en_core_web_sm')

introduction_text = ('London is the capital of the UK,'
                     ' with a population of nearly 9 millions
people.'
                     ' London is one of the most diverse cities in
the world.'
                     ' London has over 100 museums, galleries and
exhibitions.'
                     ' London has 40 universities and higher
education institutions.'
                     ' London has over 15,500 restaurants, serving
Intalian, Indian, Thai and Chinese cuisines.'
                     ' London is also one of the world''s capitals of
finance, fashion, arts and entertainment.')

doc = nlp(introduction_text)

print("1. Keywords ==================================================")
keyword = []
stopwords = list(STOP_WORDS)
pos_tag = ['PROPN','ADJ','NOUN','VERB']
for token in doc:
    if(token.text in stopwords or token.text in punctuation):
        continue
    if(token.pos_ in pos_tag):
        keyword.append(token.text)
print(keyword)

freq_word = Counter(keyword)
print(freq_word.most_common(5))

print("2. Sentence Strength =====================================")
sent_strength = {}
for sent in doc.sents:
    for word in sent:
        if word.text in freq_word.keys():
            if sent in sent_strength.keys():
                sent_strength[sent]+=freq_word[word.text]
            else:
                sent_strength[sent]=freq_word[word.text]
print(sent_strength)
```

```
print("6. Summary ============================================")
summerized_sentences = nlargest(3,sent_strength,key=sent_strength.
get)
print(summerized_sentences)
```

EXERCISE 10.2

Modify the previous code, try different text, run the code, and comment on the results.

Example 10.3 shows a Python example code of using the Gensim library for text summarization and keywords. It summarizes the text by 50 percent (`summarize(text, ratio = 0.5)`). Again, you will need to install the Gensim library first.

```
pip install gensim
```

EXAMPLE 10.3: THE GENSIM.PY PROGRAM

```
# Example 10.3: The Gensim.py Program
# https://radimrehurek.com/gensim/
# pip install gensim==3.8
# Note summarization has been removed from gensim>4.0
from gensim.summarization import summarize
# How to create a dictionary from a list of sentences?
text ='''
  Artificial intelligence (AI), is intelligence demonstrated by
machines,
  unlike the natural intelligence displayed by humans and animals.
  Leading AI textbooks define the field as the study of "intelligent
agents":
  any device that perceives its environment and takes actions that
maximize its
  chance of successfully achieving its goals.[3] Colloquially, the
term
  "artificial intelligence" is often used to describe machines (or
computers)
  that mimic "cognitive" functions that humans associate with the
human mind,
  such as "learning" and "problem solving".[4]
'''

print(summarize(text, ratio = 0.5))

from gensim.summarization import keywords
print(keywords(text))
```

This is the output of the example, which shows the summarization and keywords:

```
Artificial intelligence (AI), is intelligence demonstrated by
machines,
unlike the natural intelligence displayed by humans and animals.
Leading AI textbooks define the field as the study of "intelligent
agents":
"artificial intelligence" is often used to describe machines (or
computers)

intelligent
artificial intelligence
cognitive
humans
human
machines
```

EXERCISE 10.3

Modify the previous code, try different summarization ratios and different text, run the code, and comment on the results.

Example 10.4 shows some Python example code of how to read the content of a Wikipedia page and perform text summarization by using the Gensim library.

EXAMPLE 10.4:   THE GENSIMWIKI.PY PROGRAM

```
# Example 10.4: Summarize Wiki page with gensim
#!pip install wikipedia

from gensim.summarization.summarizer import summarize
from gensim.summarization import keywords
import wikipedia

wikisearch = wikipedia.page("Artificial_intelligence")
wikicontent = wikisearch.content

# Summary (0.5% of the original content).
summ = summarize(wikicontent, ratio = 0.05)
print(summ)
```

This is a selection of the output of the example, which shows the 0.05 percent summarization:

```
Colloquially, the term "artificial intelligence" is often used to
describe machines (or computers) that mimic "cognitive" functions that
humans associate with the human mind, such as "learning" and "problem
solving".As machines become increasingly capable, tasks considered to
```

```
require "intelligence" are often removed from the definition of AI, a
phenomenon known as the AI effect.

... ...

Dick considers the idea that our understanding of human subjectivity is
altered by technology created with artificial intelligence.
```

Example 10.5 shows another version of the previous Python example code, which reads the content of a Wikipedia page, saves the content in a text file, reads the content of the text file, and performs text summarization by using the Gensim library.

EXAMPLE 10.5:   THE GENSIMWIKI2.PY **PROGRAM**

```python
# Example 10.5: Summarize Wiki page with gensim
#!pip install wikipedia

from gensim.summarization.summarizer import summarize
from gensim.summarization import keywords
import wikipedia

wikisearch = wikipedia.page("Artificial_intelligence")
wikicontent = wikisearch.content

# Save the content to a text file
with open("wiki.txt", 'w', encoding='utf-8') as f:
    print(wikicontent, file=f)

from smart_open import smart_open
text = " ".join((line for line in smart_open('wiki.txt',
encoding='utf-8')))

# Summary (0.5% of the original content).
summ = summarize(text, ratio = 0.05)
print(summ)
```

EXERCISE 10.4

Modify the previous code, try different summarization ratios and different Wikipedia topics, run the code, and comment on the results.

Example 10.6 shows some Python example code of how to use the TextBlob library to analyze the text; to display the tags, nouns, words, and sentences; and to do sentiment analysis.

EXAMPLE 10.6:   THE `TEXTBLOB.PY` **PROGRAM**

```
#Example 10.6 TextBlob
# https://textblob.readthedocs.io/en/dev/
#!pip install textblob
#!pip install nltk
#!python -m textblob.download_corpora

from textblob import TextBlob

text = '''
Artificial intelligence (AI), is intelligence demonstrated by
machines,
  unlike the natural intelligence displayed by humans and animals.
  Leading AI textbooks define the field as the study of "intelligent
agents":
  any device that perceives its environment and takes actions that
maximize its
  chance of successfully achieving its goals.[3] Colloquially, the
term
  "artificial intelligence" is often used to describe machines (or
computers)
  that mimic "cognitive" functions that humans associate with the
human mind,
  such as "learning" and "problem solving".[4]
'''

blob = TextBlob(text)
print(blob.tags)
print(blob.noun_phrases)

#Tokenization
print(blob.words)
print(blob.sentences)

#Sentiment Analsys
blob = TextBlob("This is a cool gadget!")
print(blob.sentiment)
blob = TextBlob("I am not really interested!")
print(blob.sentiment)
```

This is the output of the example, which shows the summarization and key-words:

```
[('Artificial', 'JJ'), ('intelligence', 'NN'), ('AI', 'NNP'), ('is', 'VBZ'),
('intelligence', 'NN'), ('demonstrated', 'VBN'), ('by', 'IN'), ('machines',
'NNS'), ('unlike', 'IN'), ('the', 'DT'), ('natural', 'JJ'), ('intelligence',
'NN'), ('displayed', 'VBN'), ('by', 'IN'), ('humans', 'NNS'), ('and', 'CC'),
('animals', 'NNS'), ('Leading', 'VBG'), ('AI', 'NNP'), ('textbooks', 'NNS'),
('define', 'VBP'), ('the', 'DT'), ('field', 'NN'), ('as', 'IN'), ('the', 'DT'),
```

```
('study', 'NN'), ('of', 'IN'), ('intelligent', 'JJ'), ('agents', 'NNS'),
('any', 'DT'), ('device', 'NN'), ('that', 'WDT'), ('perceives', 'VBZ'), ('its',
'PRP$'), ('environment', 'NN'), ('and', 'CC'), ('takes', 'VBZ'), ('actions',
'NNS'), ('that', 'IN'), ('maximize', 'VB'), ('its', 'PRP$'), ('chance', 'NN'),
('of', 'IN'), ('successfully', 'RB'), ('achieving', 'VBG'), ('its', 'PRP$'),
('goals', 'NNS'), ('[', 'RB'), ('3', 'CD'), (']', 'NNP'), ('Colloquially',
'NNP'), ('the', 'DT'), ('term', 'NN'), ('artificial', 'JJ'), ('intelligence',
'NN'), ('is', 'VBZ'), ('often', 'RB'), ('used', 'VBN'), ('to', 'TO'),
('describe', 'VB'), ('machines', 'NNS'), ('or', 'CC'), ('computers', 'NNS'),
('that', 'IN'), ('mimic', 'JJ'), ('cognitive', 'JJ'), ('functions', 'NNS'),
('that', 'WDT'), ('humans', 'NNS'), ('associate', 'VBP'), ('with', 'IN'),
('the', 'DT'), ('human', 'JJ'), ('mind', 'NN'), ('such', 'JJ'), ('as', 'IN'),
('learning', 'VBG'), ('and', 'CC'), ('problem', 'NN'), ('solving', 'NN'), ('[',
'RB'), ('4', 'CD'), (']', 'NNS')]
['artificial', 'ai', 'natural intelligence', 'ai', 'intelligent agents',
'colloquially', 'artificial intelligence', 'describe machines', 'human mind']

['Artificial', 'intelligence', 'AI', 'is', 'intelligence', 'demonstrated',
'by', 'machines', 'unlike', 'the', 'natural', 'intelligence', 'displayed',
'by', 'humans', 'and', 'animals', 'Leading', 'AI', 'textbooks', 'define',
'the', 'field', 'as', 'the', 'study', 'of', 'intelligent', 'agents', 'any',
'device', 'that', 'perceives', 'its', 'environment', 'and', 'takes', 'actions',
'that', 'maximize', 'its', 'chance', 'of', 'successfully', 'achieving', 'its',
'goals', '3', 'Colloquially', 'the', 'term', 'artificial', 'intelligence',
'is', 'often', 'used', 'to', 'describe', 'machines', 'or', 'computers', 'that',
'mimic', 'cognitive', 'functions', 'that', 'humans', 'associate', 'with',
'the', 'human', 'mind', 'such', 'as', 'learning', 'and', 'problem', 'solving',
'4']

[Sentence("
Artificial intelligence (AI), is intelligence demonstrated by machines,
  unlike the natural intelligence displayed by humans and animals."),
Sentence("Leading AI textbooks define the field as the study of "intelligent
agents":
  any device that perceives its environment and takes actions that maximize its
  chance of successfully achieving its goals."), Sentence("[3] Colloquially,
the term
  "artificial intelligence" is often used to describe machines (or computers)
  that mimic "cognitive" functions that humans associate with the human mind,
  such as "learning" and "problem solving"."), Sentence("[4]")]

Sentiment(polarity=0.4375, subjectivity=0.65)
Sentiment(polarity=-0.15625, subjectivity=0.5)
```

Example 10.7 shows some Python example code that can read an RSS (RDF Site Summary or Really Simple Syndication) news feed from the Google and BBC websites. You will need to install a few libraries to be able to parse XML/HMTL:

```
pip install beautifulsoup4
pip install lxml
```

EXAMPLE 10.7:   THE GOOGLENEWS.PY **PROGRAM**

```
#Example 10.7 Read RSS news feeds
# https://www.w3resource.com/python-exercises/basic/python-basic-1-
exercise-8.php
# pip install BeautifulSoup4
# pip install lxml

import bs4
from bs4 import BeautifulSoup as soup
from urllib.request import urlopen

url="https://news.google.com/news/rss"
url="http://feeds.bbci.co.uk/news/rss.xml"
Client=urlopen(url)
page=Client.read()
Client.close()

soup_page=soup(page,"xml")
news_list=soup_page.findAll("item")
word = "UK"
# Print news contains key words
for news in news_list:
    if word in news.title.text:
        #print(news)
        print(news.title.text)
        print(news.description.text)
        print(news.link.text)
        print(news.pubDate.text)
        print("="*80)
```

The following is a selection of the output. As you can see, it reads and displays all the latest BBC news feeds that contain the keyword "UK" in the title.

```
Climate change: Is the UK on track to meet its targets?
As the UK prepares to host a global climate summit, is the government on
track to meet its own commitments?
https://www.bbc.co.uk/news/58160547?at_medium=RSS&at_campaign=KARANGA
Fri, 22 Oct 2021 13:19:46 GMT
================================================================================
Is the UK's green plan enough to halt climate change?
Support for roads, aviation and fossil fuel drilling could undermine UK's
green credentials at COP26.
https://www.bbc.co.uk/news/science-environment-
58973826?at_medium=RSS&at_campaign=KARANGA
Wed, 20 Oct 2021 09:10:54 GMT
================================================================================
What is net zero and how are the UK and other countries doing?
```

```
Experts have recommended developed countries adopt targets to reduce
emissions to net zero by 2050.
https://www.bbc.co.uk/news/science-environment-
58874518?at_medium=RSS&at_campaign=KARANGA
Tue, 19 Oct 2021 15:31:27 GMT
============================================================================
What is Covid Plan B and what are the rules across the UK this winter?
Health service figures are calling for stricter Covid restrictions in
England to protect the NHS.
https://www.bbc.co.uk/news/explainers-52530518?at_medium=RSS&at_
campaign=KARANGA
Mon, 25 Oct 2021 08:19:01 GMT
============================================================================
Covid-19 in the UK: How many coronavirus cases are there in my area?
Explore the data on coronavirus in the UK and find out how many cases there
are in your area.
https://www.bbc.co.uk/news/uk-51768274?at_medium=RSS&at_campaign=KARANGA
Mon, 25 Oct 2021 16:42:40 GMT
============================================================================
Covid: Why are UK cases so high?
The UK has higher infections than most of its neighbours, as scientists
fear a difficult winter.
https://www.bbc.co.uk/news/health-58954793?at_medium=RSS&at_campaign=KARANGA
Fri, 22 Oct 2021 13:37:29 GMT
============================================================================
```

EXERCISE 10.5

Modify the previous code, try different RSS news feeds and searching different news, run the code, and comment on the results.

If you have a list of keywords, you can use regular expression library or the `any()` function to search the text to see if it contains the keywords. See Example 10.8.

EXAMPLE 10.8:   THE `GOOGLENEWS1.PY` PROGRAM

```python
#Example 10.8 Search keywords in news feed import re

search_list = ['bbc', 'google', 'yahoo']
long_string = 'Read RSS news from bbc and '
if re.compile('|'.join(search_list),re.IGNORECASE).
search(long_string):
    print("Key words present")
else:
    print("Key words not present")
```

```
results = any(item in long_string for item in search_list)
print(results)
```

Example 10.9 is another example of reading and displaying news feeds from Google and BBC. You will need to install the `feedparser` library first by typing this:

```
pip install feedparser
```

EXAMPLE 10.9:   THE `GOOGLENEWS2.PY` **PROGRAM**

```
# Example 10.9 feedparser to read news feeds
# https://codeloop.org/how-to-read-google-rss-feeds-in-python/
# pip install feedparser
import feedparser

def getHeadlines(rss_url):
    headlines = []
    feed = feedparser.parse(rss_url)
    for newsitem in feed['items']:
        #print(newsitem)
        item = newsitem['title']+"\n"+newsitem['link']+"\
n"+newsitem['published']
        headlines.append(item)
    return headlines


allheadlines = []
newsurls = {
    'googlenews': 'https://news.google.com/news/rss/',
    'bbcnews':"http://feeds.bbci.co.uk/news/rss.xml"
}

for key, url in newsurls.items():
    allheadlines.extend(getHeadlines(url))

for hl in allheadlines:
    print(hl)
    print("="*80)
```

The following is a selection of the output. As you can see, it reads and displays all the latest news feeds.

```
{"Five dead in US Capitol riot after Donald Trump's supporters storm
Washington - everything we know - The Telegraph", 'https://news.google
.com/__i/rss/rd/articles/CBMibGh0dHBzOi8vd3d3LnRlbGVncmFwaC5jby51
ay9uZXdzLzIwMjEvMDEvMDgvdXMtY2FwaXRvbC1yaW90LXByb3Rlc3Qtd2hhdC1oYXBw
ZW5lZC13aG8tZGllZC10cnVtcC1zdXBwb3J0ZXJzL9IBcGh0dHBzOi8vd3d3LnRlbGVncmVm
FwaC5jby51ay9uZXdzLzIwMjEvMDEvMDgvdXMtY2FwaXRvbC1yaW90LXByb3Rlc3Qtd2hhd
```

```
CloYXBwZW51ZC13aG8tZGllZC10cnVtcC1zdXBwb3J0ZXJzL2FtcC8?oc=5', 'Fri, 08
Jan 2021 08:34:00 GMT'}
========================================================================



... ...


========================================================================
Covid-19 in the UK: How many coronavirus cases are there in your area?
https://www.bbc.co.uk/news/uk-51768274
Thu, 07 Jan 2021 17:45:07 GMT
========================================================================
Jimmy Carter: The story behind the Premier League's first British Asian
player
https://www.bbc.co.uk/sport/football/55536025
Wed, 06 Jan 2021 00:00:03 GMT
========================================================================
```

The following is an example of NLP by using the NLTK library. You will need to install the NLTK library and the WordCloud library first by typing this:

```
pip install nltk
pip install wordcloud
```

Example 10.10 reads the text from a text file called london.txt, gets all the sentences, gets all the words, and plots the most frequently used words as a word cloud.

EXAMPLE 10.10:   THE NLTK 1.PY PROGRAM

```
# Example 10.10 NLTK example with wordcloud
# pip install wordcloud

#Open the text file :
text_file = open("london.txt")

#Read the data :
text = text_file.read()

#Import required libraries :
import nltk
from nltk import sent_tokenize
from nltk import word_tokenize

import nltk
nltk.download("popular")

#Tokenize the text by sentences :
sentences = sent_tokenize(text)
```

```
#How many sentences are there? :
print (len(sentences))

#Print the sentences :
print(sentences)

#Tokenize the text with words :
words = word_tokenize(text)

#Print words :
print (words)

#Import required libraries :
from nltk.probability import FreqDist

#Find the frequency :
fdist = FreqDist(words)

#Print 10 most common words :
print(fdist.most_common(10))

#Library to form wordcloud :
from wordcloud import WordCloud
import matplotlib.pyplot as plt
wordcloud = WordCloud().generate(text)

#Plot the wordcloud :
plt.figure(figsize = (12, 12))
plt.imshow(wordcloud)

#To remove the axis value :
plt.axis("off")
plt.show()
```

Figure 10.1 shows the word cloud output of the previous NLTK example code.

EXERCISE 10.6

Modify the previous code, try different text and generate your own word cloud, run the code, and comment on the results.

10.3   Text Sentiment Analysis

Text sentiment analysis is another important natural language processing task. Text sentiment analysis analyzes the text, such as movie reviews or Twitter messages, and tries to predict the emotion (positive, negative, and neutral) of the text.

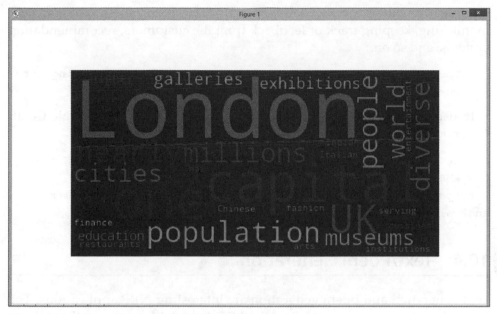

Figure 10.1: The word cloud output of the NLTK example code

Example 10.11 shows an example of text sentiment analysis by using the NLTK library.

As you can see in the example, the NLTK library makes it simple to analyze text sentiment; it takes only three lines of code.

EXAMPLE 10.11:   THE `NLTK SENTIMENT.PY` **PROGRAM**

```
# Example 10.11 NLTK Sentiment
from nltk.sentiment import SentimentIntensityAnalyzer
sia = SentimentIntensityAnalyzer()
print(sia.polarity_scores("London is really beautiful!"))
```

This is the output of the code, which shows the text is positive, with more than 59.9 percent confidence.

```
{'neg': 0.0, 'neu': 0.401, 'pos': 0.599, 'compound': 0.6689}
```

EXERCISE 10.7

Modify the previous code, use a `while` loop to input a sentence from the keyboard and perform sentiment analysis, run the code, and comment on the results. *Hint: Use `line = input("Enter your sentence: ")` to get text from keyboard.*

The following link shows an interesting NLP tutorial on sentiment analysis (opinion mining) with Python. It also shows an example of sentiment analysis on women's clothing review. Sentiment analysis has been widely used in market monitoring, keeping track of feedback from the customers, recommendation systems, and so on.

```
https://pub.towardsai.net/sentiment-analysis-opinion-mining-with-
python-nlp-tutorial-d1f173ca4e3c
```

It also provides an IPython Notebook and corresponding Google Colab Notebook.

```
https://colab.research.google.com/drive/1eosolvfJqXi9xQHMLtmE91_
pfq_RM8zF?usp=sharing
https://github.com/towardsai/tutorials/tree/master/sentiment_
analysis_tutorial
```

10.4 Text/Poem Generation

Text generation and poem generation are interesting NLP applications. The following is an example of using the LSTM model to train on the *Alice in Wonderland* text and to generate new text based on the trained model. It has two Python programs, modified based on the example code (`https://machinelearning-mastery.com/text-generation-lstm-recurrent-neural-networks-python-keras/`).

The first Python program is to train a character-by-character LSTM model on *Alice in Wonderland* text, which can be downloaded from Project Gutenberg. See Example 10.12.

```
https://www.gutenberg.org/ebooks/11
```

EXAMPLE 10.12: THE `WONDERLAND1.PY` **PROGRAM**

```
# Example 10.12 Train a character-by-character LSTM prediction model
# Modified based on:
# https://machinelearningmastery.com/text-generation-lstm-recurrent-
neural-networks-python-keras/
# Text Generation With LSTM Recurrent Neural Networks in Python with
Keras
# Larger LSTM Network to Generate Text for Alice in Wonderland
import numpy
from keras.models import Sequential
from keras.layers import Dense
from keras.layers import Dropout
from keras.layers import LSTM
from keras.callbacks import ModelCheckpoint
from keras.utils import np_utils

# load ascii text and covert to lowercase
# prepare the dataset of input to output pairs encoded as integers
def get_textdata(filename):
```

```python
        raw_text = open(filename, 'r', encoding='utf-8').read()
        raw_text = raw_text.lower()
        # create mapping of unique chars to integers
        chars = sorted(list(set(raw_text)))
        char_to_int = dict((c, i) for i, c in enumerate(chars))
        # summarize the loaded data
        n_chars = len(raw_text)
        n_vocab = len(chars)
        print ("Total Characters: ", n_chars)
        print ("Total Vocab: ", n_vocab)

        seq_length = 100
        dataX = []
        dataY = []
        for i in range(0, n_chars - seq_length, 1):
                seq_in = raw_text[i:i + seq_length]
                seq_out = raw_text[i + seq_length]
                dataX.append([char_to_int[char] for char in seq_in])
                dataY.append(char_to_int[seq_out])
        n_patterns = len(dataX)
        print ("Total Patterns: ", n_patterns)
        # reshape X to be [samples, time steps, features]
        X = numpy.reshape(dataX, (n_patterns, seq_length, 1))
        # normalize
        X = X / float(n_vocab)
        # one hot encode the output variable
        y = np_utils.to_categorical(dataY)
        return X, y

# define the LSTM model
def get_model(X, y):
        model = Sequential()
        model.add(LSTM(256, input_shape=(X.shape[1], X.shape[2]),
return_sequences=True))
        model.add(Dropout(0.2))
        model.add(LSTM(256))
        model.add(Dropout(0.2))
        model.add(Dense(y.shape[1], activation='softmax'))
        model.compile(loss='categorical_crossentropy',
optimizer='adam')
        # define the checkpoint
        filepath="weights-improvement-{epoch:02d}-{loss:.4f}-bigger.
hdf5"
        checkpoint = ModelCheckpoint(filepath, monitor='loss',
verbose=1, save_best_only=True, mode='min')
        callbacks_list = [checkpoint]
        return model,callbacks_list

# Main function
```

```
filename = "wonderland.txt"
X,y = get_textdata(filename)
model,callbacks_list = get_model(X, y)
# fit the model
model.fit(X, y, epochs=50, batch_size=64, callbacks=callbacks_list)
```

The second Python program, shown in Example 10.13, uses a trained LSTM model to generate new text.

EXAMPLE 10.13:   THE WONDERLAND2.PY **PROGRAM**

```
# Example 10.13 Text generation from model trained in Example 10.12
# Modified based on:
# https://machinelearningmastery.com/text-generation-lstm-recurrent-
neural-networks-python-keras/
# Text Generation With LSTM Recurrent Neural Networks in Python with
Keras
# Larger LSTM Network to Generate Text for Alice in Wonderland
import numpy
import sys
from keras.models import Sequential
from keras.layers import Dense
from keras.layers import Dropout
from keras.layers import LSTM
from keras.callbacks import ModelCheckpoint
from keras.utils import np_utils




# load ascii text and covert to lowercase
# prepare the dataset of input to output pairs encoded as integers
def get_textdata(filename):
        raw_text = open(filename, 'r', encoding='utf-8').read()
        raw_text = raw_text.lower()
        # create mapping of unique chars to integers
        chars = sorted(list(set(raw_text)))
        char_to_int = dict((c, i) for i, c in enumerate(chars))
        int_to_char = dict((i, c) for i, c in enumerate(chars))
        # summarize the loaded data
        n_chars = len(raw_text)
        n_vocab = len(chars)
        print ("Total Characters: ", n_chars)
        print ("Total Vocab: ", n_vocab)

        seq_length = 100
        dataX = []
        dataY = []
        for i in range(0, n_chars - seq_length, 1):
                seq_in = raw_text[i:i + seq_length]
```

```
                seq_out = raw_text[i + seq_length]
                dataX.append([char_to_int[char] for char in seq_in])
                dataY.append(char_to_int[seq_out])
        n_patterns = len(dataX)
        print ("Total Patterns: ", n_patterns)
        # reshape X to be [samples, time steps, features]
        X = numpy.reshape(dataX, (n_patterns, seq_length, 1))
        # normalize
        X = X / float(n_vocab)
        # one hot encode the output variable
        y = np_utils.to_categorical(dataY)
        return X, y, dataX,int_to_char,n_vocab

# define the LSTM model
def get_model(X, y):
        model = Sequential()
        model.add(LSTM(256, input_shape=(X.shape[1], X.shape[2]),
return_sequences=True))
        model.add(Dropout(0.2))
        model.add(LSTM(256))
        model.add(Dropout(0.2))
        model.add(Dense(y.shape[1], activation='softmax'))
        model.compile(loss='categorical_crossentropy', optimizer='adam')
        # define the checkpoint
        filepath="weights-improvement-{epoch:02d}-{loss:.4f}-bigger.
hdf5"
        checkpoint = ModelCheckpoint(filepath, monitor='loss',
verbose=1, save_best_only=True, mode='min')
        callbacks_list = [checkpoint]
        return model,callbacks_list
def get_prediction(filename,dataX,int_to_char,n_vocab):
        model.load_weights(filename)
        model.compile(loss='categorical_crossentropy', optimizer='adam')
        # pick a random seed
        start = numpy.random.randint(0, len(dataX)-1)
        pattern = dataX[start]
        print ("Seed:")
        print ("\"", ''.join([int_to_char[value] for value in pattern]),
"\"")
        # generate characters
        for i in range(1000):
          x = numpy.reshape(pattern, (1, len(pattern), 1))
          x = x / float(n_vocab)
          prediction = model.predict(x, verbose=0)
          index = numpy.argmax(prediction)
          result = int_to_char[index]
          seq_in = [int_to_char[value] for value in pattern]
          sys.stdout.write(result)
          pattern.append(index)
          pattern = pattern[1:len(pattern)]
```

```
        print ("\nDone.")
# Main function
filename = "wonderland.txt"
X,y,dataX,int_to_char,n_vocab = get_textdata(filename)
model,callbacks_list = get_model(X, y)

# load the network weights and get prediction
filename = "weights-improvement-49-1.3079-bigger.hdf5"
get_prediction(filename,dataX,int_to_char,n_vocab)
```

The training of the previous example takes a long time on a standard desktop computer. There is also an IPython Notebook of the previous two examples called Wonderland1.ipynb, which you can upload to your Google Colab to run it on a GPU and TPU, which will be much faster.

Figure 10.2 (top) shows the training of the LSTM model on the *Alice in Wonderland* text. As you can see, it takes 50 epochs, and an intermediate model is saved at each epoch. Figure 10.2 (bottom) shows the using the trained model for text generation, or predictions. Just make sure the model filename matched one of the saved intermediate models.

EXERCISE 10.8

Modify the previous two Python programs, try different LSTM parameters and training the model on different texts, run the code, and comment on the results.

The following is an interesting Backus-Naur (context-free grammars) poetry generator; it also has a live demo page.

```
https://github.com/schollz/poetry-generator
```

EXERCISE 10.9

Clone the previous GitHub repository, follow the instructions, run the code, and comment on the results.

The following is the corresponding live demo of the Poetry generator website, which can generate different types of poems, with source code provided.

```
http://www.poetrygenerator.ninja/
```

Figure 10.3 is an interesting Chinese poem generator, which is trained on thousands of poems from the Tang Dynasty of ancient China and can generate really realistic, random, new poems.

Figure 10.2: The training of the LSTM model for the *Alice in Wonderland* text (top) and using the trained model for text generation (bottom)

Text to speech means to convert the text into voice, and speech to text is to detect the voice and convert it to text. By combining text to speech and speech to text, you can create really cool and useful applications.

10.5.1   Text to Speech

Example 10.14 shows a Python example code that can convert text into speech. You need to install the Pyttsx3 library.

```
pip install pyttsx3
```

Figure 10.3: The GitHub site for the Poems_generator_Keras.project

(Source: `https://github.com/youyuge34/Poems_generator_Keras`)10.5 Text to Speech and Speech to Text

EXAMPLE 10.14:   THE `TEXTTOSPEECH1.PY` PROGRAM

```
#Example 10.14 Text to Speech
#pip install pyttsx3


import pyttsx3


text = "Welcome to London!"


engine = pyttsx3.init()
engine.say(text)
engine.runAndWait()
```

EXERCISE 10.10

Modify the previous code, use a `while` loop to input a sentence from keyboard and perform text to speech, run the code, and comment on the results. *Hint: Use `line = input("Enter your sentence: ")` to get text from keyboard.*

Example 10.15 shows a revised version of the previous program, which reads the text from a text file and then converts it to speech.

EXAMPLE 10.15:   THE `TEXTTOSPEECH2.PY` **PROGRAM**

```
#Example 10.15 Text to Speech 2
#pip install pyttsx3
#pip install googletrans==3.1.0a0

import pyttsx3

file_name = 'Bolna.txt'
text = open(file_name).read()

engine = pyttsx3.init()
engine.say(text)
engine.runAndWait()
```

EXERCISE 10.11

Modify the previous code, try different text files, run the code, and comment on the results.

10.5.2   Speech to Text

Example 10.16 shows some Python example code that can recognize speech from a microphone. You need to install the PyAudio library.

EXAMPLE 10.16:   THE `SPEECH RECOGNITION.PY` **PROGRAM**

```
#Example 10.16 Speech Recognition through Microphone
#pip3 install pyaudio
#pip install googletrans--3.1.0a0

import speech_recognition as sr
print(sr.__version__)

r = sr.Recognizer()
with sr.Microphone() as source:
    print(source)
    audio_data = r.record(source, duration=5)
    #audio_data = r.listen(source,timeout=1,phrase_time_limit=10)
    print("Recognizing...")
    # convert speech to text
    text = r.recognize_google(audio_data)
    #text = r.recognize_google(audio_data, language="es-ES")
    print(text)
```

Example 10.17 shows a Python example code that can recognize speech from an audio file. You need to install the `SpeechRecognition` and `PyAudio` libraries.

```
pip install SpeechRecognition
pip install pyaudio
```

EXAMPLE 10.17:   THE `SPEECH RECOGNITION 1.PY` **PROGRAM**

```python
# Example 10.17 Speech Recognition from an audio file
# pip install SpeechRecognition

# pip install pyaudio
# https://www.lfd.uci.edu/~gohlke/pythonlibs/#pyaudio
# PyAudio-0.2.11-cp37-cp37m-win_amd64.whl
# pip install PyAudio-0.2.11-cp37-cp37m-win_amd64.whl

import speech_recognition as sr
print(sr.__version__)

r = sr.Recognizer()
'''
recognize_bing(): Microsoft Bing Speech
recognize_google(): Google Web Speech API
recognize_google_cloud(): Google Cloud Speech - requires installation
of the google-cloud-speech package
recognize_houndify(): Houndify by SoundHound
recognize_ibm(): IBM Speech to Text
recognize_sphinx(): CMU Sphinx - requires installing PocketSphinx
recognize_wit(): Wit.ai
'''
#mic = sr.Microphone()
#print(sr.Microphone.list_microphone_names())
#==================================================================
harvard = sr.AudioFile('harvard.wav')
with harvard as source:
    audio = r.record(source)
    #audio = r.record(source, duration=4)
    #audio = r.record(source, offset=4, duration=3)

print(type(audio))
print(r.recognize_google(audio))
```

EXERCISE 10.12

Modify the previous code, try a different speech recognition API, run the code, and comment on the results.

If you have the MP4 format video file, you need first to convert it to MP3 format audio file and then convert the MP3 format audio file to a WAV format audio file, before you do the speech recognition. You can use the FFmeg library to do that. For more details, see the following:

```
https://ffmpeg.org/
```

Just download the FFmeg latest release and unzip it to a folder. Then you can run the following commands to convert MP4 to MP3 to WAV:

```
E:\ffmpeg\bin\ffmpeg -i Goal-GAN.mp4 Bolna.mp3
E:\ffmpeg\bin\ffmpeg -i Bolna.mp3 Bolna.wav
```

EXERCISE 10.13

Modify the previous code, try to convert different MP4 video files, run the code, and comment on the results.

Example 10.17a shows how to use some Python code with the os library.

EXAMPLE 10.17A: THE COVERT_WAV_1.PY PROGRAM

```python
# Example 10.17a Convert an mp4 file to a wav file

import os

cmd1 = "E:\\ffmpeg\\bin\\ffmpeg -i Goal-GAN.mp4 Bolna.mp3"
failure = os.system(cmd1)
if failure:
    print ('Execution of "%s" failed!\n' % cmd1)

cmd2 = "E:\\ffmpeg\\bin\\ffmpeg -i Bolna.mp3 Bolna.wav"
failure = os.system(cmd2)
if failure:
    print ('Execution of "%s" failed!\n' % cmd2)
```

Example 10.17b shows how to use some Python code with the subprocess library.

EXAMPLE 10.17B: THE COVERT_WAV_2.PY PROGRAM

```python
# Example 10.17b Convert an mp4 file to a wav file
import subprocess

cmd1 = "E:\\ffmpeg\\bin\\ffmpeg -i Goal-GAN.mp4 Bolna.mp3"
```

```
failure = subprocess.call(cmd1, shell=True)
if failure:
    print ('Execution of "%s" failed!\n' % cmd1)

cmd2 = "E:\\ffmpeg\\bin\\ffmpeg -i Bolna.mp3 Bolna.wav"
failure = subprocess.call(cmd2, shell=True)
if failure:
    print ('Execution of "%s" failed!\n' % cmd2)
```

Example 10.18 shows some Python example code that can recognize speech from an MP4 video file. Again, you need to install the `SpeechRecognition` and `PyAudio` libraries.

EXAMPLE 10.18:   THE `SPEECH RECOGNITION 3.PY` **PROGRAM**

```
#Example 10.18 Speech Recognition from MP4

import os
import speech_recognition as sr

cmd1 = "E:\\ffmpeg\\bin\\ffmpeg -i Goal-GAN.mp4 Bolna.mp3"
failure = os.system(cmd1)
if failure:
    print ('Execution of "%s" failed!\n' % cmd1)


cmd2 = "E:\\ffmpeg\\bin\\ffmpeg -i Bolna.mp3 Bolna.wav"
failure = os.system(cmd2)
if failure:
    print ('Execution of "%s" failed!\n' % cmd2)

r = sr.Recognizer()
audio = sr.AudioFile('Bolna.wav')

with audio as source:
    audio = r.record(source, duration=100)
print(r.recognize_google(audio))

file1 = open("Bolna.txt","w")
file1.writelines(r.recognize_google(audio))
file1.close() #to change file access modes
```

EXERCISE 10.14

Modify the previous code, try different MP4 videos, run the code, and comment on the results.

Example 10.19 shows how to record audio from a microphone and save it to an audio file. You need to install the `wave` and `PyAudio` libraries.

EXAMPLE 10.19: THE `SAVE_RECORDING_TO_AUDIO_FILE.PY` **PROGRAM**

```python
# Example 10.19 Save microphone recording to wav audio file
#https://realpython.com/playing-and-recording-sound-
python/#recording-audio
import pyaudio
import wave


chunk = 1024  # Record in chunks of 1024 samples
sample_format = pyaudio.paInt16  # 16 bits per sample
channels = 2
fs = 44100  # Record at 44100 samples per second
seconds = 3
filename = "output.wav"


p = pyaudio.PyAudio()  # Create an interface to PortAudio

print('Recording')

stream = p.open(format=sample_format,
                channels=channels,
                rate=fs,
                frames_per_buffer=chunk,
                input=True)


frames = []  # Initialize array to store frames

# Store data in chunks for 3 seconds
for i in range(0, int(fs / chunk * seconds)):
    data = stream.read(chunk)
    frames.append(data)


# Stop and close the stream
stream.stop_stream()
stream.close()
# Terminate the PortAudio interface
p.terminate()

print('Finished recording')

# Save the recorded data as a WAV file
wf = wave.open(filename, 'wb')
wf.setnchannels(channels)
wf.setsampwidth(p.get_sample_size(sample_format))
wf.setframerate(fs)
wf.writeframes(b''.join(frames))
wf.close()
```

10.6 Machine Translation

Machine translation is an important application for natural language processing. Example 10.20 shows example code that uses Google Translate to translate the text into another language. You need to install the `googletrans` library by typing the following:

```
pip install googletrans==3.1.0a0
```

EXAMPLE 10.20: THE GOOGLETRANSLATE1.PY PROGRAM

```
#Example 10.20 Google Translate
#pip install googletrans==3.1.0a0

text = "Welcome to London!"

#translates into the mentioned language
from googletrans import Translator
p = Translator()
# translates the text into german language
k = p.translate(text,dest='ja')
print(k)
```

EXERCISE 10.15

Modify the previous code, try different text and different languages, run the code, and comment on the results.

EXERCISE 10.16

Modify the previous code, read the text from a text file, translate it into another language, run the code, and comment on the results.

Example 10.21 shows a revised version of the previous program, which can detect the language of the text and also translate the text into another language.

EXAMPLE 10.21: THE GOOGLETRANSLATE2.PY PROGRAM

```
#Example 10.21 language detection and translation
#pip install googletrans==3.1.0a0
from googletrans import Translator

translator = Translator()
translator = Translator(service_urls=[
    'translate.google.com',
```

```
        'translate.google.co.kr',
    ])

translator.detect('이 문장은 한글로 쓰여졌습니다.')


translator.translate('안녕하세요.')
# <Translated src=ko dest=en text=Good evening. pronunciation=Good
evening.>
```

EXERCISE 10.17

Modify the previous code, try different texts and different languages, run the code, and comment on the results.

10.7   Optical Character Recognition

Example 10.22 shows some Python example code that can read text from an image file, i.e., optical character recognition (OCR). You need to install the `pytesseract` library, which is a wrapper of the Google `tesseract` program, which you can install from here:

```
https://github.com/tesseract-ocr/tesseract
https://tesseract-ocr.github.io/tessdoc/Downloads
```

EXAMPLE 10.22:   THE GOOGLEOCR1.PY PROGRAM

```
# Example 10.22 OCR and Google Translate
# import the following libraries
# will convert the image to text string
import pytesseract

# adds image processing capabilities
from PIL import Image

# converts the text to speech
import pyttsx3

#translates into the mentioned language
from googletrans import Translator

# opening an image from the source path
img = Image.open('text1.png')
```

```
# describes image format in the output
print(img)
# path where the tesseract module is installed
pytesseract.pytesseract.tesseract_cmd ='C:/Program Files (x86)/
Tesseract-OCR/tesseract.exe'
# converts the image to result and saves it into result variable
result = pytesseract.image_to_string(img)
print(result)
# write text in a text file and save it to source path
with open('abc.txt',mode ='w') as file:

                        file.write(result)
                        print(result)

p = Translator()
# translates the text into german language
k = p.translate(result,dest='german')
print(k)
engine = pyttsx3.init()

# an audio will be played which speaks the text if pyttsx3 recognizes
it
engine.say(k.text)
engine.runAndWait()
```

EXERCISE 10.18

Modify the previous code, try different OCR images, run the code, and comment on the results.

10.8 QR Code

A quick response (QR) code is a two-dimensional version of the barcode able to store up to 7,089 digits or 4,296 characters, including punctuation marks and special characters. The code can equally encode words and phrases such as the Internet addresses. As more data is added, a QR code's structure becomes more complex. A QR code's structure also provides redundancies that allow up to 30 percent of the code structure to be damaged without affecting its readability on scanners.

QR codes were invented by Masahiro Hara and his team from Denso Wave, a subsidiary manufacturing company in Japan, in 1994. QR codes offer a better, faster, stronger technology to the barcode to process higher amounts of characters in tracking vehicles and parts in a company.

Example 10.23 shows a Python example code that can generate a QR code image that is linked to a URL. You need to install the `qrcode` library.

```
pip install qrcode
```

EXAMPLE 10.23:   THE `QRCODE1.PY` **PROGRAM**

```python
# Example 10.23 QR code generation
# https://pypi.org/project/qrcode/
# https://en.wikipedia.org/wiki/QR_code
# pip install qrcode

import qrcode

#Create a QRcode
qr = qrcode.QRCode(
        version=1,
        box_size=10,
        border=5)
qr.add_data("https://www.bioxsystems.com/")
qr.make(fit=True)
img = qr.make_image(fill='black', back_color='white')
img.save('qrcode001.png')
```

Figure 10.4 shows the QR code image generated by the example.

Figure 10.4: The QR code image generated by the example

EXERCISE 10.19

Modify the previous code, try to generate the QR code for different websites, run the code, and comment on the results.

Example 10.24 shows a Python example code that can read a QR code image and decode its URL. You need to install the `qrcode` library.

EXAMPLE 10.24:   THE `QRCODE2.PY` **PROGRAM**

```
# Detect QRCode using the cv2 QRCode detector
import cv2

img = cv2.imread('qrcode001.png')
detector = cv2.QRCodeDetector()

# detect and decode
data, bbox, straight_qrcode = detector.detectAndDecode(img)
# if there is a QR code
if bbox is not None:
    print(f"QRCode data:\n{data}")
    # display the image with lines
    # length of bounding box
    n_lines = len(bbox)
    for i in range(n_lines):
        point1 = tuple(bbox[i][0].astype(int))
        point2 = tuple(bbox[i][2].astype(int))
        cv2.rectangle(img, point1, point2, (255, 0, 0), 2)# display
the result
cv2.imshow("img", img)
cv2.waitKey(0)
cv2.destroyAllWindows()
```

The following is the output of the program:

```
QRCode data:
https://www.bioxsystems.com/
```

EXERCISE 10.20

Modify the previous code so that it can take the QR code filename from the command line, run the code, and comment on the results. *Hint: The following is Python example code to get command-line parameters:*

```
# cmd.py - Command line example
import sys
print 'Number of arguments:', len(sys.argv), 'arguments.'
print 'Argument List:', str(sys.argv)
This is how to test the code:
python cmd.py arg1 arg2 arg3
```

10.9   PDF and DOCX Files

Example 10.25 shows some Python example code that can read image files and convert them to PDF files.

EXAMPLE 10.25:   THE `PDF1.PY` PROGRAM

```python
# Example 10.25 Image to PDF
# --- Save one image to pdf ------------------------------------
#https://datatofish.com/images-to-pdf-python/
from PIL import Image

image1 = Image.open(r'images\000_000.jpg')
im1 = image1.convert('RGB')
im1.save(r'myFirstImage1.pdf')


# --- Save several images to pdf ------------------------------------
image1 = Image.open(r'images\000_000.jpg')
image2 = Image.open(r'images\000_010.jpg')
image3 = Image.open(r'images\000_020.jpg')
im1 = image1.convert('RGB')
im2 = image2.convert('RGB')
im3 = image3.convert('RGB')
imagelist = [im2,im3]
im1.save(r'mySecondImage1.pdf',save_all=True, append_images=
imagelist)
```

EXERCISE 10.21

Modify the previous code, try different image files, run the code, and comment on the results.

Example 10.26 shows a Python example code that can convert a PDF file in a directory and save it to a DOCX file by using the PDF2DOCX library.

EXAMPLE 10.26:   THE `PDF2.PY` PROGRAM

```python
# Example 10.26 Convert pdf to word

from pdf2docx import Converter

pdf_file = 'source.pdf'
docx_file = 'source1.docx'
```

```
# convert pdf to docx
cv = Converter(pdf_file)
cv.convert(docx_file)        # all pages by default
cv.close()
```

Example 10.26a shows a variation of the previous Python example code that can convert all PDF files in a directory to DOCX files by using the PDF2DOCX and GLOB libraries.

EXAMPLE 10.26A: THE `PDF2A.PY` **PROGRAM**

```
# Example 10.26a Convert pdf to word

from pdf2docx import Converter
import glob
import os


pdfs_path = "" # folder where the .pdf files are stored
for i, pdf_file in enumerate(glob.iglob(pdfs_path+"*.pdf")):
    print(pdf_file)
    filename = pdf_file.split('\\')[-1]
    in_file = os.path.abspath(pdf_file)
    docx_file = os.path.abspath(filename[0:-4]+ ".docx")
    print(in_file)
    cv = Converter(in_file)
    cv.convert(docx_file)
    cv.close()
```

Example 10.27 shows another Python example code that can select and convert a PDF file to a DOC file by using the PyPDF2 and Tkinter libraries.

EXAMPLE 10.27:   THE `PDF3.PY` **PROGRAM**

```
# Example 10.27 Convert pdf to word

from tkinter import *
from tkinter import filedialog
from tkinter.filedialog import askopenfilename,asksaveasfile
from PyPDF2 import PdfFileReader

# Select an input pdf file
input_file = askopenfilename(defaultextension=".pdf",
                             filetypes=[("Pdf files","*.pdf")])
text = ""

pdfFile = open(input_file, 'rb')
```

```
# creating a pdf reader object
read_pdf = PdfFileReader(pdfFile)

c = read_pdf.numPages
for i in range(c):
    page = read_pdf.getPage(i)
    text+=(page.extractText())

# closing the pdf file object
pdfFile.close()

# Select an output Doc file
wordfile = asksaveasfile(mode='w',defaultextension=".doc",
                         filetypes=[("word file","*.doc"),
                                    ("text file","*.txt")])

# convert the pdf file to doc file
wordfile.write(text)
wordfile.close()
print("saved: ",wordfile)
```

Example 10.28 shows a Python example code that can merge PDF files to one file.

EXAMPLE 10.28:   THE `PDF4.PY` PROGRAM

```
# Example 10.28 Merge pdf files
# https://stackoverflow.com/questions/3444645/merge-pdf-files
#
from PyPDF2 import PdfFileMerger

#pdfs = ['file1.pdf', 'file2.pdf', 'file3.pdf', 'file4.pdf']
pdfs = ['file1.pdf', 'file2.pdf']
merger = PdfFileMerger()

for pdf in pdfs:
    merger.append(pdf)

merger.write("result.pdf")
merger.close()
```

EXERCISE 10.22

Modify the previous code, try to merge different PDF files, run the code, and comment on the results.

10.10   Chatbots and Question Answering

Chatbots and question answering have many practical applications and have been implemented in many online banking, online shopping, flight and hotel booking websites, and so on. In this section, we will take a look at how to create chatbot and question answering applications in Python.

10.10.1   ChatterBot

ChatterBot is a simple, user-friendly library that allows you to develop your own chatbot and question answering applications. It supports SQL (Structured Query Language) databases such as MongoDB and can be used to process and evaluate mathematical and time-based questions. To use it, you will need to install the following libraries and packages:

```
pip install spacy
pip install https://github.com/explosion/spacy-models/releases/download/
en_core_web_sm-2.2.0/en_core_web_sm-2.2.0.tar.gz
python -m spacy download en
pip install chatterbot, chatterbot_corpus
```

See the following link for more details.

```
https://chatterbot.readthedocs.io/en/stable/examples.html
```

Example 10.29 shows some Python example code of a basic ChatterBot demo.

EXAMPLE 10.29:   THE `CHATTERBOT1.PY` PROGRAM

```python
# Example 10.29 Chatterbot basic demo
# https://chatterbot.readthedocs.io/en/stable/setup.html
# https://chatterbot.readthedocs.io/en/stable/examples.html

# pip install spacy
# pip install https://github.com/explosion/spacy-models/releases/
download/en_core_web_sm-2.2.0/en_core_web_sm-2.2.0.tar.gz
# python -m spacy download en
# pip install chatterbot_corpus

from chatterbot import ChatBot
from chatterbot.trainers import ChatterBotCorpusTrainer

chatbot = ChatBot('Ron Obvious')

# Create a new trainer for the chatbot
trainer = ChatterBotCorpusTrainer(chatbot)
```

```
# Train the chatbot based on the english corpus
trainer.train("chatterbot.corpus.english")

# Get a response to an input statement
#chatbot.get_response("Hello, how are you today?")

while True:
    message = input('You:')
    if message.strip() != 'Bye':
        reply = chatbot.get_response(message)
    print('ChatBot:',reply)
    if message.strip() =='Bye':
        print('ChatBot:Bye')
        break
```

Example 10.30 shows some Python example code of a ChatterBot best match demo.

EXAMPLE 10.30:   THE `CHATTERBOT2.PY` **PROGRAM**

```
# https://chatterbot.readthedocs.io/en/stable/setup.html
# https://chatterbot.readthedocs.io/en/stable/examples.html

from chatterbot import ChatBot
from chatterbot.trainers import ListTrainer


# Create a new instance of a ChatBot
bot = ChatBot(
    'Example Bot',
    storage_adapter='chatterbot.storage.SQLStorageAdapter',
    logic_adapters=[
        {
            'import_path': 'chatterbot.logic.BestMatch',
            'default_response': 'I am sorry, but I do not
understand.',
            'maximum_similarity_threshold': 0.90
        }
    ]
)

trainer = ListTrainer(bot)

# Train the chat bot with a few responses
trainer.train([
    'How can I help you?',
    'I want to create a chat bot',
    'Have you read the documentation?',
    'No, I have not',
```

```
      'This should help get you started: http://chatterbot.rtfd.org/en/
    latest/quickstart.html'
    ])

    # Get a response for some unexpected input
    response = bot.get_response('can I help you')
    print(response)
    response = bot.get_response('read the documentation')
    print(response)
    response = bot.get_response('How do I make an omelette?')
    print(response)
```

EXERCISE 10.23

Modify the previous code, try your own questions and answers, run the code, and comment on the results.

10.10.2 Transformers

Transformers are new types of recurrent neural networks that are particularly suitable for natural language processing. Transformers have become the state-of-the-art approach in natural language processing since 2017. With transformers you can build chatbot and question answering applications easily.

Example 10.31 shows an example of text sentiment analysis by using the Transformers library.

```
pip install transformers
```

As you can see in the example, the Transformers library makes it simple to analyze text sentiment; it takes only three lines of code.

EXAMPLE 10.31: THE TRANSFORMERS1.PY PROGRAM

```
# Example 10.31 Sentiment analylsis with transformers
# https://github.com/huggingface/transformers
from transformers import pipeline

# Allocate a pipeline for sentiment-analysis
classifier = pipeline('sentiment-analysis')
classifier('We are very happy to visit London.')
```

This is the output of the code, which shows the text is positive, with more than 99.9 percent confidence.

```
[{'label': 'POSITIVE', 'score': 0.9998719096183777}]
```

Example 10.32 shows some Python example code of using transformers for question answering.

EXAMPLE 10.32:   THE `TRANSFORMERS2.PY` **PROGRAM**

```
# Example 10.32 Q&A with transformers
from transformers import pipeline
question_answerer = pipeline('question-answering')
question_answerer({
    'question': 'What is the name of the company?',
    'context': 'We created Biox Systems Ltd company back in the year
of 2000.'
})
```

This is the output of the example, which shows the answer to the question:

```
{'answer': 'Biox Systems Ltd',
 'end': 27,
 'score': 0.7553602457046509,
 'start': 11}
```

EXERCISE 10.24

Modify the previous code, try different text and different questions, run the code, and comment on the results.

Example 10.33 shows another version of the previous Python example; in this case, it asks the user to input the question from the keyboard.

EXAMPLE 10.33:   THE `TRANSFORMERS3.PY` **PROGRAM**

```
# Example 10.33 open question answering with transformers
from transformers import pipeline

context = '''
We created Biox Systems Ltd company back in the year of 2000.
'''
Question = input('Ask a question:')
question_answerer = pipeline('question-answering')
result = question_answerer(question=Question, context=context)
print("Answer:", result['answer'])
print("Score:", result['score'])
```

EXERCISE 10.25

Modify the previous code, read the text from a text file, use a `while` loop to ask user to input the questions, run the code, and comment on the results.

Example 10.34 shows another Python example on text generation by using Generative Pre-trained Transformer 2 (GPT-2) model Transformers. GPT-2 is a large transformer-based language model developed by OpenAI. The latest version is GPT-3. GPT-2 has 1.5 billion parameters and is trained on a dataset of 8 million web pages. GPT-2 is trained to predict the next word, given the previous words within the text. Access to GPT-3 is limited, access to GPT-2 is free.

EXAMPLE 10.34:   THE `TRANSFORMERS4.PY` **PROGRAM**

```
# Example 10.34 Text Generation with transformers (GPT-2 Model)
# pip install transformers
from transformers import pipeline, set_seed
generator = pipeline('text-generation', model='gpt2')
set_seed(20)
generator("I feel amazing about", max_length=20,
num_return_sequences=5)
```

The following is the output of the code, very impressive results.

```
[{'generated_text': 'I feel amazing about how this whole project is
making sense and I am incredibly proud of how it got'},
 {'generated_text': 'I feel amazing about this. I am a proud believer.
You can do great things, but I'},
 {'generated_text': 'I feel amazing about my relationship with women,"
said her former assistant, who declined to be identified,'},
 {'generated_text': "I feel amazing about this, and I think there's good
reason for it. We love these guys"},
 {'generated_text': 'I feel amazing about that," she said. "I\'d rather
sleep with somebody who\'s more comfortable'}]
```

EXERCISE 10.26

Modify the previous code, use different phrases or sentences for text generation, run the code, and comment on the results.

See the following link for details about GPT-2 model.
`https://huggingface.co/transformers/model_doc/gpt2.html`

10.10.3   J.A.R.V.I.S.

J.A.R.V.I.S. (Just A Rather Very Intelligent System) is an artificial intelligence system in the Hollywood blockbuster movie *Iron Man* that can hold conversations and answer questions.

Example 10.35 shows some PySimpleGUI-based Python J.A.R.V.I.S. example code that allows users to ask a question, searches WolframAlpha and Wikipedia, and then returns the answers. When you run the code, please replace "XXX-XXXX" with your own WolframAlpha ID. For more details on how to get the ID, check the following:

```
https://products.wolframalpha.com/simple-api/documentation/
```

EXAMPLE 10.35: THE JAVIS 1.PY PROGRAM

```python
# Example 10.35 Jarvis 1.py
# pip install wolframalpha
# pip install pyttsx3

import wolframalpha
client = wolframalpha.Client("XXX-XXXX")

import wikipedia

import PySimpleGUI as sg
sg.theme('LightGreen')

searchpanel = [[sg.InputText()],[sg.Button('Search'),
sg.Button('Cancel')]]
resultspanel =[[sg.Text('Wolfram Result:', size =(20, 1))],
               [sg.Multiline("", key='Wolfram')],
               [sg.Text('Wikipedia Result:', size =(20, 1))],
               [sg.Multiline("", key='Wikipedia')],
               [sg.Frame('Search the Web:', searchpanel, font='Any
12', title_color='blue')],
               ]
layout = [[sg.Column(resultspanel)]]
window = sg.Window('Javis 1 ',location=(100, 100))
window.Layout(layout).Finalize()

#layout =[[sg.Text('Enter a command'), sg.InputText()],[sg
.Button('Ok'), sg.Button('Cancel')]]
#window = sg.Window('PyDa', layout)

import pyttsx3
engine = pyttsx3.init()

searching = False
while True:
    event, values = window.read(timeout=20, timeout_key='timeout')
    if event == sg.WIN_CLOSED:
        break
```

```
        elif event == 'Search':
            searching = True
        if event in (None, 'Cancel'):
            break
        if searching:
            wiki_res = wikipedia.summary(values[0], sentences=2)
            wolfram_res = next(client.query(values[0]).results).text
            engine.say(wiki_res)
            engine.say(wolfram_res)
            #sg.PopupNonBlocking("Wikipedia Result: "+wiki_res)
            window['Wolfram'].update(wolfram_res)
            window['Wikipedia'].update(wiki_res)

            engine.runAndWait()
            searching = False
            print (values[0])

    window.close()
```

Figure 10.5 shows the output of the previous PySimpleGUI-based example program, which shows the questions and the answers from WolframAlpha and from Wikipedia.

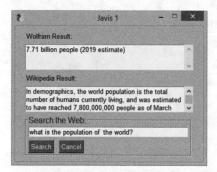

Figure 10.5: The PySimpleGUI-based example program

EXERCISE 10.27

Modify the previous code to allow users to ask the questions using their voice through a microphone, run the code, and comment the results. *Hint: See the speech to text examples.*

Example 10.36 shows more J.A.R.V.I.S. Python example code that can hold voice conversations with a user.

EXAMPLE 10.36:   **THE** JARVIS DEMO.PY **PROGRAM**

```
# Example 10.36 Jarvis conversation
# Modified based on:
# https://www.geeksforgeeks.org/personal-voice-assistant-in-python/
# pip install speechrecognition
# pip install playsound
# pip install gtts
# pip install selenium
# pip install pyaudio


# importing speech recognition package from google api
import speech_recognition as sr
import playsound # to play saved mp3 file
from gtts import gTTS # google text to speech

import os # to save/open files
import wolframalpha # to calculate strings into formula
from selenium import webdriver # to control browser operations
#driver = webdriver.Firefox(executable_path=r'E:\\geckodriver.exe')

num = 1
def assistant_speaks(output):
        global num

        # num to rename every audio file
        # with different name to remove ambiguity
        num += 1
        print("PerSon : ", output)

        toSpeak = gTTS(text = output, lang ='en', slow = False)
        # saving the audio file given by google text to speech
        file = str(num)+".mp3 "
        toSpeak.save(file)

        # playsound package is used to play the same file.
        playsound.playsound(file, True)
        os.remove(file)



def get_audio():

        rObject = sr.Recognizer()
        audio = ''

        with sr.Microphone() as source:
                print("Speak...")

                # recording the audio using speech recognition
```

```
                    audio = rObject.listen(source, phrase_time_limit = 5)
        print("Stop.") # limit 5 secs

        try:

                text = rObject.recognize_google(audio, language
='en-US')
                print("You : ", text)
                return text

        except:

                assistant_speaks("Could not understand your audio,
PLease try again !")
                return 0


def process_text(input):
        try:
                if 'search' in input:
                        # a basic web crawler using selenium
                        driver = webdriver.Chrome()
                        driver.implicitly_wait(1)
                        driver.maximize_window()

                        indx = input.lower().split().index('google')
                        query = input.split()[indx + 1:]
                        driver.get("https://www.google.com/search?q
=" + '+'.join(query))

                        return

                elif "calculate" in input.lower():

                        # write your wolframalpha app_id here
                        app_id = "XXX-XXXX"
                        client = wolframalpha.Client(app_id)

                        indx = input.lower().split().
index('calculate')
                        query = input.split()[indx + 1:]
                        res = client.query(' '.join(query))
                        answer = next(res.results).text
                        assistant_speaks("The answer is " + answer)
                        return

                elif 'open microsoft word' in input:

                        # another function to open
                        # different application availaible
                        assistant_speaks("Opening Microsoft Word")
```

```
                        os.startfile('C:\ProgramData\Microsoft\
Windows\Start Menu\Programs\Microsoft Office\\Microsoft Word 2010
.lnk')
                    return

            else:
                    assistant_speaks("....")

        except :

                assistant_speaks("I don't understand, please try
again.")

# Driver Code
if __name__ == "__main__":
        assistant_speaks("What's your name, Human?")
        name ='Human'
        name = get_audio()
        assistant_speaks("Hello, " + name + '.')

        while(1):

                assistant_speaks("What can i do for you?")
                text = get_audio().lower()

                if text == 0:
                        continue

                if "exit" in str(text) or "bye" in str(text) or
"sleep" in str(text):
                        assistant_speaks("Ok bye, "+ name+'.')
                        break

                # calling process text to process the query
                process_text(text)
```

The following is the output, which shows the conversation between the program and a user:

```
PerSon :  What's your name, Human?
Speak...
Stop.
You :  Perry
PerSon :  Hello, Perry.
PerSon :  What can i do for you?
Speak...
Stop.
You :  search python
PerSon :  I don't understand, please try again.
```

```
PerSon :  What can i do for you?
Speak...
Stop.
You :  open Microsoft Word
PerSon :  Opening Microsoft Word
PerSon :  What can i do for you?
Speak...
Stop.
You :  calculate 2 + 3
PerSon :  The answer is 5
PerSon :  What can i do for you?
Speak...
Stop.
You :  search
PerSon :  I don't understand, please try again.
PerSon :  What can i do for you?
Speak...
Stop.
You :  bye
PerSon :  Ok bye, Perry.
```

EXERCISE 10.28

Modify the previous code, add a graphical user interface to the program using libraries such as PySimpleGUI, run the code, and comment on the results.

10.10.4   Chatbot Resources and Examples

The following is the list of interesting Chatbot resources and example projects:

- Build Your Own AI (ARTIFICIAL INTELLIGENCE) Assistant 101

    ```
    https://www.instructables.com/id/Build-Your-Own-AI-Artificial-
    Intelligence-Assistan/
    ```

- Leon

    ```
    https://github.com/leon-ai/leon
    ```

- Wit.Ai

    ```
    https://wit.ai/
    ```

- Mycroft – Open Source Voice Assistant (include Raspberry Pi version)

    ```
    https://mycroft.ai/
    https://mycroft-ai.gitbook.io/docs/using-mycroft-ai/get-mycroft/
    picroft
    ```

- Open Assistant

  `https://openassistant.org/`

- 10+ Top Open source Voice Assistants Projects

  `https://www.google.com/amp/s/medevel.com/10-open-source-voice-`
  `assistants/amp/`

- The Top 18 Personal Assistant Open Source Projects

  `https://awesomeopensource.com/projects/personal-assistant`

- Healthcare. ai

  `https://healthcareai-py.readthedocs.io/en/master/`

- GEEKSFORGEEKS Personal Voice Assistant in Python

  `https://www.google.com/amp/s/www.geeksforgeeks.org/personal-`
  `voice-assistant-in-python/amp/`

- Simple AI Chatbot

  `https://techwithtim.net/tutorials/ai-chatbot/part-1/`

- How To Convert Your Computer Into JARVIS

  `https://www.youtube.com/watch?v=fm8MGPKgUPk`
  `https://mega-voice-command.com/`
  `https://jarvis.ai-dot.net/betaRelease/publish.html`

- MELISSA, A LOVELY VIRTUAL ASSISTANT!

  `https://www.youtube.com/watch?v=r1yoaq3BcUA`
  `https://github.com/Melissa-AI`

10.11   Summary

This chapter covered the topics of natural language processing, which is a popular research field about developing applications and services that are able to understand the human language.

NLP typically includes lexical analysis, syntactic analysis, semantic analysis, disclosure analysis, and pragmatic analysis. The most commonly used NLP libraries are Natural Language Toolkit (NLTK), SpaCy, Gensim, and TextBlob.

Text summarization summarizes the given long text into shorter text. Text sentiment analysis analyzes the text, such as customer feedback and social media comments, to determine whether the user sentiment is positive, negative, or neutral.

Text generation generates new text based on the existing texts. Poem generation generates new poems based on the existing poems. Text to speech is the process of converting text data into voice data. Speech to text converts the voice data into text data; this includes voice detection, voice analysis, and voice recognition. Translation translates one human language to another language.

Optical character recognition detects and recognizes the characters and words in an image. A QR code is a 2D version of barcode for fast, convenient storing of information.

PDF and DOCX files can be easily converted to each other, as well as merged together with Python libraries.

Chatbots and question answering applications are commonly used in many online commercial websites. There are many examples and resources in Python of chatbot and question answering.

10.12   Chapter Review Questions

Q10.1.   What is natural language processing (NLP)?

Q10.2.   Describe the differences between rule-based NLP and statistical NLP.

Q10.3.   Explain the concepts of syntactic analysis, semantic analysis, disclosure analysis, and pragmatic analysis in the context of natural language processing.

Q10.4.   What is text summarization?

Q10.5.   What is text sentiment analysis?

Q10.6.   What is text generation and poem generation?

Q10.7.   What is text to speech, and what is speech to text?

Q10.8.   What is machine translation?

Q10.9.   What is optical character recognition?

Q10.10. What is a QR code?

Q10.11. What is chatbot, and what is question answering?

Data Analysis

"Data is the new oil."
—Clive Robert Humby (British mathematician
and entrepreneur in data science)

CHAPTER OUTLINE

11.1   Introduction

As Clive Robert Humby said, data is the new oil. Every day, business is generating enormous amounts of data, whether it is the data from social media, sales and marketing data from retailers, or data from manufacturers. Properly analyzing and utilizing the data can tremendously benefit the business.

That is why data analysts and data scientists are among the highest paid professions. But you don't have to change your job to get this benefit. As Andrew Ng (British-born American computer scientist) once recommended, don't change your job; just add AI to it. Data is everywhere, data is in every discipline, and adding AI data analysis ability to your expertise will no doubt enhance your career prosperity and benefit you financially.

So, how to get started? Data analysis can be divided into three steps: collecting data, analyzing data, and writing a report.

1. **Collecting data:** First is to collect the data, which can be scientific measurement data or business data. The collected data can be saved in plain-text files, such as Comma Separated Values (CSV) format, or Microsoft Excel format. Large data can also be saved in databases. Based on the data structure, databases can be divided into SQL or NoSQL databases. Traditional databases are typical Structured Query Language (SQL) databases, such as Oracle and MySQL, where data is saved in the format of tables, and there are relationships between tables. NoSQL is a relatively new type of database, such as MongoDB, which has more flexible data structures, can scale horizontally, handles incredibly fast queries, and is easy for developers to work with. For more details, see section 11.8.
Data cleaning is also an important part of the data collection, which involves correcting the wrong data and removing or conditioning incomplete data, outlier data, or null data. Many machine learning algorithms also require data normalization, which means re-scaling the values to between 0 and 1.

2. **Analyzing data:** After you have the data ready, next is to analyze the data. A range of techniques can be employed, such as regression, time-series prediction, anomaly detection, and classification. This is the main focus of this chapter.

3. **Writing a report:** After analyzing the data, the final step is to write a report. A good report can summarize the results, share your findings with others, and enhance your research reputations.

In this chapter, we will walk you through a number of commonly used techniques for data analysis.

11.2   Regression

Regression is one of the most widely used data analysis techniques. We saw some simple regression examples in Chapter 3. Here we have more examples. Traditional regression techniques include linear regression, logistic regression, polynomial regression, and so on. A much more modern approach is to use machine learning for regression, such as support vector regression, nearest neighbors regression, Gaussian process regression (GPR), and random forest regression. There are also partial least squares regression and principal component regression for analyzing the spectral data.

Linear regression can also be divided into simple linear regression (or single linear regression), multiple linear regression, and multivariate linear regression. In simple linear regression, there is just one dependent variable (Y) and one independent variable (X), and X and Y follow a linear relationship, such as Y = A*X + B. In multiple linear regression, there is one dependent variable (Y), but there is more than one independent variable (X1, X2, . . . Xn). In multivariate linear regression, there is more than one dependent variable (Y1, Y2, . . . Yn), and there is more than one independent variable (X1, X2, . . . Xn).

In Python, you can use the Numpy, Scikit-Learn, Statsmodels, and Scipy libraries to implement regression.

11.2.1   Linear Regression

Example 11.1 shows how to read the data from a CSV file called `data.csv` and then use the Scipy library's `stats.linregress(x, y)` function to perform the linear regression.

EXAMPLE 11.1:   THE `LINEAR REGRESSION1.PY` PROGRAM

```python
#Example 11.1 Linear Regression
import matplotlib.pyplot as plt
from scipy import stats
import pandas

df = pandas.read_csv('data.csv')
print(df)
x = df['Time']
y = df['Voltage']


slope, intercept, r, p, std_err = stats.linregress(x, y)
print("slope: ", slope)
print("intercept: ", intercept)
print("std_err: ", std_err)
def myfunc(x):
    return slope * x + intercept

mymodel = list(map(myfunc, x))

plt.scatter(x, y,label="data")
plt.plot(x, mymodel, "r",label="fitted line")
plt.xlabel("Time")
plt.ylabel("Voltage")
plt.legend()
plt.show()
```

The following is the output of the program, which shows the content of the data.csv file and the linear squares fitting results, the slope, the intercept, and the standard error:

```
     Time   Voltage
0     0        10
1     1        12
2     2        12
3     3        14
4     4        13
5     5        15
6     6        16
7     7        18
8     8        17
9     9        19


slope:   0.9333333333333333
intercept:   10.399999999999999
std_err:   0.08287754140107488
```

Figure 11.1 shows the plotting results.

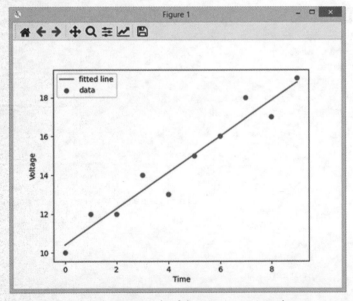

Figure 11.1: The plotting result of the previous example.

EXERCISE 11.1

Modify the previous code so that it uses a file open dialog to choose the data file, run the code, and comment on the results. *Hint: You can use the Tkinter library to select files through a file open dialog box, as shown here:*

```
import tkinter as tk
from tkinter import filedialog
root = tk.Tk()
root.withdraw()
file_path = filedialog.askopenfilename()
print(file_path)
```

11.2.2 Support Vector Regression

As we showed in Chapter 2, you can also use machine learning algorithms for regression, for example, support vector regression. Example 11.2 shows how to read the data from a CSV file and then perform the SVR regression. SVR supports different types of kernels, such as linear, poly, and radial basis function (RBF).

EXAMPLE 11.2: THE SVR REGRESSION.PY **PROGRAM**

```
#Example 11.2 SVR Regression
import matplotlib.pyplot as plt
from scipy import stats
import pandas

df = pandas.read_csv('data.csv')
print(df)
x1 = df['Time'].values.reshape(-1,1)
y1 = df['Voltage'].values.reshape(-1,1)
print(x1)
print(y1)


from sklearn.svm import SVR
lr = SVR(kernel = 'linear', C =1000.0)
pr = SVR(kernel = 'poly', C =1000.0, degree = 2)
rr = SVR(kernel = 'rbf', C =1000.0, gamma = 0.85)
lr.fit(x1,y1)
pr.fit(x1,y1)
rr.fit(x1,y1)

plt.figure()
plt.scatter(x1, y1, color='r', label='Data')
plt.plot(x1, lr.predict(x1),label='linear SVR')
plt.plot(x1, pr.predict(x1),label='poly SVR')
plt.plot(x1, rr.predict(x1),label='rbf SVR')
plt.legend()
plt.show()
```

Figure 11.2 shows the output of the previous program.

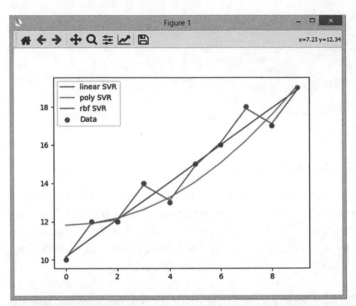

Figure 11.2: The differences of the linear, poly, and RBF kernels in SVR regression.

EXERCISE 11.2

Modify the previous code, add linear regression to the code so that it can compare SVR regression with linear regression, run the code, and comment on the results.

For more details, see the following:

```
https://scikit-learn.org/stable/modules/generated/sklearn.svm
.SVR.html
```

Besides local CSV files, you can also read CSV files over the Internet, as long as you know the full uniform resource locator (URL). Example 11.3 shows how to read the CSV data from a URL and then perform the linear regression.

EXAMPLE 11.3:   THE `LINEAR REGRESSION 2.PY` **PROGRAM**

```
#Example 11.3 Linear Regression
import matplotlib.pyplot as plt
from scipy import stats
import pandas as pd

#df = pd.read_csv('data.csv')
#wine_names = ['Class', 'Alcohol', 'Malic acid', 'Ash', 'Alcalinity
of ash', 'Magnesium', 'Total phenols', 'Flavanoids', 'Nonflavanoid
phenols', 'Proanthocyanins', 'Color intensity', 'Hue', 'OD280/OD315',
'Proline']
#df = pd.read_csv('https://archive.ics.uci.edu/ml/machine-learning-
databases/wine/wine.data', names = wine_names)
```

```
#df = pd.read_csv('https://archive.ics.uci.edu/ml/machine-learning-
databases/adult/adult.data')
#df = pd.read_csv('https://archive.ics.uci.edu/ml/machine-learning-
databases/car/car.data', header=None)
df = pd.read_csv('https://archive.ics.uci.edu/ml/machine-
learning-databases/00291/airfoil_self_noise.dat', sep="\t",
names = ['Frequency','Angle of attack','Chord length','Free-stream
velocity','Suction/side','Scaled/sound'])

print(df)
#print(df.head())
#print(df.describe())


x = df['Frequency']
y = df['Scaled/sound']


slope, intercept, r, p, std_err = stats.linregress(x, y)
print("slope: ", slope)
print("intercept: ", intercept)
print("std_err: ", std_err)
def myfunc(x):
  return slope * x + intercept

mymodel = list(map(myfunc, x))

plt.scatter(x, y, label='original data')
plt.plot(x, mymodel, "r", label='fitted line')
plt.xlabel("Time")
plt.ylabel("Voltage")
plt.legend()
plt.show()
```

The following is the output of the program, which shows the content of the remote CSV file and the linear squares fitting results, the slope, the intercept, and the standard error:

	Frequency	Angle of attack	...	Suction/side	Scaled/sound
0	800	0.0	...	0.002663	126.201
1	1000	0.0	...	0.002663	125.201
2	1250	0.0	...	0.002663	125.951
3	1600	0.0	...	0.002663	127.591
4	2000	0.0	...	0.002663	127.461
...	...	...	...	...	...
1498	2500	15.6	...	0.052849	110.264
1499	3150	15.6	...	0.052849	109.254
1500	4000	15.6	...	0.052849	106.604
1501	5000	15.6	...	0.052849	106.224

```
1502        6300               15.6  ...        0.052849        104.204

[1503 rows x 6 columns]


slope:  -0.000854979012525303
intercept:  127.30373759248681
std_err:  5.199230158034171e-05
```

Figure 11.3 shows the result.

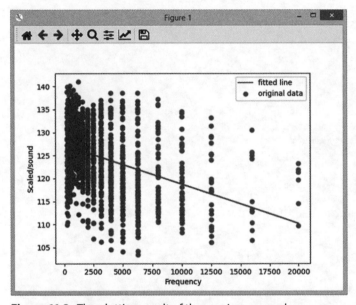

Figure 11.3: The plotting result of the previous example.

EXERCISE 11.3

Modify the previous code, choose a different dataset from the UCI website (https://archive.ics.uci.edu/ml/index.php), **run the code, and comment on the results.**

The Pandas library also allows you to read table data from a web page. Example 11.4 shows how to read the table data from a website. You will need to install the html5lib library by typing the following:

```
pip install html5lib
```

EXAMPLE 11.4:   THE `HTML5LIB1.PY` **PROGRAM**

```
#Example 11.4 - html5lib library
import matplotlib.pyplot as plt
from scipy import stats
import pandas as pd
import numpy as np

#pip install html5lib
df = pd.read_html('https://cn.wikipedia.org/wiki/World_population')
print(f'Total tables: {len(df)}')
df = pd.read_html('https://en.wikipedia.org/wiki/World_population',
match='Global annual population growth')
df =df[0]

x = df['Year'].astype('float')
y = df['Population'].astype('float')

plt.scatter(x, y)
plt.show()
```

Figure 11.4 shows the result.

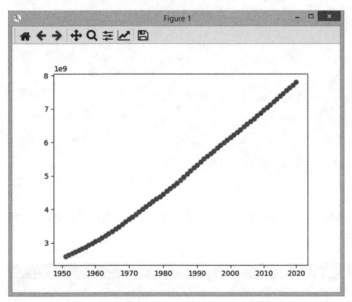

Figure 11.4: The plotting result of the previous example.

BeautifulSoup is another library that allows you to read table data from a web page. Example 11.5 shows how to read the table data from a Wikipedia website. You will need to install the `beautifulsoup4` library and the `requests` library by typing the following:

```
pip install requests beautifulsoup4
```

EXAMPLE 11.5:   THE `BeautifulSoup1.PY` PROGRAM

```python
#Example 11.5 Wiki table scrap with Beautiful Soup
#pip install requests beautifulsoup4
from bs4 import BeautifulSoup
import requests
import csv

#url = "https://en.wikipedia.org/wiki/List_of_countries_by_GDP_
(nominal)"
url = "https://en.wikipedia.org/wiki/World_population"
soup = BeautifulSoup(requests.get(url).text, 'html.parser')

tables = soup.find_all('table', class_='sortable')
print(len(tables))

for table in tables:
    ths = table.find_all('th')
    headings = [th.text.strip() for th in ths]
    #print(headings)

table = tables[4]
population = []
for tr in table.find_all('tr'):
    tds = tr.find_all('td')
    #print(tds)
    if not tds:
        continue
    population.append(tds[0].text.replace('\n', ' ').strip())
print(population)
```

Example 11.6 shows how to get finance data of a list of companies from the Yahoo Finance website.

EXAMPLE 11.6:   THE `BeautifulSoup2.PY` PROGRAM

```python
#Example 11.6 Web scrap Finance with Beautiful Soup
#pip install requests beautifulsoup4
import pandas as pd
from bs4 import BeautifulSoup
import requests

def get_stock(t):
    url = f'http://finance.yahoo.com/quote/{t}?p={t}'
```

```
        res = requests.get(url)
        soup = (BeautifulSoup(res.content, 'lxml'))
        table = soup.find_all('table')[0]
        labels, data = pd.read_html(str(table))[0].values.T
        return pd.Series(data, labels, name = t)


stock_name = ["AAPL","AMZN","GOOG","TSLA"]
df = pd.concat(map(get_stock, stock_name), axis=1)
print(df.T)
```

Example 11.7 shows an example of how to read all the CSV data files from a folder and then perform the linear regression on all the data files and plot all the results.

EXAMPLE 11.7:   THE FIT1.PY PROGRAM

```
# Example 11.7 Linear Regression from a folder
import matplotlib.pyplot as plt
from scipy import stats
import pandas as pd

from os import listdir
from os.path import isfile, join

def myFit(file):
    df = pd.read_csv(file)
    #print(df.columns)
    x = df[df.columns[0]]
    y = df[df.columns[1]]

    slope, intercept, r, p, std_err = stats.linregress(x, y)
    print(file)
    print("slope: ", slope)
    print("intercept: ", intercept)
    print("std_err: ", std_err)
    def myfunc(x):
        return slope * x + intercept
    mymodel = list(map(myfunc, x))
    plt.figure()
    plt.scatter(x, y, label='original data')
    plt.plot(x, mymodel, "r", label='fitted line')
    plt.title(file)
    plt.xlabel(df.columns[0])
    plt.ylabel(df.columns[1])
    plt.legend()

mypath = "./datasets"
files = [join(mypath, f) for f in listdir(mypath) if f.split(".")[-1]
=="csv"]
```

```
#print(files)

for file in files:
    myFit(file)
plt.show()
```

Another way of getting all the files from a folder is to use the Glob library.

```
import glob
mypath = "./datasets"
files = glob.glob(join(mypath,"*.csv"))
```

The following is the output of the program, which shows the least squares fitting of three CSV files in the folder:

```
./datasets\data0.csv
slope:  0.9030303030303031
intercept:  20.636363636363637
std_err:  0.08549536957373294
Index(['Time', 'Voltage'], dtype='object')
./datasets\data1.csv
slope:  0.9333333333333333
intercept:  10.399999999999999
std_err:  0.08287754140107488
Index(['Time', 'Voltage'], dtype='object')
./datasets\data2.csv
slope:  0.9515151515151515
intercept:  30.21818181818182
std_err:  0.1087536875450082
```

Figure 11.5 shows the plotting results, which show the data and fitted lines of three different data files.

EXERCISE 11.4

Modify the previous code, use the Glob library to get all the data file in a folder, run the code, and comment on the results.

11.2.3 Partial Least Squares Regression

Partial least squares (PLS) regression is a technique that is widely used to analyze spectroscopy data. Instead of performing the regression on the original raw data, it works on a smaller set of uncorrelated components and performs least squares regression on these components. PLS is useful especially in the case where the number of independent variables is significantly larger than the number of dependent variables. PLS regression is primarily used in the chemical, drug, food, and plastic industries. A common application is to study the relationship between spectral measurement (NIR, IR, UV) data and chemical composition in the sample, called *chemometrics*.

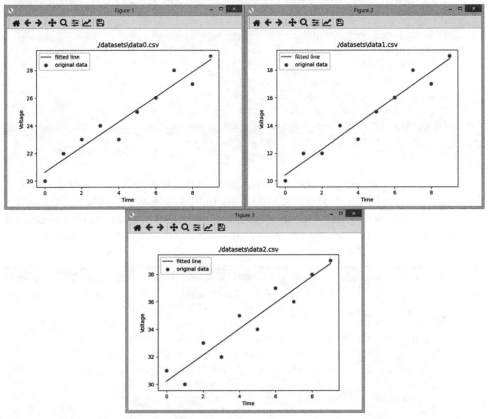

Figure 11.5: The plotting result of the previous example, which shows the data and fitted lines of three different data files.

The following is the NIRPY Research website, which has many interesting articles on near infrared (NIR) spectroscopy analysis by using various techniques, such as PLS regression.

```
https://nirpyresearch.com/
```

The following is the corresponding GitHub site for NIRPY Research.

```
https://github.com/nevernervous78/nirpyresearch
```

Example 11.8 shows how to use the Scikit-Learn library to perform PLS regression on different NIR spectral data. It is modified based on the Python code provided by the NIRPY research website. We will show the example code section by section; the whole code is available in an IPython Notebook file called `Python_PLS.ipynb`.

Example 11.8a shows how to import all the libraries.

EXAMPLE 11.8A: **THE** `PYTHON_PLS.IPYNB` **PROGRAM (PART 1)**

```
#Example 11.8 Partial Least Squares
from sys import stdout
import numpy as np
import pandas as pd
import matplotlib.pyplot as plt
from scipy.signal import savgol_filter
from sklearn.cross_decomposition import PLSRegression
from sklearn.model_selection import cross_val_predict
from sklearn.metrics import mean_squared_error, r2_score
```

The following section of code shows how to get the NIR spectral data from the NIRPY GitHub site and plot out the data. In this case, we get the milk powder spectra. Please note different spectra have different wavelength ranges, so please check the NIRPY website and choose the right range. See Example 11.8b.

EXAMPLE 11.8B: **THE** `PYTHON_PLS.IPYNB` **PROGRAM (PART 2)**

```
data = pd.read_csv('https://raw.githubusercontent.com/nevernervous78/
nirpyresearch/master/data/milk-powder.csv')
#data = pd.read_csv('https://raw.githubusercontent.com/
nevernervous78/nirpyresearch/master/data/milk.csv')
#data = pd.read_csv('https://raw.githubusercontent.com/
nevernervous78/nirpyresearch/master/data/plums.csv')

y = pd.DataFrame.as_matrix(data)[:,1].astype('uint8')
X = pd.DataFrame.as_matrix(data)[:,2:]
wl = np.linspace(350,2500, num=X.shape[1], endpoint=True)
# wl = np.arange(1100,2300,2) # wavelengths

import matplotlib.pyplot as plt
plt.plot(wl,X.T)
plt.ylabel('Absorption')
plt.title('NIR Spectra')
plt.figure()
plt.plot(y)
plt.title('Milk %')
plt.ylabel('Measured Values')
plt.show()
```

Figure 11.6 shows the corresponding outputs, which includes the spectra of milk powder (top) and the milk concentration levels (bottom).

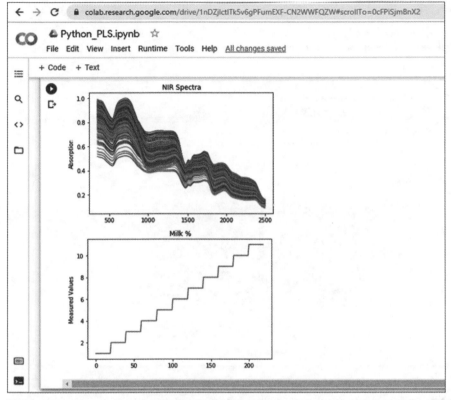

Figure 11.6: The spectra of milk powder (top) and the milk concentration levels (bottom).

Example 11.8c shows how to calculate the second derivative of the NIR spectral and how to plot them out.

EXAMPLE 11.8C: THE `PYTHON_PLS.IPYNB` **PROGRAM (PART 3)**

```
# Calculate second derivative
X2 = savgol_filter(X, 17, polyorder = 2,deriv=2)
# Plot second derivative
plt.figure(figsize=(8,4.5))
with plt.style.context(('ggplot')):
  plt.plot(X2.T)
  plt.xlabel('Wavelength (nm)')
  plt.ylabel('D2 Absorbance')
  plt.show()
```

Figure 11.7 shows the corresponding plot output of the second derivative of the milk powder spectral data.

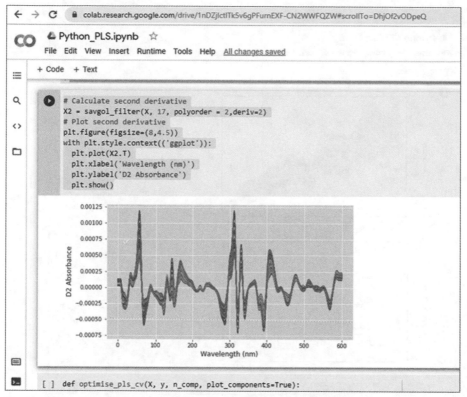

Figure 11.7: The second derivative of the milk powder spectral data.

Example 11.8d shows how to perform the partial least squares regression on milk powder spectral data and how to find out the optimum number of components that give the lowest mean squared error (MSE). Once it finds the optimum number of components, it then plots the PLS regression results.

EXAMPLE 11.8D: THE `PYTHON_PLS.IPYNB` PROGRAM (PART 4)

```python
def optimise_pls_cv(X, y, n_comp, plot_components=True):
    '''Run PLS including a variable number of components, up to n_comp,
        and calculate MSE '''
    mse = []
    component = np.arange(1, n_comp)
    for i in component:
        pls = PLSRegression(n_components=i)
        # Cross-validation
        y_cv = cross_val_predict(pls, X, y, cv=10)
        mse.append(mean_squared_error(y, y_cv))
        comp = 100*(i+1)/40
        # Trick to update status on the same line
        stdout.write("\r%d%% completed" % comp)
        stdout.flush()
    stdout.write("\n")
```

```
        # Calculate and print the position of minimum in MSE
        msemin = np.argmin(mse)
        print("Suggested number of components: ", msemin+1)
        stdout.write("\n")
        if plot_components is True:
            with plt.style.context(('ggplot')):
                plt.plot(component, np.array(mse), '-v', color = 'blue',
mfc='blue')
                plt.plot(component[msemin], np.array(mse)[msemin], 'P',
ms=10, mfc='red')
                plt.xlabel('Number of PLS components')
                plt.ylabel('MSE')
                plt.title('PLS')
                plt.xlim(left=-1)
            plt.show()
        # Define PLS object with optimal number of components
        pls_opt = PLSRegression(n_components=msemin+1)
        # Fir to the entire dataset
        pls_opt.fit(X, y)
        y_c = pls_opt.predict(X)
        # Cross-validation
        y_cv = cross_val_predict(pls_opt, X, y, cv=10)
        # Calculate scores for calibration and cross-validation
        score_c = r2_score(y, y_c)
        score_cv = r2_score(y, y_cv)
        # Calculate mean squared error for calibration and cross
validation
        mse_c = mean_squared_error(y, y_c)
        mse_cv = mean_squared_error(y, y_cv)
        print('R2 calib: %5.3f'  % score_c)
        print('R2 CV: %5.3f'  % score_cv)
        print('MSE calib: %5.3f' % mse_c)
        print('MSE CV: %5.3f' % mse_cv)
        # Plot regression and figures of merit
        rangey = max(y) - min(y)
        rangex = max(y_c) - min(y_c)
        # Fit a line to the CV vs response
        z = np.polyfit(y, y_c, 1)
        with plt.style.context(('ggplot')):
            fig, ax = plt.subplots(figsize=(9, 5))
            ax.scatter(y_c, y, c='red', edgecolors='k')
            #Plot the best fit line
            ax.plot(np.polyval(z,y), y, c='blue', linewidth=1)
            #Plot the ideal 1:1 line
            ax.plot(y, y, color='green', linewidth=1)
            plt.title('$R^{2}$ (CV): '+str(score_cv))
            plt.xlabel('Predicted $^{\circ}$Brix')
            plt.ylabel('Measured $^{\circ}$Brix')
            plt.show()
    return
optimise_pls_cv(X2,y, 40, plot_components=True)
```

Figure 11.8 shows the number of PLS components against the mean squared error (MSE), and it clearly indicates that the best number of components is 13.

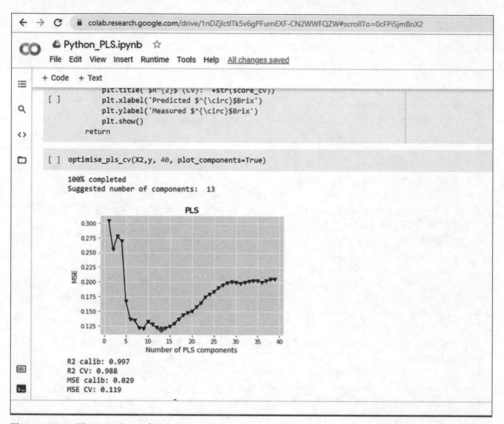

Figure 11.8: The number of PLS components against the MSE.

Figure 11.9 shows the corresponding PLS regression plotting result of the milk powder spectral data, with real milk powder concentration levels against predicted concentration levels. The results show that PLS regression can effectively group the data points according to different milk powder concentration levels.

Example 11.8e shows how to perform the partial least squares regression on milk powder spectral data, with five components, and then plots the PLS regression results.

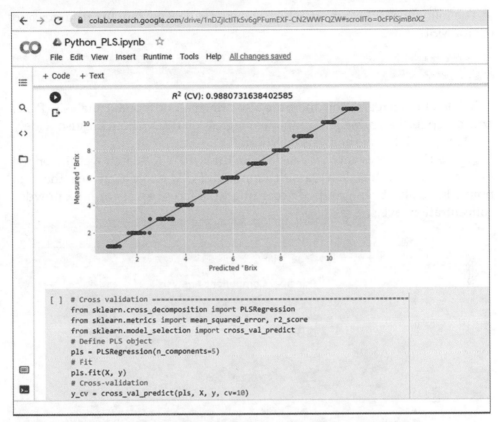

Figure 11.9: The PLS regression plotting result of the milk powder spectral data.

EXAMPLE 11.8E: THE PYTHON_PLS.IPYNB PROGRAM (PART 5)

```
# Cross validation =================================================
from sklearn.cross_decomposition import PLSRegression
from sklearn.metrics import mean_squared_error, r2_score
from sklearn.model_selection import cross_val_predict
# Define PLS object
pls = PLSRegression(n_components=5)
# Fit
pls.fit(X, y)
# Cross-validation
y_cv = cross_val_predict(pls, X, y, cv=10)
# Calculate scores
score = r2_score(y, y_cv)
mse = mean_squared_error(y, y_cv)
print(score)
print(mse)
```

The following is the output, which shows about 98 percent for accuracy and 0.2 for MSE.

```
0.9799675085710466
0.2003249142895337
```

Related to PLS regression, there are also principal component analysis (PCA) and, a step further, principal component regression (PCR). Both are also widely used in the qualitative analysis of NIR data.

Figure 11.10 shows another article from the NIRPY Research website on the milk powder spectral data classification with PCA. As you can see, the data points have also been grouped according to different levels of milk powder concentration levels.

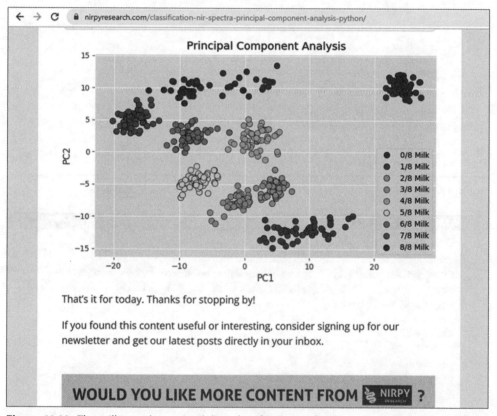

Figure 11.10: The milk powder spectral data classification with PCA.

(Source:`https://nirpyresearch.com/classification-nir-spectra-principal-component-analysis-python/`)

EXERCISE 11.5

From a web browser, log in to your Google Colab account, upload the previous IPython file, run the code, and comment on the results.

11.3 Time-Series Analysis

Time-series data is a collection of measurement values over a period of time. It is one of the most commonly available types of data in our daily life. For example, stock market share prices, time-dependent sensor measurement data, global temperature and CO_2 level changes, seasonal customer numbers and shopping patterns, and so on, are all time-series data.

11.3.1 Stock Price Data

You can get the finance stock price data from the Yahoo website, and on the Historical Data tab, you can choose the period of the data. Click the Apply button to apply the changes and click the Download button to download the data as a CSV file.

```
https://finance.yahoo.com/quote/GOOG/history?p=GOOG
```

Example 11.9 shows how to get the stock price data of a particular company from the Yahoo or Google website, calculate the 20-day rolling average and the 100-day rolling average, and plot the data. It uses the `pandas_datareader` library to read the data from the website.

EXAMPLE 11.9: THE STOCK1.PY PROGRAM

```python
#Example 11.9 Get Stock Data from Yahoo
from pandas_datareader import data
import matplotlib.pyplot as plt
import pandas as pd


symbol = 'MSFT'           #'AMZN','AAPL', 'GOOGL'
data_source='yahoo'       #'google'
start_date = '2016-01-01'
end_date = '2021-01-01'

df = data.DataReader(symbol, data_source, start_date, end_date)
#print(df)
close = df['Close']
#print(close)
#print(close.head(10))
#print(close.describe())
```

```
# Calculate the 20 and 100 days moving averages
short_rolling = close.rolling(window=20).mean()
long_rolling = close.rolling(window=100).mean()

from pandas.plotting import register_matplotlib_converters
register_matplotlib_converters()

# Calculate the 'buy' and 'sell' signals and positions
df['Signal'] = 0.0
df['Signal'] = np.where(short_rolling > long_rolling, 1.0, 0.0)
df['Position'] = df['Signal'].diff()

# Plot the data
fig, ax = plt.subplots(figsize=(16,9))
ax.plot(close.index, close, label=symbol)
ax.plot(short_rolling.index,  short_rolling, label='20 days rolling')
ax.plot(long_rolling.index, long_rolling, label='100 days rolling')

# plot 'buy' signals
plt.plot(df[df['Position'] == 1].index,
         short_rolling[df['Position'] == 1],
         '^', markersize = 15, color = 'g', label = 'buy')

# plot 'sell' signals
plt.plot(df[df['Position'] == -1].index,
     short_rolling[df['Position'] == -1],
     'v', markersize = 15, color = 'r', label = 'sell')
ax.set_xlabel('Date')
ax.set_ylabel('Closing price ($)')
ax.legend()
plt.show()
```

Figure 11.11 shows the output of the previous example, which shows the MSFT (Microsoft) stock price from 2010 to 2020, as well as the 20-day rolling average and the 100-day rolling average with a number of Buy and Sell signals. The Buy signals are generated when the 20-day rolling average overtakes the 100-day rolling average. The Sell signals are generated when the 20-day rolling average undertakes the 100-day rolling average.

The results show that the rolling average can effectively smooth the data. The 20-day rolling average (short rolling average) is much closer to the original data than the 100-day rolling average (long rolling average). The crossover points between the short rolling average and the long rolling average are often used as buying and selling points in algorithm trading. For example, when the short rolling average starts to become lower than the long rolling average, it is the signal to sell. When the short rolling average starts to overtake the long rolling average, it is the signal to buy.

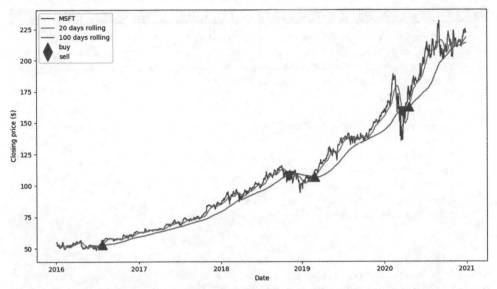

Figure 11.11: The MSFT stock price from 2016 to 2020, as well as the 20-day rolling average and 100-day rolling average with a number of Buy and Sell signals.

EXERCISE 11.6

Modify the previous code, try different stocks from Yahoo as well as from Google, run the code, and comment on the results.

For more information about the Python algorithmic trading, check the following:

```
https://www.datacamp.com/community/tutorials/finance-python-trading
https://www.freecodecamp.org/news/algorithmic-trading-in-python/
```

11.3.2   Stock Price Prediction

The following example shows how to make predictions for stock prices. It is modified based on the following:

```
https://machinelearningmastery.com/time-series-prediction-lstm-
recurrent-neural-networks-python-keras/
```

The program first reads the stock price data from a CSV file and then splits the data into X and Y values, trains it on a simple LSTM model, and makes a prediction. It uses the first 90 percent of the data as training data and uses the other 10 percent of the data as test data. See Example 11.10.

EXAMPLE 11.10:   THE STOCK2.PY **PROGRAM**

```python
# Example 11.10 Stock Prediction with LSTM
# Modified from
# https://machinelearningmastery.com/time-series-prediction-lstm-
recurrent-neural-networks-python-keras/
import numpy
import matplotlib.pyplot as plt
from pandas import read_csv
import math
from keras.models import Sequential
from keras.layers import Dense
from keras.layers import LSTM
from sklearn.preprocessing import MinMaxScaler
from sklearn.metrics import mean_squared_error


def create_dataset(dataset, xback=1):
    dataX, dataY = [], []
    for i in range(len(dataset)-xback-1):
        a = dataset[i:(i+xback), 0]
        dataX.append(a)
        dataY.append(dataset[i + xback, 0])
    return numpy.array(dataX), numpy.array(dataY)
def getData(file, col):
    # load the dataset
    dataframe = read_csv(file,usecols=[col], engine='python')
    dataset = dataframe.values
    dataset = dataset.astype('float32')
    # normalize the dataset
    dataset = scaler.fit_transform(dataset)
    # split into train and test sets
    train_size = int(len(dataset) * ratio)
    test_size = len(dataset) - train_size
    train, test = dataset[0:train_size,:], dataset[train_size:len
(dataset),:]

    trainX, trainY = create_dataset(train, xback)
    testX, testY = create_dataset(test, xback)
    # reshape input to be [samples, time steps, features]
    trainX = numpy.reshape(trainX, (trainX.shape[0], trainX.shape[1],
1))
    testX = numpy.reshape(testX, (testX.shape[0], testX.shape[1], 1))
    return trainX, trainY,testX, testY, dataset

def train(trainX, trainY,testX, testY):
    # create and fit the LSTM network
    model = Sequential()
    model.add(LSTM(4, input_shape=(xback, 1)))
```

```
    model.add(Dense(1))
    model.compile(loss='mean_squared_error', optimizer='adam')
    model.fit(trainX, trainY, epochs=10, batch_size=1, verbose=2)
    return model

def predict(model, trainX, trainY,testX, testY, dataset):
    # make predictions
    trainPredict = model.predict(trainX)
    testPredict = model.predict(testX)
    # invert predictions
    trainPredict = scaler.inverse_transform(trainPredict)
    trainY = scaler.inverse_transform([trainY])
    testPredict = scaler.inverse_transform(testPredict)
    testY = scaler.inverse_transform([testY])
    # calculate root mean squared error
    trainScore = math.sqrt(mean_squared_error(trainY[0],
trainPredict[:,0]))
    print('Train Score: %.2f RMSE' % (trainScore))
    testScore = math.sqrt(mean_squared_error(testY[0],
testPredict[:,0]))
    print('Test Score: %.2f RMSE' % (testScore))
    # shift train predictions for plotting
    trainPredictPlot = numpy.empty_like(dataset)
    trainPredictPlot[:, :] = numpy.nan
    trainPredictPlot[xback:len(trainPredict)+xback, :] = trainPredict
    # shift test predictions for plotting
    testPredictPlot = numpy.empty_like(dataset)
    testPredictPlot[:, :] = numpy.nan
    testPredictPlot[len(trainPredict)+(xback*2)+1:len(dataset)-1, :]
= testPredict
    # plot baseline and predictions
    plt.plot(scaler.inverse_transform(dataset),'o',label='origial
data')
    plt.plot(trainPredictPlot,label='predict train')
    plt.plot(testPredictPlot,label='predict test')
    plt.legend()
    plt.show()


# reshape into X=5 and Y=5+1
xback = 5
#numpy.random.seed(7)
scaler = MinMaxScaler(feature_range=(0, 1))
ratio = 0.9
file = 'AAPL.csv'
col = 4

trainX, trainY,testX, testY, dataset = getData(file,col)
model = train(trainX, trainY,testX, testY)
predict(model, trainX, trainY,testX, testY, dataset)
```

The following is the output of the program:

```
Epoch 1/10
1127/1127 - 1s - loss: 0.0050
Epoch 2/10
1127/1127 - 1s - loss: 1.4707e-04
Epoch 3/10
1127/1127 - 1s - loss: 1.4058e-04
Epoch 4/10
1127/1127 - 1s - loss: 1.2915e-04
Epoch 5/10
1127/1127 - 1s - loss: 1.2593e-04
Epoch 6/10
1127/1127 - 1s - loss: 1.1901e-04
Epoch 7/10
1127/1127 - 1s - loss: 1.2254e-04
Epoch 8/10
1127/1127 - 1s - loss: 1.2025e-04
Epoch 9/10
1127/1127 - 3s - loss: 1.1931e-04
Epoch 10/10
1127/1127 - 1s - loss: 1.0878e-04
Train Score: 1.06 RMSE
Test Score: 4.79 RMSE
```

Figure 11.12 shows the plotting results of the previous example. The right side with 10 percent of the data shows the prediction data, based on the left's 90 percent training data. The results show that the prediction matches reasonably with the real stock price data.

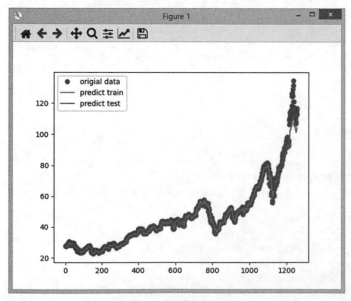

Figure 11.12: The plotting result of the previous example.

EXERCISE 11.7

Modify the previous code, add more layers to the LSTM mode, run the code, and comment on the results.

Streamlit Stock Price Web App

Example 11.11 shows a really cool example of the stock price web app by using the Streamlit library.

EXAMPLE 11.11:   THE `GOOGLE-APP.PY` **PROGRAM**

```python
# Example 11.11
import yfinance as yf
import streamlit as st
from datetime import datetime
from datetime import date
import datetime as dt
import pandas as pd
import numpy as np
import altair as alt


st.write("""
# Simple Stock Price App

Shown are the stock **closing price** and ***volume*** of a Company!

""")


@st.cache
def load_data():
    url = 'https://en.wikipedia.org/wiki/List_of_S%26P_500_companies'
    html = pd.read_html(url, header = 0)
    df = html[0]
    return df

@st.cache
def load_ftse100data():
    url = 'https://en.wikipedia.org/wiki/FTSE_100_Index'
    html = pd.read_html(url, header = 0)
    df = html[3]
    return df

start = date.today()-dt.timedelta(days=365)
st.sidebar.markdown("# Start and End Date:")
w1 = st.sidebar.date_input("Start", start, min_value=date(1970, 1, 1))
#st.write("Value 1:", w1)
```

```python
w2 = st.sidebar.date_input("End", date.today(), min_value=date(1970,
1, 1))
#st.write("Value 1:", w2)


tickerSymbol = 'GOOGL'
name = 'Google'

option = st.sidebar.selectbox(
    'Select a Stock Market:',
    ["S&P 500","FTSE 100"], index=0)
st.sidebar.write('You selected:', option)
if option == "S&P 500":
    df = load_data()
    #print(df)
    #coms = df.groupby('EPIC')

    #coms = df['Symbol'].unique()
    #names = df['Security'].unique()
    coms = df['Symbol']
    names = df['Security']
    #print(coms)

    # Sidebar - Sector selection
    #selected_scoms = st.sidebar.multiselect('Companies', coms , coms
)

    option1 = st.sidebar.selectbox(
     'Select a Company:',
     coms, index=0)
    #st.sidebar.write('You selected:', option1)
    i=[i for i, j in enumerate(coms) if j == option1]
    #i = np.where(coms == option1)
    name = names[i]
    #print(i)
    #print(name)
    tickerSymbol = option1
    st.sidebar.write(option1)

elif option == "FTSE 100":
    df = load_ftse100data()
    #print(df)
    #coms = df.groupby('EPIC')

    coms = df['EPIC']
    names = df['Company']
    #print(coms)
```

```
    # Sidebar - Sector selection
    #selected_scoms = st.sidebar.multiselect('Companies', coms , coms
)

    option2 = st.sidebar.selectbox(
        'Select a Company:',
        coms, index=0)
    #st.sidebar.write('You selected:', option2)
    i=[i for i, j in enumerate(coms) if j == option2]
    #i = np.where(coms == option2)
    name = names[i]
    tickerSymbol = option2
    st.sidebar.write(option2)


# https://towardsdatascience.com/how-to-get-stock-data-using-python-
c0de1df17e75
#define the ticker symbol
#tickerSymbol = 'GOOGL'
#get data on this ticker
tickerData = yf.Ticker(tickerSymbol)
#get the historical prices for this ticker
tickerDf = tickerData.history(period='1d', start=w1, end=w2)
# Open        High      Low       Close     Volume    Dividends
Stock Splits

st.write(name)
st.write("""
## Closing Price
""")
if (len(tickerDf)>1):
    st.line_chart(tickerDf.Close)
    st.write("Percentage Change : " +str(int((tickerDf.Close[-1] -
tickerDf.Close[0])/tickerDf.Close[0]*1000)/10.0) + "%")
else:
    st.write("Data not available...")
st.write("""
## Volume Price
""")
if (len(tickerDf)>1):
    st.line_chart(tickerDf.Volume)
else:
    st.write("Data not available...")


toplist = []
if ( st.button("Top Performers")):
    #for i in coms:
    for i in range(len(coms)):
```

```
        tickerData = yf.Ticker(coms[i])
        #get the historical prices for this ticker
        tickerDf = tickerData.history(period='1d', start=w1, end=w2)
        print(len(tickerDf))
        if (len(tickerDf)<1):
            continue
        percentChange = int((tickerDf.Close[-1] - tickerDf.Close[0])/
tickerDf.Close[0]*1000)/10.0
        name = names[i]
        toplist.append([coms[i],name,percentChange])
        print(coms[i])
        print(name)
        print(percentChange )


    results = sorted(toplist,key=lambda l:l[2], reverse=True)
    st.write(results[0:19])
    #https://docs.streamlit.io/en/stable/api.html
    #chart_data = pd.DataFrame(
    #    np.random.randn(50, 3),
    #    columns=["a", "b", "c"])
    #st.bar_chart(chart_data)


    #https://discuss.streamlit.io/t/sort-the-bar-chart-in-descending-
order/1037/2
    #import streamlit as st
    #import pandas as pd
    #import altair as alt

    x = [x[0] for x in results[0:19]]
    print(x)
    y = [x[1] for x in results[0:19]]
    print(y)
    z = [x[2] for x in results[0:19]]
    print(z)
    data = pd.DataFrame({
        'Company Symbol': x,
        'Company Name': y,
        'Percentage Change': z,
    })

    st.write(data)
    st.write(alt.Chart(data).mark_bar().encode(
        x=alt.X('Company Symbol', sort=None),
        y='Percentage Change',
    ))
```

To run the program, just type the following:

```
streamlit run google-app.py
```

Figure 11.13 is the web page output of the previous program, from which you can select the start and end dates of the stock price, the stock market index of S&P 500 or FTSE 100, and a constituent stock of the index.

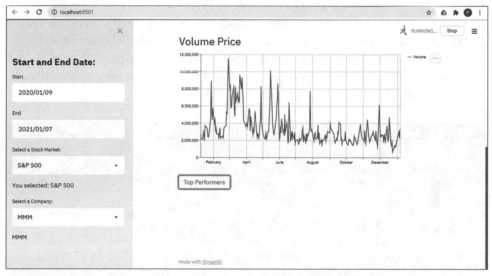

Figure 11.13: The web page output of the Streamlit stock price web app example.

11.3.4   Seasonal Trend Analysis

Seasonal-trend decomposition using LOESS, or STL, is a versatile and robust mathematical algorithm for decomposing time series. STL was developed by Cleveland, McRae, and Terpenning in 1990. STL can decompose a time series into three components: trend, seasonal, and residual. STL uses locally estimated scatterplot smoothing (LOESS) to extract smooth estimates of the three components. There are three key input parameters for STL.

- **Season:** The length of the seasonal smoother. Must be odd.
- **Trend:** The length of the trend smoother, usually around 150 percent of the season. Must be odd and larger than the season.
- **Low_pass:** The length of the low-pass estimation window, usually the smallest, odd number larger than the periodicity of the data.

The easiest way to use STL is through the Statsmodels library, as we saw in Chapter 3. You will need to install it first.

```
pip install statsmodels
```

Example 11.12 shows a simple example of how to use STL to decompose the global CO_2 yearly data into trend and seasons. In this code, it first retrieves the global CO_2 data from the NOAA Earth System Research Laboratories (ESRL) website as a CSV file format. It then uses STL to decompose it into Trend, Season, and Residual components. Finally, it also shows how to predict the future 24 months of data by using the ARIMA model.

EXAMPLE 11.12:   THE STL1.PY PROGRAM

```python
import pandas as pd
#Global CO2 data
df = pd.read_csv('https://www.esrl.noaa.gov/gmd/webdata/ccgg/trends/
co2/co2_mm_gl.csv', comment='#')

print(df.head())
dl = df['average'].values.tolist()
df = pd.Series(dl, index=pd.date_range('1-1-1980', periods=len(df),
freq='M'), name = 'CO2')
print(df.head())
df.describe()


from statsmodels.tsa.seasonal import STL
stl = STL(df)
res = stl.fit()
fig = res.plot()
fig.show()


#Predition =============================================================
from statsmodels.tsa.forecasting.stl import STLForecast
from statsmodels.tsa.arima.model import ARIMA
import matplotlib.pyplot as plt

data = df
stlf = STLForecast(data , ARIMA, model_kwargs={"order": (2, 1, 0)})
res = stlf.fit()

forecast = res.forecast(24)
plt.figure()
plt.plot(data)
plt.plot(forecast)
plt.show()
```

The following is the text output of the program. It first shows the first five rows of the global CO_2 data since January 1980. It then shows the first five rows of the data serials for STL analysis.

```
     year   month   decimal   average   trend
0    1980       1   1980.042   338.56  337.93
1    1980       2   1980.125   339.27  338.22
2    1980       3   1980.208   339.60  338.25
3    1980       4   1980.292   340.00  338.38
4    1980       5   1980.375   340.43  338.91
1980-01-31       338.56
1980-02-29       339.27
1980-03-31       339.60
1980-04-30       340.00
1980-05-31       340.43
```

Figure 11.14 shows the output of the program, which shows the original CO_2 data and the Trend, Season, and Residual components. The Trend data shows a steady increase of CO_2, and the Season data shows the up and down oscillation throughout the year. It tends to have higher CO_2 during the winter and lower CO_2 during the summer.

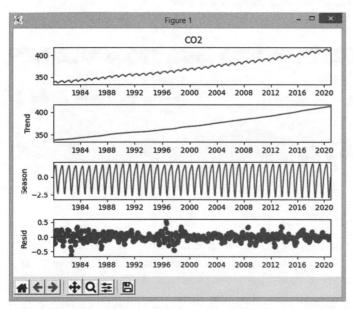

Figure 11.14: The original CO_2 data and the Trend, Season, and Residual components.

Figure 11.15 shows the original CO_2 data and the prediction. The prediction clearly follows the trend and seasonal oscillations.

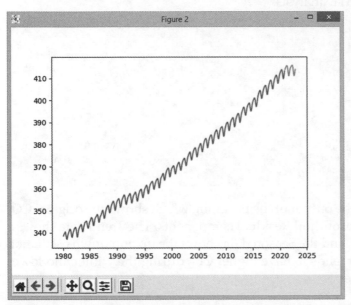

Figure 11.15: The original CO_2 data and the prediction.

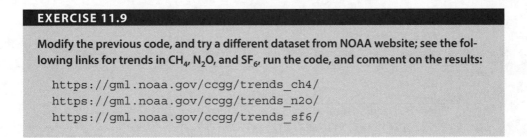

EXERCISE 11.9

Modify the previous code, and try a different dataset from NOAA website; see the following links for trends in CH_4, N_2O, and SF_6, run the code, and comment on the results:

```
https://gml.noaa.gov/ccgg/trends_ch4/
https://gml.noaa.gov/ccgg/trends_n2o/
https://gml.noaa.gov/ccgg/trends_sf6/
```

11.3.5   Sound Analysis

Sound is another type of time-series data that has attracted many research interests. The types of sound that have been studied include natural environmental sounds, respiratory sounds, heartbeat sounds, ultrasound, and so on. With sound analysis you can identify the activities, such as bird chirping, dog barking, or human activities, meaning a type of human activity recognition (HAR). In the industry, sound has long been used for gas pipe or water pipe leakage detection.

Sound analysis in AI is typically a classification problem. There are two common approaches. One is working directly on the sound numerical data and using recurrent neural networks to train and to classify the sounds. Another approach is to convert the sound data into 2D images, through spectrogram, mel-frequency cepstral coefficients (MFCCs), and cross-recurrence plot (CRP). Then use convolutional neural networks to train and classify the images.

Example 11.13 shows a Python code that can record five seconds of voice data from your computer microphone, play it, save it into a file called test.wav, and plot both channels of the sound. It uses the SoundDevice library for recording and playing the sound and uses the SoundFile library to save the sound into a WAV file. So, you will need to install the two libraries, as shown here:

```
pip install sounddevice soundfile
```

EXAMPLE 11.13:   THE SOUND1.PY PROGRAM

```python
# Example 11.13
# pip install sounddevice soundfile

import sounddevice as sd
import soundfile as sf
import numpy as np
import scipy.io.wavfile as wav
import matplotlib.pyplot as plt
from scipy import signal

fs=44100
duration = 5  # seconds
myrecording = sd.rec(duration * fs, samplerate=fs, channels=2,
dtype='float64')
print ("Recording ...")
sd.wait()
print ("Playing Audio ...")
sd.play(myrecording, fs)
sd.wait()
print ("Writing Audio: test.wav")
filename = "test.wav"
sf.write(filename, myrecording, fs)

# plot wave by audio frames
plt.figure(figsize=(10, 5))
plt.subplot(2,1,1)
plt.plot(myrecording[:,0], 'r-', label='Left');
plt.legend()
plt.subplot(2,1,2)
plt.plot(myrecording[:,1], 'g-', label='Right');
plt.legend()
plt.show()
```

Figure 11.16 shows the plot results, which displays the left and right channels of the five-second sound; in this case, three Hellos were spoken during the recording.

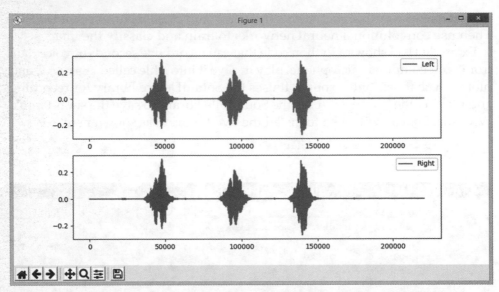

Figure 11.16: The left and right channels of the five-second sound with three Hellos.

EXERCISE 11.10

Modify the previous code, try saying different words, run the code, and comment on
the results.

Short-time Fourier transform (STFT) is an interesting technique for analyzing sound data. STFT divides the sound time signal into shorter segments
of equal length and then computes the Fourier transform separately on each
shorter segment. By plotting the different frequencies against time, you can get
a spectrogram.

Example 11.14 shows some simple Python code that reads the sound data
from a WAV file and uses the `matplotlib.pyplot` function to plot the left
channel's sound amplitude and the corresponding spectrogram.

EXAMPLE 11.14:   THE `SOUND2.PY` **PROGRAM**

```
# Example 11.14

import soundfile as sf
import matplotlib.pyplot as plt

path = 'test.wav'
data, rate = sf.read(path)
# Plot the signal read from wav file
plt.subplot(211)
plt.title('Spectrogram of a wav file')
plt.plot(data[:,0])
```

```
plt.xlabel('Sample')
plt.ylabel('Amplitude')

plt.subplot(212)
plt.specgram(data[:,0],Fs=rate)
plt.xlabel('Time')
plt.ylabel('Frequency')
plt.show()
```

Figure 11.17 shows the amplitude (top) and the spectrogram (bottom) of the left channel's sound data from the `test.wav` file.

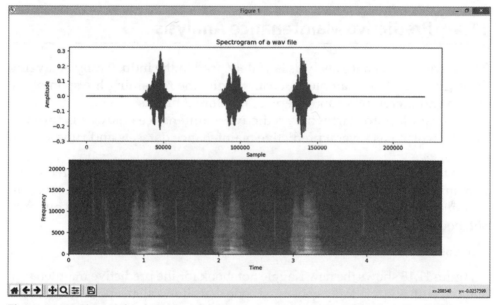

Figure 11.17: The amplitude (top) and the spectrogram (bottom) of the left channel sound data from the `test.wav` file.

EXERCISE 11.11

Modify the previous code, try different sound files, run the code, and comment on the results.

See the following links for more information about STFT and spectrograms. As you can see, apart from the `matplotlib.pyplot` library, you can use the `scipy.signal` library and the `librora` library for plotting the spectrogram.

https://matplotlib.org/stable/api/_as_gen/matplotlib.pyplot
.specgram.html

https://docs.scipy.org/doc/scipy/reference/generated/scipy.signal
.spectrogram.html

```
https://librosa.org/doc/main/generated/librosa.feature
.melspectrogram.html
```

The following is a list of interesting sound datasets on Kaggle along with the corresponding Python example code:

```
https://www.kaggle.com/mmoreaux/environmental-sound-
classification-50
https://www.kaggle.com/vbookshelf/respiratory-sound-database
https://www.kaggle.com/kinguistics/heartbeat-sounds
https://www.kaggle.com/pavansanagapati/ultrasound-dataset
https://www.kaggle.com/pavansanagapati/spotify-music-data
```

11.4 Predictive Maintenance Analysis

Predictive maintenance analysis is widely used in the industry. By analyzing the engine data, for example, you can predict the remaining life span of the engine and therefore repair or replace it before it breaks down.

The best place to start with predictive maintenance analysis is through Kaggle, which has several predictive maintenance datasets and runs several challenges.

The following website shows a Kaggle challenge, which aims to predict the remaining useful life (RUL) of turbofan engines. Let's use this data set as an example. Click the New Notebook button at the top right to create your own notebook.

```
https://www.kaggle.com/c/predictive-maintenance/code
```

Figure 11.18 shows the new Kaggle notebook for the predictive maintenance dataset, with automatically generated code that shows all the data files that are available in the default data folder `/kaggle/input/`. You can also see all the files in the right-side panel, which shows four training data files, four testing data files, and four RUL files. Each data file contains the following 32 columns or features:

```
'engine_no',
'time_in_cycles',
'op_setting_1',
'op_setting_2',
'op_setting_3',
```

```
'sensor_1',

'sensor_2',

'sensor_3',

... ...

'sensor_25',

'sensor_26',

'sensor_27'
```

Figure 11.18: The new Kaggle notebook for a predictive maintenance dataset, with automatically generated code.

The complete code of this is available in a file called `predictivemaintenance-tutorial.ipynb`, which you can upload or copy and paste to your new Kaggle notebook. Here we show only a few key outputs.

Figure 11.19 shows the last few columns of the dataset with the RUL column added at the end.

Figure 11.20 shows the code for plotting the sensor data and first three sensor plots.

Figure 11.21 shows the code to use a random forest regressor to predict the RUL from the engine data and the code to plot the results.

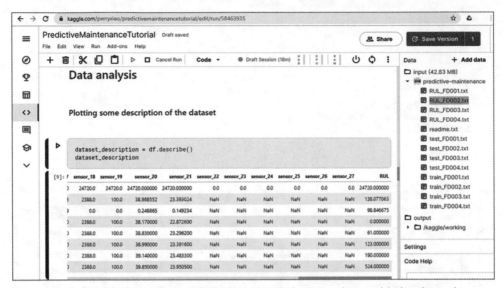

Figure 11.19: The last few columns of the dataset with the RUL column added at the end.

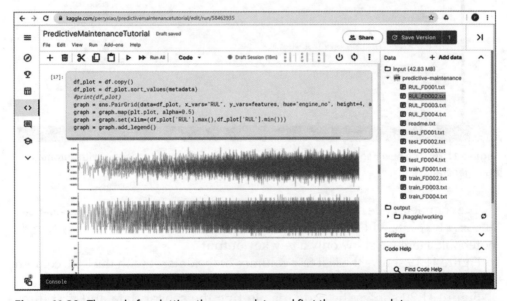

Figure 11.20: The code for plotting the sensor data and first three sensor plots.

Figure 11.22 shows the ideal RUL result plot (top) and predicted RUL result plot (bottom). The horizontal axis is the real RUL data, and the vertical axis is the predicted RUL; ideally, it should be a straight line as shown in the top plot. The results show that the predicted RUL, although pretty noisy, is close to a straight line.

Training a random forest

```
In [24]: from sklearn.ensemble import RandomForestRegressor
         rf_reg = RandomForestRegressor()
         rf_reg.fit(X_train, y_train)

         print("Score on train data : " + str(rf_reg.score(X_train, y_train)))
         print("Score on test data : " + str(rf_reg.score(X_val, y_val)))
```

```
/opt/conda/lib/python3.6/site-packages/sklearn/ensemble/forest.py:246: FutureWarning: The default val
ue of n_estimators will change from 10 in version 0.20 to 100 in 0.22.
  "10 in version 0.20 to 100 in 0.22.", FutureWarning)
```

```
Score on train data : 0.9335086350869007
Score on test data : 0.6310047761108404
```

Plotting the result

```
In [29]: df_pred = data_train.copy()
         df_pred['pred'] = rf_reg.predict(X_train)
         #print(df_pred['pred'])
         df_pred['error'] = df_pred['pred'] - df_pred['RUL']
         df_plot = df_pred.copy()
         df_plot = df_plot.sort_values(['engine_no', 'time_in_cycles'])
         g = sns.PairGrid(data=df_plot, x_vars="RUL", y_vars=['RUL', 'pred', 'error'], hue="engine_no", height=6
         g = g.map(plt.plot, alpha=0.5)
         g = g.set(xlim=(df_plot['RUL'].min(),df_plot['RUL'].max()))
         g = g.add_legend()
```

Figure 11.21: The code to use a random forest regressor to predict the RUL from the engine data and the code to plot the results.

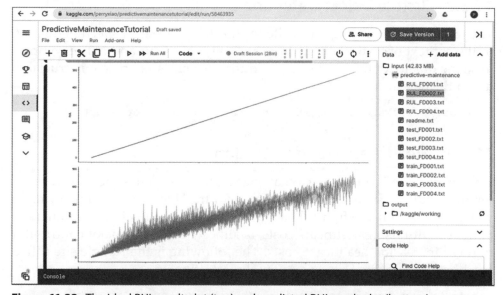

Figure 11.22: The ideal RUL result plot (top) and predicted RUL result plot (bottom).

EXERCISE 11.12

From a web browser, log in to your Kaggle account, repeat the previous steps to build your own IPython notebook code, run the code, and comment on the results.

11.5   Anomaly Detection and Fraud Detection

Anomaly detection and fraud detection are practical applications in finance, healthcare, and other businesses. Again, we will use Kaggle dataset examples.

11.5.1   Numenta Anomaly Detection

The following is the Kaggle website for the Numenta Anomaly Benchmark (NAB) dataset. The NAB is a novel benchmark for evaluating algorithms for anomaly detection in streaming online applications. It is comprised of more than 50 labeled real-world and artificial time-series data files plus a novel scoring mechanism designed for real-time applications.

```
https://www.kaggle.com/boltzmannbrain/nab
```

EXERCISE 11.13

From a web browser, log in to your Kaggle account, find the NAB dataset, choose an IPython notebook, run the code, and comment on the results.

11.5.2   Textile Defect Detection

The following is the Kaggle website for the Textile Defect Detection dataset. In the context of textile fabric, a rare anomaly can occur and hence compromise the quality of the textile. To avoid that in some scenarios, it is crucial to detect the defect.

```
https://www.kaggle.com/belkhirnacim/textiledefectdetection
```

11.5.3   Healthcare Fraud Detection

Healthcare fraud is considered a challenge for many societies. Healthcare funding that could be spent on medicine, care for the elderly, or emergency room visits is instead lost to fraudulent activities by materialistic practitioners or patients. With rising healthcare costs, healthcare fraud is a major contributor to these increasing healthcare costs. The following is the Kaggle site called Healthcare Providers Data For Anomaly Detection.

```
https://www.kaggle.com/tamilsel/healthcare-providers-data
```

11.5.4   Santander Customer Transaction Prediction

The following is the Kaggle site called Santander Customer Transaction Prediction Challenge.

```
https://www.kaggle.com/c/santander-customer-transaction-prediction
```

The aim of this challenge is to develop new machine learning algorithms for binary classification problems such as the following: Is a customer satisfied? Will a customer buy this product? Can a customer pay this loan?

In this challenge, it aims to identify which customers will make a specific transaction in the future. The data provided for this competition has the same structure as the real data.

The following website shows an interesting article called "Introduction to Fraud Detection Systems" on the KDnuggets website.

```
https://www.kdnuggets.com/2018/08/introduction-fraud-detection-
systems.html
```

The following is the corresponding IPython notebook example:

```
https://github.com/miguelgfierro/sciblog_support/blob/master/Intro_
to_Fraud_Detection/fraud_detection.ipynb
```

11.6   COVID-19 Data Visualization and Analysis

The COVID-19 pandemic that began in 2020 has sparked much interest in developing Python code to visualize and to analyze the COVID-19 data.

Example 11.15 shows some simple Python code that reads the COVID-19 data from the John Hopkins University GitHub site, finds out the sum of each country, and chooses a country (United Kingdom) to display the total confirmed cases and daily cases. You can also set the minimum case numbers, which is used as the threshold for a starting plot. By uncommenting the corresponding statements, the example can also read the number of deaths, the number of recoveries, and the latest data.

EXAMPLE 11.15:   THE `COVID-19.PY` **PROGRAM**

```python
# Example 11.15 Covid-19.py

import pandas as pd
import numpy as np
import matplotlib.pyplot as plt
#import seaborn as sns

from matplotlib.ticker import MaxNLocator

# Number of Covid Death
#path = 'https://raw.githubusercontent.com/CSSEGISandData/COVID-19/
master/csse_covid_19_data/csse_covid_19_time_series/time_series_
covid19_deaths_global.csv'
# Number of Covid Recoveries
#path = 'https://raw.githubusercontent.com/CSSEGISandData/COVID-19/
master/csse_covid_19_data/csse_covid_19_time_series/time_series_
covid19_recovered_global.csv'
```

```
# The latest Covid data
#path = 'https://raw.githubusercontent.com/CSSEGISandData/COVID-19/
master/csse_covid_19_data/csse_covid_19_daily_reports/08-19-2021.csv'

# Number of Confirmed Covid Cases
path = 'https://raw.githubusercontent.com/CSSEGISandData/COVID-19/
master/csse_covid_19_data/csse_covid_19_time_series/time_series_
covid19_confirmed_global.csv'
df = pd.read_csv(path)
df.info()
df.head()

# The country to plot the data for.
country = 'United Kingdom'

# Group by country and sum over the different states/regions of each
country.
grouped = df.groupby('Country/Region')
df2 = grouped.sum()
print(df2)

# Start the plot on the day when the number of confirmed cases
reaches MIN_CASES.
MIN_CASES = 1

def make_plot(country):
    """Make the bar plot of case numbers and change in numbers line
plot."""

    # Extract the Series corresponding to the case numbers for
country.
    confirmed = df2.loc[country, df2.columns[3:]]
    print(confirmed)
    # Discard any columns with fewer than MIN_CASES.
    confirmed = confirmed[confirmed >= MIN_CASES].astype(int)
    # Convet index to a proper datetime object
    confirmed.index = pd.to_datetime(confirmed.index)
    n = len(confirmed)
    if n == 0:
        print('Too few data to plot: minimum number of cases is {}'
                .format(MIN_CASES))
        sys.exit(1)

    fig = plt.Figure()

    # Arrange the subplots on a grid
    ax2 = plt.subplot2grid((2,1), (0,0))
    ax1 = plt.subplot2grid((2,1), (1,0))
    ax1.bar(confirmed.index, confirmed.values)
```

```
        # Force the x-axis to be in integers (whole number of days)
        ax1.xaxis.set_major_locator(MaxNLocator(integer=True))

        confirmed_change = confirmed.diff()
        # Running average of daily cases
        sevenday_rolling = confirmed_change.rolling(window=7).mean()
        ax2.plot(confirmed.index, confirmed_change.values, label = 'Daily
Cases')
        ax2.plot(confirmed.index, sevenday rolling.values,'-r', label =
'7 Day Average')
        ax2.set_xticks([])
        ax2.legend()

        ax1.set_xlabel('Date ')
        ax1.set_ylabel('Total Confirmed cases, $N$')
        ax2.set_ylabel('Daily Cases $\Delta N$')

        # Add a title reporting the latest number of cases available.
        title = '{}\nTotal {} cases on {}'.format(country, confirmed[-1],
                  confirmed.index[-1].strftime('%d %B %Y'))
        plt.suptitle(title)

make_plot(country)
plt.show()
print('Today New Cases:', confirmed_change[-1])
print('Today Total Cases:', confirmed[-1])
```

Figure 11.23 shows the plots of the previous program, which shows the total confirmed cases (bottom), the daily cases (top), and the corresponding seven-day running average.

EXERCISE 11.14

Modify the previous example code, and try different COVID-19 data, such as the number of deaths, the number of recoveries, the latest data, as well as different countries. Run the code and comment on the results.

EXERCISE 11.15

Modify the previous example code, and use the stock data prediction algorithms, as seasonal trend analysis, to predict the COVID-19 data. Run the code, and comment on the results.

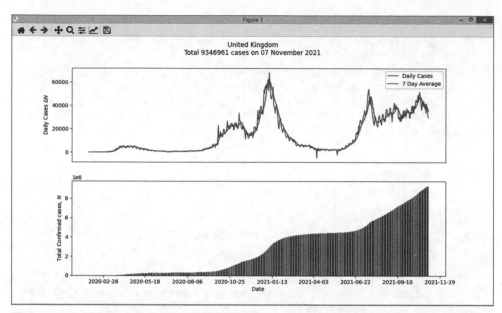

Figure 11.23: The total confirmed cases (bottom), the daily cases (top), and the corresponding seven-day running average in the United Kingdom.

The following is the GitHub website for the PySimpleGUI-COVID19 project, which is an impressive graphical user interface (GUI)–based Python program that can display and analyze the COVID-19 data. It uses the Johns Hopkins Time-Series data.

```
https://github.com/PySimpleGUI/PySimpleGUI-COVID19
```

The following is the Kaggle website for the COVID-19 Open Research Dataset Challenge (CORD-19). CORD-19 is the most extensive machine-readable coronavirus literature resource with over 500,000 scholarly articles about COVID-19, SARS-CoV-2, and related coronaviruses. It calls the global research community to apply recent advances in AI techniques to generate new insights in support of the ongoing fight against this infectious disease.

```
https://www.kaggle.com/allen-institute-for-ai/CORD-19-research-
challenge
```

11.7 KerasClassifier and KerasRegressor

KerasClassifier and KerasRegressor are Keras wrapper classes that aim to make it easier to perform classification and regression tasks.

11.7.1   KerasClassifier

Let's use an example to illustrate how to use KerasClassifier for classification. The following is the Kaggle website for the Pima Indians Diabetes Database. Click the New Notebook button to create your own IPython notebook.

```
https://www.kaggle.com/uciml/pima-indians-diabetes-database
```

Then copy or upload the following Example 11.16a code into your Kaggle notebook. Here we show the code section by section, and the full code is in a file called `KerasClassifier1.ipynb`.

The first part of the code is automatically generated when you create a new notebook on Kaggle, which simply shows what data files are there in the Kaggle data folder `/kaggle/input`.

EXAMPLE 11.16A: THE `KerasClassifier1.IPYNB` PROGRAM (PART 1)

```python
# This Python 3 environment comes with many helpful analytics
libraries installed
# It is defined by the kaggle/python Docker image: https://github
.com/kaggle/docker-python
# For example, here's several helpful packages to load

import numpy as np # linear algebra
import pandas as pd # data processing, CSV file I/O (e.g.
pd.read_csv)

# Input data files are available in the read-only "../input/"
directory
# For example, running this (by clicking run or pressing Shift+Enter)
will list all files under the input directory

import os
for dirname, _, filenames in os.walk('/kaggle/input'):
    for filename in filenames:
        print(os.path.join(dirname, filename))

# You can write up to 20GB to the current directory (/kaggle/
working/) that gets preserved as output when you create a version
using "Save & Run All"
# You can also write temporary files to /kaggle/temp/, but they won't
be saved outside of the current session
```

Example 11.16b shows the code to import all the libraries.

EXAMPLE 11.16B: THE `KerasClassifier1.IPYNB` **PROGRAM (PART 2)**

```
from keras.models import Sequential
from keras.layers import Dense
from keras.layers import Dropout
from keras.wrappers.scikit_learn import KerasClassifier
from sklearn.model_selection import StratifiedKFold
from sklearn.model_selection import cross_val_score
from sklearn.metrics import accuracy_score
from sklearn.preprocessing import StandardScaler

import numpy
import pandas as pd
import matplotlib.pyplot as plt
from sklearn.model_selection import train_test_split
from pandas.plotting import scatter_matrix
```

Example 11.16c defines a function called `get_data()` and another function called `create_model()`. The `get_data()` function will load the diabetes CSV data, plot the histogram, and plot the scatterplot. The `create_model()` function will create a deep learning model for the purpose of classification by using KerasClassifier.

EXAMPLE 11.16C: THE `KerasClassifier1.IPYNB` **PROGRAM (PART 3)**

```
# Get the data
def get_data():
        # load pima indians dataset
        dataset=pd.read_csv("/kaggle/input/pima-indians-diabetes-
database/diabetes.csv", delimiter=",")
        print(dataset.shape )
        print(dataset.head())

        # Plotting Histogram
        dataset.hist(figsize=(10,8))
        plt.show()

        # Plotting Scatterplot Matrix
        plt.rcParams['figure.figsize'] = [20, 20]
        scatter_matrix(dataset)
        plt.show()

        X = dataset.drop(['Outcome'],axis=1).values
        y = dataset['Outcome'].values

        X_train, X_test, y_train, y_test = train_test_split(X, y,
test_size=0.3)
        sc = StandardScaler()
        X_train = sc.fit_transform(X_train)
```

```
        X_test = sc.transform(X_test)
        return X_train, X_test, y_train, y_test

# Function to create model, required for KerasClassifier
def create_model():
    # create model
    model = Sequential()
    model.add(Dense(12, input_dim=8, activation='relu'))
    model.add(Dropout(rate = 0.1))
    model.add(Dense(8, activation='relu'))
    model.add(Dropout(rate = 0.1))
    model.add(Dense(1, activation='sigmoid'))
    # Compile model
    model.compile(loss='binary_crossentropy', optimizer='adam',
metrics=['accuracy'])
    return model
```

Example 11.16d calls the `get_data()` function, which loads in the diabetes CSV data, plots the histogram, and plots the scatterplot. It also uses KerasClassifier to create a model based on the `create_model()` function.

EXAMPLE 11.16D: THE `KerasClassifier1.IPYNB` **PROGRAM (PART 4)**

```
# get data
X_train, X_test, y_train, y_test = get_data()
# create model
model = KerasClassifier(build_fn=create_model, epochs=150, batch_
size=10, verbose=0)
```

The following shows the text output of the diabetes dataset information, which shows it has 768 samples and nine columns of features. The "Outcome" column indicates whether it is diabetic or not diabetic. It also shows the first five rows of the data.

```
(768, 9)
   Pregnancies  Glucose  BloodPressure  SkinThickness  Insulin   BMI  \
0            6      148             72             35        0  33.6
1            1       85             66             29        0  26.6
2            8      183             64              0        0  23.3
3            1       89             66             23       94  28.1
4            0      137             40             35      168  43.1

   DiabetesPedigreeFunction  Age  Outcome
0                     0.627   50        1
1                     0.351   31        0
2                     0.672   32        1
3                     0.167   21        0
4                     2.288   33        1
```

Figure 11.24 shows the scatterplot of the nine features of the Pima Indians Diabetes data, from which you can see the correlations of the different features against each other.

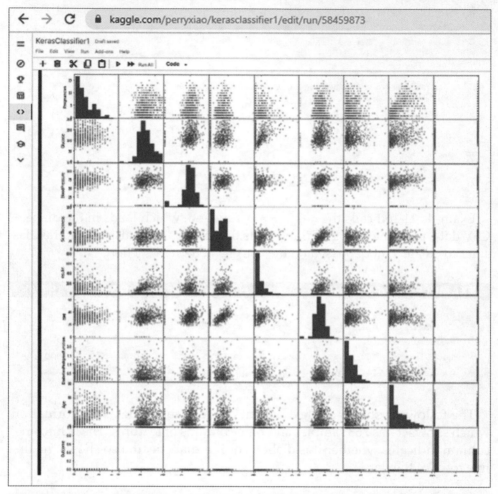

Figure 11.24: The scatterplot of the nine features of the Pima Indians Diabetes data.

Example 11.16e performs a cross validation of the KerasClassifier model.

EXAMPLE 11.16E: THE `KerasClassifier1.IPYNB` **PROGRAM (PART 5)**

```
seed = 7
numpy.random.seed(seed)
# evaluate using 10-fold cross validation
kfold = StratifiedKFold(n_splits=10, shuffle=True, random_state=seed)
results = cross_val_score(model, X_train, y_train, cv=kfold)
print("Mean: ", results.mean())
print("Variance: ", results.var())
```

The following is the output, which shows 75 percent accuracy and 0.002 variance:

```
Mean:  0.7578965842723846
Variance:  0.0024074942801846433
```

Example 11.16f shows the code for the KerasClassifier model with training data and performs the prediction on the testing data.

EXAMPLE 11.16F: THE `KerasClassifier1.IPYNB` **PROGRAM (PART 6)**

```
model.fit(X_train, y_train)
prediction = model.predict(X_test)
print(accuracy_score(y_test, prediction))
```

The output shows it has about 76 percent accuracy.

```
0.7575757575757576
```

EXERCISE 11.16

From a web browser, log in to your Kaggle account, follow the previous steps to build your own IPython notebook code, run the code, and comment on the results.

11.7.2   KerasRegressor

Example 11.17 shows a simple example of how to use KerasRegressor to perform regression on the physical exercise Linnerud dataset data. The Linnerud dataset has 20 samples of physical exercise data, with three features (Chins, Situps, Jumps) and three targets (Weight, Waist, Pulse). The Linnerud dataset is typically suitable for multiple output regressions.

In this example, it first builds a simple baseline deep learning model and then uses KerasRegressor to create an estimator based on the baseline model.

EXAMPLE 11.17: THE `KerasRegressor1.PY` **PROGRAM**

```
# Example 11.17
from sklearn import datasets, linear_model
from sklearn.model_selection import cross_val_score, KFold
from keras.models import Sequential
#from sklearn.metrics import accuracy_score
from keras.layers import Dense
from keras.wrappers.scikit_learn import KerasRegressor
from sklearn.preprocessing import StandardScaler
from sklearn.pipeline import Pipeline
```

```
import numpy as np

linnerud = datasets.load_linnerud()
print(linnerud.DESCR)
print(linnerud.data.shape)
print(linnerud.feature_names)
print(linnerud.target_names)
print(linnerud.target)

# Use only one feature
#linnerud_X = linnerud.data[:, np.newaxis, 0]
X = linnerud.data
# Choose one target 0: 'Weight', 1: 'Waist', 2:'Pulse'
#y = linnerud.target[:,1]
y = linnerud.target

# Split the data into training/testing sets
X_train = X[:-10]
X_test = X[-10:]
# Split the targets into training/testing sets
y_train = y[:-10]
y_test = y[-10:]

def baseline_model():
    model = Sequential()
    model.add(Dense(10, input_dim=3, activation='relu'))
    model.add(Dense(3))
    model.compile(loss='mean_squared_error', optimizer='adam')
    return model

seed = 1
estimator = KerasRegressor(build_fn=baseline_model, nb_epoch=100,
batch_size=100, verbose=False)
kfold = KFold(n_splits=10, random_state=seed, shuffle=True)
results = cross_val_score(estimator, X, y, cv=kfold)
print("Results: %.2f (%.2f) MSE" % (results.mean(), results.std()))

estimator.fit(X, y)
prediction = estimator.predict(X)

import numpy as np
train_error =  np.abs(y - prediction)
print("Mean Prediction Error: ", np.mean(train_error))
```

The following is the console output, which shows the details of the Linnerud dataset and the means and standard deviations of the regressor and the mean prediction error. Because we use only a simple model here, the errors are quite large.

```
Using TensorFlow backend.
.. _linnerrud_dataset:

Linnerud dataset
-----------------

**Data Set Characteristics:**

    :Number of Instances: 20
    :Number of Attributes: 3
    :Missing Attribute Values: None

The Linnerud dataset is a multi-output regression dataset. It consists
of three
excercise (data) and three physiological (target) variables collected
from
twenty middle-aged men in a fitness club:

- *physiological* - CSV containing 20 observations on 3 physiological
variables:
    Weight, Waist and Pulse.
- *exercise* - CSV containing 20 observations on 3 exercise variables:
    Chins, Situps and Jumps.

.. topic:: References

  * Tenenhaus, M. (1998). La regression PLS: theorie et pratique. Paris:
    Editions Technic.

(20, 3)
['Chins', 'Situps', 'Jumps']
['Weight', 'Waist', 'Pulse']
[[191.  36.  50.]
 [189.  37.  52.]
 [193.  38.  58.]
 [162.  35.  62.]
 [189.  35.  46.]
 [182.  36.  56.]
 [211.  38.  56.]
 [167.  34.  60.]
 [176.  31.  74.]
 [154.  33.  56.]
 [169.  34.  50.]
 [166.  33.  52.]
 [154.  34.  64.]
 [247.  46.  50.]
 [193.  36.  46.]
 [202.  37.  62.]
 [176.  37.  54.]
 [157.  32.  52.]
```

```
[156.  33.  54.]
[138.  33.  68.]]

Warning (from warnings module):
  File "C:\Program Files\Python36\lib\site-packages\sklearn\model_
selection\_split.py", line 297
    FutureWarning
FutureWarning: Setting a random_state has no effect since shuffle is
False. This will raise an error in 0.24. You should leave random_state
to its default (None), or set shuffle=True.
Results: -19721.18 (8690.13) MSE
Mean Prediction Error:  128.35342439015707
```

Example 11.18 shows an improved version of the previous example, which uses a larger deep learning model; it also uses Scikit-Learn's `Pipeline` to perform the regression. `Pipeline` is often used to assemble multiple estimators into one and automate the machine learning process.

EXAMPLE 11.18:   THE `KerasRegressor2.PY` PROGRAM

```python
# Example 11.18
from sklearn import datasets, linear_model
from sklearn.model_selection import cross_val_score, KFold
from keras.models import Sequential
#from sklearn.metrics import accuracy_score
from keras.layers import Dense
from keras.wrappers.scikit_learn import KerasRegressor
from sklearn.preprocessing import StandardScaler
from sklearn.pipeline import Pipeline

import numpy as np
import matplotlib.cm as cm

linnerud = datasets.load_linnerud()
#print(linnerud.DESCR)
#print(linnerud.data.shape)
#print(linnerud.feature_names)
#print(linnerud.target_names)
#print(linnerud.target)

# Use only one feature
#linnerud_X = linnerud.data[:, np.newaxis, 0]
X = linnerud.data
# Choose one target 0: 'Weight', 1: 'Waist', 2:'Pulse'
#y = linnerud.target[:,1]
y = linnerud.target

# Split the data into training/testing sets
X_train = X[:-10]
X_test = X[-10:]
```

```python
# Split the targets into training/testing sets
y_train = y[:-10]
y_test = y[-10:]


# define the model
def larger_model():
    # create model
    model = Sequential()
    model.add(Dense(20, input_dim=3, activation='relu'))
    model.add(Dense(10, activation='relu'))
    model.add(Dense(6, activation='relu'))
    model.add(Dense(3))
    # Compile model
    model.compile(loss='mean_squared_error', optimizer='adam')
    return model

seed = 1
np.random.seed(seed)
estimators = []
estimators.append(('standardize', StandardScaler()))
estimators.append(('mlp', KerasRegressor(build_fn=larger_model,
epochs=50, batch_size=5, verbose=0)))
pipeline = Pipeline(estimators)
kfold = KFold(n_splits=10, random_state=seed, shuffle=True)
results = cross_val_score(pipeline, X, y, cv=kfold, n_jobs=1)
print("Larger: %.2f (%.2f) MSE" % (results.mean(), results.std()))


pipeline.fit(X, y)
prediction = pipeline.predict(X)

import numpy as np
train_error = np.abs(y - prediction)
print("Mean Prediction Error: ", np.mean(train_error))
#print(np.min(train_error))
#print(np.max(train_error))
#print(np.std(train_error))

import matplotlib.pyplot as plt
plt.figure()
plt.subplot(2,1,1)

ys = [i for i in range(3)]
colors = cm.rainbow(np.linspace(0, 1, len(ys)))
for i, c in zip(ys, colors):
plt.scatter(y[:,i], prediction[:,i], color=c)

#plt.scatter(y,prediction)
plt.title('Prediction')
```

```
plt.subplot(2,1,2)
plt.scatter(y,train_error)
plt.title('Error')
plt.show()
```

The following is the console output, which shows a reduced prediction error:

```
Larger: -10523.43 (2416.25) MSE
Mean Prediction Error:  80.99469582041105
```

Figure 11.25 shows the output plot. The top shows the prediction results; the horizontal axis is the real data, and the vertical axis is the predicted data. By using random forest regression, as you can see, different target outputs have different performances. The bottom is the error of regression. The results show that "Waist" data gives the best regression results, with the predicted data close to a straight line with real data and with small errors. But the overall error is still large due to the small dataset.

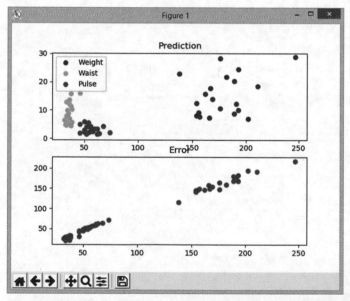

Figure 11.25: The prediction (top) and the error (bottom) of the random forest regression.

EXERCISE 11.17

Modify the previous code, try different Scikit-Learn datasets, see the following links, run the code, and comment on the results:

```
https://scikit-learn.org/stable/datasets/toy_dataset.html
https://scikit-learn.org/stable/datasets/real_world.html
```

11.8 SQL and NoSQL Databases

SQL or NoSQL, that is the question!

When you have a large amount of data, it is often better to save it into a database. Traditionally, this is done by using relational databases, in which data is saved in table format, and there are relationships between tables. You can work with the traditional relational databases with Structured English Query Language (SEQUEL), which is now commonly referred to as Structured Query Language (SQL). The relational databases are also called SQL databases.

The following are the popular SQL databases:

- MySQL

  `https://www.mysql.com/`

- PostgreSQL

  `https://www.postgresql.org/`

- Oracle

  `https://www.oracle.com/uk/database/`

- Microsoft SQL Server

  `https://www.microsoft.com/en-us/sql-server`

NoSQL is a relatively new type of database. Different from SQL, NoSQL is nonrelational and can handle more complex structures. With NoSQL, you can create documents without having to first define their structure, you can allow each document to have its own unique structure, you can have the syntax vary from database to database, and you can add fields as you go.

SQL is vertically scalable, which means you can increase the load by increasing CPU, RAM, and hard drive space on the server. NoSQL is horizontally scalable, which means you can handle more traffic by scaling up your database cluster, such as adding more servers. This is called *sharding*. This can be more powerful, making NoSQL databases the preferred choice for large or ever-changing datasets.

Table 11.1 shows a quick comparison of SQL and NoSQL.

Table 11.1: SQL vs. NoSQL

SQL	NOSQL
Relational	Nonrelational
Use the SQL language and have a predefined schema	Have dynamic schemas for unstructured data
Vertically scalable	Horizontally scalable
Table based	Document, key-value, graph, or wide-column stores based
Better for multirow transactions	Better for unstructured data like documents or JSON

Figure 11.26 shows the data differences between SQL and NoSQL.

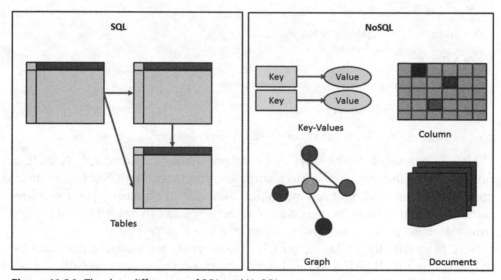

Figure 11.26: The data differences of SQL and NoSQL.

The following are the popular NoSQL databases:

- MongoDB

  https://www.mongodb.com/

- Apache Cassandra

  https://cassandra.apache.org/

- Google Cloud BigTable

  https://cloud.google.com/bigtable/

- XPlenty

  https://www.xplenty.com/

Next, let's look at some Python database examples.

SQLite3 is a Python integrated module for creating and managing small, lightweight SQL databases that can easily run on your local computer. See the following SQLite3 link for more details:

```
https://docs.python.org/3/library/sqlite3.html
```

Example 11.19 shows a simple SQLite3 example that shows how to create and connect to a database file, in this case called `test.db`, how to create a table called COURSE, how to insert a record into the table, and how to search the table and display the results.

EXAMPLE 11.19: THE `SQLite3 DEMO.PY` **PROGRAM**

```python
# Example 11.19 SQLite3
import sqlite3
# Create and Connect to the SQLite3 Database
conn = sqlite3.connect('test.db')
print ("Opened database successfully")


# Insert a Table ========================================
conn.execute('''CREATE TABLE IF NOT EXISTS COURSE
        (ID INT PRIMARY KEY     NOT NULL,
        NAME            TEXT    NOT NULL,
        STUDENT_NO      INT     NOT NULL,
        ADDRESS         CHAR(50),
        MARK            REAL);''')
print ("Table created successfully")


# Insert an record ========================================
conn.execute("INSERT INTO COURSE (ID,NAME,STUDENT_NO,ADDRESS,MARK) \
      VALUES (1, 'Billy', 202119, '103 Borough Road, London', 75.00
)");

#conn.commit()
print ("Records created successfully")

# Search the Table ========================================
cursor = conn.execute("SELECT id, name, address, mark from COURSE")
for row in cursor:
   print ("ID = ", row[0])
   print ("NAME = ", row[1])
   print ("ADDRESS = ", row[2])
   print ("MARK = ", row[3], "\n")

print ("Operation done successfully")
conn.close()
```

The following is the console output of the example:

```
Opened database successfully
Table created successfully
Records created successfully
ID = 1
NAME = Billy
ADDRESS = 103 Borough Road, London
MARK = 75.0

Operation done successfully
```

EXERCISE 11.18

Modify the previous code, add email and gender information into the database, run the code, and comment on the results.

MongoDB Altas is a cloud-based NoSQL database platform based on Amazon AWS, Microsoft Azure, and Google Cloud Platform (GCP). From its website, as shown in Figure 11.27, you can create an account or sign in with your Google account.

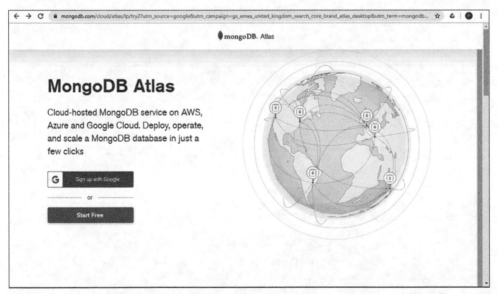

Figure 11.27: The MongoDB Atlas database website.
(Source: `https://cloud.mongodb.com/`)

Once you've created the account or signed in, you can name your organization, create your project, and choose the preferred language on the MongoDB cloud website.

After creating the project, you can choose clusters on the MongoDB cloud website; Shared Clusters is chosen here since it is free, as shown in Figure 11.28.

For the clusters you have chosen, you also need to choose providers, such as AWS, Azure, or GCP, as well as the region, such as Europe, North America, Asia or Australia.

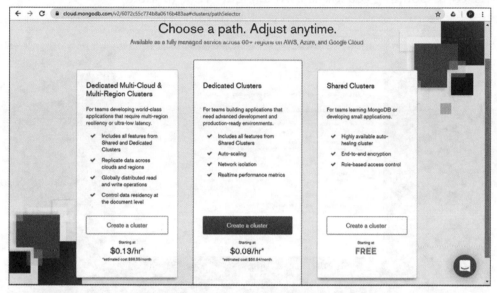

Figure 11.28: Choose Shared Clusters on the MongoDB cloud website.

The new cluster will now be created, which will take a few minutes. After the new cluster is created, click the Connect button to set up the connection, as shown in Figure 11.29.

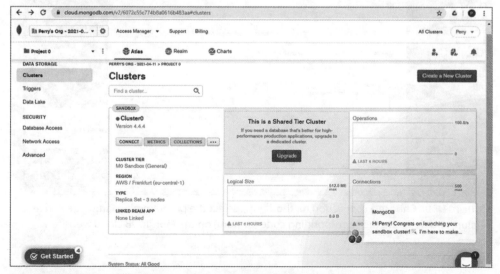

Figure 11.29: Creating the cluster on the MongoDB cloud website.

For the connection, you need to add a connection IP address and create a database user to the cluster.

Then you need to choose a connection method; for this you choose the "Connect your application" method, as shown in Figure 11.30 (top). Then you need to select the programming language and its version and generate the corresponding code, as shown in Figure 11.30 (bottom).

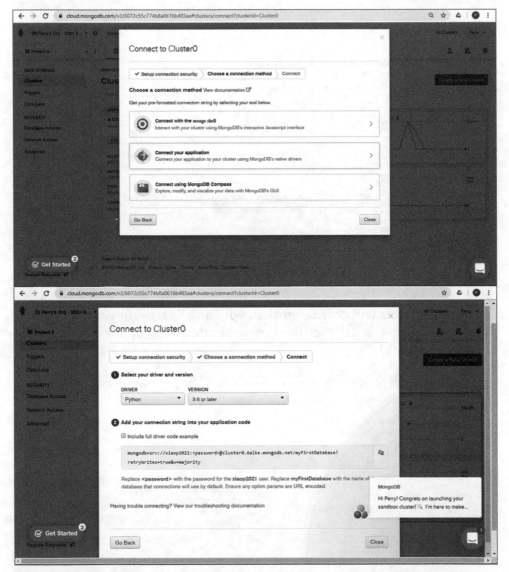

Figure 11.30: Choose a connection method (top), select the programming language and its version, and generate the corresponding code (bottom) on the MongoDB cloud website.

Now you are ready to connect to your MongoDB cloud database with Python.

Example 11.20 shows a simple MongoDB example code, which shows how to connect to a MongoDB database cluster in the cloud, how to create a database called `test`, how to insert records (called *posts*) into the `test` database, and how to search the database. In this case, the posts are in JavaScript Object Notation (JSON) format, which is popular with web applications.

You will need to install two libraries for the example.

```
pip install pymongo
pip install dnspython
```

Also, remember to replace the content inside `MongoClient("...")` with your own generated code, and replace `<username>` and `<password>` with your own username and password for the MongoDB database.

EXAMPLE 11.20: **THE** `MongoDB TEST.PY` **PROGRAM**

```
# Example 11.20
# pip install pymongo
# pip install dnspython
import pymongo
from pymongo import MongoClient

# Replace the content inside MongoClient("...") with your own
generated code
# Replace <username> and <password> with your own username and
password
cluster = MongoClient("mongodb+srv://<username>:<password>@cluster0.6
alke.mongodb.net/myFirstDatabase?retryWrites=true&w=majority")
db = cluster.test
collection = db['test']

post1 = {"_id": 0, "name": "Tom", "mark": 54}
post2 = {"_id": 1, "name": "John", "mark": 78}
#collection.insert_one(post1)
collection.insert_many([post1,post2])

#results = collection.find()
results = collection.find({"name":"John"})
for result in results:
    print(result)
```

The following is the console output, which shows the search results:

```
{'_id': 1, 'name': 'John', 'mark': 78}
```

From your MongoDB cloud website, click the Collections tab. You can see the corresponding changes: a `test` database will be created, and two posts will be inserted, as shown in Figure 11.31.

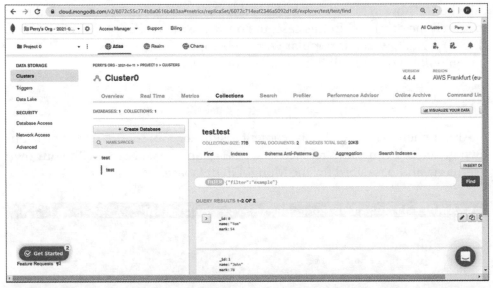

Figure 11.31: The corresponding changes on the MongoDB cloud website.

EXERCISE 11.19

Modify the previous code, add more records to the MongoDB, run the code, and comment on the results.

Example 11.21 shows how to save image files into MongoDB by using the GridFS library.

Also, remember to replace the content inside `MongoClient("...")` with your own generated code, and replace `<username>` and `<password>` with your own username and password for the MongoDB database.

EXAMPLE 11.21: THE `MongoDB TEST2.PY` **PROGRAM**

```
# Example 11.21
# pip install pymongo
# pip install dnspython
import pymongo
from pymongo import MongoClient


# Replace the content inside MongoClient("...") with your own
generated code
# Replace <username> and <password> with your own username and
password
```

```
cluster = MongoClient("mongodb+srv://<username>:<password>@cluster0.6
alke.mongodb.net/myFirstDatabase?retryWrites=true&w=majority")
db = cluster.test
collection = db['test']

#Save image to MongoDB
import gridfs

#Create an object of GridFs for the above database.
fs = gridfs.GridFS(db)

#define an image object with the location.
file = "child.jpg"

#Open the image in read-only format.
with open(file, 'rb') as f:
    contents = f.read()

#Now store/put the image via GridFs object.
fs.put(contents, filename="file")
```

Figure 11.32 shows the corresponding image file has been created in the MongoDB cloud website.

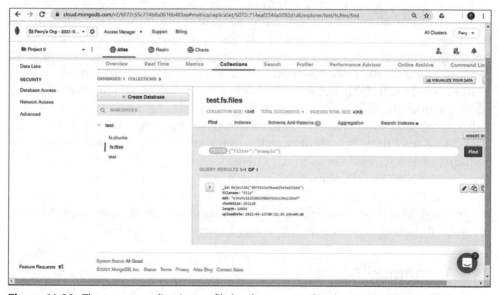

Figure 11.32: The corresponding image file has been created in the MongoDB cloud website.

EXERCISE 11.20

Modify the previous code, add more image files to MongoDB, run the code, and comment on the results.

The following are a few related tutorials:

```
https://www.mongodb.com/blog/post/getting-started-with-python-
and-mongodb
https://pymongo.readthedocs.io/en/stable/tutorial.html
https://www.w3schools.com/python/python_mongodb_getstarted.asp
https://realpython.com/introduction-to-mongodb-and-python/
```

11.9   Immutable Database

Traditional databases are not immutable, which means they do not record the changes. So, when something has changed or is being hacked, you do not know what has been changed or when it was changed. In the other words, there is no way to know whether your database has been compromised. This is not desirable for many applications, such as bank transactions, supply chain records, art and antique records, and so on.

To solve this problem, the immutable database was introduced. Nothing is ever deleted or changed without a record in an immutable database. All the database operations are recorded in a blockchain-based ledger with the cryptographic verification. With immutable databases, you can track changes in sensitive data in your databases and then record those changes indelibly in a tamperproof immutable database. This allows you to keep an indelible history of all the operations.

Immutable databases are centralized database systems where information is stored in a way that its integrity can be cryptographically verified. Every data change is tracked, and the complete history of changes is maintained so that the "integrity of the database" can be verified over time. This is why we call them *immutable*, because the history of all changes performed in the data store is maintained so that whenever there is an unintended or malicious modification, it can be detected, reported, and in many cases even recovered.

11.9.1   Immudb

Immudb is a lightweight, high-speed immutable database for systems and applications. It is an open source database under the Apache v2.0 license and claims to be the fastest immutable database.

Immudb is immutable, which means you can only add records but never change or delete records. Data stored in Immudb is encrypted and verifiable, just like blockchains, but without the complexity. Immudb is simple and easy to use, and it supports programming languages such as node.js, Java, Python, Golang, .NET, and more. You can run Immudb on Linux, Windows, and macOS, as well as Kubernetes and Docker.

For more details, check the following Immudb GitHub and official websites:

```
https://github.com/codenotary/immudb
https://www.codenotary.com/technologies/immudb/
https://docs.immudb.io/master/
```

Immudb also has an impressive online playground for you to play with without the hassle of installation and configuration, see the following link for details.

```
https://play.codenotary.com/
```

The following are the Linux commands to log in and get started with the Immudb database:

```
Bash-5.1#immuclient login immudb
Password: immudb
Bash-5.1#immuclient
immuclient>set balance 9000
immuclient>get balance
immuclient>history balance
immuclient>safeget balance
```

The following is the simple Python code to save a key-value pair in the Immudb database and to retrieve it:

```
from immudb.client import ImmudbClient
ic = ImmudbClient("localhost:3322")
ic.login(username = "immudb", password = "immudb")
key = "Hello".encode('utf8')
value = "Immutable world".encode('utf8')
ic.set(key, value)
readback = ic.get(key)
saved_value = readback.value.decode('utf8')
key = key.decode('utf8')
print(key, saved_value)
print("The transaction number was ", readback.tx)
```

11.9.2   Amazon Quantum Ledger Database

Amazon also provides its own immutable database called Amazon Quantum Ledger Database (QLDB), which is a fully managed ledger database that provides a transparent, immutable, and cryptographically verifiable transaction log owned by a central trusted authority. With Amazon QLDB, you can track every application data change and maintain a complete and verifiable history of changes over time.

For more details about QLDB, visit the following:

```
https://aws.amazon.com/qldb/
```

11.10   Summary

This chapter covers topics of data analysis. The most commonly used data analysis technique is regression, which investigates the relationship between the dependent and independent sets of variables. Traditional regression techniques include linear regression, logistic regression, polynomial regression, and so on. Modern approaches use machine learning for regression, such as support vector regression, nearest neighbors regression, Gaussian process regression (GPR), and random forest regression. You can also use partial least squares regression and principal component regression for analyzing the spectral data.

With time-series data, you can use deep learning recurrent neural network models to predict future data. You can also use seasonal-trend decomposition using LOESS, or STL, for decomposing time-series data into trend, seasonal, and residual.

Predictive maintenance analysis is to analyze the data and predict the remaining useful life (RUL) of an equipment.

Anomaly detection is to detect abnormal data in a dataset. It is widely used as fraud detection in banking, healthcare, and many other businesses.

KerasClassifier and KerasRegressor are convenient wrapper classes in Keras for deep learning models to train classification or regression estimators in the Scikit-Learn library.

NoSQL is a relatively new type of databases, different from traditional SQL databases. NoSQL is nonrelational and is more powerful in processing complex, unstructured data.

With immutable databases, you can track changes in your databases and keep an indelible history of all the operations.

11.11   Chapter Review Questions

Q11.1.   What is data analysis? Give a few examples in your life and work.

Q11.2.   What is regression? What is multiple linear regression?

Q11.3.   What is support vector regression (SVR)? Explain the differences between linear SVR, poly SVR, and RBF SVR.

Q11.4.   What is the difference between regression and classification?

Q11.5.   What is time-series data? Give a few examples.

Q11.6.   What is predictive maintenance analysis?

Q11.7.   What is remaining useful life?

Q11.8.   What is anomaly detection?

Q11.9.   What is fraud detection?

Q11.10. What is KerasClassifier?

Q11.11. What is KerasRegressor?

Q11.12. What is a SQL database?

Q11.13. What is a NoSQL database?

Q11.14. What is an immutable database?

CHAPTER

12

Advanced AI Computing

"AI is neither good nor evil. It's a tool. It's a technology for us to use."

—Oren Etzioni (American computer scientist)

CHAPTER OUTLINE

12.1 Introduction
12.2 AI with Graphics Processing Unit
12.3 AI with Tensor Processing Unit
12.4 AI with Intelligence Processing Unit
12.5 AI with Cloud Computing
12.6 Web-Based AI
12.7 Packaging the Code
12.8 AI with Edge Computing (Raspberry Pi, Google TPU Kit)
12.9 Create a Mobile AI App
12.10 Quantum AI
12.11 Summary
12.12 Chapter Review Questions

12.1   Introduction

Artificial intelligence algorithms are often computationally intensive and resource hungry; therefore, they are commonly run on graphic processing units (GPUs) and tensor processing units (TPUs). GPU and TPU hardware

are often expensive; therefore, it is popular to utilize GPU and TPU capabilities through online platforms such as Google Colab and Kaggle.

Apart from running artificial intelligence algorithms on local computers, laptops, or desktops, artificial intelligence algorithms are also being increasingly run on remote servers; this is called *cloud computing*, or cloud AI. Whey they run on embedded devices, such as Raspberry Pi, microcontrollers, or your mobile phones, this is called *edge computing*, or edge AI.

Cloud AI and edge AI are getting more attention due to the fast development of the Internet of Things (IoT).

In this chapter, we will first introduce AI with GPUs and TPUs and then introduce cloud AI; we'll also show how to develop web-based AI applications. We will also cover packaging your AI code, using Kubernetes (K8s) and Docker, understanding edge AI, developing mobile AI applications, and finally understanding quantum AI.

12.2   AI with Graphics Processing Unit

A GPU is an electronic graphics acceleration card, a term popularized by Nvidia. Unlike a CPU, which is designed to perform general-purpose computing and sequential computing tasks, a GPU is designed for processing large blocks of data in parallel. Figure 12.1 shows the key differences between CPU and GPU architectures, where a GPU has a vast number of arithmetic logic units (ALUs). GPUs were originally designed for gaming for fast processing the images and now is being increasingly used for AI, due to its massive parallel data processing capabilities. It is fair to say that GPU has ignited a worldwide AI boom and has become a key part of modern supercomputing infrastructure.

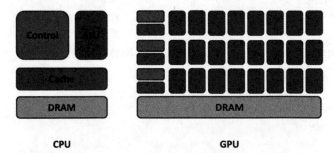

Figure 12.1: The CPU and GPU architectures where GPU has a vast number of ALUs

The following shows the NVidia website for its latest GeForce RTX 3080 GPU.

```
https://www.nvidia.com/en-gb/geforce/graphics-cards/30-series/
rtx-3080/
```

Figure 12.2 shows the Dive to Deep Learning (D2L) website for selecting servers and GPUs for AI computing. For the chart you can see the best performance for the price is the NVidia GTX 9XX series and then the GTX 10XX series, RTX 20XX. The Titan series gives the best performance but also is the most expensive option.

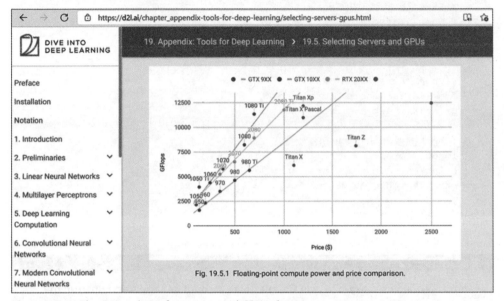

Figure 12.2: The D2L website for servers and GPU selection

(Source: `https://d2l.ai/chapter_appendix-tools-for-deep-learning/ selecting-servers-gpus.html`)

According to the following article, the best GPU performance per dollar is the latest NVidia GeForce RTX 3080 (10GB):

`https://timdettmers.com/2020/09/07/which-gpu-for-deep-learning/`

To use GPUs on your local computer, you need to follow these steps:

1. Download and install the Nvidia GPU drivers.

   `https://www.nvidia.com/Download/index.aspx`

2. Download and install the Nvidia CUDA Toolkit.

   `https://developer.nvidia.com/cuda-toolkit`

3. Download and install the GPU and install the cuDNN library.

   `https://docs.nvidia.com/deeplearning/cudnn/install-guide/index .html`

4. Install the TensorFlow-GPU library.

   `https://www.tensorflow.org/install/gpu`

After installation, you can run the code shown in Example 12.1 to test if GPUs are working for TensorFlow, Keras, or PyTorch. Example 12.1 shows a simple GPU test example.

EXAMPLE 12.1:   THE `GPUTest.PY` **PROGRAM**

```
# Example 12.1 GPUTest.py
# Check TensorFlow with GPU
from tensorflow.python.client import device_lib
print(device_lib.list_local_devices())

# Check Keras with GPU
from keras import backend as K
print(K._get_available_gpus())

#Check PyTorch with GPU
import torch
print(torch.cuda.is_available())
print(torch.cuda.get_device_name())
```

EXERCISE 12.1

From a web browser, log in to your Google Colab account or Kaggle account, run the previous code, and comment on the results.

For more details about GPU for AI computing, see the following:

```
https://developer.nvidia.com/deep-learning
https://www.quora.com/What-is-currently-the-best-GPU-for-deep-learning
https://lambdalabs.com/blog/choosing-a-gpu-for-deep-learning/
https://www.tomshardware.com/uk/reviews/gpu-buying-guide,5844.html
```

The following shows the Google Colab Notebook example for using TensorFlow with GPU.

```
https://colab.research.google.com/notebooks/gpu.ipynb
```

Example 12.2 shows a simple GPU test example, which not only shows what GPU you have on your computer but also shows how long it takes to run a simple MNIST data classification code on GPU and on CPU.

EXAMPLE 12.2:   THE `GPUTest2.py` **PROGRAM**

```
# Example 12.2 GPUTest2.ipynb
#import tensorflow and print the version
import tensorflow as tf
print(tf.__version__)
```

```
#Display GPU info
device_name = tf.test.gpu_device_name()
if device_name != '/device:GPU:0':
  raise SystemError('GPU device not found')
print('Found GPU at: {}'.format(device_name))

import time
def current_milli_time():
    return round(time.time() * 1000)

#Test MNIST data on GPU
t0 = current_milli_time()
mnist=tf.keras.datasets.mnist
(x_train, y_train), (x_test, y_test) = mnist.load_data()
x_train, x_test = x_train / 255.0, x_test/255.0
with tf.device('/GPU:0'):
  model=tf.keras.models.Sequential([
      tf.keras.layers.Flatten(input_shape=(28,28)),
      tf.keras.layers.Dense(512, activation=tf.nn.relu),
      tf.keras.layers.Dropout(0.2),
      tf.keras.layers.Dense(10, activation=tf.nn.softmax)
  ])
  model.compile(optimizer='adam',
                loss='sparse_categorical_crossentropy')
  #              metices=['accuracy'])
  model.fit(x_train, y_train, epochs=5)
  model.evaluate(x_test, y_test)
  dt = current_milli_time() - t0
  print("time: ",dt)


  #Test MNIST data on CPU
  t0 = current_milli_time()
  with tf.device('/CPU:0'):
    model=tf.keras.models.Sequential([
        tf.keras.layers.Flatten(input_shape=(28,28)),
        tf.keras.layers.Dense(512, activation=tf.nn.relu),
        tf.keras.layers.Dropout(0.2),
        tf.keras.layers.Dense(10, activation=tf.nn.softmax)
  ])
  model.compile(optimizer='adam',
                loss='sparse_categorical_crossentropy')
  model.fit(x_train, y_train, epochs=5)
  model.evaluate(x_test, y_test)
  dt = current_milli_time() - t0
  print("time: ",dt)

from tensorflow.python.client import device_lib
device_lib.list_local_devices()
```

12.3 AI with Tensor Processing Unit

A TPU is a new type of hardware developed by Google for the purpose of AI computing. It is specially designed for tensor operations. In AI computing, a tensor is a multidimensional object that describes a multilinear relationship between sets of algebraic objects related to a vector space. Figure 12.3 shows the differences between scalars, vectors, matrixes, and tensors.

Scalar	Vector	Matrix	Tensor
3	$\begin{bmatrix} 5 \\ 4 \\ 7 \end{bmatrix}$	$\begin{bmatrix} 1 & 7 & 2 \\ 3 & 2 & 4 \\ 2 & 1 & 7 \end{bmatrix}$	$\begin{bmatrix} 4 & 6 & 9 \\ 3 & 9 & 3 \\ 5 & 7 & 5 \end{bmatrix} \begin{bmatrix} 1 & 7 & 2 \\ 3 & 2 & 4 \\ 2 & 1 & 7 \end{bmatrix}$ $\begin{bmatrix} 6 & 3 & 3 \\ 1 & 2 & 6 \\ 2 & 5 & 1 \end{bmatrix} \begin{bmatrix} 4 & 3 & 2 \\ 8 & 2 & 4 \\ 7 & 1 & 3 \end{bmatrix}$

Figure 12.3: The differences between scalars, vectors, matrixes, and tensors

Figure 12.4 shows the Google Cloud website for TPU architecture.

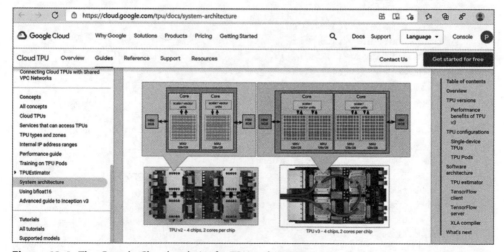

Figure 12.4: The Google Cloud website for TPU architecture

(Source: https://cloud.google.com/tpu/docs/system-architecture)

The following shows the Google Colab Notebook example for using TPUs in Colab. It uses a flower classification example to show how to use TPUs in Google Colab for training models as well as performing classifications.

```
https://colab.research.google.com/notebooks/tpu.ipynb
```

Example 12.3 shows a simple TPU test example, which first initializes the TPUs, displays the TPUs information, and then performs a simple matrix calculation on TPUs and CPUs. You need to upload this code to your Google Colab to run it.

EXAMPLE 12.3:   THE TPU_TEST.PY PROGRAM

```python
# Example 12.3 TPU Test
#import tensorflow and print the version
import tensorflow as tf
print(tf.__version__)

#Display TPU info
resolver = tf.distribute.cluster_resolver.TPUClusterResolver(tpu='')
tf.config.experimental_connect_to_cluster(resolver)
# This is the TPU initialization code that has to be at the
beginning.
tf.tpu.experimental.initialize_tpu_system(resolver)
print("All devices: ", tf.config.list_logical_devices('TPU'))

import time
def current_milli_time():
    return round(time.time() * 1000)

#Test Matrix calculation on TPU
t0 = current_milli_time()
a = tf.constant([[1.0, 2.0, 3.0], [4.0, 5.0, 6.0]])
b = tf.constant([[1.0, 2.0], [3.0, 4.0], [5.0, 6.0]])
with tf.device('/TPU:0'):
  c = tf.matmul(a, b)
print("c device: ", c.device)
print(c)
dt = current_milli_time() - t0
print("TPU time: ",dt)

#Test calculation on CPU
t0 = current_milli_time()
a = tf.constant([[1.0, 2.0, 3.0], [4.0, 5.0, 6.0]])
b = tf.constant([[1.0, 2.0], [3.0, 4.0], [5.0, 6.0]])
with tf.device('/CPU:0'):
  c = tf.matmul(a, b)
print("c device: ", c.device)
print(c)
```

```
dt = current_milli_time() - t0
print("CPU time: ",dt)

#Display the CPU GPU TPU information
from tensorflow.python.client import device_lib
device_lib.list_local_devices()
```

EXERCISE 12.3

From a web browser, log in to your Google Colab account, run the previous code, and comment on the results.

For more information about TPUs, check the following:

```
https://www.kdnuggets.com/2019/03/train-keras-model-20x-faster-
tpu-free.html
```

The following is a quick comparison of CPU, GPU, and TPU:

Performance

- A CPU can handle tens of operations per cycle.
- A GPU can handle tens of thousands of operations per cycle.
- A TPU can handle up to 128,000 operations per cycle.

Purpose

- A CPU is a processor designed to solve a general-purpose computational problem. The cache and memory are also designed to be optimal for general programming problems.
- A GPU is a processor designed to accelerate the rendering of graphics. It also has been used for machine learning model training and inference.
- A TPU is a processor designed to accelerate deep learning tasks developed using TensorFlow. It is not for general-purpose programming.

AI Computing

- A CPU achieves the highest floating-point operations per second (FLOPS) utilization for RNNs and supports the largest model because of a large memory capacity.
- A GPU is optimized for training a model in deep learning requires a huge amount of parallel data, due to its parallel computing capability.
- A TPU is highly optimized for large batches and CNNs and has the highest training throughput.

Manufacturers

- **CPU:** Intel, AMD, Qualcomm, NVIDIA, IBM, Samsung, Hewlett-Packard, VIA, Atmel and many others
- **GPU:** NVIDIA, AMD, Broadcom Limited, Imagination Technologies (PowerVR)
- **TPU:** Google

12.4 AI with Intelligence Processing Unit

As discussed in Chapter 1, an intelligence processing unit (IPU) is a new form of artificial intelligence computing infrastructure, developed by Graphcore, a company based in Bristol, United Kingdom. An IPU has shown improved performances and is more cost effective than the traditional GPU. It is particularly suitable for natural language processing and computer vision.

Graphcore's entry-level product is the IPU-Machine: IPU-M2000. It is built with the powerful Colossus MK2 IPU, packed with 1 petaFLOP of AI compute with up to 526GB Exchange-Memory in a slim 1U blade.

The IPU-Machine: IPU-M2000 `https://www.graphcore.ai/products/`
`mk2/ipu-m2000-ipu-pod4`

There are also more advanced products, such as IPU-POD$_{16}$, which is basically preconfigured with a four-petaFLOPS AI system, and IPU-POD$_{64}$, which is a 16-petaFLOPS AI system. See the following links for details:

`https://www.graphcore.ai/products/mk2/ipu-pod16`
`https://www.graphcore.ai/products/mk2/ipu-pod64`

Graphcore provides a cloud-based AI computing service called Graphcloud, which is a secure, cloud-based, commercial machine learning (ML) platform running on Graphcore MK2 IPU-POD systems hosted by Cirrascale in partnership with Graphcore and available to customers worldwide.

Graphcloud `https://www.graphcore.ai/graphcloud`
Graphcore also runs an academic program, which is designed to support professors, researchers, principal investigators, and graduate students conducting and publishing research using IPUs or in their coursework or teaching.

- Graphcore academic program:
  `https://www.graphcore.ai/academic`

- Graphcore resources:
  `https://www.graphcore.ai/resources`

- Graphcore software documents:
  `https://docs.graphcore.ai/en/latest/`

12.5   AI with Cloud Computing

Cloud computing is the online computing platform that provides services such as virtual machines (VMs) (Linux or Windows), databases (SQL and NoSQL), storage, applications, and other services, typically with pay-as-you-go pricing. Cloud computing is no doubt the future, with more and more businesses relying on cloud computing. The largest three clouding computing providers are Amazon AWS, Microsoft Azure, and Google GCP, followed by IBM, Oracle, Baidu, and others.

Cloud computing typically offers their services according to the following three standard models:

- Infrastructure as a service (IaaS)
- Platform as a service (PaaS)
- Software as a service (SaaS)

Figure 12.5 shows the differences between on-premises, infrastructure as a service (IaaS), platform as a service (PaaS), and software as a service (SaaS). On-premises is the traditional way of providing computing services, in which the organization is responsible for all the hardware and software; this approach can be expensive and difficult to scale. With cloud computing, the organization can choose IaaS, PaaS, or SaaS, according to its requirements. This can be cheaper, more flexible, and easier to scale.

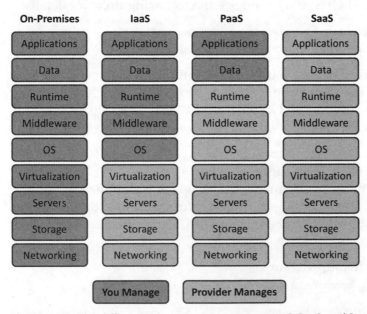

Figure 12.5: The differences between on-premises, IaaS, PaaS, and SaaS

12.5.1   Amazon AWS

Amazon Web Services (Amazon AWS) is the largest cloud computing provider. Started in 2006, Amazon AWS provides more than 175 services, in 190 countries around the world.

The following shows the Amazon AWS website for machine learning.

```
https://aws.amazon.com/machine-learning/
```

To use Amazon AWS, first you need to create a free AWS account; it might ask for your bank information, but it is free for one year:

```
https://aws.amazon.com/free/
```

The following are a list of tasks I recommend for getting familiar with Amazon AWS.

Please remember to do each task within the same day, and when you finish, delete the services you created; otherwise, you might get charged.

Task 1 Run a serverless `Hello, World!` with AWS Lambda.

```
https://aws.amazon.com/getting-started/hands-on/run-serverless-code/
```

Task 2 Store and retrieve a file.

```
https://aws.amazon.com/getting-started/hands-on/backup-files-
   to-amazon-s3/
```

Task 3 Remotely run commands on an EC2 instance with AWS systems Manager.

```
https://aws.amazon.com/getting-started/hands-on/remotely-run-
   commands-ec2-instance-systems-manager/
```

Task 4 Create and query a NoSQL table with Amazon DynamoDB.

```
https://aws.amazon.com/getting-started/hands-on/create-nosql-table/
```

Task 5 Detect, analyze, and compare faces with Amazon Rekognition.

```
https://aws.amazon.com/getting-started/hands-on/detect-analyze-
   compare-faces-rekognition/
```

Task 6 Create an audio transcript with Amazon Transcribe.

```
https://aws.amazon.com/getting-started/hands-on/create-audio-
   transcript-transcribe/
```

Task 7 Analyze sentiment in text with Amazon Comprehend.

```
https://aws.amazon.com/getting-started/hands-on/analyze-sentiment-
   comprehend/
```

Task 8 Create a simple web application using AWS Amplify.

```
https://aws.amazon.com/getting-started/hands-on/deploy-react-app-
   cicd-amplify/
```

Please note the following tasks using Amazon Lightsail, which is free for one month only:

Task 9 Launch and configure a WordPress instance with Amazon Lightsail.

```
https://aws.amazon.com/getting-started/hands-on/launch-a-wordpress-
website/?trk=gs_card
```

Task 10 Launch a Linux virtual machine with Amazon Lightsail.

```
https://aws.amazon.com/getting-started/hands-on/launch-a-virtual-
   machine/
```

Task 11 Launch a Windows virtual machine in Amazon Lightsail.

```
https://aws.amazon.com/getting-started/hands-on/launch-windows-vm/
```

Also, here is a PDF version of the AWS Getting Started guide:

```
https://awsdocs.s3.amazonaws.com/gettingstarted/latest/
awsgsg-intro.pdf
```

Here are a few YouTube links from `Simplilearn` and `Edureka!` to get started:

```
https://www.youtube.com/watch?v=r4YIdn2eTm4&list=PLEiEAq2VkUUL1N
tIFhEQHo8gacvme35rz
https://www.youtube.com/watch?time_continue=15&v=RY5FdAk7jp4&
feature=emb_logo
https://www.youtube.com/watch?v=k1RI5locZE4
```

12.5.2   Microsoft Azure

Microsoft Azure is a cloud computing platform, launched in February 2010. It is an open and flexible cloud platform that helps in development, data storage, service hosting, and service management. Microsoft Azure has more than 50 worldwide data centers, and 90 percent of Fortune 500 companies now rely on Microsoft Azure.

The following shows the Microsoft Azure website.

```
https://azure.microsoft.com/en-us/
```

To get started with Microsoft Azure, you can also apply for a 12-month free account. The following are the Microsoft Azure sites for machine learning, as well as a step-by-step tutorial on how to create no-code predictive models with Azure machine learning.

```
https://azure.microsoft.com/en-gb/services/machine-learning/
https://docs.microsoft.com/en-us/learn/paths/create-no-code-
predictive-models-azure-machine-learning/
```

The following are some more tutorials about Microsoft Azure:

```
https://www.tutorialspoint.com/microsoft_azure/index.htm
https://mindmajix.com/microsoft-azure-tutorial
```

12.5.3   Google Cloud Platform

Google Cloud Platform (GCP) is relatively new and relatively small compared with Amazon AWS and Microsoft Azure. Started in 2011, Google GCP provides a suite of cloud computing services including computing, data storage, data analytics, and machine learning. Google Cloud Platform is available in 24 regions and 73 zones around the world. The following shows the Google GCP website.

```
https://cloud.google.com/gcp/getting-started
```

The following are some interesting tutorials:

```
https://www.freecodecamp.org/news/google-cloud-platform-from-
zero-to-hero/
```

```
https://www.javatpoint.com/google-cloud-platform
```

```
https://www.edureka.co/blog/google-cloud-platform-tutorial/
```

12.5.4   Comparison of AWS, Azure, and GCP

The following are some major differences between Amazon AWS versus Microsoft Azure versus Google Cloud Platform (GCP):

- Amazon AWS charges for its VMs per hour. It uses a pay-as-you-go model. Microsoft Azure VMs are charged per minute. Google GCP VMs are charged per minute.

- Amazon AWS uses ECS as Docker management, while Microsoft Azure uses Container Services, and Google GCP uses Container Engine.

- Amazon AWS uses the Glacier for archive storage. Microsoft Azure uses Archive Storage, and Google GCP uses Coldline Storage.

- Amazon AWS uses Amazon Cloud Search for the search service. Microsoft Azure uses Azure Search. Google GCP uses Google Cloud Search.

- Amazon AWS uses Amazon Kinesis for analytics. Microsoft Azure uses Azure Stream Analytics. Google GCP uses Cloud Dataflow and Cloud Data prepare for analytics.

- Amazon AWS uses AWS OpsWorks for automation. Microsoft Azure uses Azure Automation. Google GCP uses Compute Engine management with Puppet, Chef, and so on.

- Amazon AWS uses AWS cloud HSM compliance. Microsoft Azure uses the Azure Trust Center. Google GCP uses Cloud Platform Security for compliance.

- Amazon AWS uses the AWS key management service for security credentials. Microsoft Azure uses Azure Key Vault. Google GCP uses Google Cloud Platform Security.

Table 12.1 compares the top features between AWS versus Azure versus GCP.

Table 12.1: Top Feature Comparison Between AWS vs. Azure vs. GCP

FEATURES	AWS	AZURE	GCP
Website	https://aws.amazon.com	https://azure.microsoft.com	https://cloud.google.com
Revenue (2020)	$12B	$8B	$2B
Market share (2019)	33%	18%	8%
Global coverage	Regions: 25	Regions: 60+	Regions: 24
	Zones: 80	Countries: 140	Zone: 73
	Countries: 245		Countries: 35
High-profile customers	Netflix	eBay	HSBC
	Unilever	Apple	Snapchat
	Samsung	Pixar	HTC
	MI	HP	Phillips
	Airbnb	Honeywell	Spotify
	BMW	Pearson	
	ESPN	Ford	
	AstraZeneca	NBC News	
	Financial Times	Easyjet	
	Dow Jones		
	Nasdaq		
	Nike		
	Pfizer		
	McDonald's		
Number of services	212	100+	60+
Processors	128	128	96

Table 12.2 compares the compute services between AWS versus Azure versus GCP.

Table 12.2: Compute Services Comparison Between AWS vs. Azure vs. GCP

COMPUTE SERVICES	AWS	AZURE	GCP
Infrastructure as a service	Amazon EC2	Virtual Machines	Google Compute Engine
Platform as a service	AWS Elastic Beanstalk	App Service and Cloud Services	Google App Engine
Container services	Amazon Elastic Container Service	Azure Kubernetes Service or AKS	Google Kubernetes Engine
Serverless computing	Amazon Lambda	Azure Functions	Cloud Functions
Media services	Amazon Elastic Transcoder	Azure Media Services	Cloud Video Intelligence API
AI/ML	1) SageMaker 2) Comprehend 3) Lex 4) Polly 5) Rekognition 6) Machine Learning 7) Translate 8) Transcribe 9) DeepLens 10) Deep Learning AMIs 11) Apache MXNet on AWS 12) TensorFlow on AWS	1) Machine Learning 2) Azure Bot Service 3) Cognitive Services	1) Cloud Machine Learning Engine 2) Dialogflow Enterprise Edition 5) Cloud Natural Language 6) Cloud Speech API 7) Cloud Translation API 8) Cloud Video Intelligence 9) Cloud Job Discovery (Private Beta)

Table 12.3 shows the storage services comparison between AWS versus Azure versus GCP.

Table 12.3: Storage Comparison Between AWS vs. Azure vs. GCP

STORAGE	AWS	AZURE	GCP
Object storage	Amazon S3	Azure Disk Storage	Google Cloud Storage
Block store	Amazon EBS	Azure Blob Storage	Google Compute Engine (Persistent Disks)
Archival/cold storage	Amazon Glacier	Azure Archive Blob Storage	Google Nearline/ Coldline
File system storage	Amazon EFS	Azure File Storage	Google ZFS

Table 12.4 shows the database services comparison between AWS versus Azure versus GCP.

Table 12.4: Database Comparison Between AWS vs. Azure vs. GCP

DATABASE	AWS	AZURE	GCP
Relation DB	Amazon RDS	SQL DB	Google Cloud SQL
NoSQL DB: Key-value	Amazon DynamoDB	Table Storage	Google Cloud Datastore, Google Cloud Bigtable
NoSQL DB: With Indexing	Amazon SimpleDB	Azure Cosmos DB	Google Cloud Datastore
Relation DB	Amazon RDS	SQL DB	Google Cloud SQL

Table 12.5 compares the pricing between AWS versus Azure versus GCP.

Table 12.5: Pricing Comparison Between AWS vs. Azure vs. GCP

PRICING	AWS	AZURE	GCP
A small virtual instance with minimum RAM and virtual CPU	$69 per month	$70 to 75 per month	$50 to 55 per month
A small virtual instance with 4TB of RAM, and around 128 virtual CPUs	$2,700 to $3,000 per month	$5,000 per month	$3,800 to $4,000 per month
Price calculator	`https://calculator.s3.amazonaws.com/index.html`	`https://azure.microsoft.com/en-gb/pricing/calculator/?cdn=disable`	`https://cloud.google.com/products/calculator/`

12.6   Web-Based AI

As we saw earlier, web-based applications, or web apps, have become increasingly popular. Different from traditional static web pages, or dynamic web pages developed with PHP or JSP or ASP, web apps run like mobile apps and can automatically adjust the layout to fit the mobile device. With Python, you can develop web apps with several libraries, such as Django, Flask, Streamlit, and so on. With web apps, you don't need to worry about the version of programming language and the version of libraries or frameworks, and there is no need to have the hassles of installing any software on your computer. All these make the web apps particularly suitable for AI applications.

12.6.1   Django

Django is a Python-based powerful comprehensive web framework, built by experienced developers. Django claims it makes it easier to build better web apps more quickly and with less code. Django is free and open source. It is also ridiculously fast, reassuringly secure, and exceedingly scalable.

The following are the Django website and some tutorials:

```
https://www.djangoproject.com/
https://docs.djangoproject.com/en/3.1/intro/tutorial01/
https://realpython.com/lessons/web-frameworks-and-django/
https://developer.mozilla.org/en-US/docs/Learn/Server-side/Django
```

12.6.2   Flask

Flask is a lightweight web framework written in Python. It is designed to make web apps quick and easy, with the ability to scale up to complex applications. It has become one of the most popular Python web app frameworks. If you think of Django as a toolbox, Flask is just a hammer. Django provides a complete full set of functionalities, and Flask provides just a few simple functions.

The following shows the Full Stack Python Flask website.

```
https://www.fullstackpython.com/flask.html
```

The following are the Flask documentation website and Quick Start tutorials:

```
https://flask.palletsprojects.com/en/1.1.x/
https://flask.palletsprojects.com/en/1.1.x/quickstart/#quickstart
```

Example 12.4 shows a simple Flask web app program, which simply prints "Hello World" on the web page.

EXAMPLE 12.4:   THE `FlaskApp.PY` **PROGRAM**

```
# Example 12.4
from flask import Flask
app = Flask(__name__)


@app.route('/')
def hello_world():
    return 'Hello, World!'

if __name__ == '__main__':
    app.run()
```

To run the program, just type the following command at the Windows command prompt:

```
C:\>python FlaskApp.py
```

The following is the corresponding output, which indicates the Flask web server is running on the following uniform resource locator (URL): `http://127.0.0.1:5000/`.

```
* Serving Flask app "FlaskApp" (lazy loading)
 * Environment: production
   WARNING: This is a development server. Do not use it in a
nt.
   Use a production WSGI server instead.
 * Debug mode: off
 * Running on http://127.0.0.1:5000/ (Press CTRL+C to quit)
```

From a web browser, copy and paste the URL `http://127.0.0.1:5000/`; you will see "Hello World" has been displayed on the web page, as shown in Figure 12.6.

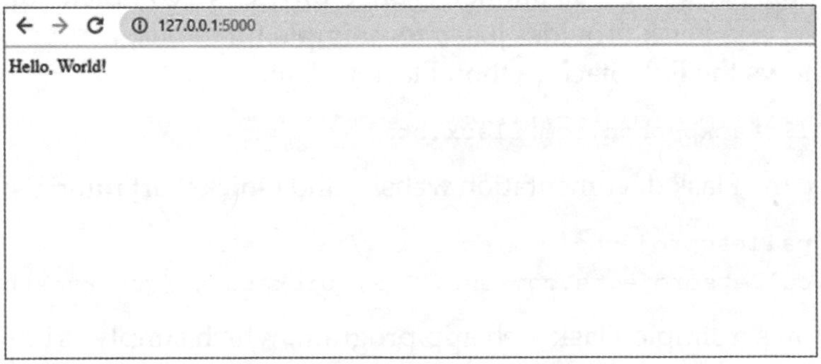

Figure 12.6: The web page output of the `FlaskApp.py` program

Example 12.5 is an improved version of the previous Flask web app program, which will run the web service at `http://127.0.0.1:5000/hello/<name>`. Then it will print "Hello <name>" on the web page, where <name> is a name you change with the URL.

EXAMPLE 12.5:   THE `FlaskApp2.PY` **PROGRAM**

```
# Example 12.5
from flask import Flask
app = Flask(__name__)

# routing the decorator function hello_name
@app.route('/hello/<name>')
def hello_name(name):
    return 'Hello %s!' % name

if __name__ == '__main__':
    app.run(debug = True)
```

Figure 12.7 shows the web page output of the `FlaskApp2.py` program.

Figure 12.7: The web page output of the `FlaskApp2.py` program

Example 12.6 shows another version of the Flask web app program, which will run the web service at `http://127.0.0.1:5000/`. But it displays the web page from a file called `index.html` located in a folder called `template`.

EXAMPLE 12.6:   THE `FlaskApp2.PY` **PROGRAM**

```
# Example 12.6
from flask import Flask, render_template
app = Flask(__name__)

@app.route("/")
def index():
    return render_template("index.html")

if __name__ == '__main__':
    app.run(debug = True)
```

This is the file structure of the program:

```
flask/
    |-->FlaskApp2.py
        |-->template/
                |-->index.html
```

EXERCISE 12.4

Modify the previous code, add another web page called `help.html`, **load the web page when the URL is** `http://127.0.0.1:5000/help/`, **run the previous code, and comment on the results.**

Example 12.7 shows the webcam version of the Flask web app program, which will display the webcam live stream images through the web service at `http://127.0.0.1:5000/`. It has three files, `FlaskWebcam.py`, `camera.py`, and `indexwc.html`, located in a folder called `template`.

EXAMPLE 12.7: THE `FlaskWebcam.PY` PROGRAM

```python
# Example 12.7

from flask import Flask, render_template, Response
from camera import VideoCamera

app = Flask(__name__)

@app.route('/')
def index():
    return render_template('indexwc.html')

def gen(camera):
    while True:
        frame = camera.get_frame()
        yield (b'--frame\r\n'
                b'Content-Type: image/jpeg\r\n\r\n' + frame +
b'\r\n\r\n')

@app.route('/video_feed')
def video_feed():
    return Response(gen(VideoCamera()),
                    mimetype='multipart/x-mixed-replace;
boundary=frame')

if __name__ == '__main__':
    app.run(host='0.0.0.0', debug=True)
```

The `camera.py` file defines the `Webcam` class, as shown in Example 12.8.

EXAMPLE 12.8:   THE `CAMERA.PY` **PROGRAM**

```python
# Example 12.8
import cv2

class VideoCamera(object):
    def __init__(self):
        self.video = cv2.VideoCapture(0)


    def __del__(self):
        self.video.release()

    def get_frame(self):
        success, image = self.video.read()
        ret, jpeg = cv2.imencode('.jpg', image)
        return jpeg.tobytes()
```

The `indexwc.html` file specifies the web page, as shown in Example 12.9.

EXAMPLE 12.9:   THE `INDEXWC.HTML` **PROGRAM**

```html
# Example 12.9
<html>
  <head>
    <title>Video Streaming Demonstration</title>
  </head>
  <body>
    <h1>Video Streaming Demonstration</h1>
    <img src="{{ url_for('video_feed') }}">
  </body>
</html>
```

The following is the file structure:

```
flask/
    |-->FlaskWebcam.py
    |-->camera.py
        |-->template/
            |-->indexwc.html
```

Figure 12.8 shows the web page output. As you can see, it has the webcam live stream within the page.

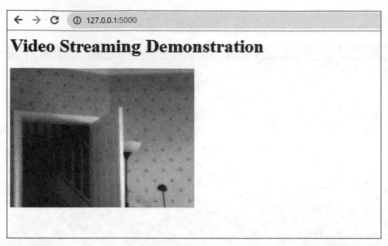

Figure 12.8: The web page output of the `FlaskWebcam.py` program

EXERCISE 12.5

Modify the previous code so that it converts the webcam images to grayscale first and then displays it on the web page, run the previous code, and comment on the results.

The following links show some more tutorials on deep learning web app deployment with Flask:

```
https://www.kdnuggets.com/2020/05/build-deploy-machine-learning-
web-app.html
https://realpython.com/flask-by-example-part-3-text-processing-
with-requests-beautifulsoup-nltk/
```

12.6.3   Streamlit

Streamlit is my favorite library for creating Python web apps. It is simple and fast, and best of all, it is purposely designed for creating machine learning applications. It also allows you to share your project online. We have seen many Streamlit examples throughout the chapters, so we will not cover more here. For more details, see the following:

```
https://streamlit.io/
https://share.streamlit.io/
```

12.6.4   Other Libraries

There are libraries for developing web-based AI applications, such as ML5.js and TensorFlow.js, both based on JavaScript.

As shown in Chapter 8, ML5.js is an impressive, friendly machine learning web framework, which provides many interesting AI models; it also allows you to edit and run the code online.

```
https://learn.ml5js.org/#/
https://editor.p5js.org/ml5/sketches/
```

TensorFlow.js is a library for machine learning in JavaScript, which allows you to run AI models directly in a web browser or in Node.js.

```
https://www.tensorflow.org/js
```

12.7   Packaging the Code

After you have developed your code, you can package your code to give it to others to use. Packaging the code is important and useful, as it makes it easier for the other people to use it without the hassle of rebuilding the application. It can also protect your source code if you choose not to give it away. In this section, we will introduce several popular ways of packaging your code.

Pyinstaller

Pyinstaller is probably the most powerful tool to convert your Python program into EXE files. In addition to Windows, it also supports Unix/Linux and macOS. Pyinstaller allows you to bundle your Python application and all its dependencies into a single package. You can then run the packaged app without installing a Python interpreter or any modules. Using it is also remarkably simple; just install it first and run the Pyinstaller on your Python file.

```
pip install pyinstaller
pyinstaller yourprogram.py
```

For more details, see the following:

```
https://www.pyinstaller.org/
https://pypi.org/project/pyinstaller/
```

Nbconvert

Nbconvert is a simple library that can convert IPython Jupyter files (.ipynb) to Python files (.py) and then from Python files (.py) to executable files (.exe). You need to install two libraries:

```
pip install ipython
pip install nbconvert
```

For example, if you have a file called `test.ipynb`, you can run the following command to convert it to a Python file, `test.py`:

```
ipython nbconvert --to script test.ipynb
```

Then you can use the Pyinstaller library to convert `test.py` to `test.exe`.

```
pyinstaller test.py
```

The following is the file structure. You can find the `test.exe` file in the `dist/test/` subfolder.

```
test.ipynb
test.py
__pycahce__/
build/
dist/
  |-->test/
        |-->test.exe
        |-->test.exe.manifest
      ... ...
```

For more details, see the following:

```
https://nbconvert.readthedocs.io/en/latest/
```

Py2Exe

Py2exe is a library that converts Python scripts into executable Windows programs and is compatible with Python 2.4+ including Python 3.0 and 3.1.

```
https://sourceforge.net/p/py2exe/svn/HEAD/tree/trunk/py2exe-3/
py2exe/
```

Py2app

Py2app is a Python setup tool command to create stand-alone macOS applications with Python. It is similar in purpose and design to Py2exe, which is for Windows.

```
https://py2app.readthedocs.io/en/latest/
```

Auto-Py-To-Exe

The Auto-Py-To-Exe library is a Python (`.py`) to executable (`.exe`) converter using a simple graphical interface and Pyinstaller in Python (see Figure 12.9). To install the application, run this line at the Windows command prompt:

```
pip install auto-py-to-exe
```

To open the application, run this line at the Windows command prompt:

```
auto-py-to-exe
```

Figure 12.9: The graphical user interface of the Auto-Py-To-Exe program

For more details, see the following:

```
https://pypi.org/project/auto-py-to-exe/
```

cx_Freeze

cx_Freeze is a cross-platform library for freezing Python scripts into executables with the same performance, in much the same way that Py2exe and Py2app do. But unlike these two tools, cx_Freeze should work on any platform that Python itself works on. It supports Python 3.6 up to 3.9.

The following command converts the Python file `hello.py` into an executable file stored in the `dist/` subfolder:

```
cxfreeze -c hello.py --target-dir dist
```

For more details, see the following:

```
https://pypi.python.org/pypi/cx_Freeze
http://cx-freeze.readthedocs.io/en/latest/overview.html
```

Cython

Cython is a programming language that can compile Python-like code into C programming language code. Cython is a superset of the Python language, which allows you to add typing information and class attributes that can then be translated to C code and to C-Extensions for Python.

Cython code must be compiled. This is done in two stages:

■ A Python `.pyx` file is compiled by Cython to a `.c` file.

■ The `.c` file is compiled by a C compiler to a `.pyd` file on Windows or `.so` file on Linux/Unix, which can be imported directly into a Python session. `Distutils` or `setuptools` takes care of this part.

Let's use an example to illustrate the process. Create a Python file called `hello.pyx` with the content shown in Example 12.10a.

EXAMPLE 12.10A: THE `HELLO.PYX` **PROGRAM**

```
def say_hello(name):
    print("Hello %s!" % name)
def say_bye(name):
    print("Goodbye %s!" % name)
```

Then create a Python file called `setup.py` with the content shown in Example 12.10b.

EXAMPLE 12.10B: THE `SETUP.PY` **PROGRAM**

```
from setuptools import setup
from Cython.Build import cythonize

setup(
    name='Hello world app',
    ext_modules=cythonize("hello.pyx"),
    zip_safe=False,
)
```

To compile it, type the following:

```
python setup.py build_ext --inplace
```

If successful, a file called `hello.c` and a file called `hello.cp36-win_amd64 .pyd` (in Windows) or `hello.so` (in Unix/Linux) will be generated. The `hello.c` file is the C file of the `hello.pyx` file. The `.pyd` file or the `.so` file is the binary file that `hello.c` has been compiled into. You can now distribute the `.pyd` file or the `.so` file to others without revealing your original Python code defined in the `hello.pyx` file.

To test the `.pyd` file or the `.so` file, create another Python test file called `hellotest.py` with the content shown in Example 12.10c.

EXAMPLE 12.10C: THE `HELLOTEST.PY` **PROGRAM**

```
import pyximport; pyximport.install()
import hello

hello.say_hello("Perry")
hello.say_bye("Tony")
```

To run the program, type the following:

```
python hellotest.py
```

You should see the following output on the screen:

```
Hello Perry!
Goodbye Tony!
```

EXERCISE 12.6

Repeat the previous steps, create your own Cython program, run the service, and comment on the results.

For more details, see the following:

```
https://cython.org/
https://cython.readthedocs.io/en/latest/
```

Kubernetes

Kubernetes, also shortened to K8S, is an open source platform for managing containerized services. The word *kubernete* originates from Greek, meaning helmsman or pilot. Developed by Google, Kubernetes has a large, rapidly growing ecosystem.

Figure 12.10 shows the Kubernetes website on the history of software deployment. Traditionally, the software code needs to be compiled according to the operating system; therefore, for different operating systems, such as Windows and Linux/Unix, you will need to compile the code differently. The operating system provides all the libraries, dependencies, and runtime environment for the software to run. The main problem with this approach is scalability; as the number of applications increase, you will also need to increase the hardware capabilities.

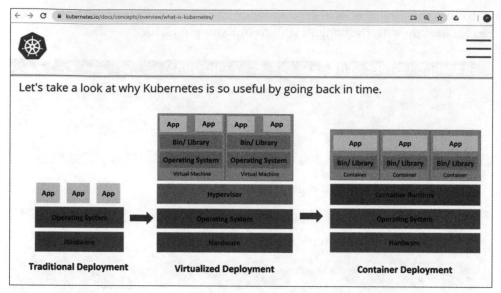

Figure 12.10: The Kubernetes website on the history of software deployment

(Source: `https://kubernetes.io/docs/concepts/overview/what-is-kubernetes/`)

Then came the virtual machine, in which software code needs to be compiled and run within the operating system of each virtual machine, and the virtual machine runs within the hypervisor of the operating system. This approach has improved scalability, but each virtual machine is a complete operating system, which is still large in size, complex, and resource hungry.

The latest is container technology, in which the software code is compiled and packaged into an isolated, lightweight unit, called a *container*. The container has all the necessary libraries and dependencies for the software to run, and the container runs in the container runtime. Compared to a virtual machine, a container is much smaller, more portable, more scalable, and less resource hungry.

Figure 12.11 shows the schematic diagram of the Kubernetes architecture. A Kubernetes cluster contains a master node and a number of worker nodes. On the master node, there are the API server (kube-apiserver), controller manager (kube-controller-manager), cloud controller manager (cloud-controller-manager), scheduler (kube-scheduler), and etcd, which is used as a backing store for all the cluster data. The API server is the brain of the Kubernetes cluster, which orchestrates the whole operation. Users can interact with the API server through the user interface (UI), application programming interface (API), and command-line interface (CLI).

On the worker node, there are the agent (kubelet), proxy (kube-proxy), and container runtime and pods. Pods are the smallest deployable units of computing that you can create and manage in Kubernetes. Inside each pod, there are containers.

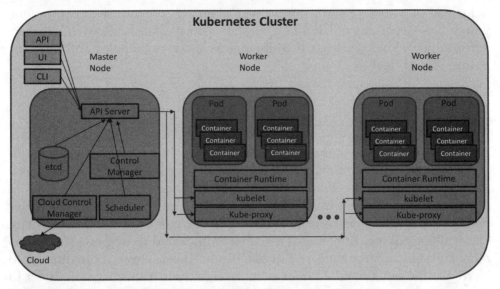

Figure 12.11: The schematic diagram of the Kubernetes architecture

The best way to get started with Kubernetes is to follow its online interactive tutorial, which has step-by-step interactive instructions on how to create a Kubernetes cluster, how to deploy and run an app, and so on, as shown in Figure 12.12.

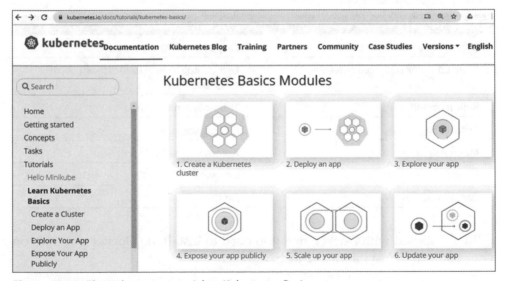

Figure 12.12: The Kubernetes tutorial on Kubernetes Basics

(Source: `https://kubernetes.io/docs/tutorials/kubernetes-basics/`)

Instead of installing and configuring Kubernetes on your own computers, you can also try it online. The following shows the website for Play with Kubernetes, which allows you to create Kubernetes clusters and deploy and run apps online. All for free!

```
https://labs.play-with-k8s.com/
```

Docker

Docker is another open source containerization tool used for spinning up isolated, reproducible application environments. It was developed by Docker and is a popular development tool for Python developers.

Many people get confused with Kubernetes and Docker. As a container platform, you can either use Kubernetes on its own or use Docker on its own. Generally speaking, Kubernetes is more complex and more powerful and is more suitable for large clusters. But as a result, Kubernetes is more difficult to learn. On the other hand, Docker is lightweight, much simpler, and easier to use, but has fewer functionalities. Docker is more suitable for small clusters. You can also use Kubernetes and Docker together, that is, using Docker to create containers and using Kubernetes to orchestrate the containers.

Docker also has its own orchestration software, called Docker Swarm. Table 12.6 shows a quick comparison of Kubernetes and Docker Swarm.

Table 12.6: Kubernetes vs. Docker Swarm

KUBERNETES	DOCKER SWARM
Difficult to install and configure	Easy to install and configure
More complex but more powerful	Less complex, easy to use, fewer functionalities
Built-in monitoring	Third-party monitoring
Autoscaling	No autoscaling
Manual load balancer	Automatic load balancer
Need for a separate CLI tool	Integrated Docker CLI
Dashboard GUI	No GUI

To get started with Docker, first you need to install the Docker program on your computer; just follow the instructions here:

```
https://docs.docker.com/get-docker/
```

The simplest way to install and get started with Docker is using Ubuntu, such as version 20.04 (LTS), 18.04 (LTS), and 16.04 (LTS). The following commands are to install Docker and get Docker running:

```
sudo apt-get update
sudo apt install docker.io
sudo systemctl start docker
sudo systemctl enable docker
```

The following commands are to check the Docker version, list of containers, Docker information, and Docker images:

```
docker --version
docker ps
docker info
docker images
```

Then, create a folder, say `docker`, and inside the folder create a file called `main.py`, a file called `requirements.txt`, and another file called `dockerfile`.

The `main.py` file is the Python program. For example, the example code shown in Example 12.11 plots the Sin function.

EXAMPLE 12.11:   THE `MAIN.PY` PROGRAM

```
# Example 12.11
import numpy as np
import matplotlib.pyplot as plt

x = np.linspace(-np.pi, np.pi, 50)
y1 = np.sin(x)
plt.plot(x, y1, color = 'blue', marker = "s", label='Sin')
plt.legend()
plt.show()
```

The `requirements.txt` file, shown in Example 12.12, has all the libraries that are needed by the Python program.

EXAMPLE 12.12:   THE `REQUIREMENTS.TXT` PROGRAM

```
numpy
matplotlib
```

The `dockerfile` file, shown in Example 12.13, has all the instructions on how to set up and run the Python program using Docker.

EXAMPLE 12.13: **THE** DOCKERFILE **PROGRAM**

```
# set base image (host OS)
FROM python:3.7

# set the working directory in the container
WORKDIR /docker

# copy the dependencies file to the working directory
COPY requirements.txt .

# install dependencies
RUN pip install -r requirements.txt

# copy the content of the local src directory to the working
directory
COPY . .

# command to run on container start
CMD [ "python", "main.py" ]
```

The following is the file structure:

```
docker/
  |-->main.py
  |-->requirements.txt
  |-->Dockerfile
       ... ...
```

To build a Docker image, run the following command from the folder:

```
docker build -t myimage .
```

After it's built, run the following command to view all the Docker images:

```
docker images
```

To run the Python program within Docker, type the following:

```
docker run myimage
```

To view the status of all the running images, type the following:

```
docker ps
```

Example 12.14 is the Streamlit version of the previous example. Again, it has three files. The `main2.py` file is the Streamlit Python program that plots the Sin or Cos function on the web app depending on the selection in the left panel.

EXAMPLE 12.14:   THE `MAIN2.PY` **PROGRAM**

```python
# Example 12.14
import streamlit as st
import numpy as np
import matplotlib.pyplot as plt
st.title('Streamlit Plotting')
selectbox = st.sidebar.selectbox(
    "What you do like to plot?",
    ("Sin", "Cos")
)
x = np.linspace(-np.pi, np.pi, 50)
if selectbox == "Sin":
    y1 = np.sin(x)
    plt.plot(x, y1, color = 'blue', marker = "s", label='Sin')
else:
    y1 = np.cos(x)
    plt.plot(x, y1, color = 'red', marker = "d", label='Cos')
plt.legend()
plt.show()
st.pyplot()
```

The `requirements.txt` file, shown in Example 12.15, has all the libraries that are needed by the Python program.

EXAMPLE 12.15:   THE `REQUIREMENTS.TXT` **PROGRAM**

```
numpy
matplotlib
cython
streamlit
```

The `dockerfile` file, shown in Example 12.16, has all the instructions on how to set up and run the Python program using Docker.

EXAMPLE 12.16:   THE `DOCKERFILE` **PROGRAM**

```
# set base image (host OS)
FROM python:3.7

# set the working directory in the container
WORKDIR /docker

# copy the dependencies file to the working directory
COPY requirements.txt .
```

```
# install dependencies
RUN pip install -r requirements.txt

# copy the content of the local src directory to the working
directory
COPY . .

# exposing default port for streamlit
EXPOSE 8501
# command to run on container start
CMD [ "streamlit", "run", "main2.py" ]
```

The Docker building and running processes are the same. You can view the web app at the usual `https://localhost:8501/`, as shown in Figure 12.13. By selecting Sin or Cos from the selection box, you can plot the function accordingly.

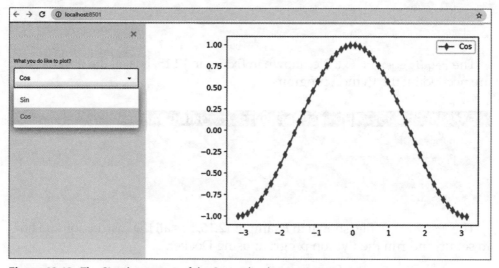

Figure 12.13: The Sin plot output of the Streamlit plot program

---

EXERCISE 12.7

Repeat the previous steps, create your own Streamlit web app Docker service, run the service, and comment on the results.

For more details on getting started with Docker, check out the following:

```
https://www.docker.com/blog/containerized-python-development-part-1/
https://kubernetes.io/blog/2019/07/23/get-started-with-kubernetes-
using-python/
```

PIP

PIP is the coolest Python tool that makes it so simple to install and uninstall Python packages. You can also make your code available as a PIP installable package through the `PyPI.org` website.

```
https://python-packaging-user-guide.readthedocs.io/
https://docs.python-guide.org/shipping/packaging/
```

The following shows the RealPython tutorial called "How to Publish on Open-Source Python Package to PyPI."

```
https://realpython.com/pypi-publish-python-package/
```

12.8   AI with Edge Computing

Edge computing means to run your software programs on the edge, namely, microcontrollers, embedded systems, single-board computers, or mobile phones. Different from cloud computing, where there are powerful servers, edge devices tend to have limited computing powers, have limited memory resources, and are often constrained with battery power. To run AI models on the edge, first you will need to train the models on the cloud, then reduce the models to lightweight versions, and finally deploy them to the edges. This section will show a few examples on how to run AI models on edge devices.

12.8.1   Google Coral

Google Coral provides a range of tools built on Google's Edge TPU technology, which allows you to run AI on your local devices, or the edge. The prototyping devices include a single-board computer and USB accessory, and production-ready devices include a system-on-module and PCIe module.

The following shows the Google Coral website, which provides a Coral USB stick and Edge TPU single-board computer.

```
https://coral.ai/
```

You can find many interesting project tutorials and example code (see the following link).

```
https://coral.ai/examples/#project-tutorials
```

The following shows the Teachable Machine tutorial. In this example, it teaches you how to build a teachable machine and to recognize different chess pieces by using TensorFlow.js, a Coral USB Accelerator, and a Raspberry Pi.

```
https://coral.ai/projects/teachable-machine/
```

12.8.2   TinyML

TinyML is another interesting technology that allows you to run TensorFlow on an Arduino board, such as Arduino Nano 33 BLE Sense and Arduino Portenta H7. TinyML uses Edge Impulse, which enables developers to create the next generation of intelligent device solutions with embedded machine learning. See the following link for details.

```
https://store.arduino.cc/arduino-nano-33-ble-sense
```

The following are the Edge Impulse website and its corresponding GitHub website for Arduino Nano 33 BLE Sense:

```
https://docs.edgeimpulse.com/docs/arduino-nano-33-ble-sense
https://github.com/edgeimpulse/firmware-arduino-nano-33-ble-sense
```

The best way to get started with TinyML is to follow the interesting Arduino blog, as shown in the following blog. It shows you step-by-step how to train a TensorFlow Lite Micro model on an Arduino Nano 33 board, how to recognize a voice command, and hand gestures such as fist, punch, and hook.

```
https://blog.arduino.cc/2019/10/15/get-started-with-machine-
learning-on-arduino/
```

The following are steps to train a model for gesture recognition with TinyML:

Step 1. Downloading and Setting Up the Arduino IDE
Download and install the Arduino IDE:

```
https://arduino.cc/downloads
```

From the Arduino IDE, search and install the Nano BLE board from Boards Manager.
Search for and install the `Arduino_TensorFlowLite` library and the `Arduino_LSM9DS1` library from Library Manager.

Step 2. Streaming Sensor Data from the Arduino Board
Download `IMU_Capture.ino` from the following link, and open it in the Arduino IDE. Compile and upload it to the board.

```
https://github.com/arduino/ArduinoTensorFlowLiteTutorials/blob/
master/GestureToEmoji/ArduinoSketches/IMU_Capture/IMU_Capture.ino
```

In the Arduino IDE, open the Serial Monitor.
Make 10 punch gestures with the board in your hand and then copy and paste the data from the Serial Monitor to a new text file called `punch.csv`. Clear the console window output, make 10 flex gestures, and save the data in a file called `flex.csv`.

Repeat the previous step, make 10 hook gestures, and save the data in a file called `hook.csv`.

Step 3. Training in TensorFlow

Open the following Google Colab Notebook; copy it to your own Google Colab account; upload the three files `punch.csv`, `flex.csv`, and `hook.csv`; and run the code.

```
https://colab.research.google.com/github/arduino/ArduinoTensor
FlowLiteTutorials/blob/master/GestureToEmoji/arduino_tinyml_work-
shop.ipynb
```

The code should generate two files, `model.h` and `gesture_model.tflite`. Download the two files to a local folder.

Step 4. Gesture Recognition

Download `IMU_Classifier.ino` from the following link. Save it into a directory. Copy in the `model.h` file and `gesture_model.tflite` file. Compile and run the code using the Arduino IDE.

```
https://github.com/arduino/ArduinoTensorFlowLiteTutorials/
blob/master/GestureToEmoji/ArduinoSketches/IMU_Classifier/IMU_
Classifier.ino
```

Now from the Arduino IDE Serial Monitor, you should be able to see the gesture recognition.

Arduino Portenta H7   Another impressive Arduino board that can run TensorFlow Lite models is the Arduino Portenta H7 board. It has two parallel cores in its main processor, with a Cortex M7 running at 480 MHz and a Cortex M4 running at 240 MHz. The two cores communicate seamlessly via a Remote Procedure Call (RPC). The main processor also has an on-chip GPU and a dedicated JPEG encoder and decoder. Portenta H7 comes with 3× ADCs with 16-bit resolution (up to 36 channels, up to 3.6 MSPS), 2× 12-bit DAC (1 MHz), USB-C, as well as built-in WiFi 802.11b/g/n and Bluetooth 5.1 BR/EDR/LE. It supports both the MicroPython and JavaScript languages.

```
https://store.arduino.cc/portenta-h7
https://github.com/ARM-software/developer/tree/master/projects/
portenta_person_detection
```

12.8.3   Raspberry Pi

The Raspberry Pi is one of my favorite single-board computing devices. With Raspberry Pi and its camera, you can build a teachable machine to recognize your body gestures, such as this tutorial, shown in the following link.

```
https://developer.arm.com/solutions/machine-learning-on-arm/
developer-material/how-to-guides/teach-your-raspberry-pi-yeah-world/
run-your-new-network
```

The following are the steps:

1. Install all the libraries.

```
sudo apt update
sudo apt install python3-dev python3-pip
sudo apt install libatlas-base-dev      # required for numpy
sudo apt install libhdf5-dev
sudo pip3 install -U virtualenv          # system-wide install
sudo pip3 install --no-cache-dir tensorflow
```

2. Verify TensorFlow.

```
python3 -c "import tensorflow as tf; tf.enable_eager_execution();
print(tf.reduce_sum(tf.random_normal([1000, 1000])))"
```

3. Install the ARM training scripts.

```
git clone https://github.com/ARM-software/ML-examples.git
cd ML-examples/yeah-world
```

4. Preview the Raspberry Pi camera.

```
python3 preview.py
```

5. Record 15 seconds of video with your hands up.

```
mkdir example
python record.py example/yeah 15
```

6. Record 15 seconds of video with your hands down.

```
python3 record.py example/sitting 15
```

7. Record 15 seconds of video with random positions.

```
python3 record.py example/random 15
```

8. Train a network on the data.

```
python3 train.py example/model.h5 example/yeah example/sitting
example/random
```

9. Run your new network.

```
python3 run.py example/model.h5
```

Next, wave your hands in the air, put your hands down, and do some random positions. From the console it should print the prediction:

0: Cheering.
1: Sitting in view but not cheering.
2: Random behaviors.

The following shows another example, using Raspberry Pi as an image classifier.

https://www.instructables.com/Image-Recognition-With-TensorFlow-on-Raspberry-Pi/

The following are the steps:

1. Update the system.

```
sudo apt-get update
sudo apt-get upgrade
```

2. Display the Python 3 version.

```
python3 --version
```

3. Install the libatlas library (ATLAS - Automatically Tuned Linear Algebra Software).

```
sudo apt install libatlas-base-dev
```

4. Install TensorFlow.

```
pip3 install tensorflow
```

5. Clone the TensorFlow repository.

```
git clone https://github.com/tensorflow/models.git
cd models/tutorials/image/imagenet
```

6. Run the image classification code on a default image.

```
python3 classify_image.py
```

Or, run the image classification code on a customized image

```
python3 classify_image.py --image_file=/home/pi/Downloads/
TensorImageTest1.jpg
```

12.9   Create a Mobile AI App

MIT App Inventor 2 is an online platform developed by Google and MIT. With MIT App Inventor 2, you can easily develop mobile phone apps by using block programming. It supports only Android phone apps at the moment, but with the intention to expand to Apple iOS phones.

The following shows the artificial intelligence with the MIT App Inventor website, in which it shows several AI examples.

```
https://appinventor.mit.edu/explore/ai-with-mit-app-inventor
```

The following is a simple personal image classification example with step-by-step instructions:

```
https://appinventor.mit.edu/explore/resources/ai/personal-image-
classifier-part1
```

Step 1. Train the model.

Open your browser and go to `https://classifier.appinventor.mit.edu/oldpic/`.

Follow the instructions and create several personal image classes, such as `Smile`, `Superised`, and `Frown`. Train the model and download the `model.mdl` model file.

Step 2. Perform the Personal Image Classification.

Download the Personal Image Classification (PIC) project template file called `PIC.aia` from the following link:

```
http://bit.ly/2BYiNoG
```

Go to `http://appinventor.mit.edu/` and import the `PIC.aia` file into your projects.

Upload the model file `model.mdl` into the project.

Build the project and create a QR code. Scan the QR code to download and install the app on your phone.

Here is more information about MIT App Inventor 2 extensions:

```
http://ai2.appinventor.mit.edu/reference/other/extensions.html
```

Here is more information about Google Teachable machine:

```
https://teachablemachine.withgoogle.com/
```

Here is more information about AI for kids' resources:

```
https://machinelearningforkids.co.uk/#!/links
```

`Thunkable.com` is another web-based platform for mobile app development, which supports Google Android, Apple iOS, and Windows phones (see the following link). Similar to MIT App Inventor 2, no code is needed.

```
https://thunkable.com/#/
```

You can also use the following software to develop mobile apps:

- OpenCV for Android

  `https://opencv.org/android/`

- TensorFlow for Android

  `https://www.tensorflow.org/lite/guide/android`

- Mediapipe for Android and iOS

  `https://google.github.io/mediapipe/getting_started/android.html`
  `https://google.github.io/mediapipe/getting_started/ios.html`

12.10   Quantum AI

Quantum computing has been a hot research topic for some years now. Quantum computing is based on quantum phenomena such as superposition and entanglement to perform the calculation. The computers based on quantum physics are called *quantum computers*.

Conventional computers are based on the binary system, called *bits*. You can imagine a bit is like a switch, which can be switched on and off, to represent zero and one. All the software programs, all the photos, and all the files are eventually represented in computers as bits, in a combination of ones and zeros.

Instead of using bits, quantum computers use qubits. See Figure 12.14 for bits and qubits. Rather than being just zero or one, qubits can also be in superposition, where they can be both zero and one, or somewhere on a spectrum between the two. Quantum computers use particles that possess quantum properties to represent qubits, which usually need to be cooled down to near absolute zero degrees. You can imagine a qubit as a spinning coin; it could be either heads or tails, or somewhere in between, until you stop the coin. Then it will become just a head or just a tail. A qubit can be more than just zeros and ones, and that is what makes quantum computers so powerful.

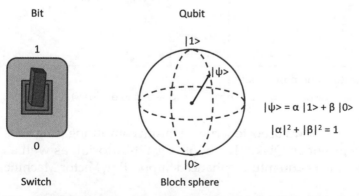

Figure 12.14: The bit in conventional computing and the qubit in quantum computing

Quantum computing could change our lives. It could transform medicine, break encryption, and revolutionize communications and artificial intelligence. Around the world, companies like IBM, Microsoft, Google, and Baidu are all racing to build their own quantum computers.

IBM is the first company to build quantum computers on an impressive scale. The latest IBM quantum computer has 53 qubits. The qubits are achieved by trapping atoms in a vacuum environment, with an ambient temperature close to absolute zero (−273°C), and insulated from the earth's magnetic field.

The following shows the IBM Quantum Computing Tools website.

```
https://www.ibm.com/quantum-computing/tools
```

IBM has developed a quantum computing toolkit called Qiskit, as shown in the following link. With Qiskit, you can write quantum computing simulation code offline or run the code on real IBM quantum computers online.

```
https://qiskit.org/
```

Based on Qiskit, IBM provides the IBM Quantum Composer and the IBM Quantum Lab, the two online platforms that allow public and premium access to cloud-based quantum computing services.

The IBM Quantum Composer allows users to compose quantum computing programs using symbols, like composing the music; see Figure 12.15.

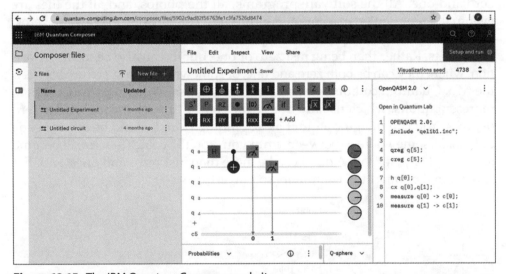

Figure 12.15: The IBM Quantum Composer website

(Source: `https://quantum-computing.ibm.com/composer/files/new`)

The IBM Quantum Lab allows users to write quantum computing programs using Python; it also provides Qiskit-Textbook, Qiskit-Tutorial, as well as many useful examples, such as quantum-enhanced Supporting Vector Machine

(QSVM). It also allows users to run the code on real IBM Quantum computers, as illustrated in Figure 12.16.

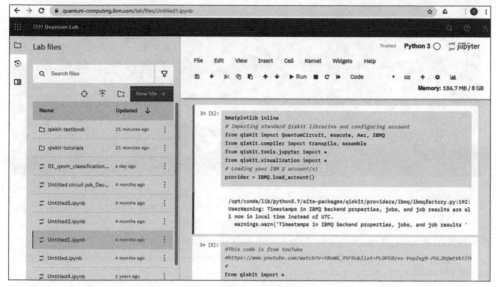

Figure 12.16: The IBM Quantum Computing Lab website

(Source: `https://quantum-computing.ibm.com/lab`)

Google is another company heavily invested in quantum computing; see the following link.

`https://quantumai.google/`

Google claimed quantum supremacy in October 2019, when Google developed a 54-qubit processor, named Sycamore, that performed the target computation in 200 seconds in an experiment that would take the world's fastest supercomputer 10,000 years to produce a similar output; see Figure 12.17 for a detailed report.

The following shows the Google TensorFlow Quantum Computing website.

`https://www.tensorflow.org/quantum`

In December 2020, a team from the University of Science and Technology of China also claimed quantum supremacy, when it used a 76-qubit system known as Jiuzhang, which performed calculations at 100 trillion times the speed of classical supercomputers. Different from IBM's and Google's quantum computers, which need to be cooled down to near absolute zero degrees, Jiuzhang is based on photons, which can work at the ambient temperature; see Figure 12.18 for the detailed report.

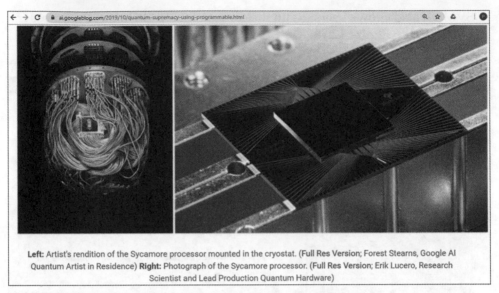

Left: Artist's rendition of the Sycamore processor mounted in the cryostat. (**Full Res Version**; Forest Stearns, Google AI Quantum Artist in Residence) **Right:** Photograph of the Sycamore processor. (**Full Res Version**; Erik Lucero, Research Scientist and Lead Production Quantum Hardware)

Figure 12.17: Google claimed quantum computing supremacy in 2019.

(Source: https://ai.googleblog.com/2019/10/quantum-supremacy-using-programmable.html)

Figure 12.18: The news report on China claiming quantum supremacy at the University of Science and Technology of China

(Source: https://www.futuretimeline.net/blog/2020/12/5-quantum-supremacy-china-2020.htm)

Baidu also provides quantum computing through the Baidu PaddlePaddle framework; see the following link. It provides a platform to construct and train quantum neural networks (QNNs), supporting combinatorial optimization, quantum chemistry, and other cutting-edge quantum applications. It claimed to be the first deep learning framework in China that supports quantum machine learning.

```
https://github.com/PaddlePaddle/Quantum
```

12.11   Summary

This chapter introduced some advanced topics in AI. For simple AI applications, you can train and run the models on standard computers based on the CPU. To train larger models, it is better to run on a GPU and a TPU. An IPU is a new form of AI computing hardware infrastructure that has improved performances and is more cost effective.

Cloud computing is the future trend for many businesses, and the biggest three cloud computing services providers are Amazon AWS, Microsoft Azure, and Google GCP, followed by Oracle, IBM, and Baidu.

Web apps are also getting trendy. You can develop web-based AI applications with Django, Flask, Streamlit, and many other libraries and frameworks.

There are several ways you can package and deploy your Python programs, such as Nbconvert, Pyinstaller, Py2Exe, Py2app, Auto-Py-To-Exe, Cx_Freeze, Cython, and PIP.

Kubernetes (K8s) and Docker are container-based technologies for packaging and deploying software programs.

Edge AI means to run AI applications on the edge devices such as embedded systems, single-board computers, and mobile phones.

There are also several ways to develop mobile AI apps, such as MIT App Inventor 2, Thunkable, OpenCV, TensorFlow, and Mcdiapipe.

Quantum computing is getting a lot of attention in recent years, and there are quantum AI services provided by IBM, Google, and Baidu.

12.12   Chapter Review Questions

Q12.1.   What is a GPU, and what is the advantage of a GPU over a CPU?

Q12.2.   What is a TPU? Use a table to compare CPUs, GPUs, and TPUs.

Q12.3.   What is an IPU?

Q12.4.   What is cloud computing?

Q12.5. What AI services does AWS provide?

Q12.6. What AI services does Azure provide?

Q12.7. What AI services does GCP provide?

Q12.8. What are Django, Flask, and Streamlit?

Q12.9. Compare the different Python packaging techniques, such as Nbconvert, Pyinstaller, Py2Exe, Py2app, Auto-Py-To-Exe, Cx_Freeze, Cython, and PIP.

Q12.10. What is Kubernetes? What are containers?

Q12.11. Compare the traditional computers, virtual machines, and container-based technologies.

Q12.12. What is Docker, and what is Docker Swarm?

Q12.13. What is edge computing?

Q12.14. What is TinyML?

Q12.15. How do you develop a mobile AI app?

Q12.16. What is quantum computing, and what is quantum AI?

Index